THE
NAG HAMMADI LIBRARY

IN ENGLISH

THE
NAG HAMMADI LIBRARY

IN ENGLISH

TRANSLATED BY

MEMBERS OF THE COPTIC GNOSTIC LIBRARY PROJECT
OF THE INSTITUTE FOR ANTIQUITY AND CHRISTIANITY

James M. Robinson, Director

HARPER & ROW, PUBLISHERS, San Francisco
Cambridge, Hagerstown, Philadelphia, New York,
London, Mexico City, São Paulo, Sydney

CONTRIBUTORS

Harold W. Attridge

Hans-Gebhard Bethge

Alexander Böhlig

James Brashler

Roger A. Bullard

Peter A. Dirkse

Joseph A. Gibbons

Søren Giversen

Charles W. Hedrick

Wesley W. Isenberg

Helmut Koester

Thomas O. Lambdin

Bentley Layton

George W. MacRae

Dieter Mueller†

William R. Murdock

Elaine H. Pagels

Douglas M. Parrott

Birger A. Pearson

Malcolm L. Peel

James M. Robinson

William C. Robinson, Jr.

William R. Schoedel

John H. Sieber

John D. Turner

Francis E. Williams

R. McL. Wilson

Orval S. Wintermute

Antoinette Clark Wire

Frederik Wisse

Jan Zandee

Marvin W. Meyer, Managing Editor

First Harper & Row paperback edition published in 1981.

Library of Congress Cataloging in Publication Data

Main entry under title:

The Nag Hammadi Library in English.

    1. Gnosticism—Collected works.   I. Coptic Gnostic Library Project.   II. Title.
BT1390.C4713   1981   299'.932   77-7853
ISBN 0-06-066933-0

Composition by E. J. Brill, The Netherlands

83   84   85   10 9 8

TABLE OF CONTENTS

Preface IX
  MARVIN W. MEYER

Table of Tractates in the Nag Hammadi Library XIII

Textual Signs XVI

Introduction 1
  JAMES M. ROBINSON

The Prayer of the Apostle Paul (I, 1) 27
  DIETER MUELLER

The Apocryphon of James (I, 2) 29
  FRANCIS E. WILLIAMS and DIETER MUELLER

The Gospel of Truth (I, 3 and XII, 2) 37
  GEORGE W. MACRAE

The Treatise on Resurrection (I, 4) 50
  MALCOLM L. PEEL

The Tripartite Tractate (I, 5) 54
  HAROLD W. ATTRIDGE, ELAINE H. PAGELS, and DIETER MUELLER

The Apocryphon of John (II, 1, III, 1, IV, 1, and BG 8502, 2) . . 98
  FREDERIK WISSE

The Gospel of Thomas (II, 2) 117
  HELMUT KOESTER and THOMAS O. LAMBDIN

The Gospel of Philip (II, 3) 131
  WESLEY W. ISENBERG

The Hypostasis of the Archons (II, 4) 152
  ROGER A. BULLARD and BENTLEY LAYTON

On the Origin of the World (II, 5 and XIII, 2) 161
  HANS-GEBHARD BETHGE and ORVAL S. WINTERMUTE

The Exegesis on the Soul (II, 6) 180
  WILLIAM C. ROBINSON, Jr.

The Book of Thomas the Contender (II, 7) 188
  JOHN D. TURNER

The Gospel of the Egyptians (III, 2 and IV, 2) 195
  ALEXANDER BÖHLIG and FREDERIK WISSE

Eugnostos the Blessed (III, 3 and V, 1) and The Sophia of Jesus
Christ (III, 4 and BG 8502, 3) 206
    DOUGLAS M. PARROTT

The Dialogue of the Savior (III, 5) 229
    HELMUT KOESTER, ELAINE H. PAGELS, and HAROLD W. ATTRIDGE

The Apocalypse of Paul (V, 2) 239
    GEORGE W. MACRAE, WILLIAM R. MURDOCK, and
    DOUGLAS M. PARROTT

The First Apocalypse of James (V, 3) 242
    WILLIAM R. SCHOEDEL and DOUGLAS M. PARROTT

The Second Apocalypse of James (V, 4) 249
    CHARLES W. HEDRICK and DOUGLAS M. PARROTT

The Apocalypse of Adam (V, 5) 256
    GEORGE W. MACRAE and DOUGLAS M. PARROTT

The Acts of Peter and the Twelve Apostles (VI, 1) 265
    DOUGLAS M. PARROTT and R. MCL. WILSON

The Thunder, Perfect Mind (VI, 2) 271
    GEORGE W. MACRAE and DOUGLAS M. PARROTT

Authoritative Teaching (VI, 3) 278
    GEORGE W. MACRAE and DOUGLAS M. PARROTT

The Concept of our Great Power (VI, 4) 284
    FRANCIS E. WILLIAMS, FREDERIK WISSE, and
    DOUGLAS M. PARROTT

Plato, Republic 588B-589B (VI, 5) 290
    JAMES BRASHLER and DOUGLAS M. PARROTT

The Discourse on the Eighth and Ninth (VI, 6) 292
    JAMES BRASHLER, PETER A. DIRKSE, and DOUGLAS M. PARROTT

The Prayer of Thanksgiving (VI, 7) 298
    JAMES BRASHLER, PETER A. DIRKSE, and DOUGLAS M. PARROTT

Asclepius 21-29 (VI, 8) 300
    JAMES BRASHLER, PETER A. DIRKSE, and DOUGLAS M. PARROTT

The Paraphrase of Shem (VII, 1) 308
    FREDERIK WISSE

The Second Treatise of the Great Seth (VII, 2) 329
    JOSEPH A. GIBBONS, ROGER A. BULLARD, and FREDERIK WISSE

Apocalypse of Peter (VII, *3*) 339
    JAMES BRASHLER, ROGER A. BULLARD, and FREDERIK WISSE
The Teachings of Silvanus (VII, *4*) 346
    MALCOLM L. PEEL, JAN ZANDEE, and FREDERIK WISSE
The Three Steles of Seth (VII, *5*) 362
    JAMES M. ROBINSON and FREDERIK WISSE
Zostrianos (VIII, *1*) 368
    JOHN H. SIEBER
The Letter of Peter to Philip (VIII, *2*) 394
    FREDERIK WISSE
Melchizedek (IX, *1*) 399
    BIRGER A. PEARSON and SØREN GIVERSEN
The Thought of Norea (IX, *2*) 404
    BIRGER A. PEARSON and SØREN GIVERSEN
The Testimony of Truth (IX, *3*) 406
    BIRGER A. PEARSON and SØREN GIVERSEN
Marsanes (X, *1*) 417
    BIRGER A. PEARSON
The Interpretation of Knowledge (XI, *1*) 427
    ELAINE H. PAGELS and JOHN D. TURNER
A Valentinian Exposition (XI, *2*), with On the Anointing,
  On Baptism A and B, and On the Eucharist A and B 435
    ELAINE H. PAGELS and JOHN D. TURNER
Allogenes (XI, *3*) 443
    ANTOINETTE CLARK WIRE, JOHN D. TURNER, and
      ORVAL S. WINTERMUTE
Hypsiphrone (XI, *4*) 453
    JOHN D. TURNER
The Sentences of Sextus (XII, *1*) 454
    FREDERIK WISSE
Fragments (XII, *3*) 460
    FREDERIK WISSE
Trimorphic Protennoia (XIII, *1*) 461
    JOHN D. TURNER
The Gospel of Mary (BG 8502, *1*) 471
    GEORGE W. MACRAE, R. MCL. WILSON, and
      DOUGLAS M. PARROTT
The Act of Peter (BG 8502, *4*) 475
    JAMES BRASHLER and DOUGLAS M. PARROTT
Index of Proper Names 478

PREFACE

This volume has been a long time in coming. Since the Nag Hammadi library was discovered in December 1945 by Muḥammad ʿAlī al-Sammān Muhammad Khalīfah, the publication of the tractates has encountered a number of obstacles of a political and scholarly sort. As a result, though it has been some thirty-two years since their discovery, the Nag Hammadi tractates have not previously been available in their entirety in English translation—nor, for that matter, in any other modern language. Even the publication of *The Facsimile Edition of the Nag Hammadi Codices* is a task only now reaching completion. With the completion of the *Facsimile Edition* and the appearance of the present volume, the Nag Hammadi library is at last available to the reading public.

The Nag Hammadi Library in English is only one facet of the work of the Coptic Gnostic Library Project of the Institute for Antiquity and Christianity, Claremont Graduate School, Claremont, California. Since the Project began in 1966, the goals and projected publications of the Project have expanded considerably, so that at present three publishing ventures have been undertaken. In addition to the present one-volume edition, two series of volumes are in the process of being published. The first is the aforementioned *Facsimile Edition*, published (Leiden: E. J. Brill, 1972 ff.) under the auspices of the Department of Antiquities of the Arab Republic of Egypt, in conjunction with UNESCO. This set of twelve volumes contains photographic reproductions of the papyrus pages and leather covers, and is an invaluable tool for the scholarly study of the Nag Hammadi codices. The introductory volume, to be published last, will contain a history of the discovery and subsequent research, and a number of photographs of the persons, places, and artifacts connected with the Nag Hammadi library, as well as corrections and additions to the *Facsimile Edition*. The second series of volumes is *The Coptic Gnostic Library*, a set to number eleven volumes when complete. These volumes, published in the Nag Hammadi Studies series by E. J. Brill, will provide Coptic transcriptions, English translations, introductions, notes, and indices for all the tractates and the cartonnage in the Nag Hammadi library, and will include the Berlin Gnostic Codex 8502. To date one volume in this set has appeared: *The Gospel of the Egyptians* (*The Holy Book of the Great Invisible Spirit*) (Nag Hammadi Studies 4, 1975), edited by Alexander Böhlig and Frederik Wisse in cooperation with Pahor Labib. A second volume is in the press: *Nag Hammadi Codices V, 2-5 and VI with Codex Berolinensis 8502, 1 and 4*, edited by Douglas M. Parrott. Furthermore, two additional tasks are being undertaken by the members of the Coptic Gnostic Library Project: the archaeological investigation of the Jabal al-Ṭārif (the site of the discovery), the Pachomian monastery and basilica at Faw Qiblī, and nearby sites; and the establishment of a permanent Nag Hammadi Archive at the Institute for Antiquity and Christianity, so that the scholarly investigation of the Nag Hammadi tractates may be encouraged in the future.

The Nag Hammadi Library in English seeks to provide, within the scope of a single volume, English translations of the Nag Hammadi tractates. To these English translations have been added very brief introductions, so that the reader may become aware of the main features and issues to be noted within each tractate. In most cases the translations utilized are up-to-date drafts of the translations to be used in *The Coptic Gnostic Library*; similarly, the introductions are usually abbreviations of those to be used in that same set of volumes. Like *The Coptic Gnostic Library*, the present volume includes the tractates from BG 8502 (sometimes shortened to BG), since both the Gnostic character of the codex and the specific tractates within it parallel the Nag Hammadi library. The textual signs employed in the translations (see "Textual Signs") are designed to aid the reader by indicating such helpful information as line and page sequence, lacunas in the text, and the like. These signs, however, have been kept to a minimum, to facilitate ease of reading.

There are, of course, limitations within a volume of this sort. Restrictions in the space, time, and personnel which were available have prevented the inclusion of extensive indices and scriptural references. Only an index of proper names and an indication of a few scriptural quotations have proved feasible for this volume. In addition, since the edition is confined to a single volume, the use of all the texts of a tractate with parallel versions has been impossible. In such cases it has proved necessary to choose the version which would be more lucid and helpful to the reader. Hence, where possible, the longer and more complete versions have been utilized. Again, for reasons of brevity and readability, the lacunas usually have been handled in a rather standardized fashion. Such limitations as these may be remedied by referring to the more expansive volumes in *The Coptic Gnostic Library*.

There are a goodly number of contributors who have provided materials for this volume, and each of these individuals has brought a unique perspective to the contribution. Thus, although a degree of standardization has been possible within this volume, the reader should expect that the introductions and translations reflect the work of the individual contributors: variations in English style and translational policy should be anticipated.

For further discussion of the codices and tractates the reader is referred to the appropriate volumes in *The Coptic Gnostic Library*, where additional bibliography is given. A few works, however, may also be cited here. A comprehensive bibliography on Gnostic studies, with an emphasis upon the Nag Hammadi library, is provided by David M. Scholer, *Nag Hammadi Bibliography 1948-1969* (Nag Hammadi Studies 1; Leiden: E. J. Brill, 1971), updated annually in *Novum Testamentum*. An excellent introduction to Gnosticism is given by Hans Jonas, *The Gnostic Religion* (Boston: Beacon Press, 1958; second paperback edition, 1963). For a lively account of the discovery of the Nag Hammadi library, the developments within recent scholarship, and the major themes of the tractates, the general reader is referred to John Dart, *The Laughing Savior* (New York: Harper and Row, 1976). John Dart's book updates an earlier work describing the first phase of research about the discovery and the library: Jean Doresse, *The Secret Books of the Egyptian Gnostics* (New York: Viking Press, 1960). For a more detailed consideration of major segments of the history of scholarship and the remarkable circumstances surrounding the discovery of the Nag Hammadi library, the reader may consult the provocative article by James M. Robinson, "The Jung Codex: The Rise and Fall of a Monopoly," *Religious Studies Review* 3 (1977) 17-30.

Finally, it should be noted with appreciation that numerous people have contributed over the years to this volume. To those people who have assisted as team members, advisors, editors, and typists, we offer a hearty word of thanks. A special word of appreciation is extended to the officials of UNESCO, the Egyptian Antiquities Organization, and the American Research Center in Egypt who assisted in the work during the past several years. The National Endowment for the Humanities, the John Simon Guggenheim Memorial Foundation, the American Philosophical Society, the Smithsonian Institution, UNESCO, and Claremont Graduate School have made major grants in support of the work of the project. The devotion, generosity, and cooperation of many persons have made this edition possible, and to all we express our gratitude. It is our hope that this volume itself may contribute to mutual cooperation among those who read and study the documents within the Nag Hammadi library.

Marvin W. Meyer

TABLE OF TRACTATES IN
THE NAG HAMMADI LIBRARY

The table of tractates lists the following for the thirteen Nag Hammadi Codices and the Berlin Gnostic Codex 8502: the codex and tractate numbers; the tractate titles as used in this edition (the titles found in the tractates themselves, often simplified and standardized, or, when the tractate bears no surviving title, one supplied by the contributors); and the page and line numbers from the Coptic manuscripts.

I, 1	The Prayer of the Apostle Paul	A, 1-B, 10
	(+ colophon)	(+ B, 11-12)
I, 2	The Apocryphon of James	1, 1-16, 30
I, 3	The Gospel of Truth	16, 31-43, 24
I, 4	The Treatise on Resurrection	43, 25-50, 18
I, 5	The Tripartite Tractate	51, 1-138, 25
II, 1	The Apocryphon of John	1, 1-32, 9
II, 2	The Gospel of Thomas	32, 10-51, 28
II, 3	The Gospel of Philip	51, 29-86, 19
II, 4	The Hypostasis of the Archons	86, 20-97, 23
II, 5	On the Origin of the World	97, 24-127, 17
II, 6	The Exegesis on the Soul	127, 18-137, 27
II, 7	The Book of Thomas the Contender	138, 1-145, 19
	(+ colophon)	(+ 145, 20-23)
III, 1	The Apocryphon of John	1, 1-40, 11
III, 2	The Gospel of the Egyptians	40, 12-69, 20
III, 3	Eugnostos the Blessed	70, 1-90, 13
III, 4	The Sophia of Jesus Christ	90, 14-119, 18
III, 5	The Dialogue of the Savior	120, 1-147, 23
IV, 1	The Apocryphon of John	1, 1-49, 28
IV, 2	The Gospel of the Egyptians	50, 1-81, 2
		(+ missing end)
V, 1	Eugnostos the Blessed	1, 1-17, 18
V, 2	The Apocalypse of Paul	17, 19-24, 9
V, 3	The First Apocalypse of James	24, 10-44, 10
V, 4	The Second Apocalypse of James	44, 11-63, 32
V, 5	The Apocalypse of Adam	64, 1-85, 32

VI, 1	The Acts of Peter and the Twelve Apostles	1, 1-12, 22
VI, 2	The Thunder, Perfect Mind	13, 1-21, 32
VI, 3	Authoritative Teaching	22, 1-35, 24
VI, 4	The Concept of Our Great Power	36, 1-48, 15
VI, 5	Plato, Republic 588B-589B	48, 16-51, 23
VI, 6	The Discourse on the Eighth and Ninth	52, 1-63, 32
VI, 7	The Prayer of Thanksgiving (+ scribal note)	63, 33-65, 7 (+ 65, 8-14)
VI, 8	Asclepius 21-29	65, 15-78, 43
VII, 1	The Paraphrase of Shem	1, 1-49, 9
VII, 2	The Second Treatise of the Great Seth	49, 10-70, 12
VII, 3	Apocalypse of Peter	70, 13-84, 14
VII, 4	The Teachings of Silvanus (+ colophon)	84, 15-118, 7 (+ 118, 8-9)
VII, 5	The Three Steles of Seth (+ colophon)	118, 10-127, 27 (+ 127, 28-32)
VIII, 1	Zostrianos	1, 1-132, 9
VIII, 2	The Letter of Peter to Philip	132, 10-140, 27
IX, 1	Melchizedek	1, 1-27, 10
IX, 2	The Thought of Norea	27, 11-29, 5
IX, 3	The Testimony of Truth	29, 6-74, 30 (+ missing end)
X, 1	Marsanes	1, 1-68, 18
XI, 1	The Interpretation of Knowledge	1, 1-21, 35
XI, 2	A Valentinian Exposition	22, 1-39, 39
XI, 2a	On the Anointing	40, 1-29
XI, 2b	On Baptism A	40, 30-41, 38
XI, 2c	On Baptism B	42, 1-43, 19
XI, 2d	On the Eucharist A	43, 20-38
XI, 2e	On the Eucharist B	44, 1-37
XI, 3	Allogenes	45, 1-69, 20
XI, 4	Hypsiphrone	69, 21-72, 33 (+ missing end)
XII, 1	The Sentences of Sextus	15, 1-34, 28 (+ missing beginning and missing end)
XII, 2	The Gospel of Truth	53, 19-60, 30 (+ missing beginning and missing end)

XII, 3	*Fragments*	
XIII, 1	*Trimorphic Protennoia*	35, 1-50, 24
XIII, 2	*On the Origin of the World*	50, 25-34 (+ missing end)
BG 8502, 1	*The Gospel of Mary*	7, 1-19, 5 (+ missing beginning)
BG 8502, 2	*The Apocryphon of John*	19, 6-77, 7
BG 8502, 3	*The Sophia of Jesus Christ*	77, 8-127, 12
BG 8502, 4	*The Act of Peter*	128, 1-141, 7

TEXTUAL SIGNS

Small strokes above the line indicate line divisions. Every fifth line a small number is inserted in place of the stroke; the frequency of these numbers, however, may vary in tractates which are quite fragmentary. A new page is indicated with a number in bold type. When the beginning of a new line or page coincides with the opening of a paragraph, the line divider or number is placed at the end of the previous paragraph.

[ ] Square brackets indicate a lacuna in the manuscript. When the text cannot be reconstructed, three dots are placed within the brackets, regardless of the size of the lacuna; a fourth dot, if appropriate, may function as a period. An exception to this rule is the occasional use of a different number of dots to estimate the extent of the missing portion of a proper noun. In a few instances the dots are used without brackets to indicate a series of Coptic letters which do not constitute a translatable sense unit. A bracket is not allowed to divide a word, except for a hyphenated word or a proper noun. Other words are placed entirely inside or outside the brackets, depending on the certainty of the Coptic word and the number of Coptic letters visible.

⟨ ⟩ Pointed brackets indicate a correction of a scribal omission or error. The translator has either inserted letters unintentionally omitted by the scribe, or replaced letters erroneously inserted with what the scribe presumably intended to write.

{ } Braces indicate superfluous letters or words added by the scribe.

( ) Parentheses indicate material supplied by the editor or translator. Although this material may not directly reflect the text being translated, it provides useful information for the reader.

INTRODUCTION

by

JAMES M. ROBINSON

1. The Stance of the Texts

The Nag Hammadi library is a collection of religious texts that vary widely from each other as to when, where, and by whom they were written. Even the points of view diverge to such an extent that the texts are not to be thought of as coming from one group or movement. Yet these diversified materials must have had something in common which caused them to be chosen by those who collected them. The collectors no doubt contributed to this unity by finding in the texts hidden meanings not fully intended by the original authors. After all, one of them, the *Gospel of Thomas*, begins with a word to the wise: "Whoever finds the interpretation of these sayings will not experience death." Thus the texts can be read at two levels: what the original author may have intended to communicate and what the texts may subsequently have been taken to communicate.

The focus that brought the collection together is an estrangement from the mass of humanity, an affinity to an ideal order that completely transcends life as we know it, and a life-style radically other than common practice. This life-style involved giving up all the goods that people usually desire and longing for an ultimate liberation. It is not an aggressive revolution that is intended, but rather a withdrawal from involvement in the contamination that destroys clarity of vision.

As such, the focus of this library has much in common with primitive Christianity, with eastern religions, and with holy men of all times, as well as with the more secular equivalents of today, such as the counter-culture movements coming from the 1960's. Disinterest in the goods of a consumer society, withdrawal into communes of the like-minded away from the bustle and clutter of big-city distraction, non-involvement in the compromises of the political process, sharing an in-group's knowledge both of the disaster-course of the culture and of an ideal, radical alternative not commonly known—all this in modern garb is the real challenge rooted in such materials as the Nag Hammadi library.

To be sure, these roots, fascinating and provocative as they are, can also be confusing and even frustrating, not only for the person scarcely open to what they have to say, but also to the more attentive who seek to follow the light glimmering through the flow of language. For the point of the Nag Hammadi library has been battered and fragmented by the historical process through which it has finally come to light. A salvage operation is needed at many levels if that point is to be grasped clearly today. The ancient world's religious and philosophical traditions and mythology were all that was available to express what was in fact a quite untraditional stance. Yet the stance was too radical to establish itself within the organized religions or philosophical schools of the day, and hence was hardly able to take advantage of the culture's educational institutions to develop and clarify its implications. Gnostic schools began to emerge within Christianity and Neoplatonism, until both agreed in excluding them as the "heresy" of Gnosticism. Thus meaningful and eloquent myths and philosophic formulations of that radical stance became in their turn garbled traditions, reused by later and lesser authors whose watered-down, not to say muddied, version may be most of what has survived ... though there are several "classics" in the Nag Hammadi library.

The texts were translated one by one from Greek into Coptic, and not always by a translator capable of grasping the profundity or sublimity of what he had before him. The translator of a brief section of Plato's *Republic* clearly did not understand the philosophy before his eyes, though he did find something edifying and worth translating. Fortunately, most texts are better translated, but when there are duplications one can sense what a difference the better translation makes in comparison to the poorer translation—which leads one to wonder about the bulk of the texts that exist only in a single version. There is the same kind of hazard in the transmission of the texts by a series of scribes who copied them, generation after generation, from increasingly corrupt copies, first in Greek and then in Coptic. The number of unintentional errors is hard to estimate, since such a thing as a clean control copy does not exist; nor does one have, as in the case of the Bible, a quantity of manuscripts of the same text that tend to correct each other when compared. Only when the error can be detected as such in the copy we have can it be corrected. In addition there is the physical deterioration of the books themselves, which began no doubt before they were buried around 400 C.E., advanced steadily while they remained buried, and unfortunately was not completely halted in the period between their discovery in

1945 and their final conservation some thirty years later. When only a few letters are missing, they can often be filled in adequately, but larger holes must simply remain blank. The present translation also has its own limitations. Many of the texts have not been previously translated, much less fully analyzed and interpreted. They are here presented to the public at large precisely to facilitate that process, which should lead to improved understanding and ultimately improved translations.

The reader should not be misled by such impediments to understanding into thinking that the stance inherent in these essays is unworthy of serious consideration. Rather, we have to do here with an understanding of existence, an answer to the human dilemma, an attitude toward society, that is worthy of being taken quite seriously by anyone able and willing to grapple with such ultimate issues. This basic stance has until now been known almost exclusively through the myopic view of heresy-hunters, who often quote only to refute or ridicule. Thus the coming to light of the Nag Hammadi library gives unexpected access to the Gnostic stance as Gnostics themselves presented it. It provides new roots for the uprooted.

Those who collected this library were Christians, and many of the essays were originally composed by Christian authors. In a sense this should not be surprising, since primitive Christianity was itself a radical movement. Jesus called for a full reversal of values, announcing the end of the world as we have known it and its replacement by a quite new, utopian kind of life in which the ideal would be the real. He took a stand quite independent of the authorities of his day ... and did not last very long before they eliminated him. Through a remarkable experience of his vindication, his followers reaffirmed his stand—for them he came to personify the ultimate goal. Yet some of his circle, being a bit more practical, followed a more conventional way of life. The circle gradually became an established organization with a quite natural concern to maintain order, continuity, lines of authority, and stability. But this concern could encourage a commitment to the status quo, rivalling, and at times outweighing, the commitment to the ultimate goal far beyond any and every attained achievement. Those who cherished the radical dream, the ultimate hope, would tend to throw it up as an invidious comparison to what was achieved, and thus seem to be disloyal, and to pose a serious threat to the organization.

As the cultural situation changed with the passage of time and the shift of environments, the language for expressing such radical transcendence itself underwent change. The world of thought from which

Jesus and his first followers had come was the popular piety of the Jewish synagogue, focussed in terms of John the Baptist's apocalyptic rite of transition from the old regime to the new ideal world whose dramatic arrival was forthcoming. In this way of thinking, the evil system that prevails is not the way things inherently are. In principle, though not in practice, the world is good. The evil that pervades history is a blight, ultimately alien to the world as such. But increasingly for some the outlook on life darkened; the very origin of the world was attributed to a terrible fault, and evil was given status as the ultimate ruler of the world, not just a usurpation of authority. Hence the only hope seemed to reside in escape. For humans, or at least some humans, are at heart not the product of such an absurd system, but by their very nature belong to the ultimate. Their plight is that they have been duped and lured into the trap of trying to be content in the impossible world, alienated from their true home. And for some a mystical inwardness undistracted by external factors came to be the only way to attain the repose, the overview, the merger into the All which is the destiny of one's spark of the divine.

Christian Gnosticism emerged as a reaffirmation, though in somewhat different terms, of the original stance of transcendence central to the very beginnings of Christianity. Such Gnostic Christians surely considered themselves the faithful continuation, under changing circumstances, of that original stance which made Christians Christians. But the "somewhat different terms" and "under changing circumstances" also involved real divergences, and other Christians surely considered Gnosticism a betrayal of the original Christian position. This was the conviction not just of those who had accommodated themselves to the status quo, but no doubt also of some who retained the full force of the original protest and ultimate hope. But as Christianity became organized and normalized, this divergence between the new radicals and those who retained the more traditional Christian language became intolerable.

Gnostics came to be excluded from the Church as heretics. In the New Testament two such Gnostic Christians are repudiated at the beginning of the second century (2 Timothy 2:16-18):

> Avoid empty and worldly chatter; those who indulge in it will stray further and further into godless courses, and the infection of their teaching will spread like a gangrene. Such are Hymenaeus and Philetus; they have shot wide of the truth in saying that our resurrection has already taken place, and are upsetting people's faith.

This view, that the Christian's resurrection has already taken place as a spiritual reality, is advocated in the *Treatise on Resurrection*, the *Exegesis on the Soul*, and the *Gospel of Philip* in the Nag Hammadi library!

But the Nag Hammadi library also documents the fact that the rejection was mutual, in that Christians described as "heretical" seem to be more like what is usually thought of as "orthodox." The *Apocalypse of Peter* has Christ criticize the orthodox as follows:

> They will cleave to the name of a dead man, thinking that they will become pure. But they will become greatly defiled and they will fall into a name of error and into the hand of an evil, cunning man and a manifold dogma, and they will be ruled heretically. For some of them will blaspheme the truth and proclaim evil teaching. And they will say evil things against each other. . . . But many others, who oppose the truth and are the messengers of error, will set up their error and their law against these pure thoughts of mine, as looking out from one (perspective), thinking that good and evil are from one (source). They do business in my word. . . . And there shall be others of those who are outside our number who name themselves bishop and also deacons, as if they have received their authority from God. They bend themselves under the judgment of the leaders. These people are dry canals.

With the conversion of the Roman Empire to Christianity of the more conventional kind, the survival chances of Gnostic Christianity, such as that reflected in the Nag Hammadi library, were sharply reduced. The Bishop of Cyprus, Epiphanius, whose main work was a "Medicine Chest" against all heresies, describes his encounter with Gnosticism in Egypt about the same time the Nag Hammadi library was being collected:

> I have had a brush with this sect myself, beloved, and got my information about its customs in person, straight from the mouths of its members. Women who believed this nonsense offered it to me, and told me the kind of thing I have been describing. In their brazen impudence, what is more, they tried to seduce me, like that vicious, wicked Egyptian woman who was married to the chief cook—I was young, and this made me attractive to them. . . . For the women who told me about this salacious myth were outwardly very charming, but all the devil's ugliness was in their vile minds. However, the merciful God saved me from their depravity. Then, while I was at it, I read their books, understood what they really intended, and was not entrapped as they had been; their literature left me unmoved. And I promptly reported these people to the local bishops, and found which of them were masquerading as members of the church. And so they were driven out of the city, about eighty of them, and it was cleansed of their rank, thorny growth.

Gnosticism was ultimately eradicated from Christendom, except for occasional underground movements, affinities in medieval mysticism, and an occasional tamed echo that stays just within the limits of propriety, for example within English romanticism:

> Our birth is but a sleep and a forgetting:
> The Soul that rises with us, our life's Star,
>   Hath had elsewhere its setting
>   And Cometh from afar.
>   . . .
> The world is too much with us; late and soon,
> Getting and spending, we lay waste our powers.

Gnosticism of sorts was also able to continue beyond the frontiers of the Roman-Empire-become-Christendom. It is still extant in the form of a small sect of peasants in Iraq called Mandaeans, which is their word for "Knowers," that is to say "Gnostics."

This same withdrawal to inwardness or despair of the world from which the Gnostic stance emerged swept not only through early Christianity to produce Christian Gnosticism, but also through late antiquity in general, thus producing forms of Gnosticism outside of Christianity. There is a long-standing debate among historians of religion as to whether Gnosticism is to be understood as only an inner-Christian development or as a movement broader than, and hence independent of, and perhaps even prior to Christianity. This debate seems to be resolving itself, on the basis of the Nag Hammadi library, in favor of understanding Gnosticism as a much broader phenomenon than early Christian heresy-hunters would lead one to think.

Some of the Gnostic essays do not seem to reflect Christian tradition, but do build upon the Old Testament, which was of course also the Jewish Bible. In this sense one often hears reference to Jewish Gnosticism. Such a concept is often rejected as a contradiction in terms. How could Jews designate their God as the malevolent force whose misguided blunder produced the world, a God who was ignorant of the hidden good God beyond? Since Christians worship the same God as do Jews, this argument could also be made against the very idea of Christian Gnosticism. But since early Christian heresy-hunters clearly identified Gnostics as Christians, though of course heretical Christians, the concept of Christian Gnosticism is firmly established. To use another analogy, Simon Magus, one of the earliest known Gnostics, was from Samaria, although the Samaritans worshipped in their own way the same God as did the Jews and Christians. Hence by analogy the concept of Jewish

Gnostics is intelligible, even if, from a given normative point of view, the validity of using the word Jewish, Christian, or Samaritan for such a person or text may be contested.

The discovery of the Dead Sea Scrolls has already drawn attention to the fact that first century Judaism was quite pluralistic in its theological positions, and contained a number of divergent sects. The Essenes, prior to the discovery of the Dead Sea Scrolls, were in a situation much like the Gnostics prior to the discovery of the Nag Hammadi library; they too were a movement about which too little was known to be treated with the seriousness it deserved. Now we know that the Essenes were a Jewish sect that had broken with the official Judaism of the Jerusalem temple and had withdrawn to the desert at the Wadi Qumran. They understood their situation in terms of the antithesis of light and darkness, truth and the lie, a dualism that ultimately went back to Persian dualism—and then moved forward toward Gnosticism. The latest of the Dead Sea Scrolls meet in time and space one of the earliest of the Nag Hammadi texts, the *Apocalypse of Adam*, in which Gnosticism is transmitted to Seth by Adam on his deathbed as his last will and testament. Thus the history of Gnosticism, as documented in the Nag Hammadi library, takes up about where the history of the Essenes, as documented by the Dead Sea Scrolls, breaks off. Later Jewish mystical traditions, traced especially by Gershom Scholem, have shown that, inconsistent though it seems, Gnostic trends have continued to carry on a clandestine existence within the context of normative Judaism.

It may be that there is a vestige of historical truth to the view of Christian heresy-hunters that some Christian heresies go back to Jewish sects. After all, Christianity itself grew up within Judaism, and it would be surprising if it did not reflect various strands of the Judaism of the day. Primitive Christianity itself first became a Jewish sect, until it became largely Gentile and, after the fall of Jerusalem, was excluded. For Judaism was first standardized in response to the threat to Jewish identity posed by the destruction of Jerusalem in 70 C.E. In the process a repudiation of heretics was added to the prayers used in the synagogue, to make sure such sectarians would not attend.

It is not inconceivable that such a Christian Gnostic movement as the Sethians may simply be a Christian outgrowth of a Jewish Gnostic group. One text in the Nag Hammadi library, the *Paraphrase of Shem*, represents a Gnostic viewpoint, but without clear Christian traditions. Hippolytus, a Christian heresy-hunter, cites a "Paraphrase of Seth" that is very similar except that it is now clearly Christian. The *Apocalypse of*

Adam is clearly a Sethian text. Although this mythological adaptation of the book of Genesis includes a Gnostic Savior, the presentation does not seem to be based on the tradition of Jesus—indeed the nearest parallel in the New Testament is the very mythological childbirth in Revelation 12, which itself seems less dependent on the story of Mary and Jesus than upon some such previously unknown mythological tradition. Yet this Jewish Gnostic *Apocalypse of Adam* stands in the same tradition as another Nag Hammadi text, the *Gospel of the Egyptians*, which clearly is Christian. A Sethian liturgical text in the Nag Hammadi library entitled the *Three Steles of Seth* presents a kind of Neoplatonic Gnosticism, without a clearly Christian overlay on the Jewish point of departure. Yet it gives a prominent place to the feminine deity Barbelo, familiar in Christian Gnosticism.

There are other texts in the Nag Hammadi library that seem more philosophic and Neoplatonic in orientation than Christian or Jewish, although such religious roots and interpolations do appear at times. Plotinus, the leading Neoplatonist of the third century C.E., does in fact refer to Gnostics within his school:

> We feel a certain regard for some of our friends who happened upon this way of thinking before they became our friends, and, though I do not know how they manage it, continue in it.

But the school turned against Gnosticism, as Plotinus' polemics indicate. His pupil Porphyry reports in his *Life of Plotinus*:

> There were in his time many Christians and others, and sectarians who had abandoned the old philosophy, men . . . who . . . produced revelations by Zoroaster and Zostrianos and Nicotheus and Allogenes and Messos and other people of the kind, themselves deceived and deceiving many, alleging that Plato had not penetrated to the depths of intelligible reality. Plotinus hence often attacked their position in his lectures, and wrote the treatise to which we have given the title "Against the Gnostics"; he left it to us to assess what he passed over. Amelius went to forty volumes in writing against the book of Zostrianos.

The Nag Hammadi library contains treatises entitled *Zostrianos* and *Allogenes*, which may well be those refuted by Amelius and other Neoplatonists. And such Nag Hammadi texts as the *Trimorphic Protennoia* and *Marsanes* are quite similar in philosophic orientation. Plotinus' own attack on Gnostic "magic chants" addressed to the "higher powers" may have in view hymnic texts like the *Three Steles of Seth*. Thus the Nag Hammadi library makes an important contribution not only to the history of religion, but also to the history of philosophy.

The Nag Hammadi library also includes material drawing upon other religious traditions than the Judeo-Christian heritage. There are, for example, Hermetic texts that build on Egyptian lore. Typically they present dialogues of initiation between the deities Hermes Trismegistus and his son Tat. One such *Discourse on the Eighth and Ninth* in the Nag Hammadi library is a previously unknown Hermetic text. And, whereas one could debate whether a good number of the texts in the library are actually Gnostic or not, depending on how one defines Gnosticism and interprets the texts, a few, such as the *Sentences of Sextus*, clearly are not Gnostic. But, just as a Gnostic interpretation of the Bible became possible, one may assume that these moralistic maxims could also be fitted into a Gnostic orientation.

Since the Nag Hammadi library seems to have been collected in terms of Christian Gnosticism, it is sometimes difficult to conceive of some of the texts, such as the Hermetic ones, being used by persons who thought of themselves as Christian. One text even claims a Zoroastrian heritage, in that it is ascribed to his grandfather (or, possibly, uncle) Zostrianos and in a cryptogram even mentions Zoroaster. Yet Gnostics were more ecumenical and syncretistic with regard to religious traditions than were orthodox Christians, so long as they found in them a stance congenial to their own. If they could identify Seth with Jesus, they probably could produce Christianizing interpretations of Hermes and Zoroaster as well. In another instance, it is possible to observe the Christianizing process taking place almost before one's eyes in the Nag Hammadi library itself. The non-Christian philosophic treatise *Eugnostos the Blessed* is cut up somewhat arbitrarily into separate speeches, which are then put on Jesus' tongue, in answer to questions the disciples address to him during a resurrection appearance—and both forms of the text occur side by side in Codex III. In other cases the text, as it stands in the Nag Hammadi library, has an occasional but unmistakable Christian reference which, however, seems so external to the main thrust of the text that one may be inclined to think it was added by a Christian editor, translator, or scribe to what had been originally composed as a non-Christian text. This has been thought to be the case, for example, with the *Apocryphon of John*, the *Hypostasis of the Archons*, and the *Trimorphic Protennoia*. It must be part of this Christianizing trend when "the Holy Book of the Great Invisible Spirit" is also given by some scribe the title *Gospel of the Egyptians.*

Thus Gnosticism seems not to have been in its essence just an alternate form of Christianity. Rather it was a radical trend of release from the dominion of evil or of inner transcendence that swept through late antiquity and emerged within Christianity, Judaism, Neoplatonism, the mystery religions, and the like. As a new religion it was syncretistic, drawing upon various religious heritages. But it was held together by a very decided stance, which is where the unity amid the wide diversity is to be sought.

It is no doubt this stance, rather than the myths and doctrines of the texts themselves, that explains the association of the Nag Hammadi library with Christian monasticism, where the withdrawal from the world into a commune in which utopia could be anticipated was strikingly similar to the Gnostic way of life. It may be no coincidence that the Nag Hammadi library was discovered in sight of the Basilica of Saint Pachomius, the founder of Christian monasticism. Indeed the copies of the texts that survived seem to have been produced in a Pachomian monastery. The following section will sketch what is currently known about these copies themselves. The Nag Hammadi library is not only of inestimable importance for the content of the many lost Greek works it has preserved in Coptic translation. It also sheds significant light upon the production of the books themselves and hence upon those who copied and buried them.

2. The Manuscripts

The Nag Hammadi library consists of twelve books, plus eight leaves removed from a thirteenth book in late antiquity and tucked inside the front cover of the sixth. These eight leaves comprise a complete text, an independent treatise taken out of a book of collected works. In fact, each of the books, except the tenth, consists of a collection of relatively brief works. Thus there is a total of fifty-two tractates. Since a single book usually contains several tractates, one may suspect that, like the books of the Bible, the texts were composed with a small format in mind, but that a larger format had come into use by the time these extant copies were made. This can be explained in terms of the history of the manufacture of books.

The roll was the usual form of a book up until the first centuries C.E., when it began to be replaced by a more economical format that permitted writing on both sides, namely the modern book with individual leaves. Technically speaking, a book in the form of a roll is a "scroll" or "volume" (from the Latin verb meaning "to roll"). But a book in the form of a modern book is a "codex" (plural: "codices"), the Latin word for a set of wooden waxed tablets tied together as a scratch pad, which was the ancestor of the book with papyrus, parchment, or paper leaves. Whereas literary works continued to be written in the more prestigious form of the scroll, Christians (but not Jews) soon came to prefer the more economical codex. The codex was also more practical than the scroll, as anyone who has worked with microfilm knows. The inconvenience and wear-and-tear of unrolling and then rerolling the scroll every time one wanted to resume reading or look up a reference led to the replacement of the scroll with the codex, just as today there is a trend away from microfilm and toward microfiche.

In Egypt the most common writing material was papyrus. The triangular stalk of the papyrus plant is filled with a fibrous pith that can be cut or peeled off in long thin strips. These strips are laid side by side and then a second layer is placed at right angles on top. When this is pressed, dried, and polished it becomes a flexible, smooth, and durable writing surface. Whereas these papyrus sheets were usually about twenty centimeters long, those used in the Nag Hammadi library were often over a meter in length. Since this was a technological feat for that time, it indicates the importance of the books for those who made them. A series of such papyrus writing surfaces was placed side by side so as to overlap a couple of centimeters where they were pasted together. The result was the papyrus roll, often about three meters long. Sheets ranging in breadth from twenty to forty centimeters would be cut from such rolls, from the right end of the roll to the left. A stack of from twenty to forty sheets, when folded down the middle, formed the quire of a codex. Since each strip of papyrus has a fiber pattern as distinctive as a fingerprint, the more fragmentary books in the Nag Hammadi library were reassembled by locating the fiber position of a fragment or a leaf on the original papyrus sheet that had been made from the papyrus strips. Then its position within the roll and ultimately within the codex could be calculated. The fact that from two to six rolls were used to manufacture a single codex helps to explain the fact that a codex could contain more than one text which had originally been composed with the size of the roll in view.

The Coptic Museum in Cairo, where the Nag Hammadi library is kept, has assigned a number to each book. At the time this was done, the numeration was thought to be the order in which they would be published, which in turn reflected a value judgment in terms of their importance and state of preservation. Only the very fragmentary fourth book is an exception to this tendency—it was given its position because the two tractates it contains are duplicates of tractates in the third book. For convenience of reference the tractates are numbered consecutively in each book. Although the numeration systems used for the books, tractates, and even pages have varied widely over the past generation, the numeration used here is that of the official facsimile edition and hence should supersede older numerations.

Of the fifty-two tractates, six that are duplicates (III, *1*, IV, *1* and *2*, V, *1*, XII, *2*, and XIII, *2*) are not included in the present work since there is a better copy that is included. Six more were already extant when the Nag Hammadi library was discovered, either in the original Greek (VI, *5* and *7*, and XII, *1*), or in translation, in Latin (VI, *8*) or Coptic (II, *1* and III, *4*). The two in Coptic are from a papyrus codex, now in Berlin, called BG 8502, which to this extent is a codex similar to the Nag Hammadi library. For this reason the other two tractates it contains are included at the end of the present work. To get an impression of the amount of literature that has survived only in the Nag Hammadi library, one may subtract the total of twelve duplications and thus reach the figure of forty newly-recovered texts. To be sure, a few fragments existed of three of these, one in Greek (II, *2*) and two in Coptic (II, *5* and VII, *4*), but they had not been identified as such until the complete text became available in the Nag Hammadi library. Now that the whole library is accessible, fragments of still others may be identified. But such vestiges of a tractate are more tantalizing than useful. Hence a more serious limitation on the figure of forty new texts is the fact that some of these are themselves quite fragmentary (VIII, *1*, IX, *1*, *2*, and *3*, X, *1*, XI, *1*, *2*, *3*, and *4*, and XII, *3*). It would be safe to think of the Nag Hammadi library as adding to the amount of literature that has survived from antiquity thirty more-or-less complete texts, and ten that are rather fragmentary.

Although the Nag Hammadi library is in Coptic, the texts were originally composed in Greek. Hence the fact that they were discovered in Upper Egypt may be misleading. Some may of course have been composed in Egypt, for several contain specific allusions to Egypt: *Asclepius* calls Egypt the "image of heaven"; *On the Origin of the World* appeals to "the crocodiles in Egypt" and "the two bulls in Egypt" as witnesses; and the *Discourse on the Eighth and Ninth* instructs the son to "write this book for the temple at Diospolis (Magna near Luxor or Parva near Nag Hammadi) in hieroglyphic characters." Yet the Greek-writing authors may have been located anywhere in the ancient world where Greek was used, such as Greece itself (VI, *5*), or Syria (II, *2*), or Jordan (V, *5*). Much the same is the case with the Bible and other ancient texts written in various parts of the ancient world and preserved in the "dry sands of Egypt." Thus the Nag Hammadi library involves the collecting of what was originally a Greek literary production by largely unrelated and anonymous authors spread through the Eastern half of the ancient world and covering a period of almost half a millennium (or more, if one takes into consideration a brief section of Plato's *Republic*, VI, 5).

Almost nothing is known about the different persons who translated the tractates into Coptic, or those who commissioned and copied the extant copies, or those who buried them, other than what may be inferred from the books themselves. The Egyptian reading public in this period was largely familiar with Greek, and hence Greek literature was imported and copied extensively. A Roman garrison town, Diospolis Parva, with Greek-speaking Galatian troops from Asia Minor, was just across the Nile from the site where the Nag Hammadi library was buried. A Greek inscription reading "In behalf of the [good] fortune of Emperor [Caesar] Trajan Hadrian [Augustus]" has been found at Chenoboskeia, on the right bank of the Nile in sight of the place of the burial. Greek prayers to Zeus Sarapis mentioning Antioch are found in two caves in the cliff near where the books were buried. But, more and more, Greek texts such as the Bible and the Nag Hammadi library were translated into the native Egyptian language. The *Life of Saint Pachomius*, which itself exists in both Greek and Coptic, tells that a Greek-speaking monk from Alexandria came to Pachomius, who "made him live in the same dwelling with an old brother who knew the Greek language," while he learned the native tongue. Meanwhile Pachomius "made every effort to learn Greek by the grace of God in order to discover the way of offering him solace frequently. Then Pachomius appointed him house manager of the Alexandrian and other foreign brothers who came after him."

When the Egyptian language is written with the Greek alphabet (plus a few letters for sounds Greeks did not make), it is called Coptic. The Nag Hammadi library is written in two Coptic dialects. Even among the texts translated into the same dialect, minor divergences point to a plurality of translators, who do not correspond to the plurality of scribes responsible for the surviving copies. In the case of duplicates, different translators were involved, working from divergent Greek texts. The translation process may have been spread over a wide area of Egypt, and several centuries.

Each codex was bound in leather. The outline of the desired book size was often scored onto the leather, whereupon the flesh side of the outlined area was lined with used papyrus pasted into thick cardboards called cartonnage, producing a hardback effect. This used papyrus consisted of Greek and Coptic letters and business documents, and has produced names of persons and places as well as dates that help to determine the time and place of the manufacture of the covers. After a cover was thus lined with cartonnage, a strip of the cover was turned in at the head and foot of the front and back cover and at the fore edge of the back cover. Since the line of the animal's spine usually ran horizontally across the cover, the narrowing of the skin leading to the animal's tail could be retained to form a flap extending from the fore edge of the front cover. To this was added a thong to encircle horizontally the closed book. This may have been a practice taken over from the manufacture of a papyrus scroll, where a parchment wrapper and thong were traditionally used to protect it and hold it closed. A thong was also needed to hold a codex closed. For each of the Nag Hammadi books has a single quire, that is to say, a single stack of sheets folded down the center to produce the writing surfaces, although in Codex I the main quire is supplemented with two smaller quires. Such large quires would tend to gape at the fore edge unless securely tied. Shorter thongs extending from the head and foot of the front and back covers were tied together to aid in holding the codex closed.

Two of the covers (IV and VIII) lack a flap on the fore edge of the front cover, though they do have the usual thong. A third cover of a similar construction (V) has such a flap added to the fore edge of the front cover. These three books thus seem to have been made from smaller skins, and the poor quality of the papyrus used for their quires confirms the impression of economy. Others of the covers include a leather reinforcement (called by book-binders a mull) that lines the spine and protects the cover and the quire from the pressure of the binding thongs that run through the cover at the spine and through the fold at the center of the quire, as well as two horizontal supportive thongs lying between the cover and the mull. Three covers have such a construction (VI, IX, and X). They form a second group among the covers, together with another similarly-constructed cover (II), which however is now lacking whatever lining it may have had. This group is characterized both by such advances in technique as have been discussed above and by a higher aesthetic quality. Indeed, the cover of Codex II has rather beautiful tinted tooling. The four other covers do not share distinctive traits except for a certain primitiveness that would make it possible to assign them to a group.

The handwriting of the scribes is quite similar in a number of cases, and there seem to be few clear instances of a single scribe working on more than one codex. One scribe copied most of Codex I, but a second scribe copied tractate *4* of Codex I; this second scribe also copied tractates *1* and *2* of Codex XI. A third scribe copied in a different dialect tractates *3* and *4* of Codex XI and also Codex VII. Thus three of the books that seem unrelated to each other in terms of the way the covers were made do seem interrelated in terms of the scribes who wrote them.

The two groups of covers plus four miscellaneous covers, and the one group of scribal hands plus miscellaneous scribes, may indicate that the Nag Hammadi library is a secondary merging of what was originally a series of smaller libraries or isolated books. This would seem to be confirmed by the distribution of the duplicates. No one codex contains two copies of the same work, nor did any one scribe copy the same work twice, nor is there a duplicate tractate among the books of one group of covers. There seems to have been an awareness of the wastefulness of such duplication. A scribal note in Codex VI expresses concern not to displease whoever commissioned the work by duplicating something already owned. When duplication does turn up in terms of the whole library, one is inclined to think the books were not produced with the whole library in view. Both of the tractates in Codex IV are also in Codex III, so that Codex IV is wholly superfluous in the present library. And there are a total of three copies of the Apocryphon of John (II, *1*, III, *1*, and IV, *1*). Thus one may conjecture that the present library derives from at least three smaller collections.

The dating of Coptic literary hands such as those who inscribed the texts in the quires is much less certain than is the dating of Greek literary hands, or the dating of the cursive business hands of the day. A thorough study of the hands in the Nag Hammadi library has not yet been made, although dates ranging at least from the beginning to the end of the fourth century C.E. have been proposed. The texts themselves do not normally contain dates or datable historical references. But the *Concept of our Great Power* may provide one reference that can serve as a point of departure for dating Codex VI:

> Cease from the evil lusts and desires and (the teachings of) the Anomoeans, evil heresies that have no basis!

While the Archbishop of Alexandria, Athanasius, was in hiding in the Pachomian monasteries around 360 C.E., "Anomoean" heretics were flourishing for a brief period in Alexandria. Probably this text received its final form no earlier than at this time.

The papyrus used for letters and business documents and reused to thicken the leather covers may be located in time and space with more ease than can the quires themselves. Dates found in such cartonnage of Codex VII are 333, 341, 346, and 348 C.E. This indicates that the cover of Codex VII was manufactured after these dates. The cursive scribal hand of some of this discarded papyrus used to line the cover of the same codex may be dated as late as 360 C.E. A document fou.'d in the cartonnage of Codex I mentions "Chenobos[keia]" and "Dio. [polis Parva]." Other locations in the same general region also occur in the cartonnage of other covers. Personal names, titles, forms of address, and the like that are present in the cartonnage tend to indicate it came from the Pachomian monasteries founded in this region up and down the Nile during the first half of the fourth century. In fact the cartonnage in the cover of Codex VII seems to have belonged to a monk named Sansnos who was in charge of the cattle of a monastery, which would no doubt account for his close relationship to the manufacture of the leather covers. The headquarters monastery of the Pachomian order at Pabau, where the Basilica of Saint Pachomius was located, as well as the third Pachomian monastery at Chenoboskeia, where Pachomius himself began his Christian life as a hermit, are only 8.7 and 5.3 kilometers (5.4 and 3.3 miles) respectively from the place where the library was buried.

In view of the orthodoxy of the Pachomian monasteries reflected in the *Life of Saint Pachomius* and other monastic legends, some have hesitated to associate the Nag Hammadi library with these monasteries, unless it be that such texts were copied for ready reference in refuting heresy. But such a defender of orthodoxy would not bother to collect the non-Christian texts in the Nag Hammadi library. And some of the Christian texts are not explicitly "heretical" and hence would hardly have been included in such a blacklist. Nor would duplicates have been needed. The very fact that the library seems to have been made up by combining several smaller collections tends to point toward individual Christian Gnostics or monasteries producing the individual books or small collections for their own spiritual enlightenment, rather than to a heresy-hunting campaign. Since the familiar heresy-hunting literature is in Greek, one should hesitate to postulate such a widespread heresy-hunting activity in Coptic.

Of course it is conceivable that book manufacture could have been one of the handicrafts common in monasteries to produce commodities to trade or sell for the necessities of life. Hence one could conjecture that uninscribed books were produced in the monastery and were sold to

Gnostics (or anyone else) to inscribe as they saw fit. But there is some evidence from that period that books were first inscribed and then bound, as when a line of writing passes through the fold at the spine. And in the Nag Hammadi library blotting is usually present on the first and last pages but not elsewhere, which may perhaps be explained as due to the dampness of the paste in the cartonnage at the time of binding, in which case the quire would have to have been inscribed before being bound.

The care and religious devotion reflected in the manufacture of the Nag Hammadi library hardly suggest that the books were produced out of antagonism or even disinterest in their contents, but rather reflect the veneration accorded to holy texts. The leather covers are not very ornate, compared, for example, with the Manichaean books of a century later, that are thought to have been studded with jewels. But this simplicity would be appropriate to the Pachomian monasteries. The *Life of Saint Pachomius* reports:

> He also taught the brothers to pay no attention to the loveliness and beauty of this world, whether it be beautiful food or clothing, or a cell, or an outwardly seductive book.

The simple tooling of some of the leather covers does include crosses (II, IV, and VIII). The ankh hieroglyph of life that became the Christian cross ansata is on the beautifully-tooled cover of Codex II and at the end of the *Prayer of the Apostle Paul*. The acrostic "fish" symbol standing for the creed "Jesus Christ, Son of God, Savior" occurs in two scribal notes (in Codices III and VII). In the first case the name of the scribe is preserved in the comment "in the flesh my name is Gongessos," which is probably the Latin name Concessus. He also had a spiritual name or title of Eugnostos. Thus he had some spiritual status, and referred to his "fellow lights in incorruptibility." Within this spiritual circle he described the text as "God-written." Even if such a scribal note was not composed by the scribe who copied the codex that has survived, but rather came from an earlier scribe who wrote an ancestor of the copy that survived, nevertheless the scribe of Codex III did not feel called upon to eliminate it, much less to replace it with a warning against heresy in the text. Some scribal notes, however, since they were written at the end of an extant codex, may be assumed to have been composed by the scribe of that particular codex. They reflect the godliness he found in what he was copying. Codex II concludes with this note:

> Remember me also, my brethren, [in] your prayers: Peace to the Saints and the Spiritual.

Codex VII ends on a similar note:

> This book belongs to the fatherhood. It is the son who wrote it. Bless me, O father. I bless you, O father, in peace. Amen.

The term fatherhood may refer to the leadership of a monastery. In any case, these scribal notes, together with the scribes' care to correct errors and even add small explanatory glosses and reading aids, tend to indicate that the scribes were of a religious persuasion congenial to the contents they were copying.

Perhaps the common presentation of the monastic movement of the fourth century C.E. as solidly orthodox is an anachronism, and more nearly reflects the situation of the later monasticism that recorded the legends about the earlier period. When a hermit withdrew from civilization into the desert he also tended to be out of contact with the Church, for example with its fellowship, sacraments, and authority. Early in the fourth century there was a monk in the Delta named Hierakas, a scribe by trade and a learned interpreter of the Bible, who was so ascetic in his views as to argue that marriage was limited to the old covenant, for no married person "can inherit the kingdom of heaven." Although this led to him being classified as a heretic, it did not prevent him from having a following. The *Testimony of Truth* in the Nag Hammadi library represents a similar view:

> For no one who is under the Law will be able to look up to the truth, for they will not be able to serve two masters. For the defilement of the Law is manifest; but undefilement belongs to the light. The Law commands (one) to take a husband (or) to take a wife, and to beget, to multiply like the sand of the sea. But passion which is a delight to them constrains the souls of those who are begotten in this place, those who defile and those who are defiled, in order that the Law might be fulfilled through them. And they show that they are assisting the world; and they [turn] away from the light, who are unable [to pass by] the archon of [darkness] until they pay the last [penny].

The *Life of Saint Pachomius* narrates that a "philosopher" from Panopolis (Akhmim), where Pachomius built a monastery just 108 kilometers (67 miles) downstream from where the Nag Hammadi library was buried, came to test the monks' "understanding of the scriptures." Pachomius sent his assistant Theodore to meet him:

> The philosopher queried him on something for which the answer was not difficult to find, "Who was not born but died? Who was born but did not die? And who died without giving off the stench of decomposition?" Theodore replied that Adam was not born but died, Enoch was born but

did not die, and Lot's wife died but, having become a pillar of salt, did not give off the stench of decomposition. The philosopher accepted these answers and departed.

This may well be a faint echo of Pachomian debates with Christian Gnostics before the middle of the fourth century C.E. Epiphanius' efforts to run Christian Gnostics out of town took place in Egypt about the same time.

In 367 C.E. Archbishop Athanasius wrote an Easter letter that condemns heretics and their "apocryphal books to which they attribute antiquity and give the name of saints." Theodore, by then head of the Pachomian monasteries, had the letter translated into Coptic, and "deposited it in the monastery to serve them as a rule." There must still have been Gnostics or Gnostic books influencing the Pachomian monastic movement which made this act necessary. Of course many of the Nag Hammadi texts are indeed pseudonymous, that is to say, ascribed in their titles to some "saint" of the past. In another of the Pachomian legends one of "these books that the heretics write" but "give out under the name of saints" is quoted:

> After Eve was deceived and had eaten the fruit of the tree, it is of the devil that she bore Cain.

The *Hypostasis of the Archons* in the Nag Hammadi library has a narrative that points in this direction:

> Then the Authorities came to their Adam. And when they saw his female counterpart speaking with him, they became agitated with great agitation; and they became enamored of her. They said to one another, "Come, let us sow our seed in her," and they pursued her. And she laughed at them for their witlessness and their blindness; and in their clutches, she became a tree, and left them her shadowy reflection resembling herself; and they defiled [it] foully.—And they defiled the form that she had stamped in her likeness, so that by the form they had modelled, together with [their] (own) image, they made themselves liable to condemnation.

Early in the fifth century C.E. Shenoute, Abbot of the White Monastery at the same Panopolis where Pachomius had founded monasteries and from which the "philosopher" had come, attacked a group at the nearby temple of Pneueit that called itself "kingless," worshipped the "demiurge," and would not accept Cyril, Archbishop of Alexandria, as their "illuminator." These terms, which Shenoute seems to borrow from the group, are so well-known in the Nag Hammadi library that it may have been a Christian Gnostic, perhaps a Sethian group, even though in his polemic Shenoute calls them pagan heretics. He seized their "books full of abomination" and "of every kind of magic." Series of vowels and unintelligible magic words—Plotinus called it "hissing"—occur in the Nag Hammadi library itself—and Pachomius too wrote to the heads of his monasteries using a code that even his successors could not decipher! Hence the Nag Hammadi library and Pachomius' "books of spiritual letters" may not have been entirely different in appearance from what Shenoute would call a book of magic. Shenoute threatened the heretics:

> I shall make you acknowledge . . . the Archbishop Cyril, or else the sword will wipe out most of you, and moreover those of you who are spared will go into exile.

Just as the Dead Sea Scrolls were put in jars for safekeeping and hidden at the time of the approach of the Roman Tenth Legion, the burial of the Nag Hammadi library in a jar may also have been precipitated by the approach of Roman authorities, who by now have become Christian.

The fact that the Nag Hammadi library was hidden in a jar suggests the intention not to eliminate but to preserve the books. For not only were the Dead Sea Scrolls put in such jars for safekeeping, but biblical manuscripts have been found similarly preserved up and down the Nile, in some cases dating from the same period and buried in the Nag Hammadi region. The Bible refers to burial in a jar as the way to preserve, and to burning as the way to eliminate a book (Jeremiah 32:14-15; 36:23). The *Life of Saint Pachomius* reports that he got rid of a book by Origen, whom he considered a heretic, by throwing it in the water with the comment that if the Lord's name had not been in it he would have burned it. The burning of the greatest library in antiquity at Alexandria by Christians late in the fourth century C.E. suggests that such a ready solution would hardly have been overlooked if the intent had been to get rid of the Nag Hammadi library. It must have been buried in the jar for safekeeping, perhaps for posterity.

Two of the texts in the Nag Hammadi library refer to their being stored for safekeeping in a mountain until the end of time. The *Gospel of the Egyptians* concludes:

> The great Seth wrote this book with letters in one hundred and thirty years. He placed it in a mountain that is called Charaxio, in order that, at the end of the times and the eras, . . . it may come forth and reveal this incorruptible, holy race of the great savior, and those who dwell with them in love, and the great, invisible, eternal Spirit, and his only begotten Son. . . .

Near the end of *Allogenes* a similar idea occurs:

> Write down [the things that I] shall [tell] you and of which I shall remind
> you for the sake of these who will be worthy after you. And you will
> leave this book upon the mountain and you will call up the guardian,
> "Come, O Dreadful One."

On each side of the Nile valley cliffs rise abruptly to the desert above.
The section of the cliff on the right bank marking the limit of the Nile
valley and the arable land between Chenoboskeia and Pabau is called
the Jabal al-Ṭārif. A protruding boulder shaped somewhat like a stalag-
mite had broken off some time in antiquity from the face of the cliff
and fallen down onto the talus below (the inclined plane of fallen rock
that over the ages naturally collects like a buttress at the foot of a cliff).
Under the northern flank of one of the huge barrel-shaped pieces of this
boulder the jar containing the Nag Hammadi library was secreted.

In the face of the cliff, just at the top of the talus, sixth dynasty tombs
from the reigns of Pepi I and II (2350-2200 B.C.E.) had in antiquity long
since been robbed. Thus they had become cool solitary caves where a
monk might well hold his spiritual retreats, as is reported of Pachomius
himself, or where a hermit might have his cell. Greek prayers to Zeus
Sarapis, opening lines of biblical Psalms in Coptic, and Christian crosses,
all painted in red onto the walls of the caves, show that they were indeed
so used. Perhaps those who cherished the Nag Hammadi library made
such use of the caves, which would account for the choice of this site
to bury them. The jar rested there a millennium and a half....

3. The Discovery

In the month of December peasants of the Najʿ Ḥammādī region
fertilize their fields by carrying nitrates from the talus of the Jabal
al-Ṭārif to their fields, using the saddle-bags of their camels. Two brothers,
Muḥammad and Khalīfah ʿAlī of the al-Sammān clan, hobbled their
camels on the south side of the fallen boulder and came upon the jar
as they were digging around its base. Muḥammad ʿAlī reports that at
first he was afraid to break the jar, whose lid may have been sealed on
with bitumen, for fear that a jinn might be closed up inside it; but, on
reflecting that the jar might contain gold, he recovered his courage and
smashed it with his mattock. Out swirled golden-like particles that
disappeared into the sky—neither jinns nor gold but perhaps papyrus
fragments! He wrapped the books in his tunic, slung it over his shoulder,
unhobbled his camel, and carried the books home, a hovel in the hamlet

of al-Qaṣr, which was the ancient site of Chenoboskeia where Pachomius had begun his life as a Christian.

Half a year earlier, during the night of 7 May 1945, the father of the two brothers, whose name was ʿAlī, while on his job as night watchman guarding irrigation equipment in the fields, had killed a marauder. By mid-morning he had been in turn murdered in blood vengeance. About a month after the discovery of the books, a peasant named Aḥmad fell asleep sitting in the heat of the day on the side of the dirt road near Muḥammad ʿAlī's house, a jar of sugar-cane molasses for sale beside him. A neighbor pointed him out to Muḥammad ʿAlī as the murderer of his father. He ran home and alerted his brothers and widowed mother, who had told her seven sons to keep their mattocks sharp. The family fell upon their victim, hacked off his limbs bit by bit, ripped out his heart, and devoured it among them, as the ultimate act of blood revenge.

Aḥmad was the son of the sheriff, Ismāʿīl Husayn, a strong man imposed on al-Qaṣr from outside, indeed, a member of the Hawāra tribe, which is so alienated from society that it considers itself non-Arabic though directly descended from the Prophet. The village of the Hawāra, Ḥamrah Dūm, is just at the foot of the Jabal al-Ṭārif, and Muḥammed ʿAlī has been afraid to return to the site of the discovery lest his vengeance be in turn avenged. In fact Aḥmad's brother did avenge the death by killing two members of the al-Sammān clan. Even a decade later, Aḥmad's young son, who by then was a teenager, heard that there was to be at dusk in al-Qaṣr a funeral procession of the family of Muḥammed ʿAlī. He proved his manhood by sneaking into town and shooting up the procession, with a score killed and wounded. Muḥammad ʿAlī proudly shows a wound just above his heart, to prove that they tried but failed in vengeance. But he stoutly refused to return to the cliff to identify the site of the discovery until a camouflage costume, a governmental escort, and of course a financial consideration combined to persuade him to change his mind.

The village of al-Qaṣr was so glad to be rid of the sheriff's son that no eye-witnesses could be found to testify at the hearing. But during this period the police tended to search Muḥammad ʿAlī's home every evening for weapons. Having been told that the books were Christian, no doubt simply on the basis of the Coptic script, Muḥammad ʿAlī asked the Coptic priest of al-Qaṣr, Bāsīlīyūs ʿAbd al-Masīḥ, if he could deposit the books in his house. A priest's home would hardly be searched. Coptic priests marry, and this priest's wife had a brother, Rāghib Andrawus, who went from village to village in a circuit teaching English and history in the parochial schools of the Coptic Church. Once a week when he taught in al-Qaṣr he stayed in his sister's home. On seeing one of the books (Codex III), he recognized its potential value and persuaded the priest to give it to him. He took it to Cairo and showed it to a Coptic physician interested in the Coptic language, George Sobhi, who called in the authorities from the Department of Antiquities. They took control of the book, agreeing to pay Rāghib £ 300. After what seemed endless delays, Rāghib finally received £ 250 upon agreeing to make a gift of the balance of £ 50 to the Coptic Museum, where the book was deposited. The Register of the Museum records the date as 4 October 1946.

Thinking the books were worthless, perhaps even a source of bad luck, the widow of ʿAlī had burned part of them in the oven (probably Codex XII, of which only a few fragmentary leaves remain). Illiterate Muslim neighbors purchased the remainder for next to nothing. Nāshid Bisādah had one, and entrusted it to a gold merchant of Nag Hammadi to sell in Cairo, whereupon they divided the profit. A grain merchant is reported to have acquired another and sold it in Cairo at such a high price that he was able to set up his shop there. The villagers of al-Qaṣr identify him as Fikrī Jibrāʾīl, today the proprietor of the "Nag Hammadi Store" in Cairo; however, he denies any involvement. Bahīj ʿAlī, a one-eyed outlaw of al-Qaṣr, got most of the books. Escorted by a well-known antiquities dealer of the region, Dhakī Basṭā, he went to Cairo. They first offered the books to Mansoor's shop at Shepheards Hotel, and then to the shop of Phocion J. Tano, who bought their whole stock and then went to Nag Hammadi to get whatever was left.

Most of Codex I was taken out of Egypt by a Belgian antiquities dealer in Cairo, Albert Eid. It was offered for sale unsuccessfully in New York and Ann Arbor in 1949, and then on 10 May 1952 was acquired in Belgium from Eid's widow by the Jung Institute of Zürich and named the "Jung Codex." It has been gradually returned after publication to Cairo, where it is conserved in the Coptic Museum of Old Cairo. Meanwhile Tano's collection was taken into custody by the Egyptian Department of Antiquities to prevent it from leaving the country. After Nasser came to power it was nationalized, with a token compensation of £ 4,000. Today the Nag Hammadi library is back together again, conserved in the Coptic Museum.

The Director of the Coptic Museum at the time of the discovery, Togo Mina, had studied in Paris under the Abbot Étienne Drioton, who had subsequently become Director of the Department of Antiquities of Egypt. Togo Mina had been a classmate of the wife of Jean Doresse, a young French scholar who came to Egypt to study Coptic monasteries. Togo Mina was glad to give him access to Codex III and to make plans with him for a predominantly French edition of the library, plans cut short by his death in 1949. In 1956 a meeting of some members of an international committee in Cairo led to the publication of the *Gospel of Thomas* in 1959. And the Jung Codex was gradually published in six volumes from 1956 through 1975. Meanwhile the new Director of the Coptic Museum, Pahor Labib, who had received his doctorate from the Humboldt University in Berlin, made plans to publish the better part of the library with the German scholars Alexander Böhlig and Martin Krause.

The General Director of UNESCO, René Maheu of France, worked out an agreement in the early 1960's with the Minister of Culture and National Guidance of the United Arab Republic, Saroite Okacha, to publish a complete edition through an international committee jointly chosen by Egypt and UNESCO. But when it was discovered that many of the choicest texts had already been assigned for publication, the UNESCO plan was limited to a fácsimile edition. The project was rather dormant until an International Committee for the Nag Hammadi Codices was appointed at the end of 1970. The twelve-volume *Facsimile Edition of the Nag Hammadi Codices* began to appear in 1972, and is expected to be completed with the publication of the cartonnage and an introductory volume in 1978. A number of the earlier assignments have by now been published, and complete editions in English, German, and French are currently being prepared. The present volume is a preprint of the translations from the eleven-volume English edition, entitled *The Coptic Gnostic Library.*

With the publication of *The Nag Hammadi Library in English* the work has only begun, for it marks a new beginning in the study of Gnosticism. Over a century ago students began to study Gnosticism in order to know what the heresy-hunting Church fathers were talking about. Around the turn of this century the History of Religions School broadened the issue by seeking the origins of Gnosticism throughout the Ancient Near East. Between the two World Wars Hans Jonas produced a philosophical interpretation of Gnosticism that for the first time made sense of it as a possible way to understand existence. Rudolf Bultmann then reinterpreted the New Testament in terms of an interaction with Gnosticism involving appropriation as well as confrontation. Yet the results of this century of research into the origin, nature, and influence of Gnosticism stand in a certain ambivalence, as if hanging in suspense.

One cannot fail to be impressed by the clairvoyance, the constructive power, the learned intuitions of scholars who, from limited and secondary sources, were able to produce working hypotheses that in fact worked so well. Yet the discovery of the Nag Hammadi library has drawn attention to how meager those sources were. For even though the discovery of the Nag Hammadi library was quite accidental and its contents somewhat arbitrary, the flood of new source material it contains cannot fail to outweigh the constructions and conjectures of previous scholarship. But for a generation the flood of new source material has at best been a trickle, and the suspense has produced stagnation, as the scholarly community waited and waited. Now the time has come for a concentrated effort, with the whole Nag Hammadi library accessible, to rewrite the history of Gnosticism, to understand what it was really all about, and of course to pose new questions. Rarely has a generation of students had such an opportunity! May the readers of this book share this exhilaration, and this responsibility, with those who produced it.

THE PRAYER OF THE APOSTLE PAUL (I, *1*)

Introduced and translated by

DIETER MUELLER

The *Prayer of the Apostle Paul* occupies the front flyleaf of Codex I, also known as the Jung Codex. Apparently the scribe added this prayer to the collection of tractates in the Jung Codex after he had finished copying the *Tripartite Tractate* (I, 5). The title, followed by a brief colophon, is placed at the end of the prayer, and retains the Greek language of the original. Though this short text is of unknown date and provenance, its Gnostic and probably Valentinian character may suggest a date of origin between the second half of the second century and the end of the third century.

In form and content the *Prayer of the Apostle Paul* echoes various other compositions. It displays a striking resemblance not only to prayers in the Corpus Hermeticum but also to invocations found in magical texts. Furthermore, its beginning is rather similar to that of the hymn on the First Stele of the *Three Steles of Seth* (VII, 5); both of these documents may use a common tradition. Again, the thoughts expressed in the present tractate have parallels in the *Gospel of Philip* (II, 3). In general, the *Prayer of the Apostle Paul* is heavily indebted to the Psalms and the Pauline letters. Thus the author asks to be granted "what no angel-eye has seen and no archon-ear has heard and what has not entered into the human heart" (cf. 1 Corinthians 2:9).

THE PRAYER OF THE APOSTLE PAUL

I A, 1-B, 10
B, 11-12

[... ³ your] light, give me your [mercy]!

[My] ' Redeemer, redeem me, for ⁵ [I am] yours: from you have I come ' forth.

You are [my] mind: bring me forth! '

You are my treasure-house: open for me!

You ' [are] my fullness: take me to you! '

You are ⟨my⟩ repose: give me ¹⁰ [the] perfection that cannot be grasped! '

I invoke you, the one who is ' and preexisted, by the name ' [which is] exalted above every name, through Jesus Christ ' [the Lord] of Lords, the king of the ages: ¹⁵ give me your gifts which you do not regret ' through the Son of man, ' the Spirit, the Paraclete of ' [truth].

Give me authority ' [when I] ask you; give ²⁰ healing for my body when I ask ' you through the Evangelist, ' [and] redeem my eternal light-soul ' and my spirit.

And the ' [First]-born of the pleroma of grace — ²⁵ [reveal] him to my mind!

Grant ' what no angel-eye has ' [seen] and no archon-ear ' ⟨has⟩ heard and what ' [has not] entered into the human heart, ³⁰ which came to be angelic and (came to be) ' after the image of the psychic God ' when it was formed ' in the beginning, since I have ' faith and hope.³⁵ And place upon me your ' beloved, elect, ' and blessed greatness, the ' First-born, the First-begotten, [...] **B³** and the [wonderful] mystery ' of your house; [for] ⁵ yours is the power [and] ' the glory and the blessing ' and the [greatness] ' for ever and ever. [Amen. (?)] '

Prayer of Paul ¹⁰
(the) Apostle '

* * * * * * *

In Peace '

Christ is holy

THE APOCRYPHON OF JAMES (I, *2*)

Introduced and translated by

FRANCIS E. WILLIAMS

Edited by

DIETER MUELLER

Untitled in the original, the *Apocryphon of James* has received its modern title from the reference to the "secret book" (Greek: apocryphon) allegedly revealed to James and Peter by the Lord and recorded in Hebrew by James—James the Just, the brother of Jesus. This tractate assumes the form of a letter, and opens in typical epistolary fashion. An identification of the recipient of the letter is impossible, though it has been suggested that the name of the addressee might be restored as "[Cerin]thos." The letter proceeds to describe the circumstances surrounding the composition of this "secret book," and emphasizes the need for care in its circulation.

The major section of the *Apocryphon of James* relates a dialogue between the two apostles and the resurrected Christ. James and Peter are selected to receive special revelation, and the Savior discourses on such topics as diminution and fullness, persecution and death, prophecy and parables. Appeals and warnings are given for the sake of salvation. The Savior tells the apostles that he wishes them to know themselves and to live as sons of God, filled with the kingdom. Finally, after Jesus ascends in his "chariot of spirit," James and Peter themselves experience an ecstatic trip to the heavens, a trip depicted in an apocalyptic fashion; then James sends each of the disciples out, while he himself goes to Jerusalem. The tractate closes with an exhortation to the addressee: "I pray that the beginning may come from you."

The *Apocryphon of James* may be a Gnostic document, and some scholars have suggested that it reflects certain Valentinian ideas, though there is no full agreement concerning the precise nature of the document. The emphasis upon knowledge, and the use of such typically Gnostic themes as sleep, drunkenness, and sickness, suggest that the tractate would be at home within Christian Gnosticism. The *Apocryphon of James* may have been written in Egypt in the third century C.E., though some would place it earlier.

THE APOCRYPHON OF JAMES

I 1, 1-16, 30

James writes to ' [...]thos: Peace ' [be with you from] Peace, ' [love from] Love,[5] [grace from] Grace, ' [faith] from Faith, ' life from Holy Life! '

Since you asked ' that I send [10] you a secret book ' which was revealed to me ' and Peter by the Lord, ' I could not turn you away ' or gainsay (?) you; [15] but I have written it in ' the Hebrew alphabet and ' sent it to you, and you ' alone. But since you are ' a minister of the salvation [20] of the saints, endeavor earnestly ' and take care not to rehearse ' this text to many—this ' that the Savior did not wish ' to tell to all of us, his [25] twelve disciples. ' But blessed will they be ' who will be saved through ' the faith of this discourse.

I ' also sent you,[30] ten months ago, another secret ' book which the Savior ' had revealed to me. Under the circumstances, however, ' regard that one ' as revealed [35] to me, James; but this one [. . .]. **2**[7] Now when ' the twelve disciples ' were all sitting together [10] and recalling ' what the Savior had said ' to each one of them, whether ' in secret or openly, ' and [setting it in order] [15] in books—but I ' was writing that which was in [my book]— ' lo, the Savior appeared, [after] ' he had departed from us, and we had waited ' for him. And after five hundred [20] and fifty days since he had risen ' from the dead, we said ' to him, "Have you departed and removed yourself from us?" '

But Jesus said, "No, but ' I shall go to the place from whence I came.[25] If you wish to come ' with me, come!"

They all answered ' and said, "If you bid ' us, we come."

He said, ' "Verily I say unto you,[30] no one will ever enter ' the kingdom of heaven at my ' bidding, but (only) because ' you yourselves are full. Leave ' James and Peter to me [35] that I may fill them." And ' having called these two ' he drew them aside and bade ' the rest occupy themselves ' with that which they were about.[40]

The Savior said, "You have received mercy [. . .]. **3**[8] Do you not, then, desire to be filled? ' And your heart is drunken; [10] do you not, then, desire to be sober? ' Therefore be ashamed! Henceforth, waking ' or sleeping, remember ' that you have seen ' the Son of Man, and [15] spoken with him in person, ' and listened to him in person. ' Woe to those who have seen the ' son of man; ' blessed will they be who [20] have not seen the man, and they ' who have not consorted with him, and ' they who have not spoken with him, ' and they who have not listened to ' anything from him: yours is [25] life! Know, then, that he healed ' you when you were ill ' that you might reign. Woe ' to those who have found relief from ' their illness, for they will [30] relapse into illness. Blessed will ' they be who have not been ill, and ' have known relief before ' falling ill: yours is the ' kingdom of God. Therefore I [35] say to you, become ' full and leave no space within ' you empty, for he who is coming ' can mock you."

Then ' Peter replied, "Lo,[40] three times you have told us, **4** 'Become filled'; [but] ' we are full."

[The Savior answered] ' and said, "[For this cause I have said] ' to you, '[Become filled],' that [5] [you] may not [be in want. They who are in want], ' however, will not [be saved]. For it is good to be full, ' and bad to be in want. Hence, just as ' it is good that you (sing.) be in want and, ' conversely, bad that you be full, so [10] he who is full is in want, ' and he who is in want does not become full as ' he who is in want becomes full, and ' he who has been filled, in turn, attains ' due perfection. Therefore you must be in want [15] while it is possible to fill you (pl.), and ' be full while it is possible for you to be in want, ' so that you may be able [to fill] ' yourselves the more. Hence become ' full of the Spirit [20] but be in want of ' reason, for it is reason; ' the soul, in turn, is soul." '

But I answered and said to him, "Lord, ' we can obey you [25] if you wish, for we have forsaken ' our fathers ' and our mothers and our villages ' and followed you. Grant us ' not to be tempted [30] by the devil, the evil one." '

The Lord answered ' and said, "What is your merit ' if you do the will of the Father ' and it is not given to you from him [35] as a gift while ' you are tempted by ' Satan? But if ' you are oppressed by ' Satan and [40] persecuted and you do his (the Father's) **5** will, I [say] that he will ' love you, and make you equal ' with me, and reckon ' [you] to have become [5] beloved through his providence ' by your own choice. So ' will you not cease ' loving the flesh and being ' afraid of sufferings? Or do [10] you not know that you have yet ' to be abused and to be ' accused unjustly; ' and have yet to be shut ' up in prison, and [15] condemned ' unlawfully, and ' crucified ⟨without⟩ ' reason, and buried ' ⟨shamefully⟩, as (was) I myself,[20] by the evil one? ' Do you dare to spare the flesh, ' you for whom the Spirit is an ' encircling wall? If you consider ' how long the world existed [25] ⟨before⟩ you, and how long ' it will exist after you, you will find ' that your life is one single day ' and your sufferings one ' single hour. For the good [30] will not enter into the world. ' Scorn death, therefore, ' and take thought for life! ' Remember my cross ' and my death, and you will [35] live!"

But I answered and ' said to him, "Lord, ' do not mention to us the cross ' and death, for they are far **6** from you."

The Lord answered ' and said, "Verily I say ' unto you, none will be saved ' unless they believe in my cross.[5] But those who have believed in my ' cross, theirs is the kingdom of ' God. Therefore become seekers ' for death, like the dead ' who seek for life, [10] for that which they seek is revealed to them. ' And what is there ' to trouble them? As for you, when you examine ' death, it will ' teach you election. Verily [15] I say unto you, none ' of those who fear death will be saved; ' for the kingdom of death ' belongs to those who put themselves to death. ' Become better than I; make [20] yourselves like the son of the Holy Spirit!" '

Then I asked him, ' "Lord, how shall we be able ' to prophesy to those who request ' us to prophesy [25] to them? For there are many who ' ask us, and look ' to us to hear an oracle ' from us."

The Lord ' answered and said, "Do you not [30] know that the head of ' prophecy was cut off with John?" '

But I said, "Lord, ' can it be possible to remove ' the head of prophecy?"

The Lord [35] said to me, "When you ' come to know what 'head' means, and ' that prophecy issues from the ' head, (then) understand the meaning of 'Its head was 7 removed.' At first I spoke ' to you in parables ' and you did not understand; ' now I speak to [5] you openly, and ' you (still) do not perceive. Yet ' it was you who served me ' as a parable in ' parables, and as that which is open [10] in the (words) that are open.

"Hasten ' to be saved without being urged! ' Instead, be ' eager of your own accord and, ' if possible, arrive even before me,[15] for thus ' the Father will love you. '

"Come to hate ' hypocrisy and the evil ' thought; for it is the thought [20] that gives birth to hypocrisy; ' but hypocrisy is far from ' truth.

"Do not allow ' the kingdom of heaven to wither; ' for it is like a palm shoot [25] whose fruit has poured down ' around it. It put forth ' leaves, and after they had sprouted ' they caused the pith to dry up. ' So it is also with the fruit which [30] had grown from this single root; ' when it had been picked (?), ' fruit was borne by many (?). ' It (the root) was certainly good, (and) if ' it were possible to produce the [35] new plants now, you (sing.) would find it (?).

"Since ' I have already been glorified in this fashion, ' why do you (pl.) hold me back ' in my eagerness to go? 8 For after the [end] you have ' compelled me to stay with ' you another eighteen days for ' the sake of the parables. It was enough [5] for some ⟨to listen⟩ to the ' teaching and understand 'The Shepherds' and ' 'The Seed' and 'The Building' and 'The Lamps of ' the Virgins' and 'The Wage of the ' Workmen' and 'The Didrachmae' and 'The [10] Woman.'

"Become earnest about ' the word! For as to the word, ' its first part is faith, ' the second, love, the ' third, works; [15] for from these comes life. ' For the word is like a ' grain of wheat: when someone ' had sown it, he had faith in it; and ' when it had sprouted, he loved it because he had seen [20] many grains in place of one. And ' when he had worked, he was saved because he had ' prepared it for food, (and) again he ' left (some) to sow. So also ' can you yourselves receive [25] the kingdom of heaven; ' unless you receive this through knowledge, ' you will not be able to find it.

"Therefore ' I say to you, ' be sober; do not be deceived! [30] And many times have I said to you all together, ' and also to you alone, ' James, have I said, ' be saved! And I have commanded ' you (sing.) to follow me,[35] and I have taught you ' what to say before the archons. ' Observe that I have descended ' and have spoken and undergone tribulation ' and carried off my crown [9] after saving you (pl.). For ' I came down to dwell with ' you so that you in turn ' might dwell with me. And,[5] finding your houses ' unceiled, I have made my abode ' in the houses that could receive me ' at the time of my descent. '

"Therefore trust [10] in me, my brethren; understand ' what the great light is. The Father ' has no need of me, ' for a father does not need a son; ' but it is the son who needs [15] the father. To him I go, ' for the Father ' of the Son has no need of you. '

"Hearken to the word; ' understand knowledge; love [20] life, and no one will persecute ' you, nor will anyone ' oppress you, other ' than you yourselves. '

"O you wretches; O [25] you unfortunates; O ' you pretenders to the truth; ' O you falsifiers of knowledge; ' O you sinners against the Spirit: ' can you still bear to [30] listen when it behooved you ' to speak from the first? ' Can you still bear to ' sleep, when it behooved you to be awake ' from the first, so that [35] the kingdom of heaven might receive you? [10] Verily I say unto you, ' it is easier for a pure one ' to fall into defilement, and for ' a man of light to fall [5] into darkness, than for you to reign ' or not reign.

"I remembered ' your tears and your mourning ' and your anguish; they are far ' behind us. But now, you who are [10] outside of the Father's inheritance, ' weep where it is necessary, ' and mourn and ' preach what is good, ' as the Son is ascending as he should.[15] Verily I say ' unto you, had I been sent ' to those who listen to me, and ' had I spoken with them, ' I would never have come [20] down to earth. So, ' then, be ashamed before (?) them now! '

"Behold, I shall depart from you ' and go away, and do not wish ' to remain with you any longer, just as [25] you yourselves have not wished it. ' Now, therefore, follow ' me quickly. This is why ' I say to you, for your sakes ' I came down. You are [30] the beloved; you are they ' who will be the cause of life ' in many. Invoke the Father, ' implore God often, ' and he will give to you. Blessed [35] is he who has seen you with Him ' when He was proclaimed among the ' angels, and glorified among ' the saints; yours is life. ' Rejoice and be glad as 11 sons of God. Keep (his) will ' that you may be saved; ' accept reproof from me and ' save yourselves. I intercede [5] on your behalf with the Father, and he will ' forgive you much."

And when we ' had heard these words, we became glad, ' for we had been grieved ' at the words we have mentioned [10] before. But when he saw us ' rejoicing, he said, "Woe to you, ' you who lack an advocate! ' Woe to you, you who stand in need ' of grace! Blessed will they be [15] who have ' spoken out and obtained ' grace for themselves. Liken ' yourselves to foreigners; ' of what sort are they in the eyes of your [20] city? Why are you disturbed ' when you cast yourselves away ' of your own accord and ' separate yourselves from your city? Why ' do you abandon your dwelling place [25] of your own accord, ' making it ready for those who want ' to dwell in it? O you ' outcasts and fugitives: woe ' to you, for you will be caught! Or [30] do you perhaps think that the Father ' is a lover of mankind, or that he is ' won over without prayers, or that he ' grants remission to one on another's behalf, or ' that he bears with one who asks? [35]—For he knows the desire and ' also what it is that the flesh needs!— ' (Or do you think) that it is not this (flesh) that desires ' the soul? For without the soul ' the body does not sin, just as 12 the soul is not saved without [the] ' spirit. But if the soul ' is saved (when it is) without evil, and ' the spirit is also saved, then the body [5] becomes free from sin. For it is the spirit ' that quickens the soul, but the body that ' kills it; ' that is, it is it (the soul) which kills ' itself. Verily I say unto you,[10] he will not forgive the soul the sin ' by any means, nor the flesh ' the guilt; for none of those who have ' worn the flesh will be saved. ' For do you think that many have [15] found the kingdom of heaven? ' Blessed is he who has seen himself as ' a fourth one in heaven!" '

When we heard these words, we were distressed. ' But when he saw that we were distressed,[20] he said, "For this cause I tell ' you this, that you may ' know yourselves. For the kingdom ' of heaven is like an ear of grain after it ' had sprouted in a field. And [25] when it had ripened, it scattered its ' fruit and again filled the field ' with ears for another year. You ' also: hasten to reap ' an ear of life for yourselves that [30] you may be filled with the kingdom! '

"And as long as I am ' with you, give heed to me ' and obey me; but ' when I depart from you,[35] remember me. And remember me ' because I was with you (and) ' you did not know me. ' Blessed will they be who have ' known me; woe to those who have [40] heard and have not believed. ' Blessed will they be who **13** have not seen yet [have believed]. '

"And once more I prevail upon you, ' for I am revealed to you ' building a house which is of great value to [5] you since you find shelter ' beneath it, just as it will be able ' to stand by your neighbors' house ' when it threatens to fall. Verily ' I say unto you, woe [10] to those for whose sakes I was sent ' down to this place; blessed ' will they be who ascend ' to the Father. Once more I ' reprove you, you who are: [15] become like those who are not, ' that you may be with those who ' are not.

"Do not make ' the kingdom of heaven a desert ' within you. Do not be proud [20] because of the light that illumines, but ' be to yourselves ' as I myself am ' to you. For your sakes I have ' placed myself under the curse, that you [25] may be saved." '

But Peter replied ' to these words and said, ' "Sometimes you urge ' us on to the kingdom of [30] heaven, and then again you turn ' us back, Lord; sometimes ' you persuade and draw ' us to faith and promise ' us life, and then again you cast [35] us forth from the kingdom ' of heaven."

But the Lord answered ' and said to us, "I have given you (pl.) ' faith many times; moreover, ' I have revealed myself to you (sing.), **14** James, and you (pl.) have not ' known me. Now again I ' see you (pl.) rejoicing many times; ' and when you are elated [5] at the promise of life, ' are you yet sad, and do you ' grieve when you are instructed ' in the kingdom? But you, through ' faith [and] knowledge, have received [10] life. Therefore disdain ' the rejection when you ' hear it, but when you hear ' the promise, rejoice the more. ' Verily I say unto you,[15] he who will receive life and ' believe in the kingdom will ' never leave it, not even if ' the Father wishes ' to banish him.

"These are the things that I shall tell [20] you so far; now, however, I shall ' ascend to the place from whence I came. ' But you, when I was eager ' to go, have cast me out, and ' instead of accompanying me,[25] you have pursued me. ' But pay heed to the glory that awaits ' me and, having opened ' your heart, listen to the hymns ' that await me up in the heavens; [30] for today I must ' take (my place at) the right hand of the Father. ' But I have said (my) last word to ' you, and I shall depart from you, ' for a chariot of spirit has borne me aloft,[35] and from this moment on I shall strip myself ' that I may clothe myself. ' But give heed: blessed ' are they who have proclaimed ' the Son before his descent [40] that, when I have come, I might ascend (again). ' Thrice blessed 15 are they who [were] ' proclaimed by the Son ' before they came to be, that ' you might have a portion [5] among them."

Having said these words, ' he departed. But we bent (our) knee(s), ' I and Peter, and gave thanks ' and sent our heart(s) upward ' to heaven. We heard with [10] our ears, and saw with ' our eyes, the noise of wars ' and a trumpet blare ' and a great turmoil.

And ' when we had passed beyond [15] that place, we sent our ' mind(s) farther upward and ' saw with our eyes and heard ' with our ears hymns ' and angelic benedictions and [20] angelic rejoicing. And ' heavenly majesties were ' singing praises, and we too ' rejoiced.

After this ' again we wished to send our [25] spirit upward to the ' Majesty, and after ascending we ' were not permitted to see or hear ' anything, for the other ' disciples called us and [30] asked us, "What did you ' hear from the ' Master? And what did he ' say to you? And where has he gone?" '

But we answered [35] them, "He has ascended, and ' he has given us a pledge and ' promised life to us all and ' revealed to us children (?) ' who are to come after us, after bidding 16 [us] love them, as we would be ' [saved] for their sakes."

And ' when they heard (this), they indeed believed ' the revelation, but were displeased [5] about those to be born. And so, not wishing ' to arouse their resentment, ' I sent each one to another ' place. But I myself went ' up to Jerusalem, praying that I [10] might obtain a portion among the beloved, ' who will appear. '

And I pray that ' the beginning may come from you, ' for thus I shall be capable of [15] salvation, since they will be ' enlightened through me, by my faith— ' and through another (faith) that is ' better than mine, for I would that ' mine be the lesser.[20] Endeavor earnestly, then, to make ' yourself like them and ' pray that you may obtain a portion ' among them. For apart from the persons ' I have mentioned, the Savior did [25] not give us the revelation. ' For their sake we proclaim, indeed, ' a portion among those ' for whom the proclamation was made, ' those whom the Lord has made his [30] sons.

THE GOSPEL OF TRUTH (I, *3* AND XII, *2*)

Introduced and translated by
GEORGE W. MACRAE

The *Gospel of Truth* is a Gnostic and perhaps a Valentinian tractate which discusses, in the manner of a meditation, the person and work of Christ. The title of the work, taken from the opening of the Coptic text, may correspond to the "Gospel of Truth" mentioned in Irenaeus. If this is the case, the Greek original of the Coptic *Gospel of Truth* may be dated in the middle or second half of the second century, and may have been written by a member of the Valentinian school. Some scholars have even suggested that Valentinus himself may have been the author of the tractate.

In spite of the title, this work is not a gospel of the same sort as the New Testament gospels: it does not focus upon the words and deeds of the historical Jesus. Yet the *Gospel of Truth* is "gospel" in the sense of "good news" about Jesus, about the eternal and divine Son, the Word who reveals the Father and passes on knowledge, particularly self-knowledge. For through this self-knowledge the Gnostics know who they are, where they have come from, and where they are going; they realize that they themselves are essentially sons of the Father, that they are of divine origin, that their past and future rest in the divine. Hence it can be said that this "gospel" is a joy for those who have received the gift of knowing the Father. By means of such salvific knowledge the Gnostic achieves joy and wholeness: the nightmare of living in ignorance is transformed into the joyful life in union with the Father.

Although the *Gospel of Truth* does not explicitly cite either the Old Testament or the New Testament, it does clearly allude to many themes and passages in the New Testament. Like the Valentinians, the *Gospel of Truth* uses and interprets the New Testament as a witness to Christian Gnosticism; and the result is a work of power and beauty.

The following translation is based on the text of Codex I; the text of Codex XII is very fragmentary.

THE GOSPEL OF TRUTH

I 16, 31-43, 24

The gospel of truth is a joy ' for those who have received from ' the Father of truth the gift of knowing him, ' through the power of the Word that came forth from [35] the pleroma—the one who is in the thought ' and the mind of the Father, that is, ' the one who is addressed as ' the Savior, (that) being the name of the work he is ' to perform for the redemption of those who were **17** ignorant of the Father, while the name

[of] ' the gospel is the proclamation ' of hope, being discovery ' for those who search for him.

Indeed [5] the all went about searching for the one ' from whom it (pl.) had come forth, and the all was ' inside of him, the ' incomprehensible, inconceivable one ' who is superior to every thought.[10] Ignorance of the Father brought about anguish ' and terror. And the anguish ' grew solid like a fog ' so that no one was able to see. ' For this reason error [15] became powerful; it fashioned its own matter ' foolishly, ' not having known the truth. ' It set about making a creature, ' with (all its) might preparing, in [20] beauty, the substitute for the truth. '

This was not, then, a humiliation for him, ' the incomprehensible, inconceivable one, ' for they were nothing—the anguish ' and the oblivion and the creature [25] of lying—while the established ' truth is immutable, ' imperturbable, perfect in beauty. ' For this reason, despise ' error.

Being thus [30] without any root, it fell into ' a fog regarding the Father, while it was involved in ' preparing works and ' oblivions and terrors in order that ' by means of these it might entice those [35] of the middle and capture them. ' The oblivion of error was ' not revealed. It is not a **18** [. . .] under the Father. Oblivion ' did not come into existence under the Father, ' although it did indeed come into existence because of him. ' But what comes into existence in him is knowledge,[5] which appeared in ' order that oblivion might vanish ' and the Father might be known. Since ' oblivion came into existence because ' the Father was not known, then if [10] the Father comes to be known, oblivion ' will not exist from that moment on.

This ' ⟨is⟩ the gospel of the one who is searched ' for, which ⟨was⟩ revealed to those who ' are perfect through the mercies [15] of the Father— the hidden mystery, ' Jesus, the Christ. Through it ' he enlightened those who were in darkness. ' Out of oblivion he enlightened ' them, he showed (them) a way.[20] And the way is the truth ' which he taught them.

For this reason ' error grew angry at him, ' persecuted him, was distressed at him, ' (and) was brought to naught. He was nailed to a tree; he [25] became a fruit of the knowledge of ' the Father, which did not, however, become destructive because ' it ⟨was⟩ eaten, but to those who ate it ' it gave (cause) to become glad ' in the discovery. For he [30] discovered them in himself, ' and they discovered him in themselves, the ' incomprehensible, inconceivable one, the ' Father, the perfect one, the one who ' made the all, while the all is [35] within him and the all has need of him, ' since he retained its (pl.) perfection ' within himself which he did not give ' to the all. The Father was not jealous. ' What jealousy indeed (could there be) [40] between himself and his members? **19** For if the aeon had thus [received] their [perfection], ' they could not have come [...] ' the Father, since he retained ' their perfection within him-self,[5] granting it to them as a return to him ' and a knowledge unique in ' perfection. It is he who fashioned ' the all, and the all is within ' him and the all had need [10] of him.

As in the case ' of one of whom some ' are ignorant, who ' wishes to have them know him and ' love him, so— [15] for what did the all have need of ' if not knowledge regarding ' the Father?—he became a guide, ' restful and leisurely. ' He went into the midst of the schools (and) he spoke [20] the word as a teacher. ' There came the wise men— ' in their own estimation— ' putting him to the test. ' But he confounded them because they [25] were foolish. They hated ' him because they were not really ' wise.

After all these, ' there came the little ' children also, those to whom [30] the knowledge of the Father belongs. Having been strengthened, ' they learned about the impressions ' of the Father. They knew, ' they were known; they were glorified, they ' glorified. There was revealed in their [35] heart the living book ' of the living—the one written ' in the thought and the mind **20** [of the] Father, and which from before the ' foundation of the all was within ' the incomprehensible (parts) of him—that (book) ' which no one was able to take [5] since it is reserved for the one who will take it and ' will be slain. No one could have appeared ' among those who believed ' in salvation unless ' that book had intervened.[10] For this reason the merciful one, the faithful one, ' Jesus, was patient in accepting sufferings ' until he took that book, ' since he knows that his death ' is life for many.[15]

Just as there lies hidden in a will, before ' it ⟨is⟩ opened, the fortune ' of the deceased master of the house, ' so (it is) with the all, which ' lay hidden while the Father of the all was [20] invisible, the one ' who is from himself, from whom ' all spaces come forth. ' For this reason Jesus appeared; ' he put on that book; [25] he was nailed to a tree; ' he published the edict ' of the Father on the cross. O ' such great teaching! He draws ' himself down to death though life [30] eternal clothes him. Having stripped ' himself of the perishable rags, ' he put on imperishability, ' which no one ' can possibly take away from him. Having entered [35] the empty spaces of ' terrors, he passed through ' those who were stripped naked by ' oblivion, being knowledge ' and perfection, proclaiming the things that are in the heart **21** of the [Father] in order to [...] ' teach those who will receive teaching. '

But those who are to receive teaching [are] ' the living who are in-scribed in the book [5] of the living. They receive teaching ' about them-selves. They receive it (pl.) ' from the Father, turning ' again to him. Since the ' perfection of the all is in the Father,[10] it is necessary for the all to ' ascend to him. Then, if ' one has knowledge, he receives what are ' his own and draws ' them to himself. For he who is [15] ignorant is in need, and ' what he lacks is great ' since he lacks that which will ' make him perfect. Since the perfection of ' the all is in the Father [20] and it is necessary for the all to ' ascend to him and for each ' one to receive what are his own, ' he enrolled them in advance, having ' prepared them to give to those [25] who came forth from him.

Those ' whose name he knew in advance ' were called at the end, ' so that one who has knowledge is ' the one whose name the Father [30] has uttered. For he whose name ' has not been spoken is ignorant. ' Indeed, how is one ' to hear if his name has not ' been called? For he who is [35] ignorant until the end is a creature ' of oblivion, and he will ' vanish along with it. If not, ' how is it that these miserable ones have [22] no name, (how is it that) they do not have ' the call? Therefore ' if one has knowledge, he is ' from above. If he is called,[5] he hears, he answers, ' and he turns to him who is calling ' him, and ascends to him. And ' he knows in what manner he ' is called. Having knowledge, he does [10] the will of the one who called ' him, he wishes to be pleasing to him, he ' receives rest.

Each one's name ' comes to him. He who is to have knowledge ' in this manner knows where he comes [15] from and where he is going. ' He knows as one ' who having become drunk has turned away from ' his drunkenness, (and) having returned to himself, ' has set right what [20] are his own. He has brought many ' back from error. He has gone ' before them to their places, ' from which they had moved away ' when they received error,[25] on account of the depth of the one who encircles ' all spaces while there is none ' that encircles him. It was a great ' wonder that they were in the Father, ' not knowing him, and (that) they were [30] able to come forth by themselves, ' since they were unable to ' com-prehend or to know the one ' in whom they were. If ' his will had not thus emerged from him— [35] for he revealed it ' in view of a knowledge in which ' all its emanations concur. '

This is the knowledge of ' the living book which he revealed to the [23] aeons to the last of its [letters], ' revealing how ' they are not vowels ' nor are they [5] consonants, ' so that one might read them and ' think of something foolish, ' but they are letters of the ' truth which they alone speak [10] who know them. ' Each letter is a complete ⟨thought⟩ ' like a complete ' book, since they are ' letters written by [15] the Unity, the Father having ' written them for the aeons in order that by ' means of his letters ' they should know the Father. His wisdom ' contemplates [20] the Word, his teaching ' utters it, his knowledge ' has revealed ⟨it⟩. ' His forbearance is ' a crown upon it,[25] his gladness is in harmony ' with it, his glory ' has exalted it, his image ' has revealed it, ' his repose has [30] received it into itself, his love ' has made a body over it, ' his fidelity has embraced ' it. In this way the Word ' of the Father goes [35] forth in the all, as the fruit **24** [of] his heart and ' an impression of his will. ' But it supports the all; it ' chooses it (pl.) and also receives [5] the impression of the all, ' purifying it (pl.), bringing it (pl.) back ' into the Father, into the Mother, ' Jesus of the infiniteness of ' gentleness.

The Father reveals [10] his bosom—now his bosom ' is the Holy Spirit. He ' reveals what is hidden of him— ' what is hidden of him is ' his Son—so that through [15] the mercies of the Father ' the aeons may know him ' and cease laboring in search of ' the Father, resting there ' in him, knowing [20] that this is rest. Having ' filled the deficiency, he abolished ' the form—the form of ' it is the world, that ' in which he served.[25] For the place where there is envy ' and strife is a deficiency, ' but the place where (there is) Unity ' is a perfection. Since the deficiency ' came into being because the [30] Father was not known, therefore when ' the Father is known, ' from that moment on the deficiency will no longer exist. As ' with the ignorance ' of a person, when he comes [35] to have knowledge his ignorance ' vanishes of itself, ' as the darkness vanishes ' when light appears, **25** so also ' the deficiency vanishes ' in the perfection. So ' from that moment on the form is not apparent,[5] but it will vanish ' in the fusion of Unity, ' for now their works ' lie scattered. In ' time Unity will perfect [10] the spaces. It is within ' Unity that each one ' will attain himself; within ' knowledge he will purify himself ' from multiplicity into [15] Unity, consuming ' matter within himself ' like fire, and ' darkness by light, death by ' life.

If indeed these things have happened [20] to each one of us, ' then we must ' see to it above all that ' the house will be holy ' and silent for the Unity.[25] (It is) as in the case of some people ' who moved out of dwellings ' where there were ' jars that in ' spots were not good.[30] They would break them, and ' the master of the house does not suffer loss. ' Rather ⟨he⟩ is glad because ' in place of the bad jars ' there are full ones which are made [35] perfect. For such is ' the judgment which has come from **26** above. It has passed judgment on ' everyone; it is a drawn sword, ' with two edges, cutting ' on either side. When the [5] Word came into the midst, the one that is ' within the heart of those who utter it— ' it is not a sound alone ' but it became a body—a great ' disturbance took place among [10] the jars because some had ' been emptied, others filled; ' that is, some had been supplied, ' others poured out, ' some had been purified, still [15] others broken up. All the spaces ' were shaken and disturbed ' because they had no order ' nor stability. ' Error was upset, not knowing [20] what to do; ' it was grieved, in mourning, ' afflicting itself because it knew ' nothing. When ' knowledge drew near it—this [25] is the downfall of (error) and all its emanations— ' error is empty, ' having nothing inside. '

Truth came into the midst; ' all its emanations knew it.[30] They greeted the Father in truth ' with a perfect power ' that joins them with the Father. ' For everyone loves the truth ' because the truth is the mouth [35] of the Father; his tongue is the ' Holy Spirit. He who is joined 27 to the truth is joined ' to the Father's mouth ' by his tongue, whenever he is to ' receive the Holy Spirit.[5] This is the manifestation of the ' Father and his revelation ' to his aeons: he manifested ' what was hidden of him; he explained it. ' For who contains [10] if not the Father alone? ' All the spaces are his emanations. ' They have known that they came forth ' from him like children ' who are from a grown [15] man. They knew ' that they had not yet ' received form nor yet ' received a name, each one of which ' the Father begets.[20] Then when they receive form ' by his knowledge, ' though truly within him, they ' do not know him. But the Father ' is perfect, knowing [25] every space within him. ' If he wishes, ' he manifests whomever he wishes ' by giving him form and giving ' him a name, and he gives a name [30] to him and brings it about ' that those come into existence who ' before they come into existence are ' ignorant of him who fashioned them. '

I do not say, then, that [35] they are nothing (at all) who have not ' yet come into existence, but they are 28 in him who will wish ' that they come into existence when he ' wishes, like ' the time that is to come.[5] Before all things appear, ' he knows what he will ' produce. But the fruit ' which is not yet manifest ' knows nothing, nor [10] does it do anything. Thus ' also every space which is ' itself in the Father is from ' the one who exists, who ' established it [15] from what does not exist. ' For he who has no ' root has no ' fruit either, but ' though he thinks to himself,[20] "I have come into being," yet ' he will perish by himself. ' For this reason, he who did not exist ' at all will ' never come into existence. What, then, did he [25] wish him to think of himself? ' This:

"I have come into being like the ' shadows and phantoms ' of the night."
When ' the light shines on the terror [30] which that person had experienced, ' he knows that it is nothing. '

Thus they were ignorant ' of the Father, he being the one **29** whom
they did not see. Since ' it was terror and disturbance ' and instability '
and doubt and [5] division, there were many ' illusions at work ' by means
of these, and ' (there were) empty fictions, as if ' they were sunk in
sleep [10] and found themselves in ' disturbing dreams. Either (there is) a
place ' to which they are fleeing, or ' without strength they come (from)
having chased ' after others, or they are involved in [15] striking blows,
or they are receiving ' blows themselves, or they have ' fallen from high
places, ' or they take off into ' the air though they do not even have
wings.[20] Again, sometimes (it is as) if people ' were murdering them,
though there is ' no one even pursuing them, or they themselves ' are
killing their neighbors, ' for they have been stained with [25] their blood. '
When those who ' are going through ' all these things wake up, they see
nothing, ' they who were in the midst [30] of all these disturbances, ' for
they are nothing. ' Such is the way ' of those who have cast ' ignorance
aside [35] from them like sleep, ' not esteeming it as anything, ' nor do
they esteem its **30** works as solid ' things either, but they ' leave them
behind like ' a dream in the night. The [5] knowledge of the Father they
value ' as the dawn. This is the way ' each one has acted, ' as though
asleep at the time ' when he was ignorant.[10] And this is the way ' he has
come to knowledge, as if ' he had awakened. {And} Good ' for the man
who will come to ' and awaken. And [15] blessed is he who has opened '
the eyes of the blind. And ' the Spirit ran after him, ' hastening from '
waking him up. Having extended his hand [20] to him who lay upon the '
ground, he set him up ' on his feet, for ' he had not yet risen. ' He gave
them the means of knowing [25] the knowledge of the Father and the '
revelation of his Son. '

For when they had seen him and had ' heard him, he granted them to '
taste him and [30] to smell him and ' to touch the ' beloved Son. When he
had appeared ' instructing them about the Father, ' the incomprehensible one, when he had breathed into them [35] what is in the mind, doing '
his will, when many had ' received the light, they turned **31** to him. For
the material ones were strangers ' and did not see his likeness ' and had
not known ' him. For he came [5] by means of fleshly ' appearance while
nothing blocked ' his course because it was ' incorruptibility (and)
irresistibility. ' Again, speaking [10] new things, still speaking about ' what
is in the heart of the Father, he ' brought forth the flawless word. '

Light spoke ' through his mouth,[15] and his voice ' gave birth to life. He ' gave them thought and understanding ' and mercy and salvation and the powerful spirit ' from the infiniteness [20] and the gentleness of the Father. ' He made punishments ' and tortures cease, for it was they which ' were leading astray from his face some ' who were in need of mercy, in [25] error and in bonds; ' and with power he destroyed them ' and confounded them with knowledge. ' He became a ' way for those who were lost [30] and knowledge for those who were ' ignorant, a discovery for those ' who were searching, and a support ' for those who were wavering, ' immaculateness for those who [35] were defiled.

He is the shepherd ' who left behind the ninety-nine [32] sheep which were not lost. ' He went searching for the one which ' was lost. He rejoiced when he ' found it, for 99 [5] is a number that is in the left hand ' which holds it. But ' when the one is found, ' the entire number ' passes to the right (hand). Thus (it is with) [10] him who lacks the one; that is, ' the entire right which ' draws what was deficient and ' takes it from the ' left-hand side and brings (it) to the [15] right, and thus the number ' becomes 100. It is the sign of the one who is in ' their sound; it is the Father. ' Even on the Sabbath, he labored for the sheep ' which he found fallen into the [20] pit. He gave life to ' the sheep, having brought it up ' from the pit in order that you ' might know interiorly— [38] you, the sons of interior [39] knowledge— [24] what is the Sabbath, on which it is not fitting ' for salvation to be idle, ' in order that you may speak ' from the day from above, ' which has no night, ' and from the light [30] which does not sink because it is perfect. ' Say, then, from the heart that ' you are the perfect day ' and in you dwells ' the light that does not fail.[35]

Speak of the truth with those who ' search for it, and (of) knowledge to those ' who have committed sin in their error. [33] Make firm the foot of those ' who have stumbled and stretch out ' your hands to those who are ill. Feed ' those who are hungry and [5] give repose to those who are weary, and ' raise up those who wish to ' rise, and awaken those who ' sleep. For you are the ' understanding that is drawn forth. If [10] strength acts thus, it becomes ' even stronger. Be concerned with yourselves; ' do not be concerned with ' other things which you have ' rejected from yourselves.[15] Do not return to what you have vomited ' to eat it. Do not be moths, ' do not be worms, for you have already ' cast it off. ' Do not become a [20] (dwelling) place for the devil, for ' you have already destroyed him. ' Do not strengthen (those who are) obstacles to you ' who are collapsing, as though (you were) a support (for them). ' For the unjust one is someone to treat [25] ill rather than the just one. ' For the former ' does his works as an ' unjust person; the latter as ' a righteous person does his [30] works among others. So ' you, do the will of the Father, ' for you are from him. '

For the Father is gentle and in ' his will there are good [35] things. He took cognizance of ' the things that are yours that you might find rest ' in them. For by the ' fruits does one take cognizance of ' the things that are yours because the children of the Father [34] are his fragrance, for ' they are from the grace of his ' countenance. For this reason the Father loves ' his fragrance and manifests it [5] in every place, and if it mixes ' with matter he gives his fragrance ' to the light and in his repose ' he causes it to surpass every form ' (and) every sound. For it is not the ears that [10] smell the fragrance, but ' (it is) the breath that has ' the sense of smell and attracts the fragrance ' to itself and is submerged ' in the fragrance of the Father. It [15] shelters it, then, takes it to the place ' where it came from, ' the first fragrance which ' is grown cold. It is something in a ' psychic form, being [20] like cold water ' which has [. . .], which is on earth ' that is not solid, of which those ' who see it think it ' is earth; afterwards it dissolves [25] again. If a breath ' draws it, it gets hot. The fragrances ' therefore that are cold are from the division. ' For this reason [faith] came; ' it did away with the division,[30] and it brought the warm pleroma ' of love in order that ' the cold should not come again ' but there should be the unity of ' perfect thought.[35]

This ⟨is⟩ the word of the gospel ' of the discovery of the pleroma, for ' those who await [35] the salvation which is coming ' from on high. While their ' hope which they ' are waiting for is waiting—they whose image [5] is light with no shadow ' in it—then at that time ' the pleroma ' is about to come. The deficiency ' of matter has not arisen through [10] the limitlessness of ' the Father, who is about to bring the time of ' the deficiency, although no one ' could say that the incorruptible one will ' come in this way. But [15] the depth of the Father was multiplied ' and the thought of ' error did not exist ' with him. It is a thing that falls, ' it is a thing that easily stands upright (again) [20] in the discovery of him ' who has come to him whom he shall bring back. ' For the bringing back ' is called repentance. '

For this reason incorruptibility [25] breathed forth; it pursued the one ' who had sinned in order that he might ' rest. For forgiveness is ' what remains for the light in the deficiency, ' the word of the pleroma.[30] For the physician runs to the place ' where a sickness is because ' that is his will that is ' in him. He who has a deficiency, then, does not ' hide it, because one has what [35] the other lacks. So with the ' pleroma, which has no deficiency; ' it fills up his deficiency—(it is) that which he **36** provided for filling up ' what he lacks, in order that ' therefore he might receive the grace. When ' he was deficient he did not have [5] the grace. That is why ' there was diminution existing in ' the place where there is no grace. ' When that which was diminished ' was received, he revealed what he [10] lacked, as a pleroma; ' that is the discovery of the light ' of truth which rose upon him because ' it is immutable.

That is why ' Christ was spoken of in their [15] midst, so that those who were ' disturbed might receive a bringing back, and he ' might anoint them with the ointment. The ointment is ' the mercy of the Father who will have mercy ' on them. But those whom he has anointed [20] are the ones who have become perfect. ' For full jars are the ' ones that are usually anointed. But when ' the anointing of one (jar) is dissolved, ' it is emptied, and the [25] reason for there being a deficiency is the thing ' through which its ointment goes. ' For at that time ' a breath draws it, one ' by the power of the one with it.[30] But from him who ' has no deficiency no seal is removed, ' nor is anything emptied. ' But what he lacks ' the perfect Father fills again.[35] He is good. He knows ' his plantings because it is he ' who planted them in his paradise. ' Now his paradise ' is his place of rest.

This **37** is the perfection in the thought ' of the Father, and these are ' the words of his meditation. ' Each one of his words [5] is the work of his ' one will in the revelation ' of his Word. While they were still in ' the depth of his thought, the Word ' which was first to come forth revealed [10] them along with a mind that ' speaks the one Word in ' silent grace. It (masc.) was called ' thought since they ' were in it (fem.) before being revealed.[15] It came about, then, that it ' was first to come forth at the ' time that was pleasing to the ' will of him who willed. ' And the will is what the Father [20] rests in and ' is pleased with. Nothing ' happens without him, nor does anything ' happen without the will of ' the Father, but his will [25] is incomprehensible. His trace ' is the will, and no one ' will know it, nor is it possible ' for one to scrutinize it in order to ' grasp it. But [30] when he wills, ' what he wills is this—even if ' the sight does not please them ' in any way—before God (it is) the ' will, the Father. For he knows the [35] beginning of all of them and their end. ' For at their end he will question them ' directly (?). Now the end is receiving knowledge ' about the one who is hidden, and this is the Father, **38** from whom the beginning came ' forth, to whom all will ' return who have ' come forth from him.[5] And they have appeared for the glory and the ' joy of his name. '

Now the name of the Father is the Son. It is he ' who first gave a name to the one ' who came forth from him, who was himself,[10] and he begot him as a son. ' He gave him his name which ' belonged to him; he is the one to whom ' belongs all that exists around ' him, the Father. His is the name; [15] his is the Son. It is possible ' for him to be seen. But the name ' is invisible because ' it alone is the ' mystery of the invisible [20] which comes to ears that are completely filled ' with it. For indeed ' the Father's name is not spoken, ' but it is apparent through a ' Son.

In this way, then, the name is a great thing.[25] Who therefore will be able to utter a name for him, ' the great name, except him ' alone to whom ' the name belongs and the sons of the name ' in whom rested [30] the name of the Father, ' (who) in turn themselves rested ' in his name? Since the ' Father is unengendered, he alone is the one ' who begot a name for himself [35] before he brought forth the ' aeons in order that the name ' of the Father should be over their head as ' lord, that is, the **39** name in truth, which is firm in his ' command through perfect power. ' For the name is not from ' (mere) words, nor [5] does his name consist of appellations, ' but it is invisible. ' He gave a name to himself ' since he sees himself, he ' alone having [10] the power to give himself a name. ' For he who does not exist ' has no name. ' For what name is given to him ' who does not exist? [15] But the one who exists ' exists also with his name, and ' he knows himself. ' And to give himself a name ' is (the prerogative of) the Father. The Son [20] is his name. He did ' not therefore hide it in the work, ' but the Son ' existed; he alone was given the name. ' The name therefore is that of the Father,[25] as the name of ' the Father is the Son. Where ' indeed would mercy find a name ' except with the Father?

But ' no doubt one will say [30] to his neighbor, "Who is it ' who will give a name to him who ' existed before himself, ' as if offspring did not receive a name **40** from those ' who begot them?" First, ' then, it is fitting for us ' to reflect on this matter: what [5] is the name? It is the name ' in truth; it is not therefore ' the name from the father, for ' it is the one which is the proper ' name. Therefore he did not receive the name [10] on loan as (do) others, according to the form ' in which each one ' is to be produced. ' But this is the proper name.[15] There is no one else who gave it to him. ' But he is unnameable, ' indescribable, ' until the time when he ' who is perfect spoke of himself.[20] And it is he who ' has the power to speak ' his name and to see ' it.

When therefore it pleased ' him that his name [25] which is uttered should be his Son, and ' he gave the name to him, that is, him ' who came forth from the depth, he ' spoke about his secret things, knowing ' that the Father is a being without evil.[30] For that very reason he brought him ' forth in order to speak ' about the place and his ' resting-place from which he had come forth, **41** and to glorify the pleroma, ' the greatness of his name and ' the gentleness of the Father. About ' the place each one came from [5] he will speak, and to the ' region where he received his essential being ' he will hasten to return ' again, and to be taken from ' that place—the place where he [10] stood—receiving a taste ' from that place and ' receiving nourishment, receiving growth. And ' his own resting-place ' is his pleroma.

Therefore [15] all the emanations of the Father ' are pleromas, and ' the root of all his emanations is in ' the one who made them all ' grow up in himself. He assigned them [20] their destinies. Each one then ' is apparent ' in order that through their ' own thought [. . .]. ' For the place to which they send [25] their thought, that place ' (is) their root, which takes them ' up in all the heights ' to the Father. They possess his ' head which is rest for them [30] and they hold on ' close to him, ' as though to say that ' they have participated in his face ' by means of kisses.[35] But they do not appear **42** in this way, ' for they did not surpass themselves ' nor lack the glory ' of the Father nor think of him [5] as small nor that he is harsh ' nor that he is wrathful, but ' a being without evil, imperturbable, ' gentle, knowing ' all spaces before they have come into existence, and [10] having no need to be instructed. '

This is the manner of ' those who possess (something) ' from above of the ' immeasurable greatness, as they [15] stretch out after the one alone ' and the perfect one, the one who is ' there for them. And they do not go down ' to Hades nor have they ' envy nor [20] groaning nor death ' within them, but they ' rest in him who is at rest, ' not striving nor ' being involved in the [25] search for truth. But they ' themselves are the truth; and ' the Father is within them and ' they are in the Father, being perfect, ' being undivided in [30] the truly good one, being ' in no way deficient in anything, but ' they are set at rest, refreshed in the ' Spirit. And they will heed their ' root. They will be concerned with those (things) [35] in which he will find his root ' and not suffer loss to his ' soul. This is the place of the ' blessed; this is their ' place.

For the rest, then, may they [40] know, in their places, that ' it is not fitting for me, **43** having come to be in the resting-place, ' to speak of anything else. But ' it is in it that I shall come to be, to ' be concerned

at all times with the Father of [5] the all and the true brothers, ' those
upon whom the love of ' the Father is poured out and ' in whose midst
there is no lack of him. ' They are the ones who appear [10] in truth since
they exist in ' true and eternal life and ' speak of the light which ' is
perfect and filled with ' the seed of the Father, and [15] which is in his
heart and in the ' pleroma, while his ' Spirit rejoices in it and glorifies '
the one in whom it existed ' because he is good. And [20] his children are
perfect and ' worthy of his name, ' for he is the Father: it is children
of this kind that he ' loves.

THE TREATISE ON RESURRECTION (I, 4)

Introduced and translated by

MALCOLM L. PEEL

The *Treatise on Resurrection* was written by an anonymous teacher to his pupil, Rheginos, in response to questions regarding death and the afterlife. Accordingly, this tractate is of great importance in illuminating Christian Gnostic thought about the resurrection in the late second century. Though permeated with Valentinian symbols and imagery, the document's most striking feature is the similarity of its teaching to the view of Hymenaeus and Philetus combatted in 2 Timothy 2:18 that "the resurrection (of believers) has already occurred."

Debate continues over whether the *Treatise on Resurrection* is a general epistle addressed to a brotherhood or a more personal letter, though lacking an opening naming sender and receiver (like Ptolemy's *Letter to Flora*). Whatever may be the case, the main teachings are clear: the resurrection, though philosophically undemonstrable and seemingly fantastic, is a "necessity" and assuredly real: even now the elect participate proleptically in Christ's own death, resurrection, and ascension (cf. the use of Romans 8:17 and Ephesians 2:5-6 in 45, 24-28). Immediately following death a "spiritual resurrection" of the believer occurs, involving the ascension of a spiritual body composed of invisible "members" covered with a "spiritual flesh." A citation of Mark 9:2-8 (48, 3-11) demonstrates a continuity of identification between the deceased and the resurrected person. Finally, after much assurance, the believer is exhorted to live as if already resurrected (49, 19-36)!

Though some have suggested that the author of the letter may have been Valentinus himself, most scholars would now deny this. Rather, the author seems to be a late second century Christian Gnostic who is certainly influenced by Valentinianism but whose views on several crucial points are closer to the apostle Paul than to Valentinus.

THE TREATISE ON RESURRECTION

I 43, 25-50, 18

Some there are, my son Rheginos, ' who want to learn much. ' They have this goal ' when they are occupied with questions ' whose answer is lacking.[30] If they succeed with these, they usually ' think very highly of ' themselves. But I do not think ' that they have stood within ' the Word of Truth. They seek [35] rather their own rest, which ' we have received through our ' Savior, our Lord Christ. **44** We received it (Rest) when we knew ' the truth and rested ' ourselves upon it. But ' since you ask us [5] pleasantly what is proper ' concerning the resurrection, I am writing ' you (to say) that it is necessary. ' To be sure, many are ' lacking faith in it, but there are a few [10] who find it. ' So then, let us discuss ' the matter. '

How did the Lord make use ' of things while he existed [15] in flesh and after ' he had revealed himself as Son ' of God? He lived ' in this place where you ' remain, speaking [20] about the Law of Nature—but I call ' it "Death"! Now the Son ' of God, Rheginos, ' was Son of Man. ' He embraced them [25] both, possessing the ' humanity and the divinity, ' so that on the one hand he might vanquish ' death through his ' being Son of God,[30] and that on the other through the Son of ' Man the restoration ' to the Pleroma ' might occur; because ' he was originally from above,[35] a seed of the Truth, before ' this structure (of the cosmos) had come into being. ' In this (structure) many dominions and ' divinities came into existence. '

I know that I am presenting **45** the solution in difficult terms, ' but there is nothing ' difficult in the Word ' of Truth. But since [5] the Solution appeared ' so as not to leave anything hidden, ' but to reveal all ' things openly concerning ' existence—the destruction [10] of evil on the one hand, the revelation ' of the elect on the other—this is ' the emanation of Truth and ' Spirit; Grace is that which belongs to Truth. '

The Savior swallowed up [15] death—(of this) you are not reckoned as being ignorant— ' for he put aside the world ' which is perishing. He transformed [himself] ' into an imperishable Aeon ' and raised himself up, having [20] swallowed the visible ' by the invisible, ' and he gave us ' the way of our immortality. Then, ' indeed, as the Apostle [25] said (Romans 8:17, Ephesians 2:5-6),

"We suffered ' with him, and we arose ' with him, and we went to heaven ' with him."

Now if we are ' manifest in [30] this world wearing ' him, we are that one's beams, ' and we are ' embraced by ' him until our setting, that is [35] to say, our death in this life. ' We are drawn to heaven ' by him, like beams ' by the sun, not being restrained ' by anything. This is [40] the spiritual resurrection **46** which swallows up the psychic ' in the same way as the fleshly. '

But if there is one who ' does not believe, he does not have [5] the (capacity to be) persuaded. For it is the position of faith, ' my son, and not that which belongs ' to persuasion: the dead shall ' arise! There is one who believes ' among the philosophers who are in this world.[10] At least he will arise. And let not the philosopher ' who is in this world

have cause to ' believe that he is one who returns himself ' by himself—
and (that) because of our faith! ' For we have known the Son of [15] Man,
and we have believed ' that he rose from among the ' dead. This is he
of whom we say, ' "He became the destruction ' of death, as he is a great
one [20] in whom they believe." ' ⟨Great⟩ are those who believe. '

The thought of those ' who are saved shall not perish. ' The mind of
those who have known him shall not perish.[25] Therefore, we are elected
to ' salvation and redemption since ' we are predestined from the
beginning ' not to fall into the ' foolishness of those who are without
knowledge,[30] but we shall enter into the ' wisdom of those who have
known the ' Truth. Indeed, the Truth which is guarded ' cannot be
abandoned, ' nor has it been.[35]

"Strong is the system of the ' Pleroma; small is that which ' broke
loose (and) became ' [the] world. But the All is ' what is encompassed. It has [not] **47** come into being; it was existing."

Therefore, ' never doubt concerning ' the resurrection, my son Rheginos. ' For if you were not existing [5] in flesh, you received flesh when
you ' entered this world. Why ' will you not receive flesh when you '
ascend into the Aeon? ' That which is better than the flesh, which is [10]
for it (the) cause of life, ' that which came into being on your account,
is it not ' yours? Does not that which is yours ' exist with [you]? ' Yet,
while you are in this world, what is it that you [15] lack? This is what '
you have been making every effort to learn. '

The afterbirth of the body is ' old age, and you ' exist in corruption.
You have [20] absence as a gain. ' For you will not give up what ' is better
if you depart. That which is worse ' has diminution, ' but there is grace
for it.

Nothing,[25] then, redeems us from ' this world. But the All which ' we
are—we are saved. We have received ' salvation from end ' to end. Let
us think in this way! [30] Let us comprehend in this way!

But ' there are some (who) wish to understand, ' in the inquiry about '
those things they are looking into, whether ' he who is saved, if he
leaves [35] his body behind, will ' be saved immediately. Let ' no one be
given cause to doubt concerning this. ' . . . indeed, the visible members '
which are dead **48** shall not be saved, for (only) the living [members] '
which exist within ' them would arise.

What, ' then, is the resurrection? [5] It is always the disclosure of ' those
who have risen. For if you ' remember reading in the Gospel ' that
Elijah appeared ' and Moses [10] with him, do not think the resurrection '
is an illusion. ' It is no illusion, but ' it is truth. Indeed, it is more '

fitting to say that [15] the world is an illusion, ' rather than the resurrection which ' has come into being through ' our Lord the Savior, ' Jesus Christ.[20]

But what am I telling ' you now? Those who are living ' shall die. How ' do they live in an illusion? ' The rich have become poor,[25] and the kings have been overthrown. ' Everything is prone ' to change. The world ' is an illusion!—lest, ' indeed, I rail at [30] things to excess!

But ' the resurrection does not have ' this aforesaid character; for ' it is the truth which stands firm. ' It is the revelation of [35] what is, and the transformation ' of things, and a ' transition into ' newness. For imperishability **49** [descends] upon ' the perishable; the light flows ' down upon the darkness, ' swallowing it up; and the Pleroma [5] fills up the deficiency. ' These are the symbols and ' the images of the resurrection. ' This is what makes the ' good.

Therefore, do not [10] think in part, O Rheginos, ' nor live ' in conformity with this flesh for the sake of ' unanimity, but flee ' from the divisions and the [15] fetters, and already you have ' the resurrection. For if ' he who will die knows ' about himself that he ' will die—even if he spends many [20] years in this life he is ' brought to this— ' why not consider yourself ' as risen and (already) ' brought to this? [25] If you have ' the resurrection but continue as if ' you are to die—and yet that one knows ' that he has died—why, then, ' do I ignore your [30] lack of exercise? It is fitting for each ' one to practice ' in a number of ways, and ' he shall be released from this Element ' that he may not be misled but shall himself [35] receive again ' what at first was. '

These things I have received from ' the magnanimity of my **50** Lord Jesus Christ. [I have] taught ' you and your [brethren], my sons, concerning them, ' while I have not omitted any of ' the things suitable for strengthening you (pl.).[5] But if there is one thing written ' which is obscure in my exposition of ' the Word, I shall interpret it for you (pl.) ' when you (pl.) ask. But now, ' do not be envious of anyone who is in your number [10] when he is able to help. '

Many are looking forward to ' this which I have written ' to you. To these I say: ' peace (be) among them and grace.[15] I greet you and those who love ' you (pl.) in brotherly love. '

The Treatise on the '
Resurrection

THE TRIPARTITE TRACTATE (I, 5)

Introduced by

HAROLD W. ATTRIDGE and ELAINE H. PAGELS

Translated by

HAROLD W. ATTRIDGE and DIETER MUELLER

The *Tripartite Tractate*, named for the three parts of the text, narrates the origin and history of the universe from the beginning to the anticipated "restoration of all things." The first part begins by describing what is transcendent ("the things that are exalted"), above all, the Father "who is the root of everything," the "depth, the abyss, and the Unengendered One." While such language shows affinity with the language of Valentinian Gnostics, this author, unlike Valentinus, declares that the Father is "alone, without any companion," encompassing within himself all the qualities that other Valentinian sources attribute to feminine elements of the divine being (that is, the Mother, Silence, Grace). The Father, "out of the abundance of his sweetness," desires to share himself, and so engenders the Son, the "only begotten," who exists "from the beginning" in the Father's thought. With the Son, "preexisting from the beginning," is the church which comes forth from the love between the Father and the Son. Thereby the author of the *Tripartite Tractate* interprets the divine being (here called the pleroma, literally the "fullness") in terms of only three primary members—Father, Son, and Church—a theological innovation that Tertullian attributes to the western Valentinian teacher Heracleon.

The text goes on to relate the process of devolution and precreation known from Valentinian sources in the form of the myth of Sophia. Unlike any known Valentinian teacher, however, this author transposes the myth into a myth of the Word (Logos). Here it is the divine Logos who undergoes suffering, and brings forth from himself the elements involved in creation. This author insists, perhaps in response to "orthodox" criticism, that the Logos' "rash act," far from violating the Father's will, actually fulfills it in bringing forth the dispensation.

The second part of the *Tripartite Tractate*, interpreting the Genesis account, relates the creation of the human race and explains how the fall led to the dominion of death. From this account the author explains that there came into existence three different types of human beings: those identified with spirit (the pneumatics, or spiritual ones), those identified with matter (the hylics, or material ones), and those identified with soul (the psychics, composed of a mixture of spirit and matter).

The third part of the tractate describes how the Savior came into the world to release humankind from death, to redeem the church, and to "restore all things" to the Father. Human response to Christ's coming depends on each person's essential nature. Those whose inclination is material reject him, and face ultimate destruction; those who are spiritual, together with those of the psychics who believe in Christ and obey him, are to be redeemed and restored to God. The text closes with praise to the Father through "Jesus the Lord" and through the "Holy Spirit."

While the language and teaching of this text show affinities with Valentinian theology, it offers radically different interpretations of such major themes as the nature of God the Father, and the activity of the Logos in creation and redemption. Thus, the *Tripartite Tractate* offers a remarkable new source for understanding how a Gnostic teacher interprets the major themes of Christian theology.

THE TRIPARTITE TRACTATE

I 51, 1-138, 25

As for what we can say about the things which are exalted, ' it is fitting that we ' begin with the Father, who is the root of ' everything, the one from whom we have received [5] grace to ' say of him that he existed ' before anything other than himself ' came into being.

The Father is a ' unity, like a [10] number, for he is the first and is that which ' he alone is. Yet he is ' not like a solitary individual. ' Otherwise, how could he be a father? ' For whenever there is a "father," [15] it follows that there is a "son." But the single ' one, who alone is ' the Father, is like a root ' with tree, branches, ' and fruit. It is said [20] of him that he is ' a father in the proper sense, since he is ' inimitable ' and immutable, because ' he is a sole lord [25] and is a god, because no ' one is a god for him nor ' is anyone a father to him. ' For he is unbegotten and there is no other ' who begot him, nor [30] another who created him. ' For whoever is someone's father ' or someone's creator, ' he, too, has a father and ' creator. It is certainly possible [35] for him to be the father and the creator ' of the one who came into being ' from him and the one whom he created. ' Yet he is not a father ' in the proper sense, nor [40] a god, because he has **52** someone who begot [him and] who ' created him. In the proper sense, then, ' the only Father and God ' is the one whom no one else begot. As for the universe,[5] he is the one who begot it and ' created it.

He is without beginning ' and without end; for not only ' is he without end—he is immortal for this reason, ' that he is unbegotten— [10] but he is also invariable in ' his eternal existence, ' in his identity, in that ' by which he is established, and in that ' by which he is great. Neither [15] will he remove himself from what he ' is, nor will anyone else ' force him to approach ' a goal which he has not ever desired, ' since he has

not had [20] anyone who initiated his own existence. ' Likewise he is himself unchanged, ' and no one else ' can remove him from his ' existence
and [25] his identity, that by which he is, ' and his greatness. Thus ' he cannot be grasped, nor is it possible ' for anyone else to change him into a
different ' form or to reduce him, alter him,[30] or diminish him, because
this, ' in the fullest sense, is the truth: ' he is the unalterable, unchangeable one, ' with immutability clothing him. '

Not only is he the one [35] called ' "without a beginning" and "without
an end," ' because he is unbegotten ' and immortal. ' But just as he
has [40] no beginning and no ' end, so he is ' unattainable [53] in his greatness, inscrutable ' in his wisdom, incomprehensible ' in his power, ' and
unfathomable in his [5] sweetness.

In the proper sense ' he alone is the good, ' the unbegotten Father
and the ' complete perfect one. He is the one filled ' with all his offspring [10] and with every virtue and with ' everything of value. And he
has ' more, that is, lack of any ' evil. In order that it may be discovered '
that he has everything that he has,[15] he gives it away, being unsurpassed '
and not wearied ' by that which he gives, but wealthy ' (precisely) in the
gifts which he bestows ' and at rest [20] in the favors which he grants. '

He is of such kind and ' such form and such great magnitude '
that no one else has been with ' him from the beginning;
nor is there a place [25] in which he is, or from which he has come
forth, ' or into which he will go; '
nor is there a primordial form ' which he uses as a model ' in his
work;
nor is there any difficulty [30] which accompanies him in what ' he
does;
nor is there any material set ' out for him, from which he creates '
what he creates; '
nor any substance within him from [35] which he begets what he
begets; '
nor a co-worker ' who, along with him, does what he does. '

To say anything of this sort ' is ignorant. Rather,[40] as one who is good,
blameless, perfect, and [54] complete, he by himself is everything. '

Not one of ' the names which are conceived, ' spoken, seen, or [5]
grasped, ' not one of them, applies to him, ' even if they are exceedingly
glorious, great, ' and honored. However, ' it is possible to utter these
names for his glory [10] and honor, in accordance with the capacity ' of
each of those who give him glory. ' Yet as for him, in his own ' existence, being, ' and form,[15] it is impossible for mind to conceive ' him,

nor can any work ' express him,
nor can any eye ' see him,
nor can any body ' grasp him,
 because of [20] his inscrutable greatness, '
 and his incomprehensible depth, '
 and his immeasurable height, '
 and his illimitable will. '

This is the nature of the [25] unbegotten one, which does not touch ' anything else, nor is it joined (to anything) ' in the manner of something which is limited. ' Rather, he possesses this constitution, ' without having a [30] face or a form, things which ' are understood through ' perception, which the incomprehensible one transcends. ' If he is incomprehensible, ' then it follows that [35] he is unknowable, that he is the one who is inconceivable ' by any thought, ' invisible in any thing, ' ineffable by any word, ' untouchable by any hand.[40] He alone ' is the one who knows himself as he [55] is, along with his form ' and his greatness and his magnitude, ' and who has the ability to ' conceive of himself, to see himself, to name [5] himself, to comprehend himself, since he ' alone is the one who is his own mind, ' his own eye, ' his own mouth, his own ' form, and the one who conceives [10] of himself, who sees himself, ' who speaks of himself, who comprehends ' himself, ' namely, the inconceivable, ' ineffable, the incomprehensible, unchanging one.[15]

He is sustenance;
he is joy; '
he is truth;
he is rejoicing; '
he is rest.
That which he conceives, '
that which he sees,
that about which he speaks, '
the thought which he has,[20]
 transcends ' all wisdom,
 and is ' above all intellect,
 and is ' above all glory,
 and is ' above all honor,
  and [25] all sweetness,
  and all greatness, '
  and any depth,
  and any height. '

If this one, who is ' unknowable in his ' nature, to whom pertain all the greatnesses which [30] I already mentioned, ' if in the abundance of his sweetness he wishes to grant knowledge ' so that he might be known, ' he has the ability to do so. ' He has his power,[35] which is his will. Now, however, ' it is in silence that he keeps himself, ' he who is ' the great one, who is the cause ' of bringing the Totalities into their [40] eternal being. **56**

He himself, '

>since in the proper sense he begets ' himself as ineffable one, '
>since he is self-begotten,[5]
>since he conceives of himself,
>and since he ' knows himself as he is, '
>>(namely as) the one who is worthy of ' his admiration, and
>>glory, and honor, ' and praise,
>since he produces himself [10]
>>because of the boundlessness ' of his greatness,
>>and the ' unsearchability of his ' wisdom,
>>and the immeasurability ' of his power,
>>and his [15] untasteable sweetness, '

he is the one who projects himself ' in this manner of generation, thus having ' honor and a wondrous glory ' of love; the one who [20] gives himself glory, ' who wonders, who ' honors, who also loves; ' the one who has ' a Son,

>who subsists [25] in him,
>who is silent concerning him;
>who is ' the ineffable one ' in the ineffable one,
>the ' invisible one,
>the incomprehensible one, '
>the inconceivable one in [30] the inconceivable one.

Thus, ' the Father exists forever, ' as we said earlier, ' in an unbegotten way, the one who ' knows himself,[35] who begot himself, who ' has a thought, ' which is the thought ' of himself, that is, the **57** perception of himself, which is the [foundation] ' of his constitution ' forever. That is, ' in the proper sense,[5] the silence and the wisdom ' and the grace which is designated ' properly ' in this way.

Just as [the] ' Father exists in the fullest sense,[10] the one before whom [there was no one] ' else and [the one] ' after [whom] there is no other unbegotten one, so ' too the [Son] ' exists in the fullest sense,[15] the one before whom there is no other ' and after whom ' no other son exists. ' Therefore he is a first-born ' and an only Son,[20] the first-born because no one ' exists before him and the only Son ' because no one is after ' him. Furthermore, he has ' his own fruit,[25] that which is unknown because ' of its surpassing greatness. Yet ' he wanted it to be known, ' because of the riches of his ' sweetness.[30] And he revealed the unsurpassable power and ' he combined with it ' the great abundance of his generosity. '

Not only does the Son exist ' from the beginning, but the Church,[35] too, exists from the beginning. ' Now he who thinks that the discovery ' that the Son is an only son ' opposes the word (about the church)— ' because of the mysterious quality of the matter [40] it is not so. For just as **58** the Father is a unity ' and has revealed himself ' as a father for him (the Son) ' alone, so too [5] the Son was found ' to be a brother to him (the Father) alone, ' in virtue of the fact that he is unbegotten ' and without beginning. He ' wonders at himself [10] [along with the] Father, and he gives ' [him(self)] glory and honor and ' [love]. Furthermore, he too ' is the one who conceives of himself ' as Son, in accordance with the [15] conditions: "without ' beginning" and "without end." ' The matter (of the Son) exists just as ' something which is fixed. ' His offspring, the things which exist, being innumerable,[20] illimitable, and inseparable, ' have, ' like kisses, come ' forth from the Son and the Father, ' (like kisses) because of the multitude [25] of those who kiss one ' another with a ' good, insatiable thought, ' the kiss being a unity, although it involves ' many. Such is the [30] Church consisting of many men, which ' exists before the aeons, ' and which is called, in the proper ' sense, "the aeons of the aeons." ' Such is the nature of the [35] holy imperishable spirits, ' upon which the Son rests, ' since his essence is like ' that of the Father who rests **59** upon the Son.

[. . .] ' the Church exists in the ' conditions and properties ' in which the Father and the Son exist,[5] as I mentioned previously. ' Therefore it subsists ' in the innumerable aeonic procreations. ' Also in an uncountable way [they] ' too beget, by [the] properties [and] [10] the conditions in which it (the Church) [exists]. ' These [comprise the] ' constitution which [they form] ' with one another and [with those] ' who have come forth from them [15] toward the Son, for whose glory they exist. ' Therefore ' it is not possible for mind to conceive ' them. They were the perfection of that place, ' and no word [20] designates them, for they are ineffable ' and unnameable ' and inconceivable. They ' alone have the ability ' to name themselves in order to conceive [25] of themselves. For they have not been planted ' in these places.

The things which pertain to that place ' are ineffable, ' (and) innumerable in ' the system, which is [30]

the manner and
the ' size and
the joy and
the gladness '
    of the unbegotten, '
    nameless,
    unnameable, '
    inconceivable,
    invisible,[35]
    incomprehensible one. '

It is the fullness of the Fatherhood, ' so that his abundance ' is a begetting. **60**

[. . .] all of the aeons ' were forever in ' the thought of the Father, ' who was like a thinking [5] of them and a place (for them). When the generations had been established, ' the one who controls everything ' wished to take, ' to lay hold of, and to bring ' forth those who were deficient in the [10] [. . ., and he brought] forth those who ' [are] in him. But since he is ' [as] he is, ' [he is like] a spring which is not ' diminished by the water which [15] abundantly flows from it. ' At the time that they were ' in the Father's thought, that ' is, in the hidden depth, ' the depth knew them,[20] but they ' were unable to know ' the depth in which they were; ' nor could ' they know [25] themselves; nor ' could they know anything else. In ' other words, they were ' with the Father; they did not exist by ' themselves. Rather,[30] they only had ' existence in the manner ' of a seed. Thus it has been discovered ' that they existed like a ' fetus. Like the word,[35] he begot them, and they subsisted ' spermatically, before ' the ones whom he was to beget came into being. **61** Therefore the Father who ' first thought of them— ' not only so that they might exist for him, ' but also that they might exist for themselves as well,[5] that they might then exist in [his] thought ' with the mode of existence proper to thought, ' and that they might exist for themselves too—he ' sowed a thought like a seed ' of [knowledge], so that [they] [10] might know [what it is that has come into being] ' for them. He graciously [granted the] ' initial form that they might [think about] ' who is the Father who exists [. . .]. ' He gave them the name "father" [15] by means of a voice proclaiming to them ' that what exists exists through ' that name which they have ' by virtue of the fact that they come into being.

The exalted one, ' whom they have forgotten, is in the name.[20]—While in the ' form of a fetus, the infant is ' self-sufficient ' before ever seeing the one who ' sowed him.—Therefore, they had [25] the sole task ' of

searching for him, realizing ' that he exists, ever wishing to find out '
what it is that exists. Since, however, ' the perfect Father is good,[30] just
as he did not hear ' them until they came into being ' in his thought,
but (then) granted that ' they too might come into being, so ' also will
he give them grace [35] to know what it is that exists, ' that is, the one
who knows ' himself eternally, 62 [and the one who has given them a] '
form to [know] what it is that ' exists. As they are begotten in this '
place, when they are born, they are in [5] the light, so that they see those
who have begotten them. '

The Father brought forth everything. '

Like a little child, '
like a drop from a ' spring,
like a blossom [10] from a [vine],
like a ' [flower], ·
like a planting, '

[they are] in need of gaining ' [knowledge] and growth and ' faultlessness. He withheld it [15] for a time, he who had thought ' of it from the
very beginning. He ' has possessed it from the very beginning, ' he saw
it, and he closed it ' to those who first came from [20] him. (He did this),
not out of envy, but ' in order that the aeons might not receive their
faultlessness ' from the very beginning ' and might not exalt themselves
to the ' Father in glory and might not think [25] that from themselves
alone ' they have this. But ' just as he wished ' to grant that they might
come into being, so ' too (he wished to grant) that they might come into
being as [30] faultless ones. When he wished, he gave them ' the perfect
idea of ' beneficence ' toward them.

The one whom he took up ' as a light for those who came [35] from himself, the one ' from whom they take their name, ' he is the Son, who is
full, complete, ' and blameless. He (the Father) brought him forth '
united with the one who came forth from 63 him [. . .] ' partaking of
the [glory from] ' the Totality, in so [far] as each ' one can receive [him]
for himself,[5] since his greatness is not such ' before they receive him,
but ' he does certainly exist, as ' he is, in his own manner and ' form
and greatness.[10] Since it is possible for them to see him ' and for them to
say that which they know ' of him since they bear ' him while he bears
them [. . .], ' it is possible for them to comprehend him.[15] He, however,
is as he is, ' the incomparable one. ' In order that he might receive '
honor from each one, ' the Father reveals himself,[20] and yet in his
ineffability ' he is hidden as an invisible ' one, while he mentally wonders
at himself. ' Therefore the ' greatness of his loftiness consists in the fact

that they [25] speak about him and see him. ' He becomes manifest, ' so that he may be hymned because of the abundance ' of his sweetness, with the grace ' of. . . . Just as [30] the admirations ' of the silences ' are eternal generations ' and they are mental offspring, ' so too the dispositions [35] of the word are spiritual ' emanations. Both of them (admirations and dispositions), ' since they belong to a word, **64** are [. . .] and ' thoughts [of] his begetting, ' and roots which live ' forever, showing that [5] they are offspring which have come forth from ' him, being minds and ' spiritual offspring to ' the glory of the Father.

There is no need ' for voice and spirit, for mind and [10] word, [. . .] nor is there need to ' [work at] that which they desire ' [to do], but as ' [he] was, so ' have they come forth from him,[15] begetting everything which they desire. And ' the one whom they conceive of,
> and ' whom they speak about,
> and the one ' toward whom they move,
> and ' the one in whom they are,
> and [20] the one whom they hymn,
to him do they give glory. ' They have ' sons—for this is their power ' as begetters—even like ' those from whom they have come,[25] according to their mutual assistance, ' since they assist one another ' like the unbegotten ones. '

The Father, in accordance with his ' exalted position over the Totalities, being [30] an unknown and incomprehensible one, ' has greatness ' of the sort and magnitude, such that ' if he had formerly revealed himself ' suddenly [35] to all the exalted ones among the aeons ' who had come forth from him, they ' would have perished. Therefore he ' withheld his power and his ease ' within that which he **65** is. [He is] ' ineffable [and] unnameable ' and exalted above every mind ' and every word. He, however, reached [5] out from himself, ' and what he spread out ' is what gave a confirmation and ' a place and a dwelling to ' the universe, a name of his being "the [10] one by whom," since he is ' the Father of the universe. Therefore [he] ' labored for those who exist, ' having sown himself into their thought so that [they] ' might seek after him. The abundance of [their . . .] [15] is the fact that they think that he ' exists and that they seek after what it is ' [that] he was. This one was ' given to them for enjoyment and ' nourishment and joy and an abundance [20] of the illumination, which ' consists in his fellow laboring, ' his knowledge, and his mingling ' with them. This is the one ' who is called and is, in fact,[25] the Son, since he is the Totality ' and the one whose identity is known ' and the one who clothes himself with them. ' He is the one who is called '

"Son," and the one of whom they think [30] that he exists and they were seeking ' after him. This is the one who is ' a Father, and the one whom they are not able to speak about, ' and the one of whom they do not conceive; ' he is the one who first exists.[35]

It is impossible for anyone to conceive ' of him or think of him. Who can ' approach there, toward the exalted one, ' toward the preexistent in the proper ' sense? But all the names conceived **66** or spoken ' about him are produced ' for an honor, as a trace ' of him, according to the power of each [5] of those who glorify him. Now he ' who arose from him stretches ' himself out for begetting and ' for knowledge on the part of the Totalities. He ' [also], without falsification, is all of the names,[10] and he is, ' in the proper sense, the sole first one, ' [the] man of the Father. He it is whom I ' call the form of the formless, '

    the body of the bodiless,
    the face [15] of the invisible,
    the word of [the] ' unutterable,
    the mind of the inconceivable, '
    the fountain which flows from ' him,
    the root of those who are planted, '
    and the god of those who exist,
    the light [20] of those whom he illuminates,
    the love of those ' whom he loved,
    the providence of those for whom he ' providentially cares,
    the wisdom ' of those whom he made wise,
    the power ' of those to whom he gives power,
    the assembly [25] of those whom he assembles,
    the revelation ' of the things which are sought after,
    the eyes ' of those who see,
    the breath of those who breathe, '
    the life of those who live,
    the unity ' of those who are mixed with the Totalities.[30]

All of these are in the single one, ' as he clothes himself completely. ' By his single name ' he is never called. ' And in [35] this unique way they are equally ' a single individual and the Totalities. ' He is neither divided as a body, ' nor is split up into the names ' which he has.[40] He is different in one way and different **67** in another. [Yet] ' he does not change by [. . .] nor ' is he changed into [the] names ' which he has. He is now this, now [5] something else, with each ' item being different. ' Yet he is entirely and completely himself. [He] ' is each and every one of the Totalities ' forever at the same time. He is what [10] all of them are. He, as '

the Father of the Totalities, also is the Totalities, ' for he is the one who
is knowledge ' for himself and he is ' each one of the qualities. He [15]
has the powers and he is beyond ' all that which he knows, ' while seeing
himself ' completely and having a ' Son and a form. Therefore [20] his
powers and properties are innumerable ' and inaudible, ' because of the
begetting by which he ' begets them. Innumerable ' and indivisible are [25]
the begettings of his words, and ' his commands and his Totalities. ' He
knows them—which things he himself is, ' since they are in ' the single
name, and [30] are all speaking within him. And ' he brings (them) forth,
in order that ' it might be discovered that they ' exist according to their
individual properties in a unified way. ' And he did not reveal the
multitude [35] to the Totalities at once, ' nor did he reveal his equality ' to
those who had come forth from him. '

All those who came forth from him, ' who are the aeons of the aeons,
68 they are emanations, they are offspring of ' his procreative nature. '
They too, in their procreative ' nature, have given glory to [5] the Father,
since he was ' the cause of their ' establishment. This is what ' we said
originally, namely that he created ' the aeons as roots and [10] springs and
fathers, and that he ' to whom they give glory has begotten, for ' he has
knowledge ' and wisdom, ' and the Totalities know [15] that it is from
knowledge ' and wisdom that they have come forth. ' They would have
brought forth ' a semblance of honor—"The Father is the one ' who is
the Totalities"— [20] if the aeons had risen up to give ' honor individually. ' Therefore, in the ' song of glorification and ' in the power of the
unity [25] of him from ' whom they have come, they were drawn into a
mingling ' and a combination and a unity ' with one another. ' They
offered glory worthy of [30] the Father from the pleromatic ' congregation,
which is a ' single image although many, ' because it was brought forth
as a glory ' for the single one and because [35] they came forth toward the
one who ' is himself the Totalities. Now this **69** is their praise [. . .] to '
the one who brought forth the Totalities, ' being a first fruit of the
immortals ' and an eternal one, because [5] it was from the living aeons
that it came forth, ' perfect and full, because of the one who is perfect '
and full. It left them full ' and perfect, those who have given glory in ' a
perfect way because of the [10] fellowship. For like the faultless Father
(that he is), ' when he is glorified he ' hears the glory of those who
glorify him, ' so as to make them manifest as that which ' he is.

The cause of the second [15] honor which accrued to them ' was that
which was returned ' to them from the Father when they had known '
the grace by which they bore fruit for one another ' because of the

Father.[20] As a result, just as they ' came forth in glory for the Father, ' so too (have they come forth) in order to appear ' perfect, as a manifestation, ' acting by giving glory.

They [25] are fathers in the third glory ' according to the independence and ' the power which was begotten with them, ' since each one of them individually does not ' exist so as to give glory [30] in a unitary way to him whom he desires (to glorify). '

They are the first and the ' second, and thus they are both perfect and ' full, for they are manifestations ' of the Father who is perfect [35] and full, as well as of those who came forth, ' who are perfect by the fact that they glorify ' the perfect one. The third fruit, however, ' consists of honors of ' the will of each one of the aeons [40] and each one of the properties. ' The Father has power. He is **70** [in] a Pleroma which ' is perfect [in the thought], which is a product of a ' combination as much as it is a product ' of the individuality [5] of the aeons. It is this which he desires ' and over which he has power, ' as it gives glory to the Father. '

For this reason they are minds of ' minds, which are found to be [10] words of words, ' elders of ' elders, depths ' of depths, which are exalted above ' one another. Each one [15] of those who give glory has ' his place and his ' exaltation and his dwelling and his ' rest, which consists of the glory ' which he brings forth.[20]

All those who glorify the Father ' have their begetting ' eternally— they beget in ' the act of assisting one another— ' since the emanations are limitless and [25] immeasurable, and since there is ' no envy on the part ' of the Father toward those who come forth from ' him (so as to prevent) their begetting something ' equal or similar to him, since he is the one who [30] is in the Totalities, begetting ' and revealing himself. ' Whomever he wishes he makes into a father, ' of whom he in fact is Father, ' and a god, of whom he in fact [35] is God, and he makes them ' the Totalities, whose entirety he is. '

All the names which **71** are fair are kept there ' with these (aeons) in the proper sense, ' these (names) which the angels share, ' who have come into being in [5] the cosmos along with the archons, although they do not have ' any resemblance ' to the eternal beings.

The entire system ' of the aeons has ' a love and a longing [10] for the perfect, complete discovery ' of the Father, and this is their unimpeded union. ' Though the Father reveals ' himself eternally, ' he did not wish [15] that they should know him, since he grants that he be ' conceived in such a way as to be sought for, while ' keeping to himself his unsearchable, ' primordial being.

However, ' the Father is the one who has given a start [20] to the aeonic roots, since they are places ' on the peaceful path toward him, ' as toward a school of ' behavior. He has extended to them ' faith in and prayer to him whom [25] they have not seen, and a firm hope ' in him whom they have not conceived, ' and a fruitful love ' which looks toward that which it does not ' see, and an acceptable understanding [30] of the eternal mind, ' and a blessing, ' which is riches and freedom, ' and a wisdom of the one ' who desires the glory of the Father [35] for his thoughts.

It is by virtue of his will that the Father, ' the one who is exalted, is known, **72** that is, ' (by virtue of) the spirit which breathes in the Totalities ' and which gives them an ' idea of seeking after the [5] unknown one, just as one is drawn ' by a pleasant ' aroma to search for the thing ' from which the aroma arises, ' since the aroma [10] of the Father surpasses these ordinary ones. ' For his sweetness ' exists in the aeons in an ' ineffably pleasurable way, ' and it gives them their idea [15] of mingling with him who ' wants them to know him in ' a united way, and (an idea) of assisting ' one another in the spirit which ' is sown within them. Though existing [20] under a great weight, ' they are renewed in an inexpressible way, ' since it is impossible ' for them to be separated from that ' in which they are set in ignorance,[25] because they do not speak, ' being silent about the Father's glory, ' about the one who has power ' to speak, and yet they take form from ' him. He became manifest,[30] though it is impossible to speak of him. ' They have him, hidden in ' their thoughts, since (they are) from ' this one. They are silent about ' the way the Father is [35] in his form, and his nature, ' and his greatness, **73** while the aeons have become worthy of knowing ' through his spirit ' that he is unnameable and ' incomprehensible, through [5] his spirit, which is the trace ' of the discovery of him, providing ' them the ability to conceive of him and ' to speak about him.

Each one ' of the aeons is a name, each of which is [10] a virtue and power of ' the Father. Since he is in many names, which are ' mixed yet harmonious with one another, ' it is possible to speak of him because ' of the wealth of speech, just as the Father [15] is a single name because ' he is a unity, yet is innumerable ' in his properties and ' names.

The emanation of ' the Totalities, which have come into being from the one [20] who exists, did not at all come into being ' separate from one another, ' as something cast off from the one who begets ' them. Rather, their begetting is like ' a process of extension,[25] as the Father extends himself ' to those whom he desires, so that ' those who have come forth from him might ' become him as well.

Just as ' the present aeon, although a [30] unity, is divided into ages, ' and ages are divided into ' years, and years are divided into ' seasons, and seasons into months, ' and months into days, and days [35] into hours, and hours ' into moments, so **74** too the aeon of the Truth, ' being a unity ' and multiplicity, is honored with little ' and great names according to the [5] power of each to grasp it—by way ' of analogy, like a spring ' which is what it is, ' yet flows into rivers ' and lakes and canals [10] and branches, or like a ' root which extends into ' trees with branches and ' fruit, or like a ' human body, which is partitioned [15] in an indivisible way into members ' of members, primary members ' and secondary, great [and] ' small.

The aeons have been brought forth ' in accord with the third [20] fruit by the ' freedom of the will ' and by the wisdom ' which he graciously gave them for their thought. ' They do not wish to honor [25] the one who comes from an agreement, ' though he was produced for words of [praise] ' for each of the Pleromas. ' Nor do they wish ' to give glory with the Totality. Nor do [30] they wish (to do so) with anyone else, ' who was originally above ' the depth of that one, or (above) its ' place, except for the one who exists ' in the exalted name and [35] the exalted place, and only if he receives ' from the one who wished (to praise), **75** taking it to him(self) for the one above ' him. And he begets ' himself, so to speak, and ' through that one, he begets him [5] along with that which he is. He renews ' himself along with the one who came upon him, ' by his brother. He sees him ' and asks him about the matter. '

He who wished to ascend to him,[10] so that it might be in this way, ' he, the one who ' wished to give honor, did not say anything to him about this ' except it alone. For there is a boundary ' to speech set in the Pleroma, so [15] that they are silent about the incomprehensibility ' of the Father, but they speak about the one ' who wishes to comprehend him. It came to ' one of the aeons that it should attempt ' to grasp the incomprehensibility.[20] He gives glory to it, and ' especially to the ineffability of the Father. ' Since he is a Logos of the unity, ' he is one, though he is not from ' the Father of the Totalities, nor [25] from him who brought them forth (the Son). ' For the one who brought forth the Totality is the Father. '

This aeon is among those ' to whom was given wisdom, ' each one of whom preexisted [30] in his thought. By that which he wills ' are they produced. Therefore ' he took a nature of wisdom ' in order to examine the hidden establishment, ' as a fruit of [35] wisdom, for the free will ' which was begotten with ' the Totalities was a cause ' of this one, so that he would do **76** what he desired, with no one ' to restrain him.

The ' intent of the Logos ' was something good.[5] When he had come forth, he gave ' glory to the Father, although he ' had attempted an act beyond his power, ' wishing to bring forth one ' who is perfect, from a [10] harmony in which he had not been, ' and without having a ' command. '

This aeon was last to have been brought ' forth by [15] mutual assistance—and he was young ' in age. And before ' he begot anything else for the glory ' of the will and in harmony with the Totalities, ' he acted magnanimously,[20] from an abundant love, ' and set out ' for the one who is within ' perfect glory, ' for it was not without the will of the Father [25] that the Logos was produced, which ' is to say, not without him (the Father) ' does he (the Logos) go forth. But ' the Father himself had brought him forth ' for those of whom he knew that it was [30] fitting that they should come into being.

The Father ' and the Totalities drew away from him, ' so that the limit, ' which the Father had set, ' might be established—for [35] it is not from the attainment of ' incomprehensibility but by the will **77** of the Father—and furthermore, (they withdrew) so that ' the things which have come to be might become ' a system which would ' be bitter if it did not come into being [5] by the revelation of the Pleroma. ' Therefore it is not fitting to ' criticize the movement which is the Logos, ' but it is fitting that we should say about ' the movement of the Logos, that it is a cause [10] of a system, which has been destined to ' come about.

The Logos begot himself ' as a perfect unity ' for the glory of the Father, the one who ' desired him and who takes pleasure in him,[15] but those whom he (the Logos) wished to take hold ' as an establishment, he begot in shadows, ' models, and likenesses. ' For he was not able to bear the sight ' of the light, but he looked into [20] the depth and he doubted. ' Therefore it was an extremely painful division ' and a turning away because of his ' self-doubt and division, forgetfulness ' and ignorance of himself and [25] of that which is.

His self-exaltation and ' his expectation of comprehending ' the incomprehensible became firm for him ' and was in him. But the sicknesses ' which followed him [30] when he went beyond ' himself came into being ' from self-doubt, namely the fact ' that he did not attain to ' the glory of the Father, the one whose exalted status [35] is unlimited. This one ' did not attain him, for he did not receive him. '

The one whom he brought forth from himself **78** as a unitary aeon ' rushed up to ' that which is his and to his kin ' in the Pleroma. He abandoned [5] that which exists defectively, ' those who had come forth from him in ' an imaginary way, since they are not his. '

When he who produced ' himself as perfect actually did bring [10] himself forth, ' he became weak like a female nature ' which has abandoned its ' virility.

From that ' which was deficient in itself there [15] came those things which came into being ' from his thought and [his] ' arrogance. Because of this ' his perfect (self) left him and raised [itself] ' up to those who are his. He was [20] in the Pleroma as ' a reminder to him that he [would be] ' saved from [his . . .]. '

The one who ran on high and ' the one who drew him to himself were not [25] barren, but brought ' forth a fruit in the Pleroma. ' They upset those who ' were in the defect. '

Like the Pleromas are the things which came into being from the [30] arrogant thought, ' which are their (the Pleromas') ' likenesses, ' models, shadows, ' and phantasms, lacking [35] reason and the light, these ' which belong to the vain thought, ' since they are not products of anything. Therefore [79] their end will be like ' their beginning: (they are) from that which did ' not exist, (and are) to return once again to ' that which will not be. The ones, however,[5] who by themselves ' are great (the Pleromas), are more powerful ' and beautiful than the names ' which are given to them, which are [their] shadows. ' In the manner of a likeness are they (the names) beautiful.[10] For the [face] of the image normally takes its beauty ' from that of which it is an image. '

They thought of themselves, ' that they are beings existing by themselves ' and are without a source,[15] since they do not see anything else ' existing before them. Therefore they ' [live] in disobedience ' [and] acts of rebellion, without ' having humbled themselves before the one because of whom they came into being.[20]

They wanted to command ' one another, outrivalling one another ' in their vain ambition, ' while the glory which they possess ' contains a cause [25] of the system which was to be. '

They are likenesses of the things which are exalted. ' They were brought to a lust for power ' over one another ' according to the glory of the name [30] of which each is a shadow, ' each one imagining that it is superior ' to the others.

The thought of these ' others was not barren, ' but just like those [35] of which they are shadows, all that ' they think about they have as sons [80] and those of whom they thought ' they had ' as offspring. Therefore ' it happened that many offspring came forth from them,[5]

as fighters '
as warriors,
as ' troublemakers,
as apostates ' in disobedience,
as ' lovers of power and [10]
all others such as (derive) ' from these.

The Logos was ' a cause of these [who] ' came into being. He also, to a greater degree, ' was embarrassed and astonished: [15]

instead of perfection, he saw a defect, '
instead of unification, he saw division, '
instead of stability, he [saw] ' disturbances,
instead of [rest], ' tumults.

Neither was it [possible] [20] for him to make them cease from [loving] ' disturbance, nor was it possible for him ' to destroy it. He was powerless, ' once his Totality and his exaltation ' abandoned him.

The things which had come into being [25] unaware of themselves ' both did not know ' the Pleroma from which they came forth, ' and did not know ' the one who was the cause of [30] their existence.

The Logos, ' being in ' such unstable conditions, ' did not continue to bring ' forth anything like emanations,[35] the things which are in the Pleroma, ' the glories which exist for the honor ' of the Father. Rather, he brought **81** [forth] in [...] weakness (things) small and ' [hindered] by their illnesses, ' by which he too was hindered. ' It was the imitation of the system which was [5] a unity, that which ' was the cause of the things ' which do not exist from the first, by ' themselves.

Until the one who brought ' forth these things in the way which was [10] responsible for the defect, until he ' judged those who have come into being because ' of him, contrary to reason, and until that judgment ' was a condemnation, ' he struggled against them for their destruction.[15] These are the ones who struggled against the condemnation ' and whom the wrath pursues, while ' it (the wrath) helps and ' redeems (them) from their (false) opinion and ' apostasy. From it [20] [also] comes the conversion which is ' called "metanoia." ' The Logos turned to [another] opinion ' and another thought, ' turning away from evil and [25] turning toward good. ' Following the conversion, ' the remembrance of the things which exist ' and the prayer came to the one who converted ' himself to the good.[30]

That which is in the Pleroma ' was what he first prayed to, and ' remembered; then (he remembered) his brothers ' individually and (yet) always ' with one another; then all of them together; [35] but before all of them, the Father. **82**

The prayer of the Totality ' helped him to ' return to himself ' and (to) the Totality, for it caused ⁵ him to remember ' those who have existed from the first, ' and them to remember him. This ' is the thought which calls out ' from afar, bringing him back.¹⁰

All his prayer and ' remembering were ' numerous powers according to that limit. ' For there is nothing ' barren in his thought.¹⁵

The powers were good ' and greater than those of the ' likeness. For those belonging to the ' likeness also belong to a [...]. ' From an illusion ²⁰ of similarity and a thought ' of arrogance has [come about] ' that which they became. And they ' originate from the one ' who first knew [them].²⁵

The former ' are like forgetfulness ' and a heavy sleep, being ' like those who dream ' troubled dreams, to whom ³⁰ sleep comes while they— ' those who dream—are oppressed. ' The others are ' like some creatures of light ' for him, looking for ³⁵ the rising of the sun. It happened that ' they saw dreams in it, ' (dreams) which are truly sweet. However, **83** immediately it put a stop ' [to] the emanations of the thought. ' They [did] not any longer have ' their substance, and also they did ⁵ not have honor any longer. '

Though he is not equal to those who ' preexisted, if they were superior to ' the likenesses, it was he alone ' through whom they were more exalted than those,¹⁰ for they are not from a good intent. '

It was not ' from the sickness which came into being that they were produced, ' which (sickness) is the good intent ' from [...], which ¹⁵ sought after the preexistent. ' Once he had prayed, he both exalted ' himself to the good ' and sowed in them ' their predisposition to seek ²⁰ and pray to the ' glorious preexistent one, ' and he sowed in them their thought ' about him and an idea that they should ' think that there is something greater than themselves and that he ²⁵ exists prior to them, although they did not understand ' what he was. Begetting ' agreement and mutual love ' through that thought, ' they acted in ³⁰ unity and unanimity, ' since from ' unity and from unanimity ' they have received their very being. '

They were stronger than them ³⁵ in the lust for power, ' for they were more honored **84** than the first ones, who had raised themselves ' above them. Those had not ' humbled themselves. They thought about themselves ' that they were beings originating from themselves ⁵ alone and were ' without a source. As they brought [forth] ' at first according to their own birth, ' the two orders assaulted one another, ' fighting for ¹⁰ command because of their manner of ' being. As a result they were submerged in ' acts of violence and cruelty, ' as is normal in cases of mutual assault, ' since they have a [15] lust for power ' and all other things ' of this sort. From these the ' vain love of glory draws ' all of them to [20] the desire of the lust ' for power, while none ' of them remembers the ' exalted one nor acknowledges ' him.

The powers [25] of this thought were prepared ' for the works of the preexistent ' ones, those of which they are ' images. For the order ' of those of this sort [30] had mutual ' harmony, and also it ' fought against the order ' of those of the likeness, while the order ' of those of the likeness wages war [35] against the representations and acts ' against it alone, because of its ' wrath. **85** Therefore it [...] ' them [...] ' against one another, in respect [to ...] ' necessity appointed so [that they might ...] [5] and might prevail [over them and ...] ' was not great, [...] ' and their envy and their malice ' and wrath and violence and ' desire and prevailing ignorance [10] produce empty matters and ' powers of various sorts, mixed in ' great number with one another; while the mind of the Logos, which was ' a cause of their begetting, was open to ' a revelation of the hope [15] which would come to him from above.

The Logos ' which moved had ' the hope and the expectation of him ' who is exalted. As for those of the shadow, he separated ' himself from them in every way,[20] since they fight against him and are not at all humble ' before him. He was content ' with the beings of the thought. And the one who [...] ' up in this way and who is within the ' exalted boundary, remembering [25] the one who is defective, the Logos knew ' him in an invisible way ' among those who came into being according to the thought, according ' to the one who was with them, ' until the light shone upon him from [30] above as a life-giver, the one who was begotten ' by the thought of brotherly love ' of the preexistent Pleromas. '

The stumbling, which happened to the aeons ' of the Father of the Totalities who did [35] not suffer, was brought to them, as if it were their own, ' in a careful and non-malicious ' and immensely sweet way. **86** [... the] Totalities so that they might receive ' [instruction] from the single one, the one ' from whom they all [received strength] ' to eliminate the defects.

The order [5] [which] was his came into being from ' him who ran [on] high and that which brought itself forth ' from him and from the entire perfection. ' The one who ran on high became ' for the one who was defective an intercessor with the [10] emanation of the aeons which had come into being in accord with ' the things which exist. When he prayed ' to them, they consented joyously and ' willingly, since they were in agreement, and with harmonious ' consent, to aid the [15] defective one. They gathered together, ' asking the Father with a beneficent intent, ' that there be aid from ' above, from the Father, for his glory, ' since the defective one could not become perfect in any other way,[20] unless it was the will of ' the Pleroma of the Father, who had drawn him to himself, ' who revealed himself and who gave to the defective ' one. Then from the agreement in a ' joyous willingness which had come into being they [25] brought forth the fruit, which was a begetting ' from the agreement, a ' unity, a possession of the Totalities ' revealing the countenance of ' the Father, of whom the aeons thought [30] as they gave glory and prayed for help for their ' brother with a wish in which the Father counted himself ' with them. Thus it was willingly and ' gladly that they bring forth ' the fruit. And he made manifest the agreement of the [35] revelation of his union ' with them—which is the Son ' of his will. **87** But the Son in whom the Totalities are pleased ' put himself on them as a garment, ' through which ' he gave perfection to the defective one,[5] and gave strength to those who are perfect, ' the one who is properly called ' "Savior" and "the Redeemer" ' and "the Pleasing One" and "the Beloved," ' "the one to whom prayers have been offered" and "the Christ" and [10] "the Light of those appointed," in accordance with the ones from whom ' he was brought forth, since he has become ' the names of the positions which were given ' to him. Yet what other name may be applied ' to him except "the Son," as we previously [15] said, since he is the knowledge ' of the Father, whom he wanted them ' to know?

Not only did the aeons ' generate the countenance of the Father to whom ' they gave praise, which was written previously, but also [20] they generated that which is theirs. For the aeons, ' those who give glory, generated this countenance ' and their face. They were produced as an army ' for him, as for a king, ' since the beings of the thought have a [25] powerful fellowship and an intermingled ' harmony. They came forth ' in a multifaceted form in ' order that the one to whom help was to be given might ' see those to whom he had prayed [30] for help. He also sees the one who gave ' it to him.

The fruit ' of the agreement with him, of which I previously spoke, ' is subject to the power of the Totalities. ' For the Father has set the Totalities within him,[35] both the ones which preexist ' and the ones which are and the ones which will be. **88** He was capable (of doing it). He revealed ' those which he had placed within him ' in his breast. Having entrusted (it) to him, ' he directed the administration of the universe [5] according to the authority which was given him ' from the first and the power of the task. ' Thus he began and effected ' his revelation.

He created first the one ' in whom the Father is and the one [10] in whom the Totalities are, ' earlier than the one who lacked ' sight. He gave instruction about himself to those who searched ' for their sight, by ' means of the shining of that perfect light.[15] He first perfected it ' in ineffable joy. He ' perfected it for himself as a perfect one, ' and he also gave to it what is appropriate to each ' individual. For this is the determination of [20] the first joy.—Also we were sown ' in him in an invisible way ' as a word which is destined to be ' knowledge.—And he gave him power ' to separate. He cast out from himself [25] those who are disobedient to him. ' Thus he made himself manifest ' to him. But to those ' who came into being because of him he ' revealed a form surpassing [30] them. They acted in a hostile way ' toward one another. Suddenly he revealed himself to them, ' approaching them ' in the form of lightning. And ' in putting an end to the entanglement which they have with [35] one another, he stopped it **89** by the sudden revelation ' which they were not informed about, ' did not expect, ' and did not know of. Because of this they [5] were afraid and fell down, since they were not able to bear ' the blow of the light which struck ' them. The one who appeared was an ' assault for the two orders. Just as ' the beings of thought had been given the name [10] "little one," so they have ' a faint notion that they have the ' exalted one. He exists before them, and they ' have sown within them an attitude of ' amazement at the exalted one who [15] will become manifest. Therefore they welcomed ' his revelation and ' they worshiped him. They became ' convinced witnesses to him. They acknowledged ' the light which had come into being as [20] one stronger than those who fought against them. The ' beings of the likeness, however, were exceedingly afraid, ' since they were not able to hear about him ' in the beginning, that there is a vision of this sort. ' Therefore they fell down [25] to the pit of ignorance ' which is called "the Outer Darkness" ' and "Chaos" and ' "Hades" and "the Abyss." He set up what ' was beneath the order of the beings [30] of thought, as it had ' become stronger than they. They were worthy of ' ruling over the unspeakable darkness, ' since it is theirs ' and is the lot which was assigned to them. He [35] granted them that they, too, should be of use ' for the organization which was to come, **90** to which he had assigned them.

There is a great ' difference between the revelation to the one who had come into being ' and the one who was defective and those things which are to come into being because of ' the latter. For he revealed himself to him within [5] him, since he is with him, is ' a fellow sufferer with him, gives ' him rest little by little, makes ' him grow, lifts him up, gives himself ' to him completely for enjoyment from [10] the vision. But to those who are outside ' he revealed himself quickly and ' in a striking way, and he withdrew to himself beyond them, ' without having let them see him. '

When the Logos which was defective was illumined,[15] his Pleroma began. ' He escaped those who had disturbed ' him at first. He became ' unmixed with them. He stripped off ' that arrogant thought.[20] He received mingling with the Rest, ' when those who had been disobedient to him at first ' bent down and humbled themselves before him. ' And he rejoiced ' over the visitation of his brothers [25] who had visited him. He gave ' honor and praise to those who had become manifest ' as a help to him, while he gave thanks, ' because he had escaped those who revolted against him, ' and admired and honored the greatness [30] and those who had appeared to him in a ' determined way. He generated manifest images ' of the living forms, beautiful ' in that which is good, existing ' among the things which exist, resembling [35] them in beauty, but unequal to them ' in truth, since they are not from ' an agreement with him, between the one who brought them **91** forth and the one who revealed himself to him. But ' in wisdom and knowledge ' he acts, mixing the Logos with ' him(self) entirely. Therefore those which came [5] forth from him are great, just as ' that which is is truly great. '

After he was amazed at the beauty ' of the ones who had appeared to him, ' he professed gratitude for their [10] visitation. The Logos performed this activity, ' through those from whom he had received ' aid, for the stability ' of those who had come into being because of him, and ' so that they might receive something good,[15] thinking to pray for the organization ' of all those who came forth from him, ' which is stabilized, so that it might make them established. ' Therefore those whom he intentionally produced ' are in chariots,[20] just as those who came into being, those who ' have shown that they would pass through ' every place of things which are below, ' so that each one might be given the place ' which is constituted as he [25] is. This is destruction ' for the beings of the likeness, yet is an act of beneficence ' for the beings of the thought ' and a revelation ' for those who are from [30] the Ordinance, which was a unity ' while suffering, while they are seeds, ' which have not come to be by themselves. '

The one who appeared was a countenance ' of the Father and of the agreement, and he was [35] a garment (composed) of every grace, and food ' which is for those whom the Logos ' brought forth while praying and receiving glory and ' honor. **92** This is the one whom he glorified and honored ' while looking to those to whom he prayed, ' so that he might perfect them through the ' images which he had brought forth.

The Logos added [5] even more to ' their mutual assistance and ' to the hope of the promise, since ' they have the joy and great rest ' and undefiled pleasures.[10] He generated those whom ' he thought of ' at first, when they were not with ' him, (he generated them) having the perfection. ' Now, while he who belongs to the vision is with him,[15] he exists in hope and ' faith in the perfect Father, as much as the Totalities. ' He appears to him before he ' mixes with him in order that the things which have ' come into being might not perish by looking [20] upon the light, for they can ' not accept the great, exalted stature. '

The thought of the Logos, ' which had returned to his stability ' and ruled over those who had [25] come into being because of him, was called ' "Aeon" and "Place" of ' all those whom he had brought forth ' in accord with the ordinance, and he is also called ' "Synagogue of [30] Salvation," because he healed himself from ' the dispersal, which is the multifarious thought. ' He returned to ' the single thought. Similarly, ' he is called "Storehouse," [35] because of the rest which he ' obtained, giving (it) to himself alone. **93** And he is also called "Bride," ' because of the joy in the one ' who gave himself to him in the hope of fruit ' from the union, and who appeared to him.[5] He is also called "Kingdom" ' because of the stability which he received, while he ' rejoices at the domination over those who fought him. ' And he is called "the Joy ' of the Lord" because of the gladness in [which he] [10] clothed himself. With him is the light, ' giving him recompense for the ' good things which are in him, ' and (with him is) the thought of freedom. '

The aeon, of whom we previously spoke,[15] is above the two orders ' of those who fight against one another. ' He is not a companion of those who hold dominion and ' is not implicated in the illnesses and weaknesses, ' things belonging to the thought and to the likeness.[20]

The one in whom the Logos set ' himself, perfect in joy, ' was an aeon, having ' the form of matter, but also having ' the constitution of the cause, which [25] is the one who revealed himself, being an image ' of those things which are in the Pleroma, ' those things which came into being from the abundance ' of the enjoyment of the one who exists ' joyously. He, moreover, is [30] the countenance of the one who revealed himself ' in sincerity and attentiveness ' and the promise concerning ' the things for which he asked. He had ' the designation of the Son [35] and his essence and his power and his ' form, who is the one (whom) he loved ' and in whom he was pleased, **94** who was entreated in a loving way. ' He was light and was a desire ' to be established and an openness ' for instruction and an eye and a vision,[5] qualities which he had ' from the exalted ones. He was also wisdom ' for his thinking in opposition to the things beneath the ' organization. He was also a word for ' speaking and the perfection of the things [10] of this sort. It is these who ' took form with him, but according to the image ' of the Pleroma, having ' fathers who are the ones who gave them life, ' each one being a copy [15] of each one of the faces, ' which are forms of maleness, ' since they are not from the illness which ' is femaleness, but are from ' this one who already has left behind [20] the sickness, and who has the name ' "the Church," for in harmony ' they resemble the harmony in the assembly ' of those who have revealed themselves.

The one ' who came into being in the image of the [25] light, he too is perfect, ' inasmuch as he is an image of the ' one existing light which is the ' Totalities. Even if he was inferior to the one of whom ' he is an image, nevertheless he has [30] his indivisibility, because ' he is a countenance of the ' indivisible light. Those, however, ' who came into being in the image ' of each one of the aeons,[35] they in their essence are in the one whom we ' previously mentioned, but in power they are not equal ' because it (the power) is in each ' of them. In ' this mingling with one another [40] they have equality, **95** but each one has not cast off what is peculiar to him. ' Therefore they are passions, ' for passion is sickness, since ' they are productions not of the union [5] of the Pleroma but of this one, ' prematurely, before he received the Father. Hence ' the agreement with his (the Father's) Totality and his will ' was something beneficial for the organization ' which was to come. It was granted them [10] to pass through the places which are below, ' since the places are unable ' to accommodate their coming ' quickly, unless (they come) individually, ' one by one.[15] Their coming is necessary, since ' by them will everything be perfected. '

In short, the Logos received the vision of all things, ' those which preexist and those which are now ' and those which will be,[20] since he has been entrusted ' with the administration of all that which ' exists. Some things are already ' in things which are worthy of ' coming into being, but the seeds which are to [25] be he has with himself, ' because of the promise which belonged to the one ' whom he conceived, as something belonging ' to seeds which are to be. And ' he produced his offspring, that [30] is, the revelation of the one who ' conceived him. However, for a while the seed of ' promise is guarded ' so that those who have been appointed for a mission ' might be appointed [35] by the coming of the Savior and of those who ' are with him, the ones who are first ' in knowledge and glory of ' the Father.

It is fitting from **96** the prayer which he made and the ' conversion which occurred because of it, ' that some should perish, ' while others benefit,[5] and still others be ' set apart. He first prepared ' the punishment of those who are ' disobedient, making use of the power ' of the one who appeared, the one from whom he received [10] authority over all things, ' so as to separate from himself that ' which is below. He also kept it ' apart from the exalted one until he ' prepares the arrangement of all those things [15] which are external, and gives to each the place ' which is assigned to it. '

The Logos established himself at ' first, when he beautified the Totalities, as ' a basic principle and cause [20] and ruler of the things which ' came to be, like the Father, the one who ' was the cause of his (the Logos') establishment, ' which was the first to exist after him (the Father). ' He created the preexistent images,[25] which he brought forth ' in thanks and glorification. Then ' he beautified the place of those whom he had ' brought forth in glory, (the place) which is called ' "Paradise" and [30] "the Enjoyment" and "the Joy full ' of sustenance" and "the Joy," which ' preexist. And of ' every goodness which exists in ' the Pleroma, he preserves the image.[35] Then he beautified the kingdom, ' like a city ' filled with everything of beauty, ' which is brotherly love and ' the great generosity, which is filled **97** with the holy spirits and [the] ' mighty powers which govern ' them, those which the Logos ' produced and confirmed [5] in power. Then (he beautified) the place of ' the Church which assembles in this region, ' having the form of the ' Church which exists in the aeons, which glorifies ' the Father. After these (he beautified) the place [10] of the faith and obedience (which arises) from ' hope, which things the Logos received ' when the light appeared; ' then (he beautified the place of) the disposition, which is prayer [and] ' supplication, which were followed by forgiveness [15] and the word concerning ' the one who will appear.

All the spiritual places ' are in spiritual power. ' They are separate from those ' of the thought, while the power of an image is established,[20] which separates ' the Pleroma from the Logos, while the power ' is active in prophesying about ' the things which will be, and leaves ' to the preexistent one the things belonging to the thought, which have already come into being,[25] and does not permit them to mix with the

things which ' have come into being through a vision of the things which
are ' in his presence.

Things which belong to the thought which ' is transcendent are
humble, they ' preserve the representation of the pleromatic,[30] especially
because of the sharing ' in the names by which they are beautiful. '

The conversion is ' humble toward the things of thought, and the
law, ' too, is humble toward them,[35] (the law) of the judgment, which is
their condemnation and ' wrath. Also humble toward them ' is the
power which separates those ' below them, sends them ' far off, and
does not allow them **98** [to] lay hold of those belonging to thought and '
the conversion, which (power) consists in fear and ' perplexity and
forgetfulness and astonishment and ' ignorance and the things which
have come into being [5] in the manner of a likeness, through phantasy. '
Those things too, which are in fact lowly, ' are given the exalted names. '
There is no knowledge for those who have come ' forth from them with
arrogance [10] and lust for power, ' and disobedience and falsehood. '

He named each one ' of the two orders. ' Those belonging to the
thought and those of the representation [15] are called ' "the Right" and
"Psychic" and ' "the Flames" and "the Middle Ones." ' Those who
belong to the arrogant thought and those of the likeness ' are called "the
Left," [20] "Hylic," "the Dark Ones," and "the Last." '

After the Logos established ' each one in his order, ' both the images
and the representations and the likenesses, ' he kept the aeon of the
images [25] pure from all those who ' fight against it, as a place of joy. '
However, to those of the thought he revealed ' the thought which he
had stripped ' from himself, desiring to draw them [30] into a material
union, for the sake ' of their organization and dwelling place, ' and in
order that they might bring forth ' an impulse for diminution from '
their attraction to evil, so that they might not any more [35] rejoice in the
glory ' of their environment and be dissolved, ' but might rather see '
their sickness in which they suffer, **99** so that they might beget love ' and
continuous searching after ' the one who is able to heal them ' of the
inferiority. Also over those [5] who belong to the likeness he set ' the word
of beauty, so that he might ' bring them into a form. He also set ' over
them the law of judgment. ' Again, he set over them [the] [10] powers
which the roots had produced ' [in] their lust for power. He [appointed] '
those who rule over them, so that ' either by the support of the word
which instructs ' them or by the threat of the [law] [15] or by the power of
lust for ' power they might keep the order ' of those who have reduced
it to evil, ' until the Logos is pleased with them, ' since they are useful
for the administration.

The Logos knows the agreement [20] in the lust for power of the ' two orders. ' To these and to all the others he ' graciously granted their desire. He gave ' to each one the appropriate rank,[25] and it was ordered ' that each one ' be a ruler over a ' place and an activity, yielding to the place ' more exalted than himself, in order to command [30] the other places in an activity ' which is in the allotted activity ' which falls to him to have control over ' because of his mode of being. ' As a result, there are commanders and [35] subordinates in positions of domination ' and subjection among the angels **100** and archangels, while the activities ' are of various types and are different. ' Each one of the archons with his ' race and his perquisites to which his lot [5] has claim, just as they ' appeared, each was on guard, since they have been entrusted ' with administration, and none ' lacks a command, and ' none is without kingship from [10] the end of the heavens to the end of the ' [earth], even to the foundations of the [earth] ' and to the places beneath the earth. There are ' kings, there are lords, and those who give ' commands, some [15] for administering punishment, others ' for administering justice, still others for ' giving rest and healing, others ' for teaching, others for guarding. '

Over all the images he established an Archon [20] with no one commanding ' him, since he is the lord of all of them, ' the countenance which the Logos ' brought forth in his thought ' as a representation of the Father of the Totalities. Therefore [25] he is adorned with all names ' which are a representation of him (the Father), since he is characterized by every property ' and glorious quality. For he too is called ' "father" and "god" and "demiurge" and ' "king" and "judge" and "place" [30] and "dwelling" and "law." '

The Logos uses him (the Archon) ' as a hand, to beautify and ' work on the things below, and he ' uses him as a mouth,[35] to say the things which will be prophesied. '

The things which he has spoken he does. ' When he (the Archon) saw that they are great and ' good and wonderful, he was ' pleased and rejoiced, as **101** if he himself in his own thought ' had been the one to say them and do ' them, not knowing that the movement ' within him is from the spirit who moves [5] him in a determined way toward those things which he (the spirit) wants. '

In regard to the things which came into being from him, he uttered them ' and they came into being as a representation of the spiritual ' realms which we mentioned previously ' in the discussion about the images.

Not only [10] does he work, but also, as ' he is father of [his] organization, ' he engenders by himself and by the seeds, yet also [by ' the spirit] which is elect and which will descend ' through him to the places which are below.[15] Not only does he speak spiritual words ' of his own, ⟨but⟩ in ' an invisible way ' (he speaks) through the spirit which calls out ' and produces things greater than his own essence.[20]

Since in his ' essence he is a "god" ' and "father" and all the rest of ' the honorific titles, he was ' thinking that they were elements [25] of his own essence. He established ' a rest for those who obey ' him, but for those who ' disobey him he also established punishments. ' With him too [30] there is a paradise and a ' kingdom and everything else ' which exists in the aeon ' which exists before him. (The latter) are more valuable ' than the imprints, because of the thought which [35] is connected with them, which is like **102** a shadow and a garment, so to ' speak, because he does not see ' in what way the things which exist actually do exist.

He established ' workers and [5] servants for ' what he will do and what he will say, ' for in every place where he worked ' he left his countenance ' in his beautiful name,[10] effecting and speaking of ' the things which he thinks about.

He ' established in his place ' images of the light ' which appeared and of [those things which are] [15] spiritual, while (the images) were of ' his own essence.

Thus they were ' honored in every place by him, ' being pure, from the countenance ' of the one who appointed them, and they were [20] established: paradises ' and kingdoms and rests ' and promises and multitudes ' of servants of his will, ' and though they are lords of dominions,[25] they are set beneath the one who is ' (truly) lord, the one who made them. '

After he heard ' in this way, properly, about the lights, ' which are the source [30] and the structure, he set them over ' the beauty of the things below. ' The invisible spirit moved him in this way ' so that he would **103** wish to administer through ' his own servant, ' whom he too used, ' as a hand and [5] as a mouth and as if ' he were his face, (and his servant is) the things which he brings, ' order and threat and ' fear, in order that those who have done ' what is ignorant [along with him] [10] might despise the order which [was given for them to] ' keep as they are fettered in the [bonds of ' the archons], which are on them [securely]. ' The whole establishment of matter ' [is divided] into three. The [strong] powers [15] which the spiritual Logos ' brought forth from fantasy ' and arrogance, he established ' in the first spiritual rank. ' Then those (powers) which these produced by [20] their lust for power, he set ' in the middle area, since they are powers ' of ambition, so that they ' might exercise dominion and give commands with compulsion and force ' to the establishment which is beneath them.[25] Those ' which came into being through envy ' and jealousy and all the other offspring ' from dispositions of this sort, he set ' in a servile order [30] controlling the extremities, commanding ' all those which exist and all (the realm of) generation, ' from whom come ' rapidly destroying illnesses, ' who eagerly desire begetting, who are something [35] in the place where they are from ' and to which they will return. ' Therefore he set over ' them authoritative powers, ' acting [continuously] in matter, in order that **104** the offspring of that which exists might also exist ' continuously. For this is their ' glory. '

* * * * *

The matter which flows through its form [5] (is) a cause by which the ' invisibility which exists through the powers ' [belongs] to them all, to [. . .] ' begetting before them and ' [destroying].

The thought which is set [10] between those of the right [and] ' those of the left is a power of [. . .]. ' All those which we have [. . .] ' will wish to make them, so to ' speak, a projection of theirs,[15] like a shadow cast from ' and following a body. Those who ' are the roots of the visible creations, ' namely the entire preparation of the ' adornment of the images and representations [20] and likenesses, have come ' into being precisely because of those who need ' education and teaching and formation, ' so that the smallness ' might grow, little [25] by little, as through a mirror image. ' Therefore at the very end did he create ' man, having first ' prepared and ' provided for him the things which he had created [30] for his sake. '

Like that of all else is the creation of man. ' The spiritual Logos ' also moved him ' invisibly, as he perfected [35] him through the **105** Demiurge and his angelic servants, ' who shared in the act of fashioning in [multitudes. He] ' took counsel with his archons, being ' like a shadow of an earthly man,[5] so that he might be like [those] ' who are cut off from the Totalities. Also ' he is something prepared by all of them, those of the right ' and those of the left, since each one in [the] ' orders gives a form to the [. . .],[10] in which it exists.

The [. . .] which ' the Logos brought forth, the Logos [who was] ' defective, as he had [been] ' in the sickness, (that form) was not like him ' because he brought it forth [forgetfully],[15] ignorantly, and [defectively], '

and in all the other weak ways, ' when the Logos gave the first form '
through the Demiurge ' in ignorance, so that he [20] would learn that the
exalted one exists ' and would know that he needs [him]. ' This is what
the prophet called ' "Living Spirit" and "the Mind ' of the exalted
aeons" and "[the] [25] Invisible," and this is the living soul ' which has
given life to the power ' which was dead at first. For that which ' is dead
is ignorance. '

It is fitting that we explain [30] about the soul of the first man, ' that it
is from the spiritual Logos, ' while the creator thinks ' that it is his,
since it is from ' him, as from a mouth through which [35] one breathes.
The creator also sent ' down souls ' from his substance, since he ' too
has a power of procreation, **106** because he is a being in the image ' of
the Father. Also those of the left brought forth, ' as it were, men ' of
their own, since they have [5] the likeness of being. '

The spiritual substance is a ' name and a single image, ' [and] its
weakness is the determination ' [in many] forms. As for the substance [10]
of the psychics, its determination ' is double, since it has the knowledge '
and the confession of the exalted one, ' and it is not inclined to evil,
which ' is the inclination of thought. As for the material substance,[15] its
way is different ' and in many forms, and it was a weakness ' which
existed in many types ' of inclination.

The first man is a ' mixed formation, and a [20] mixed creation, and a
deposit ' of those of the left and those of the right, ' and a spiritual word '
whose attention is divided between each of the two ' substances from
which he takes [25] his being. Therefore ' it is said that ' a paradise was
planted for him, so that he might ' eat of the food of three ' kinds of
tree, since it is a garden of the [30] threefold order, ' and since it is that
which gives enjoyment.

The ' noble elect substance ' which is in him was more exalted. ' It
created and it did not wound [35] them. Therefore they issued ' a command, making a threat ' and bringing upon him a great **107** danger,
which is death. Only the ' enjoyment of the things which are evil ' did
he allow him to taste, ' and from the other tree with [5] the double (fruit)
he did not allow him ' to eat, much ' less from the tree of life, so that
[they would not] ' acquire honor [. . .] ' them and so that [they would
not be . . .] [10] by the evil power [which] ' is called "the serpent." And he
is more cunning ' than all the evil powers. ' He led man astray [through] '
the ordinance of those which belong to the thought [15] and the desires.
He made him transgress ' the command, so that he would die. ' And he
(man) was expelled from ' every enjoyment of that place. '

This is the expulsion which was made [20] for him, when he was expelled from the enjoyments ' of the beings of the likeness and those of the representation. ' It was a work of providence, so that ' it might be found that it is a short time ' until man will receive the enjoyment [25] of the things which are eternally good, ' in which is the place of rest. ' This the spirit ordained when ' he first planned ' that man should experience the [30] great evil, which is death, ' that is complete ignorance of the Totality, ' and that he (man) should experience ' all the evils which ' come from this and,[35] after the deprivations and cares which are in these (evils), ' that he should receive of the greatest **108** good, which is ' life eternal, that is ' firm knowledge of the Totalities ' and the reception of all good things.[5] Because of the transgression of the first man ' death ruled. It was accustomed ' to slay every man ' in the manifestation of its ' [domination] which had been given it [10] [as] a kingdom, because of the organization ' of the Father's will, ' of which we spoke previously. '

* * * * *

If both of the orders, ' those on the right and those on the left,[15] are brought together with one another by ' the thought which is set between them, ' which gives them their organization ' with each other, it happens ' that they both act with the same [20] emulation of their deeds, with ' those of the right resembling those of the left ' and those of the left resembling ' those of the right. And at times when the evil order ' begins to do [25] evil in a ' foolish way, ' the wise order emulates ' in the form of a man of violence, ' even doing what is evil [30] as if it were a power of a man ' of violence. At other times ' the foolish order ' attempts to do good, ' imitating the hidden order,[35] when it is jealous to do it (good). ' As it is in ' the things which are established, [or] in the **109** things which have come to resemble ' the things which are unlike one another, ' they are unable to know the course ' of the things which exist, namely those [5] who were not instructed.

Therefore ' other types (of explanation) have been introduced, ' some saying that ' it is according to providence that the things which exist have their being. ' These are the people who observe [10] the stability and the conformity of the movement of creation. ' Others say ' that it is something extraneous (by which existents exist). ' These are people who observe the ' diversity and the lawlessness and the evil of the powers.[15] Others say ' that the things which exist are what ' is destined to happen. These are the people who were ' occupied with this matter. Others say ' that it (what exists) is something in accordance with nature.[20] Others say that ' it is a self-existent. The majority, however, ' all who have gone as far as the visible elements, ' do not know anything more ' than them.

Those who were wise [25] among the Greeks and the barbarians ' have advanced to the powers which have ' come into being by way of imagination and ' empty speculation. Those who have ' come from these (sages), in accord with the mutual conflict [30] and rebellious manner ' active in them (the sages), ' also spoke in a likely, ' arrogant, and ' imaginary way concerning the things [35] which they thought of as wisdom, ' although they were deceived by the likeness, ' thinking that they had attained the truth, **110** when they had (only) attained error. ' (They did so) not simply in minor appellations, but ' the powers themselves seem to hinder them, ' (appearing) as if they were the Totality.[5] Therefore, it happened that the ' order was caught up in fighting ' itself alone, because of the ' arrogant hostility of ' one [of the offspring] of the archon who is [10] superior, who exists before him. ' Therefore nothing ' is in agreement with its fellows, ' nothing, neither ' philosophy nor types of medicine [15] nor types of rhetoric nor types ' of music nor types of ' logic, but they are opinions and ' theories. It happened that ' ineffability ruled,[20] in confusion because of the inarticulateness ' of those who hold sway, who give them ' thoughts.

What has come ' from the race of the ' Hebrews and what is written by [25] the hylics, who speak in the fashion of the Greeks, ' ⟨are⟩ the powers of those who think ' of attributing them to the right, powers ' which move them all to think of ' words and images for them. And they [30] grasped so as to attain ' the truth. They used the confused powers ' which act in them. ' Afterwards they attained to the order ' of the unmixed, the one who is established, the [35] unity, who exists in the ' image of the Father's image. He is not invisible **111** in his nature, but ' a wisdom envelops him so that ' he might preserve the form of the ' truly invisible one. Therefore [5] many angels have not been able to see him. ' Also other men of ' the Hebrew race, of whom we ' already spoke, namely the righteous ones ' and the prophets, did not think of anything,[10] and did not say anything ' from imagination or from ' analogy or from esoteric thinking, ' but each one ' by the power which was at work in him,[15] and while listening to the things which he saw ' and heard, spoke of them in faith. ' Having a unified agreement ' with one another after the manner ' of those who worked in them,[20] they preserve the connection and the ' mutual agreement primarily ' by the confession of the one more exalted ' than they. And there is one who is greater than they, ' who was appointed since they have need [25] of him,

begotten by the spiritual Logos ' along with them as one who needs '
the exalted one, (begotten) in hope and ' expectation in accord with the
thought which ' is the seed of salvation.[30] And he is an illuminating
word, which ' consists of the thought and his offspring and ' his emanations. Since the just ones and ' the prophets, whom we have previously
mentioned, ' preserve the confession and the [35] testimony concerning '
the one who is great made by their fathers who were **112** looking for the
hope and ' the hearing, in them is sown ' the seed of prayer and the
searching, ' which is sown in many [5] who have searched for strengthening. ' It appears and draws them to ' love the exalted one, to proclaim '
these things as pertaining to a unity. ' And it was a unity which [10]
worked in them when they spoke. ' Their vision and their words do not
differ ' because of the multitude ' of those who have given them the
vision and ' the word. Therefore those who have [15] listened to what they
have said ' concerning this do not reject any ' of it, but have accepted
the scriptures ' in an altered way. By interpreting ' them they established [20] many heresies which ' have existed to the present among the '
Jews. Some ' say that God is one, ' who made a proclamation [25] in the
ancient scriptures. Others ' say that he is many. ' Some say ' that God
is simple ' and was a simple mind [30] in nature. Others say ' that his
activity is linked with ' the origin of good ' and evil. Still others ' say
that he is the [35] creator of that which has come into being. Still others '
say that **113** it was by his angels that he created. '

   The multitude of ideas of ' this sort, the multitude of forms and the
abundance ' of types of scripture, is what produced [5] their teachers of the
Law. The ' prophets, however, did not say anything of ' their own
accord, ' but each one of them ' (spoke) of the things which he had seen
and [10] heard through the proclamation of ' the Savior. This is what he
proclaimed, ' with the main subject of their ' proclamation being that
which each said concerning ' the coming of the Savior, which is this
coming.[15] Sometimes the prophets speak about it ' as if it will be. '
Sometimes (it is) as if the Savior speaks ' from their mouths, saying that
the Savior will come ' and show favor to those who have not [20] known
him. They (the prophets) have not all joined ' with one another in confessing anything, ' but each one thinks on the basis of the ' activity from
which he received power ' to speak about him,[25] and on the basis of the
place which he saw, ' that it is from it (the activity) ' that he (the Savior)
will be begotten and that he will ' come from that place. Not ' one of
them knew [30] whence he would come nor by whom he ' would be begotten, but he alone ' is the one of whom it is worthy to speak, the one

who ' will be begotten and ' who will suffer. Concerning [35] that which he previously was ' and that which he is eternally, ' an unbegotten, impassible ' Logos who came into being in flesh, 114 he did not come into their (the prophets') thought. And this ' is the account, which they received an impulse ' to give, concerning his flesh ' which was to appear. They say that [5] it is from all of them (the archons), ' but before all things, for it is from ' the spiritual Logos ' who is the cause of the things which ' have come into being, from whom the Savior received [10] his flesh. He ' conceived him at the revelation ' of the light, according to the ' word of the promise, at his revelation ' from the seminal state.[15] For the one who exists is not a seed of the things which exist, ' since he was begotten at the end. But to the one ' by whom the Father ordained the manifestation ' of salvation, who is ' the fulfillment of the promise,[20] to him belonged all these instruments for ' entry into life, through which he ' descended. His Father is one, ' and alone is ' truly a father to him, the [25] invisible, unknowable, ' the incomprehensible in his nature, who ' alone is God in his will ' and his form, who ' has granted that he might be seen,[30] known, and comprehended. '

He it was who is our Savior ' in willing compassion, ' who is that which ' they were. So, for their sake he became [35] manifest in an involuntary suffering. ' They became flesh and soul— ' that is, eternally— which (things) hold ' them, and in corruptibility ' they die. And as for those who [came into being, 115 the] invisible one ' taught them invisibly about himself. '

Not ' only did he take upon himself the death of [5] those whom he thought ' to save, but also he accepted their smallness ' to which they had descended, when they had fasted ' in body and soul. ' (He did so) because he had let himself be conceived [10] and born as an infant, in ' body and soul.

Among all the others ' who shared in them (body and soul) ' and those who fell and received the light, ' he appeared being exalted, because [15] he had let himself be conceived without sin, ' stain, and ' defilement. ' He was begotten in life, being in life ' because the former and the latter are in [20] passion and changing opinion ' from the Logos who moved, ' who established them to be body ' and soul. He it is who has taken ' to himself the one who came for those whom we previously [25] mentioned.

He came into being from the ' glorious vision and the unchanging thought, ' from the Logos who had ' returned to himself after his movement ' from the organization, just as [30] those who came with him

took body and soul ' and a confirmation ' and stability and judgment of '
things. They too intended ' to come.

When they thought of [35] the Savior they came, and they came when he
knew; ' they also came more exalted in the ' emanation according to the
flesh than those ' who had been brought forth from a defect, because **116**
in this way ' they received their bodily emanation along with ' the body
of the Savior through ' the revelation and [5] the mingling with him. The '
others were those of one substance ' and it indeed is the spiritual (substance). ' The organization ' is different. This is one thing,[10] that is
another. Some ' come forth from passion ' and division, needing '
healing. Others are from ' prayer so that they heal [15] the sick, when they
have been appointed ' to treat those who have fallen. These ' are the
apostles and the evangelists. ' They are the disciples ' of the Savior, and
teachers [20] who need instruction. Why then ' did they, too, share in the
passions ' in which ' those who have been brought forth ' from passion
share, if indeed they are bodily productions [25] in accordance with the
organization and ' the Savior, who did not ' share in the passions? '

The Savior was a bodily image ' of the unitary one. He [30] is the Totality
in bodily form. ' Therefore he preserved the form of ' indivisibility, from
which ' comes impassibility. ' They, however, are images [35] of each
thing which ' became manifest. Therefore they ' assume division from '
the pattern, having taken form for the planting which ' exists beneath
[the heaven]. This also **117** is what shares in the evil which exists ' in the
places which they have reached. ' For the will ' held the Totality under
sin so that [5] by that will he might have mercy ' on the Totality and they
might be saved, while a single one ' alone is destined to give life and all
the rest ' need salvation. Therefore ' it was from (reasons) of this sort
that [10] he began to receive grace to give the ' honors which were proclaimed ' by Jesus, which were suitable for ' him to proclaim to the rest, '
since a seed of the [15] promise of Jesus Christ was set up, whom we have '
served in (his) revelation and union. ' Now the promise possessed ' the
instruction and the return ' to what they were from [20] the first, from
which they possess ' the drop, so as to return ' to him, which is that
which is called ' "the redemption." And it is the release ' from the
captivity and the acceptance [25] of freedom. In its places the captivity of '
those who were slaves of ignorance ' holds sway. ' The freedom is the
knowledge of ' the truth which existed before [30] the ignorance came to
be, ruling ' forever without beginning and ' without end, being something good ' and a salvation of things ' and a release from [35] the servile
nature ' in which they have suffered. '

Those who have been brought forth in a lowly thought ' of vanity, ' that is, (a thought) which goes to things which are evil **118** through the thought which [draws] them ' down to the lust for power, these have ' received the possession which is freedom, ' from the abundance of the grace which looked [5] upon the children. However, it (the possession) was disturbance of the ' passion and destruction of ' those things which he cast off from ' himself at first, when the Logos separated them ' from himself, (the Logos) who [10] was the cause of their being destined for ' destruction, though he kept them at the end of the organization ' and allowed them to exist ' because even they were useful for the things which were ' ordained.

Mankind came [15] to be in three essential types, ' the spiritual, the psychic, ' and the material, conforming ' to the triple arrangement ' of the Logos, from which [20] were brought forth the material ones and the ' psychic ones and the spiritual ones. Each ' of the three essential types ' is known by its fruit. ' They were not known at first [25] but only at the coming of the Savior, ' who shone upon the saints ' and revealed what each ' was.

The ' spiritual race, being [30] like light from ' light and like spirit from ' spirit, when its head ' appeared, it ran toward him ' immediately. It immediately became a body [35] of its head. It suddenly received knowledge ' in the revelation. ' The psychic race is like light ' from a fire, since it hesitated to accept knowledge **119** of him who appeared to it. (It hesitated) even ' more to run toward him in faith. ' Rather, through a voice it was instructed ' and this was sufficient, since it is not far [5] from the hope according to the promise, ' since it received, so to speak as a ' pledge, the assurance of the things ' which were to be. The material ' race, however, is alien in [10] every way; since it is dark, it ' shuns the shining of the light ' because its appearance destroys ' it. And since it has not received its unity, ' it is something excessive and [15] hateful toward the Lord at his ' revelation.

The spiritual race ' will receive complete salvation in ' every way. The material will receive ' destruction in every way, just as [20] one who resists him. The psychic ' race, since it is in the middle ' when it is brought forth and also when it is established, ' is double in its determination ' for both good and evil. It takes its [25] appointed departure ' suddenly and its complete escape ' to those who are good, ' whom the Logos brought forth ' in accordance with the first element of his [30] thought, when he remembered the ' exalted one and prayed for salvation. ' It (the saved psychic race) has salvation [immediately]. ' It will be saved completely [because of] ' the salvific thought. As he [35] was brought forth, so [too] ' were these brought forth from ' him, **120** whether angels or men. ' In accordance with the confession that there is ' one who is more exalted than themselves, ' and in accordance with the prayer and the search for [5] him, they also will attain the ' salvation of those who have been brought forth, since ' they are from the disposition ' which is good. They were appointed for ' service in proclaiming the coming [10] of the Savior who was to be and ' his revelation which had come. ' Whether angels or men, when ' he was sent as a service to them, they in fact received ' the essence of their being.[15] Those, however, who are from ' the thought of lust for ' power, who have come into being from ' the blow of those who fight ' against him, those whom the thought [20] brought forth, ' since they are mixed, they will receive their end ' suddenly. Those who will be brought forth ' from the lust for ' power which is given to them for a [25] time and for certain periods, and who will give glory to ' the Lord of glory, and who will relinquish ' their wrath, they will receive the reward for ' their humility, which is to remain ' forever. Those, however, who [30] are proud because of the desire ' of ambition, and who love temporary ' glory and who forget that ' it was only for certain periods and times which they have ' that they were entrusted with power,[35] and for this reason ' did not acknowledge that the Son of God **121** is the Lord of all and ' Savior, and were not brought ' out of the wrath and the ' resemblance to the evil ones, they [5] will receive judgment for their ignorance ' and their senselessness, ' which is suffering, along with those ' who went astray, anyone ' of them who turned away; and [10] even more (will they be judged for their) wickedness in ' doing to the Lord things ' which were not fitting, ' which the powers of the left did to him, ' even including his death. They persevered,[15] saying, "We shall become rulers ' of the universe if ' the one who has been proclaimed king of the universe ' is slain," (they said this) when they labored to do ' this, namely the men and angels [20] who are not from the good organization ' of the right ones but ' from the mixture. And ' they first chose for themselves ' honor, though it was only a temporary wish [25] and desire, while the ' path to eternal rest is by way ' of humility for the salvation of ' those who will be saved, those of ' the right ones. After they confess [30] the Lord and the thought of that which ' is pleasing to the church and the song of ' those who are humble along with her to the full extent ' possible, in that which is pleasing to do ' for her, in sharing in her sufferings [35] and her pains in the manner of ' those who understand what is good ' for the Church, they will have a share ' in [her] hope. This (needs be) said **122** on the subject of how the path of men and angels ' who are from the ' order of the left ' leads to error: [5] not only that they denied the Lord ' and plotted evil against him, ' but also toward the Church, too, ' is directed their hatred ' and envy and jealousy; [10] and this is the reason for the condemnation ' of those who have moved and have aroused themselves ' for the trials of the church.

The election ' shares body ' and essence with [15] the Savior, since it is like a bridal ' chamber because of its unity ' and its agreement with him. For before ' every place the Christ came for her sake. ' The calling,[20] however, has the place ' of those who rejoice at the bridal chamber ' and who are glad and happy ' at the union of the bridegroom ' and the bride.[25] The place which the election will have is the aeon ' of the images, where ' the Logos has not yet joined with the Pleroma. And ' since the man of the Church was glad and ' happy at this, as he hoped for [30] it, ' he separated spirit, soul, and body in ' the organization of the one who thinks that ' he is a unity, though within him ' is the man, who is [35] the Totality—and he is all of them. ' And, since he has ' the effluence from the [. . .] which **123** the places will receive, he also has ' the members about which we spoke ' earlier. When the redemption was proclaimed, ' the perfect man received knowledge [5] immediately ' so as to return in haste to his ' unitary state, to the place from ' which he came, to return ' there joyfully, to the place [10] from which he came, to the place from which ' he flowed forth. His ' members, however, needed a place of instruction, ' which is in the places which ' are prepared, so that they, like mirrors, might receive from them forms resembling [15] the images and archetypes, ' until ' all the members of the body of ' the church are in a single place ' and receive the restoration at one [20] time, when they have been manifested as the ' sound body—the restoration ' (is) into the Pleroma. ' It has a prior assent ' to a mutual agreement,[25] which is the assent which belongs to the Father, ' until the Totalities receive a countenance ' like him. The restoration is at the ' end, after the Totality ' reveals what it is, the Son,[30] who is the redemption, that ' is the path toward the ' incomprehensible Father, that is the return to ' the pre-existent, and ' (after) the Totalities reveal themselves [35] in this one in the proper way, the one who ' is the inconceivable one and the ' ineffable one, **124** and the invisible one and the ' incomprehensible one, so that it (the Totality) ' receives redemption. It (redemption) was not only release ' from the domination of the [5] left ones, nor was it only escape ' from the power ' of those of the right, to each of which ' we thought ' that we were slaves and [10] sons, from whom none ' escapes who does not quickly ' become theirs again, but ' the redemption also is an ascent ' and (it is) the depths which are in the [15] Pleroma and those who have named ' themselves and who conceive of themselves ' according to the power of each of ' the aeons, and (it is) an entrance ' into what is silent, where there is no [20] need for voice nor for ' knowing nor for forming a concept ' nor for illumination, ' but (where) all things are ' light which does not need to be [25] illumined.

Not only ' do humans need ' redemption but also the angels, ' too, need redemption along with ' the image and the rest of the Pleromas of [30] the aeons and the wondrous powers of ' illumination. So that we might not be in doubt in regard to ' the others, even the Son himself, ' who has the position of ' redeemer of the Totality, [needed] redemption **125** as well—he who had become ' man—when he gave ' himself for each thing which we need, ' we in the flesh, who are [5] his Church. Now when he ' first received redemption from ' the Logos who had descended upon him, ' all the rest received redemption from ' him, namely those who had taken him to themselves.[10] For those who received the one who had received (redemption) ' also received what was in him.

Among ' the men who are in the flesh he ' began to give redemption, his first-born, ' and his love, the [15] Son who was incarnate. ' The angels who are in heaven ' asked for a constitution, so that they might form an association ' with him upon the earth. Therefore ' he is called "the Redemption [20] of the angels of the Father," he who ' comforted those who were laboring ' under the Totality for his knowledge, ' because he was given the grace ' before anyone else.

The Father was the first [25] to know him, since he was ' in his thought before ' anything came into being and since he had ' those to whom he has revealed him. ' He set the deficiency on the one who [30] remains for a certain period of time, ' as a glory for his Pleroma, since ' the fact that he is unknown ' is a cause ' of his production from his [35] agreement [. . .] **126** of him. Just as reception of ' knowledge of him is a manifestation of his ' lack of envy and the revelation ' of the abundance of his sweetness,[5] which is the second glory, ' so too he has been found ' to be a cause ' of ignorance, although he is also ' a begetter of knowledge.

In a [10] hidden and incomprehensible wisdom ' he kept the knowledge to the end, ' until the Totalities became weary in their search for ' God the Father, whom no one ' found through his own wisdom [15] or power. ' In his abundant thought he gives himself so that they might receive knowledge ' of his great glory, which ' he has given, and the cause, which he has ' given, which is his unceasing thanksgiving,[20] which is

from ' the immobility of his counsel. ' From eternity he reveals himself '
to those who are worthy of the Father ' who is unknown in his nature,
so that they [25] might receive knowledge of him through his desire ' that
they should come to experience the ' ignorance and its pains. '

Those of whom he first thought ' that they should attain knowledge
and [30] the good things which are in it, ' they were planning—which is
the wisdom ' of the Father—that they might experience ' the evil things
and might ' train themselves in them,[35] as a [. . .] for a time ' [. . . so
that they might] receive the enjoyment ' [of good things] for ' eternity.
127 They hold change and ' persistent renunciation and the ' cause of
those who fight against them as an adornment ' and marvelous quality
of those who [5] are exalted, so that it is made manifest ' that the ignorance
of ' those who are ignorant of the Father was ' something of their own.
He who gave them ' knowledge of him (the Father) was one of his
powers [10] for enabling them to grasp that ' knowledge in the fullest sense
is ' called "the knowledge of ' all that which is thought of" and "the '
treasure" and "the addition for the [15] increase of knowledge," "the
revelation ' of those things which were first known," ' and "the path
toward assent ' and toward the ' preexistent one," which is the [20] increase of those who have ' abandoned the greatness which was theirs ' in
the organization of ' the will, so that the end ' might be like the beginning.[25]

As for the baptism which exists ' in the fullest sense, into ' which the
Totalities will descend ' and in which they will be, there is no other '
baptism apart from this one alone,[30] which is the redemption into ' God,
Father, Son, and ' Holy Spirit, when ' confession is made through '
faith in those names,[35] which are a single name of ' the gospel, **128** when
they have come to believe what has been said to them, ' namely that
they (Father, Son, and Holy Spirit) exist. From ' this they have their '
salvation, those who have [5] believed that they exist. This ' is attaining in
an invisible way ' to the Father, Son, ' and Holy Spirit in an ' un-
doubting faith. And when they [10] have borne witness to them, it is also
with a ' firm hope that they ' attain them, so that the return to them
might ' become the perfection of those who have believed ' in them and
(so that) [15] the Father might be one with them, the Father, ' God,
whom they have confessed ' in faith and who ' gave (them) their union
with him in ' knowledge.

The baptism which we [20] previously mentioned is called ' "garment of
those who do not ' strip themselves of it," for those who ' will put it on
and those who have ' received redemption wear it. It is also [25] called

"the confirmation of the ' truth which has no fall." ' In an unwavering and ' immovable way he grasps those ' who have received the restoration [30] while they grasp him. (Baptism) is ' called "silence" because of ' the quiet and the tranquility. ' It is also called "bridal chamber" ' because of the agreement and the [35] individual state of those who know ' that they have known him. It is also called 129 "the light which does not set ' and is without flame," since it does not give light, ' but those who have worn it ' are made into light. They [5] are the ones whom he wore. ' (Baptism) is also called "the ' eternal life," which is ' immortality; and it is called ' "all that which it is," simply,[10] in the proper sense of what is pleasing, ' inseparably and irremovably ' and faultlessly and ' imperturbably, to that which belongs ' to those who have received a beginning. For what else is there [15] to name it ' apart from the designation "it is the Totalities"; ' that is, if it is given ' numberless names, ' they are spoken simply as a reference to it.[20] Just as it transcends every word ' and it transcends every voice ' and it transcends every mind ' and transcends everything ' and it transcends every silence,[25] so ' it is ' with those who are that ' which it is. This is that which they find ' it to be,[30] ineffably and ' inconceivably in (its) visage, for the coming into being in those who ' know, through him whom they have comprehended, ' who is the one to whom ' they gave glory.

Even if on the matter of the election 130 there are many more things for ' us to say as it is fitting to ' say, nonetheless, to the matters ' concerning the call—for [5] those of the right are so named— ' it is necessary ' for us to turn once again ' and it is not profitable ' for us to forget them. We have spoken [10] about them, if there is enough in ' what preceded at some length. How have we ' spoken? In a partial way, ' since I said that all those who came ' forth from the Logos,[15] either from the judgment of ' the evil ones or from ' the wrath which fights against them and the ' separation from them, which ' is the separation toward [20] the exalted ones, or from the prayer and ' the remembrance of those who pre-existed ' or from hope and ' faith that they would receive their salvation ' from good work,[25] since they have been deemed worthy because ' they are beings from the good ' dispositions, they have ' the cause of their begetting ' which is an opinion from the one who [30] exists. Still further (I said) that before the ' Logos concerned himself with ' them in an invisible way, ' willingly, the exalted one added ' to this thought, because [35] they were [. . .] to him, 131 who was the cause of ' their being. They did not exalt themselves, ' when they were saved, as if there were nothing ' existing before them, but they [5] confess that they have a beginning ' to their existence and they ' desire this: to know him ' who exists before them. ' Most of all (I said) that they worshipped [10] the revelation of the light ' in the form of lightning and ' they bore witness that it appeared ' as salvation for them. '

Not only those who have come forth [15] from the Logos, about whom ' alone we said that ' they would accomplish the good work, ' but also those whom these brought forth ' according to the good dispositions [20] will share ' in the rest according to the abundance ' of the grace. Also those who have been ' brought forth from the desire ' of lust for [25] power, having the ' seed in them which is the ' lust for power, will receive ' the reward for (their) good deeds, ' namely those who acted and those [30] who have the predisposition ' toward the good, if they ' intentionally desire and wish ' to abandon the ' vain, temporal ambition [35] and [they] keep the commandment of the Lord **132** of glory, instead of the ' momentary honor. They will inherit ' the eternal kingdom.

Now ' it is necessary that we unite [5] the causes and the effects on them ' of the grace and the impulses, ' since it is fitting that we say what ' we mentioned previously about the salvation ' of all those of the right,[10] of all those unmixed and those mixed, ' to join them with ' one another. And as for the rest, [which] ' is the revelation of [the] ' form (in) which they believed,[15] (it is fitting) that we should treat it with a ' suitable discussion. For when we ' confessed the kingdom ' which is in Christ, we escaped from ' the whole multiplicity of forms and from [20] inequality and change. For the end ' will receive a unitary existence ' just as the beginning, ' where there is no ' male nor female, nor slave [25] and free, nor circumcision ' and uncircumcision, neither angel ' nor man, but ' Christ is all in all. What is the form ' of the one who did not exist at first? [30] It will be found that he will exist, and ' what is the nature of the one who was not a slave? ' He will take a place with a **133** free man. For they will receive the vision ' more and more by nature ' and not only by word, ' so that they believe only through [5] a voice (saying) that this is the way ' it is. '

The restoration to that which used to be is a unity. ' Even if some are ' exalted because of the organization, since they have been appointed [10] as causes of the things which have come into being, ' since they are more active as natural forces, ' and since they are desired because of these things, ' yet angels and men will receive the kingdom and the confirmation ' [and] the salvation.[15] These, then, are the causes. '

About the one who appeared in flesh they believed ' without any doubt ' that he is the Son of the unknown ' God, who [20] was not previously spoken of ' and who could not be seen. Then ' they abandoned their gods ' whom they had previously worshipped ' and the lords who are [25] in heaven and on ' earth. Before ' he had taken them up, and while he was still ' a child, they testified that he had already ' begun to preach,[30] and when he was in the tomb ' as a dead man the ' [angels] thought that he was alive ' [and received] life **134** from the one who had died. ' They first desired their numerous services ' and wonders ' which were in the temple on their behalf [5] to be performed continuously as the confession. ' That is, it can ' be done on their behalf through ' their (very) approach to him. '

That preparation which they did not accept,[10] they rejected ' because of the one who had not been sent ' from that place, but [they accepted] ' the Christ who they thought ' existed in [that] place [15] from which they had come ' along with him, a place of gods ' and lords whom they served, ' worshipped, ' and ministered to [20] in the names which they had received on loan. ' —They were given to the one who is designated ' by them properly.— ' However, after his ' assumption, they had the experience [25] to know that he is their Lord, ' over whom no one else is lord. ' They gave him a kingdom; ' they rose from their thrones; ' they were kept from their [30] crowns. He, however, revealed himself to them, ' for the reasons which we have already spoken of, ' their salvation and the [return to a] ' good thought until [. . .] **135** companion and the angels ' [. . .] and the abundance of good ' [which they did] with it. Thus ' they were entrusted with the services [5] which benefit the elect, ' bringing their iniquity ' up to heaven. They tested them eternally ' for the lack of humility from the inerrancy ' of the creation, continuing on their [10] behalf until all come to life and ' leave life, while their ' bodies [remain] on earth. They (the angels) serve ' all their [. . .], sharing ' [with them] in their sufferings [15] [and] persecutions and ' tribulations, which were brought ' upon the saints in every place. '

As for the servants of the ' evil one, though [20] evil is worthy of destruction, they are in ' [. . .]. But because of the ' [polity] which is above ' all the worlds, which is ' their good thought [25] and the fellowship, ' the Church will remember them ' as good friends ' and faithful servants, once she has received ' redemption [. . .] requital.[30] Then the [gladness] which is in ' the bridal [chamber] and the [. . .] ' in her house [. . .] ' in the thought [. . .] ' the giving and the one who [. . .]. **136** Christ is the one with her [and the] ' expectation of the Father [of] ' the Totality, since she will produce for them ' angels as guides and [5] servants.

They will ' think pleasant thoughts. ' They are services for her. She will ' give them their requital for all that which ' the aeons will think about.[10] The exalted one is an emanation from them. ' Just as Christ [did] his ' will which he brought [forth and] ' exalted the greatnesses of the Church [to] ' give them to her, so [15] will she be a thought for ' [these]. And to men he gives [their] ' dwelling places forever, in ' which they will dwell [leaving] ' behind the attraction toward [20] the defect, while ' the power of the Pleroma pulls them up ' in the greatness of the ' generosity and [the] sweetness of ' the aeon which preexists. This [25] is the nature of the entire begetting of those ' whom he had when he shone ' on them [in] a light which he ' revealed [. . .]. ' Just as this one [. . .] [30] who will be [. . .] ' so too his [lord ' while] the change alone is ' in those who have changed [. . .] **137**[4] which [. . .] by ' him [. . .] give praise ' as I have said, ' while the hylics will remain until ' the end for destruction, since they will not give ' forth for their [. . .], if [10] [they would] return once again to that which ' [. . .]. As they were ' [. . .] they were not ' [. . .] but they were of use ' [in the] time that they were [15] [in it] among them, although they were not ' [. . .] at first. If ' [. . .] to do something else concerning ' the control which ' they have of the preparation.[20] [. . .] before them. ' —For though I continually use ' these words, I have not understood ' his meaning.—Some ' [elders . . .] him [25] [greatness. . . .] **138**[4] all [. . .] angels ' [. . .] word ' and [the sound of] a trumpet ' he will proclaim the great, ' complete amnesty ' from the beauteous east, in the [10] bridal chamber which is the love ' of God the Father [. . .] ' according to the power which [. . .] ' of the greatness [. . .] ' the sweetness of [. . .] [15] of him, since he reveals ' himself to the greatnesses [. . .] ' his goodness [. . .] ' the praise, the dominion, [and] the [glory] ' through [. . .] the Lord, the [20] Savior, the Redeemer of all those belonging to the one filled ' with Love, ' through his Holy Spirit ' from now through all ' generations for ever [25] and ever. Amen.

THE APOCRYPHON OF JOHN
(II, *1*, III, *1*, IV, *1*, AND BG 8502, *2*)

Introduced and translated by

FREDERIK WISSE

The *Apocryphon of John* is an important work of mythological Gnosticism. Using the framework of a revelation delivered by the resurrected Christ to John the son of Zebedee, this tractate offers a remarkably clear description of the creation, fall, and salvation of humanity; the mythological description is developed largely in terms of the early chapters of Genesis. Reports of the church fathers indicate that some of them were familiar with the contents of the *Apocryphon of John:* the teachings of certain Gnostics described by Irenaeus are very similar to the cosmological teachings of the present tractate. Though Irenaeus apparently did not know the *Apocryphon of John* in its present form, it is certain that the main teachings of the tractate existed before 185 C.E., the date of Irenaeus' work *Against Heresies.* The *Apocryphon of John* was still used in the eighth century by the Audians of Mesopotamia.

The *Apocryphon of John* supplies answers to two basic questions: What is the origin of evil? How can we escape from this evil world to our heavenly home? The cosmogony, in spite of its exotic details, also seeks to answer these questions. The highest deity is defined in terms of an abstract Greek concept of perfection, a perfection which excludes all anthropomorphism and all involvement in the world. From this supreme deity emanates a series of light-beings, including Christ and Sophia.

According to the *Apocryphon of John*, the fall occurs when Sophia desires to bring forth a being without the approval of the great Spirit or her consort. Consequently, she produces the monstrous creator-god Yaldabaoth, who still possesses some of the light-power of his mother. Yaldabaoth creates angels to rule over the world and aid in the creation of man; man himself is fashioned after the perfect Father's image, which was mirrored on the water. Man comes to life when Yaldabaoth is tricked into breathing light-power into him. Thus begins a continuous struggle between the powers of light and the powers of darkness for the possession of the divine particles in man. The evil powers put man in a material body to keep him imprisoned, and also create woman and sexual desire to spread the particles of light and make escape more difficult. Finally Christ is sent down to save humanity by reminding people of their heavenly origin. Only those who possess this knowledge and have lived ascetic lives can return to the realm of light; the others are reincarnated until they also come to saving knowledge.

The *Apocryphon of John* was composed both in a short recension (III, *1* and BG, *2*) and a long recension (II, *1* and IV, *1*). In cases where the copy translated here (II, *1*) has a corrupt text or a lacuna, the text is corrected or, where possible, the lacuna filled (without use of brackets) from IV, *1*.

THE APOCRYPHON OF JOHN
II 1, 1-32, 9

The teaching [of the savior] and [the revelation] ' of the mysteries [and the] things hidden in ' silence, [all these things which] he taught ' John, [his] disciple. ⁵

It happened [one day], when ' Jo[hn, the brother] of James, ' —who are the sons of Ze[bed]ee—went up and came to ' the temple, that a [Ph]arisee ' named Arimanius approached him and ¹⁰ said to him, "[Where] is your master whom ' you followed?" And he [said] to him, ' "He has gone to the place from which he came." The Pharisee ' said to him, "[This Nazarene] ' deceived you (pl.) with deception ¹⁵ and filled [your ears with lies] ' and closed [your hearts and turned you] ' from the traditions [of your fathers]."

[When] I, ' [John], heard these things, [I turned] ' away from the temple [to a desert place], ²⁰ and I became [greatly] grieved [and said in my heart], ' "How [then was] the savior [chosen], ' and why was he sent [into the world] ' by [his Father, and who is his] ' Father who [sent him, and of what sort] ²⁵ is [that] aeon [to which we shall go]? ' For what did he [mean when he said to us], ' 'This aeon to which [you will go is of the] ' type of the [imperishable] aeon,' [but he did not] ' teach us concerning [that one of what sort it is]." ³⁰

Straightway, [while I was contemplating these things], ' behold the [heavens opened and the whole] ' creation [which is] under heaven ' shone and [the world] was shaken. 2 [And I was afraid, and behold I] saw in ' the light [a youth who stood] by me. ' While I looked [at him he became] like an ' old man. And he [changed his] form (again), becoming like ⁵ a servant. There was [not a plurality] before me, ' but there was a [likeness] with multiple forms ' in the light, and the [forms] appeared ' through each other, [and] the likeness had three ' forms.

He said to me, "John, ¹⁰ Jo[h]n, why do you doubt, and why ' are you afraid? You are not unfamiliar with this likeness, are you? ' That is to say, be not timid! I am the one who ' [is with you (pl.)] for ever. I ' [am the Father], I am the Mother, I am the Son. ¹⁵ I am the unpolluted and incorruptible one. ' Now [I have come to teach] you what is ' [and what was] and what will come to ' [pass], that [you may know the] things which are not revealed ' [and the things which are revealed, and to teach] you the ²⁰ [. . . about the] perfect [Man]. Now, ' [then, lift up] your [face, that] you may ' [receive] the things which I [shall tell you] today, [and ' that you may tell them to your] fellow spirits who are ' [from] the [unwavering] race of the perfect ²⁵ Man."

[And when I] asked to ' [know it he said] to me, "The Monad ' [is a] monarchy with nothing above it. ' It is [he who] exists as [God] and Father of ' everything, [the invisible one] who is above [30] [everything, who is] imperishability, existing ' [as] pure light which no ' [eye] can behold. '

"He [is the] invisible [Spirit]; it is not right ' [to think] about him as a god, or something [35] similar. For he is more than a god, ' since there is no one above him, nor does anyone 3 lord it over him. [He exists] in nothing ' inferior, [for everything] exists in him; (IV 4, 9-10 adds: [he, however], ' stands) ' alone. [He is . . .] because ' he has [no] need [of anyone]. For [he] is completely perfect; [5] he did not [lack] anything that he might ' be completed by it. [But at] all times he is completely ' perfect in [light]. He is [illimitable] because ' there is no one [prior to him to] limit him. ' He is unsearchable [because there] exists no one [10] prior to him to [examine him. He is] immeasurable ' because there [was] no one [prior to him to measure] ' him. He is [invisible because] ' no one saw [him. He is eternal] who [exists] ' eternally. He is [ineffable because] [15] no one could comprehend him to speak [about him]. He is ' unnameable because [there is no one prior to him] ' to name him.

"[He] is [the immeasurable light] ' which is pure, holy, [and immaculate]. He is ' ineffable, [being perfect] in [20] imperishability, not in [perfection] nor in ' blessedness nor in ' divinity, but being far superior. ' He is not corporeal [nor] incorporeal. ' He is not great [and not] small. [It is not] [25] possible to say, 'What is his quantity' or 'What [is his quality],' ' for no one can [know him]. ' He is not one of [the existing ones, but he is] far [superior. ' Not] as if [he is superior], but his ' essence does not belong to the aeons nor [30] to time. For he who belongs to [an aeon] ' was first constructed. Time [was not] ' apportioned to him, [because] he cannot receive anything ' [from] another. [For what is] received is a ' loan. For he who exists prior to someone [35] has [no need] which might be fulfilled [by him]. ' For that one [rather] looks expectantly up to him in 4 his light.

"For the [perfect one] is majestic; ' he is pure and immeasurable [greatness]. ' He is an aeon-giving Aeon, ' [life]-giving Life, a blessedness-giving [5] Blessed One, knowledge-giving ' Knowledge, goodness-giving ' Goodness, mercy and redemption-giving Mercy, ' grace-giving Grace, not because he possesses ' it, but because he gives immeasurable and [10] incomprehensible [light].

"[How shall I speak] with you about him? His ' aeon is indestructible, at rest and ' being in [silence, reposing] and being ' prior [to everything.

He] is the head of [all] the ' aeons, [and] it is he who gives them strength through [15] his goodness. For we [know] not ' [the things which are . . . and] we know not ' [the immeasurable things] except for him who came forth ' from him, namely (from) [the] Father. For it is he ' [alone] who told it to us, and it is he alone who looks at [20] him in his light which surrounds ' [him]. This is the spring of the water of life ' which gives to [all] the aeons and in every form. He ' [gazes upon] his image which he sees ' in the spring of the [Spirit. He] puts his desire in his [25] light-[water, that is] the spring of the [pure] ' light-water [which] surrounds him.

"And ' [his Ennoia performed a] deed and she came forth, ' [namely] she who had [appeared] before him ' in [the shine of] his light. This is [30] the first [power which was] before all of them ' (and) [which came] forth from his mind, that ' [is the Pronoia of the All]. Her light ' [is the likeness of the] light, the [perfect] ' power which is [the] image of the invisible, [35] virginal Spirit who is perfect. ' [The first power], the glory, Barbelo, the perfect **5** glory in the aeons, the glory of the ' revelation, she glorified the virginal ' Spirit and praised him, because thanks to him ' she had come forth. This is the first thought, [5] his image; she became the womb of everything ' for she is prior to them all, the ' Mother-Father, the first Man, the holy Spirit, ' the thrice-male, the thrice-powerful, ' the thrice-named androgynous one, and the [10] eternal aeon among the invisible ones, and ' the first to come forth.

"⟨She⟩ requested from ' the invisible, virginal Spirit, ' that is Barbelo, to give her foreknowledge. ' And the Spirit consented. And when he had [consented], [15] the foreknowledge came forth, and ' it stood by the Pronoia; it originates from ' the thought of the invisible, ' virginal Spirit. It glorified him [and] ' his perfect power, Barbelo, for [20] thanks to her it had come into being.

"And she requested again ' to grant her [indestructibility], and he ' consented. When he had [consented], indestructibility ' [came] forth, and it stood by ' the thought and the foreknowledge. It glorified [25] the invisible One and Barbelo ' thanks to whom they had come into being.

"And Barbelo requested ' to grant her eternal life. And ' the invisible Spirit consented. And ' when he had consented, eternal life [30] came forth, and [they stood] and they glorified ' the invisible [Spirit] and Barbelo ' thanks to whom they had come into being.

"And she requested again ' to grant her truth. And the invisible Spirit ' consented. Truth came forth, [35] and they stood and glorified the invisible, **6** excellent Spirit and his Barbelo ' thanks to whom they had come into being.

"This is the five-aeon ' of the Father which is the first ' Man, the image of the invisible Spirit; [5] it is the Pronoia which is Barbelo, ' the thought and the foreknowledge and ' the indestructibility and the eternal life and ' the truth. This is the androgynous five-aeon, ' which is the ten-aeon, which is [10] the Father.

"And he looked within Barbelo ' with the pure light which surrounds the invisible ' Spirit and (with) his spark, and she conceived ' from him. He begot a spark of light with a light ' of a blessed likeness. But it does not equal [15] his greatness. This was an only-begotten one ' of the Mother-Father which had come forth; ' it is his only begetting, the only-begotten one of ' the Father, the pure Light.

"And ' the invisible, virginal Spirit rejoiced [20] over the light which came forth, that which ' was brought forth first by the first power ' of his Pronoia who is Barbelo. ' And he anointed it with his goodness ' until it became perfect, not lacking [25] in any goodness, because he had anointed it ' with the goodness of the invisible Spirit. And ' it stood before him as he poured upon ' it. And immediately when it had received from ' the Spirit, it glorified the holy Spirit [30] and the perfect Pro[n]oia {. . .} [32] thanks to whom it had ' come forth.

"And it requested to give it a fellow worker, ' which is the mind, and he consented. [35] And when the invisible Spirit had consented, [7] the mind came forth, and it stood ' by Christ glorifying him and ' Barbelo. And all these came into being ' in silence.

"And the mind wanted [5] to perform a deed through the word ' of the invisible Spirit. And his will became ' a deed and it appeared with ' the mind; and the light glorified it. ' And the word followed the will. [10] For because of the word, Christ ' the divine Autogenes created everything. And the ' eternal life ⟨and⟩ his will and the mind ' and the foreknowledge stood and glorified ' the invisible Spirit and Barbel[o], [15] for thanks to her they had come into being.

"And the holy ' Spirit completed the divine Autogenes, ' his son, together with Barbel[o], ' that he may stand before the mighty and invisible, ' virginal Spirit as the divine [20] Autogenes, the Christ, whom he had ' honored with a mighty voice. He came forth ' through the Pronoia. And the invisible, ' virginal Spirit placed the ' divine Autogenes of truth over everything. [25] And he subjected to him every authority ' and the truth which is in him, ' that he may know the all which ' has been called with a name exalted above ' every name. For they will mention that name [30] to those who are worthy of it.

"For from the light, ' which is the Christ, and the indestructibility, ' through the gift of the Spirit and the four ' lights, from the divine Autogenes, ' he looked out that they may be stationed **8** by him. And the three (are) will, ' thought, and life. And the four ' powers (are) understanding, grace, perception, ' and prudence. And grace exists with [5] the light-aeon Armozel, who ' is the first angel. And there are ' three other aeons with this aeon: grace, ' truth, and form. And the second ' light (is) Oriel, who has been placed [10] on the second aeon. And there are ' three other aeons with him: conception, perception, ' and memory. And the third light ' is Daveithai, who has been placed ' on the third aeon. And there are [15] three other aeons with him: understanding, ' love, and idea. And the fourth ' aeon was placed on the fourth ' light Eleleth. And there are ' three other aeons with him: perfection, [20] peace, and Sophia. These are the four lights ' which stand by the divine Autogenes, ' (and) these are the twelve aeons which stand ' by the son of the mighty one, the Autogenes, the Christ, ' through the will and the gift of the invisible [25] Spirit. And the twelve aeons belong to ' the son, the [A]utogenes. And all things had been ' established by the will of the holy Spirit ' through the Autogenes.

"And from ' the foreknowledge of the perfect mind, [30] through the revelation of the will of the invisible ' Spirit and the will of the Autogenes, ' (came into being the) perfect Man, the first revelation, ' and the truth. It is he whom ' the virginal Spirit called Pigeraadama(s), [35] and he placed him on **9** the first aeon with the mighty one, the Autogenes, ' the Christ, by the first light Armozel; ' and his powers are with him. ' And the invisible one gave him an intelligible, [5] invincible power. And he spoke ' and glorified and praised the invisible ' Spirit, saying, 'It is thanks to thee that everything ' has come into being and everything will return to thee. ' And I shall praise and glorify thee and [10] the Autogenes and the aeons, the three: the Father, ' the Mother, and the Son, the perfect power.'

"And he ' placed his son S[e]th on the second ' aeon in the presence of the second light ' Oroiel. And in the third aeon [15] the seed of Seth was placed ' on the third light Daveitha[i]. ' And the souls of the saints were placed (there). ' And in the fourth aeon ' the souls were placed of those who do not know the [20] Pleroma and who did not repent at once, ' but who persisted for a while and repented ' afterwards; they are by the fourth ' light Eleleth. These are ' creatures which glorify the invisible Spirit. [25]

"And the Sophia of the Epinoia, being an aeon, ' conceived a thought from herself with ' the reflection of the invisible Spirit and ' foreknowledge. She wanted to bring forth ' a likeness out of herself without the consent of the Spirit [30]—he had not approved—and without her consort ' and without his consideration. And though the personage of her ' maleness had not approved, ' and she had not found her agreement, ' and she had thought without the consent of the Spirit [35] and the knowledge of her agreement, (yet) she brought forth. **10** And because of the invincible power which is in her, ' her thought did not remain idle and ' a thing came out of her ' which was imperfect and different from her appearance, [5] because she had created it without her consort. ' And it was dissimilar to the likeness of its mother ' for it has another form.

"And when she saw (the consequence of) her ' desire, it had changed into a form ' of a lion-faced serpent. And its eyes [10] were like lightning fires which ' flash. She cast it away from her, outside ' that place, that no one ' of the immortal ones might see it, for she had created it ' in ignorance. And she surrounded it with [15] a luminous cloud, and she placed a throne ' in the middle of the cloud that no ' one might see it except the holy Spirit ' who is called the mother of the living. ' And she called his name Yaltabaoth.

"This [20] is the first archon who took a great ' power from his mother. And he ' removed himself from her and moved ' away from the places in which he was born. He ' became strong and created for himself other aeons with [25] a flame of luminous fire which (still) exists now. ' And he joined with his madness ' which is in him and begot ' authorities for himself. The name of the first one ' is Athoth, whom the generations call [30] [. . .]. The second one is Harmas, ' who [is the eye] of envy. The third one ' is Kalila-Oumbri. The fourth one is Yabel. ' The fifth one is Adonaiou, who is called ' Sabaoth. The sixth one is Cain, [35] whom the generation of men call ' the sun. The seventh is Abel. The ' eighth is Abrisene. The ninth is Yobel. **11** The tenth is Armoupieel. The eleventh ' is Melcheir-Adonein. The twelfth ' is Belias, who is over the depth ' of Hades. And he placed seven kings [5]—corresponding to the firmaments of heaven—over the ' seven heavens and five over the depth of the abyss, ' that they may reign. And he shared his fire ' with them, but he did not send out from ' the power of the light which he had taken from his mother, [10] for he is ignorant darkness.

"And ' when the light had mixed with the darkness, it caused the ' darkness to shine. And when the darkness had mixed with ' the light, it darkened the light and it became ' neither light nor dark, but it became [15] weak.

"Now the archon who is weak has ' three names. The first name is Yaltaba[oth], ' the second is Saklas, and the third is ' Samael. And he is impious in his madness ' which is in him. For he said, [20] 'I am God and there is no other God ' beside me,' for he is ignorant of his strength, ' the place from which he had come.

"And the archons ' created seven powers for themselves, and ' the powers created for themselves six angels for [25] each one until they became 365 angels. ' And these are the bodies belonging with the names: the first is Athoth, ' he has a sheep's face; the second is Eloaiou, ' he has a donkey's face; the third ' is Astaphaios, he has a [hyena's] face; the [30] fourth is Yao, he has a [serpent's] face with ' seven heads; the fifth is Sabaoth, ' he has a dragon's face; the sixth is Adonin, ' he has a monkey's face; the seventh is Sabbede, ' he has a shining fire-face. This is the [35] sevenness of the week.

"But Yaltabaoth ' had a multitude **12** of faces in addition to all of them ' so that he could bring a face before ' all of them, according to his desire, being in ' the middle of seraphs. He shared [5] his fire with them; ' therefore he became lord over them, because of the power of ' the glory he possessed of his mother's ' light. Therefore he called ' himself God. And he did not [10] put his trust in the place from which he came. And ' he united with the authorities which were ' with him, the seven powers, through his thought. ' And when he spoke it happened. And ' he named each power beginning [15] with the highest: the first is ' goodness with the first one, Athoth; ' the second is foreknowledge with ' the second one, Eloaio; and the third is divinity with the third one, ' Astraphaio; the fourth is [20] lordship with the fourth one, Yao; ' the fifth is kingdom with the fifth one, ' Sanbaoth; the sixth is envy with ' the sixth one, Adonein; the seventh ' is understanding with the seventh one, [25] Sabbateon. And these have ' a firmament corresponding to each aeon-heaven. They were ' given names according to the glory which belongs to heaven ' for the [destruction of the] powers. And in the names which were ' given to [them by] their Originator [30] there was power. But the names which were given ' them according to the glory which belongs to heaven mean ' for them destruction and powerlessness. ' Thus they have two names.

"And ' everything he organized according to the model of the first [35] aeons which had come into being so that he might **13** create them like the indestructible ones. Not because ' he had seen the indestructible ones, but the power ' which is in him which he took from ' his mother produced in him the likeness of [5] the cosmos. And when he saw the

creation which surrounds ' him and the multitude of the angels around '
him which had come forth from him, ' he said to them, 'I am a ' jealous
God and there is no other God beside me.' But by [10] announcing this
he indicated to the angels ' who attended to him that there exists another
God, ' for if there were no other one, of whom ' would he be jealous?
Then the mother began ' to move to and fro. She became aware of the
deficiency when [15] the brightness of her light diminished. And she '
became dark because her consort ' had not agreed with her."

—But I ' said, "Lord, what does it mean that she moved to and fro?"
And he ' smiled and said, "Do not think it is, as [20] Moses said, 'above '
the waters.' No, but when she had seen ' the wickedness which had
happened, and the theft which ' her son had committed, she repented. '
And forgetfulness overcame her in the darkness of [25] ignorance and she
began to be ashamed. (IV 21, 13-14 adds: And she did not dare ' to return,
but she was moving) ' about. And the moving is the going to and fro.—

"And the ' arrogant one took a power from ' his mother. For he was
ignorant, ' thinking that there existed no other except [30] his mother
alone. And when he saw the multitude ' of the angels which he had
created, then he felt ' exalted above them.

"And when ' the mother recognized that the cover of darkness ' was
imperfect, then she knew [35] that her consort had not agreed ' with her.
She repented **14** with much weeping. And the whole ' pleroma heard
the prayer of her repentance ' and they praised on her behalf ' the
invisible, virginal [5] Spirit. (IV 22, 5-7 adds: And ' he consented; and when
the invisible Spirit ' had consented,) the holy Spirit poured ' over her
from their whole fullness. ' For her consort had not come to her, ' but
he came to her through the pleroma ' in order that he might correct
her deficiency. And she was taken [10] up not to her own aeon ' but
above her son, that she might be ' in the ninth until she has corrected
her ' deficiency.

"And a voice came forth from the exalted ' aeon-heaven: 'The Man
exists and [15] the son of Man.' And the chief archon, Yaltabaoth, '
heard (it) and thought that the ' voice had come from his mother, ' and
he did not know from where she (or: it) came. And ' the holy Mother-
Father taught them, [20] and the perfect, complete foreknowledge, '
the image of the invisible one who is the Father ' of the all through
whom everything came into being, ' the first Man, for he revealed his
appearance ' in a human form.

"And the [25] whole aeon of the chief archon trembled, ' and the foundations of the abyss shook. And ' of the waters which are above '

matter, the underside was illuminated by ' the appearance of his image which [30] had been revealed. And when all the authorities ' and the chief archon looked, they ' saw the whole part of the underside which was ' illuminated. And through the light they saw ' the form of the image in the water. **15**

"And he said to the authorities which attend to him, ' 'Come, let us create a man according to ' the image of God and according to our likeness, that ' his image may become a light for us.' [5] And they created by means of each other's powers ' in correspondence with the indications which were given. And ' each authority supplied a characteristic ' by means of the form of the image which he had seen ' in its psychic (form). He created a being [10] according to the likeness of the first, perfect Man. ' And they said, 'Let us call him ' Adam, that his name may become ' a power of light for us.'

"And the powers ' began: the first one, goodness, created [15] a bone-soul; and the second, foreknowledge, ' created a sinew-soul; the third, ' divinity, created a flesh-soul; ' and the fourth, the lordship, created ' a marrow-soul; the fifth, kingdom, [20] created a blood-soul; the sixth, ' envy, created a skin-soul; ' the seventh, understanding, created ' an eyelid-soul. And the multitude ' of the angels stood by him and they received [25] from the powers the seven substances ' of the psychic (form) in order to create ' the composition of the limbs and the composition of the rump ' and the connection of each ' of the parts.

"The first one began to create [30] the head: Eteraphaope-Abron created ' his head; Meniggesstroeth created ' the brain; Asterechme the right eye; ' Thaspomocha the left eye; ' Yeronumos the right ear; Bissoum [35] the left ear; Akioreim the nose; **16** Banen-Ephroum the lips; Amen ' the teeth; Ibikan the molars; Basiliademe ' the tonsils; Achchan the uvula; Adaban ' the neck; Chaaman the vertebrae; [5] Dearcho the throat; Tebar the (IV 25, 4-5 adds: right shoulder; ' [. . . the]) left ' shoulder; Mniarchon the (IV 25, 6-7 adds: right ' elbow; [. . . the]) left ' elbow; Abitrion the right underarm; ' Evanthen the left underarm; Krys the right hand; ' Beluai the left hand; [10] Treneu the fingers of the right hand; Balbel ' the fingers of the left hand; Kriman the nails ' of the hands; Astrops the right breast; ' Barroph the left breast; Baoum the right ' shoulder joint; Ararim the left shoulder joint; Areche [15] the belly; Phthave the navel; Senaphim ' the abdomen; Arachethopi the right ' ribs; Zabedo the left ribs; ' Barias the (IV 25, 19-20 adds: right ' hip; Phnouth the) left hip; Abenlenarchei ' the marrow; Chnoumeninorin the bones; [20] Gesole the stomach; Agromauma ' the heart; Bano the lungs; Sostrapal ' the liver; Anesimalar the spleen; Thopithro ' the intestines; Biblo the kidneys; ' Roeror the sinews; Taphreo the spine [25] of the body; Ipouspoboba the veins; ' Bineborin the arteries; Atoimenpsephei, ' theirs is the breath which is in all the limbs; ' Enthollei[n] all the flesh; Bedouk ' the right womb; Arabeei the left penis; [30] Eilo the testicles; Sorma the genitals; Gormakaiochlabar ' the right thigh; Nebrith ' the left thigh; Pserem the kidneys of ' the right leg; Asaklas the left ' kidney; Ormaoth the right leg; [35] Emenun the left leg; Knyx the **17** right shin-bone; Tupelon the left shin-bone; ' Achiel the right knee; Phneme the ' left knee; Phiouthrom the right foot; ' Boabel its toes; Trachoun [5] the left foot; Phikna its toes; ' Miamai the nails of the feet; Labernioum—. '

"And those who were appointed over all of these ' are: Zathoth, Armas, Kalila, Yabel, (IV 26, 19-20 adds: Sabaoth, Cain, ' Abel). And ' those who work particularly in the limbs: [10] (in) the head Diolimodraza, the neck Yammeax, ' the right shoulder Yakouib, the ' left shoulder Verton, the right hand ' Oudidi, the left one Arbao, the fingers of the right hand ' Lampno, the fingers of the left hand [15] Leekaphar, the right breast Barbar, the ' left breast Imae, the chest Pisandriaptes, ' the right shoulder joint Koade, the left shoulder joint ' Odeor, the right ribs Asphixix, the left ' ribs Synogchouta, the belly Arouph, [20] the womb Sabalo, the right thigh ' Charcharb, the left thigh Chthaon, ' all the genitals Bathinoth, the right ' leg Choux, the left leg Charcha, ' the right shin-bone Aroer, the left shin-bone [25] Toechea, the right knee Aol, the left ' knee Charaner, the right foot ' Bastan, its toes Archentechtha, the ' left foot Marephnounth, its toes ' Abrana.

"Seven ruled over [30] all of these: Michael, Ouriel, ' Asmenedas, Saphasatoel, Aarmouriam, ' Richram, Amiorps. And the ones who are over the senses ' (are) Archendekta; and he who is over the receptions ' (is) Deitharbathas; and he who is over the imagination [35] (is) Oummaa; and he who is over the composition **18** Aachiaram, and he who is over the whole impulse ' Riaramnacho.

"And the origin of the demons ' which are in the whole body is ordained to be four: ' heat, cold, wetness, [5] and dryness. And the mother of all of them is matter. ' And he who reigns over the heat (is) Phloxopha; ' and he who reigns over the cold ' is Oroorrothos; and he who reigns over ' what is dry (is) Erimacho; and he who reigns [10] over the wetness (is) Athuro. And the mother of all of these ' sets in their midst Onorthochras, ' since she is illimitable, and she mixes ' with all of them. And she is truly matter, ' for they are nourished through her.

"The four [15] chief demons are: Ephememphi who ' belongs to pleasure,

Yoko who belongs to desire, ' Nenentophni who belongs to grief, Blaomen ' who belongs to fear. And the mother of them all is ' Aesthesis-Ouchepiptoe. And from the four [20] demons passions came forth. ' And from grief (came) envy, jealousy, ' distress, trouble, pain, ' callousness, anxiety, mourning, ' etc. And from pleasure [25] much wickedness arises, and empty ' pride, and similar things. ' And from desire (comes) anger, wrath ' and bitterness and bitter passion ' and unsatedness and similar things. [30] And from fear (comes) dread, ' fawning, agony, and shame. All of these ' are like useful things as well as evil things. ' But the insight into their true (character) is Anaro, ' who is the head of the material soul, **19** for she belongs with the seven senses, Ouchepiptoe. '

"This is the number of the angels: ' together they are 365. They ' all worked on it until, [5] limb for limb, the psychic and ' material body was completed by them. Now there are ' other ones over the remaining passions ' whom I did not mention to you. But if you ' wish to know them, it is written in [10] the book of Zoroaster. And ' all the angels and demons worked ' until they had constructed the psychic body. ' And their product was completely ' inactive and motionless for a long time. [15]

"And when the mother wanted to retrieve ' the power which she had given to the chief archon, ' she petitioned the Mother-Father ' of the all who is most merciful. He sent, ' by means of the holy decree, the five lights [20] down upon the place of the angels of ' the chief archon. They advised him that they should ' bring forth the power of the mother. And they said ' to Yaltabaoth, 'Blow into his ' face something of your spirit and [25] his body will arise.' And he blew ' into his face the spirit which is the power ' of his mother; he did not know (this), for he exists ' in ignorance. And the power ' of the mother went out of [30] Yaltabaoth into the psychic soul ' which they had fashioned after the image of the One who ' exists from the beginning. The body moved and gained strength, ' and it was luminous. '

"And in that moment the rest of the powers **20** became jealous, because he had come into being ' through all of them and they had given their ' power to the man, and his ' intelligence was greater than that of those who had made him, and [5] greater than that of the chief archon. And when they recognized ' that he was luminous, and that he could think better ' than they, and that he was free from wickedness, they took ' him and threw him into the lowest region ' of all matter.

"But the blessed One, the Mother-Father, [10] the beneficent and merciful One, ' had mercy on the power of the mother ' which was brought forth out of the chief archon, ' for they (the archons) might again gain power over the ' psychic and perceptible body. And he[15] sent, through his beneficent ' Spirit and his great mercy, a ' helper to Adam, luminous Epinoia ' which comes out of him, who was called ' Life. And she assists the whole creature,[20] by toiling with him and by restoring ' him to his fullness and by ' teaching him about the descent of his ' seed (and) by teaching him about the way of ascent, ' (which is) the way he came down. [25] And the luminous Epinoia was hidden in Adam, ' in order that the archons might not know her, ' but that the Epinoia might be a correction ' of the deficiency of the mother.

"And the man came forth ' because of the shadow of the light [30] which is in him. And his thinking ' was superior to all those who had made him. ' When they looked up they saw ' that his thinking was superior. And they took ' counsel with the whole array of archons [35] and angels. They took fire and earth 21 and water and mixed them together ' with the four fiery winds. And they wrought them ' together and caused a great ' disturbance. And they brought him (Adam) into the shadow [5] of death in order that they might form (him) again ' from earth and water and fire ' and the spirit which originates in matter, which is ' the ignorance of darkness and desire, ' and their opposing spirit which [10] is the tomb of the newly-formed body ' with which the robbers had clothed the man, ' the bond of forgetfulness; and he became a ' mortal man. This is the first one who came down ' and the first separation. But the [15] Epinoia of the light which was in him, ' she is the one who will awaken his thinking.

"And ' the archons took him and placed ' him in paradise. And they said to him, ' 'Eat, that is, at leisure,' for [20] their luxury is bitter and their beauty is depraved. ' And their luxury is deception and ' their trees are godlessness and their fruit ' is deadly poison and their ' promise is death. And the tree of their [25] life they had placed in the middle of paradise. '

"And I shall teach you (pl.) ' what is the mystery of their life, ' which is the plan which they made together, ' which is the likeness of their spirit. [30] The root of this tree is bitter and its branches ' are death, its shadow is hate ' and deception is in its leaves, ' and its blossom is the ointment of evil, ' and its fruit is death and [35] desire is its seed, and ' it sprouts in darkness. The 22 dwelling place of those who taste from it is ' Hades and the darkness is their place of rest. '

"But what they call ' the tree of knowledge of good and [5] evil, which is the Epinoia of the light, ' they stayed in front of it in order that he

(Adam) might not ' look up to his fullness and ' recognize the naked-ness of his shamefulness. ' But it was I who brought about that they ate."

And [10] I said to the savior, "Lord, was it not the serpent ' that taught Adam to eat?" ' The savior smiled and said, "The serpent taught them ' to eat from wickedness, begetting, ' lust, (and) the destruction, that he might [15] be useful to him. And he (Adam) knew that he was ' disobedient to him (the chief archon) due to the light of the Epinoia ' which is in him, which corrected him in his ' thinking (to be) superior to the chief archon. And (the latter) ' wanted to bring out the power which he himself had given [20] him. And he brought a forgetfulness ' over Adam."

And I said to the savior, "What is ' the forgetfulness?" And he said, "It is not the way Moses ' wrote (and) you heard. For he said in ' his first book, 'He put him to sleep' (Genesis 2:21), but [25] (it was) in his per-ception. For he said through the ' prophet, 'I will make their ' hearts heavy that they may not pay attention and may not ' see' (Isaiah 6:10).

"Then the Epinoia of the light ' hid herself in him (Adam). And the chief archon wanted [30] to bring her out of his rib. ' But the Epinoia of the light cannot be grasped. ' Although darkness pursued her, it did not catch her. And ' he brought a part of his power ' out of him. And he made another creature [35] in the form of a woman according to the likeness of the Epinoia ' which had appeared to him. And he brought **23** the part which he had taken from the power ' of the man into the female creature, ' and not the way Moses said, ' 'his rib-bone.'

"And he (Adam) saw the woman by [5] him. And in that moment ' the luminous Epinoia appeared, and she lifted ' the veil which lay over his mind. ' And he became sober from the drunkenness of darkness. ' And he recognized his counter-image, and he said, [10] 'This is indeed bone from my bones ' and flesh from my flesh.' Therefore ' the man will leave his father and his ' mother and he will cleave to his wife and they will ' both be one flesh, for they [15] will send him his consort, ' and he will leave his father and his mother. {. . . .} [20]

"And our sister ' Sophia (is) she who came down in innocence ' in order to rectify her deficiency. ' Therefore she was called Life which is ' the mother of the living. Through the foreknowledge [25] of the sovereignty and through her ' they have tasted the perfect Knowledge. I appeared ' in the form of an eagle on ' the tree of knowledge, which is the Epinoia ' from the foreknowledge of the pure light, [30] that I might teach them and awaken ' them out of the depth of sleep. For they ' were both in a fallen state and they ' recognized their nakedness. The

Epinoia ' appeared to them as a light (and) she awakened [35] their thinking.

"And when Aldabaoth ' noticed that they withdrew from him, ' he cursed his earth. He found the woman as she was **24** preparing herself for her husband. He was lord ' over her though he did not know the mystery ' which had come to pass through the holy decree. ' And they were afraid to blame him. And [5] he showed his angels his ' ignorance which is in him. And ' he cast them out of paradise and ' he clothed them in gloomy darkness. And the ' chief archon saw the virgin who stood [10] by Adam, and that the luminous ' Epinoia of life had appeared in her. ' And Yaldabaoth was full of ignorance. ' And when the fore-knowledge of the all ' noticed (it), she sent some and they snatched [15] Life out of Eve.

"And the chief archon ' seduced her and he begot in her ' two sons; the first and the second ' (are) Eloim and Yave. Eloim has a bear-face ' and Yave has a cat-face. The one [20] is righteous but the other is un-righteous. (IV 38, 4-6 adds: Yave ' is righteous but Eloim is ' unright-eous.) ' Yave he set ' over the fire and the wind, and Eloim he set ' over the water and ' the earth. And these he called with the names [25] Cain and Abel with a view to deceive. '

"Now up to the present day ' sexual intercourse continued due to the chief archon. ' And he planted sexual desire ' in her who belongs to Adam. And he produced through [30] intercourse the copies of the bodies, ' and he inspired them with his opposing spirit. '

"And the two archons he set ' over principalities so that ' they might rule over the tomb. [35] And when Adam recognized the likeness of his own ' foreknowledge, he begot the likeness **25** of the son of man. He called him Seth ' according to the way of the race in the aeons. Like-wise ' the mother also sent down her spirit ' which is in her likeness and a [5] copy of those who are in the pleroma, for she will ' prepare a dwelling place for the aeons which will come ' down. And he made them drink water of forgetfulness, ' from the chief archon, in order that they might not ' know from where they came. Thus [10] the seed remained for ' a while assisting (him) in order that, when ' the Spirit comes forth from ' the holy aeons, he may raise him up and ' heal him from the deficiency, that the [15] whole pleroma may (again) become holy and ' faultless."

And I said to the savior, ' "Lord, will all the souls then be brought safely ' into the pure light?" He answered ' and said to me, "Great things [20] have arisen in your mind, for it is ' difficult to explain them to others ' except to those who are from ' the immovable race. Those on whom the Spirit of life ' will descend and (with whom) he will be with the power, [25] they will be saved and become perfect ' and be worthy of the greatnesses and ' be purified in that place from ' all wickedness and the involvements in evil. ' Then they have no other care than [30] the incorruption alone, to which they direct their attention ' from here on, without anger or envy or jealousy ' or desire and greed of ' everything. They are not affected by ' anything except the state of being in [35] the flesh alone, which they bear while looking expectantly ' for the time when they will be ' met **26** by the receivers. Such ' then are worthy of the imperishable, ' eternal life and the calling. For they endure ' everything and bear up under [5] everything, that they may finish ' the good fight and inherit ' eternal life."

I said to him, "Lord, ' the souls of those who did not do these works, ' (but) on whom the power and Spirit [10] of life descended, (IV 40, 24-25 adds: will they be rejected?" He ' answered and said to me, "If) the ' Spirit (IV 40, 26 adds: descended upon them), they will in any case be saved ' and they will change (for the better). For the ' power will descend on every man, ' for without it no one can stand. [15] And after they are born, then, ' when the Spirit of life increases and ' the power comes and strengthens that soul, ' no one can lead it astray ' with works of evil. [20] But those on whom the opposing spirit ' descends are drawn by ' him and they go astray."

And I ' said, "Lord, where will the souls of these go ' when they have come out of their [25] flesh?" And he smiled ' and said to me, "The soul in which the power ' will become superior to the despicable spirit, ' she is strong and she flees from ' evil and, through [30] the intervention of the incorruptible one, she is saved ' and she is taken up to the rest ' of the aeons."

And I said, "Lord, ' those, however, who have not known ' to whom they belong, where will their souls [35] be?" And he said to me, ' "In those the despicable spirit has **27** gained strength when they went astray. And he ' burdens the soul and draws her ' to the works of evil, and he casts ' her down into forgetfulness. And after she [5] comes out of (the body), she is handed over to the authorities, ' who came into being through the archon, and ' they bind her with chains and cast ' her into prison and consort with her ' until she is liberated from the forgetfulness and [10] acquires knowledge. And if thus she ' becomes perfect, she is saved."

And I ' said, "Lord, how can the soul become smaller ' and return into the nature ' of its mother or into man?" Then [15] he rejoiced when I asked him this, and ' he said to me, "Truly, you are blessed, ' for you have understood! That soul ' is made to follow another one (fem.), since the Spirit of ' life is in her. She is saved through ²⁰ him. She is not again cast ' into another flesh.''

And I said, ' ''Lord, these also who did know but ' have turned away, where will their ' souls go?'' Then he said to me, ''To that place ²⁵ where the angels of poverty go ' they will be taken, the place ' where there is no repentance. And ' they will be kept for the day on which ' those who have blasphemed the spirit will be tortured, ³⁰ and they will be punished with eternal punishment.'' '

And I said, ''Lord, ' from where did the despicable spirit come?'' ' Then he said to me, ''The Mother-Father ' who is rich in mercy, the holy Spirit ³⁵ in every way, the One who is merciful and **28** who sympathizes with you (pl.), i.e. the ' Epinoia of the foreknowledge of light, ' he raised up the offspring of the perfect ' race and his thinking and the eternal ⁵ light of man. When ' the chief archon realized that they were exalted ' above him in the height—and they surpass ' him in thinking— then he wanted to seize their ' thought, not knowing that they surpassed ¹⁰ him in thinking and that he will not be able ' to seize them.

''He made a plan ' with his authorities, which are his powers, and ' they committed together adultery with Sophia, and ' bitter fate was begotten through them, ¹⁵ which is the last of the terrible bonds. ' And it is of a sort that ' they are dreadful to each other. And it is harder and ' stronger than she with whom ' the gods are united and the angels and the demons ²⁰ and all the generations until this day. ' For from that fate ' came forth every sin and ' injustice and blasphemy and the chain ' of forgetfulness and ignorance and every ²⁵ difficult command and serious sins ' and great fear. And thus ' the whole creation was made blind, ' in order that they may not know God who is ' above all of them. And because of the chain of forgetfulness ³⁰ their sins were hidden. For they are bound with ' measures and times and moments, ' since it (fate) is lord over everything.

''And he ' repented for everything which had come into being ' through him. This time he planned ³⁵ to bring a flood **29** over the work of man. But the greatness ' of the light of the foreknowledge informed ' Noah, and he proclaimed (it) to all the offspring ' which are the sons of men. But ⁵ those who were strangers to him did not listen to him. ' It is not as Moses said, ' 'They hid themselves in an ark' (Genesis 7:7), but ' they hid themselves in a place, not ' only Noah but also many other people ¹⁰ from the immovable race. They went ' into a place and hid themselves in a ' luminous cloud. And he recognized his authority, ' and she who belongs to the light was with him, ' having shone on them because [15] he had brought darkness upon the whole earth. '

"And he made a plan with his powers. ' He sent his angels to the daughters ' of men, that they might take some of them for themselves ' and raise offspring [20] for their enjoyment. And at first they did not succeed. ' When they had no success, they gathered ' together again and they made ' a plan together. They created ' a despicable spirit, who resembles the Spirit who had descended, [25] so as to pollute the souls through it. ' And the angels changed themselves in their ' likeness into the likeness of their (the daughters of men) mates, ' filling them with the spirit of darkness, ' which they had mixed for them, and with evil. [30] They brought gold and silver ' and a gift and copper and iron ' and metal and all kinds ' of things. And they steered the people ' who had followed them **30** into great troubles, by leading them astray ' with many deceptions. They (the people) became old without having enjoyment. ' They died, not having found truth and ' without knowing the God of truth. And [5] thus the whole creation became enslaved forever, ' from the foundation of the world ' until now. And they took women ' and begot children out of the darkness according to ' the likeness of their spirit. And they closed their hearts, [10] and they hardened themselves through the hardness ' of the despicable spirit until now.

"I, ' therefore, the perfect Pronoia of the all, ' changed myself into my seed, for I existed ' first, going on every road. [15] For I am the richness of the light; ' I am the remembrance of the pleroma.

"And I ' went into the realm of darkness and ' I endured till I entered the middle ' of the prison. And the foundations of chaos [20] shook. And I hid myself from them because of ' their wickedness, and they did not recognize me.

"Again ' I returned for the second time ' and I went about. I came forth from those who belong to the light, ' which is I, the remembrance of the Pronoia. [25] I entered into the middle of darkness and ' the inside of Hades, since I was seeking (to accomplish) ' my task. And the foundations of chaos ' shook, that they might fall down upon those who ' are in chaos and might destroy them. [30] And again I ran up to my root of light ' lest they be destroyed before ' the time.

"Still for a third time ' I went—I am the light ' which exists in the light, I am [35] the remembrance of the Pronoia—that I might ' enter into the middle of darkness and the inside **31** of Hades. And I filled my face with ' the light of the completion of their aeon. ' And I entered into the middle of their prison ' which is the prison of the body. And [5]

I said, 'He who hears, let him get up from the deep ' sleep.' And he wept and shed tears. ' Bitter tears he wiped from ' himself and he said, 'Who is it that calls my ' name, and from where has this hope come to me, [10] while I am in the chains of the prison?' And ' I said, 'I am the Pronoia of the pure light; ' I am the thinking of the virginal ' Spirit, he who raised you up to the honored ' place. Arise and remember [15] that it is you who hearkened, and follow ' your root, which is I, the merciful one, and ' guard yourself against ' the angels of poverty and the demons ' of chaos and all those who ensnare you, [20] and beware of the ' deep sleep and the enclosure of the inside ' of Hades.'

"And I raised him up ' and sealed him in the light ' of the water with five seals, in order that [25] death might not have power over him from this time on.

"And ' behold, now I shall go up to the perfect ' aeon. I have completed everything for you ' in your hearing. And I ' have said everything to you that you might write [30] them down and give them secretly to your fellow spirits, ' for this is the mystery of the immovable race." '

And the savior presented these things to him that ' he might write them down and keep them ' secure. And he said to him, "Cursed be [35] everyone who will exchange these things for a gift ' or for food or for ' drink or for clothing or for any other such thing." [32] And these things were presented to him ' in a mystery, and immediately ' he disappeared from him. ' And he went to his fellow disciples and related [5] to them what the savior had told him. '

Jesus Christ, Amen. '

The '
Apocryphon '
According to John

THE GOSPEL OF THOMAS (II, *2*)

Introduced by

HELMUT KOESTER

Translated by

THOMAS O. LAMBDIN

The *Gospel of Thomas* is a collection of traditional sayings, prophecies, proverbs, and parables of Jesus. The Coptic *Gospel of Thomas* was translated from the Greek; in fact, several fragments of this Greek version have been preserved, and can be dated to about 200 C.E. Thus the Greek (or even Syriac or Aramaic) collection was composed in the period before about 200 C.E., possibly as early as the second half of the first century, in Syria, Palestine, or Mesopotamia. The authorship of the *Gospel of Thomas* is attributed to Didymos Judas Thomas, that is, Judas "the Twin," who was identified particularly within the Syrian church as the apostle and twin brother of Jesus.

The relationship of the *Gospel of Thomas* to the New Testament gospels has been a matter of special interest: many of the sayings of the *Gospel of Thomas* have parallels in the synoptic gospels (Matthew, Mark, and Luke). A comparison of the sayings in the *Gospel of Thomas* with their parallels in the synoptic gospels suggests that the sayings in the *Gospel of Thomas* either are present in a more primitive form or are developments of a more primitive form of such sayings. Indeed, the *Gospel of Thomas* resembles the synoptic sayings source, often called "Q" (from the German word Quelle, "source"), which was the common source of sayings used by Matthew and Luke. Hence, the *Gospel of Thomas* and its sources are collections of sayings and parables which are closely related to the sources of the New Testament gospels.

The influence of Gnostic theology is clearly present in the *Gospel of Thomas*, though it is not possible to ascribe the work to any particular school or sect. The collected sayings are designated as "the secret sayings which the living Jesus spoke." Thus the collection intends to be esoteric: the key to understanding is the interpretation or secret meaning of the sayings, for "whoever finds the interpretation of these sayings will not experience death." According to the *Gospel of Thomas*, the basic religious experience is not only the recognition of one's divine identity, but more specifically the recognition of one's origin (the light) and destiny (the repose). In order to return to one's origin, the disciple is to become separate from the world by "stripping off" the fleshly garment and "passing by" the present corruptible existence; then the disciple can experience the new world, the kingdom of light, peace, and life.

The numeration of one hundred fourteen sayings is not in the manuscript but is followed by most scholars today.

THE GOSPEL OF THOMAS

II 32, 10-51, 28

These are the secret sayings which the living Jesus ' spoke and which Didymos Judas Thomas wrote down. '

(1) And he said, ' "Whoever finds the interpretation of these sayings will ' not experience death."

(2) Jesus said, [15] "Let him who seeks continue seeking until he ' finds. When he finds, he will ' become troubled. When he becomes troubled, he will ' be astonished, and he will ' rule over the All."

(3) Jesus said, "If [20] those who lead you say to you, ' 'See, the Kingdom is in the sky,' ' then the birds of the sky will precede you. ' If they say to you, 'It is in the sea,' ' then the fish will precede you. [25] Rather, the Kingdom is inside of you, and ' it is outside of you. When you come to ' know yourselves, then you will become known, [33] and you will realize that it is you who are ' the sons of the living Father. But if ' you will not know yourselves, you ' dwell in poverty and it is you [5] who are that poverty."

(4) Jesus said, "The man old in days will not ' hesitate to ask ' a small child seven ' days old about the place of life, and ' he will live. For many who are first will become last, [10] and they will become one and the same."

(5) Jesus said, ' "Recognize what is in your sight, ' and that which is hidden from you will become plain ' to you. For there is nothing hidden which will ' not become manifest."

(6) His disciples questioned Him [15] and said to Him, "Do You want us to fast? ' How shall we pray? Shall we give alms? ' What diet shall we observe?" '

Jesus said, "Do not tell lies, ' and do not do what you hate, for [20] all things are plain in the sight of Heaven. ' For nothing hidden will not ' become manifest, and nothing covered ' will remain without being uncovered."

(7) Jesus said, ' "Blessed is the lion which [25] becomes man when consumed by ' man; and cursed is the man ' whom the lion consumes, and ' the lion becomes man."

(8) And He said, ' "The man is like a wise fisherman [30] who cast his net ' into the sea and drew it up ' from the sea full of small fish. ' Among them the wise fisherman found a fine large fish. ' He threw [35] all the small fish [34] back into the sea and chose the large ' fish without difficulty. Whoever has ears ' to hear, let him hear."

(9) Jesus said, "Now ' the sower went out, took a handful (of seeds), [5] and scattered them. Some fell on the road; ' the birds came and gathered them up. Others ' fell on rock, did not take root ' in the soil, and did not produce ears. ' And others fell on thorns; [10] they choked the seed(s) and worms ate them. ' And others fell on the good soil ' and produced good fruit: ' it bore sixty per measure and a hundred and twenty per measure." '

(10) Jesus said, "I have cast fire upon [15] the world, and see, I am guarding it ' until it blazes."

(11) Jesus said, "This heaven will ' pass away, and the one above it will pass away. ' The dead are not alive, and the living ' will not die. In the days when you consumed [20] what is dead, you made it what is alive. ' When you come to dwell in the light, ' what will you do? On the day when you ' were one you became two. But when ' you become two, what [25] will you do?"

(12) The disciples said to Jesus, ' "We know that You will depart from us. Who is ' to be our leader?"

Jesus said to them, ' "Wherever you are, you are to ' go to James the righteous, [30] for whose sake heaven and earth came into being."

(13) Jesus said ' to His disciples, "Compare me to someone and ' tell Me whom I am like."

Simon Peter ' said to Him, "You are like a ' righteous angel."

Matthew said to Him, **35** "You are like a wise philosopher." '

Thomas said to Him, ' "Master, my mouth is wholly incapable ' of saying whom You are like."

Jesus said, [5] "I am not your master. Because you have drunk, you have become intoxicated ' from the bubbling spring which I ' have measured out."

And He took him and withdrew ' and told him three things. ' When Thomas returned to his companions, they asked him, [10] "What did Jesus say to you?"

Thomas said to them, ' "If I tell you one of the things ' which he told me, you will pick up stones and ' throw them at me; a fire will come out of ' the stones and burn you up." [15]

(14) Jesus said to them, "If you fast, you will ' give rise to sin for yourselves; and if you ' pray, you will be condemned; and ' if you give alms, you will do ' harm to your spirits. When you [20] go into any land and ' walk about in the districts, if they receive ' you, eat what they will set before you, ' and heal the sick among them. ' For what goes into your mouth [25] will not defile you, but that which ' issues from your mouth—it is that which ' will defile you."

(15) Jesus said, "When ' you see one who was not born ' of woman, prostrate yourselves on [30] your faces and worship him. That one ' is your Father."

(16) Jesus said, ' "Men think, perhaps, that it is peace which I have come to cast ' upon the world. ' They do not know that it is dissension which I have come to cast [35] upon the earth: fire, sword, ' and war. For there will be five **36** in a house: three will be against ' two, and two against three, the father ' against the son, and the son against the father. ' And they will stand solitary." [5]

(17) Jesus said, "I shall give you what ' no eye has seen and what no ' ear has heard and what no hand has touched ' and what has never occurred to the human ' mind."

(18) The disciples said to Jesus, "Tell [10] us how our end will be." ' Jesus said, "Have you discovered, then, ' the beginning, that you look for ' the end? For where the beginning is, ' there will the end be. Blessed is [15] he who will take his place in the beginning; ' he will know the end and will not experience ' death."

(19) Jesus said, "Blessed is ' he who came into being before he came into being. ' If you become My disciples [20] and listen to My words, these stones ' will minister to you. ' For there are five trees for you in Paradise ' which remain undisturbed summer and winter ' and whose leaves do not fall. [25] Whoever becomes acquainted with them will not experience death." '

(20) The disciples said to Jesus, "Tell ' us what the Kingdom of Heaven is ' like."

He said to them, "It is like ' a mustard seed, the smallest of [30] all seeds. But when it ' falls on tilled soil, it ' produces a great plant and becomes ' a shelter for birds of the sky." '

(21) Mary said to Jesus, "Whom are Your disciples [35] like?"

He said, "They are like [37] children who have settled in a field ' which is not theirs. When the owners of the field come, ' they will say, 'Let us have back our field.' ' They (will) undress in their presence [5] in order to let them have back their field and to give ' it back to them. Therefore I say to you, ' if the owner of a house knows that the thief is coming, ' he will begin his vigil before he comes and will not ' let him dig through into his house of his [10] domain to carry away his goods. You, ' then, be on your guard against the world. Arm ' yourselves with great strength ' lest the robbers find a way to come ' to you, for the difficulty which you expect [15] will (surely) materialize. Let there be ' among you a man of understanding. ' When the grain ripened, he came quickly ' with his sickle in his hand and reaped it. ' Whoever has ears to hear, let him hear." [20]

(22) Jesus saw infants being suckled. He said to ' His disciples, "These infants being suckled ' are like those who enter the ' Kingdom."

They said to Him, "Shall we then, as children, ' enter the Kingdom?"

Jesus said to them, [25] "When you make the two one, and ' when you make the inside like the outside ' and the outside like the inside, and the above ' like the below, and when ' you make the male and the female one and the same, [30] so that the male not be male nor ' the female female; and when you fashion ' eyes in place of an eye, and a hand ' in place of a hand, and a foot in place ' of a foot, and a likeness in place of a likeness; [35] then will you enter [the Kingdom]." [38]

(23) Jesus said, "I shall choose you, one out ' of a thousand, and two out of ten thousand, and ' they shall stand as a single one." '

(24) His disciples said to Him, "Show us the place [5] where You are, since it is necessary for us ' to seek it."

He said to them, "Whoever has ' ears, let him hear. There is light ' within a man of light, ' and he (or: it) lights up the whole world. If he (or: it) [10] does not shine, he (or: it) is darkness."

(25) Jesus said, "Love ' your brother like your soul, guard him ' like the pupil of your eye."

(26) Jesus said, "You see the mote ' in your brother's eye, ' but you do not see the beam in your own eye. When [15] you cast the beam out of your own ' eye, then you will see clearly to cast the mote ' from your brother's eye."

(27) ⟨Jesus said,⟩ "If you do not fast ' as regards the world, you will not find the Kingdom. ' If you do not observe the Sabbath as a Sabbath, [20] you will not see the Father." '

(28) Jesus said, "I took My place in the midst of the world, ' and I appeared to them in flesh. ' I found all of them intoxicated; I found none ' of them thirsty. And My soul became afflicted [25] for the sons of men, because they are blind ' in their hearts and do not have sight; ' for empty they came into the world, ' and empty too they seek to leave the world. ' But for the moment they are intoxicated. [30] When they shake off their wine, then they will ' repent."

(29) Jesus said, "If the flesh ' came into being because of spirit, it is a wonder. ' But if spirit came into being because of the body, ' it is a wonder of wonders. Indeed, I am amazed [39] at how this great wealth ' has made its home in this poverty."

(30) Jesus said, ' "Where there are three gods, ' they are gods. Where there are two or one, I [5] am with him."

(31) Jesus said, "No prophet ' is accepted in his own village; no physician heals ' those who know him."

(32) Jesus said, ' "A city being built on a high mountain ' and fortified cannot fall, ^{10} nor can it be hidden."

(33) Jesus said, "Preach from your housetops ' that which you will ' hear in your ear {(and) in the other ear}. ' For no one lights a lamp and ' puts it under a bushel, nor does he put it in a ^{15} hidden place, but rather he sets it on a lampstand ' so that everyone who enters ' and leaves will see its ' light."

(34) Jesus said, "If a blind man leads ' a blind man, they will both fall ^{20} into a pit."

(35) Jesus said, "It is not possible ' for anyone to enter the house of a strong man ' and take it by force unless he binds ' his hands; then he will (be able to) ransack ' his house."

(36) Jesus said, "Do not be concerned from ^{25} morning until evening and from evening ' until morning about what you will wear." '

(37) His disciples said, "When ' will You become revealed to us and when ' shall we see You?"

Jesus said, "When ^{30} you disrobe without being ' ashamed and take up your garments ' and place them under your feet ' like little children and ' tread on them, then [will you see] **40** the Son of the Living One, and you will not be ' afraid."

(38) Jesus said, "Many times have you ' desired to hear these words ' which I am saying to you, and you have ^{5} no one else to hear them from. There will be days ' when you will look for Me and ' will not find Me."

(39) Jesus said, "The Pharisees ' and the scribes have taken the keys ' of Knowledge and hidden them. They themselves have not entered, ^{10} nor have they allowed to enter those who wish to. You, however, be as wise ' as serpents and as innocent as ' doves."

(40) Jesus said, "A grapevine has been ' planted outside of the Father, but being ^{15} unsound, it will be pulled up by its roots and ' destroyed."

(41) Jesus said, "Whoever has something in his ' hand will receive more, and whoever has nothing ' will be deprived of even the little he has." '

(42) Jesus said, "Become passers-by." ^{20}

(43) His disciples said to him, ' "Who are You, that You should say these things to us?"

⟨Jesus said to them,⟩ "You do not realize who I am ' from what I say to you, ' but you have become like ' the Jews, for they (either) love the tree and hate [25] its fruit (or) love the fruit ' and hate the tree."

(44) Jesus said, "Whoever ' blasphemes against the Father will be forgiven, and ' whoever blasphemes against the Son will be forgiven, ' but whoever blasphemes against the Holy Spirit [30] will not be forgiven either on earth ' or in heaven."

(45) Jesus said, "Grapes are not harvested ' from thorns, nor are figs gathered ' from thistles, for they do not produce fruit. ' A good man brings forth **41** good from his storehouse; an evil ' man brings forth evil things from ' his evil storehouse, which is in his heart, and ' says evil things. For out of [5] the abundance of the heart he brings forth evil ' things."

(46) Jesus said, "Among those born of women, ' from Adam until John ' the Baptist, there is no one so superior to John the Baptist ' that his eyes should not be lowered (before him). [10] Yet I have said, whichever one of you ' comes to be a child will be acquainted with the Kingdom ' and will become superior to John."

(47) Jesus said, ' "It is impossible for a man to mount two horses ' or to stretch two bows. And it is impossible [15] for a servant to serve two masters; ' otherwise, he will honor the one ' and treat the other contemptuously. No man drinks old wine ' and immediately desires to drink new wine. ' And new wine is not put into old wineskins, [20] lest they burst; nor ' is old wine put into a new wineskin, lest ' it spoil it. An old patch is not sewn onto a new garment, ' because a tear would result." '

(48) Jesus said, "If two make peace with [25] each other in this one house, they will say ' to the mountain, 'Move away,' and it will move ' away."

(49) Jesus said, "Blessed are the ' solitary and elect, for you will ' find the Kingdom. For you are from it, [30] and to it you will return." '

(50) Jesus said, "If they say to you, ' 'Where did you come from?', say to them, ' 'We came from the light, the place ' where the light came into being on [35] its own accord and established [itself] **42** and became manifest through their image.' ' If they say to you, 'Is it you?', say, ' 'We are its children, and we are the elect ' of the Living Father.' If they ask you, [5] 'What is the sign of your Father in ' you?', say to them, 'It is movement and ' repose.' "

(51) His disciples said to Him, ' "When will the repose of ' the dead come about, and when [10] will the new world come?"

He said to them, ' "What you look forward to has already come, but ' you do not recognize it." '

(52) His disciples said to Him, "Twenty-four ' prophets spoke in Israel, [15] and all of them spoke in You." '

He said to them, "You have omitted the one living in ' your presence and have spoken (only) of the ' dead."

(53) His disciples said to Him, ' "Is circumcision beneficial or not?"

He said [20] to them, "If it were beneficial, their father ' would beget them already circumcised from their mother. ' Rather, the true circumcision in spirit has ' become completely profitable."

(54) Jesus said, "Blessed are the poor, ' for yours is the Kingdom of Heaven." [25]

(55) Jesus said, "Whoever does not hate his father ' and his mother cannot become a disciple to Me. ' And whoever does not hate his brothers and ' sisters and take up his cross in My way ' will not be worthy of Me." [30]

(56) Jesus said, "Whoever has come to understand the world has found (only) ' a corpse, and whoever has found a corpse ' is superior to the world." '

(57) Jesus said, "The Kingdom of the Father is like ' a man who had [good] seed. [35] His enemy came by night **43** and sowed weeds among the good seed. ' The man did not allow them to pull up ' the weeds; he said to them, 'I am afraid that ' you will go intending to pull up the weeds [5] and pull up the wheat along with them.' ' For on the day of the harvest the weeds will be plainly visible, ' and they will be pulled up and burned."

(58) Jesus said, ' "Blessed is the man who has suffered ' and found life."

(59) Jesus said, "Take heed of the [10] Living One while you are alive, lest you die ' and seek to see Him and be unable ' to do so."

(60) ⟨They saw⟩ a Samaritan carrying ' a lamb on his way to Judea. ' He said to his disciples, "(Why does) that man (carry) the [15] lamb around?"

They said to Him, "So that he may ' kill it and eat it."

He said to them, "While ' it is alive, he will not eat it, but only when he has ' killed it and it has become a corpse."

They said to Him, ' "He cannot do so otherwise."

He said to them, [20] "You too, look for a ' place for yourselves within Repose, ' lest you become a corpse and be ' eaten."

(61) Jesus said, "Two will rest ' on a bed: the one will die, and other [25] will live."

Salome said, "Who are You, ' man, that You, as though from the

One, (or: as ⟨whose son⟩, that You) have come up on ' my couch and eaten from my ' table?"

Jesus said to her, "I am He ' who exists from the Undivided. [30] I was given some of the things of My father."

⟨Salome said,⟩ "I ' am Your disciple."

⟨Jesus said to her,⟩ "Therefore I say, ' if he is ⟨undivided⟩, he will be filled ' with light, but if he is ' divided, he will be filled with darkness."

(62) Jesus said, "It [35] is to those [who are worthy of **44** My] mysteries that I tell My mysteries. Do not let your left hand know ' what your right hand is doing."

(63) Jesus said, ' "There was a rich man who had ' much money. He said, 'I shall put [5] my money to use so that I may sow, reap, ' plant, and fill my storehouse with produce, ' with the result that I shall lack nothing.' Such were ' his intentions, but ' that same night he died. Let him who has ears [10] hear."

(64) Jesus said, "A man ' had received visitors. And when he had prepared ' the dinner, he sent his servant to ' invite the guests. He went to ' the first one and said to him, 'My master invites [15] you.' He said, 'I have claims ' against some merchants. They are coming to me this evening. ' I must go and give them my orders. I ask to be excused ' from the dinner.' He went to another ' and said to him, 'My master has invited you.' [20] He said to him, 'I have just bought a house and ' am required for the day. I shall not have any spare time.' ' He went to another and said to him, 'My master ' invites you.' He said to him, 'My friend ' is going to get married, and I am to prepare the banquet. [25] I shall not be able to come. I ask to be excused from the dinner.' ' He went to another and said to him, 'My master ' invites you.' He said to him, 'I have just bought ' a farm, and I am on my way to collect the rent. I shall not be able to come. ' I ask to be excused.' The servant returned and said [30] to his master, 'Those whom you invited to ' the dinner have asked to be excused.' The master said to ' his servant, 'Go outside to the streets ' and bring back those whom you happen to meet, so that ' they may dine.' Businessmen and merchants [35] will not enter the Places of My Father." **45**

(65) He said, "There was a good man who owned ' a vineyard. He leased it to tenant farmers ' so that they might work it and he might collect the produce ' from them. He sent his servant so that [5] the tenants might give him the produce of ' the vineyard. They seized his servant ' and beat him, all but killing him. ' The servant went back and told his master. ' The master said, 'Perhaps ⟨they⟩ did not recognize ⟨him⟩.' [10]

He sent another servant. The tenants beat ' this one as well. Then the owner sent ' his son and said, 'Perhaps they will show respect ' to my son.' Because the tenants ' knew that it was he who was the heir [15] to the vineyard, they seized him and killed him. ' Let him who has ears hear." '

(66) Jesus said, "Show me the stone which ' the builders have rejected. That one is the ' cornerstone."

(67) Jesus said, "Whoever believes that the All [20] itself is deficient is (himself) completely deficient." '

(68) Jesus said, "Blessed are you when ' you are hated and persecuted. ' Wherever you have been persecuted ' they will find no Place." [25]

(69) Jesus said, "Blessed are they who have been persecuted ' within themselves. It is they ' who have truly come to know the Father. ' Blessed are the hungry, for ' the belly of him who desires will be filled."

(70) Jesus said, [30] "That which you have will save you ' if you bring it forth from yourselves. ' That which you do not have within you will kill you ' if you do not have it within you." '

(71) Jesus said, "I shall destroy [this] house, [35] and no one will be able to rebuild it." **46**

(72) [A man said] to Him, "Tell my brothers ' to divide my father's possessions ' with me."

He said to him, "O man, who ' has made Me a divider?"

He turned to [5] His disciples and said to them, "I am not a divider, ' am I?"

(73) Jesus said, "The harvest ' is great but the laborers are few. ' Beseech the Lord, therefore, to send out laborers ' to the harvest."

(74) He said, "O Lord, there are [10] many around the drinking trough, but there is nothing in ' the cistern."

(75) Jesus said, "Many are standing ' at the door, but it is the solitary who will enter ' the bridal chamber."

(76) Jesus said, ' "The Kingdom of the Father is like a [15] merchant who had a consignment of merchandise ' and who discovered a pearl. That merchant ' was shrewd. He sold the merchandise ' and bought the pearl alone for himself. ' You too, seek [20] his unfailing and enduring treasure ' where no moth comes near ' to devour and no worm destroys." '

(77) Jesus said, "It is I who am the light which is above ' them all. It is I who am the All. [25] From Me did the All come forth, and unto Me did the All ' extend. Split a piece of wood, and I ' am there. Lift up the stone, and you will ' find Me there."

(78) Jesus said, "Why ' have you come out into the desert? To see a reed [30] shaken by the wind? And to see ' a man clothed in fine garments ' like your kings and your great **47** men? Upon them are the fine [garments], ' and they are unable to discern ' the truth."

(79) A woman from the crowd said to Him, ' "Blessed are the womb which [5] bore You and the breasts which ' nourished You."

He said to her, ' "Blessed are those who have heard ' the word of the Father and have truly kept it. ' For there will be days [10] when you will say, 'Blessed are the womb ' which has not conceived and the breasts which have not ' given milk.' "

(80) Jesus said, "He who has recognized ' the world has found the body, but he who has found ' the body is superior to the world." [15]

(81) Jesus said, "Let him who has grown rich ' be king, and let him who possesses power ' renounce it."

(82) Jesus said, "He who is near ' Me is near the fire, and he who is far ' from Me is far from the Kingdom."

(83) Jesus said, [20] "The images are manifest to man, ' but the light in them remains concealed ' in the image of the light of the Father. ' He will become manifest, but his image will remain concealed ' by his light."

(84) Jesus said, [25] "When you see your likeness, you ' rejoice. But when you see ' your images which came into being before you, ' and which neither die nor become manifest, ' how much you will have to bear!"

(85) Jesus said, [30] "Adam came into being from a great ' power and a great wealth, ' but he did not become worthy of you. ' For had he been worthy, [he would] not [have experienced] ' death."

(86) Jesus said, "[The foxes **48** have their holes] and the birds have ' [their] nests, but the Son of Man ' has no place to lay his head and ' rest."

(87) Jesus said, "Wretched [5] is the body that is dependent upon a body, ' and wretched is the soul that is dependent ' on these two."

(88) Jesus said, "The angels ' and the prophets will come to you and ' give to you those things you (already) have. And [10] you too, give them those things which you have, ' and say to yourselves, 'When ' will they come and take what is theirs?' " '

(89) Jesus said, "Why do you wash the outside ' of the cup? Do you not realize that [15] he who made the inside is the same one ' who made the outside?"

(90) Jesus said, ' "Come unto me, for My yoke is easy ' and My lordship is mild, ' and you will find repose for [20] yourselves."

(91) They said to Him, "Tell us ' who You are so that we may believe in You." '

He said to them, "You read the face of the sky ' and of the earth, but you have not recognized ' the one who (or: that which) is before you, and ²⁵ you do not know how to read this moment." '

(92) Jesus said, "Seek and you will find. Yet, what ' you asked Me about in former times and which I did not ' tell you then, now ' I do desire to tell, but you do not inquire after ³⁰ it."

(93) ⟨Jesus said,⟩ "Do not give what is holy to dogs, lest ' they throw them on the dung-heap. Do not throw the ' pearls to swine, lest they grind it ' [to bits]."

(94) Jesus [said], "He who seeks will find, ' and [he who knocks] will be let in." ³⁵

(95) [Jesus said], "If you have money, **49** do not lend it at interest, but give [it] to one ' from whom you will not get it back."

(96) Jesus [said], ' "The Kingdom of the Father is like a certain woman. She ' took a little leaven, [concealed] it in ⁵ some dough, and made it into large loaves. ' Let him who has ears hear." '

(97) Jesus said, "The Kingdom of the [Father] is like ' a certain woman who was carrying a jar ' full of meal. While she was walking [on] a road, ¹⁰ still some distance from home, the handle of the jar broke ' and the meal emptied out behind her on the road. ' She did not realize it; she had noticed no ' accident. When she reached her house, ' she set the jar down and found it ¹⁵ empty."

(98) Jesus said, "The Kingdom of the Father ' is like a certain man who wanted to kill ' a powerful man. In his own house he drew ' his sword and stuck it into the wall ' in order to find out whether his hand could carry through. ²⁰ Then he slew the powerful man." '

(99) The disciples said to Him, "Your brothers ' and Your mother are standing outside." '

He said to them, "Those here ' who do the will of My Father are ²⁵ My brothers and My mother. It is they who will ' enter the Kingdom of My Father." '

(100) They showed Jesus a gold coin and said to Him, ' "Caesar's men demand taxes from us." '

He said to them, "Give Caesar what belongs ³⁰ to Caesar, give God what belongs to God, ' and give Me what is Mine." '

(101) ⟨Jesus said,⟩ "Whoever does not hate his father and his ' mother as I do cannot become a disciple to Me. ' And whoever does [not] love his father and his ³⁵ mother as I do cannot become a [disciple] '

to Me. For My mother [gave me falsehood], **50** but [My] true [Mother] gave me life." '

(102) Jesus said, "Woe to the Pharisees, for ' they are like a dog sleeping in the ' manger of oxen, for neither does he eat [5] nor does he let the oxen eat."

(103) Jesus said, ' "Fortunate is the man who knows ' where the brigands will enter, ' so that he may get up, muster his ' domain, and arm himself [10] before they invade." '

(104) They said [to Jesus], "Come, let us pray today ' and let us fast." Jesus said, "What ' is the sin that I have committed, or wherein have I been defeated? ' But when the bridegroom leaves [15] the bridal chamber, then let them ' fast and pray."

(105) Jesus said, ' "He who knows the father and the mother will be called ' the son of a harlot."

(106) Jesus said, ' "When you make the two one, you will become [20] the sons of man, and when you ' say, 'Mountain, move away,' it will ' move away."

(107) Jesus said, "The Kingdom is like ' a shepherd who had a hundred ' sheep. One of them, the largest, went astray. [25] He left the ninety-nine and looked for that one ' until he found it. When he had gone to such trouble, he said ' to the sheep, 'I care for you more than the ninety-nine.' " '

(108) Jesus said, "He who will drink from My mouth ' will become like Me. I myself shall become [30] he, and the things that are hidden will be revealed to him." '

(109) Jesus said, "The Kingdom is like a man ' who had a ' [hidden] treasure in his field without knowing it. ' And [after] he died, he left it to his [35] son. The son did not know (about the treasure). He inherited **51** the field and sold [it]. And the one who bought it ' went plowing and found the treasure. ' He began to lend money at interest to whomever he wished." '

(110) Jesus said, "Whoever finds the world [5] and becomes rich, let him renounce the world." '

(111) Jesus said, "The heavens and the earth will be rolled up ' in your presence. And the one who lives from ' the Living One will not see death." Does not Jesus ' say, "Whoever finds himself [10] is superior to the world"?

(112) Jesus said, "Woe ' to the flesh that depends on the soul; woe ' to the soul that depends on the flesh." '

(113) His disciples said to Him, ' "When will the Kingdom come?"

⟨Jesus said,⟩ "It will not come by [15] waiting for it. It will not be a matter of saying 'Here ' it is' or 'There it is.' Rather, the Kingdom ' of the Father is spread out upon the earth, and ' men do not see it."

(114) Simon Peter said ' to them, "Let Mary leave us, [20] for women are not worthy of Life."

Jesus said, ' "I myself shall lead her ' in order to make her male, so that ' she too may become a living spirit resembling ' you males. For every woman who will make herself [25] male will enter the Kingdom ' of Heaven." '

The Gospel '
According to Thomas

THE GOSPEL OF PHILIP (II, *3*)

Introduced and translated by

WESLEY W. ISENBERG

The *Gospel of Philip* is a collection of theological statements or excerpts concerning sacraments and ethics. Generally Valentinian in character, this collection was named for Philip the apostle, and was probably written in Syria in the second half of the third century C.E. The various sorts of statements comprising the collection are not organized in a way that can be conveniently outlined by the use of headings and subheadings. Though the line of thought is often rambling and disjointed, some continuity of thought is maintained by means of an association of ideas or through catchwords. This collection of excerpts seems to derive largely from a Christian Gnostic sacramental catechesis. In fact, the voice of the original author may still be heard as he speaks to catechumens preparing for the initiation rite.

While emphasizing the place of the sacraments, the *Gospel of Philip* concerns itself in particular with the bridal chamber: "The Lord did everything in a mystery, a baptism and a chrism and a eucharist and a redemption and a bridal chamber." According to this tractate, the existential malady of humanity results from the differentiation of the sexes. When Eve separated from Adam, the original androgynous unity was broken. The purpose of Christ's coming is to reunite "Adam" and "Eve." Just as a husband and wife unite in the bridal chamber, so also the reunion effected by Christ takes place in a bridal chamber, the sacramental, spiritual one, where a person receives a foretaste and assurance of ultimate union with an angelic, heavenly counterpart. "Christ came to repair the separation which was from the beginning and again unite the two," so that restoration may be accomplished and rest achieved.

The *Gospel of Philip* makes an important contribution to our rather limited knowledge of Gnostic sacramental theology and practice. The sacraments exhibited in the *Gospel of Philip* are similar to those used by Christians in the Great Church for the initiation of candidates. Thus the Gnostics who wrote and used the present text had not departed radically from orthodox sacramental practice; yet the interpretation provided for the sacraments clearly remains Gnostic.

THE GOSPEL OF PHILIP

II 51, 29-86, 19

A Hebrew makes another Hebrew, [30] and such a person is called ' "proselyte." But a proselyte does not ' make another proselyte. [Some] both exist ' just as they [are] ' and make others like themselves, **52** while [others] simply exist. '

The slave seeks only to be ' free, but he does not hope to acquire the estate ' of his master. But the son is not only [5] a son but lays claim to the inheritance of the father. ' Those who are heirs to ' the dead are themselves dead, ' and they inherit the dead. Those ' who are heirs to what is living are alive, [10] and they are heirs to both what is living and the dead. ' The dead are heirs to ' nothing. For how can he who is dead inherit? ' If he who is dead inherits ' what is living he will not die, but he who is dead [15] will live even more.

A Gentile ' does not die, for he has never lived in order that ' he may die. He who has believed in the truth ' has found life, and this one is in danger of dying, for he is alive. ' Ever since Christ came the world is [20] created, the cities adorned, ' the dead carried out. When we were ' Hebrews we were orphans and ' had only our mother, but when we became ' Christians we had both father and mother. [25]

Those who sow in winter reap in summer. ' The winter is the world, the summer the other aeon. ' Let us sow in the world that ' we may reap in the summer. Because of this it is fitting ' for us not to pray in the winter. Summer [30] follows winter. But if any man reap ' in winter he will not actually reap but only ' pluck out, since this sort of thing will not provide ' [him] a harvest. It is not only [now] that ' the fruit will [not] come forth, but also on the Sabbath [35] [his field] is barren.

Christ came **53** to ransom some, ' to save others, to ' redeem others. He ransomed those who were strangers and ' made them his own. And he set [5] his own apart, those whom he gave as a pledge ' in his will. It was not only when he ' appeared that he voluntarily laid down his life, ' but he voluntarily laid down his life ' from the very day the world came into being. [10] Then he came forth in order to take it, since ' it had been given as a pledge. It fell into the hands of ' robbers and was taken captive, but he ' saved it. He redeemed the good people ' in the world as well as the evil.

Light and darkness, [15] life and death, right and left, ' are brothers of one another. They are inseparable. ' Because of this neither are the good ' good, nor the evil evil, ' nor is life life, nor death death. [20] For this reason each one will dissolve ' into its original nature. But those who are exalted ' above the world are indissoluble, ' eternal.

Names given ' to worldly things are very deceptive, [25] for they divert our thoughts ' from what is correct to what is incorrect. ' Thus one who hears the word "God" does not perceive ' what is correct, but perceives ' what is incorrect. So also with "the Father" [30] and "the Son" and "the Holy Spirit" and ' "life" and "light" and "resurrection" ' and "the Church" and all the rest—' people do not perceive what is correct but they ' perceive what is incorrect, [unless] they [35] have come to know what is correct. The [names which are heard] ' are in the world [to [54] deceive. If they] were in the aeon, they would ' at no time be used as names in the world. ' Nor were they set among ' worldly things. They have an end in [5] the aeon.

One single name is not uttered ' in the world, the name which the Father gave ' to the Son, the name above all things: ' the name of the Father. For the Son ' would not become Father unless he wears [10] the name of the Father. ' Those who have this name know it, but they do ' not speak it. But those who do not have it ' do not know it.

But truth brought names into existence ' in the world because it is not possible [15] to teach it without names. Truth is one single thing ' and it is also many things for our sakes who ' learn this one thing in love through ' many things. The powers wanted to deceive ' man, since they saw that he had [20] a kinship with those that are ' truly good. They took the name of those that are good ' and gave it to those that are not good, ' so that through the names they might deceive ' him and bind them to those that are [25] not good. And afterward, if they do ' them a favor, they will be made to remove them ' from those that are not good and place them ' among those that are good. These things they knew, ' for they wanted to [30] take the free man and make him a ' slave to them forever.

There are powers ' which [contend against] man, not wishing ' him to be [saved], in order that they may ' [...]. For if man [35] is [saved, there will not] be any sacrifices ' [...] and animals will not be offered [55] to the powers. The [very ones] who [...] the animals are they ' who sacrifice to them. They were indeed offering ' them up alive, but when they ' offered them up they died. As for man, they offered [5] him up to God dead, and he lived. '

Before Christ came there was no bread ' in the world, just as paradise, the place ' where Adam was, had many trees ' to nourish the animals but no wheat [10] to sustain man. Man used to feed ' like the animals, but when Christ ' came, the perfect man, he brought bread ' from heaven in order that man might be nourished ' with the food of man. The powers [15] thought that it was by their own power and will ' that they were doing what they did, ' but the Holy Spirit in secret ' was accomplishing everything through them ' as it wished. Truth, [20] which existed since the beginning, is sown everywhere. And ' many see it as it is sown, ' but few are they who see it as it is reaped. '

Some said, "Mary conceived by ' the Holy Spirit." They are in error. ²⁵ They do not know what they are saying. When ' did a woman ever conceive by a woman? ' Mary is the virgin whom no ' power defiled. She is a ' great anathema to the Hebrews, who ³⁰ are the apostles and [the] apostolic men. ' This virgin whom no power ' defiled [...] the powers ' defile themselves. And the Lord [would] not have said ' "My [Father who is in] heaven" (Matthew 16:17) ³⁵ unless [he] had had another father, ' but he would have said simply "[My father]." '

The Lord said to the disciples, "[Bring **56** out] from every (other) house. Bring into the house ' of the Father. But do not take (anything) in the house ' of the Father nor carry it off."

"Jesus" is a hidden name, ' "Christ" is a revealed name. ⁵ For this reason "Jesus" does not exist ' in any (other) language, but his name is always "Jesus," ' as he is called. "Christ" ' is also his name: in Syriac it is "Messiah," ' in Greek it is "Christ." Certainly ¹⁰ all the others have it ' according to their own language. ' "The Nazarene" is he who reveals ' what is hidden. Christ has everything ' in himself, whether man or angel ¹⁵ or mystery, and the Father.

Those who say ' that the Lord died first and (then) ' rose up are in error, for he rose up ' first and (then) died. If one does not first attain ' the resurrection will he not die? As God ²⁰ lives, he would be (already) ⟨dead⟩.

No one ' will hide a large valuable object ' in something large, but many a time ' one has tossed countless thousands ' into a thing worth a penny. Compare ²⁵ the soul. It is a precious thing (and) it came to be ' in a contemptible body.

Some ' are afraid lest they rise naked. ' Because of this they wish to rise ' in the flesh, and [they] do not know that it is those who ³⁰ wear the [flesh] who are naked. ' [It is] those who [...] to unclothe ' themselves who are not naked. "Flesh ' [and blood shall] not [be able] to inherit the kingdom ' [of God]" (1 Corinthians 15:50). What is this which will **57** not inherit? This which is on us. But what ' is this very thing which will inherit? It is that which belongs to Jesus ' and his blood. Because of this he said, ' "He who shall not eat my flesh and drink ⁵ my blood has not life in him" (John 6:53). What ' is it? His flesh is the word, and his blood ' is the Holy Spirit. He who has received these has ' food and he has drink and clothing. ' I find fault with the others who say ¹⁰ that it will not rise. Then both of them ' are at fault. You say ' that the flesh will not rise. But tell me ' what will rise, that we may honor you. ' You say the spirit in the flesh, ¹⁵ and it is also this light in the flesh. (But) this too is a matter ' which is in the flesh, for whatever you shall, say, ' you say nothing outside the flesh. ' It is necessary to rise in this flesh, since ' everything exists in it. In this world [20] those who put on garments are better than the ' garments. In the kingdom of heaven the garments ' are better than those who have put them on.

It is through ' water and fire that the whole place is purified—' the visible by the visible, [25] the hidden by the hidden. There are some things ' hidden through those visible. ' There is water in water, there is fire ' in a chrism.

Jesus took them all by stealth, ' for he did not reveal himself in the manner [30] [in which] he was, but it was ' in the manner in which [they would] be able to see ' him that he revealed himself. He revealed himself to [them all. ' He revealed himself] to the great ' as great. He [revealed himself] [35] to the small as small. He [revealed himself **58** to the] angels as an angel, and ' to men as a man. Because of this his ' word hid itself from everyone. Some ' indeed saw him, thinking that they were seeing [5] themselves, but when he appeared ' to his disciples in glory ' on the mount he was not small. He ' became great, but he made the disciples ' great, that they might be able to see [10] him in his greatness.

He said on that day ' in the Thanksgiving, "You who have joined ' the perfect, the light, with the Holy Spirit, ' unite the angels with us also, ' the images." Do not despise the lamb, for without it [15] it is not possible to see the king. No one ' will be able to go in to the king if he is ' naked.

The heavenly man has many more sons ' than the earthly man. If the sons of Adam ' are many, although they die, [20] how much more the sons of the perfect man, ' they who do not die but are ' always begotten. The father makes a son, ' and the son has not the power to make ' a son. For he who has been begotten has not the power [25] to beget, but the son gets ' brothers for himself, not sons. All who ' are begotten in the world ' are begotten in a natural way, and ' the others in a spiritual way. [Those who] are begotten [30] by him [cry out] from that place ' to the (perfect) man [because they are nourished] on the ' promise [concerning] the heavenly [place. ' ...] from the mouth, ' [because if] the word has gone out from that place **59** it would be nourished from the mouth and ' it would become perfect. For it is ' by a kiss that the perfect conceive and give birth. For this reason ' we also kiss one another. [5] We receive conception from the grace which is in ' each other.

There were three who always walked with ' the Lord: Mary his mother ' and her sister and Magdalene, the one ' who was called his companion. [10] His sister and his mother ' and his companion were each a Mary.

"The Father" and "the Son" ' are single names, "the Holy Spirit" ' is a double name. For they are ' everywhere: they are above, they are below; [15] they are in the concealed, they are in the revealed. ' The Holy Spirit is in the revealed: ' it is below. It is in the concealed: ' it is above.

The saints are served ' by evil powers, [20] for they are blinded by the Holy Spirit ' into thinking that they are serving ' an (ordinary) man whenever they do (something) for the saints. ' Because of this a disciple ' asked the Lord one day for something [25] of this world. He said to him, ' "Ask your mother and she will give you ' of the things which are another's."

The apostles said ' to the disciples, "May our whole offering ' obtain salt." [30] They called [Sophia] "salt." Without it ' no offering [is] acceptable. But Sophia ' is barren, [without] child. For this reason ' she is called "a trace of ' salt." [But] where they will be [35] in their own way, the Holy Spirit [will (also) be, **60** and] her children are many.

What the father possesses ' belongs to the son, and the son ' himself, so long as he is small, is not ' entrusted with what is his. But when [5] he becomes a man his father gives him ' all that he possesses.

Those who have gone astray, whom ' the Spirit (itself) begets, usually go astray also ' because of the Spirit. Thus, by this one and the same breath, ' the fire blazes and is put out. [10]

Echamoth is one thing and Echmoth another. ' Echamoth is Wisdom simply, ' but Echmoth is the Wisdom of death which is ' {the Wisdom of death which is} the one which ' knows death, which is called [15] "the little Wisdom."

There are ' domestic animals, like the bull ' and the ass and others of this kind. ' Others are wild ' and live apart in the deserts. Man ploughs [20] the field by means of the domestic animals, ' and from this he feeds (both) himself and ' the animals, whether tame or ' wild. Compare the perfect ' man. It is through powers which are submissive [25] that he ploughs, preparing for everything to come into being. ' For it is because of this that the whole place stands, ' whether the good or the evil, ' the right and the left. The Holy Spirit ' shepherds every one and rules [30] [all] the powers, the "tame" ones ' and the "wild" ones, as well as those which are unique. ' For indeed he [gathers them (and)] shuts them in, ' in order that [these, even if they] wish, will not be able ' [to escape].

[He who] has been created is [35] [beautiful and] you would find his sons **61** noble creations. If he was not ' created but begotten, you would find ' that his seed was noble. But now ' he was created (and) he begot. What [5] nobility is this? First adultery ' came into being, afterward murder. And he ' was begotten in adultery, for he was the child ' of the serpent. So he became ' a murderer, just like his father, and [10] he killed his brother. Indeed every act of sexual intercourse ' which has occurred between those unlike ' one another is adultery.

God ' is a dyer. As the good dyes, ' which are called "true," dissolve [15] with the things dyed in them, so ' it is with those whom God has dyed. ' Since his dyes are immortal, they are ' immortal by means of his colors. ' Now God dips what he dips [20] in water.

It is not possible ' for anyone to see anything of the things that actually exist ' unless he becomes like ' them. This is not the way with man ' in the world: he sees the sun without being a sun; [25] and he sees the heaven and the earth and ' all other things, but he is not these things. ' This is quite in keeping with the truth. But you (sing.) saw ' something of that place and you became ' those things. You saw the Spirit, you [30] became spirit. You saw Christ, you became ' Christ. You saw [the Father, you] shall become Father. ' So [in this place] you see ' everything and [do] not [see] yourself, ' but [in that place] you do see yourself—and what [35] you see you shall [become]. '

Faith receives, love gives. [No one will be able **62** to receive] without faith. No one will be able to give without ' love. Because of this, in order that we may indeed receive, ' we believe, but it is so that we may love and give, since ' if one does not give in love, he has no [5] profit from what he has given. He who ' has not received the Lord is still a Hebrew. '

The apostles who were before us had these names for him: ' "Jesus, the Nazorean, Messiah," that ' is, "Jesus, the Nazorean, the Christ." The last [10] name is "Christ," the first is "Jesus," that in ' the middle is "the Nazarene." "Messiah" ' has two meanings, both "the Christ" ' and "the measured." "Jesus" in Hebrew is ' "the redemption." "Nazara" is "the truth." "The [15] Nazarene," then, is "the truth." "Christ" ' has been measured. "The Nazarene" and "Jesus" ' are they who have been measured.

When the pearl is cast ' down into the mud it does not become ' greatly despised, [20] nor if it is anointed with balsam oil ' will it become more precious. But it always has ' value in the eyes of its owner. ' Compare the sons of ' God, wherever they may be. [25] They still have value in the eyes of their ' Father.

If you say, "I am a Jew," ' no one will be moved. If you say, "I am a ' Roman," no one will be disturbed. If you ' say, "I am a Greek, a barbarian, 30 a slave, [a] free man," no one ' will be troubled. [If] you [say], "I am a ' Christian," the [world] will tremble. Would ' that I [may receive] a name like that! This is the person whom ' the [powers] will not be able to endure 35 [when they hear] his name.

God is a **63** man-eater. For this reason men are [sacrificed] ' to him. Before men were sacrificed ' animals were being sacrificed, since those ' to whom they were sacrificed were not gods. 5

Glass decanters and earthenware ' jugs are both made by means of fire. ' But if glass decanters break ' they are done over, for ' they came into being through a breath. If earthenware jugs 10 break, however, they are destroyed, ' for they came into being without breath.

An ass ' which turns a millstone did a hundred miles ' walking. When it was loosed ' it found that it was still at the same place. 15 There are men who make many journeys, ' but make no progress towards ' a destination. When evening came upon them, ' they saw neither city nor ' village, neither creation nor nature, 20 power nor angel. In vain have the wretches ' labored.

The eucharist is Jesus. For ' he is called in Syriac "Pharisatha," ' which is "the one who is spread out," ' for Jesus came crucifying the world. 25

The Lord went into the dye works ' of Levi. He took seventy-two different colors ' and threw them into the vat. He took them ' out all white. And he said, "Even so ' has the Son 30 of Man come [as] a dyer."

As for the Wisdom ' who is called "the barren," she ' is the mother [of the] angels. And the ' companion of the [Savior is] Mary Magdalene. ' [But Christ loved] her 35 more than [all] the disciples [and used to] ' kiss her [often] on her [mouth]. ' The rest of [the disciples **64** were offended] by it [and expressed disapproval]. They said to him, ' "Why do you love her more than all of us?" The ' Savior answered and said to them, ' "Why do I not love you 5 like her?" When a blind man and one who sees ' are both together in darkness, they are no different from ' one another. When the light comes, then ' he who sees will see the light, and ' he who is blind will remain in darkness. 10

The Lord said, "Blessed is he who ' is before he came into being. For he who ' is, has been and shall be."

The superiority ' of man is not obvious to the eye, but ' lies in what is hidden from view. Consequently he 15 has mastery over the animals which are stronger than he is and ' great in terms of the obvious and the hidden. ' This enables them to survive. But if ' man is separated from them, they slay ' one another and bite one another. [20] They ate one another because they did not find ' any food. But now they have found food because ' man tilled the soil.

If one ' go down into the water and come up without ' having received anything and says, "I am a Christian," [25] he has borrowed the name at interest. But if he ' receive the Holy Spirit, he has ' the name as a gift. He who has received a ' gift does not have to give it back, but of him who ' has borrowed it at interest, payment is demanded. This is the way [30] [it happens to one] when one experiences ' a mystery.

Great is ' the mystery of marriage! For [without] it the world ' would [not have existed]. Now the existence of ' [the world depends on man], and the existence [35] [of man on marriage]. Think of the ' [undefiled relationship], for it possesses ' [a great] power. Its image **65** consists of a [defilement of] the form.

As for the unclean [spirits], ' there are males among them ' and there are females. The males are they which ' unite with the souls which inhabit [5] a female form, but the females ' are they which are mingled with those in a ' male form, through one who was disobedient. And none ' shall be able to escape them, since they detain him ' if he does not receive a male power or a [10] female power—the bridegroom and ' the bride.—One receives them from the ' mirrored bridal chamber. —When the wanton women ' see a male sitting ' alone, they leap down on him and [15] play with him and defile him. So ' also the lecherous men, when they see a ' beautiful woman sitting alone, ' they persuade her and compel her, ' wishing to defile her. But if they see [20] the man and his wife sitting ' beside one another, the female cannot come ' in to the man, nor can the male ' come in to the woman. So ' if the image and the angel are united [25] with one another, neither can any venture ' to go in to the man or the woman. '

He who comes out of the world ' can no longer be detained, because he was in ' the world. It is evident that he is above [30] desire [. . .] and fear. ' He is master over [nature]. He is superior to ' envy. If [any one else] comes, they seize ' him and throttle [him]. And how will [this one] ' be able to escape the [great grasping] powers? [35] How will he be able to [hide from them? Often] ' some [come and say], ' "We are faithful," in order that [they may be able to escape **66** the unclean spirits] and the demons. ' For if they had the Holy Spirit, ' no unclean spirit would cleave ' to them. Fear not the flesh nor [5] love it. If you fear it, it will gain mastery ' over you. If you love it, it will swallow and paralyze you. '

Either he will be in this world or in the ' resurrection or in the places in the middle. ' God forbid that I be found in them! [10] In this world there is good ' and evil. Its good ' is not good, and its evil ' not evil. But there is evil after ' this world which is truly evil—[15] what is called "the Middle." It ' is death. While we are in this world ' it is fitting for us to acquire the resurrection for ourselves, ' so that when we strip off the flesh ' we may be found in rest and not [20] walk in the Middle. For many go astray ' on the way. For it is good to come forth ' from the world before one ' has sinned.

Some neither desire (to sin) ' nor are able (to sin). Others, [25] (even) if they desire (to sin), are not better off ' for not having done it, for [this] desire makes ' them sinners. But (even) if some do not desire (to sin), ' righteousness will be concealed from them both—' the desire-not and the do-not.

An [30] apostolic man in a vision saw some people ' shut up in a house of fire and ' bound with fiery [chains], lying ' in flaming [ointment]. They possessed ' [...]. And he said to them, [35] "[Why are they not able] to be saved?" ' [They answered], "They did not desire it. They received ' [this place as] punishment, what is called [67] 'the [outer] darkness,' because he is [thrown] out (into it)." '

It is from water and fire that the soul ' and the spirit came into being. It is from water and ' fire and light that the son of [5] the bridal chamber (came into being). The fire is the chrism, the light ' is the fire. I am not referring to that fire ' which has no form, but to the other fire whose ' form is white, which is bright and beautiful, ' and which gives beauty.

Truth did not come [10] into the world naked, but it came in ' types and images. One will not receive truth in ' any other way. There is a rebirth and an ' image of rebirth. It is certainly necessary ' that they should be born again through the image. What [15] is the resurrection? The image must ' rise again through the image. The ⟨bridegroom⟩ and ' the image must enter through the image into ' the truth: this is the restoration. ' It is appropriate that those who do have it not only acquire the name of [20] the Father and the Son and the Holy Spirit, ' but that they have acquired it on their own. If one does not acquire ' the name for himself, the name ("Christian") will also be taken from him. ' But one receives them in the aromatic unction ' of the power of the cross. This power the apostles [25] called "the right and the left." ' For this person is no longer a Christian but ' a Christ.

The Lord [did] everything in a ' mystery, a baptism and a chrism ' and a eucharist and a redemption [30] and a bridal chamber.

[The Lord] said, ' "I came to make [the things below] ' like the things [above, and the things] ' outside like those [inside. I came to unite] ' them in that place." [He revealed himself in] [35] this place through [types and images]. ' Those who say, "[There is a heavenly man and] ' there is one above [him," are wrong. ' For] he who is revealed [in heaven is] **68** that [heavenly man], the one who is called ' "the one who is below"; and he to whom the hidden belongs ' is that one who is above him. ' For it is good that they should say, "The inner [5] and the outer, with what ' is outside the outer." Because of this the ' Lord called destruction "the outer darkness": ' there is not another outside of it. He said, ' "My Father who is in secret." He said, [10] "Go into your chamber and shut ' the door behind you, and pray to your Father ' who is in secret" (Matthew 6:6), the one who is ' within them all. But that which is within ' them all is the fullness. [15] Beyond it there is nothing else within it. ' This is that of which they say, "That which is ' above them."

Before Christ some ' came from a place they were no longer ' able to enter, and they went where they were no longer [20] able to come out. Then Christ came. ' Those who went in he brought out, and ' those who went out he brought in.

When ' Eve was still in Adam death did not exist. ' When she was separated from him death came into being. [25] If he again becomes complete and attains his former self, ' death will be no more.

"My God, my God, ' why, O Lord, have you forsaken me?" (Mark 15:34 and parallels), It was ' on the cross that he said these words, for ' it was there that he was divided.

[Everyone] who has been begotten through [30] him who [destroys did not emanate] from God. '

The [Lord rose] from the dead. ' [He became as he used] to be, but now ' [his body was] perfect. ' [He did indeed possess] flesh, but this [35] [flesh] is true flesh. ' [Our flesh] is not true, but ' [we possess] only an image of the true. **69**

A bridal chamber is not for the animals, ' nor is it for the slaves, nor for the defiled ' women; but it is for the free ' men and virgins.

Through [5] the Holy Spirit we are indeed begotten ' again, but we are begotten through ' Christ in the two. We are anointed through ' the Spirit. When we were begotten we were united. None ' shall be able to see himself either in water or in [10] a mirror without light. Nor again will you be able ' to see in light without water or mirror. ' For this reason it is fitting to baptize in the two, ' in the light and the water. Now the light ' is the chrism.

There were three buildings specifically for [15] sacrifice in Jerusalem. The one ' facing west was called ' "the Holy." Another facing ' south was called "the Holy of ' the Holy." The third facing [20] east was called "the Holy ' of the Holies," the place where only the high priest ' enters. Baptism ' is "the Holy" building. Redemption is "the Holy ' of the Holy." "The Holy of the Holies" [25] is the bridal chamber. Baptism includes ' the resurrection [and the] redemption; the redemption ' (takes place) in the bridal chamber. But the bridal chamber ' is in that which is superior to [it and the others, because] ' you will not find [anything like] it. [Those who are familiar with it] [30] are those who pray in "the Holy" in ' Jerusalem. [There are some in] ' Jerusalem who pray [only in] ' Jerusalem, awaiting [the kingdom of heaven]. ' These are called "the Holy [35] of the Holies," [because before the] ' veil was rent [we had no] other ' bridal chamber except the image [of the bridal chamber which is] **70** above. Because of this its ' veil was rent from top to ' bottom. For it was fitting for some ' from below to go upward. [5]

The powers do not see ' those who are clothed in the perfect light, ' and consequently are not able to detain them. ' One will clothe himself in this light ' sacramentally in the union.

If the [10] woman had not separated from the man, she would not die ' with the man. His separation became ' the beginning of death. Because of this ' Christ came to repair ' the separation which was from the beginning [15] and again unite the two, and to give life to those ' who died as a result of the separation ' and unite them. But the woman is united ' to her husband in the bridal chamber. ' Indeed those who have united in the bridal chamber will [20] no longer be separated. Thus Eve ' separated from Adam because she was never united with him ' in the bridal chamber.

The soul of Adam ' came into being by means of a breath, which ' is a synonym for [Spirit]. The spirit given him [25] is his mother. His soul was ' replaced by a [spirit]. When ' he was united (to the spirit), [he spoke] words incomprehensible ' to the powers. They envied him ' [because they were separated from the] spiritual union. [30] [...] hidden ' [...]. This [separation] afforded them the opportunity ' [to fashion] for themselves ' [the symbolic] bridal chamber so that ' [men would be defiled].

Jesus revealed [35] [himself at the] Jordan: it was the ' [fullness of the kingdom] of heaven. He who ' [was begotten] before everything **71** was begotten anew. He [who was] once [anointed] ' was anointed anew. He who was redeemed ' in turn redeemed (others).

Is it permitted to utter a ' mystery? The Father of everything united [5] with the virgin who came down, and ' a fire shone for him on that day. ' He appeared in the great bridal chamber. ' Therefore, his body came into being ' on that very day. It left the bridal chamber [10] as one who came into being ' from the bridegroom and the bride. So ' Jesus established everything ' in it through these. ' It is fitting for each of the disciples [15] to enter into his rest. '

Adam came into being from two virgins, ' from the Spirit and from ' the virgin earth. Christ, therefore, ' was born from a virgin [20] to rectify the fall which ' occurred in the beginning. '

There are two trees growing in Paradise. ' The one bears [animals], the other bears ' men. Adam [ate] from the tree [25] which bore animals. He became an animal ' and he brought forth animals. For this reason ' the children of Adam worship [animals]. ' The tree [whose] fruit [Adam ate] ' is [the tree of knowledge. That] [30] is why [sins] increased. [If he] ' ate the [fruit of the other tree, that is to say, the] ' fruit of the [tree of life, the one which] ' bears men, [then the gods would] worship ' man. [For in the beginning] [35] God created man. [But now men] **72** create God. That is the way it is in the world—' men make gods and worship ' their creation. It would be fitting for the gods ' to worship men!

Surely [5] what a man accomplishes ' depends on his abilities. ' We even refer to one's accomplishments as ' "abilities." Among his accomplishments are his children. They ' originate in a moment of ease. [10] Thus his abilities determine ' what he may accomplish, but this ease ' is clearly evident in the children. ' You will find that this applies directly to the image. ' Here is the man made after the image [15] accomplishing things with his physical strength, ' but producing his children with ease. '

In this world the slaves ' serve the free. In the ' kingdom of heaven the free will [20] minister to the slaves: the children of ' the bridal chamber will minister to the children ' of the marriage. The children of the bridal chamber ' have [just one] name. Together ' they [share] rest. They need take no (other) [25] form [because they have] contemplation, ' [comprehending by insight]. They are numerous ' [because they do not put their treasure] in the things ' [below, which are despised, but] in the glories which ' [are above, though they did] not (yet) [know] them.

Those [30] [who will be baptized go] down into the water. ' [But Christ, by coming] out (of the water), will consecrate it, ' [so that] they who have [received baptism] ' in his name [may be perfect]. For he said, ' "[Thus] we should fulfill all **73** righteousness" (Matthew 3:15).

Those who say they will ' die first and then rise ' are in error. If they do not first receive the ' resurrection while they live, when they die they will receive nothing. [5] So also when speaking about ' baptism they say, "Baptism ' is a great thing," because if people receive it they will ' live.

Philip the apostle ' said, "Joseph the carpenter planted [10] a garden because he needed wood ' for his trade. It was he who ' made the cross from the ' trees which he planted. His own offspring hung ' on that which he planted. His offspring was [15] Jesus and the planting was the cross." But the tree ' of life is in the middle of the garden. ' However, it is from the olive tree ' that we get the chrism, and from the chrism, ' the resurrection.

This world is a corpse-eater. [20] All the things eaten ' in it themselves die also. Truth ' is a life-eater. Therefore no one ' nourished by [truth] will die. It was ' from that place that Jesus came and brought [25] food. To those who ' so desired he gave [life, that] ' they might not die.

God [planted] a garden. ' Man [was put into the] garden. ' There were [many trees there for him], [30] and man [lived] in [this place] ' with the [blessing and in the image] ' of God. The things which are in [it I will eat as] ' I wish. This garden [is the place where] ' they will say to me, "[O man, eat] [35] this or do not eat [that, just as you] **74** wish." This is the place where I will eat all things, ' since the tree of knowledge is there. ' That one killed Adam, ' but here the tree of knowledge made men alive. [5] The law was the tree. It has power ' to give the knowledge of good ' and evil. It neither removed him from ' evil, nor did it set him in the good, ' but it created death for those who [10] ate of it. For when he said, ' "Eat this, do not eat that," it became ' the beginning of death.

The chrism is superior ' to baptism, for it is from the word "chrism" ' that we have been called "Christians," certainly not because [15] of the word "baptism." And it is because of the chrism that "the ' Christ" has his name. For the Father anointed ' the Son, and the Son anointed the apostles, ' and the apostles anointed us. He who ' has been anointed possesses everything. He possesses [20] the resurrection, the light, the cross, ' the Holy Spirit. The Father gave him this ' in the bridal chamber; he merely accepted (the gift). The Father was ' in the Son and the Son in the Father. ' This is [the] kingdom of heaven. [25]

The Lord said it well: "Some have entered the kingdom ' of heaven laughing and they have come out." ' [They do not remain there—the] one because he is [not] a Christian, ' [the other because he regrets (his action)] afterward. And as soon as ' [Christ went down into] the water he came [30] [out laughing at] everything (of this world), [not] because ' [he considers it] a trifle, but ' [because he is full of] contempt for it. He who ' [wants to enter] the kingdom of ' [heaven will attain it]. If he despises [35] [everything (of this world)] and scorns it as a trifle, ' [he will come] out laughing. So it is also **75** with the bread and the cup and the oil, ' even though there is another one superior to these.

The ' world came about through a mistake. ' For he who created it wanted to create [5] it imperishable and immortal. ' He fell short of attaining his desire. ' For the world never was imperishable, ' nor, for that matter, was ' he who made the world. [10] For things are not imperishable, ' but sons are. Nothing ' will be able to receive imperishability if it does not ' first become a son. But he who has not the ability ' to receive, how much more will he be unable to give?

The cup [15] of prayer contains wine and ' water, since it is appointed as the type of ' the blood for which thanks is given. And ' it is full of the Holy Spirit, and ' it belongs to the wholly perfect man. When [20] we drink this, we shall receive for ourselves the perfect ' man. The living water is a body. ' It is necessary that we put on the living man. ' Therefore, when he is about to go down into the water, ' he unclothes himself, in order that he may put on the living man. [25]

A horse sires a horse, a ' man begets man, a god ' brings forth a god. Compare ' [the] bridegroom and the bride. [Their children] were ' conceived in the [bridal chamber]. [30] No Jew [was ever born] ' to Greek parents [as long as the world] ' has existed. And, [as a] Christian [people],' we [ourselves do not descend] ' from the Jews. [There was] another [people and] [35] these [blessed ones] are referred to as ' "the chosen people of [the living God]" **76** and "the true man" and "the Son of ' man" and "the seed of the Son of man." ' In the world it is called ' "this true people." Where [5] they are, there are the sons of the bridal chamber. '

Whereas in this world the union ' is one of husband with wife—a case of strength complemented by ' weakness—in the aeon the form of the union ' is different, although we refer to them by the same names. There are [10] other names, however; they are superior to every name ' that is named and are ' stronger than the strong. For where there is a show of strength, ' there those who excel in strength appear. ' These are not separate things, [15] but both of them are this one ' single thing. This is the one which will not be able to rise ' above the heart of flesh.

Is it not necessary for all those who possess ' everything to know themselves? ' Some indeed, if they do not know [20] themselves, will not enjoy what they ' possess. But those who have come to know themselves will ' enjoy their possessions.

Not only ' will they be unable to detain the perfect man, ' but they will not be able to see him, for if they see him [25] they will detain him. There is no other way ' for a person to acquire this quality except ' by putting on the perfect light ' [and] becoming perfect oneself. [Every] ' one who has [put this] on will enter [30] [the kingdom]. This is the perfect ' [light, and it is necessary] that we [by all means] become ' [perfect men] before we leave ' [the world]. He who has received everything ' [and has not rid himself] of these places will [not] be able [35] [to share in] that place, but will ' [go to the Middle] as imperfect. 77 Only Jesus knows the end of this person. '

The priest is completely holy, down ' to his very body. For if he has taken the bread, ' will he consecrate it? Or the cup [5] or anything else that he gets, ' does he consecrate them? Then how will he not consecrate ' the body also?

By perfecting ' the water of baptism, Jesus ' emptied it of death. Thus we do go [10] down into the water, but we do not go ' down into death in order that we may not be poured ' out into the spirit of the world. When ' that spirit blows, it brings the winter. ' When the Holy Spirit breathes, [15] the summer comes.

He who has ' knowledge of the truth is a free man, ' but the free man does not sin, ' for "he who sins is the slave of sin" (John 8:34). ' Truth is the mother, knowledge [20] the father. Those who think that sinning does not apply to them ' are called "free" by the world. ' Knowledge of the truth merely makes ' such people arrogant, which ' is what the words "it makes them free" mean. [25] It even gives them a sense of superiority over the whole world. But "love ' builds up" (1 Corinthians 8:1). In fact, he who is really free through ' knowledge is a slave because of love ' for those who have not yet been able to attain to the ' freedom of knowledge. Knowledge [30] makes them capable of becoming ' free. Love [never calls] ' something its own, [and yet] it may actually possess [that very thing]. ' It never [says "This is mine"] ' or "That is mine," [but "All these] [35] are yours." Spiritual love ' is wine and fragrance. 78 All those who anoint themselves with it take pleasure in it. ' While those who are anointed are present, ' those nearby also profit (from the fragrance). ' If those anointed with ointment withdraw from them [5] and leave, then those not anointed, ' who merely stand nearby, still ' remain in their bad odor. The Samaritan ' gave nothing but ' wine and oil to the wounded man. It is nothing other than [10] the ointment. It healed the wounds, ' for "love covers a multitude of sins" (1 Peter 4:8). '

The children a woman bears ' resemble the man who loves her. If her ' husband loves her, then they resemble her husband. If it is an adulterer, [15] then they resemble the adulterer. Frequently, ' if a woman sleeps with her ' husband out of necessity, while her heart is with the adulterer ' with whom she usually has intercourse, the child ' she will bear is born resembling [20] the adulterer. Now you who live together with the Son ' of God, love not the world, ' but love the Lord, in order that those you will ' bring forth may not resemble the world, ' but may resemble the Lord. [25]

The human being has intercourse with the human being. ' The horse has intercourse with the horse, the ass ' with the ass. Members of a race usually have associated ' with those of like race. So spirit ' mingles with spirit, and thought [30] consorts with thought, ' and [light] shares ' [with light. If you (sing.)] are born a human being, ' it is [the human being] who will love you. If you become ' [a spirit], it is the spirit which will be joined to you. If you become [35] thought, it is thought which will mingle **79** with you. If you become light, ' it is the light which will share ' with you. If you become one of those who belong above, ' it is those who belong above who will rest [5] in you. If you become horse ' or ass or bull or dog or sheep ' or another of the animals which are outside ' or below, then ' neither human being nor spirit [10] nor thought nor light will be able to love you. Neither ' those who belong above nor those who belong within ' will be able to rest in you, ' and you have no part in them.

He ' who is a slave against his will will be able to become free. [15] He who has become free by the favor ' of his master and has sold ' himself into slavery will no longer be able ' to be free.

Farming in the ' world requires the cooperation of four essential elements. A harvest is gathered [20] into the barn only as a result of the natural action of water, ' earth, wind, and light. ' God's farming likewise ' has four elements—faith, ' hope, love, and [25] knowledge. Faith is our earth, that in which we ' take root. [And] hope ' is the water through which we are ' nourished. Love is the wind through ' which we grow. Knowledge then is the light [30] through which we [ripen]. ' Grace exists in [four ways: it is] ' earthborn; it is [heavenly; it comes from] ' the highest heaven; and [it resides] in [truth].

Blessed ' is the one who on no occasion caused a soul distress. **80** That person is Jesus Christ. He came to ' the whole place and did not burden anyone. ' Therefore, blessed is the one who is like ' this, because he is a perfect man. This indeed is [5] the Word. Tell us about it, since it is difficult ' to define. How shall we be able to accomplish ' such a great thing? How will he give everyone comfort? ' Above all, it is not proper ' to cause anyone distress—whether the person is great or small, [10] unbeliever or believer—and then give comfort ' only to those who take satisfaction in good deeds. ' Some find it advantageous to give ' comfort to the one who has fared well. He who does ' good deeds cannot give comfort [15] to such people, for it goes against his will. ' He is unable to cause distress, ' however, since he does not afflict them. To be sure, the one who ' fares well sometimes causes people distress—' not that he intends to do so; rather it is their own wickedness [20] which is responsible for their distress. He who possesses ' the qualities (of the perfect man) rejoices in the good. ' Some, however, are terribly distressed by all this. '

There was a householder who had ' every conceivable thing, be it son or slave or [25] cattle or dog or pig or corn ' [or] barley or chaff or grass or ' castor oil or meat and acorn. [Now he was] a sensible fellow ' and he knew what the food of each ' one was. He [himself] served the children bread [30] [and meat]. He served the slaves ' castor oil [and] meal. And ' [he threw barley] and chaff and grass to the cattle. ' He threw bones to [the] dogs, ' and to the pigs he threw acorns **81** and scraps of bread. Compare the disciple ' of God: if he is a sensible fellow he ' understands what discipleship is all about. The ' bodily forms will not deceive him, [5] but he will look at the condition ' of the soul of each one and speak ' with him. There are many animals in the world ' which are in human form. When ' he identifies them, to the swine he will throw [10] acorns, to the cattle he will throw ' barley and chaff and grass, to the ' dogs he will throw bones. To the slaves ' he will give only the elementary lessons, to the children he will give ' the complete instruction.

There is the Son of man [15] and there is the son of the Son of man. ' The Lord is the Son of man, ' and the son of the Son of ' man is he who is created through the Son ' of man. The Son of man received [20] from God the capacity to create. He also has the ability ' to beget. He who has received ' the ability to create is a creature. He who has received ' the ability to beget is an offspring. He who creates cannot ' beget. He who begets also has power to create. [25] Now they say, "He who creates begets." ' But his so-called "offspring" is merely a creature. [Therefore] ' his children are not offspring but [creatures]. ' He who creates works openly ' and he himself is visible. [30] He who begets begets in [private] ' and he himself is hidden, [since he is superior to every] ' image. He who creates [creates] ' openly. But one who begets [begets] ' children in private. No [one will be able] to [35] know when [the husband] **82** and the wife have intercourse with one another ' except the two of them. Indeed marriage in the ' world is a mystery for those who have taken ' a wife. If there is a hidden quality to the marriage of defilement, [5] how much more is the undefiled marriage ' a true mystery! It is not fleshly ' but pure. It belongs not to desire ' but to the will. It belongs not to the darkness ' or the night but to the day and [10] the light. If a marriage is open to the public, ' it has become prostitution, and the bride ' plays the harlot not only when she is impregnated by another man ' but even if she slips out of her bedroom ' and is seen. [15] Let her show herself only to her father and her ' mother and to the friend of the bridegroom and ' the sons of the bridegroom. These are permitted ' to enter every day into the bridal chamber. ' But let the others yearn just [20] to listen to her voice and to enjoy ' her ointment, and let them feed from the ' crumbs that fall from the table, like the ' dogs. Bridegrooms and ' brides belong to the bridal chamber. No one shall be able [25] to see the bridegroom with the bride unless ' [one become] one.

When Abraham ' [rejoiced] that he was to see what he was to see, ' [he circumcised] the flesh of the foreskin, teaching ' us that it is proper to destroy the flesh. [30]

[Most things] in the world, as long as their ' [inner parts] are hidden, stand upright and live. ' [If they are revealed] they die, as ' is illustrated by the visible man: ' [as long as] the intestines of the man are hidden, the man is alive; **83** when his intestines are exposed ' and come out of him, the man will die. ' So also with the tree: while its root ' is hidden it sprouts and grows. If its [5] root is exposed, the tree dries up. ' So it is with every birth that is in the world, ' not only with the revealed ' but with the hidden. For so long as the root ' of wickedness is hidden, it is strong. But when it is recognized [10] it is dissolved. When it is revealed ' it perishes. That is why the word says, ' "Already the ax is laid at the root ' of the trees" (Matthew 3:10). It will not merely cut—what ' is cut sprouts again—but the ax [15] penetrates deeply until it ' brings up the root. Jesus pulled out ' the root of the whole place, while others did it only ' partially. As for ourselves, let each ' one of us dig down after the root [20] of evil which is within one, and let one pluck it ' out of one's heart from the root. It will be plucked out ' if we recognize it. But if we ' are ignorant of it, it takes root in ' us and produces its fruit [25] in our heart. It masters us. ' We are its slaves. It takes us captive, ' to make us do what we do [not] want; ' and what we do want we do [not] do.

It ' is powerful because we have not recognized it. While it exists [30] it is active. Ignorance ' is the mother of [all evil]. ' Ignorance will eventuate in [death, because] ' those that come from [ignorance] ' neither were nor [are] [35] nor shall be. [But those who are in the truth] **84** will be perfect when all the truth ' is revealed. For truth is like ' ignorance: while it is hidden it rests ' in itself, but when it is revealed [5] and is recognized, it is praised inasmuch as ' it is stronger than ignorance and error. ' It gives freedom. The word said, ' "If you know the truth, ' the truth will make you free" (John 8:32). [10] Ignorance is a slave. Knowledge is ' freedom. If we know the truth, ' we shall find the fruits of the truth within ' us. If we are joined to it, it will bring our fulfillment. '

At the present time we have the manifest things [15] of creation. We say, ' "The strong are they who are held in high regard. And the obscure ' are the weak who are despised." Contrast the manifest things ' of truth: they are weak and ' despised, while the hidden things are strong and [20] held in high regard. The mysteries of truth are ' revealed, though in type and image. The bridal chamber, ' however, remains hidden. It is the holy in ' the holy. The veil at first ' concealed how God controlled [25] the creation, but when the veil is rent ' and the things inside are revealed, ' this house will be left ' desolate, or rather will be ' [destroyed]. But the whole inferior Godhead will not flee [30] [from] these places into the holies ' [of the] holies, for it will not be able to mix with the ' un-mixed [light] and the ' [flawless] fullness, but will be under the wings of the Cross ' [and under] its arms. This ark will be [35] [its] salvation when the flood **85** of water surges over them. If ' some belong to the order of the priesthood ' they will be able to go ' within the veil with the high priest. [5] For this reason the veil was not ' rent at the top only, since it ' would have been open only to those above; nor ' was it rent at the bottom only, since ' it would have been revealed only to those below. [10] But it was rent from top to bottom. Those ' above opened to us who are below, ' in order that we may go in to the secret ' of the truth. This truly is what is ' held in high regard, since it is strong! But we shall go in there [15] by means of lowly types and forms of weakness. ' They are lowly indeed when compared with the perfect glory. ' There is glory which surpasses glory. There is power which surpasses ' power. There-fore the perfect things have opened ' to us, together with the hidden things of truth. The holies [20] of the holies were revealed, and ' the bridal chamber invited us in.

As long ' as it is hidden, wickedness is indeed ineffectual, but ' it has not been removed from the midst of the seed of the Holy Spirit. ' They are slaves of evil. But when [25] it is revealed, then the ' perfect light will flow out on every ' one. And all those who are in it will [receive the chrism]. ' Then the slaves will be free [and] ' the captives ransomed. "[Every] plant [which] [30] my father who is in heaven [has not] planted [will be] ' plucked out" (Matthew 15:13). Those who are separated will be united [and] ' will be filled. Every one who will [enter] ' the bridal chamber will kindle the [light], for [it burns] ' just as in the marriages which are [observed, though they] happen [35] at night. That fire [burns] only **86** at night and is put out. But the mysteries ' of this marriage are perfected rather in ' the day and the light. Neither that day ' nor its light ever sets. If anyone becomes a son [5] of the bridal chamber, he will receive the light. ' If anyone does not receive it while he is in these places, he will not be able to receive it ' in the other place. He who will receive that light ' will not be seen, nor can he be detained. ' And none shall be able to torment [10] a person like this even while he dwells ' in the world. And again when he leaves ' the world he has already received the truth in ' the images. The world has become the aeon, ' for the aeon is fullness for him. [15] This is the way it is: it is revealed ' to him alone, not hidden in the darkness and the ' night, but hidden in a perfect day ' and a holy light.

The Gospel '
According to Philip

THE HYPOSTASIS OF THE ARCHONS (II, *4*)

Introduced by

ROGER A. BULLARD

Translated by

BENTLEY LAYTON

The *Hypostasis of the Archons* ("Reality of the Rulers") is an anonymous tractate presenting an esoteric interpretation of Genesis 1-6, partially in the form of a revelation discourse between an angel and a questioner. While the treatise illustrates a wide-ranging Hellenistic syncretism, the most evident components are Jewish, although in its present form the *Hypostasis of the Archons* shows clearly Christian features and thus can be considered a Christian work. Its theological perspective is a vigorous Gnosticism of undetermined sectarian affiliation. The tractate was originally composed in Greek, probably in Egypt; and although the date of composition is unknown, some evidence points to the third century C.E. Interestingly, the many parallels between this tractate and the tractate *On the Origin of the World* (II, 5) demonstrate some sort of close connection between the two documents.

After a brief introduction quoting "the great apostle" Paul, the *Hypostasis of the Archons* offers its mythological narrative. The main characters in the mythological drama which unfolds include the blind Ruler Samael, also called Sakla ("Fool") and Yaldabaoth, who blasphemes against the divine; the spiritual Woman, who rouses Adam and outwits the rapacious Rulers; the Snake, "the Instructor," who counsels the man and woman to eat of the fruit forbidden by the Rulers; and Norea, the daughter of Eve, a virgin pure in character and exalted in knowledge. On page 93 of the tractate the focus changes somewhat: on center stage now is the Great Angel Eleleth, who reveals to Norea the origin and destiny of the archontic powers.

The *Hypostasis of the Archons* proclaims, as its title indicates, the reality of the archontic Rulers: far from being merely fictitious, imaginary powers, the Archons are all too real. These Rulers indeed exist. This is a grim reality for the Christian Gnostics, who define their own spiritual nature in opposition to that of the ruling and enslaving Authorities. Yet, as this document promises, the Christian Gnostics can have hope, for their spiritual nature will be more lasting than the Archons, and their heavenly destiny will be more glorious. In the end the Rulers will perish, and the Gnostics, the Children of the Light, will know the Father and praise him.

THE HYPOSTASIS OF THE ARCHONS

II 86, 20-97, 23

On account of the reality (hypostasis) of the Authorities, (inspired) by the Spirit ' of the Father of Truth, the great ' apostle—referring to the "authorities of the darkness" (Colossians 1:13)—told us ' that "our contest is not against flesh and ' [blood]; rather, the authorities of the universe [25] and the spirits of wickedness" (Ephesians 6:12). ' [I have] sent (you) this because you (sing.) inquire about the reality ' [of the] Authorities.

Their chief is blind; ' [because of his] Power and his ignorance ' [and his] arrogance he said, with his [30] [Power], "It is I who am God; there is none ' [apart from me]."

When he said this, he sinned against ' [the Entirety]. And this speech got up **87** to Incorruptibility; then there was a voice that came ' forth from Incorruptibility, saying, ' "You are mistaken, Samael"—which is, "god ' of the blind."

His thoughts became blind. And, having expelled [5] his Power—that is, the blasphemy he had spoken—' he pursued it down to Chaos and ' the Abyss, his mother, at the instigation of Pistis ' Sophia (Faith-Wisdom). And she established each of his offspring ' in conformity with its power—after the pattern [10] of the realms that are above, for by starting from the ' invisible world the visible world was invented.

As Incorruptibility ' looked down into the region of the Waters, ' her Image appeared in the Waters; ' and the Authorities of the Darkness became enamored of her. [15] But they could not lay hold of that Image, ' which had appeared to them in the Waters, ' because of their weakness— since beings that merely possess a soul ' cannot lay hold of those that possess a Spirit—; for ' they were from Below, while it was from [20] Above.

This is the reason why "Incorruptibility ' looked down into the region (etc.)": ' so that, by the Father's will, she ' might bring the Entirety into union with the Light. The Rulers (Archons) laid ' plans and said, "Come, [25] let us create a man that will be soil from ' the earth." They modelled their creature ' as one wholly of the earth.

Now the Rulers ... ' body ... they have ... female ... is ... ' face(s) ... are ... bestial .... They took some [soil] [30] from the earth and modelled their [Man], ' after their body and [after the Image] ' of God that had appeared [to them] ' in the Waters.

They said, "[Come, let] us ' lay hold of it by means of the form that we have modelled, [so that] [35] it may see its male counterpart [...], **88** and we may seize it with the form that we have modelled"—not ' understanding the force of God, because of ' their powerlessness. And he breathed into ' his face; and the Man came to have a soul (and remained) [5] upon the ground many days. But they could not ' make him arise because of their powerlessness. ' Like storm winds they persisted (in blowing), that they might ' try to capture that image, which had appeared ' to them in the Waters. And they did not know [10] the identity of its power.

Now all these (events) came ' to pass by the will of the Father of the Entirety. Afterwards, ' the Spirit saw the soul-endowed Man ' upon the ground. And the Spirit came forth from ' the Adamantine Land; it descended and came to dwell within [15] him, and that Man became a living soul. '

It called his name Adam since he ' was found moving upon the ground. A voice ' came forth from Incorruptibility for the assistance of Adam; ' and the Rulers gathered together [20] all the animals of the earth and all the ' birds of heaven and brought them in to Adam ' to see what Adam would call them, ' that he might give a name to each of the birds ' and all the beasts.

They took Adam [25] [and] put him in the Garden, that he might cultivate ' [it] and keep watch over it. And the Rulers issued a command ' to him, saying, "From [every] tree ' in the Garden shall you (sing.) eat; ' yet—[from] the tree of recognizing good [30] and evil do not eat, nor ' [touch] it; for the day you (pl.) eat ' [from] it, with death you (pl.) are going to die."

They ' [. . .] this. They do not understand what ' [they have said] to him; rather, by the Father's will, **89** they said this in such a way that he ' might (in fact) eat, and that Adam might ⟨not⟩ regard them as would a man of an exclusively ' material nature.

The Rulers took counsel ' with one another and said, "Come, let us cause [5] a deep sleep to fall upon Adam." And he slept. '—Now the deep sleep that they ' "caused to fall upon him, and he slept" is Ignorance.— They opened ' his side like a living Woman. ' And they built up his side with some flesh [10] in place of her, and Adam came to be endowed ' only with soul.

And the spirit-endowed Woman ' came to him and spoke with him, saying, ' "Arise, Adam." And when he saw her, ' he said, "It is you who have given me life; [15] you will be called 'Mother of the Living.' ' —For it is she who is my mother. It is she who is the Physician, ' and the Woman, and She Who Has Given Birth."

Then the ' Authorities came up to their Adam. ' And when they saw his female counterpart speaking with him, [20] they became agitated with great agitation; ' and they became enamored of her. They said to one another, ' "Come, let us sow our seed ' in her," and they pursued her. And ' she laughed at them for their witlessness [25] and their blindness; and in their clutches, she became a tree, ' and left before them her shadowy reflection resembling herself; ' and they defiled [it] ' foully.—And they defiled the form that she had stamped in ' her likeness, so that [30] by the form they had modelled, together with [their] (own) image, they made themselves liable to condemnation. '

Then the Female Spiritual Principle came [in] ' the Snake, the Instructor; and it taught [them], ' saying, "What did he [say to] ' you (pl.)? Was it, 'From every tree in the Garden [35] shall you (sing.) eat; yet—from [the tree] **90** of recognizing evil and good ' do not eat'?"

The carnal Woman said, ' "Not only did he say 'Do not eat,' but even ' 'Do not touch it; for the day you (pl.) eat [5] from it, with death you (pl.) are going to die.' " '

And the Snake, the Instructor, said, "With death ' you (pl.) shall not die; for it was out of jealousy ' that he said this to you (pl.). Rather your (pl.) eyes ' shall open and you (pl.) shall come to be like gods, recognizing [10] evil and good." ' And the Female Instructing Principle was taken away from the Snake, ' and she left it behind merely a thing of the earth. '

And the carnal Woman took from the tree ' and ate; and she gave to her husband as well as herself; and [15] these beings that possessed only a soul, ate. And their imperfection ' became apparent in their lack of Acquaintance; and ' they recognized that they were naked of the Spiritual Element, ' and took fig leaves and bound them ' upon their loins.

Then the chief Ruler came; [20] and he said, "Adam! Where are you?"—for he did not ' understand what had happened.

And Adam ' said, "I heard your voice and was ' afraid because I was naked; and I hid." '

The Ruler said, "Why did you (sing.) hide, unless it is [25] because you (sing.) have eaten from the tree ' from which alone I commanded you (sing.) not to eat? ' And you (sing.) have eaten!" '

Adam said, "The Woman that you gave me, ' [she gave] to me and I ate." And the arrogant [30] Ruler cursed the Woman.

The Woman ' said, "It was the Snake that led me astray and I ate." ' [They turned] to the Snake and cursed its shadowy reflection, ' [. . .] powerless, not comprehending ' [that] it was a form they themselves had modelled. From that day, **91** the Snake came to be under the curse of the Authorities; ' until the All-powerful Man was to come, ' that curse fell upon the Snake.

They turned ' to their Adam and took him and expelled him from the Garden [5] along with his wife; for they have no ' blessing, since they too are ' beneath the curse.

Moreover they threw Mankind ' into great distraction and into a life ' of toil, so that their Mankind might be [10] occupied by worldly affairs, and might not have the opportunity ' of being devoted to the Holy Spirit.

Now afterwards, ' she bore Cain, their son; and Cain ' cultivated the land. Thereupon he knew his ' wife; again becoming pregnant, she bore Abel; and Abel [15] was a herdsman of sheep. Now Cain brought ' in from the crops of his field, but ' Abel brought in an offering (from) among ' his lambs. God looked upon the ' votive offerings of Abel; but he did not accept the votive offerings [20] of Cain. And carnal Cain ' pursued Abel his brother.

And God ' said to Cain, "Where is Abel your brother?" '

He answered, saying, "Am I, then, ' my brother's keeper?"

God said to [25] Cain, "Listen! The voice of your brother's blood ' is crying up to me! You have sinned with ' your mouth. It will return to you: anyone who ' kills Cain will let loose seven ' vengeances, and you will exist groaning and [30] trembling upon the earth."

And Adam [knew] ' his female counterpart Eve, and she became pregnant, and bore [Seth] ' to Adam. And she said, "I have borne [another] ' man through God, in place [of Abel]." '

Again Eve became pregnant, and she bore [Norea]. [35] And she said, "He has begotten on [me a] virgin [92] as an assistance [for] many generations ' of mankind." She is the virgin whom the ' Forces did not defile.

Then Mankind began ' to multiply and improve.

The Rulers took counsel [5] with one another and said, "Come, let ' us cause a deluge with our ' hands and obliterate all flesh, from man ' to beast."

But when the Ruler of the Forces ' came to know of their decision, he said to Noah, [10] "Make yourself an ark from some wood ' that does not rot and hide in it—you ' and your children and the beasts and ' the birds of heaven from small to large—and set it ' upon Mount Sir."

Then Orea came [15] to him wanting to board the ark. ' And when he would not let her, she blew upon the ' ark and caused it to be consumed by fire. Again he ' made the ark, for a second time.

The Rulers went to meet her ' intending to lead her astray. [20] Their supreme chief said to her, "Your mother ' Eve came to us."

But Norea turned to ' them and said to them, "It is you who are the

Rulers of ' the Darkness; you are accursed. And you did not know ' my mother; instead it was your female [25] counterpart that you knew. For I am not your descendant; ' rather it is from the World Above that I am come." '

The arrogant Ruler turned, with all his might, ' [and] his countenance came to be like (a) black ' [. . .]; he said to her presumptuously, [30] "You must render service to us, ' [as did] also your mother Eve; for . . . ' [. . .]."

But Norea turned, with the might of ' [. . .]; and in a loud voice [she] cried out ' [up to] the Holy One, the God of the Entirety, **93** "Rescue me from the Rulers of Unrighteousness ' and save me from their clutches—forthwith!"

The ⟨Great⟩ Angel ' came down from the heavens ' and said to her, "Why are you crying up [5] to God? Why do you act so boldly towards the ' Holy Spirit?"

Norea said, "Who are you?" '

The Rulers of Unrighteousness had withdrawn from ' her. He said, "It is I who am Eleleth, ' Sagacity, the Great Angel, who stands [10] in the presence of the Holy Spirit. ' I have been sent to speak with you and ' save you from the grasp of the Lawless. And I ' shall teach you about your Root."

—Now as for that angel, ' I cannot speak of his power: his appearance is like [15] fine gold and his raiment is like snow. ' No, truly, my mouth cannot bear ' to speak of his power and the appearance of his face! '

Eleleth, the Great Angel, spoke to me. ' "It is I," he said, "who am Understanding. [20] I am one of the Four Light-givers, ' who stand in the presence of the Great ' Invisible Spirit. Do you think ' these Rulers have any power over you (sing.)? None ' of them can prevail against the Root [25] of Truth; for on its account ' he appeared in the final ages (text corrupt); and ' these Authorities will be restrained. And these Authorities ' cannot defile you and that generation; ' for your (pl.) abode is in Incorruptibility, [30] where the Virgin Spirit dwells, ' who is superior to the Authorities of Chaos ' and to their universe."

But I said, ' "Sir, teach me about the [faculty of] ' these Authorities —[how] did they come into being, [35] and by what kind of genesis, [and] of **94** what material, and who ' created them and their force?"

And the ' Great Angel Eleleth, Understanding, spoke to me: ' "Within limitless realms [5] dwells Incorruptibility. Sophia, ' who is called Pistis, wanted to ' create something, alone without her consort; and ' her product was a celestial thing. '

"A veil exists between the World Above [10] and the realms that are below; and ' Shadow came into being beneath the veil; ' and that Shadow became Matter; ' and that Shadow was projected ' apart. And what she had created became [15] a product in the Matter, like an aborted fetus. ' And it assumed a plastic form molded out of Shadow, and became ' an arrogant beast resembling a lion." ' It was androgynous, as I have already said, ' because it was from Matter that it derived.

"Opening his [20] eyes he saw a vast quantity of Matter without limit; ' and he became arrogant, saying, 'It is I who am God, and there ' is none other apart from me.'

"When he said ' this, he sinned against the Entirety. ' And a voice came forth from above the realm of absolute power, [25] saying, 'You are mistaken, Samael'—' which is, 'god of the blind.'

"And he ' said, 'If any other thing exists before ' me, let it become visible to me!' And ' immediately Sophia stretched forth her finger [30] and introduced Light into ' Matter; and she pursued it down ' to the region of Chaos. And she returned ' up [to] her light; once again Darkness ' [. . .] Matter.

"This Ruler, by being androgynous, [35] made himself a vast realm, **95** an extent without limit. And he contemplated ' creating offspring for himself, and created ' for himself seven offspring, androgynous just like ' their parent.

"And he said to his offspring, [5] 'It is I who am the god of the Entirety.'

"And Zoe (Life), ' the daughter of Pistis Sophia, cried ' out and said to him, 'You are mistaken, Sakla!'—' for which the alternate name is Yaltabaoth. She ' breathed into his face, and her breath became [10] a fiery angel for her; and ' that angel bound Yaldabaoth ' and cast him down into Tartaros ' below the Abyss.

"Now when his offspring ' Sabaoth saw the force of that angel, [15] he repented and ' condemned his father and his ' mother Matter.

"He loathed her, but he ' sang songs of praise up to Sophia and her daughter Zoe. ' And Sophia and Zoe caught him up [20] and gave him charge of the seventh heaven, ' below the veil between ' Above and Below. And he is ' called 'God of the Forces, Sabaoth,' ' since he is up above the Forces [25] of Chaos, for Sophia established ' him.

"Now when these (events) had come to pass, he made ' himself a huge four-faced chariot of cherubim, ' and infinitely many angels ' to act as ministers, [30] and also harps and ' lyres.

"And Sophia took her daughter ' Zoe and had her sit upon his right ' to teach him about the things that exist ' in the Eighth (Heaven); and the

Angel [of] Wrath [35] she placed upon his left. [Since] that day, [his right] has been called **96** Life; and the left has come to represent ' the un-righteousness of the realm of absolute power ' above. It was before your (sing.) time that they came into being (text corrupt?).

"Now when ' Yaldabaoth saw him in this [5] great splendor and at this height, he envied him; ' and the envy became an androgynous product; ' and this was the origin of ' Envy. And Envy engendered Death; and Death ' engendered his offspring and gave each [10] of them charge of its heaven; and all the heavens ' of Chaos became full of their multitudes.

"But it was ' by the will of the Father of the Entirety that they all came into being—' after the pattern of all the Things Above—' so that the sum of Chaos might be attained. [15]

"There, I have taught you (sing.) about the pattern ' of the Rulers; and the Matter in which it was expressed; ' and their parent; and their universe."

But I ' said, "Sir, am I also ' from their Matter?"

—"You, together with your offspring, are from [20] the Primeval Father; ' from Above, out of the imperishable Light, ' their souls are come. Thus the Authorities ' cannot approach them because of ' the Spirit of Truth present within them; [25] and all who have become acquainted with this Way ' exist deathless in the midst ' of dying Mankind. Still that Sown Element ' will not become known now.

"Instead, ' after three generations it will come to be known, [30] and free them from the bondage of the ' Authorities' error."

Then I said, ' "Sir, how much longer?"

He said ' to me, "Until the moment when the True Man, ' within a modelled form, reveals (?) the existence of [35] [the Spirit of] Truth, which the Father has sent. **97**

"Then he will teach them about '·every thing: And he will anoint them with the ' unction of Life eternal, ' given him from the undominated generation. [5]

"Then they will be freed of ' blind thought: And they will trample under foot ' Death, which is of the Authorities: And they will ascend ' into the limitless Light, ' where this Sown Element belongs. [10]

"Then the Authorities will relinquish their ' ages: And their angels will weep ' over their destruction: And their demons ' will lament their death.

"Then all the Children ' of the Light will be truly acquainted with the Truth [15] and their Root, and the Father ' of the Entirety and the Holy Spirit: They will all say ' with a single voice, ' 'The Father's truth is just, and the Son ' presides over the Entirety': And from everyone [20] unto the ages of ages, 'Holy—Holy—' Holy! Amen!' " '

The Reality '
of the Rulers

ON THE ORIGIN OF THE WORLD (II, 5 AND XIII, 2)

Introduced by

HANS-GEBHARD BETHGE

Translated by

HANS-GEBHARD BETHGE and ORVAL S. WINTERMUTE

The modern title *On the Origin of the World* is used to name a tractate which has been transmitted without a title but which discusses what this hypothetical title suggests. *On the Origin of the World* is a compendium of essential Gnostic ideas, a work written in the form of an apologetic essay offering to the public an explanation of the Gnostic world-view. Although the treatise does not represent any known Gnostic system, there are reminiscences of Sethian, Valentinian, and Manichaean themes; the author obviously draws upon a variety of traditions and sources. For example, some sort of connection with the *Hypostasis of the Archons* (II, 4) is clear, though the precise nature of this relationship is uncertain. *On the Origin of the World* was probably composed in Alexandria at the end of the third century C.E. or the beginning of the fourth. The place and date of composition are suggested by the juxtaposition of various sorts of materials: the varieties of Jewish thought, Manichaean motifs, Christian ideas, Greek or Hellenistic philosophical and mythological concepts, magical and astrological themes, and elements of Egyptian lore together suggest that Alexandria may have been the place where the original Greek text was composed.

After opening with a reference to the philosophical controversy regarding the origin of Chaos, *On the Origin of the World* proceeds to a detailed portrayal of primeval history. The Genesis story of the creation of the world, the place of the arrogant demiurge Yaldabaoth, and the climactic creation and enlightened transgression of Adam and Eve are described from a Gnostic viewpoint. In addition, important salvific roles are played by Wisdom (Pistis Sophia and Sophia Zoe), the little blessed spirits, and Jesus the Logos and Savior. Finally, in a victorious blaze of destruction, light triumphs over darkness, and life over death.

The treatise *On the Origin of the World* is an important Gnostic work in several respects. This text provides insight into the thought, methodology, and argumentation of a Gnostic author presenting to the public at large certain information on the origin and end of the world and of man. Furthermore, the tractate also shows the freedom and skill with which such a writer could utilize various materials of a diverse character, all in the service of Gnostic proclamation. *On the Origin of the World* illustrates how the Gnostic world-view can assert itself in dialogue with other spiritual movements and in part even replace them.

The translation that follows is based on the text of Codex II. The fragmentary parallel texts from Codex XIII and from the British Library may also be consulted.

ON THE ORIGIN OF THE WORLD

II 97, 24-127, 17

Since everyone—the gods of the world [25] and men—says that nothing '
has existed prior to Chaos, I ' shall demonstrate that [they] all erred, ' '
since they do not know the [structure] ' of Chaos and its root. Here
[is the] [30] demonstration:

If it is [agreed by] **98** all men concerning [Chaos] that it is a
darkness, ' then it is something derived from a shadow. ' It was
called darkness.

But the shadow ' is something derived from a work existing [5]
from the beginning.

So it is obvious that it (the first work) existed ' before Chaos
came into being, which ' followed after the first work.

Now let us enter ' into the truth, but also into the first ' work, from
whence Chaos came; [10] and in this way the demonstration of truth
will appear. '

After the nature of the immortals ' was completed out of the boundless
one, ' then a likeness called "Sophia" flowed out of ' Pistis. ⟨She⟩
wished [15] ⟨that⟩ a work ⟨should⟩ come into being which is like ' the light
which first existed, and ' immediately her wish appeared ' as a heavenly
likeness, which possessed ' an incomprehensible greatness, [20] which is in
the middle between the immortals and those who ' came into being after
them, like what is above, which ' is a veil which separates ' men and
those belonging to the (sphere) above.

Now the aeon ' of truth has no shadow ⟨within⟩ it [25] because the
immeasurable light is ' everywhere within it. Its outside, however, is a '
shadow. It was called "darkness." From ' within it (darkness) a power
appeared (as ruler) over ' the darkness. And (as for) the shadow, the
powers [30] which came into being after them called ⟨it⟩ ' "the limitless
Chaos." And out of it ' [every] race of gods was brought forth, both '
[one and] the other and the whole place. Consequently, ' [the shadow]
too is posterior to the first **99** work [which] appeared. The abyss is
derived ' from the aforementioned Pistis.

Then ' the shadow perceived that there was one ' stronger than it.
It was jealous, and when it became self-impregnated, [5] it immediately
bore ' envy. Since that day ' the origin of envy has appeared in ' all
of the aeons and their worlds. ' But that envy was found to be a miscarriage without any [10] spirit in it. It became like the shadows ' in a
great watery substance.

Then ' the bitter wrath which came into being from the shadow ' was cast into a region of Chaos. ' Since that day ⟨a⟩ watery substance [15] has appeared, i.e. what was ⟨enclosed⟩ in it (the shadow) ' flowed forth, appearing ' in Chaos. Just as all the useless afterbirth of one who bears a little ' child falls, ' likewise the matter which came into being [20] from the shadow was cast aside. And it did not ' come out of Chaos, but matter was in Chaos, ' (existing) in a part of it. '

Now after these things happened, then Pistis came ' and appeared over the matter of [25] Chaos, which was cast off like a ' miscarriage since there was no spirit in ⟨her⟩. For ' all of that is a boundless darkness ' and water of unfathomable depth. ' And when Pistis saw what came into being [30] from her deficiency, she was disturbed. ' And the disturbance appeared as a ' fearful work. And it fled [in order to dwell] in ' the Chaos. Then she turned to it and [breathed] into ' its face in the abyss, [which is] beneath **100** all of the heavens.

Now when Pistis ' Sophia desired [to cause] the one who ' had no spirit to receive the pattern of a likeness ' and rule over the matter and over [5] all its powers, a ruler first appeared ' out of the waters, ' lion-like in appearance, androgynous, ' and having a great authority within ' himself, but not knowing [10] whence he came into being.

Then when Pistis Sophia ' saw him moving in the depth of the waters, ' she said to him, "O youth, ' pass over here," which is interpreted ' "Yaldabaoth." Since that day, the first principle [15] of the word which referred ' to the gods and angels and men has appeared. ' And the gods and angels ' and men constitute that which came into being by means of the word. ' Moreover, the ruler Yaldabaoth [20] is ignorant of the power of Pistis. ' He did not see her face, but the likeness ' which spoke with him he saw in the water. ' And from that voice he called ' himself "Yaldabaoth." But the perfect ones [25] call him "Ariael" because he ' was a lion-likeness. And after this one came ' to possess the authority of matter, ' Pistis Sophia withdrew up ' to her light.

When the ruler saw [30] his greatness—and he ' saw only himself; he did not see another one ' except water and darkness—then he thought ' that [he] alone existed. His [thought was] made complete by means of the word, **101** and it appeared as a spirit moving to and fro ' over the waters. And when that spirit ' appeared, the ruler separated the watery substance ' to one region, and the dry (substance) [5] he separated to another region. And from the (one) matter ' he created a dwelling place for himself. He called it ' "heaven." And from the (other) matter ' the ruler created a footstool. ' He called it "earth."

Afterward [10] the ruler thought within his nature, and he created an androgynous being by means of the word. He opened his mouth (and) boasted to himself. When his eyes were opened, he saw his father and he said to him "y." His [15] father called him "Yao." Again he created the second son (and) boasted to himself. He opened his eyes (and) he said to his father "e." His father called him "Eloai." Again he created [20] the third son (and) boasted to himself. He opened his eyes, (and) he said to his father "as." His father called him "Astaphaios." These are the three sons of their father.

Seven appeared in Chaos [25] as androgynous beings. They have their masculine name and their feminine name. The feminine name (of Yaldabaoth) is Pronoia Sambathas, i.e. the Hebdomad. (As for) his son called "Yao," his feminine name is "lordship." [30] Sabaoth's feminine name is "divinity." Adonaios' feminine name is "kingship." Eloaios' feminine name is "envy." Oraios' feminine name is "[riches]." Astaphaios' [feminine] name **102** is "Sophia." These [are the seven] powers of the seven heavens of Chaos. And they came into being as androgynous beings according to the deathless pattern which existed before them and in accord with [5] the will of Pistis, so that the likeness of the one who existed from the first might rule until the end.

You will find the function of these names and the masculine power in "the Archangelikē of Moses the Prophet." [10] But the feminine names are in "the First Book of Noraia."

Now since the First Father, Yaldabaoth, had great authority, he created for each of his sons by means of the word beautiful heavens as dwelling places, [15] and for each heaven great glories, seven times more exquisite (than any earthly glory), thrones and dwelling places and temples and chariots and spiritual virgins and their glories, ⟨looking⟩ up to an invisible (realm), each one [20] having these within his heaven; (and also) armies of divine, lordly, angelic, and archangelic powers, myriads without number, in order to serve.

The report concerning these you will find accurately in "the First Logos [25] of Noraia."

Now they were completed in this ⟨way⟩ up to the sixth heaven, the one belonging to Sophia. And the heaven and his earth were overturned by the troubler who was beneath all of them. And the six heavens trembled. For [30] the powers of Chaos knew ⟨not⟩ who it was who destroyed the heaven beneath them. And when Pistis knew the scorn of the troubler, she sent her breath, and she [bound him and] cast him down to Tartaros. [35]

[Since] that [day], the heaven has been consolidated along with **103** its earth by means of the Sophia of Yaldabaoth, ' the one which is beneath them all. But after ' the heavens and their powers ' and all of their government set themselves aright, the First Father [5] exalted himself, and was glorified by ' ⟨the⟩ whole army of angels. And ' all the ⟨gods⟩ and their angels gave him praise ' and glory. And he ' rejoiced in his heart, and he boasted [10] continually, saying to them, ' "I do not need anything." He said, "I ' am god and no other one exists ' except me." But when he said these things, he sinned against ' all of the immortal ⟨imperishable⟩ ones, and [15] they protected him. Moreover, when Pistis saw the ' impiety of the chief ruler, she was angry. ' Without being seen, she said, "You err, ' Samael," i.e. "the blind god." ' "An enlightened, immortal man [20] exists before you. This will appear ' within your molded bodies. He will trample upon ' you like potter's clay, ⟨which⟩ is ' trampled. And you will go with those who are yours ' down to your mother, the abyss. For in the [25] consummation of your works ' all of the deficiency which appeared ' in the truth will be dissolved. And it will cease, and it ' will be like that which did not come into being." After Pistis ' said these things, she revealed [30] the likeness of her greatness in the waters. And ' thus she withdrew up to ' her light.

But when Sabaoth, the son ' of Yaldabaoth, heard the ' voice of Pistis, he worshipped [her. He] [35] condemned the father **104** [on] account of the word of Pistis. [He] glorified her ' because she informed them of the deathless man ' and his light. Then Pistis Sophia ' stretched forth her finger, and she poured upon him [5] a light from her light for a condemnation ' of his father. Moreover when Sabaoth ' received light, he received a great authority ' against all of the powers of Chaos. ' Since that day, he has been called [10] "the lord of the powers." He hated his father, the darkness, ' and his mother, the abyss. He loathed ' his sister, the thought of the First Father, ' the one who moves to and fro over the water.

And on account ' of his light, all of the authorities of Chaos were jealous [15] of him. And when they were disturbed, ' they made a great war in the seven ' heavens. Then when Pistis Sophia ' saw the war, she sent ' seven archangels from her light to Sabaoth. [20] They snatched him away up to the seventh ' heaven. They took their stand before him as servants. ' Furthermore, she sent him three other ' archangels. She established the kingdom for him ' above every one so that he might come to be [25] above the twelve gods ' of Chaos.

But when Sabaoth received the place ' of repose because of his repentance, ' Pistis moreover gave him her daughter Zoe ' with a great authority so that she might [30] inform him about everything that exists in the ' eighth (heaven). And since he had an authority, ' he first created a dwelling place for himself. ' It is a large place which is very excellent, ' sevenfold (greater) than all those which exist [35] [in the] seven heavens.

Then in front of **105** his dwelling place he created a ' great throne on a ' four-faced chariot called ' "Cherubin." And the Cherubin has [5] eight forms for each of the four ' corners—lion forms, and ' bull forms, and human forms, ' and eagle forms—so that all ' of the forms total sixty-four forms. [10] And seven archangels stand ' before him. He is the eighth, having ' authority. All of the forms total ' seventy-two. For from this chariot ' the seventy-two gods receive a pattern; [15] and they receive a pattern so that they might rule over the seventy-two ' languages of the nations. And on that throne ' he created some other ' dragon-shaped angels called ' "Seraphin," who glorify him continually. [20]

Afterward he created an ' angelic church—thousands and myriads, without ' number, (belong to her)—being like the church which is in ' the eighth. And a first-born ' called "Israel," i.e. [25] "the man who sees god," and (also) having another ' name, "Jesus the Christ," who is like the Savior ' who is above the eighth, ' sits at his right upon ' an excellent throne. But on his left [30] the virgin of the holy spirit sits ' upon a throne praising him. ' And the seven virgins stand before her ' while thirty (other virgins) ⟨with⟩ lyres ' and harps [and] **106** trumpets in their hands glorify him. And ' all of the armies of angels glorify him ' and praise him. But he sits on a ' throne concealed by a great light-cloud. [5] And there was no one with him ' in the cloud except Sophia Pistis, ' teaching him about all those which exist in the ' eighth so that the likeness of those might be created, ' in order that the kingdom might continue [10] for him until the consummation of the heavens of Chaos ' and their powers.

Now Pistis Sophia ' separated him from the darkness. She summoned him to her right. ' But she left the First Father on her left. ' Since that day right has been called [15] "justice," but left has been called ' "injustice." Moreover, because of this they all received ' an order of the assembly of justice; ' and the injustice stands above all ⟨their⟩ creations. '

Moreover, when the First Father of Chaos [20] saw his son, Sabaoth, and that the glory ' in which he (dwells) is more exquisite than all the authorities ' of Chaos, he was jealous of him. And when he was ' angry, he begot Death from his (own) ' death. It was set up over the sixth [25] heaven. Sabaoth was snatched away from that place. ' And thus the number ⁴ of the six authorities of Chaos was completed.

Then since Death ' was androgynous, he mixed with his nature ' and begot seven androgynous sons. [30] These are the names of the males: Jealousy, Wrath, ' Weeping, Sighing, Mourning, Lamenting, ' Tearful groaning. And these are the names ' of the females: Wrath, Grief, Lust, ' Sighing, Cursing, Bitterness, Quarrelsomeness. [35] They had intercourse with one another, and each ' one begot seven so that they total **107** forty-nine androgynous demons. ' ‿

Their names and their functions you will find ' in "the Book of Solomon." '

And vis-à-vis these, Zoe, who [5] exists with Sabaoth, created seven ' androgynous good powers. ' These are the names of the males: One-who-is-not-jealous, ' the Blessed, Joy, the True One, ' One-who-is-not-envious, the Beloved, [10] the Trustworthy One. (As for) the females, however, these are their ' names: Peace, Gladness, Rejoicing, Blessedness, ' Truth, Love, Faith. And ' many good ' and guileless spirits are derived from these.

Their accomplishments [15] and their functions you will find in ' "the Schemata of the Heimarmene of the Heaven Which is ' Beneath the Twelve." '

But when the First Father saw the likeness of ' Pistis in the waters, he grieved. Especially [20] when he heard her voice, ' it was like the first voice which ' called to him out of the water, and ' when he knew that this was the one who named ' him, he groaned and was ashamed on account of his transgression. [25] And when he actually knew ' that an enlightened, immortal man ' existed before him, he was ' very much disturbed, because he had first said ' to all the gods and their angels, [30] "I am god. No other one ' exists except me." For he had been afraid lest perhaps ' they know that another one ' existed before him and condemn ' him. But he, like a fool, [35] despised the condemnation ' and acted recklessly, and said, "If **108** someone exists before me, let him appear ' so that we might see his light." And ' immediately, behold, ⟨a⟩ light came out of the ' eighth, which is above, and passed through [5] all of the heavens of the earth.

When the First Father ' saw that the light was beautiful as it shone forth, ' he was amazed and was very much ashamed. When ' the light appeared, a human likeness, ' which was very wonderful, was revealed within it; [10] and no one saw it except ' the First Father alone and

Pronoia ' who was with him. But its light appeared ' to all the powers of the heavens. Therefore ' they were all disturbed by it.

Then when ¹⁵ Pronoia saw the angel, she became enamored of him. ' But he hated her because she was in the darkness. ' Moreover she desired to embrace him, and she was not ' able. When she was unable to cease her love, ' she poured out her light upon the earth. From ²⁰ that day, that angel was called ' "Light-Adam," which is interpreted ' "the enlightened bloody (one)." And the earth ' spread over him, Holy Adamas, ' which is interpreted "the holy steel-like earth." ²⁵ At that time, ' all of the authorities began to honor the blood of the virgin. ' And the earth was purified because of ' the blood of the virgin. But especially ' the water was purified by the likeness of Pistis ³⁰ Sophia, which appeared to the ' First Father in the waters. Moreover, with ' reason they have said "through the waters." ' Since the holy water gives life to everything, **109** it purifies it too. Out of the first blood ' Eros appeared, being androgynous. ' His masculine nature is Himeros, because he is ' fire from the light. His feminine nature ⁵ which is with him is a blood-Soul, (and) is ' derived from the substance of Pronoia. He is very handsome ' in his beauty, having more loveliness than ' all the creatures of Chaos. Then when all of the gods ' and their angels saw ¹⁰ Eros, they became enamored of him. But when he appeared ' among all of them, he burned them. Just as ' many lamps are kindled from a single lamp ' and the single light (remains) there, but the lamp ' is not diminished, so also Eros ¹⁵ was scattered in all the creatures of Chaos ' and he was not diminished. Just as Eros appeared out of ' the mid-point between light and ' darkness, (and) in the midst ' of the angels and men ²⁰ the intercourse of Eros was consummated, so too ' the first sensual pleasure sprouted upon the earth. '

⟨The man followed⟩ the earth,
The woman followed ⟨the man⟩,
And marriage followed the woman,
And ' reproduction followed marriage,
And death ²⁵ followed reproduction.

After Eros, ' the grapevine sprouted up ' from the blood which was poured upon ' the earth. Therefore those who drink it (the vine) ' acquire for themselves the desire for intercourse. ³⁰ After the grapevine, a fig tree ' and a pomegranate tree sprouted up ' in the earth, together with the rest of the trees, ' according to their kind, having their ' seed in them derived from the **110** seed of the authorities and their angels. '

Then Justice created the ' beautiful Paradise. It is outside the circuit ' of the moon and the circuit of the sun [5] in the luxuriant earth, which is in the East in the midst ' of the stones. And desire is in the midst of ' the trees since they are beautiful and tall. And ' the tree of immortal life, as it ' was revealed by the will of god, is [10] in the north of Paradise in order to give ' life to the immortal saints, ' who will come out of the molded bodies of poverty ' ⟨in⟩ the consummation of the aeon. Now the color ' of the tree of life is like the sun, and [15] its branches are beautiful. Its leaves are like ' those of the cypress. Its fruit is like ' the clusters of white grapes. Its height ' rises up to heaven. And at its side is the tree ' of knowledge, possessing the power [20] of god. Its glory is like the moon ' shining forth brilliantly. And its branches are beautiful. ' Its leaves are like fig leaves. ' Its fruit is like the good, magnificent dates. ' And this is in the north side of Paradise [25] in order to raise up the souls from ' the stupor of the demons, so that they might come ' to the tree of life and eat ' its fruit and condemn the ' authorities and their angels.

The accomplishment [30] of this tree is written in "the Holy Book" (as follows): '

"You are the tree of knowledge,
which is ' in Paradise,
(from) which the first ' man ate
and which opened his mind, '
(so that) he became enamored of his co-likeness,
and condemned **111** other alien likenesses,
and loathed them." '

Now after this there sprouted up the olive tree ' which was to purify kings and ' chief priests of justice, who will [5] appear in the last days. ' Now the olive tree appeared in the light ' of the first Adam for the sake of the anointing ' which they ⟨will⟩ receive.

But the first Psyche (Soul) loved ' Eros who was with her, and poured her blood [10] upon him and upon the earth. Then from ' that blood the rose first sprouted ' upon the earth out of ' the thorn bush, for a joy in the light which ' was to appear in the bramble. After [15] this the beautiful, fragrant flowers ' sprouted up in the earth according to ' (their) kind from (the blood of) each of the virgins ' of the daughters of Pronoia. ' When they had become enamored of Eros, they poured out [20] their blood upon him and upon the earth. ' After these things, every herb sprouted up ' in the earth according to kind, and having ' the seed ⟨of⟩ the authorities and their ' angels. After these things, the authorities [25] created from the waters all species of beasts ' and reptiles and birds ' according to kind, having ' the seed ⟨of⟩ the authorities and their angels. '

But before all these (things), when he (the Light-Adam) [30] appeared on the first day, he remained ' thus upon the earth two days. He ' left the lower Pronoia in ' heaven, and began to ascend to his light. And ' immediately darkness came upon the whole world. 112 Now when Sophia, who is in the lower heaven, ' wished ⟨to⟩ receive an authority ' from Pistis, she created great luminaries ' and all the stars, and put them in the heaven in order to [5] shine upon the earth and to perfect ' chronological signs and special times and ' years and months and days ' and nights and seconds, etc. ' And thus everything above the heaven was ordered. [10]

Now when Light-Adam desired ' to enter his light, i.e. ' the eighth, he was not able because of ' the poverty which had mixed with his light. Then ' he created a great aeon for himself; and in [15] that aeon he created six aeons ' and their worlds, totaling six in number, which are sevenfold ' more exquisite than the heavens of Chaos and their worlds. ' But all these aeons and their ' worlds exist within the boundless (region), [20] which is between the eighth and Chaos, which is ' beneath it, and they are reckoned with the world which belongs ' to the poverty.

If you wish to know the ' arrangement of these, you will find it written in "the ' Seventh Cosmos of Hieralaias the Prophet." [25]

But before Light-Adam ' withdrew, the authorities saw him in Chaos. ' They laughed at the First Father because he ' lied, saying, "I am god. ' No one else exists before me." When they came to [30] him they said, "Is this not the god who ' destroyed our work?" He answered and said, ' "Yes, (but) if you desire that he not be able ' to destroy our work, come, let us ' create a man from the earth according to [35] the image of our body and according to the likeness 113 of that one, (in order) that he may serve us so that whenever ' that one sees his likeness he may become enamored of it. Then he will no longer ' ruin our work, but we shall make those who will be begotten ' from the light servants to ourselves—" [5] through all the time of this aeon. Now all of this ' which came to pass was according to the foresight of Pistis ' in order that the man might appear ' face to face with his likeness and condemn them ' from within their molded body. And their molded body [10] became a hedge for the light.

Then the authorities ' received knowledge (necessary) to create ' Man. Sophia Zoe, who is beside Sabaoth, anticipated them, ' and she laughed at ' their decision because they were blind— [15] in ignorance they created him against themselves—' and they do not know what they will ' do. Because of this she anticipated them. She created ' her man first in order to inform ' their molded body of how he would condemn [20] them. And in this way he will save them. '

Now the birth of the instructor occurred in ' this way. When Sophia cast a drop ' ⟨of⟩ light, it floated on the water. Immediately ' the man appeared, being androgynous. [25] That drop first patterned ⟨it⟩ (the water) ' as a female body. ' Afterward it patterned itself within the body ' of the likeness of the mother who appeared, ' and it fulfilled itself in twelve months. [30] An androgynous man was begotten, one whom ' the Greeks call "Hermaphrodites." ' But the Hebrews call his mother ' "Eve of Life," i.e. "the instructor ' of life." But her son is the begotten one [35] who is lord—afterward the authorities [114] called him "the beast"—in order to lead ' their molded bodies astray. The interpretation of the "beast" ' is "the instructor." For he was found to be wiser ' than all of them. Moreover Eve is the first [5] virgin, not having a husband. When she gave birth, ' she is the one who healed herself. On account of this ' it is said concerning her that she said, '

"I am the portion of my mother,
    and I am ' the mother.
I am the woman,
    and I am the virgin. [10]
I am the pregnant one.
    I am the physician.
    I am the midwife. '
My husband is the one who begot me,
    and ' I am his mother,
and he is my father ' and my lord.
He is my potency.
That which he desires ' he speaks with reason.
I am (still) in a nascent state,
    but [15] I have borne a lordly man."

Now these things ' were revealed by the will of Sabaoth ' and his Christ to the souls who will come to the molded bodies ' ⟨of⟩ the authorities; and concerning these, the holy voice ' said, "Multiply and flourish to rule [20] over all the creatures." And these are the ones who ' are taken captive ' by the First Father according to lot, and thus ' they were shut up in the prisons of the molded bodies ' ⟨until⟩ the consummation of the aeon. And then at [25] that time the First Father ' gave those who were with him a (false) intention concerning the man. ' Then each one of them cast ' his seed on the midst of the navel of the ' earth. Since that day, the seven [30] rulers have formed the man: his body ' is like their body, his likeness is ' like the man who appeared to them. ' His molded body came into being according to a portion of ' each one (of them). Their chief created [35] his head and the marrow. Afterward ' he appeared like the one who was before him. He became **115** a living man, and he who is the father was called ' "Adam," according to ' the name of the one who was before him.

Now after ' Adam was completed, he left him in a vessel since he had [5] taken form like the miscarriages, having no spirit in him. ' Because of this deed, when the chief ruler ' remembered the word of Pistis, he was afraid ' lest perhaps the man come into his ' molded body and rule over it. Because of this, he [10] left his molded body forty days without ' soul. And he withdrew and left him.

But on the ' fortieth day Sophia Zoe sent ' her breath into Adam, who was without ' soul. He began to move upon the earth. [15] And he was not able to rise. Now when the seven ' rulers came and saw him, they were ' very much disturbed. They walked up to ' him and seized him, and he (Yaldabaoth) said to ' the breath which was in him, "Who are you? And [20] from whence have you come hither?" He answered ' and said, "I came through the power ' of the (light)-man because of the destruction of your work." ' ⟨...⟩ When they heard, they glorified him because he ' gave them rest from the fear and concern in which [25] they were. Then they called that day ' "the rest," because they rested themselves ' from their troubles. And when they saw that Adam ' was not able to rise, they rejoiced. They took him ' and left him in Paradise, and withdrew [30] up to their heavens. '

After the day of rest, Sophia ' sent Zoe, her daughter, who is called ' "Eve (of Life)," as an instructor to ' raise up Adam, in whom there was no soul, [35] so that those whom he would beget might become ' vessels of the light. [When] **116** Eve saw her co-likeness cast down, she pitied ' him, and she said, "Adam, live! ' Rise up on the earth!" Immediately her word ' became a deed. For when Adam [5] rose up, immediately he opened his eyes. ' When he saw her, he said, "You will be called ' 'the mother of the living' because you are the one who ' gave me life."

Then the authorities were informed ' that their molded body was alive, and had arisen. They [10] were very much disturbed. They sent seven archangels ' to see what had happened. They came ' to Adam. When they saw Eve speaking with ' him, they said to one another, "What is this (female) light-being? ' For truly she is like the likeness which [15]

appeared to us in the light. Now come, ' let us seize her and let us cast '
our seed on her, so that when she is polluted ' she will not be able to
ascend to her light, ' but those whom she will beget will serve [20] us. But
let us not tell Adam that ⟨she⟩ is not derived from ' us, but let us bring
a stupor ' upon him, and let us teach him in his ' sleep as though she
came into being from ' his rib so that the woman will serve [25] and he
will rule over her."

Then (the Life)-Eve, since she ' existed as a power, laughed at their
(false) intention. ' She darkened their eyes and left ' her likeness there
stealthily beside Adam. She entered ' the tree of knowledge, and remained
there. [30] But they (tried to) follow her. She revealed ' to them that she
had entered the tree and become ' tree. And when ⟨the blind ones⟩ fell
into a great ' fear, they ran away.

Afterward, ' when they sobered up from the stupor, they came [35] to
[Adam. And] when they saw the likeness of that (woman) with him, **117**
they were troubled, thinking that this ' was the true Eve. And they acted
recklessly, and came ' to her and seized her and cast ' their seed upon
her. They did it [5] with a lot of tricks, not only defiling her ' naturally but
abominably, ' defiling the seal of her first voice, ' which (before) spoke
with them, saying, "What is it that exists ' before you?"—⟨But it is
impossible⟩ that they might defile those who say that [10] they are begotten
in the consummation by the true man ' by means of the word. ' And they
were deceived, not knowing ' that they had defiled their own body. It
was the likeness ' which the authorities [15] and their angels defiled in
every form.

She conceived Abel first ' from the prime ruler; and she bore the
rest ' of the sons from the seven ' authorities and their angels. Now all
this ' came to pass according to the foresight of the [20] First Father, so
that the first mother might ' beget within herself every mixed seed '
which is joined together with the Fate ' of the world and its schemata
and (Fate's) ' justice. A dispensation came into being [25] because of Eve
so that the molded body ⟨of⟩ the authorities ' might become a hedge
for the light. ' Then it will condemn them through their ' molded bodies.

Moreover the first Adam of the light ' is spiritual. He appeared [30] on
the first day. The second ' Adam is soul-endowed. He appeared ' on the
[sixth] day, and is called ' "⟨Herm⟩aphrodite⟨s⟩." The third ' Adam is
earthy, i.e. [35] "man of law," who appeared on ' the eighth day [after "the]
118 rest of poverty," which is called ' "Sunday." Now the progeny
of the ' earthy Adam multiplied and completed (the earth). ' They produced by themselves every knowledge of [5] the soul-endowed Adam.

But ⟨as for⟩ the All, he was in ' ignorance (of it). Afterwards, let me continue, ' when the rulers saw him and ' the (woman) who was with him, erring in ignorance ' like the beasts, they rejoiced greatly. [10] When they knew that the deathless man would ⟨not only⟩ ' pass by them, but that they would also fear ' the (woman) who became a tree, they were troubled ' and said, "Is perhaps this one, ' who blinded us [15] and taught us about this defiled (woman) who is like him, the true man, ' in order that we might be conquered (by her)?"

Then the seven took ' counsel. They came to Adam ' and Eve timidly. They said to him, ' "Every tree which is in Paradise, [20] whose fruit may be eaten, was created for you. But beware! ' Don't eat from the tree ' of knowledge. If you do eat, you will ' die." After they gave them a great fright, ' they withdrew up to their authorities.

Then [25] the one who is wiser than all of them, ' this one who was called "the beast," came. ' And when he saw the likeness of their mother ' Eve, he said to her, "What is it that god ' said to you? 'Don't eat from the tree [30] of knowledge'?" She said, "He not only said ' 'Don't eat from it,' but 'Don't touch it lest [you] die.'" He said ' to her, "Don't be afraid! You certainly shall ' [not die]. For [he knows] that when you eat [119] from it your mind will be sobered and ' you will become like god, ' knowing the distinctions which exist between ' evil and good men. For he [5] said this to you, lest you ' eat from it, since he is jealous."

Now Eve believed ' the words of the instructor. She looked at ' the tree. And she saw that it was beautiful and ' magnificent, and she desired it. She took some of its [10] fruit and ate, and she gave to her ' husband also, and he ate too. Then their mind ' opened. For when they ate, the light ' of knowledge shone for them. When they put ' on shame, they knew that they were naked [15] with regard to knowledge. When they sobered up, they saw ' that they were naked, and they became enamored of one another. When ' they saw their makers, they loathed them since they were ' beastly forms. They understood ' very much.

Then when the rulers knew that [20] they had transgressed their commandment, they came in an earthquake ' with a great threat into ' Paradise to Adam and Eve in order to see ' the result of the help. Then ' Adam and Eve were very much disturbed. [25] They hid under the trees which are in Paradise. ' Then because the rulers did not know where they were, ' they said, "Adam, where are you?" He said, "I am ' here. But because of fear of you I hid ' after I became ashamed." But they said to him, in [30] ignorance, "Who is the one who spoke to you of ' the shame which you put on, unless ' you ate from the tree?" He said, '

"The woman whom you gave me, she is the one who ' gave to me, and I ate." Then they [said to that (woman)], **120** "What is this you have done?" She answered and said, ' "The instructor is the one who incited me, and I ' ate." Then the rulers came to the instructor. ' Their eyes were blinded by him [5] (so that) they were not able to do anything to him. They (merely) cursed him ' since they were impotent. Afterward they came to the woman, ' and they cursed her and her sons. After ' the woman they cursed Adam, and (they cursed) the earth and the fruit because of him. ' And everything which they created [10] they cursed. There is no blessing from ' them. It is impossible that good be produced from ' evil. Since that day the authorities ' knew that truly one who is strong is ' before them. They would not have known except that [15] their command was not kept. They brought a great ' envy into the world only because of ' the deathless man.

Now when the rulers saw ' that their Adam had acquired a different knowledge, they ' desired to test him. They gathered [20] all of the domestic animals and wild beasts ' of the earth and the birds of the heaven. They brought them to Adam ' to see what he would call them. ' When he saw them, he named their ' creatures. They were troubled because Adam had sobered [25] from every ⟨ignorance⟩. They gathered together and ' took counsel, and they said, "Behold, Adam ' has become like one of us, so that he ' understands the distinction of light and darkness. ' Now lest perhaps he is deceived in the manner of [30] the tree of knowledge, and he also comes ' to the tree of life and eats from it ' and becomes immortal and rules and condemns ' us and regards [us] and all our glory as folly—' afterward he will pass judgment on [35] [us and the] world—come, let us cast him **121** out of Paradise down upon the earth, ' the place from whence he was taken, so that he will no longer ' be able to know anything more ' about us." And thus they cast Adam and his wife [5] out of Paradise. And this ' which they had done did not satisfy them; rather, they were (still) afraid. ' They came to the tree of life and they set ' great terrors around it, fiery living beings ' called "Cherubin"; and they left [10] a flaming sword in the midst, turning ' continually with a great terror, so that ' no one from among earthly men might ever enter ' that place.

After these things, when ' the rulers had become jealous of Adam, they desired to diminish their [15] lifetimes, (but) they were unable because of Fate, ' which was established since the beginning. ' For their lifetimes were determined: for each one (of the men) ' one thousand years according to the circuit of the luminaries. ' But because the rulers were not able to [20] do this, each one of those who do ' evil diminished ⟨their life-span⟩ for ten years, ' and all of this time amounts to nine hundred and ' thirty years, and these are in grief and ' weakness and in evil distractions. [25] And from that day ' the course of life thus proceeded downward until the consummation ' of the aeon.

Then when Sophia Zoe ' saw that the rulers of darkness ' cursed her co-likeness, she was angry. [30] And when she came out of the first heaven with ' every power, she chased the rulers ' from [their] heavens, and she cast them down ' to the sinful world so that they ' might become there like [35] the evil demons upon the earth. [She sent the bird] [122] which was in Paradise so that, until the consummation of the aeon, it might spend the thousand years ' in their (the rulers') world, a vital living being ' called "Phoenix," ' ⟨which⟩ kills itself and reanimates itself for a witness [5] to their judgment because they dealt unjustly with Adam and his ' race.

There are three ' men and his descendants ⟨in⟩ the world until the consummation of the aeon: ' ⟨the⟩ spiritual ' and the vital and the material. This is like [10] the three ⟨shapes⟩ of Phoenixes ⟨of⟩ Paradise: the first ' [is] immortal, the second attains one thousand ' years, as for the third it is written in "the Holy Book" ' that "he is consumed." Likewise ' three baptisms exist: the first is [15] spiritual, the second is a fire, the third ' is water.

Just as ⟨the⟩ Phoenix ' appears as a witness for the angels, ' so too the crocodiles in Egypt ' have become a witness to those who come down [20] for the baptism of a true man. ' The two bulls in Egypt, in so far as they possess ' the sun and the moon as a mystery, exist ' for a witness to Sabaoth because ⟨he exists⟩ above ' them. Sophia (of Astaphaios) received the universe, since [25] the day when she created the sun and the moon and ' sealed her heaven until ⟨the consummation of⟩ the aeon. ' Now the worm which is brought forth from ⟨the⟩ Phoenix ' is also a man. It is written of it, ' "The just will sprout up like the Phoenix." And [30] ⟨the⟩ Phoenix appears first ' alive, and dies, and again rises up, ' being a sign of the one who appeared ' in the consummation of [the aeon]. These ' great signs appeared [35] only in Egypt, not in other lands, signifying [123] that it is like the Paradise of god. '

Again let us come to the rulers ' of whom we spoke, so that we might present ' their proof. For when the seven rulers [5] were cast out of their heavens down ' upon the earth, they created for themselves angels, ' i.e. many demons, in order to serve ' them. But these (demons) taught men many errors ' with magic and potions and idolatry, [10] and shedding

of blood, and altars, and ' temples, and sacrifices, and libations to all
the demons ' of the earth, having as their co-worker ' Fate, who came
into being according to ' the agreement by the gods of injustice [15] and
justice. And thus when the world ' came to be in distraction, it wandered
astray ' throughout all time. For all the men ' who are on the earth
served the demons from the ' foundation until the consummation (of the
aeon)—the angels [20] (served) justice and the men (served) injustice. '
Thus the world came to be in a ' distraction and an ignorance and a
stupor. ' They all erred until the appearance ' of the true man.

Enough for you up [25] to here. And next we will come to our world '
so that we might complete (the discussion of) its structure ' and its
government precisely. ' Then he will appear just as ' the belief was
found in the hidden things, which appear [30] from the foundation to
the consummation ' of the aeon.

Now I will come to the praiseworthy chapters ' [about] the immortal
man. ' Concerning all [of] his own I will say why ' the forms are here.
After a multitude [35] of men came into being through [this one] **124** who
was molded from matter, ' and as soon as the world was filled, the
rulers ruled ' over it, that is to say, they possessed it ' in ignorance.
What is the cause? [5] It is this. Since the immortal Father knows ' that a
deficiency came into being in the aeons ' and their worlds out of the
truth, therefore when he desired ' to bring to naught the rulers of
destruction by means of their ' molded bodies, he sent your likenesses, [10]
i.e. the blessed little guileless spirits, down to the world of destruction. '
They are not strangers to ' knowledge. For all the knowledge is in an
angel ' who appears before them. He stands ' in front of the Father
and is not powerless to give them knowledge. [15] {For all knowledge
is in an angel ' who appears before them. He stands ' in front of
the Father and is not powerless to give them knowledge.} ' Immediately, whenever they appear in the world ' of destruction, they will first
reveal [20] the pattern of indestructibility for a condemnation ' of the rulers
and their powers. Moreover when the blessed ones ' appeared in the molded bodies ⟨of⟩ the authorities, ' they were jealous of them. And because
of the jealousy the authorities ' mixed their seed with them in order to [25]
defile them, and they were not able. Moreover when the blessed ones ' appeared in their light, ' they appeared distinctively; and each one ' of them
from their land revealed ' their knowledge of the church which appeared [30]
in the molded bodies of destruction. They found ' it to have every seed
because of the seed ' ⟨of⟩ the authorities which was mixed [with it].
Then ' the Savior created a [deliverance] from ' among all of them.

And the spirits of these [35] [appeared, being] elect and blessed **125** (but) varying in election, and many ' others are kingless and more exquisite ' than any one who was before them. Consequently four ' races exist. There are three which belong to the [5] kings of the eighth heaven. But the fourth ' race is kingless and perfect, one that is ' above all of them. For these will enter ' into the holy place of their father ' and they will rest themselves in a repose, [10] and eternal, ineffable glory, ' and a ceaseless joy. Now they ' are (already) kings as immortal within the mortal (realm). They ' will pass judgment on the gods of Chaos and ' their powers.

Moreover the Logos who is more exalted [15] than any one was sent for this work only, ' so that he might announce concerning what is unknown. ' He said, "There is nothing hidden which will not appear, ' and what was unknown ' will be known" (Matthew 10:26). Now these were sent [20] so that they might reveal that which is hidden and ' (expose) the seven authorities of Chaos and their ' impiety. And thus they were condemned ' to be killed. Moreover, when all the perfect ones ' appeared in the molded bodies [25] of the rulers, and when they revealed ' the incomparable truth, ' they put to shame every wisdom of the gods, ' and their Fate was discovered ' to be condemnable, their power [30] dried up, their dominion was destroyed, ' and their foresight [and] their glories became ' [empty].

Before the consummation ' [of the aeon], the whole place will be shaken ' by a great thunder. Then the rulers [35] will lament, [crying out on account of their] **126** death. The angels will mourn for their men, ' and the demons will weep for their times, ' and their men will mourn and cry ' out on account of their death. Then the aeon [5] will begin to ⟨... and⟩ they will be disturbed. Its kings will ' be drunk from the flaming sword and they will ' make war against one another, so that ' the earth will be drunk from the blood which is poured ' out. And the seas will be troubled by [10] that war. Then the sun will darken ' and the moon will lose its light. ' The stars of the heaven will disregard their course ' and a great thunder will come out ' of a great power that is [15] above all the powers of Chaos, the place ' where the firmament of woman is situated. When ' she has created the first work, she will ' take off her wise flame of insight. ' She will put on a senseless wrath. [20] Then she will drive out the gods ' of Chaos whom she had created together with the First Father. ' She will cast them down to the abyss. ' They will be wiped out by their (own) injustice. ' For they will become like the mountains which blaze out fire, [25] and they will gnaw at one another until they are destroyed ' by their First Father. ' When he destroys them, he will turn against ' himself and destroy himself until he ceases (to be). And ' their heavens will fall upon one another [30] and their powers will burn. Their ' aeons will also be overthrown. And his (the First Father's) heaven will ' fall and it will split in two. Likewise (the place of) his joy, [however], will ' fall down to the earth, [and the earth will not] ' be able to support them. They will fall [down] to the abyss [35] and the [abyss] will be overthrown.

The light will ' [cover the] darkness, and it will wipe it out. It will become like **127** one which had not come into being. And the work which ' the darkness followed will be dissolved. And ' the deficiency will be plucked out at its root (and thrown) down to ' the darkness. And the light will withdraw up [5] to its root. And the glory of the unbegotten ' will appear, and it will fill ' all of the aeons, when the prophetic utterance and ' the report of those who are kings are revealed and ' are fulfilled by those who are called [10] perfect. Those who were not perfected ' in the unbegotten Father will receive their glories ' in their aeons and in the kingdoms of ' immortals. But they will not ever enter ' the kingless realm.

For it is necessary that every one [15] enter the place from whence he came. ' For each one by his deed and his ' knowledge will reveal his nature.

THE EXEGESIS ON THE SOUL (II, 6)

Introduced and translated by

WILLIAM C. ROBINSON, JR.

The *Exegesis on the Soul* ("Expository Treatise on the Soul") is an anonymous treatise in the form of an exhortation to otherworldliness. This tractate must have been written in Greek, perhaps as early as 200 C.E., though only the present Coptic translation survives. The treatise contains a mythological narrative describing the fall and restoration of the soul, and concludes with a hortatory section encouraging the readers to repent. In order to support the account of the soul's fate, various quotations are included as proof-texts; these are taken particularly from the Old Testament, the New Testament, and Homer's *Odyssey*. The quotations are not integral to the narrative, but rather are catchword insertions, interruptions which in most instances have not modified their present contexts. Thus, if the quotations are removed, the narrative remains relatively intact.

The fall and deliverance of the soul are portrayed in a dramatic and graphic manner. The soul is a female (the Greek word for soul, psychē, is feminine). Originally she is a virgin, androgynous in form, living in the presence of the heavenly Father. When she falls into a body, however, she is defiled: after abandoning her Father's house and her virginity, she falls into sexuality and prostitution, and is abused by the wanton adulterers of this carnal world. Desolate and repentant, she prays to her Father for restoration, and he hears her prayer. She is returned to her former condition, and restored to androgynous union with her brother. This union is achieved through spiritual marriage: the bridegroom comes down to the bridal chamber, and the soul and her bridegroom "become a single life," inseparable from each other. Thus the ascent of the soul to the Father is accomplished, and the soul is again at home in heaven.

The *Exegesis on the Soul* shows clear affinities with some Gnostic accounts of the fate of the soul, particularly with regard to androgyny and the restoration to asexual union. The narrative itself contains nothing distinctively Jewish or Christian, but resembles Pythagorean and Platonic accounts of the exile and return of the soul. However, a precise historical setting either for the tractate or for the narrative within it cannot at present be fixed.

THE EXEGESIS ON THE SOUL

II 127, 18-137, 27

The Expository Treatise on the Soul '

Wise men of old gave [20] the soul a feminine name. ' Indeed she is female in her nature as well. ' She even has her womb.

As long as ' she was alone with the Father, ' she was virgin and in form androgynous. [25] But when she fell ' down into a body and came to this life, then she ' fell into the hands of many robbers. And ' the wanton creatures passed her from one to another ' and [. . .] her. Some made use of [30] her [by force], while others did so by seducing ' her with a gift. In short, ' they defiled her, and she [. . .] **128** virginity.

And in her body she prostituted herself ' and gave herself to one and all, ' considering each one she was about to embrace ' to be her husband. When she had given herself [5] to wanton, unfaithful adulterers, ' so that they might make use of her, then she sighed ' deeply and repented. But even when she ' turns her face from those adulterers, she runs ' to others and they compel her [10] to live with them and render service to them ' upon their bed, as if they were her masters. ' Out of shame she no longer dares ' to leave them, whereas they deceive ' her for a long time, pretending to be faithful, true husbands, [15] as if they greatly respected ' her. And after all this ' they abandon her and go.

She then ' becomes a poor desolate widow, ' without help; not even a measure [20] of food was left her from the time of her affliction. ' For from them she gained nothing except ' the defilements they gave her while they had ' sexual intercourse with her. And her offspring ' by the adulterers are dumb, [25] blind, and sickly. ' They are feeble-minded.

But when ' the Father who is above visits her ' and looks down upon her and sees her ' sighing—with her sufferings and disgrace—[30] and repenting of the prostitution ' in which she engaged, and when she begins to call ' upon [his name] ' so that he might help her, [. . .] all ' her heart, saying, "Save [35] me, my Father, for behold I will render an account ' [to thee, for I] abandoned my house and **129** fled from my maiden's quarters. ' Restore me to thyself again." When he sees her ' in such a state, then he will count ' her worthy of his mercy upon her, for many are the afflictions [5] that have come upon her because she abandoned her house.

Now concerning ' the prostitution of the soul the Holy Spirit prophesies in ' many places. For he said ' in the prophet Jeremiah (3:1-4),

"If ' the husband divorces his wife and she [10] goes and takes another man, can she return to him ' after that? Has not that woman utterly ' defiled herself? 'And you (sing.) ' prostituted yourself to many shepherds and you returned ' to me!' said the Lord. 'Take an honest [15] look and see where you ' prostituted yourself. Were you not sitting in the ' streets defiling the land with your acts of prostitution ' and your vices? And you took many shepherds for a ' stumbling block for yourself. You became shameless [20] with everyone. You did not call on me as ' kinsman or as father or author of your ' virginity.'"

Again it is written in the prophet Hosea (2:2-7), '

"Come, go to law with ' your (pl.) mother, for she is not to be a wife to me [25] nor I a husband to her. ' I shall remove her prostitution from my presence, ' and I shall remove her adultery from ' between her breasts. I shall make her naked ' as on the day she was born, and [30] I [shall] make her desolate like a land without ' [water], and I shall make her [longingly] childless. ' [I] shall show her children no pity, for ' they are children of prostitution, since their mother ' prostituted herself and [put her children to shame]. **130** For she said, 'I shall prostitute myself to ' my lovers. It was they who gave me my ' bread and my water and my garments and my ' clothes and my wine and my oil and everything [5] I needed.' Therefore behold ' I shall shut them up so that she shall not be able ' to run after her adulterers. And when she ' seeks them and does not find them, she will say, ' 'I shall return to my former husband, for [10] in those days I was better off than now.'" '

Again he said in Ezekiel (16:23-26), '

"It came to pass after much depravity, said ' the Lord, you built yourself a brothel ' and you made yourself a beautiful place [15] in the streets. And you built yourself ' brothels on every lane, and you wasted ' your beauty, and you spread your legs ' in every alley, and you multiplied your acts of prostitution. ' You prostituted yourself to the sons of Egypt, [20] those who are your neighbors, men great of flesh."

But what ' does "the sons of Egypt, men great of flesh" mean ' if not the domain of the flesh and the perceptible realm ' and the affairs of the earth, by which the soul ' has become defiled here, receiving bread from [25] them, as well as wine, oil, clothing, ' and the other external nonsense ' surrounding the body—the things she thinks ' she needs.

But as to this prostitution the ' apostles of the Savior commanded (cf. Acts 15:20, 29; 21:25; 1 Thessalonians 4:3; 1 Corinthians 6:18; 2 Corinthians 7:1), [30]

"Guard yourselves against it, purify yourselves from it," ' speaking not just of the prostitution of the ' body but especially of that of the soul. ' For this [reason] the apostles [write to the churches] of ' God, that such [prostitution] might not [35] occur among [us].

Yet the greatest ' [struggle] has to do with the prostitution **131** of the soul. From it arises the prostitution ' of the body as well. Therefore Paul, ' writing to the Corinthians (1 Corinthians 5:9), said,

"I wrote ' you in the letter, 'Do not associate with prostitutes,' [5] not at all (meaning) the prostitutes of this world ' or the greedy or the thieves or the ' idolators, since then you would have to ' go out from the world."

—here he is speaking ' spiritually—

"For our struggle is [10] not against flesh and blood"—as he ' said (Ephesians 6:12)—"but against the world rulers ' of this darkness and the spirits of ' wickedness."

As long as the soul ' keeps running about everywhere copulating with whomever [15] she meets and defiling herself, she exists suffering ' her just deserts. But when ' she perceives the straits she is in ' and weeps before the Father and repents, ' then the Father will have mercy on her and he will make [20] her womb turn from the external domain ' and will turn it again inward, so that the soul will regain her ' proper character. For it is not so with a woman. ' For the womb of the body is ' inside the body like the other internal organs, but the womb [25] of the soul is around the outside ' like the male genitalia, which are ' external.

So when the womb of the soul, ' by the will of the Father, turns itself inward, ' it is baptized and is immediately [30] cleansed of the external pollution ' which was pressed upon it, just as ' [garments, when] dirty, are put into ' the [water and] turned about until their ' dirt is removed and they become clean. And so the cleansing [35] of the soul is to regain the [newness] **132** of her former nature and to turn herself back again. ' That is her baptism.

Then she will ' begin to rage at herself like a woman ' in labor, [5] who writhes and rages in the hour of delivery. ' But since she is female, by herself she is powerless to beget ' a child. From heaven the Father sent her ' her man, who is her brother, ' the first-born. Then the bridegroom came [10] down to the bride. She gave up ' her former prostitution and cleansed herself of the pollutions ' of the adulterers, and she was renewed so as to be a bride. ' She cleansed herself in the bridal chamber; she filled it with perfume; ' she sat in it waiting [15] for the true bridegroom. No longer does she ' run about the market place, copulating with whomever she ' desires, but she continued to wait for him—' (saying) "When will he come?"—and to fear him, ' for she did not know what he looked like: [20] she no longer remembers since the time she fell ' from her Father's house. But by the will ' of the Father ⟨...⟩. And she dreamed of him like ' a woman in love with a man.

But then ' the bridegroom, according to the Father's will, [25] came down to her into the bridal chamber, ' which was prepared. And he decorated the bridal chamber. '

For since that marriage is ' not like the carnal marriage, those who are to have intercourse ' with one another will be satisfied with [30] that intercourse. And as if it were a burden ' they leave behind them the annoyance of physical ' desire and they do not [separate from] ' each other, but this marriage [...], ' but [once] they unite [35] [with one another], they become a single life. **133** Wherefore the prophet said (Genesis 2:24) ' concerning the first man and the first woman, '

"They will become a single flesh." '

For they were originally joined to one another when they were with the Father [5] before the woman led astray the man, who ' is her brother. This marriage ' has brought them back together again and the ' soul has been joined to her true love, her ' real master, as it is written (cf. Genesis 3:16; 1 Corinthians 11:1; Ephesians 5:23), [10]

"For the master of the woman is her husband."

Then gradually she recognized him, ' and she rejoiced once more, weeping ' before him as she remembered the ' disgrace of her former widowhood. ' And she adorned herself still more so that [15] he might be pleased to stay with her.

And the ' prophet said in the Psalms (45:10-11),

"Hear, ' my daughter, and see and incline your ear ' and forget your people and your father's house, ' for the king has desired your beauty, [20] for he is your lord."

For he requires her ' to turn her face from her ' people and the multitude of her adulterers, ' in whose midst she once was, to devote herself ' only to her king, her real [25] lord, and to forget the house of the ' earthly father, with whom things went ' badly for her, but to remember her Father ' who is in the heavens. Thus also it was said ' (Genesis 12:1) to Abraham,

"Come out from your [30] country and your kinsfolk and from ' your father's house."

Thus when the soul [had adorned] ' herself again in her beauty ' [...] enjoyed her beloved, ' and [he also] loved her. And [35] when she had intercourse with him, she got **134** from him the seed that is the life-giving ' Spirit, so that by him she bears good children ' and rears them. ' For this is the great, perfect marvel [5] of birth. And so this marriage is made perfect ' by the will of the Father.

Now it is fitting that the soul ' regenerate herself and become again as ' she formerly was. The soul then moves of her own accord. ' And she received the divine nature from the Father [10] for her rejuvenation, so that she might be restored to ' the place where originally she had been. This is ' the resurrection that is from the dead. ' This is the ransom from captivity. ' This is the upward journey of ascent to heaven. This [15] is the way of ascent to the Father. Therefore ' the prophet said (Psalm 103:1-5), '

"Praise the Lord, O my soul, and, all that is ' within me, (praise) his holy name. My ' soul, praise God, who forgave [20] all your sins, who healed ' all your sicknesses, who ransomed ' your life from death, who crowned ' you with mercy, who satisfies your longing ' with good things. Your youth will [25] be renewed like an eagle's."

Then when she becomes young ' again she will ascend, praising the Father ' and her brother, by whom she was rescued. ' Thus it is by being born again that the soul will ' be saved. And this [30] is due not to rote phrases ' or to professional skills or to ' book learning. Rather it [is] the grace of the [...], ' it is] the gift of the [...]. ' For such is this heavenly thing. [35] Therefore the Savior cries out (John 6:44), **135**

"No one can come to me unless ' my Father draws him and brings him to me; ' and I myself will raise him up on the last ' day."

It is therefore fitting to pray to the Father and to call [5] on him with all our soul—not externally with the lips ' but with the spirit, ' which is inward, which came forth from the ' depth—sighing; repenting for ' the life we lived; confessing [10] our sins; perceiving the empty deception ' we were in, and the empty zeal; ' weeping over how we were ' in darkness and in the wave; mourning for ourselves, ' that he might have pity on us; hating [15] ourselves for how we are now. Again ' the Savior said (cf. Matthew 5:4, 6; Luke 6:21),

"Blessed ' are those who mourn, for it is they who will be pitied; ' blessed, those who are hungry, for ' it is they who will be filled."

Again he said (cf. Luke 14:26),

"If [20] one does not hate his soul he cannot follow ' me."

For the beginning of salvation is ' repentance. Therefore (cf. Acts 13:24),

"Before ' Christ's appearance came John, ' preaching the baptism of repentance." [25]

And repentance takes place in distress ' and grief. But the Father is good and loves ' humanity, and he hears the ' soul that calls upon him and ' sends it the light of salvation. Therefore [30] he said through the Spirit to the ' prophet (cf. 1 Clement 8:3),

"Say to the children of my people, ' '[If your] sins extend ' [from earth to] heaven, and if they become ' [red] like scarlet and [35] blacker than [sackcloth and if] **136** you return to me with all your ' soul and say to me, ' "My Father," I will heed you as a ' holy people.'"

Again another place (Isaiah 30:15),

"Thus says [5] the Lord, the Holy One of ' Israel: 'If you (sing.) return and sigh, ' then you will be saved and will know where you were ' when you trusted in what is empty.'"

Again ' he said in another place (Isaiah 30:19-20),

"Jerusalem wept [10] much, saying, 'Have pity on me.' He will have pity on the sound ' of your (sing.) weeping. And when he saw he heeded you. ' And the Lord will give you (pl.) bread of ' affliction and water of oppression. ' From now on those who deceive will not approach you (sing.) again. [15] Your eyes will see those who are deceiving ' you."

Therefore it is fitting to pray to ' God night and day, spreading out ' our hands towards him as do people sailing in the middle ' of the sea: they pray to God [20] with all their heart without hypocrisy. ' For those who pray ' hypocritically deceive only themselves. ' Indeed it is in order that he might know who is worthy of salvation ' that God examines the inward parts and [25] searches the bottom of the heart. For no ' one is worthy of salvation who still loves ' the place of deception. Therefore it is written ' in the poet (Homer, *Odyssey* I, 48-59),

"Odysseus sat ' on the island weeping and grieving and turning [30] his face from the words of Calypso ' and from her tricks, longing to see ' his village and smoke coming ' forth from it. And had he not [received] ' help from heaven, [he would] not [have been able to] return [35] to his village."

Again [Helen] ⟨...⟩ saying (*Odyssey* IV, 260-261), '

"[My heart] turned itself from me. **137** It is to my house that I want to return."

For she sighed, ' saying (*Odyssey* IV, 261-264),

"It is Aphrodite who ' deceived me and brought me out of my village. My only daughter ' I left behind me, and my [5] good, understanding, handsome husband."

For when ' the soul leaves her ' perfect husband because of the

treachery of Aphrodite, ' who exists here in the act of begetting, then '
she will suffer harm. But if she sighs [10] and repents, she will be restored
to her ' house.

Certainly Israel would not have been visited ' in the first place, to be
brought out of the land of Egypt, ' out of the house of bondage, if it
had not sighed ' to God and wept for the oppression [15] of its labors.
Again it is written in the Psalms (6:6-9), '

> "I was greatly troubled in my groaning. I will ' bathe my bed and
> my cover each ' night with my tears. I have become old in the
> midst of all my enemies. ' Depart from me, all [20] you who work at
> lawlessness, for behold the ' Lord has heard the cry of my weeping
> and ' the Lord has heard my prayer."

If ' we repent, truly God will ' heed us, he who is long-suffering and
abundantly [25] merciful, to whom is the glory for ' ever and ever. Amen. '

The Expository Treatise on the Soul

THE BOOK OF THOMAS THE CONTENDER (II, 7)

Introduced and translated by

JOHN D. TURNER

The *Book of Thomas the Contender* is a dialogue between the resurrected Jesus and his brother Judas Thomas, and is allegedly recorded by a certain Mathaias (the apostle Matthew?) as he heard them speaking together. The literary genre of the tractate—a genre also represented in several other tractates from the Nag Hammadi library—is the Gnostic revelation dialogue, typically occurring between the resurrected Savior and a trusted apostle or apostles during the time between the Savior's resurrection and ascension. Here the trusted individual with whom the resurrected Jesus converses is none other than Thomas, the Savior's twin who was thought to have direct insight into the nature of the Savior and his teaching. By "knowing himself" Thomas could also know the "depth of the All" from which the Savior came and to which he was going to return; and thus Thomas could become a missionary proclaiming the true (here, the ascetic and somewhat Gnostic) teaching of the exalted Jesus. Hence, like the *Gospel of Thomas* (II, 2) and the *Acts of Thomas*, the *Book of Thomas the Contender* presents traditions about the apostle Thomas such as were prevalent within the ascetic Christianity of Syrian Edessa; the *Book of Thomas the Contender* was probably composed in Syria during the first half of the third century.

Following the introductory lines of the tractate, the text of the *Book of Thomas the Contender* can be divided into two major sections. The first section (138, 4-142, 26) consists of a revelation dialogue between Jesus and Thomas, while the second section (142, 26-145, 16) is a monologue, a homily delivered by the Savior. At the end of the tractate are added the title and a final colophon written by the scribe.

Consistently and intensely ascetic in doctrine, the tractate warns against fire—the fire of sexual passions and the fire of hellish punishment. The tractate stresses the true and divine light of the Savior, who as the emissary of the light descends to illumine the eyes and the minds of those living in a darkened world.

THE BOOK OF THOMAS THE CONTENDER

II 138, 1-145, 19
145, 20-23

The secret words that the Savior spoke to ' Judas Thomas which I, even I Mathaias, ' wrote down—I was walking, listening to them speak with ' one another.

The Savior said, "Brother Thomas, while [5] you have time in the world, listen to me ' and I will reveal to you the things you have pondered ' in your mind.

"Now since it has been said that you are my ' twin and true companion, examine yourself that you may understand ' who you are, in what way you exist, and [10] how you will come to be. Since you are called my brother, ' it is not fitting that you be ignorant ' of yourself. And I know that you have understood, ' because you had already understood that I am the knowledge of the truth. ' So while you accompany me, although you are uncomprehending, [15] you have (in fact) already come to know, and you will be called 'the one who ' knows himself.' For he who has not known himself ' has known nothing, but he who has known himself ' has at the same time already achieved knowledge about the Depth of the All. ' So then, you, my brother Thomas, have beheld what is obscure [20] to men, that is, that against which they ignorantly stumble." '

Now Thomas said to the Lord, ' "Therefore I beg you to tell me ' what I ask before your Ascension, ' and when I hear from you about [25] the hidden things, then I can speak about ' them. And it is obvious to me that the truth is difficult to ' perform before men."

The Savior answered, saying, ' "If the things that are visible to you are obscure ' to you, how can you hear [30] about the things that are not visible? If the deeds of the truth ' that are visible in the world are difficult for you to perform, ' how indeed, then, shall you perform those that pertain to the ' exalted height and to the Pleroma which are not visible? ' And how shall you be called 'Laborers'? [35] In this respect you are apprentices, and have not yet received ' the height of perfection."

Now Thomas answered ' and said to the Savior, "Tell us about these things ' that you say are not visible, [but] are hidden ' from us."

The Savior said, "[All] bodies [of men and] [40] beasts are begotten [irrational. Surely] ' it is evident in the way [a creature . . .]. ' Those, however, that are above ' [are not visible among] things that are visible, but are visible **139** in their own root, and it is their fruit ' that nourishes them. But these visible bodies ' eat of creatures similar to them ' with the result that the bodies change. Now that which changes will [5] decay and perish, and has no hope of life from then on, ' since that body is bestial. So just as the body of the beasts ' perishes, so also will these formations ' perish. Do they not derive from intercourse ' like that of the beasts? If (the body) too derives from (intercourse), [10] how will it beget anything different from ' (beasts)? So, therefore, you are babes until ' you become perfect."

And Thomas answered, ' "Therefore I say to you, Lord, that those who speak ' about things that are invisible and difficult [15] to explain are like those who shoot their arrows at a ' target at night. To be sure, they shoot their arrows as ' anyone would—since they shoot at the target—

but it is not visible. ' Yet when the light comes forth and ' hides the darkness, then the work of each will appear. [20] And you, our light, enlighten, Lord." '

Jesus said, "It is in light that light exists." '

Thomas spoke, saying, "Lord, ' why does this visible light that shines ' on behalf of men rise and set?"

The Savior [25] said, "O blessed Thomas, of course this visible light ' shone on your behalf—not in order [that] ' you remain here, but rather that you come forth—' and whenever all the elect abandon ' bestiality, then this light will withdraw [30] up to its essence, and its essence will welcome it ' since it is a good servant."

Then ' the Savior continued and said, "O ' unsearchable love of the light! O bitterness of ' the fire that burns in the bodies of men and in [35] their marrow, burning in them night and ' day, burning in the limbs of men and ' [making] their minds drunk and their souls deranged ' [and moving] them within males and females ' [by day and] night and moving them [with] a [40] [movement that moves] secretly and visibly. ' For the males [move; they move upon the females] ' and the females upon [the males. Therefore it is] **140** said, 'Everyone who seeks the truth from ' true wisdom will make himself wings so as to ' fly, fleeing the lust that scorches the spirits ' of men.' And he will make himself wings to flee [5] every visible spirit."

And Thomas answered, ' saying, "Lord, this indeed is what I am asking ' you about, since I have understood that you ' are the one who is good for us, as you say."

Again ' the Savior answered and said, "Therefore it is necessary [10] for us to speak to you, since this is the doctrine for the perfect. ' If, now, you desire to become perfect, you shall ' observe these things; if not, your name is 'Ignorant,' ' since it is impossible for a wise man to dwell with a ' fool, for the wise man is perfect in all wisdom. [15] To the fool, however, the good and bad are ' the same—for 'the wise man will be nourished by ' the truth' and 'will be like a tree growing by ' the meandering stream'—seeing that there are some who, although having wings, ' rush upon the visible things, things that [20] are far from the truth. For that which guides them, ' the fire, will give them an illusion of truth, ' [and] will shine on them with a [perishable] beauty, ' and it will imprison them in a dark ' sweetness and captivate them with fragrant pleasure. [25] And it will blind them with insatiable lust ' and burn their souls and become ' for them like a stake stuck in their heart ' which they can never dislodge. And like ' a bit in the mouth it leads them according to its [30] own desire.

"It has fettered them with its ' chains and bound all their limbs ' with the bitter bond of lust for those ' visible things that will decay and change ' and swerve by impulse. They have [35] always been attracted downwards: as they are killed, ' they are assimilated to all the beasts of ' the perishable realm."

Thomas answered and said, "It ' is obvious and has been said, '[Many are the things revealed] ' to those who do not know [that they will forfeit [40] their] soul.'"

And [the Savior] answered, saying, ' "[Blessed is] the wise man who [sought ' after the truth, and] when he found it, he rested **141** upon it forever and was unafraid of those ' who wanted to disturb him."

Thomas answered ' and said, "Is it good for us, Lord, to rest ' among our own?"

The Savior said, "Yes, it is useful. [5] And it is good for you since things visible ' among men will dissolve—for the vessel of ' their flesh will dissolve, and when it is brought to naught ' it will come to be among visible things, among things that are seen. ' And then the fire which they see gives them pain [10] on account of love for the faith they ' formerly possessed. They will be gathered back to that which is visible. ' Moreover, those who see among things that are not visible, without ' the first love they will perish in the concern for this ' life and the scorching in the fire. Only a little time [15] until that which is visible dissolves; then ' shapeless shades will emerge and ' in the midst of tombs they will forever dwell upon the corpses ' in pain and corruption of soul." '

Thomas answered and said, "What have we [20] to say in the face of these things? What shall we say to ' blind men? What doctrine should we express to these miserable ' mortals who say, 'We came to [do] ' good and not to curse,' and yet [claim], ' 'Had we not been begotten in the flesh, we would not have [25] known [iniquity]'?"

The Savior said, "Truly, as for ' [those], do not esteem them as men, but regard them [as] ' beasts, for just as beasts devour one another, ' so also men of this sort ' devour one another. On the contrary, they are deprived of [the kingdom] [30] since they love the sweetness of the fire and are ' servants of death and rush to the works of corruption. ' They fulfill the lust of their fathers. They will ⌐ be thrown down to the abyss and be afflicted ⌐ by the torment of the bitterness of their evil nature. [35] For they will be scourged so as to make them ' rush headlong to the place that they do not know, and ' they [will not recede from] their limbs patiently, but ' [with] despair. And they rejoice over [the ' concern for this life with] madness and derangement! [Some] [40] pursue [this] derangement without realizing [their ' madness, thinking] that they [are] wise. [They are beguiled by ' the] beauty of their body [as if it would not perish. And] **142** they are frenetic; their thought is occupied ' with their deeds. But it is the fire that will burn them!" '

And Thomas answered and said, "Lord, what will the one ' thrown down to them do? For I am most anxious ⁵ about them; many are those who fight them." '

The Savior answered and said, "Do you possess that which is ' visible?"

Judas—the one called ' Thomas—said, "It is you, Lord, whom it befits ' to speak, and me to listen." ¹⁰

The Savior replied, "Listen to what I am going to tell you ' and believe in the truth. That which sows and that which is sown ' will dissolve in their fire—within the fire ' and the water—and they will hide in tombs of darkness. ' And after a long time they shall appear as ¹⁵ the fruit of the evil trees, being punished, ' being slain in the mouth of beasts and men ' at the instigation of the rains and winds and air ' and the light that shines above."

Thomas ' replied, "You have certainly persuaded us, Lord. ²⁰ We realize in our heart and it is obvious that this ' is so, and that your word is sufficient. But these words ' that you speak to us are ridiculous and contemptible to the world ' since they are misunderstood. ' So how can we go ²⁵ preach them, since we are [not] esteemed ' [in] the world?"

The Savior answered and said, ' "[Truly] I tell you that he who will listen to ' [your] word and turn away his face or sneer ' at it or smirk at these things, truly ³⁰ I tell you that he will be handed over to ' the Ruler above who rules over ' all the powers as their king, and he will turn ' that one around and cast him from heaven down to ' the abyss, and he will be imprisoned in a narrow ³⁵ dark place. Moreover, he can neither turn nor move on account of ' the great depth of Tartaros and the [heavy bitterness] ' of Hades that besets [him. They are ' imprisoned] in it in [order that they might not ' escape]—their [madness] will not be forgiven. [And ⁴⁰ the Rulers who will] pursue you [will] deliver ' [them over to the] angel Tartarouchos ' [and he will take whips of] fire, pursuing them **143** [with] fiery scourges that cast a shower of sparks into ' the face of the one who is pursued. If he flees westward, he ' finds the fire. If he turns southward, he finds it there as well. ' If he turns northward, the threat ⁵ of seething fire meets him again. Nor does he find the way to the East ' so as to flee there and be saved, for he did not find it in the day ' he was in the body, so that he will find it in the day of ' Judgment."

Then the Savior continued, saying, ' "Woe to you, godless ones, who have no hope, [10] who rely on things that will not happen!

"Woe to you ' who hope in the flesh and in the prison that will ' perish! How long will you be oblivious? And the imperishables, do you ' think that they will perish too? Your hope is set ' upon the world and your god is this life! [15] You are corrupting your souls!

"Woe to you for ' the fire that burns in you, for it is insatiable! '

"Woe to you because of the wheel that turns in ' your minds!

"Woe to you because of the burning ' that is in you, for it will devour your flesh openly [20] and rend your souls secretly, ' and prepare you for your companions!

"Woe to ' you, captives, for you are bound in caverns! ' You laugh! In mad laughter you rejoice! ' You neither realize your perdition, nor [25] do you reflect on your circumstances, nor have [you] ' understood that you dwell in darkness and death! ' On the contrary, you are drunk with the fire and [full] ' of bitterness. Your mind is deranged on account of the [burning] that is in] you, and sweet to you is the crown of [30] your enemies' blows! And the darkness rose for ' you like the light, for you surrendered your freedom ' for servitude! You darkened your hearts ' and surrendered your thoughts ' to folly, and you filled your thoughts [35] with the smoke of the fire that is in you! And ' your light has hidden in the cloud ' [of darkness] and the garment that is put upon you, you [pursued ' deceitfully] and [you] were seized [by ' the hope that] does not exist. And whom is it [you [40] have] believed? Do you [not know that you] ' all dwell among those who [want you to curse] ' yourselves as if [your hope were non-existent]? **144** You baptized your souls in the water of darkness! ' You walked by your own whims!

"Woe ' to you who dwell in error, heedless ' that the sun which judges and [5] looks down upon the All will circle around all things ' so as to enslave the enemies. You do not even notice ' the moon, how by night and day it ' looks down, looking at the bodies of your corpses!

"Woe ' to you who love intimacy with womankind [10] and polluted intercourse with it!

"And woe ' to you because of the powers of your body, ' for those will afflict you!

"Woe to you because of ' the forces of the evil demons! '

"Woe to you who beguile your limbs with the fire! [15] Who is it that will rain a refreshing dew on you ' to extinguish the mass of fire from you ' along with your burning? Who is it that will cause the sun to ' shine upon you to disperse the darkness in you ' and hide the darkness and polluted water?

"The sun [20] and the moon will give a fragrance to you, together with the air and ' the spirit and the earth and the water. For if the sun does not ' shine upon these bodies, they will wither and perish ' just like weeds or grass. If ' the sun shines on (the weeds), it prevails and chokes [25] the grapevine; but if the grapevine ' prevails and shades those weeds ' [and] all that other brush growing alongside and ' [spreads] and flourishes, it alone ' inherits the land in which it grows [30] and dominates every place it shaded. ' And then when it grows up, it dominates all the land ' and is bountiful for its master, and it pleases him ' even more, for he would have suffered great pains ' on account of these plants until he uprooted them. But the [35] grapevine alone removed them and choked ' them, and they died and became like the soil."

Then ' Jesus continued and said, "[Woe to ' you], for you did not receive the doctrine, and those who are [ignorant] ' will labor at preaching [instead of you], [40] and [you] are rushing into [profligacy. ' Yet there are some who have been] sent down to [rescue ' all those whom] you killed daily [145] in order that they might rise from death.

"Blessed are you ' who have prior knowledge of the stumbling blocks and who ' flee alien things.

"Blessed are you who are reviled ' and not esteemed on account of the love [5] their Lord has for them.

"Blessed are ' you who weep and are oppressed by ' those without hope, for you will be released from ' every bondage.

"Watch and pray that you not come to be ' in the flesh, but rather that you come forth from the bondage of the bitterness [10] of this life. And as you pray, ' you will find rest, for you have left behind the suffering and the disgrace. ' For when you come forth from the sufferings and ' passion of the body, you will receive rest ' from the Good One, and you will reign with the King, [15] you joined with him and he with you, from now on, ' for ever and ever. Amen." '

The Book of Thomas '
the Contender writing '
to the Perfect. [20]

* * * * * * *

Remember me also, my brethren, '
[in] your prayers: '
Peace to the Saints '
and the Spiritual.

THE GOSPEL OF THE EGYPTIANS (III, *2* AND IV, *2*)

Introduced and translated by
ALEXANDER BÖHLIG and FREDERIK WISSE

The so-called *Gospel of the Egyptians*, existing in two versions among the tractates in the Nag Hammadi library, is not related to the well-known apocryphal *Gospel of the Egyptians*. The Coptic *Gospel of the Egyptians*, also entitled "The Holy Book of the Great Invisible Spirit," is an esoteric tractate representing mythological Gnosticism; in fact, the tractate may very well be described as a work in which Sethian Gnostics portrayed their salvation history. The author of the *Gospel of the Egyptians* is supposedly the mythological, heavenly Seth. Indeed, since Seth was made the father of the seed of the primal Father, is it not reasonable for the Gnostics to maintain that the primal Father also inspired him to write a holy book?

The tractate is divisible into four main sections. The first section (III 40, 12-55, 16 = IV 50, 1-67, 1) deals with the origin of the heavenly world: from the supreme God, dwelling in solitary height as the transcendent Great Invisible Spirit, there evolves and emanates a series of glorious beings, from the mighty trinity of Father, Mother Barbelo, and Son, through the pleroma of heavenly powers, to Adamas' great son Seth, the father and savior of the incorruptible race. The second section (III 55, 16-66, 8 = IV 67, 2-78, 10) discusses the origin, preservation, and salvation of the race of Seth: because of the arrogance and hostility of Saklas and the Archons, Seth comes from heaven, puts on Jesus as a garment, and accomplishes a work of salvation on behalf of his children. The third section (III 66, 8-67, 26 = IV 78, 10-80, 15) is hymnic in character; and the fourth section (III 68, 1-69, 17 = IV 80, 15-81, end) contains a concluding account of the Sethian origin and transmission of the tractate.

Thus, in a manner analogous to that in which the New Testament gospels proclaim the life of Jesus, the *Gospel of the Egyptians* presents the life of Seth. His pre-history, the origin of his seed, the preservation of his seed by the heavenly powers, the coming of Seth into the world, and his work of salvation, especially through baptism, are proclaimed with drama and praise.

The following translation is based primarily on the text of Codex III; the more fragmentary (though probably more reliable) text of Codex IV has been utilized for the missing pages 45-48, and the main corrupt passages of Codex III.

THE GOSPEL OF THE EGYPTIANS

III 40, 12-44, 28
IV 55, 20-60, 30
III 49, 1-69, 20

The [holy] book [of the Egyptians] ' about the great invisible [Spirit, the] Father ' whose name cannot be uttered, [he who came] ¹⁵ forth from the heights of [the perfection, the] light ' of the light of the [aeons of light], ' the light of the [silence of the] providence ' ⟨and⟩ the Father of the silence, the [light] ' of the word and the truth, the light [of the **41** incorruptions, the] infinite light, ' [the] radiance from the aeons of light ' of the unrevealable, unmarked, ' ageless, unproclaimable Father, [5] the aeon of the aeons, Autogenes, ' self-begotten, self-producing, alien, ' the really true aeon.

Three ' powers came forth from him; ' they are the Father, the Mother, (and) the Son, [10] from the living silence, what came forth from ' the incorruptible Father. These came ' [forth from] the silence of the unknown Father. '

[And] from that place ' Domedon Doxomedon came [forth, [15] the aeon of] the aeons and the [light ' of] each one of [their] powers. ' [And] thus the Son came ' [forth] fourth; the Mother [fifth; ' the Father] sixth. He was [20] [...] but unheralded; [it is he] who is unmarked among ' all [the powers], the glories, and the ' [incorruptions].

From that place ' the three powers [came] forth, **42** the three ogdoads that [the Father ' brings] forth, in silence with his providence, ' from his bosom, i.e. ' the Father, the Mother, (and) the Son. [5]

The ⟨first⟩ ogdoad, because of which ' the thrice-male child came forth, ' which is the thought, and [the] word, ' and the incorruption, and the eternal ' [life], the will, the mind, [10] and the foreknowledge, the androgynous ' Father.

The second ' ogdoad-power, the Mother, the virginal Barbelon ' epititioch[...]'ai, memeneaimen[... who] [15] presides over the heaven, karb[...] ' the uninterpretable power, ' the ineffable Mother. [She originated] ' from herself [...]; ' she came forth; [she] [20] agreed with the Father [of the] silent ' [silence].

The third ogdoad-[power], ' the Son of the [silent silence], ' and the crown of the silent silence, [and] ' the glory of the Father, and the virtue [of the **43** Mother. He] brings forth from the bosom ' the seven powers of the great ' light of the seven voices, and the word ' [is] their completion.

These are the three [5] [powers], the three ogdoads that the Father ' [through] his providence brought ' [forth] from his bosom. He brought them ' [forth] at that place.

Domedon ' Doxomedon came forth, [10] the aeon of the aeons, and the ' [throne] which is in him, and the powers ' [which surround] him, the glories and the ' [incorruptions. The] Father of the great light ' [who came] forth from the silence, he is [15] [the great] Doxomedon-aeon in which ' [the thrice]-male child rests. ' And the throne ' of his [glory] was established [in it, ' this one] on which his unrevealable name [20] [is inscribed], on the tablet ' [...] one is the word, the [Father ' of the light] of everything, he ' [who came] forth from the silence, while he rests ' in the silence, he whose **44** name [is] in an [invisible] symbol. [A] ' hidden, [invisible] mystery ' came forth iiiiiiiiiiiiiiiiiiii[iii] ' ēēēēēēēēēēēē-ēēēēēēēē[ēē o] [5]oooooooooooooooooooooo uu[uuu]'uuuuuuuuuuuuuuuuu eeeee'eeeeeeeeeeeeeeeee aaaaaaa[aaaa]'aaaaaaaaaaa ōōōōōōōōō[ōō]'ōō-ōōōōōōōōō.

And [in this] [10] way the three powers gave praise to the [great], ' invisible, unnameable, ' virginal, uncallable Spirit, and [his] ' male virgin. They asked [for a] ' power. A silence of living silence [15] came forth, namely [glories] and ' incorruptions in the aeons [... aeons] ' myriads added [on ..., the] ' three males, [the three] ' male offspring, the [male] races (IV 55, 5-7 adds: the [glories of the Father, ' the] glories of the great [Christ and ' the] male offspring, the [races]) [20] filled the great Doxomedon-[aeon with] ' the power of the word of the [whole pleroma]. '

Then the thrice-male [child of the great] ' Christ whom the [great] invisible ' Spirit had anointed—he [whose] [25] power [was called] Ainon— gave [praise to] ' the great invisible Spirit [and his] ' male virgin Yoel, [and] ' the silence of silent silence, and the [greatness] IV **55** [20] that [...] ' ineffable. [...] ' ineffable [...] ' unanswerable and ' uninterpret-able, the [25] first one who has [come forth], ' and (who is) unproclaimable, [...] **56** which is wonderful ' [...] ineffable ' [...], he who has ' all the greatnesses [of] greatness [5] [of] the silence [of] silence at ' that [place]. The thrice-[male ' child] brought ' praise and asked [for a ' power] from the [great, [10] invisible, virginal] ' Spirit.

Then there ' appeared at [that] place ' [...] who [... ' who] sees [glories [15] ...] treasures in a [... ' invisible] ' mysteries to [...] ' of the silence ' [who is the male] virgin [20] [Youel].

Then ' [the child of the] child ' Esephech [appeared]. '

And [thus] he was completed, ' namely, the [Father, the] Mother, the [Son], [25] the [five] seals, the ' unconquerable power which [is] ' the great [Christ] of all the incorruptible **57** ones. [...] ' holy [...] ' the end, [the] incorruptible [...] ' and [...], [5] they are powers [and glories ' and] incorruptions [...] ' they came forth [...]. [13] This one brought [praise] ' to the unrevealable, [15] hidden [mystery ... ' the] hidden [...] [21] him in the [... ' and] the aeons [...] thrones, ' [...] and ' each one [...] [25] myriads of [powers] ' without number surround [them, **58** glories] and ' incorruptions [...] and they ' [... of] the Father, ' [and] the [Mother, and] the Son, and [5] [the] whole [pleroma] which I [mentioned] ' before, [and the] five seals ' [and the mystery] of ' [mysteries]. They [appeared ... [13] who] presides [over ' ...] and the aeons [of [15] ... really] ' truly [...] and the [...] [18] eternal [...] [21] and the ' [really] truly [eternal] aeons. '

Then [providence came forth ' from silence], and the [living silence [25] of] the Spirit, [and] ' the Word [of] the Father, and [a] ' light. [She ... the five] 59 seals which [the Father brought] ' forth from his bosom, and she passed [through] ' all the aeons which I mentioned ' before. And she established [5] thrones of glory [and myriads] ' of angels [without] number ' [who] surrounded them, [powers ' and incorruptible] glories, who ' [sing] and give glory, all giving [10] praise with [a single voice], ' with one accord, [with ' one] never-silent [voice ... ' to] the Father, and the [Mother, ' and the] Son [... and [15] all the] pleromas [that I] ' mentioned [before], who is [the ' great] Christ, who is from [silence, ' who] is the [incorruptible] child ' Telmael Telmachael [20] [Eli Eli] Machar Machar ' [Seth, the] power which really truly lives, ' [and the] male ' [virgin] who is with [him], Youel, ' [and] Esephech, [the] holder of glory, [25] the [child] of the child ' [and the crown of] his glory ' [...] of the five ' seals, [the] pleroma [that ' I mentioned before].

There 60 the great self-begotten ' living [Word came forth, ' the] true [god], the ' unborn physis, he whose [5] name I shall tell, saying, ' [...]aia[.....]thaōthōsth[..], ' who [is the] son of the [great] ' Christ, who is the son [of ' the] ineffable silence, [who] [10] came forth from the great [invisible] ' and incorruptible [Spirit]. ' The [son] of the silence and [silence] ' appeared [... [15] invisible ... ' man ' and the] treasures [of] his glory. [Then] ' he appeared in the revealed [...]. ' And he [established] [20] the four [aeons]. ' With a word [he] established ' them.

He brought [praise] ' to the great, [invisible], ' virginal Spirit, [the silence] [25] of the [Father] in a silence [of the] ' living silence [of silence, ' the] place where the man rests. ' [...] ' through [...]. [30]

Then there came forth [at (or: from)] III 49 that [place] the cloud ' [of the] great light, the living ' power, the mother of the holy, incorruptible ones, ' the great power, the Mirothoe. [5] And she gave birth to him whose name ' I name, saying, ien ' ien ea ea ea, three times. IV 61 [8]

For this one, [Adamas], ' is [a light] which radiated [from [10] the light; he is] the eye of the [light]. ' For [this is] the first man, III 49 [10] he through whom ' and to whom everything became, ' (and) without whom nothing became. ' The unknowable, ' incomprehensible Father came forth. He [15] came down from above ' for the annulment of the deficiency.

Then ' the great Logos, the divine Autogenes, ' and the incorruptible man ' Adamas mingled with each other. [20] A Logos of man came into being. ' However, the man ' came into being through a word.

He ' gave praise to the great, invisible, ' incomprehensible, virginal [25] Spirit, and the male virgin, ' and the thrice-male child, **50** and the male [virgin] ' Youel, and Esephech, the holder of glory, ' the child of the child and ' the crown of his glory, and the great [5] Doxomedon-aeon, and ' the thrones which are in him, and the ' powers which surround him, the glories and ' the incorruptions, and their whole pleroma ' which I mentioned before, [10] and the ethereal earth, the ' receiver of God, where ' the holy men of the ' great light receive shape, ' the men of the Father [15] of the silent, living silence, the Father ' and their whole pleroma as ' I mentioned before.

The ' great Logos, ' the divine Autogenes, and [20] the incorruptible man Adamas gave praise, ' (and) they asked for a power and ' eternal strength for the Autogenes ' for the completion of the ' four aeons, in order that, [25] through them, there may appear **51** [...] the glory and the power ' of the invisible Father of ' the holy men of the great light ' which will come to the world [5] which is the image of the night. The incorruptible ' man Adamas asked for them ' a son out of himself, in order ' that he (the son) may become father of the ' immovable, incorruptible race, so [10] that, through it (the race), the silence ' and the voice may appear, ' and, through it, ' the dead aeon may raise itself, so that ' it may dissolve.

And thus [15] there came forth, from above, the power ' of the great light, the ' Manifestation. She gave birth to the four great ' lights: Harmozel, Oroiael, ' Davithe, Eleleth, [20] and the great incorruptible Seth, the son ' of the incorruptible man ' Adamas.

And thus ' the perfect hebdomad which ' exists in hidden mysteries became complete. **52** When she [receives] the [glory] ' she becomes eleven ' ogdoads.

And the Father nodded approval; ' the whole pleroma of the [5] lights was well pleased. ' Their consorts came forth ' for the completion of the ogdoad of ' the divine Autogenes: the ' Grace of the first light [10] Harmozel, the Perception of the second ' light Oroiael, the Understanding ' of the third light ' Davithe, the Prudence of the ' fourth light Eleleth. This [15] is the first ogdoad of the ' divine Autogenes.

And ' the Father nodded approval; the whole pleroma ' of the lights was well pleased. ' The ⟨ministers⟩ came forth: [20] the first one, the great ' Gamaliel (of) the first great ' light Harmozel, and the great '

Gabriel (of) the second great ' light Oroiael, and the great ²⁵ Samlo of
the great light Davithe, ' and the great Abrasax of 53 [the great light]
Eleleth. And ' [the] consorts of these came forth ' by the will of the
good pleasure ' of the Father: the Memory of the great one, ⁵ the first,
Gamaliel; the Love ' of the great one, the second, Gabriel; ' the Peace
of the third one, the great ' Samblo; the eternal Life ' of the great one,
the fourth, Abrasax. ¹⁰ Thus were the five ogdoads completed, ' a total
of forty, ' as an uninterpretable power.

Then ' the great Logos, the Autogenes, ' and the word of the pleroma
¹⁵ of the four lights gave ' praise to the great, invisible, ' uncallable,
virginal Spirit, ' and the male virgin, ' and the great Doxomedon-
aeon, ²⁰ and the thrones which are in ' them, and the powers which
surround them, ' glories, authorities, ' and the powers, ⟨and⟩ the thrice-
male ' child, and the male virgin ²⁵ Youel, and Esephech, 54 the holder
of glory, [the child] ' of the child and the crown of [his] ' glory, the
whole pleroma, and ' all the glories which are there, the ⁵ infinite
pleromas ⟨and⟩ the ' unnameable aeons, in ' order that they may name
the Father ' the fourth with the incorruptible ' race, (and) that they may
call the seed ¹⁰ of the Father the seed of the great ' Seth.

Then everything shook, ' and trembling took hold of the incorruptible ' ones. Then the three male ' children came forth ¹⁵ from above
down ' into the unborn ones, and the ' self-begotten ones, and those
who were begotten ' in what is begotten. ' The greatness came forth,
the ²⁰ whole greatness of the great Christ. He ' established thrones in
glory, ' myriads without number, ' in, the four aeons around them, '
myriads without number, ²⁵ powers and glories 55 and incorruptions.
And they came ' forth in this way.

And ' the incorruptible, spiritual ' church increased in the four ⁵ lights
of the great, living Autogenes, ' the god of truth, praising, ' singing,
(and) giving glory with one voice, ' with one accord, with a mouth '
which does not rest, to the Father, and ¹⁰ the Mother, and the Son, and
their whole ' pleroma, just as I mentioned ⟨before⟩. ' The five seals
which possess the myriads, and ' they who rule over the aeons and they
who ' bear the glory of the leaders ¹⁵ were given the command to reveal '
to those who are worthy. Amen.

Then the great ' Seth, the son of the incorruptible ' man Adamas,
gave praise ' to the great, invisible, uncallable, ²⁰ unnameable, virginal '
Spirit, and the ⟨male virgin, and the thrice-male child, and the male⟩ '
virgin Youel, and Esephech, ' the holder of glory, and the ' crown of
his glory, the child of the child, 56 and the great Doxomedon-aeons, '

and the pleroma which I mentioned ' before; and he asked for his seed. '

Then there came forth from that place [5] the great power of the great '
light Plesithea, the mother of the angels, ' the mother of the lights,
the ' glorious mother, the virgin with the ' four breasts, bringing the
fruit [10] from Gomorrah as spring and Sodom, ' which is the fruit of
the spring of ' Gomorrah which is in her. She came forth ' through the
great Seth.

Then ' the great Seth rejoiced about [15] the gift which was granted
him ' by the incorruptible ' child. He took his seed ' from her with the
four breasts, the virgin, ' and he placed it with [20] him in the fourth
aeon (or, IV 68, 3: [in] the four aeons), ' in the third great ' light
Davithe.

After five ' thousand years the great ' light Eleleth spoke: "Let someone [25] reign over the chaos and Hades." ' And there appeared a cloud **57**
[whose name is] hylic Sophia ' [. . . . She] looked out on the parts ' [of
the chaos], her face being like ' [. . . in] her form [. . .] [5] blood. And '
[the great] angel Gamaliel spoke ' [to the great Gabriel], the minister
of ' [the great light] Oroiael; ' [he said, "Let an] angel come forth [10] [in
order that he may] reign over the chaos ' [and Hades]." Then the cloud,
being ' [agreeable, came forth] in the two monads, ' each one [of which
had] light. ' [. . . the throne], which she had placed [15] in the cloud
[above. ' Then] Sakla, the great ' [angel, saw] the great demon ' [who
is with him, Nebr]uel. And they became ' [together a] begetting spirit
of the earth. [20] [They begot] assisting angels. ' Sakla [said] to the great '
[demon Neb]ruel, "Let ' [the] twelve aeons come into being in ' [the . . .]
aeon, worlds [25] [. . . ." . . .] the great angel ' [Sakla] said by the will of
the Autogenes, **58** "There shall [be] the [. . .] ' of the number of seven
[. . .]." ' And he said to the [great angels], ' "Go and [let each] [5] of you
reign over his [world]." ' Each one [of these] ' twelve [angels] went
[forth. The first] ' angel is Ath[oth. He is the one] ' whom [the great]
generations [10] of men call [. . . . The] ' second is Harmas, [who] is [the
eye of the fire]. ' The third [is Galila. The] ' fourth is Yobel. [The fifth
is] ' Adonaios, who is [called] [15] Sabaoth. The sixth [is Cain, whom] '
the [great generations of] ' men call the sun. The [seventh is Abel]; '
the eighth Akiressina; the [ninth Yubel]. ' The tenth is Harm[upiael.
The] [20] eleventh is Arch[ir-Adonin]. ' The twelfth [is Belias. These ' are]
the ones who preside over Hades [and the chaos]. '

And after the founding [of the world] ' Sakla said to his [angels], [25]
"I, I am a [jealous] god, ' and apart from me nothing has [come into
being," since he] **59** trusted in his nature.

Then a voice ' came from on high, saying, ' "The Man exists, and the Son of the Man." ' Because of the descent of the image [5] above, which is like its voice in the height ' of the image which has looked out, ' through the looking out of the image ' above, the first creature was ' formed.

Because of this [10] Metanoia came to be. She received her ' completion and her power by the will ' of the Father and his approval with which he ' approved of the great, incorruptible, ' immovable race of the great, [15] mighty men of the great Seth, ' in order that he may sow it in the aeons which ' had been brought forth, so that, through her (Metanoia), ' the deficiency may be filled up. ' For she had come forth from above down [20] to the world which is the image of the night. ' When she had come, she prayed for (the repentance of) both the seed ' of the archon of this aeon and ⟨the⟩ authorities ' who had come forth from him, that ' defiled (seed) of the demon-begetting god [25] which will be destroyed, and the seed **60** of Adam and the great Seth, ' which is like the sun.

Then the great ' angel Hormos came to prepare, ' through the virgins of the [5] corrupted sowing of this aeon, in ' a Logos-begotten, holy vessel, ' through the holy Spirit, ' the seed of the great Seth. '

Then the great Seth came and brought his [10] seed. And it was sown in the aeons ' which had been brought forth, their number being the amount of ' Sodom. Some say ' that Sodom is the place of pasture ' of the great Seth, which is Gomorrah. [15] But others (say) that the great Seth took ' his plant out of Gomorrah and ' planted it in the second place ' to which he gave the name Sodom. '

This is the race which came forth through [20] Edokla. For she gave birth through the word ' to Truth and Justice, the origin ' of the seed of the eternal life ' which is with those who will persevere ' because of the knowledge of their emanation. [25] This is the great, incorruptible ' race which has come forth through three **61** worlds to the world.

And the ' flood came as an example ' for the consummation of the aeon. But it ' will be sent into the world [5] because of this race. A conflagration will ' come upon the earth. And grace ' will be with those who belong to the race ' through the prophets ' and the guardians who guard the life [10] of the race. Because of this race ' famines will occur and plagues. ' But these things will happen because of the ' great, incorruptible race. Because of ' this race temptations will come, [15] a falsehood of false prophets. '

Then the great Seth saw the activity ' of the devil, and his many ' guises, and his schemes which will come ' upon his incorruptible, immovable race, [20] and the persecutions of his ' powers and his angels, and their ' error, that they acted against themselves. '

Then the great Seth gave ' praise to the great, uncallable, [25] virginal Spirit, and the male **62** virgin Barbelon, ' and the thrice-male child Telmael ' Telmael Heli Heli Machar ' Machar Seth, the power which really truly [5] lives, and the male virgin ' Youel, and Esephech, the ' holder of glory, and the crown of his ' glory, and the great Doxomedon-aeon, ' and the thrones which are in him, and [10] the powers which surround them, and the whole ' pleroma, as I mentioned before. ' And he asked for guards over his ' seed.

Then there came forth from the great ' aeons four hundred ethereal [15] angels, accompanied by the great ' Aerosiel and the great Selmechel, to ' guard the great, incorruptible race, ' its fruit, and the great men ' of the great Seth, from the time and [20] the moment of Truth and Justice ' until the consummation of the aeon and its ' archons, those whom the great judges ' have condemned to ' death.

Then the great Seth was [25] sent by the four ' lights, by the will of the Autogenes **63** and the whole pleroma, through ' ⟨the gift⟩ and the good pleasure of the great invisible ' Spirit, and the five seals, ' and the whole pleroma.

He passed through [5] the three parousias which I mentioned ' before: the flood, and the conflagration, ' and the judgment of the archons and the powers ' and the authorities, to save her (the race) who went astray, ' through the reconciliation of the world, and [10] the baptism through a Logos-begotten ' body which the great Seth ' prepared for himself, ' secretly through the virgin, in order that the ' saints may be begotten by the holy Spirit, through [15] invisible, secret symbols, ' through a recon-ciliation of the world with the world, ' through the renouncing of the world ' and the god of the thirteen aeons, ' and (through) the con-vocations of the saints, and [20] the ineffable ones, and the incorruptible bosom, ' and (through) the great light of the Father ' who preexisted with his Providence ' and established through her ' the holy baptism that surpasses [25] the heaven, through the incorruptible, **64** Logos-begotten one, even Jesus the living one, even ' he whom the great Seth has ' put on. And through him he nailed the powers ' of the thirteen aeons, and [5] established those who are brought forth and ' taken away. He armed them ' with an armor of knowledge of this truth, ' with an unconquerable power ' of incorruptibility.

There appeared to them [10] the great attendant Yesseus ' Mazareus Yessedekeus, the living ' water, and the great leaders, ' James the great

and Theopemptos ' and Isaouel, and they who preside over [15] the spring
of truth, Micheus and Michar ' and Mnesinous, and he who presides
over ' the baptism of the living, and the ' purifiers, and Sesengenpharanges, ' and they who preside over the gates of the waters, [20]
Micheus and Michar, and they who ' preside over the mountain Seldao
and Elainos, ' and the receivers of ' the great race, the incorruptible, '
mighty men ⟨of⟩ the great Seth, the [25] ministers of the four lights, ' the
great Gamaliel, the great Gabriel, ' the great Samblo, and the great [65]
Abrasax, and they who preside over the sun, its ' rising, Olses and
Hypneus and ' Heurumaious, and they who preside over the ' entrance
into the rest of eternal [5] life, the rulers Mixanther ' and Michanor, and
they who guard the ' souls of the elect, Akramas and ' Strempsouchos,
and the great power ' Heli Heli Machar Machar Seth, and [10] the great,
invisible, uncallable, ' unnameable, virginal ' Spirit, and the silence, and
the great light ' Harmozel, the place of the living Autogenes, ' the God
of the truth, and ⟨he⟩ who is with [15] him, the incorruptible man Adamas, '
the second, Oroiael, the place of the great ' Seth, and Jesus, who possesses the life and who came ' and crucified that which is in the law, '
the third, Davithe, the place of the [20] sons of the great Seth, the fourth, '
Eleleth, the place where the souls ' of the sons are resting, ' the fifth,
Yoel, who presides over the name ' of him to whom it will be granted
to baptize with [25] the holy baptism that surpasses the heaven, ' the
incorruptible one.

But from now on [66] through the incorruptible man Poimael, ' and
they who are worthy of (the) invocation, ' the renunciations of the five
seals in ' the spring-baptism, these will [5] know their receivers as ' they
are instructed about them, and they will ' know them (or: be known) by
them. These ' will by no means taste death.

Iē ieus ' ēō ou ēō ōua! Really truly, [10] O Yesseus Mazareus Yessedekeus, ' O living water, O child of the child, ' O glorious name, really
truly, ' aiōn o ōn (or: O existing aeon), iiii ēēēē eeee oo'oo uuuu ōōōō
aaaa{a}, really [15] truly, ēi aaaa ōō'ōō, O existing one who sees the aeons! '
Really truly, aee ēēē iiii ' uuuuu ōōōōōōōō, ' who is eternally eternal, [20]
really truly, iēa aiō, in ' the heart, who exists, u aei eis aei, ' ei o ei,
ei os ei (or: (Son) forever, Thou art what Thou art, Thou art who Thou
art)!

This great name ' of thine is upon me, O self-begotten Perfect one, '
who art not outside me. [25] I see thee, O thou who art invisible ' to
everyone. For who will be able ' to comprehend thee in another tongue?
Now [67] that I have known thee, I have mixed ' myself with the immut-

able. I have armed ' myself with an armor of light; ' I have become light. For the Mother was at [5] that place because of the ' splendid beauty of grace. Therefore ' I have stretched out my hands while they were ' folded. I was shaped in the circle ' of the riches of the light which is in [10] my bosom, which gives shape to the many ' begotten ones in the light into which no complaint ' reaches. I shall declare thy ' glory truly, for I have comprehended ' thee, sou iēs ide aeiō aeie ois, O [15] aeon, aeon, O God of silence! I ' honor thee completely. Thou art my ' place of rest, O son ēs ēs o e, the ' formless one who exists in the formless ones, ' who exists, raising up the man [20] in whom thou wilt purify me into ' thy life, according to thine imperishable name. ' Therefore the incense of life ' is in me. I mixed it with water ' after the model of all archons, [25] in order that I may live with thee in the peace ' of the saints, thou who existeth really truly **68** for ever.

This is the book ' which the great Seth wrote, and placed ' in high mountains on which ' the sun has not risen, nor is it [5] possible. And since the days of the prophets, ' and the apostles, and the ' preachers, the name has not at all risen ' upon their hearts, nor is it possible. ' And their ear has not heard it. [10]

The great Seth wrote this book ' with letters in one hundred and thirty ' years. He placed it in the mountain ' that is called Charaxio, ' in order that, at the end of the [15] times and the eras, by the ' will of the divine Autogenes ' and the whole pleroma, through the gift ' of the untraceable, unthinkable, ' fatherly love, it may [20] come forth and reveal this ' incorruptible, holy race ' of the great savior, and those who ' dwell with them in love, and ' the great, invisible, eternal [25] Spirit, and his only begotten ' Son, and the eternal light, **69** and his great, incorruptible ' consort, and the incorruptible ' Sophia, and the Barbelon, and the ' whole pleroma in eternity. [5] Amen. '

The Gospel of ⟨the⟩ Egyptians. ' The God-written, holy, secret ' book. Grace, understanding, ' perception, prudence (be) with him [10] who has written it, Eugnostos the beloved ' in the Spirit—in the flesh ' my name is Gongessos—and my ' fellow lights in incorruptibility, ' Jesus Christ, Son of God, [15] Savior, Ichthus. God-written (is) ' the holy book of the great, invisible ' Spirit. Amen. '

The Holy Book of the Great '
Invisible Spirit. [20]
Amen.

EUGNOSTOS THE BLESSED (III, *3* AND V, *1*)

and

THE SOPHIA OF JESUS CHRIST
(III, *4* AND BG 8502, *3*)

Introduced and translated by

DOUGLAS M. PARROTT

Eugnostos the Blessed is in form a religio-philosophical epistle written by a teacher to his disciples; the *Sophia of Jesus Christ* is a revelation discourse given by the risen Christ to his followers. Despite their different forms, these tractates are two versions of the same original document. The former is without apparent Christian influence, while the latter is heavily Christianized. Research thus far tends to the conclusion that *Eugnostos the Blessed* is nearer the original. On that assumption, the placing of these two versions together allows one to see how a non-Christian Gnostic tractate was modified in order to express newly-acquired Christian beliefs or to attract Christians to Gnostic teachings, or perhaps for both reasons.

The main intent of the original document, as reflected in *Eugnostos the Blessed*, seems to have been to establish the existence of an invisible, super-celestial region beyond the visible world—a region not reflected in the speculations of philosophers. Inhabiting that region are four principal divine beings: the unbegotten Father; his androgynous image, Immortal Man; Immortal Man's androgynous son, Son of Man; and Son of Man's androgynous son, the Savior. Each of these divine beings has his own sphere or aeon, and numerous attendant and subordinate beings. Gnostics have their origin and true home with the unbegotten Father. Ineffable joy and unutterable jubilation characterize existence in the super-celestial region; and from there come patterns or types for subsequent creations.

In the *Sophia of Jesus Christ* several sorts of material are added. According to this tractate, the Savior (Christ) came from the super-celestial region (III 93, 8-10; 94, 10-14; 107, 11-14; 118, 15-16). Sophia is the one responsible for the fall of drops of light from the divine realm into the visible world (III 107, 16-17; III 114, 13-BG 119, 9). Furthermore, a god exists who, with his subordinate powers, directly rules this world to the detriment of those who come from the divine realm (III 107, 3-11; BG 119, 2-121, 13). Sex, it is suggested, is the means by which enslavement to the powers is perpetuated (III 108, 10-14). But the Savior (Christ) broke the bonds imposed by the powers, and taught others to do the same (III 107, 15-108, 4; BG 121, 13-122, 3; III 118, 3-25). Two classes of persons will be saved: those who know the Father in pure knowledge (that is, as described in the *Sophia of Jesus Christ*), who will go to him; and those who know the Father defectively (III 117, 8-118, 2), who will go to the Eighth.

In Codex III the *Sophia of Jesus Christ* immediately follows *Eugnostos the Blessed*, and a connection is made between the two at the end of *Eugnostos*. There it is predicted that one will come who will speak the words written by Eugnostos "joyously and in pure knowledge."

The scheme of thought in the original document (as reflected in *Eugnostos the Blessed*), with the unbegotten Father and the three divine men, resembles most closely the theology of the Sethian-Ophite Gnostics described by Irenaeus. The additions in the *Sophia of Jesus Christ* also have significant affinities with Sethian-Ophite thought. In addition, significant Middle Platonic philosophical tendencies are present in the original document, and suggest that it was composed sometime in the first two centuries C.E.

The two versions of *Eugnostos the Blessed* and the two versions of the *Sophia of Jesus Christ* differ from each other in certain respects. The translation which follows is based on the versions of Codex III; the other versions have been employed in the three instances where pages are no longer extant (III 79-80, 109-110, and 115-116), and also have proved useful in restoring the text.

EUGNOSTOS THE BLESSED	THE SOPHIA OF JESUS CHRIST
III 70, 1-78, 23	III 90, 14-108, 25
V 7, 24-9, 11	BG 107, 4-111, 1
III 81, 2-90, 13	III 111, 1-114, 25
	BG 118, 13-122, 8
	III 117, 1-119, 18

Eugnostos the Blessed, to those ' who are his.

The Sophia of Jesus Christ

After [15] he rose from the ' dead, his twelve ' disciples and seven ' women followed him (and) ' went to Galilee onto the mountain **91** that is called "Place of Harvest-time ' and Joy." When they gathered together, ' they were perplexed about the origin (or: nature) ' of the universe, the plan, [5] the holy providence, ' the power of the authorities, and concerning ' everything that the Savior does ' with them in the secret ' of the holy plan. [10] The Savior appeared not in his ' first form, but in the ' invisible spirit. And his form ' was

like a great angel of light. ' And
his likeness I must not describe. [15]
No mortal flesh ' can endure it,
but only ' pure (and) perfect flesh
like ' that which he taught us about
on the mountain ' called [20] "Of
the Olives" in Galilee. And ' he
said, "Peace to you (pl.)! My
peace ' I give ' to you!" And they
all wondered ' and were afraid.

The Savior **92** laughed and said
to them, "What ' are you thinking
about? (Why) are you perplexed? '
What are you searching for?" '
Philip said, "For the origin (or:
nature) [5] of the universe and the
plan." '

The Savior said to them, ' "I
desire that you know ' that all men
born ' on earth from the foundation of [10] the world until now
are ' dust. Inquiring about God, '
who he is, and what he ' is like,
they have not found him. Now
the ' wisest among [15] them have
speculated on the basis of the
ordering of ' the world and (its)
movement. ' But their speculation
has not reached ' the truth. For
the ordering ' is said to be directed
in three ways [20] by all the philosophers, ' (and) hence they do not '
agree. For some of ' them say
about the world ' that it is directed
by itself. **93** Some, ' that it is
providence (that directs it). Some, '
that it is fate. ' Now, it is none of
these. [5] Again, (of) the three
opinions that I have ' just described, none ' is close to the

Rejoice in these ' things (or,
V 1, 3-4: Greetings! I wish ' [you])
to know that all men ' born from
the foundation [5] of the world until
now are ' dust. Inquiring about
God, ' who he is, and what he is
like, ' they have not found him.
The wisest ' among them have
speculated about the truth from
the ordering [10] of the world. ' But
the speculation has not reached '
the truth. For the ordering ' is
spoken of in three (different)
opinions ' by [15] all the philosophers, (and) hence ' they do not
agree. For some ' of them say '
about the world that it was
directed ' by itself. Some, [20] that
it is providence (that directs it). '
Some, that it is fate. ' Now, it is
none of these. ' Again, (of) the
three opinions that I have just '
described, none **71** is true.

For whatever is from itself ' is empty ' life, ⟨since⟩ it (only) makes itself. Providence ' is foolish. (And) the inevitable ⁵ is undiscerning.

Whoever, then, is able ' to get free of ' these three opinions that ' I have just described and come by means ' of another view to confess the ¹⁰ God of truth, and be in harmony ' with everyone because of him, he is an ' immortal who is in the midst ' of mortal men.

The one who ' is is ineffable. ¹⁵ No sovereignty knew him, no authority, ' no subjection, nor did any creature ' from the foundation of the world, ' except himself.

For he ' is immortal. He is eternal, ²⁰ having no birth; for everyone ' who has birth will perish. ' He is unbegotten, having no beginning; ' for everyone who has a beginning ' has an end. No one rules **72** over him, since he has no name; for

truth, and (they are) from ' man. But I, who came ' from the boundless Light, ¹⁰ I am here. For I am he who knows it (the Light), ' so that I might speak to you concerning the precise nature ' of the truth. For whatever is from ' itself is a polluted life ' (since it) makes itself. And providence ¹⁵ has no wisdom in it. And ' the inevitable does not discern.

"Now as for you, ' whatever is fitting for you to know, ' and those who are worthy of knowledge, ' will be given to them—whoever has been ²⁰ begotten not by the sowing of the ' unclean rubbing but by the First ' who was sent, for ' he is an immortal in the midst of ' mortal men."

Matthew said **94** to him, "Lord, ' no one can find the truth except ' through you. Therefore teach us ' the truth." The Savior said, ⁵ "He Who Is is ineffable. ' No sovereignty knew him, no authority, ' no subjection, nor did any creature ' from the foundation of ' the world until now, except ¹⁰ himself, and anyone to whom he wills ' to make revelation through him ' who is from the First ' Light. From now on ' I am the great Savior. For he ¹⁵ is immortal and eternal. ' Now he is eternal, ' having no birth; for everyone ' who has birth will perish. He is unbegotten, ' having no beginning; ²⁰ for everyone who has a beginning ' has an end. No one rules '

whoever has ' a name is the creation of another. ' He is unnameable. He has no ⸌ human form; for
whoever has [5] human form is the
creation ' of another. He has his
own semblance—' not like ' the
semblance that we have received or
seen, ' but a strange semblance [10]
that surpasses all things ' (and) is
better than the totalities. It looks '
to every side and sees itself ' from
itself. ' He is without end; he is
incomprehensible. [15] He is ever
imperishable, ' (and) has no likeness (to anything). He is ' unchanging good. He is ' faultless.
He is everlasting. ' He is blessed.
He is unknowable, [20] while he
(nonetheless) knows ' himself. He
is immeasurable. ' He is untraceable. He is ' perfect, having no
defect. 73 He is imperishably
blessed. ' He is called "the Father '
of the Universe."

Before anything was ' revealed
of those that appear, [5] the greatness and the authorities that ' are
in him, he embraced the ' totalities
of the totalities, and nothing '
embraced him. For he ' is all mind,
thought [10] and reflecting, thinking,'
rationality, and power. ' They all
are equal powers. ' They are the
sources of the totalities. ' And
their whole race, until the end, [15]
is in the foreknowledge ' of the

over him, since he has no name;
for whoever ' has a name is the
creation of ' another. (BG 84, 13-17
adds: He is unnameable. ' He has
no human form; [15] for whoever
has ' human form ' is the creation
of another.) And he has a semblance 95 of his own—not like '
what you have seen or ' received,
but a strange semblance ' that
surpasses all things [5] and is better
than the universe. ' It looks to
every side and sees itself ' from
itself. Since it has no boundary, '
he is ever incomprehensible. ' He
is imperishable, since he has no
likeness (to anything). [10] He is unchanging good. ' He is faultless.
He is eternal. ' He is blessed.
While he is not known, ' he ever
knows ' himself. He is immeasurable. He is [15] untraceable. He is
perfect, ' having no defect. He is
imperishably blessed. ' He is called'
'the Father of the Universe.' " '

Philip said, "Lord, [20] how, then,
was he revealed to the perfect
ones?" ' The perfect Savior said to
him, ' "Before anything was revealed ' of those that appear, the '
greatness and the authority were
96 in him, for he embraced the
whole of the totalities ' while nothing embraced ' him. For he is '
all mind. And he is thought, [5] and
thinking, ' and reflecting, and '
rationality, and power. They ' all
are equal powers. ' They are the
sources of the totalities. [10] And
their whole race from ' the first

Unbegotten. '

For that which appears has not
yet been arrived at. '

Now a difference existed ' between the imperishable aeons (and
the perishable ones). [20] Let us,
then, consider (it) in this way. '

Everything that came from ' the
perishable will perish, since they
came ' from the perishable. What-

until the end were ' in his foreknowledge, (that of) the boundless ' Unbegotten ' Father."

Thomas said to him, [15] "Lord,
Savior, ' why did these come to be,
and why ' were these revealed?" '
The perfect Savior said, ' "I came
from the Boundless One [20] so that
I might tell you all ' things. The
Spirit That Exists was a begetter, '
who had ' a power ⟨of⟩ a begetting
97 and form-[giving] being, so that '
the great ' abundance that was
hidden in him might be revealed.
Because of ' his mercy and his
love [5] he wished ' to bring forth
fruit by himself, so that ' he might
not ⟨enjoy⟩ his ' blessedness alone,
but other spirits ' of the unwavering generation might bring forth [10]
body and fruit, glory and ' honor
in imperishableness and ' his un-
ending grace, ' so that his blessing
might be revealed ' by the self-
begotten God, [15] the Father of
every imperishableness and ' those
that came to be after them. ' But
that which appears has not yet
been arrived at. '

"Now a great difference ' exists
between the imperishables (and
those that are perishable)." He
called [20] out, saying, "Whoever '
has an ear to hear about ' boundless things, let him hear," ' and
"It is those who are awake I have
addressed." ' Again he continued
98 and said, "Everything that
came ' from the perishable will
perish, ' since they came from '

ever came **74** from imperishableness will not ' perish but will
become ' imperishable, since it
came from ' imperishableness. Thus
a ⁵ multitude of men went astray; '
since they did not know this difference, which ' has been stated, they
died.

But let this suffice for ' now,
since it is impossible for anyone '
to dispute the nature of the words ¹⁰
that I have just spoken in regard to
the blessed, ' imperishable, true
God. ' Now, if anyone ' desires to
believe the words ' that are set
down (here), let him investigate ¹⁵
from what (sing.) is hidden to the
completion of what (sing.) is
revealed, ' and this thought ' will
instruct him how the belief ' in
those things that are not revealed
was ' found in what (sing.) is
revealed. This (thought) is a ²⁰
source of knowledge.

The Lord ' of the Universe is
not rightly ' called "Father," but
"First Father." ' For the Father
is the source **75** of what is revealed.
For he is ' the beginningless First '
Father and beholds himself ' within himself as with a ⁵ mirror. He
was revealed in his ' likeness as
Self-Father, that is, ' Self-Begetter,
and as Confronter, ' since he con-

the perishable. And whatever came
⁵ from imperishableness does not
perish ' but becomes imperishable ' (BG 89, 16-17 adds: since they
are from ' imperishableness). Thus
a multitude of men ' went astray;
since they did not know this '
difference, they died."

Mariamme said to him,¹⁰ "Lord, '
then how will we know these
things?" ' The perfect Savior
said, '

"Come (pl.) from the non-appear-
ing ' things to the completion of
those that are revealed, ¹⁵ and she,
the effluence of ' thought, will
reveal to you ' how the belief in
those ' things that are not revealed
was found ' in those that are
revealed, those that belong to ²⁰
the Unbegotten Father. ' Whoever
has an ear to hear, ' let him hear.

"The Lord of the Universe ' is
not called 'Father,' ' but 'First
Father,' the source of ²⁵ those that
were to be revealed. [Now] he **99**
is [the] beginningless First Father '
who beholds himself ' within himself ⟨as with⟩ a mirror. He was
revealed, ' resembling himself. ⁵
And his likeness was revealed ' as
a divine father ' through himself, '

fronted ' the Unbegotten First-Existing One. [10] Indeed he is of equal age with the one who is before ' his countenance, but he is not equal to him ' in power.

Afterward he revealed ' a multitude of confronting, ' self-begotten ones, equal in age [15] (and) power, being ' in glory, and without number. They are [called] ' "the generation over whom ' there is no kingdom among ' the kingdoms that exist."

And the whole multitude [20] there over which there is no ' kingdom is called ' "the Sons of the Unbegotten ' Father."

Now he is the unknowable, **76** who [is] ever [full] ' of imperishableness [and] ineffable joy. ' They all are at rest ' in him, [5] ever rejoicing in ineffable joy ' because of the unchanging glory ' and the measureless jubilation ' that was never heard or ' known among all the aeons [10] and their worlds. But ' enough for now, lest we ' go on endlessly. '

Another subject of knowledge is this, under (the heading of) ' the begotten.

and ⟨as⟩ Confronter over the confronted ones, ' the first-existing, Unbegotten [10] Father. Indeed he is of equal age ' ⟨with⟩ the light that is before ' his countenance, but he is not equal to him ' in power.

"But afterward was revealed ' a whole multitude of confronting, [15] self-begotten ones, ' equal in age and power, ' being in glory (and) without number. Their race is called ' 'the generation ' over whom there is no kingdom,' by the one [20] by whom you yourselves have been revealed (as being) ' among these ' men. And that whole multitude ' over which there is no ' kingdom is called **100** 'the Sons of the Unbegotten ' Father, God, the [Savior], ' the Son of God,' the one ' whose resemblance is with you. Now he [5] is the unknowable, ' who is full of every imperishable glory ' and ineffable joy. ' They all are at rest ' in him, [10] ever rejoicing in ineffable joy ' in his unchanging glory ' and measureless jubilation; ' this was never heard ' or known [15] among all the aeons and their worlds ' until now."

Matthew said ' to him, "Lord, ' Savior, how was Man revealed?" ' The perfect [20] Savior said, "I desire ' that you understand that

Before the universe, the First [15] was revealed. ' In the boundless-ness he is a self-grown, ' self-con-structed father ' who is full of shining, ineffable light. ' In the beginning he decided [20] to have his form come to be ' as a great power. Immediately ' the begin-ning of that light ' was revealed as an immortal, ' androgynous man.

His male name **77** is ' "the [Be-getting of the] Perfect One." ' And his female name (is) "All-wise ' Begettress Sophia." It is also said [5] that she resembles her ' brother and her consort. It is a ' truth that is uncontested; ' for here below error, which exists with it, ' con-tests the truth.

Through [10] Immortal Man ' was revealed a first designation (fem.), ' namely divinity ' and kingdom; for the Father, who is ' called "Self-Father Man," [15] revealed this (masc.). ' He created for himself a great aeon ' corresponding to his greatness. He gave it ' great au-thority, and it ruled ' over all creations. He created [20] for him-self gods and archangels ' and

he who ' was revealed before the universe in ' the boundlessness is the self-grown, **101** self-constructed Father who is full ' of shining light, ' and is ineffable. ' In the beginning he decided to have his [5] form come to be as a great power. ' Immediately the beginning ' of that light was revealed as an immortal, ' androgynous man, ' so that through that immortal [10] man they might attain ' their salvation and awake ' from forgetfulness through the interpreter ' who was sent, who ' is with you until the end [15] of the poverty of the robbers.

And his ' consort is the great Sophia, ' who was from the first ' destined in him for a yoke, through ' the self-begotten Father, from [20] Immortal Man, who first was revealed ' in divinity and king-dom; ' for the Father, who is **102** called 'Man, the Self-Father,' ' revealed him. ' He created for himself a great aeon, ' whose name is Ogdoad, [5] corresponding to his greatness. He was given ' great authority and ruled ' over the creation of poverty. ' He created for himself gods ' and angels

angels, myriads ' without number for retinue. '

Now from that man ' originated divinity **78** and kingdom. Therefore he was ' called "God of gods," "King ' of kings."

Now First Man ' is "Faith (Pistis)" for those who will come to be [5] after these. He has within ' a unique mind, thought, which is like ' it, reflecting ' and thinking, rationality ' and power. All the parts [10] that exist are perfect and immortal. ' In respect to imperishableness, they ' are equal. (However) in respect to power, there is a difference, ' like the difference between a father ' and a son, and a son and a thought, [15] and the thought and the remainder.

As ' I said earlier, among the things that were created, ' the unit is first. Two ' follows it, and three, ' up to the ten⟨s⟩. Now the ten⟨s⟩ [20] are prior to the hundred⟨s⟩. The hundred⟨s⟩ ' are prior to the thousand⟨s⟩. The thousand⟨s⟩ are prior ' to the ten thousands. This is the pattern ⟨among the⟩ ' immortals. V 7 [24] And the unit ' and the thought are those of [Immortal] Man. ' The thinkings [are] ' for the ten⟨s⟩. And the hundreds are [the teachings], ' [and the thousands] are the counsels, ' [and] the ten thousands [are] the powers. [Now] those [who] [30]

⟨and⟩ archangels, [10] myriads without number ' for retinue. (This is) from that light ' and the ' tri-male spirit, which is that of Sophia ' his consort. [15] For from this God originated ' divinity ' and kingdom. Therefore he ' was called 'God of' gods,' 'King of kings.' [20]

"First Man has ' his unique mind ' within, and thought, ' which is like it, reflecting, ' thinking, rationality, **103** power. All the parts that exist ' are perfect and ' immortal. In respect to ' imperishableness, they are equal. (However) in respect to [5] power, they are different, like the difference ' between a father and a son, ⟨and a son⟩ and a thought, ' and the thought and the remainder.

"As ' I said earlier, among ' the things that were created, the unit is [10] first.

come from [...] ' exist with their
[...] ' and every aeon [...]. **8**
[First, thought] ' and the thinkings [were revealed by] mind, '
(then) the teachings [by] the '
thinkings, the counsels [5] [by the
teachings], (and) power by ' [the
counsels]. And after everything
else, ' the universe that [appeared] '
was revealed by [power]. ' And [by]
that [which was] [10] created, that
which was [made] was revealed.
And ' that which was formed was
revealed ' by that which was
[made]. That ' which was named
was revealed ' by that which was
formed. [15] The difference among
what (pl.) was begotten ' was revealed by that which was named '
from beginning to end, by ' the
power of all the aeons.

Now Immortal Man ' is full of
every [20] imperishable glory and ineffable ' joy. His whole kingdom '
rejoices in ' everlasting rejoicing,
those who never ' have been heard
or known [25] in any aeon that '
[came] after [them], and its [worlds]. '
Afterward [First ' Source] came
from Immortal Man, ' [the one]
who is called [30] "the Perfect [Be-
getter]." '
  [Man] took his [consort ' and]
revealed ' [that first-begotten an-

And after everything else, ' that
which wholly appeared ' was revealed by his power. And by that
which ' was created ' all that was
made [15] was revealed; by ' that
which was made ' was revealed
that which was formed; ' by that
which was formed, ' that which
was named. Thus [20] came the
difference among the unbegotten
ones, ' from beginning to end." '

  Then Bartholomew ' said to him,
"How (is it that) ⟨he⟩ was designated in **104** the Gospel 'Man' '
and 'Son of Man'? ' From which
of ' them, then, is this son?" The
Holy One [5] said to him,

"I desire that you ' understand
that First Man ' is called ' 'Begetter, Mind who is complete ' in
himself.' [10] He reflected with the
great ' Sophia, his consort, and
revealed ' his first-begotten, ' an-

drogyny **9** whose ' name is] "First-begotten [Son of the ' Father]."
His female aspect ' [is (called) "First]-begotten Sophia, **5** [Mother of the Universe]," whom some ' [call] "Love." ' [Now the] First-begotten, since he has ' [his] authority from ' his [father], created a **10** great [aeon] corresponding to his greatness, ' [creating] for himself myriads of angels III **81** **2** [without] number ' for retinue. The whole multitude ' of those angels is called **5** "the Assembly of the ' Holy Ones, the shadowless lights."'
Now when these greet ' each other, their embraces ' are for angels who **10** are like them.

First-Begetter ' Father is called ' "Adam of the Light."

And the kingdom ' of Son of Man is ' full of ineffable joy **15** and unchanging jubilation because they rejoice ' continually in ineffable joy 'over their imperishable 'glory, which has ' never been heard of, nor has it been revealed to²⁰ all the aeons that came to be ' and their worlds.

drogynous son. His ' male name **15** is called 'First-Begetter ' Son of God'; his female ' name is 'First-Begettress Sophia, ' Mother of the Universe.' 'Some call her **20** 'Love.' Now the First-begotten ' is called ' 'Christ.' Since he has authority ' from his Father, he created for himself ' a multitude of angels **105** without number for retinue, ' from the spirit and the light." '

His disciples 'said to him, "Lord, the one who is **5** called 'Man,' reveal ' to us about him, so that ' we also may know his glory exactly." ' The perfect ' Savior said, "Whoever has an **10** ear to hear, let him ' hear. First-Begetter ' Father is called 'Adam, ' [the] Eye of the Light,' because he came ' from the shining light **15** [with] his holy angels, who are ineffable ' (and) shadowless. ' They rejoice continually with joy ' in their reflecting, ' which they received from their Father. (This is) the whole kingdom **20** of Son of Man, ' the one who is called 'Son ' of God.' ⟨It⟩ is full of ' ineffable and shadowless joy, ' and unchanging jubilation because they rejoice **25** over his imperishable **106** glory, which has never been heard of

Now Son ' of Man harmonized with ' Sophia, his consort, and ' revealed a great androgynous light. **82** [Some call his] masculine name ' "Savior, ' Begetter of All Things." His feminine name ' is called [5] "Sophia, All-Begettress." Some ' ,call her "Pistis." '

Then the Savior harmonized with ' his consort, Pistis Sophia. ' He revealed six androgynous spiritual beings [10] whose type ' is that of those who preceded them. ' Their male names are these. The first is ' "Unbegotten." The second is ' "Self-begotten." The third [15] is "Begetter." The fourth is ' "First Begetter." The fifth ' is "All-Begetter." The sixth ' is "Prime Begetter." Also the names ' of the females are these. The first is [20] "All-wise Sophia." The second ' is "All-Mother Sophia." The third ' is "All-Begettress Sophia." ' The fourth is "First-Begettress ' Sophia." The fifth is "Love Sophia." **83** The [sixth] is "Pistis Sophia." '

[By the] harmonizing ' of those

until ' now, nor has it been revealed ' in the aeons that came to be ' after these and their worlds. [5] I came from the ' Self-begotten and the First ' Endless Light, so that ' I might reveal ' everything to you."

Again his disciples said, [10] "Tell us clearly ' how (it happened that) from things ' invisible they came down ' from the immortal one to the world, ' since (here) they die?" The perfect [15] Savior said, "Son of ' Man harmonized with Sophia, his ' consort, and revealed ' a great androgynous light. ' His male name [20] is called 'Savior, ' Begetter of All Things.' His ' female name is called 'All-Begettress Sophia.' ' Some call her ' 'Pistis.'

of whom I have just spoken, the
thoughts were revealed ' in the
aeons that exist.⁵ By ⟨the⟩ thoughts,
the reflectings (were revealed); '
by the reflectings, ' the thinkings;
by the thinkings, ' the rationalities;
by the rationalities, ' the wills; by
the ¹⁰ wills, the words. Then the
twelve ' powers, whom I have just
spoken of, ' harmonized with each
other. ' ⟨Six⟩ males (each and)
⟨six⟩ females (each) were revealed,'
so that they make ¹⁵ seventy-two
powers. Each one of the seventy-
two ' revealed ' five spiritual
(powers), ' which makes three
hundred sixty ' powers. The union
of them all is ²⁰ the interval.

Now our aeon came to be as a
type ' in relation to Immortal
Man. ' Time came to be as ' a
type of the First Begetter, **84** his
son. [The year] came to be as ' a
type of the [Savior. The] twelve '
months came to be as a type ' of
the twelve powers. The three ⁵
hundred sixty days of the year '
came to be as a type of the three
hundred ' sixty powers who were
revealed ' by the Savior. In relation
to the angels, who ' came from
these, who are without number, ¹⁰
the hours and the moments of
them (the days) came to be as ' a
type. '

All who come ²⁵ into the world
like **107** a drop from the light ' are
sent by him ' to the world of the
Almighty, ' so that they might be
guarded ⁵ by him. And the bond

of ' its (the drop's) forgetfulness
bound it by the will ' of Sophia, so
that the matter might be ⟨revealed⟩
through it (the bond) ' to the whole
world of poverty ' concerning his
(the Almighty's) arrogance [10] and
blindness, and ' the ignorance,
because he named himself. But I '
came from the places ' above by
the will of the great ' Light, (I) who
escaped from that bond. [15] I cut
off the thing of the ' robbers. I
wakened it, namely, that drop '
that was sent from Sophia, ' so
that it ' might bear much fruit [20]
through me, and be perfected, and
not be ' lacking, but be set apart
by ' me, the great Savior, in order
that his ' glory might be revealed,
so that ' Sophia might also be
justified in regard to that [25] defect,
so that her **108** sons might not
again become defective, but '
might attain honor and ' glory,
and go up to their ' Father, and
know the words of the masculine
Light. And [5] you ' were sent by '
the son, who was sent ' so that you
might receive light and ' remove
yourselves from the forgetfulness
of [10] the authorities, and so that it
might not again come to appearance ' because of you, namely, the
unclean rubbing ' that is ' from the
fearful fire that ' came from their
fleshly part. [15] Tread upon their '
malicious intent."

Then Thomas said to [him], '
"Lord, Savior, ' how many are the
aeons of those ' that surpass the

And when those whom I have spoken of were revealed, ' the All-Begetter, their father, first ' created for them [15] twelve aeons ' for retinue and twelve ' angels. And in ' each aeon there were six (heavens), ' so that [20] there are seventy-two heavens of the seventy-two ' powers who were revealed ' by him. And in each of the heavens ' there were five firmaments, ' so that there are three hundred sixty [85] [firmaments] of the three hundred ' sixty powers that were revealed ' by them. When the firmaments ' were completed, they were named [5] "the Three Hundred Sixty Heavens," according to the name of the ' heavens that were before them. And these all ' are perfect and good. And in this ' way was revealed the defect ' of femaleness.

Now the first [10] aeon is that of Immortal Man. ' The second aeon is that of Son of ' Man, the one who is called ' "First Begetter." ⟨The third is that of the son of Son of Man,⟩ the one who ' is called "Savior." [15] The one who embraces these is the aeon ' over whom there is no kingdom in the ' divine,

heavens?" The perfect [20] Savior said, "I praise ' you because you ask about ' the great aeons, because your roots ' are in the boundless things. And when ' those whom I have spoken of were revealed, [25] the Self-Begetter Father first BG **107** [4] began to create for himself ' twelve ' aeons for retinue ' ⟨and⟩ twelve ' angels.

These ' all are perfect [10] and good. ' Through these was revealed ' the defect ' in the female."

They said ' to him, "How many are the [15] aeons from the boundless places ' of the immortals?" The perfect Savior said, ' "Whoever has ' an ear to hear, let him **108** hear. The first aeon ' is that of Son of Man, ' the one who is called ' 'First Begetter,' [5] the one who is called ' 'Savior,' ' the one who was revealed. ' The second aeon is that of ' Man, who is called [10] 'Adam, the Eye ' of the Light.' The one who embraces ' these is the aeon ' over whom boundless eternity, the ' aeon of the aeons, with the immortals ' who are in him, the one above the Eighth [20] that was revealed in ' chaos.

Now he, Immortal Man, revealed aeons ' and powers and kingdoms, ' and he gave authority to everyone [86] who was revealed by him ' to make [whatever (pl.) they desired] ' until the days that are above chaos. ' For these harmonized with each other, [5] and they revealed ' every greatness, even, by a spirit, ' a multitude of lights ' which are glorious and without number, these ' that were named in the beginning, that [10] is, the first, the middle, ⟨and⟩ the perfect, ' that is, the first aeon, ' the second, and the third. ' The first was called ' "Oneness" and "Rest"; [15] (and) each one has its (own) ' name. For they were designated "Assembly" ' from the three aeons, that is, ' from the numerous multitude that ' appeared (together) in the one multitude. [20] Because of this—the multitude ' gathering and coming to a unity—' they are called "Assembly," ' from the assembly that surpasses ' heaven. Therefore, the Assembly of [87] the [Eighth was] revealed ' as androgynous, and was named ' partly as male and

there is no kingdom, ' (the aeon) of the [15] divine, boundless eternity, ' the self-begotten aeon ' of the aeons ' that are in him, (the aeon) of the immortals, ' whom I have spoken of already, [109] (who is) above the Seventh ' that was revealed by ' Sophia, who is the ' first aeon.

"Now he, [5] Immortal Man, revealed ' aeons ' and powers and kingdoms, ' and he gave authority ' to all who are revealed [10] by him that they might ' exercise their desires until ' the last times that are above ' chaos. For these ' harmonized with each [15] other. And he revealed ' every greatness, even, ' by the spirit, a ' multitude of lights which are glorious ' (and) without number, these [110] that were designated ' in the beginning, that is, ' the first aeon, ' and two, and three. [5] The first is called ' 'Oneness,' ' and 'Rest'; ' (and) each one has ' its (own) name. For they [10] were designated 'Assembly' ' from the three aeons, ' that is, from the ' numerous multitude ' that appeared (together) [15] in one. And a multitude revealed them. ' But because ' these multitudes [111] gather together III [111] and come to a unity, (BG [111], 2-5 adds: because of this, they are called ' 'Assembly,' ' but from that assembly [5] that surpasses heaven) we call ' them the 'Assembly ' of the Eighth.' It was revealed ' as androgynous, and was named [5] partly ' as female. The male was called "Assembly," [5] the female "Life," that ' it might be shown that from ' a female came the life ' in all the aeons, since every name was received ' by (the time of) the beginning.

From his [10] good pleasure and his thought ' the powers were revealed, who were called ' "gods." And the gods ' by their thinkings revealed ' divine gods. [15] And the gods by their ' thinkings revealed lords. ' And the lords of the lords by ' their words revealed lords. ' And the lords by [20] their powers revealed ' archangels. The archangels ' revealed angels. By ' this (fem.), the semblance was revealed, **88** with structure [and form], to name ' [all] the aeons [and] their worlds. '

All the immortals, which ' I have just described, have authority—all of them—[5] by the power of ' Immortal Man and Sophia, ' his consort, who was ' called "Silence," (and) who was named ' "Silence" because in reflecting [10] without a word she perfected her ' greatness. The imperishables, since they have ' the authority, each provided for themselves ' great ' kingdoms in all the immortal heavens [15] and their firmaments, ' thrones, (and) temples ' corresponding to their greatness.

partly as male and ' partly as female. The male ' is called 'Assembly,' while the ' female is called 'Life,' ' that it might be shown that from [10] a female came the life of ' all the aeons. And every name was ' received from (the time of) the beginning.

"For by ' his concurrence and his thought the powers were first revealed, ' who [15] were called 'gods.' ' And [the] gods of the gods by their ' wisdom revealed gods. ' By their wisdom they revealed ' lords. And the lords of [20] the lords revealed lords by their thinking. ' And the lords by ' their power revealed archangels. ' The archangels ' by their words revealed angels. **112** By these, ' semblances were revealed with structure, and form, ' and name for all the aeons ' and their worlds.

"And the immortals, [5] which I have just described, all have ' authority from ' Immortal Man ⟨and Sophia, his consort, who⟩ ' is called 'Silence,' ' because in reflecting without [10] a word all her greatness was perfected. ' For the imperishables, since they have ' the authority, each created ' for themselves a great kingdom ' in the Eighth, [15] and (also) thrones, and temples, (and) firmaments corresponding to ' their greatnesses. For these all ' came from the will ' of the Mother of the Universe."

Then [20] the holy Apostles said '

Some, indeed, ' (who are) in dwelling places and in chariots, ' being in ineffable glory, [20] and not being able to be sent into any nature, ' provided for themselves ' hosts of angels, myriads ' without number for retinue **89** and glory, even ineffable virgin ' spirits of light. ' They have no sickness ' nor weakness, but it is only will, [5] so it (what is willed?) comes to be ' in an instant. ' The aeons and their heavens and the firmaments were completed ' for the glory of Immortal ' Man and Sophia, his consort. [10]

⟨This is⟩ where every aeon ⟨was⟩ and ' their worlds, and those that came ' after them, to provide ' there the types, their ' likenesses, in the heavens of chaos and [15] their worlds. And all natures, ' from the Immortal One from (the time of) the Unbegotten One ' to the revelation of (or: to) ' chaos, in the shining, shadowless light, ' and (in) ineffable joy, [20] and unutterable jubilation, ' ever delight themselves ' on account of their unchanging glory ' and the immeasurable rest ' that is impossible to speak of **90** or (even) to conceive of ' among all the aeons ' that came to be and their powers. '

But enough for now. Now all these things [5] that I have just said

to him, "Lord, Savior, ' tell us about those who are in the aeons, ' since it is necessary for us to ask ' about them." The perfect **113** Savior said, "If you ask ' about anything, I will tell you. ' They created for themselves hosts of ' angels, myriads without number [5] for retinue, and their glories. They created ' ineffable and shadowless virgin ' spirits of light. ' For they have no sickness ' nor weakness [10] but it is will. (BG 115, 14 adds: And so they came to be in an instant.)

"Thus the aeons were completed ' quickly along with the heavens ' and the firmaments in the glory ' of Immortal Man and Sophia, ' his consort—the place from which [15] every aeon, and world, ' and those that came after ' them received (their) pattern for their creation ' of likenesses in the heavens of chaos ' and their worlds. And all natures [20] from (the time of) the revelation of (or: to) chaos, ' in the shining, shadowless light, ' and (in) ineffable joy, ' and ' unutterable jubilation, ever [25] delight themselves on account of their unchanging glory **114** and the immeasurable rest ' that is impossible to speak ' of among all the aeons that ' came to be after them and all their [5] powers. Now all these things that ' I have just said to you (pl.), I have ' said so that you might shine in ' the light more than these."

to you (sing.) ' I have said in the way that you can ' accept, until the one who does not need to be taught ' is revealed among you, ' and he will say all these things to you [10] joyously and in ' pure knowledge. '

Mariamme said ' to him, "Holy Lord, [10] your disciples, whence ' came they, and where do they go, and (what) should they ' do here?" ' The perfect Savior said to them, "I desire ' that you understand that Sophia, [15] the Mother of the Universe and the consort, ' desired by herself ' to bring these to existence without ' her male (consort). But by the will ' of the Father of the Universe, so that his [20] unimaginable goodness might be revealed, ' he created that curtain ' between the immortals ' and those ' that came after them, [25] so that the consequence might follow BG **118** [13] every aeon ' and chaos, [15] so that the defect of the female ' might live, and she (the female) might ' exist, although Error fights against ' her. And these became **119** a curtain ' of a spirit. From ⟨the⟩ aeon ' above the effluences ' of light, just as [5] I said already, a ' drop from the light ' and the spirit came ' down to the lower regions ' of the Almighty [10] of chaos, so that ' he might reveal their molded ' forms from that drop, ' because it is a judgment ' on him, the Prime Begetter, [15] who is called 'Yaldabaoth.' ' That

drop ' revealed their molded forms '
through the breath for a **120**
living soul. It was withered ' and
it slumbered in the ignorance ' of
the soul. When it ' became hot
from the breath [5] of the great light '
of the male, and he took thought, '
(then) ' names were received by
all who ' are in the world of
chaos [10] and all things that are in '
it, through that ' immortal one,
when the breath ' blew into him. '
But these, when they came to be [15]
in the will of the Mother, ' Sophia,
so that Immortal Man ' might
piece together **121** the garments
there, ' were condemned ' as robbers, ' and they welcomed the
blowing [5] from that breath. ' But
since he is psychical, ' he was not
able to receive ' that power for
himself ' until [10] the number of
chaos is complete, ' and when the
time that ' is determined by the
great ' angel is complete.

"But I taught ' you about Immortal [15] Man, and I loosed ' the
bonds of the robbers ' from him. '
I broke the gates of **122** the
pitiless ones before their faces. ' I
humiliated their ' malicious intent.
They all were shamed ' and rose [5]
from their ignorance. Because ' of
this, then, I came here, ' so that
they might be joined with ' that
spirit III **117** and breath, and
might ' from two become one,
just as from ' the first, so that you
might yield much fruit ' and go
up to [5] the one who is from the

beginning, in ' ineffable joy, and glory, ' and [honor, and] grace of ' [the Father of the Universe].

"Whoever, then, knows ' [the Father in pure] knowledge [10] [will depart] to the Father ' [and repose in] the unbegotten ' [Father]. But [whoever knows] ' him [defectively] will depart ' [and repose] in [the rest [15] of the Eighth. Now] whoever knows ' [the] immortal [spirit] ' of light, in silence, through reflecting ' and desire, in truth, ' let him bring me signs [20] of the invisible one, and he will become ' a light in the spirit of silence. ' Whoever knows Son of Man ' in knowledge and love, ' let him bring me a sign **118** of Son of Man, so that he might depart ' to the dwellings with those who are in the Eighth. '

"Behold, I have revealed to you ' the name of the perfect one, the whole will [5] of the mother of the holy angels, ' so that the masculine [multitude] ' may be completed here, ' so that there [might be revealed in the aeons ' the boundless ones and] [10] those who [came to be in the] untraceable ' [wealth of the Great] ' Invisible [Spirit, so that they] all [might receive ' from his goodness] ' and wealth [the rest] [15] that has no [kingdom over it]. I ' came [from the First], who ' was sent so that I might reveal ' to you the one who is from ' the beginning, because of the arrogance [20] of the Prime Begetter and his angels, ' because they say about themselves that ' they are gods. And I ' came to remove them from their blindness ' that I might tell everyone ²⁵ about the God who is above the universe. **119** You, therefore, tread upon their ' graves, humiliate their malicious intent, ' and break their yoke, ' and arouse my own. I have given ⁵ you authority over all things ' as sons of light, ' so that you might tread upon their power with ' [your] feet."

These are the things [the] blessed ' Savior [said, ¹⁰ and he disappeared] from them. Then ' [all the disciples] were in ' [great, ineffable joy] in ' [the spirit from] that day (on). ' [And his disciples] began to preach ¹⁵ [the] Gospel of God, ' [the] eternal, imperishable [Spirit]. ' Amen. '

Eugnostos the '   The Sophia of Jesus
Blessed

THE DIALOGUE OF THE SAVIOR (III, 5)

Introduced by

HELMUT KOESTER and ELAINE H. PAGELS

Translated by

HAROLD W. ATTRIDGE

The somewhat fragmentary *Dialogue of the Savior* is an important Christian document of considerable complexity. To begin with, this tractate is composed of several sources and traditions which can be isolated. The main source used by the author was a dialogue between Jesus and several of the disciples. This dialogue is based on a traditional collection of sayings comparable to "Q" or the *Gospel of Thomas* (II, 2); in fact, many of the sayings used or alluded to in the dialogue have parallels in the *Gospel of Thomas*. The individual sayings of Jesus are quoted, expanded, and interpreted, and thus a dialogue is created. Into this dialogue are inserted various other sources and traditions: a creation myth (127, 23-131, 15) based upon Genesis 1-2, a cosmological list interpreted in the wisdom tradition (133, 16-134, 24), and a fragment of an apocalyptic vision (134, 24-137, 3). The final author has introduced this material by means of an exhortation, a prayer, and a typically Gnostic instruction about the passage of the soul through the heavenly spheres and hostile powers (120, 2-124, 22).

The author of the *Dialogue of the Savior* has one primary theological concern which he develops in continuity with his dialogue source: realized eschatology is juxtaposed with futuristic eschatology, the "already" with the "not yet." This duality is expressed in language which has many parallels in the deutero-Pauline letters, 1 Peter, and Hebrews. Like the epistle to the Ephesians, the *Dialogue of the Savior* relates metaphorical and mythical language to a cultic act for the expression of realized eschatology: in baptism the elect have already passed through death to life. Yet, paradoxically, the elect look to the future for their hope. Here the author utilizes his major source which presents the discussion of Jesus' sayings according to an order of salvation like that of the second saying in the *Gospel of Thomas*. Although the elect already have sought and found through baptism, and have marveled at visions, their rule and rest is still to come; they are still burdened by fleshly existence in the world. But they bear this burden for the sake of others, in order that they, like their Lord, may save others and "reveal the greatness of the revealer." Only when this task is completed, when they strip off the body in death and when the "works of femaleness" are dissolved, will they finally rule and rest in the "place of life," which is "pure light."

Stephen Emmel has discovered and edited a fragment of the *Dialogue of the Savior* from the Beinecke Library of Yale University. His edition of this fragment (144, 15-146, 24) has been worked into the translation given here.

THE DIALOGUE OF THE SAVIOR

III 120, 1-147, 23

The Dialogue of the Savior '

The Savior said to his disciples, ' "Already the time has come, ' brothers, that we should leave behind [5] our labor and stand in ' the rest; for he who stands ' in the rest will rest ' forever. And I ' say to you (pl.), dwell in [10] heaven always [. . .] ' time [. . . . And I say] ' to you, [that . . .]' are afraid [. . .] ' to you. I [say to you,] [15] the wrath is fearful, [and he who] ' sets the wrath in motion is a man [. . .]. ' But since you have [. . . when] ' they came from [. . .] ' they received these words [about it (fem.)] with fear [20] and trembling. And it (fem.) made ' them stand with archons, ' for from it (fem.) nothing came forth. ' But when I came, I ' opened the way; I taught them [25] the passage through which ' will pass the elect and the solitary ones **121** who have [learned of the Father], since they have ' believed the truth.

"And as for all the glories ' that you give when ' you give glory, give them in this way: [5] 'Hear us, Father, just as ' thou hast heard thine only-begotten ' Son and hast taken him to thyself ' (and) given him rest from many ' [labors. Thou] art he whose power [10] [is great, and] thy weapons are ' [. . .] light ' [. . .] living ' [. . . who] cannot be touched ' [. . .] the word of [15] [. . .] repentance of life ' [. . . from] thee. Thou art ' [the] remembrance and all the serenity ' of the solitary ones. Again hear ' us, just as thou hast heard [20] thine elect ones. These by thy sacrifice ' enter in with their ' good deeds, they who have redeemed ' their souls from these ' blind limbs in order that they might exist **122** forever. Amen.'

"I will ' teach you: When the time ' of the dissolution will come, ' the first power of the darkness will [5] come upon you. Do not be afraid ' and say, 'Behold the time ' has come.' But whenever you see ' a single staff in the ' sky, that which (or: he who) [. . .] [10] not [. . .] [12] know that [. . .] ' from the deed [. . .] ' and the archons [. . .] [15] come upon you [. . .]. ' Truly, fear is the power [of darkness]. ' If, then, you fear ' him who will come upon you, ' that one will swallow you, [20] since there is not **one** among them who will ' spare you or will have pity on you. ' But in this way look at the [. . .] ' within him, since you have overcome ' every word that is upon the earth. He **123** [will] take you up to the mountain ' [where] there is no ruling authority ' [nor] tyrant. When you ' [come to it] you will see the things that [5] [. . .]. And moreover ' [. . .] tell you that '

[. . .] the reasoning power ' [. . .] reasoning power that exists ' [. . .] the place of truth [10] [. . .] not, but they ' [. . .]. But you ' [. . .] of the truth, that ' [which . . .] living mind because of ' [. . .] and your joy [15] [. . .] you, in order that ' [. . .] your souls ' [. . .] lest he ' [. . .] the word ' [. . .] which they lift up [20] [. . . and] they could not ' [. . .] which is ' [. . .]. The [. . .] did it ' [. . .]. For the crossing-place **124** is frightful before [them]. ' But as for you, [with] ' single mind pass [it] by, ' for its depth is great [and its] [5] height [is] exceedingly great. [. . .] ' single mind [. . .] ' and the fire which [. . .] ' is. The lions [enclose . . .] ' all the powers [. . .] [10] you; they will [. . .] ' and the powers [. . .] ' they [. . .] ' beginning. I create [. . .] ' the soul from [. . .] [15] become a [. . .] ' in every one [. . .] ' you are [. . .] ' and because [. . .] ' forget not [. . .] [20] the sons of [. . .] ' and as you [. . .] ' you [. . .]."

Matthew said, "[In] ' what way [. . .]?" **125**

The Savior said, ' "[. . .] those things that are in you (sing.) ' [. . .] will remain, as for you, ' [. . .]."

Judas [said], "O Lord,[5] [. . .] the deeds ' [. . .] these souls, those ' [which . . .] these little ones, when ' [. . .] where will they be? ' [. . .] not, for the spirit [10] [. . .]."

The Lord [said, ". . .] [12] receive ' them; these do not die ' [nor] do they perish, for they knew [15] [their] consorts and him who will take ' [them] to himself. For truth seeks ' [after] the wise and the righteous one." ' The Savior said, "The lamp ' [of the] body is the mind; as long as [20] you (sing.) are upright [of heart]—which is ' [. . .]—then your (pl.) bodies are ' [lights]. As long as your mind ' is [darkness], your light which you **126** wait for [will not be]. ' As for myself, I have called [. . .] ' that I shall go [because . . .] ' my word to [him for whom] [5] I send."

His disciples [said, ' "Lord], ' who is the one who seeks [and who is the one who] ' reveals?"

[The Lord said], ' "The one who seeks [is also the one who] [10] reveals."

Matthew [said, ' "Lord], ' when I [. . .] ' what I said, who is the one who [speaks and who] ' is the one who hears?"

[The Lord] said,[15] "The one who speaks is also the one who [hears], ' and the one who sees [is] also the one who ' reveals."

Mariam said, ' "O Lord, behold, when I am ' bearing the body, [for what reason do I] [20] weep, and for what reason do [I laugh]?" '

The Lord said, "[If you (sing.)] ' weep because of its deeds [you will] ' abide, and the mind laughs [. . .] **127** spirit. If one does not ' [. . . the] darkness, he will [not] be able to see ' [the light]. Therefore [I] tell you (pl.), ' [. . . of the] light is the darkness.[5] [And if one does not] stand in ' [the darkness, he will not be able] to see the light. ' [...] the lie [...] were carried away by ' [...] you will give ' [...] and [10] [...] be for ever ' [...] in the ' [...] one ' [...] for ever. Then will ' [all] the powers [...] you,[15] those that are above and those ' [that] are below, in that place where ' [there will] be the weeping and ' [the gnashing] of teeth at the end of [all] these things." '

Judas said, "Tell [20] [us], Lord, before ' [the heaven and] the earth were, what was it that ' [existed]?"

The Lord said, ' "It was darkness and water and **128** a spirit that was upon a [water]. ' But I say to [you, as for what] ' you seek after [and] ' inquire about, [behold, it is] [5] within you, and [...] ' of the power and the [mystery ...] ' spirit, because from [...] ' the wickedness comes [...] ' the mind and [...] [10] behold [...] ' of the [...]." '

[...] said, ' "Lord, tell us where [the soul (?)] ' stands, and where the true [mind (?)] [15] is?"

The Lord said [to him], ' "As for the fire [of the] ' spirit, it was in their [...]; ' therefore the [...] ' came to be. The true mind came to be [within] [20] them. [If] ' a man [establishes his soul (?)] ' in the height, then [he will] ' be exalted."

But Matthew asked [him about **129** ...] that [...] received ' [...] he is the one who ' [...].

The Lord [said], ' "[...] steadfast against your [5] [...] outside you ' [...] him to set it ' [upon] you, and all things ' [...] your hearts. For just as ' your hearts [...] it,[10] so you will prevail over the powers that are ' [above] and those that are below. ' [But I] say to you, ' [he who is] able, let him deny ' [himself, and] repent. And he who [knows,[15] let him] seek and find and ' [rejoice]."

Judas said, "Behold, ' [...] see that everything is ' [in it] like these signs that are over ' [the earth]. For this reason they came to be like this (?)." [20]

The Lord [said], "When the Father ' [established] the world he ' [gathered] water from it. ' [His] Word came forth from him. **130** He dwelt in many [...]; ' he was more exalted than the path [of the sun that surrounds (?)] ' the whole earth. They (?) [...] ' for the water that was gathered [together] [5] was outside them. [...] ' of the water while a great fire [surrounded] ' them like walls. And [...] ' time, when many things were separating from [the] ' interior, when the [Father] [10] stood up, he looked [at the Word (?)] ' (and) said to him, 'Go, and [cast them] ' from you, in order that [the earth might not] ' be in want from generation to [generation] ' and from age to age.' Then [he] [15] cast forth from

himself [springs] ' of milk, and springs [of] ' honey, and oil, and [wine],
and good fruits, ' and a sweet taste, and ²⁰ good roots, [in order that] '
it might not be in want from generation [to] ' generation and from age
[to] ' age. But he is above [...] **131** able to stand ' [...] his beauty '
[...] the deed. And outside of ' [...] is [...] of light, being able to ⁵
[...] the one who is like him, for he ' seizes upon the aeons that are '
[above] and that are below, ' [and they] took out of the fire ' [...]. It
was scattered out of the ¹⁰ [Pleroma] that is above and ' [that is] below.
As for everything ' that depends on them, they are ' [the things which
exist] in heaven above ' [and on] earth below.¹⁵ On them all things
depend." '

[And] when Judas ' heard these things he fell down, ' [worshipped],
(and) gave glory to the Lord. ' Mariam asked, "Brothers,²⁰ [the things]
about which you ask the Son of ' [...], where will you keep them?" '

The Lord [said] to her, "Sister, ' [...] can seek out these things '
[...], since he has a place **132** to keep them in his heart [...] ' him to
go from [...] ' and enter into [the place of life (?)] ' in order that he
might not be confined [in] ⁵ this impoverished world." '

Matthew said, "Lord, I wish [to see] ' that place of life, [that place] '
in which there is no evil, but rather it is [the] ' pure light."

The Lord said,¹⁰ "Brother Matthew, ' you (sing.) cannot see it, as long
you ' wear the flesh."

Matthew said, ' "O Lord, even if [I can] ' not see it, let me [know it]." ¹⁵

The Lord said, "Every one [of you] ' who has known himself has seen
it; ' everything that is fitting for him to do, [he does] ' it. And he has
been [doing] ' it in his goodness."

Judas ²⁰ answered him and said, ' "Tell me, Lord, [the earthquake] '
that moves the earth, how does it ' move?"

The Lord took a stone [and] ' held it in his hand. [He **133** said, "What]
is this that I hold ' in my [hand]?"

He said, "[It is] a stone." '

He said to them, "He who sustains ' [the earth] is he who sustains the
heaven.⁵ When a word comes forth ' from the Greatness, it will go to
him ' who sustains the heaven and the earth. For the earth ' does not
move; if it moved, it would ' fall, but (it does not fall) in order that the
first word ¹⁰ might not be annulled, namely 'he is the one who established ' the world, and he dwelt ' in it, and he received incense from ' it.'
For everything that does not move I ' [will bring] to you, all ye sons of
men,¹⁵ for you are from [that] place. '

"As for those who speak out of ' [joy] and truth, you are in ' their heart. And if he comes from ' [the] body of the Father through men,[20] [and] they do not receive him, ' [he] turns again to his place. He who knows ' [not] the works of perfection knows ' nothing. If one does not stand ' in the darkness, he will not be able to see the light. **134** If one does not [understand] ' how the fire came to be, ' he will burn in it, because ' he does not know his root.[5] If one does not first understand the ' water, he does not know anything. For what ' is the use for him to receive baptism ' in it? If one does not understand ' how the wind that blows [10] came to be, he will run ' with it. If one does not understand ' how the body that he wears ' came to be, he will perish with ' it. And he who does not know the Son,[15] how will he know the [Father]? ' And he who will not know the root ' of all things, they (all things) are hidden from him. He who ' will not know the root of wickedness ' is not a stranger to it. He [20] who will not understand how ' he came will not understand how ' he will go, and is not a [stranger] ' to this world which [will perish and] ' which will be humbled."

Then he [took] Judas [25] and Matthew and Mariam **135** [. . . at] the end, the whole of heaven ' [and] earth. [And] when he set his ' [hand] upon them they hoped that they might ' [see] it. Judas lifted up his eyes; [5] he saw a very high place, ' and he saw the place of the pit, ' which is below.

Judas said to ' Matthew, "Brother, who can ' go up to this height or below [10] to the pit? For there is a great ' fire there, and a great terror." ' At that moment there came forth from ' it a word. While he was standing ' he saw how it came [15] [down]. Then he said to it, "Why ' have you (sing.) come down?"

And the Son ' of Man greeted them, and said to them, ' "A grain from a power ' was deficient and went down below to [20] [the] pit of the earth. And the greatness ' remembered, and sent the word ' to it. He brought it up to ' [his presence], because **136** the first word was abrogated."

[Again his] disciples ' wondered at all the [things] that ' he told them, they received them in ' faith, and they knew that it was not necessary [. . .] [5] to look at wickedness. Then he said [to] ' his disciples, "Did I not say ' to you (pl.) that just as sound and ' lightning are seen, so ' the good will be taken up to [10] the light?"

Then all his disciples ' gave glory to him. They said, "Lord, ' before you (sing.) appeared ' here, who was there to give glory to you? ' For through you are all glories.[15] And who was there to bless [you], ' since from you comes all blessing?" '

While they were standing, he saw ' two spirits bringing a single soul with them in a great flash of lightning.[20] And a word came from ' the Son of Man, saying, ' "Give them their garment." [And] ' the little one was like the big one. They were [. . .] ' to (or: of) those who had received [them. 137 The disciples said to] each other, ' "Then we [. . . his] disciples, ' those whom he [. . .]."

Mariam [said, ' ". . .] see the [5] evil one [. . .] them from the ' beginning [. . .]." '

The Lord said [to her], "When you see ' them [. . .] is great, they ' will not [. . .]. But when you [10] see Him Who Is Forever, that ' is the great vision."

Then all said to him, ' "Show it to us."

He said to them, ' "How do you wish to see it? ' [In] a vision which will cease? Or in an eternal vision?" [15] Again he said, ' "Strive to save the one ' [who] is able to follow ' [you]. Seek him and ' speak with him, in order that [20] everyone whom you seek ' [may] agree with you. For I ' [say] to you, truly ' the living God [dwells] in you 138 [and you dwell (?)] in ' him."

Judas [said to him, "Truly] I ' wish [to . . .]."

The Lord [said] to him, ' "[The] living [God (?)],[5] since he exists, the entire [. . .] ' of the deficiency."

Judas [said], ' "Who will [rule over us (?)]?" '

The Lord said, "[. . .] all the things ' that exist [. . .] the remainder,[10] it is they over which you [rule]." '

Judas said, "Behold, ' the archons dwell in heaven; ' surely, then, it is they who will rule ' over us."

The Lord said, "You [15] will rule over them. ' But when you remove ' envy from you, then ' you will clothe yourselves with the light ' and enter into the bridal [20] chamber."

Judas said, "How ' will our garments be brought to us?" '

The Lord said, "Some ' will bring (them) to you [and] ' others will receive [them], 139 for they are [the ones who bring] you your ' garments. Who [can] reach ' that place which is the reward? ' But they gave the garments of life to [5] the man, for he knows the ' way on which he will go. For indeed it is ' a burden to me as well to reach it." '

Mariam said, "Thus ' about 'The wickedness of each day,' and 'The [10] laborer being worthy of his food,' and ' 'The disciple resembling his teacher.' " ' This word she spoke as a woman who ' knew the All.

The disciples said to him, ' "What is the Pleroma and [15] what is the deficiency?"

He said to them, ' "You are from the Pleroma, ' and you dwell in the place where ' the deficiency is. And behold, ' its light was poured down [20] upon me."

Matthew said, ' "Tell me, Lord, how ' the dead die, ' and how the living live?" **140**

The Lord said, "[You (sing.) have] asked me ' for a word [about that] which eye ' has not seen, nor have I heard about it, ' except from you. But I say [5] to you (pl.), that when ' that which moves man is withdrawn he will be called ' 'dead,' and when ' the living one sets free the dead one, ' he will be called 'living.' "

Judas said,[10] "Why then, by the truth, do they die ' and live?"

The Lord said, ' "He who is from the truth ' does not die; he who is from the woman ' dies."

Mariam said,[15] "Tell me, Lord, why ' I have come to this place, to benefit ' or to suffer loss?"

The Lord said, ' "Because you (sing.) reveal the greatness of the revealer." '

Mariam said to him,[20] "Lord, is there then a place that is [...] ' or is deprived of the truth?" '

The Lord said, "The place where I ' [am] not."

Mariam said, ' "Lord, you (sing.) are fearful and wonderful **141** and [...] from ' those who do not know [you]." '

Matthew said, "Why do we not put ourselves to ' rest at once?" [5]

The Lord said, "(You will) when you lay down ' these burdens."

Matthew said, ' "In what way does the little one ' cleave to the great one?"

The Lord said, ' "When you leave behind you [10] the things that will not be able ' to follow you, then you will put yourselves to ' rest."

Mariam said, ' "I want to know ' how all things exist."

The Lord said,[15] "Whoever seeks life (knows this), ' for [this] is their wealth. ' For the [enjoyment] of this world ' is a [lie], and its gold and its silver ' is error."

His disciples said to him,[20] "What shall we do in order ' [that] our work may be perfect?" '

The Lord [said] to them, "Be ' prepared before the All. ' Blessed is the man who has found **142** the interpretation [about this thought (?)], the struggle ' with his eyes. He did not kill nor was ' [he] killed, but he came forth victorious." '

Judas said, "Tell me, Lord,[5] what is the beginning of the way?"

He said, ' "Love and goodness. For if ' there had been one of these dwelling with the ' archons, wickedness would never have come to be." '

Matthew said, "O Lord,[10] you (sing.) have spoken without pain of the end of the All." '

The Lord said, "Everything which ' I have said to you (pl.) you have understood ' and received in faith. ' If you have known them, they are [yours];[15] if not, they are not yours." '

They said to him, "What is the place ' to which we shall go?"

The Lord said, ' "The place which you can reach, ' stand there!" [20]

Mariam said, "Is everything [that] ' is established seen in this way?" '

The Lord said, "I have told you (pl.) [that] ' he who sees is he who ' reveals."

His twelve disciples asked him,[25] "Teacher, **143** as for the lack of care [...] ' teach us that [...]."

The Lord said, ' "[If you understood] everything ' which I said [to you, then] you will [5] [...], you [will know] everything." '

Mariam said, "There is one word ' that I will [say] to the Lord ' concerning the mystery of the truth, ' this in which we have stood. Moreover,[10] it is to the worldly that we appear." '

Judas said to Matthew, "We ' wish to know with what kind ' [of] garments we will be clothed, ' when we come forth from the corruption of the [15] [flesh]."

The Lord said, "The archons ' [and] the governors have ' garments that are given to them for a time, ' which do not abide. As for you, ' [however], since you are sons of the truth, it is not [20] with these temporary garments ' that you will clothe yourselves. Rather, I say ' to you that you will be blessed ' when you strip yourselves, ' for it is still a great thing **144** [...] outside." '

[...] said, "[... the] word, I ' am [...]."

The Lord said, ' "[...] your father [5] [...]."

Mariam said, ' "[What] is this mustard [seed] ' like? [Is it] from heaven [or] ' from [the] earth?"

The Lord said, ' "When [the] Father established the [10] world for himself, he left behind many things from ' the Mother of the All. Because of this he speaks ' and acts."

Judas said, "You (sing.) have ' said this [to] us from the mind of ' truth. When we pray,[15] how should we pray?"

The Lord said, ' "Pray in the place where there is no woman." '

Matthew said, ' "'Pray in the place where there ' is [no woman],' he tells us, saying, 'Destroy the [20] works of womanhood,' not because there is any other [manner of birth], ' but because they will cease [giving birth]." '

Mariam said, "They will never be obliterated." '

The Lord said, "[Who] ' knows that they will [not] dissolve **145** and [the works] ' of [womanhood here] be [destroyed as well]?" '

Judas said [to Matthew, ' "The] works of [womanhood] will dissolve ⁵ [...] the archons ' will [...]. Thus will we ' become prepared for them." '

The Lord said, "Right. For do they see you? ' [Do they see] those who receive ¹⁰ you? Now behold! A word ' [belonging to] heaven will come forth from the Father ' [to the depth], in silence with a flash of lightning, ' giving birth. Do they see it or overpower ' it? But you are all the more ¹⁵ aware of [the path], this one, ' [before] either [angel] or authority has ' [... it]. Rather it belongs to the Father and the ' [Son] because they are both a single ' [...]. And you will go via ²⁰ [the path] which you have known. Even if ' the archons become huge ' [they] will not reach it. [But listen!] I ' tell you [that] it is difficult ' even for me [to reach] it." **146**

[Mariam said to the Lord], ' "When the works [dissolve, ' ...] which (or: who) dissolves (or: dissolve) ' a [work]."

[The Lord said, "Right, for] you ⁵ know [...] if I ' dissolve [...] will go to ' his (or: its) place."

Judas said, "How (or: In what) ' is the [spirit] apparent?" '

The Lord said, "How (or: In what) [is] the sword [apparent]?" ¹⁰

Judas said, ' "How (or: In what) is the light apparent?" '

The Lord said, "[...] ' in it (or: by means of it) forever."

Judas said, ' "Who forgives the actions ¹⁵ of whom? [The] actions which [...] ' the cosmos [...] ' who forgives (or: forgive) the actions." '

The Lord [said], "Who [...]? ' It behooves whoever has understood the actions ²⁰ to do the [will] of the Father. ' And as for you, [strive] to rid yourselves of [anger] ' and [jealousy], ' and strip yourselves ' of your [...], and do not [... **147**¹³ they] will mock ' [...] for I say ¹⁵ [...] take ' [...] you many ' [...] who sought, having ' [...] understand this [...] ' will live for ²⁰ [ever]. But [I myself] say to ' [you ...] that you might not err ' [in your] spirits and your souls." '

[The] Dialogue of the Savior

THE APOCALYPSE OF PAUL (V, *2*)

Introduced and translated by

GEORGE W. MACRAE and WILLIAM R. MURDOCK

Edited by

DOUGLAS M. PARROTT

The first of the series of four apocalypses in Codex V, the *Apocalypse of Paul*, describes the ascent of Paul through the heavens. Though other ancient works of the same or similar name are known, the Coptic *Apocalypse of Paul* seems quite unique in its focus upon Paul's ascent through the fourth to the tenth heavens. The precise circumstances surrounding the composition of the document remain uncertain. Yet the polemic against the apocalyptic "old man" in the seventh heaven may indicate that the document comes from a Gnostic group with an anti-Jewish tendency. Furthermore, the portrait of Paul as one exalted above his fellow apostles resembles the portrayal of Paul in the Gnosticism, and especially the Valentinianism, of the second century C.E.

The *Apocalypse of Paul* opens with an epiphany scene: a little child, probably the risen Christ, encounters Paul on the mountain, provides a revelation, and guides Paul to the Jerusalem above. Clearly this scene with the heavenly child provides an interpretation of Galatians 1:11-17 and 2:1-2. Of course, the basis for the entire ascent narrative is to be found in 2 Corinthians 12:2-4. As Paul ascends through the heavens, he witnesses, in the fourth and fifth heavens, a scene of the judgment and punishment of souls, a scene which is reminiscent of similar pictures in Jewish apocalyptic literature but which also illustrates popular syncretism. Paul's heavenly journey seems to rely upon Jewish apocalyptic tradition, but the Gnostic character of the present ascent narrative is obvious. Finally Paul reaches the tenth heaven where, transformed, he greets his fellow spirits.

THE APOCALYPSE OF PAUL

V 17, 19-24, 9

[The Apocalypse of] Paul '

[. . .] **18**³ the road. And [he spoke to him], ' saying, "[By which] ⁵ road [shall I go] up to [Jerusalem]?" ' The little child [replied, saying], ' "Say your name, so that [I may show] ' you the road." [The little child] ' knew [who Paul was].¹⁰ He wished to make conversation with ' him through his words [in order that] he ' might find an excuse for speaking ' with him.

The little child spoke, ' saying, "I know [15] who you are, Paul. ' You are he who was blessed from ' his mother's womb. For I have [come] ' to you that you may [go up to Jerusalem] ' to your fellow [apostles. And] [20] for this reason [you were called. And] ' I am the [Spirit who accompanies] ' you. Let [your mind awaken, ' Paul], with [...]. 19 For [...] ' whole which [...] ' among the [principalities and] these authorities [and] ' archangels and powers [5] and the whole ace of demons, ' [...] the one that reveals ' bodies to a soul-seed." '

And after he brought that speech ' to an end, he spoke, saying [10] to me, "Let your mind awaken, ' Paul, and see that this mountain ' upon which you are standing is the mountain ' of Jericho, so that you may know the ' hidden things in those that are visible.[15] Now it is to the twelve apostles ' that you shall go, ' for they are elect spirits, and they will ' greet you." He raised ' his eyes and saw them [20] greeting him.

Then the ' Holy [Spirit] who was speaking ' with [him] caught him up ' on high to the third ' heaven, and he passed [25] beyond to the fourth [heaven]. ' The [Holy] Spirit spoke to him, ' saying, "Look ' and see your [likeness] ' upon the earth." And he [looked] [30] down and saw those [who were upon] ' the earth. He stared [and saw] ' those who were upon the [.... Then 20 he] gazed [upward and] saw ' [that the [twelve] apostles ' were [at] his right [and] at his left ' in the creation, and the Spirit was [5] going before them.

But I saw ' in the fourth heaven according to class—I ' saw the angels resembling ' gods, the angels bringing ' a soul out of the land of [10] the dead. They placed it at the gate ' of the fourth heaven. And ' the angels were whipping it. ' The soul spoke, saying, ' "What sin was it that I committed [15] in the world?" ' The toll collector who dwells in the ' fourth heaven replied, saying, ' "It was not right to commit all those lawless deeds ' that are in the world [20] of the dead." ' The soul replied, saying, ' "Bring witnesses! Let them [show] you ' in what body I committed lawless deeds. ' [Do you wish] to bring a book [25] [to read from]?"

And ' the three witnesses came. ' The first spoke, saying, ' "Was I [not ' in] the body the second hour [30] [...]? I rose up against you 21 until [you fell] into anger [and ' rage] and envy." And ' the second spoke, saying, ' "Was I not [5] in the world? And I entered at ' the fifth hour, and I saw you ' and desired you. And behold, ' then, now I charge you with the ' murders you committed." [10] The third spoke, saying, ' "Did I not come to you at ' the twelfth hour of the day when ' the sun was about to set? I gave you darkness ' until you should accomplish your sins." [15] When the soul heard these things, ' it gazed downward in ' sorrow. And then it gazed ' upward. It was cast down. ' The soul that had been cast down [20] [went] to [a] body which had been prepared ' [for it. And] behold ' [its] witnesses were finished.

[Then I ' gazed] upward and [saw ' the] Spirit saying [to me],[25] "Paul, come! [Proceed ' toward] me!" Then as I [went], ' the gate opened, [and] ' I went up to the fifth [heaven]. ' And I saw my fellow apostles [30] [going with me] 22 while the Spirit accompanied us. ' And I saw a great angel ' in the fifth heaven holding ' an iron rod in his [5] hand. There were three other angels with ' him, and I stared into ' their faces. But they were rivalling ' each other, with whips ' in their hands, goading the [10] souls on to the judgment. ' But I went with the Spirit ' and the gate opened for me. '

Then we went up to the sixth heaven. ' And I saw my fellow apostles [15] going with me, and the Holy Spirit ' was leading me before them. ' And I gazed up on high and saw a ' great light shining down ' on the sixth heaven. I spoke,[20] saying to the toll collector ' who was in the sixth heaven, "[Open] ' to me and the [Holy] Spirit [who ' is] before [me]." He opened [to me].

[Then ' we went] up to the seventh [heaven [25] and I saw] an old man [...] ' light [and ' whose garment] was white. [His throne], ' which is in the seventh heaven, ' [was] brighter than the sun [30] by [seven] times. 23 The old man spoke, saying to [me], ' "Where are you going, Paul, ' O blessed one and the one who was ' set apart from his mother's womb?" [5] But I looked at the Spirit, ' and he was nodding his head, saying ' to me, "Speak with him!" ' And I replied, saying ' to the old man, "I am going to the place [10] from which I came." And ' the old man responded to me, "Where are you from?" ' But I replied, saying, ' "I am going down to the world of ' the dead in order to lead captive [15] the captivity ' that was led captive ' in the captivity of Babylon." ' The old man replied to me, ' saying, "How will you be [20] able to get away from me? Look ' and see the principalities and ' authorities." [The] ' Spirit spoke, saying, "Give him [the] ' sign that you have, and [he will] [25] open for you." And then I gave [him] ' the sign. He turned his face ' downwards to his creation ' and to those who are his own authorities. '

And then the [30] ⟨seventh⟩ heaven opened and we went up to [the] 24 Ogdoad. And I saw the ' twelve apostles. They ' greeted me, and we went ' up to the ninth heaven. I [5] greeted all those who were in the ' ninth heaven, and we went up ' to the tenth heaven. And I ' greeted my fellow spirits. '

The Apocalypse of Paul

THE FIRST APOCALYPSE OF JAMES (V, *3*)

Introduced and translated by

WILLIAM R. SCHOEDEL

Edited by

DOUGLAS M. PARROTT

The *First Apocalypse of James* was actually entitled, in ancient times, "The Apocalypse of James"; the present title has been provided to distinguish this tractate from the next document (V, *4*), which was also entitled "The Apocalypse of James." The *First Apocalypse of James* is an apocalypse in the sense that it describes the secret teachings of the Lord to James the Just, the brother of the Lord. Although the framework of the document is narrative, the prevailing form is that of a dialogue between the Lord and James.

The theme of the *First Apocalypse of James* is suffering, particularly the passion and death of the Lord and the ascent of the soul after death. The passion of the Lord is symbolic of the cosmic struggle which is centered in Jerusalem, the city which is "a dwelling place of a great number of archons." Hence the Lord counsels James to leave Jerusalem. For the Gnostic, as for the Lord and James, the passion and crucifixion are expressions of the sufferings or apparent sufferings which must be endured at death. Yet, the Lord assures James, one need not be sad or afraid, for redemption is sure: in spite of the attacks of the powers, the soul will return safely to the Preexistent Father.

The *First Apocalypse of James* may be considered as a work echoing Jewish-Christian and Gnostic themes. The prominent place of James, a figure of much importance within Jewish-Christian circles, and the reference to Addai, the reputed founder of Syrian Christianity, together suggest that the document may have emerged out of Syrian Jewish Christianity. The additional use of formulas (33, 11-35, 25) connected by the heresiologists with a Valentinian rite of extreme unction illustrates the sorts of Gnostic elements which may have shaped the theology of the tractate.

THE FIRST APOCALYPSE OF JAMES

V 24, 10-44, 10

The Apocalypse of James '

It is the Lord who spoke with me: ' "See now the completion of my redemption. ' I have given you a sign of these things, James, ' my brother. For not without reason have I called ¹⁵ you my brother, although you are not my brother ' materially. And I am not ignorant ' concerning you; so that ' when I give you a sign—know and ' hear.

"Nothing existed except [20] Him Who Is. He is unnameable ' and ineffable. ' I myself also am unnameable, ' from Him Who Is, just as I have been ' [given a] number of names—two [25] from Him Who Is. And I, ' [I] am before you. Since you have ' [asked] concerning femaleness, femaleness existed, ' but femaleness was ' not [first]. And [30] [it] prepared for itself powers and gods. ' But [it did] not exist [when] I came forth, **25** since I am an image of Him Who Is. ' But I have brought forth the image of [him] ' so that the sons of Him Who Is ' might know what things are theirs [5] and what things are alien (to them). Behold, ' I shall reveal to you everything ' of this mystery. For they will seize ' me the day after tomorrow. But my ' redemption will be near." [10]

James said, "Rabbi, you have said, ' 'They will seize me.' But I, ' what can I do?" He said to me, ' "Fear not, James. ' You too will they seize.[15] But leave Jerusalem. ' For it is she who always gives the cup of bitterness ' to the sons ' of light. She is a dwelling place ' of a great number of archons.[20] But your redemption will be preserved ' from them. So that ' you may understand who they are [and] ' what kinds they are, you will [. . .]. ' And listen. They [are] not [. . .] [25] but [archons . . .]. ' These twelve [. . .] ' to raise [. . .] down [. . .] [29] archons [. . .] **26** upon his own hebdomad." '

James said, "Rabbi, are there then ' twelve hebdomads ' and not seven as [5] there are in the scriptures?" ' The Lord said, "James, he who spoke ' concerning this scripture had a limited understanding. ' I, however, shall reveal to you ' what has come forth from him [10] who has no number. I shall give a sign concerning their ' number. As for what has come forth from him ' who has no measure, I shall give a sign concerning their ' measure."

James said, ' "Rabbi, behold then, I have received [15] their number. There are seventy-two measures!" ' The Lord said, "These ' are the seventy-two heavens, which ' are their subordinates. These are the powers of ' all their might; and they were [20] established by them; ' and these are they who were distributed ' everywhere, existing under the [authority] ' of the twelve archons. ' The inferior power among them [25] [brought forth] for itself angels ' [and] unnumbered hosts. ' He Who Is, however, has been given ' [. . .] on account of ' [. . .] He Who Is [30] [. . .] they are unnumbered. **27** If you want ' to give them a number now, you [will] ' not be able to (do so) until you cast away ' from yourself blind thought,[5] this bond of flesh which encircles you. ' And then you will reach ' Him Who Is. ' And you will no longer be ' James; rather you are [10] the One Who Is. And all those who are ' unnumbered will ' all have been named." '

⟨James said, "Then,⟩ ' Rabbi, in what way shall I reach [15] Him Who Is, since ' all these powers and these ' hosts are armed against me?" ' He said to me, "These powers ' are not armed against you specifically,[20] but are armed against another. ' It is against me that they are armed. ' And they are armed with other [powers]. ' But they are armed against me [in] ' judgment. They did not give [. . .] [25] to me in it [. . .] ' through them [. . .]. ' In this place [. . .] ' sufferings, I shall [. . .]. ' He will [. . .] ' and I shall not **28** rebuke them. But there shall ' be within me a silence and ' a hidden mystery. But I ' am fainthearted before their anger." [5]

James said, "Rabbi, ' if they arm themselves against you, then ' is there no blame?

> You have come with knowledge,
>   that ' you might rebuke their forgetfulness.
> You have come with ' recollection,
>   that you might rebuke their [10] ignorance.

But I was concerned ' because of you.

> For you descended into a ' great ignorance,
>   but ' you have not been defiled by anything in it. '
> For you descended into a great mindlessness,[15]
>   and your recollection remained. '

> You walked in mud, '
>   and your garments were not soiled, '
>   and you have not been buried ' in their filth,
>   and [20] you have not been caught.

And I am ' not like them, but I have clothed myself with everything ' of theirs.

> There is in me ' forgetfulness,
>   yet I ' remember things that are not theirs.[25]
> There is in me [. . .], '
>   and I am in their ' [. . .].

[. . .] knowledge ' [. . .] not in their sufferings ' [. . .]. But I have become afraid [30] [before them], since they rule. For what **29** will they do? What will I be able ' to say? Or what word will I be able ' to say that I may escape them?" '

The Lord said, "James, I praise [5] your understanding and your fear. ' If you continue to be distressed, ' do not be concerned for anything else ' except your redemption. ' For behold, I shall complete this destiny [10] upon this earth as ' I have said from the heavens. ' And I shall reveal to you ' your redemption."

James said, ' "Rabbi, how, after these things,[15] will you appear to us again? ' After they seize you, ' and you complete this destiny, ' you will go up to Him ' Who Is." The Lord said, "James,[20] after these things I shall reveal to you ' everything, not for your sake ' alone but for the sake of [the] ' unbelief of men, ' so that [faith] may [25] exist in them. ' For [a] multitude will [attain] ' to faith [and] ' they will increase [in . . .] ' until [. . .]. **30** And after this I shall appear ' for a reproof to the archons. And I shall ' reveal to them that ' he cannot be seized. If they [5] seize him, then ' he will overpower each of them. ' But now I shall go. Remember ' the things I have spoken and let them ' go up before you." [10] James said, "Lord, I shall hasten ' as you have said." ' The Lord said farewell to him and fulfilled ' what was fitting.

When James ' heard of his sufferings [15] and was much distressed, ' they awaited the sign ' of his coming. And he came after ' several days. And James ' was walking upon the mountain, [20] which is called "Gaugelan," ' with his disciples, ' who listened to him ' [because they had been distressed], and he was ' [. . .] a comforter,[25] [saying], "This is ' [. . .] the (or: a) second [. . . .]" ' Then the] crowd dispersed, ' but James remained ' [. . .] prayer [30] [. . .], as **31** was his custom. '

And the Lord appeared to him. ' Then he stopped (his) prayer ' and embraced him. He kissed [5] him, saying, "Rabbi, ' I have found you! I have heard of your ' sufferings, which you endured. And ' I have been much distressed. My ' compassion you know.[10] Therefore, on reflection, I was wishing ' that I would not see this people. They must ' be judged for these things that they have done. ' For these things that they have done are contrary to ' what is fitting." The Lord said,[15] "James, do not be concerned ' for me or for ' this people. I am he who ' was within me. Never ' have I suffered in any way,[20] nor have I been distressed. ' And this people has done ' me no harm. ' But this (people) existed [as] ' a type of the archons,[25] and it deserved to be [destroyed] ' through them. But [. . .] ' the archons, [. . .] ' who (or: which) has [. . .] ' but since it (fem.) [. . .] [30] angry with [. . . . ' The] just [. . .] **32** is his servant. Therefore ' your name is 'James ' the Just.' You see ' how you will become sober when you see [5] me. And you stopped this prayer. ' Now since you are a just ' man of God, you have ' embraced me and kissed me. ' Truly I say to you that [10] you have stirred up great anger and ' wrath against yourself. But ' (this has happened) so that these others might come to be." '

But James was timid ' (and) wept. And he was very distressed.[15] And
they both sat down ' upon a rock. The Lord said ' to him, "James, thus '
you will undergo these sufferings. But do not ' be sad. For the flesh is [20]
weak. It will receive what has been ' ordained for it. But as for you, do
not ' be [timid] or afraid." ' The Lord [ceased].

[Now] when James ' heard these things, he [25] wiped away [the] tears
in ' [his eyes] and very bitter (?) ' [. . .] which is ' [. . .]. The Lord [said]
to [him, ' "James], behold, I shall **33** reveal to you your redemption. '
When [you] are seized, ' and you undergo these sufferings, ' a multitude
will arm themselves against you [5] that ⟨they⟩ may seize you. And in
particular ' three of them ' will seize you—they who ' sit (there) as toll
collectors. Not ' only do they demand toll, but [10] they also take away
souls ' by theft. When ' you come into their power, ' one of them who
is their guard will say ' to you,[15] 'Who are you or where are you from?' '
You are to say to him, 'I am ' a son, and I am from ' the Father.' He
will say to you, ' 'What sort of son are you, and [20] to what father do
you belong?' You are to ' say to him, 'I am from ' the Preexistent
Father, ' and a son in the ' Preexistent One.' [When he says] [25] to you,
[. . .], ' you are to [say to him, . . .] ' in the [. . .] ' that I might [. . .].

"[. . . **34** of] alien things?' You are to say to him, ' 'They are not
entirely alien, ' but they are from Achamoth, ' who is the female. And
these [5] she produced as she brought this race ' down from the ' Preexistent One. So then ' they are not alien, but they are ours. ' They are
indeed ours because she who [10] is mistress of them is from ' the Preexistent One. ' At the same time they are alien because ' the Preexistent
One did not ' have intercourse with her, when she later [15] produced
them.' When he also says to you, ' 'Where will you go?,' you are to '
say to him, 'To the place from which I have come, ' there shall I return.' '
And if you say these things, you will [20] escape their attacks.

"But when ' you come to ' [these] three detainers ' [who] take away
souls by ' theft in that place [25] [. . .] these. You ' [. . .] a vessel ' [. . .]
much more than [. . .] **35** of the one (fem.) whom ' you [. . .] for [. . .] '
her root. You ' too will [5] be sober [. . .]. But I shall call ' [upon] the
imperishable knowledge, ' which is Sophia who ' is in the Father (and)
who is the mother ' of Achamoth.[10] Achamoth had no father nor ' male
consort, but ' she is female from a ' female. She produced you (pl.) '
without a male, since she was alone [15] (and) in ignorance as to what '
[lives through] her mother because she thought ' that she alone existed. '
But [I] shall cry out ' to her mother. And then [20] they will fall into confusion (and) will ' blame their ' root and the race [of] ' their mother.

[But] you ' will go up to [what is] [25] yours [...] ' you will [...] **36** the [Preexistent One].

"[They are ' a] type [of the] twelve '.disciples and [the] twelve ' pairs, [...] [5] Achamoth, which is ' translated 'Sophia.' ' And who I myself am, ' and (who) the imperishable Sophia (is) ' through whom you will be redeemed,[10] and (who are) all the sons of Him Who ' Is—these things they have known ' and have hidden within ' them. You are to hide ⟨these things⟩ within you, ' and you are to keep silence.[15] But you are to reveal them to ' Addai. When you [depart], ' immediately war will be [made] ' with this land. [Weep], ' then, for him who dwells in Jerusalem.[20] But let Addai take these things ' to heart. In the tenth ' year let Addai sit ' and write them down. ' And when he writes them down [25] [...] and they are to give them ' [...] he has the [...] **37**[6] he is [called] ' Levi. Then he is to bring ' [...] word ' [...] from [10] [what I] said earlier ' [...] a woman ' [...] Jerusalem in her ' [... and] he begets ' [two] sons through her.[15] [They are to] inherit these things ' [and] the understanding of him who ' [...] exalts. And they are to receive ' [...] through him from his ' intellect. Now, the younger of them [20] is greater. And ' may these things remain ' hidden in him until [he] ' comes to the age of ' seventeen years [...] **38**[3] beginning [...] [5] through [them]. They will pursue ' him exceedingly, since [they are] from ' his [...] companions. He will be ' proclaimed [through] them, ' and [they will] proclaim this word.[10] [Then he will become] ' a seed of [...]." '

James said, "[I am] ' satisfied [...] ' and they are [...] [15] my soul. Yet [another thing] ' I ask of you: who are the [seven] ' women who have [been] your disciples? ' And behold, ' all women bless you.[20] I also am amazed ' how [powerless] vessels ' have become strong by a perception ' which is in them." ' [The] Lord [said], "You [...] well [...] **39**[3] a spirit [of ...], ' a [spirit] of thought, [a spirit] [5] of counsel of [a ...], ' a spirit [..., a] spirit ' of knowledge [...] of their ' fear. [...] when we had passed ' through [the breadth] of [10] [this] archon who ' is [named] Adonaios ' [...] him and ' [...] he was ignorant ' [...] when I came forth from him,[15] [he] remembered that I ' am [a] son of his. He was gracious ' [to me] at that time as ' his son. And then, ' before ⟨I⟩ [20] appeared here, ⟨he⟩ ' cast them among [this] ' people. And from the [place] ' of heaven the prophets [...]." **40**[4]

James [said], "Rabbi, [...] [6] I [...] all together ' [...] in them ' especially [...]." ' The Lord said, "[James], I [10] praise [you ...] ' walk upon the earth [...] ' the words while he [...] ' on the [...]. ' For cast away from [you the] [15] cup, which is the bitterness [...]. ' For some from

[...] ' set themselves against you. For [through] ' you ⟨they are to⟩ understand [their roots] ' from beginning to end. Cast [20] away from yourself all lawlessness. ' And beware lest ' they envy you. When you ' speak these words of this ' [perception], encourage these [25] [four]: Salome and Mariam ' [and Martha and Arsinoe ...] **41**[6] since he takes ' some [...] to me ' he is [...] burnt offerings ' and [...]. But I [10] [...] not in this way; but ' [...] first fruits of the ' [...] upward ' [...] so that ' the power [of God might] appear.[15] The perishable has [gone ' up] to the imperishable and ' the female element has ' attained to this male element." '

James said,[20] "Rabbi, into these three (things), then, ' has their [...] been cast. ' For they have been reviled, [and they have been] ' persecuted [...]. **42**[5] Behold ' [...] everything ' [...] from ' anyone [...]. ' For you have received [...] of [10] knowledge. [And ...] ' that what is the [...] ' go [...] ' you will [find ...]. ' But I shall go [forth] [15] and shall reveal ' that they believed in you [that they may] ' be content with their [blessing] ' and salvation, and ' this revelation may come to pass." [20] And he went at that time ' [immediately] and rebuked the ' twelve, and cast ' [out] of them contentment ' [concerning the] way of knowledge [...].

[...]. **43**[7] And the majority ' of [them ...] when they ' [saw that the] messenger took in [10] [...]. The others [...] [12] said, "[...] [14] him from this earth. ' For [he is] not [worthy] of life." ' These, then, [were] afraid. They arose, ' saying, "We ' have no part in this blood, ' for a just man [20] will perish through ' injustice." James departed ' so that [...] **44**[6] look ' [...] for ' we (?) [...] him. '

The Apocalypse [10]
of James

THE SECOND APOCALYPSE OF JAMES (V, *4*)

Introduced and translated by

CHARLES W. HEDRICK

Edited by

DOUGLAS M. PARROTT

Like the preceding tractate, the *Second Apocalypse of James* was entitled in ancient times "The Apocalypse of James." The presence in Codex V of two apocalypses linked with the James tradition is noteworthy; furthermore, the order seems deliberate. While the *First Apocalypse of James* stresses the period prior to the martyrdom of James and offers certain predictions, the *Second Apocalypse of James* describes the suffering and death of James in line with these predictions. Thus, the present order of these two apocalypses, far from being merely accidental, probably reflects the scribal understanding of the tractates and their complementary relationship.

The *Second Apocalypse of James* may be considered as an apocalypse in the sense of a revelation discourse: James relates a special revelation delivered by the resurrected Jesus. It must be noted, however, that the actual structure of the tractate is that of a report by Mareim, priest and relative of Theuda, father of James. It is obvious that the author of the *Second Apocalypse of James* made extensive use of Jewish-Christian traditions. Such is particularly clear with regard to the account of the martyrdom of James, which is quite similar to the account in the *Memoirs* of Hegesippus. Yet it is also clear that, as it now stands, the tractate is Gnostic in character, although it shows a remarkable restraint in treating certain general Gnostic themes.

The portrait of James the Just in the tractate is particularly significant. It is well known that James held a position of honor and importance within several Jewish-Christian traditions. In the *Second Apocalypse of James*, however, James is also the escort guiding the Gnostic through the heavenly door, the "illuminator" and "redeemer" who astonishes people with his "powerful deeds," the one whom the heavens bless and on whose account the people "reign and become kings." In short, James seems to function practically as a Gnostic redeemer.

THE SECOND APOCALYPSE OF JAMES

V 44, 11-63, 32

The Apocalypse '
of [James] '

This is [the] discourse that James ' [the] Just spoke [15] in Jerusalem, [which] ' Mareim, one [of] the priests, ' wrote. He had told it to ' Theuda, the father of the Just One, ' since he was a relative [20] of his. He said, '

"[Hasten]! Come with ' [Mary], your wife and ' your relatives [...] **45** therefore [...] ⁵ of this [...] ' to him. Hasten then! Perhaps ' [after] you yourself [have led] ' us to [him, he will] understand. ' For behold, a multitude ¹⁰ are disturbed over ' his [...], and they are very ' angry [at him. ...] ' and they pray [....].¹⁵ For ' [he would] often say these words ' and others ' also.

"He used to speak these words ' while the multitude of people ²⁰ were seated. But (on this occasion) he entered ' and did ⟨not⟩ sit down ' in the place, as was his custom. ' Rather he sat above ' the fifth flight of steps, [which] ²⁵ is (highly) esteemed, while all our people [...] ²⁷ the words [...].

" '[...]. **46**⁶ I am he who ' received revelation from ' the Pleroma [of] Imperishability. ' (I am) he who was first summoned ¹⁰ by him who is great, and ' who obeyed the [Lord]— ' he who passed [through] ' the [worlds ...] ' he who [... he who] ¹⁵ stripped [himself and] ' went about naked, ' he who was found in a ' perishable (state), though he was about to be brought ' up into imperishability.— ²⁰ This Lord who is present ' [came] as a son who sees, ' and as a brother ' [was he sought]. He will come to ' [...] produced him because ²⁵ [...] and he unites ' [...] make him free [...] **47** in [...] ' he who came [to ...]. ⁷

" 'Now again am I rich in ' knowledge [and] I have ' a unique [understanding],¹⁰ which was produced only from ' above and the [...] ' comes from a [...]. ' I am the [...] ¹⁵ whom I ' knew. That which was revealed ' to me was hidden from everyone ' and shall (only) be revealed ' through him. These ²⁰ two who see, I ⟨...⟩ ' (and) they have already proclaimed ' through these [words]: ' "He shall be judged with the [unrighteous]." ' He who lived [without] ²⁵ blasphemy died by means of [blasphemy]. ' He who was cast out ' they [...].

" ' "[... **48**⁵ the] flesh ' [and] it is by knowledge ' that I shall come forth from the [flesh]. ' I am surely dying, ' but it is in life that I shall be found.¹⁰ I entered ' in order that they might judge [... I] ' shall come forth [in ...] ' judge [... I do] ' not bring blame against the ¹⁵ servants of his [...] ' I hasten ' to make them free and ' want to take them above ' him who wants to rule ²⁰ over them. If ' they are helped, ' I am the brother in ' secret, who prayed ' to the Father [until ²⁵ he ...] in [...] **49**² reign: [... ' imperishability ...] first ' in [...].⁵

> I [am the] first [son] ' who was begotten.—
> He will destroy ' the dominion of [them] all.— '
> I am the beloved. '

I am the righteous one.[10]
I am the son of ' [the Father].

I speak even as ' [I] heard.
I command ' even as I [received] the order.
I ' show you (pl.) even as [15] I have [found].

Behold, I speak ' in order that I may come forth. Pay ' attention to me
in order that you ' may see me!

" ' "If I ' have come into existence, who then am I? [20] For I did ⟨not⟩
come as I am, ' nor would I have appeared ' as I am. ' For I used to
exist ' for a brief period [25] of time [. . .]." **50**[5]

" 'Once when I was sitting ' deliberating, ' [he] opened [the] door. '
That one ' whom you hated [10] and persecuted came in to me. ' He said
to me, "Hail, my ' brother; my brother, hail." ' As I raised my [face] '
to stare at him,[15] (my) mother said to me, "Do not ' be frightened, my
son, because ' he said 'My brother' to you (sing.). ' For you (pl.) were
nourished with ' this same milk. Because of [20] this he calls ' me 'My
mother.' ' For he is not a stranger to us. ' He is your [step-brother. . . .]."

" ' "[. . .] **51**[2] these words [. . .] [5] great [. . .] ' I shall [find] them, and
[they shall come] ' forth. [However], I am the stranger, ' and they have
no knowledge ' of me in [their] thoughts,[10] for they know me in ' [this
place]. But it ' was fitting that others ' know through you. '

" ' "⟨This is⟩ what I say to you: [15] Hear and understand— ' for a
multitude, when they ' hear, will be slow-witted. ' But you, understand
as I ' shall be able to tell you. Your father [20] is not my father. But ' my
father has become a father ' to [you].

" ' "This virgin ' about whom you hear— ' this is how [. . .] [27] virgin
[. . .] **52** namely, the virgin. ' [. . .],How ' [. . .] to me for ' [. . .] to know [5]
[. . .] not as ' [. . .] whom I [. . .]. For this one (masc.) ' [. . .] to him, ' and
this also is profitable ' for you. Your father, whom you [10] consider to
be [rich], ' shall grant that you inherit ' all these (things) that you ' see.

" ' "I proclaim ' to you to tell you [15] these (words) that I shall speak.
When ' you hear, therefore, ' open your ears ' and understand and walk
(accordingly)! ' It is because of you that they pass by,[20] activated by '
that one who is glorious. ' And if they want to make a ' disturbance and
(seize) possession [. . .] **53** he began [. . .] ' not, nor those who are
[coming], ' who were sent forth [by] ' him to make this present [crea-
tion].[5] After [these things, ' when he] is ashamed, he shall be disturbed '
that his labor, which is far [from] ' the aeons, is nothing. And ' his
inheritance,[10] which he boasted ' to be great, shall appear ' small. And
his ' gifts are not ' blessings. His promises are evil [15] schemes. For you

are not an (instrument) ' of his compassion, ' but it is through you '
that he does violence. He wants ' to do injustice to us, and [20] will exercise
dominion for a time ' allotted to him.

" ' "But ' understand and know the Father ' who has compassion. '
He was not given [25] an inheritance that was unlimited, ' [nor] does it
(his inheritance) [have] ' a (limited) number of days, ' but it is as [the]
eternal [day . . .] [30] it is [. . .] **54** perceive [. . .]. ' And he used ' [. . .].
For in fact he is not ' one (come) from [them], (and) because of this he [5]
[is despised]. Because of this he [boasts], so ' that he may not be reproved. ' For because of this he is superior to ' those who are below,
those ' through whom you [10] were looked down upon. After he imprisoned ' those from [the] Father; ' he seized them ' and fashioned
them to resemble ' himself. And it is [15] with him that they exist.

" ' "I ' saw from the height ' those (things) that happened, and I have
explained ' how they happened. ' They were visited while they [20] were
in another form, and, ' while I was watching, ' [they] came to know
⟨me⟩ as I am, ' through those whom I know. '

" ' "Now before those (things) [25] [happened] they will make a ' [. . .].
I know ' [how] they attempted ' [to come] down to this place **55** [that]
he might approach [. . .] ' the small children, [but ' I] wish to reveal '
through you and the [Spirit [5] of Power], in order that he might reveal '
[to those] who are yours. And ' those who wish to enter, ' and who seek
to ' walk in the way that is [10] before the door, ' open the good door
through you. And they ' follow you; they enter ' [and you] escort them
inside, and give a reward ' to each one who is ready for it.[15]

> For you are not the redeemer '
> nor a helper of strangers. '
> You are an illuminator ' and a redeemer '
> of those who (are) mine,
> and now [20] of those who (are) yours.
> You shall ' reveal (to them);
> you shall bring good ' among them all.
>
> You [they shall] ' admire
> because of every powerful (deed). '
> You are he whom the heavens [25] bless.
> You ' he shall envy,
> he [who has] ' called himself your [Lord]. '
> I am the [. . .] **56**
> [those who] are instructed in these
> (things) with [you]. '

For your sake
   they will be told ' [these (things)],
   and will come to rest. '
For your sake
   they will reign,
   [and will] [5] become kings.
For [your] sake '
   they will have pity
   on whomever they pity. '

For just as ' you are first
   having clothed ' yourself,
you are also the [10] first who will strip himself, '
and you shall become ' as you were '
   before you were stripped." '

" 'And he kissed [15] my mouth. He took hold of me, saying, ' "My beloved! ' Behold, I shall reveal ' to you those (things) that (neither) ' [the] heavens nor their archons [20] have known. Behold, ' I shall reveal to you ' those (things) that he did not know, ' he who [boasted, '... [26] there is no] **57** other except me. Am I not alive? ' Because I am a father, ' [do] I [not have power] for everything?' ' Behold, I shall reveal to you [5] everything, my beloved. ' [Understand] and know [everything, ' that] you may come forth just as ' I am. Behold, I ' [shall] reveal to you him who [10] [is hidden]. But now, stretch out your ' [hand]. Now, take hold of me." ' [And] then I stretched out my ' hands and I did not find him ' as I thought (he would be). But [15] afterward I heard him ' saying, "Understand and ' take hold of me." Then I understood, ' and I was afraid. And ' I was exceedingly joyful.[20]

" 'Therefore, I tell ' you (pl.), judges, you ' have been judged. And you ' did not spare, but you were spared. ' Be sober and [...] **58** you did not [know]. '

He was that one ' whom he who created ' the heaven and the earth,[5]
   and dwelled in it, ' did not see.
He was [this one who] ' is the life.
He ' was the light.
He ' was that one who will come to be.[10]

And again he shall provide
   [an] ' end for what ' has begun
   and a beginning ' for what is about to be ended. '

He was the Holy Spirit [15] and the Invisible One, ' who did not
descend ' upon the earth.
He was ' the virgin, and that which ' he wishes happens [20] to him.
I saw ' that he was naked, ' and there was no garment clothing ' him.
That which he wills ' happens to him [. . .]. **59**

" '[Renounce] this difficult way, ' which is (so) variable, ' [and] walk
in accordance with him who desires ' [that] you become free men [5]
[with] me, after you have passed above ' every [dominion]. For he will
not [judge] (you) ' for those (things) that you did, ' but will have mercy
on you. ' For (it is) not you that did them, but it is [10] [your] Lord (that
did them). [He was not] ' a wrathful one, but he was a kind Father. '

" 'But you have judged [yourselves], ' and because of this you will
remain ' in their fetters. You [15] have oppressed yourselves, and you '
will repent, (but) you will ' not profit at all. Behold him ' who speaks
and seek ' him who is silent. Know him [20] who came to this place, and
understand ' him who went forth (from it). I am ' the Just One, and I do
⟨not⟩ judge. ' I am not a master, then, but ' I am a helper. He was cast [25]
out before he ' stretched out his hand. I [. . .].

" '[. . .] **60** and he allows me to hear. ' And play your trumpets, '
your flutes ' and your harps [of [5] this house]. The Lord has taken ' you
captive ' from the Lord, having closed ' your ears, that ' they may not
hear the sound of [10] my word. Yet you [will be able to pay] ' heed in
your hearts, [and] ' you will call me "the Just One." ' Therefore, I tell '
you: Behold, I gave [15] you your house, which ' you say that God ' has
made. Did he who dwells ' in it promise to give you ' an inheritance
through it? [20] This (house) I shall doom to ' destruction and derision of
those ' who are in ignorance. ' For behold, ' those who judge deliberate
[. . .].' **61**

"[On] that day ' all the [people] and the crowd ' were disturbed, and
they ' showed that they had not been persuaded.[5] And he arose and
went ' forth speaking in this [manner]. ' And he entered (again) on that
same day and ' spoke a few hours. ' And I was with the priests [10] and
revealed nothing ' of the relationship, ' since all of them were saying '
with one voice, 'Come, ' let us stone the Just One.' [15] And they arose, '
saying, 'Yes, let ' us kill this man, that ' he may be taken from our
midst. ' For he will be of no use to us.' [20]

"And they were there and found him ' standing beside the columns
of ' the temple beside the mighty corner ' stone. And they decided to
throw ' him down from [25] the height, and they cast ' him down. And '

they [...] they [...]. **62** They seized him and [struck] ' him as they dragged him upon the ground. ' They stretched him out, and placed ' a stone on his abdomen.[5] They all placed their feet on him, ' saying, ' 'You have erred!'

"Again ' they raised him up, since he was alive, and made him ' dig a hole. They made him stand [10] in it. After having covered him ' up to his abdomen, they stoned ' him in this manner.

"And ' he stretched out his hands ' and said this prayer— [15] not that (one) which it is his custom to say: '

'My God and my Father, '
   who saved me from ' this dead hope, '
   who made me alive through a [20] mystery of what he wills, '
do not let these days of this world ' be prolonged for me, '
but the day of your (sing.) ' [light ...] remains [25]
in [...] **63** salvation.
Deliver me from this ' [place of] sojourn!
Do not let your grace be left behind ' in me,
   but may ' your grace become pure! [5]
Save me from an ' evil death!
Bring me from ' a tomb alive,
   because your grace— ' love—is alive in me '
   to accomplish a work of fullness! [10]
Save me from ' sinful flesh,
   because I trusted ' in you with all my strength!
   Because you ' are the life of the life,
save me ' from a humiliating [15] enemy!
Do not give me into the hand ' of a judge
   who is severe ' with sin!
Forgive me ' all my debts of the ' days (of my life)!
Because I am alive in [20] you, your grace is alive in me. '
I have renounced everyone, '
   but you I have confessed. '
Save me from evil ' affliction!
But now is the [time] [25] and the hour.
O Holy ' [Spirit], send [me] '
   salvation [...] the light [...] '
   the light [...] ' in a power [...].' [30]

"After he [spoke, he] fell silent [...] ' word [... afterward ' ...] the discourse [...]."

THE APOCALYPSE OF ADAM (V, 5)

Introduced and translated by

GEORGE W. MACRAE

Edited by

DOUGLAS M. PARROTT

The *Apocalypse of Adam* may be termed a Sethian tractate in the sense that Seth and his descendants figure prominently as the recipients and bearers of the Gnostic tradition. Whether there is any connection with the Sethians as depicted by the heresiologists, however, remains uncertain. It is obvious that the *Apocalypse of Adam* depends heavily on Jewish apocalyptic traditions; in fact, the document may represent a transitional stage in the development from Jewish to Gnostic apocalyptic. If this be the case, its date may be very early, perhaps as early as the first or second century C.E. Most interestingly, the *Apocalypse of Adam* does not disclose any explicitly Christian themes. Hence some have concluded that this tractate demonstrates the existence of a sort of Gnosticism which, though non-Christian, yet contains a well-developed myth proclaiming a heavenly redeemer.

In content this work consists of a revelation received by Adam and taught to his son Seth. Father Adam explains how in the fall he and Eve lost their glory and knowledge, and came under the enslaving power of the lowly creator and of death itself. Through the revelation imparted to Adam by three heavenly visitors, however, this knowledge is passed on to Seth and his seed; and in spite of the attacks of the creator, who tries to destroy mankind with a flood and with fire, the knowledge is preserved. Finally, when the mighty "illuminator" comes, "the man upon whom the holy spirit has come," he will be persecuted by the worldly powers. But in the end he will triumph, and those who have truly known the living God will live forever.

THE APOCALYPSE OF ADAM

V 64, 1-85, 32

The Apocalypse of Adam [1]

The revelation which Adam [1] taught his son Seth in [1] the seven hundredth year, saying,[5] "Listen to my words, my [1] son Seth. When [1] God had created me out of [1] the earth along with Eve your mother, [1] I went about with her in a [10] glory which she had seen in [1] the aeon from which we had come ' forth. She taught me a word ' of knowledge of the eternal God. ' And-we resembled [15] the great eternal angels, ' for we were higher than ' the God who had created us and ' the powers with him, whom ' we did not know.[20]

"Then God, ' the ruler of the aeons ' and the powers, divided us in wrath. Then ' we became two aeons. ' And the glory in our heart(s) [25] left us, ' me and your mother Eve, ' along with the first knowledge ' that breathed within us. And ' it (glory) fled from us; [30] it entered into [...] great [... **65** had come] forth, not from this aeon from which [we had] ' come forth, I ' and Eve your mother. But ' it (knowledge) entered into the seed of [5] great aeons. For this reason ' I myself have called you ' by the name of that man ' who is the seed of the great generation ' or from whom (it comes). After [10] those days the eternal knowledge ' of the God of truth ' withdrew from me ' and your mother Eve. ' Since that time we [15] learned about dead things, ' like men. Then ' we recognized the God who had ' created us. For we were not ' strangers to his powers. And [20] we served him in fear ' and slavery. ' And after these (events) we became ' darkened in our heart(s). ' Now I slept in the [25] thought of my heart. '

"And I saw three ' men before me ' whose likeness I was unable ' to recognize, since they [30] were not from the powers ' of the God who had [created ' us]. They surpassed [...] ' glory, and [...] ' men [...] **66** saying to me, 'Arise, ' Adam, from the sleep ' of death, and hear ' about the aeon and the seed [5] of that man ' to whom life has come, ' who came from you and ' from Eve, your wife.' '

"When I had heard these [10] words from the great men ' who were standing ' before me, then we ' sighed, I and Eve, in ' our heart(s). And the Lord, the God [15] who had created us, stood ' before us. He said to us, ' 'Adam, why were you (pl.) ' sighing in your heart? ' Do you not know that I [20] am the God who created ' you? And I breathed into ' you a spirit of life ' as a living soul.' ' Then darkness came upon our [25] eyes.

"Then the God, who ' created us, created a ' son from himself [and] Eve, ' [your mother], for [... **67** in] the thought [of] ' my [...]. I knew ' a sweet desire ' for your mother. Then [5] the vigor of ' our eternal knowledge ' was destroyed in us, ' and weakness ' pursued us.[10] Therefore the days of ' our life became few. ' For I knew that I had ' come under the authority ' of death.

"Now then,[15] my son Seth, I will ' reveal to you the things ' which those men ' whom I saw ' before me [20] at first ' revealed to me: ' after I have completed ' the times ' of this generation [25] and [the] years of ' [the generation] ' have been accomplished, [then ' . . .] slave [. . .]. (p. 68 blank) **69**[2]

"For rain-showers ' of [God] the ' almighty [5] will be poured forth [so that] he ' might destroy [all] flesh {of ' God the almighty, ' so that he might destroy all flesh} ' from the earth [10] by means of that (pl.) which is around ' them, along with [those from] ' the seed [of] the men ' to whom passed ' the life of [15] the knowledge, that ' came from me [and] Eve, ' your mother. For they were ' strangers to him. ' Afterwards great [20] angels will come ' on high clouds, ' who will bring those men ' into the place ' where the spirit [of] life dwells [. . .] **70** glory ' [. . .] there. ' [. . .] come from heaven ' to earth. [Then] [5] the whole [multitude] of flesh ' will be left behind in the [waters].

"Then God ' will rest from ' his wrath. And he will cast ' his power upon the waters,[10] and [he will] give power to his sons ' and their wives by means of the ark ' [along with] the animals, ' whichever he pleased, and the ' birds of heaven, which he [15] called and released ' upon the earth. And God ' will say to Noah— ' whom the generations will call ' Deucalion—, 'Behold,[20] I have protected ⟨you⟩ in the ark ' along with your wife and your sons ' and their wives and their ' animals and the birds of ' [heaven], which you called [25] [and released upon the earth]. **71** Therefore I will give the [earth] to you— ' you and your sons. In ' kingly fashion you will rule over it—you ' and your sons. And no [5] seed will come from you ' of the men who will not ' stand in my presence in ' another glory.'

"Then they will ' become as the cloud of the [10] great light. Those ' men will come who have ' been cast forth from the knowledge ' of the great aeons and the ' angels. They will stand [15] before Noah and the aeons. ' And God will say to ' Noah, 'Why have you departed from ' what I told you? You have ' created another generation so that you [20] might scorn my power.' Then ' Noah will say, 'I shall ' testify before your ' might that the generation ' of these men did not come [25] [from me] nor [from ' my sons. . . .] **72** knowledge.

"And [he] will ' [. . .] those men ' and bring them into their proper ' land and build them a [5] holy dwelling place. And ' they will be called by that ' name and dwell there ' six hundred years in a ' knowledge of imperishability.[10] And angels of the great ' light will dwell with them. ' No foul deed ' will dwell in their heart(s), but ' only the knowledge of God.[15]

"Then Noah will divide the ' whole earth among his sons, ' Ham and Japheth and Shem. ' He will say to them, 'My sons, ' listen to my words.

Behold,[20] I have divided the earth among you. But ' serve him in fear and ' slavery all the days ' of your life. Let not ' your seed depart from the face [25] of God the almighty. ' [. . .] I and your [. . .] **73** son of Noah, '[My] ' seed [will be] pleasing before you ' and before your power. ' Seal it by your [5] strong hand with fear and ' commandment, so that the whole ' seed which came forth from me ' may not be inclined away from you ' and God the almighty, [10] but it will serve ' in humility and ' fear of its knowledge.' '

"Then others ' from the seed of Ham and [15] Japheth will come, four hundred ' thousand men, and enter into ' another land and sojourn ' with those men who ' came forth from the great [20] eternal knowledge. For ' the shadow of their power will ' protect those who have sojourned ' with them from every evil thing ' and every unclean desire.[25] Then the seed of Ham and ' Japheth will form twelve ' kingdoms, and their ' seed [also] will enter into ' the kingdom of another people.[30]

"[Then . . .] will take counsel [. . .] ' aeons [. . .] **74** who are dead, of the great ' aeons of imperishability. ' And they will go to Sakla ' their God. They will go in [5] to the powers, accusing the great ' men who are in their ' glory.

"They will say to Sakla, ' 'What is the power of these men who ' stood in your presence,[10] who were taken from the ' seed of Ham and Japheth, ' who will number four hundred ⟨thousand⟩ men? ' They have been received into another aeon ' from which they had come forth, and [15] they have overturned all the glory of your ' power and the dominion of your hand. ' For the seed of Noah through ' his son has done ' all your will, and (so have) all the powers [20] in the aeons over which your might ' rules, while both those ' men and the ones who are ' sojourners in their glory ' have not done your will.[25] [But] they have turned (aside) your ' whole throng.'

"Then the God ' of the aeons will give them ' (some) of those who serve [him . . .] [30] they will come upon that land **75** where the great men ' will be who ' have not been defiled, nor will be ' defiled by any desire.[5] For their soul did not come ' from a defiled hand, but it ' came from a great commandment ' of an eternal angel. ' Then fire [10] and sulphur and asphalt will be cast upon ' those men, and ' fire and (blinding) mist will come over ' those aeons, and ' the eyes of the powers of the illuminators will be darkened,[15] and the aeons will not see by ' them in those days. ' And great clouds of light ' will descend, and ' other clouds of light [20] will come down upon them from ' the great aeons. '

"Abrasax and Sablo and ' Gamaliel will descend and bring ' those

men out of [25] the fire and the wrath, and ' take them above the aeons '
and the rulers of the [powers], and ' [take] them away [. . .] ' of life
[. . .] [30] and take them away [. . .] ' aeons [. . . **76** dwelling place] of the
[great . . .] ' there with the holy angels ' and the aeons. ' The men will
be like [5] those angels, for they ' are not strangers to them. But ' they
work in the imperishable seed. '

"Once again, for the ' third time, the illuminator [10] of knowledge will
pass by in great ' glory, in order to leave ' (something) of the seed of
Noah ' and the sons of Ham and Japheth— ' to leave for himself [15]
fruit-bearing trees. And he will ' redeem their souls from the ' day of
death. For the whole creation ' that came from ' the dead earth will be [20]
under the authority of death. ' But those who reflect upon the knowledge ' of the eternal God ' in their heart(s) will not perish. ' For they
have not received spirit [25] from this kingdom alone, ' but they have
received (it) from one ' of the eternal angels. ' [. . .] illuminator ' [. . .
will] come upon [30] [. . . that is] dead [. . .] **77** of Seth. And he will perform ' signs and wonders in order to ' scorn the powers and their ruler. '

"Then the God [5] of the powers will be disturbed, saying, 'What ' is
the power of this man who ' is higher than we?' Then he will ' arouse a
great wrath against ' that man. And [10] the glory will withdraw and '
dwell in holy houses which ' it has chosen for itself. And ' the powers
will not see it ' with their eyes, nor will they [15] see the illuminator either. '
Then they will punish the flesh ' of the man upon whom the ' holy
spirit has come.

"Then ' the angels and all the [20] generations of the powers ' will use
the name ' in error, asking, ' 'Where did it (the error) come from?' or '
'Where did the [25] words of deception, which ' all the powers have failed '
to discover, come from?'

"[Now] the first ' kingdom [says of him] '
  [that] he came [from . . .]. **78** A spirit [. . .] to heaven.
  He was nourished ' in the heavens.
  He received the glory ' of that one and the power. He came '
    to the bosom of his mother.[5]
  And thus he came to the water. '

"And the second kingdom says ' about him
    that he came ' from a great prophet. ' And a bird came, took [10]
      the child who was born and brought him ' onto a high
      mountain. '

And he was nourished by ' the bird of heaven. An angel ' came
forth there. He said to him,[15] 'Arise! God has given glory ' to
you.'
He received glory and strength. '
And thus he came to the water. '

"The third kingdom says ' of him
that he came [20] from a virgin womb. ' He was cast out of his
city, ' he and his mother; he was brought ' to a desert place.
He was nourished ' there.
He came and received [25] glory and power.
And thus ' he came to the water. '

"[The fourth] kingdom says ' [of him]
[that] he came ' [from a virgin.[30] ... Solomon **79** sought] her, he
and Phersalo ' and Sauel and his armies, ' which had been sent
out. Solomon ' himself sent his army [5] of demons to seek out
the ' virgin. And they did not find ' the one whom they sought,
but ' the virgin who was given to them. ' It was she whom they
fetched.[10] Solomon took her. ' The Virgin became pregnant and
gave birth to ' the child there. '
She nourished him on a border ' of the desert. When [15] he had
been nourished,
he received glory ' and power from the seed ' from which he had
been begotten. '
And thus he came to the ' water.

"And the fifth [20] kingdom says of him
that ' he came from a ' drop from heaven. He was thrown ' into
the sea. The abyss ' received him, gave birth to him,[25] and
brought him to heaven.
He received ' glory and power.
And ' thus he came to [the water]. '

"And [the] sixth kingdom ' [says]
that a [... [30] down] to the aeon **80** which is below, in order to
[gather] ' flowers. She became pregnant from ' the desire of the
flowers. She ' gave birth to him in that place.[5]
The angels of the ' flower garden nourished him.
He received ' glory there ' and power.
And thus he came ' to the water.

"And the [10] seventh kingdom says ' of him
    that he is a drop. ' It came from heaven to earth. ' Dragons
    brought him down to caves. ' He became a [15] child. A spirit
    came upon him and ' brought him on high to the place where
    the ' drop had come forth. '
    He received glory and power ' there.
    And thus [20] he came to the water.

"And the ' eighth kingdom says ' of him
    that a cloud came ' upon the earth and enveloped a ' rock. He
    came [25] from it.
    The angels ' who were above the cloud ' nourished him.
    He [received] glory ' [and] power [there]. '
    And [thus he] came to [the water]. **81**

"And the [ninth] kingdom says ' of him
    that from the nine ' Muses one separated away. ' She came to a
    high mountain and spent [5] (some) time seated there, so that '
    she desired herself alone ' in order to become androgynous. '
    She fulfilled her desire ' and became pregnant from her desire.[10]
    He was born.
    The ' angels who were over the desire nourished him. '
    And he received glory there ' and power.
    And ' thus he came to the water.

"The [15] tenth kingdom says of him '
    that his god loved a cloud ' of desire. He begot him ' in his hand
    and cast ' upon the cloud above him [20] (some) of the drop,
    and ' he was born.
    He received glory and ' power there.
    And ' thus he came to the water. '

"And the eleventh [25] kingdom says
    that the father ' desired his [own] ' daughter. She herself became
    pregnant ' [from] her father. She cast [. . .] ' tomb **82** out in the
    desert.
    The angel ' nourished him there. '
    And thus he came ' to the water.

"The [5] twelfth kingdom says ' of him
    that he came from ' two illuminators.
    He was ' nourished there.

He received glory ' and power.
And thus he came [10] to the water.

"And the ' thirteenth kingdom says ' of him
that every birth ' of their ruler is a word. '
And this word received [15] a mandate there.
He ' received glory and power. '
And thus he came to the water, '
      in order that the desire ' of those powers might be satisfied.

"But the generation [20] without a king over it says ' that God chose ' him from all the aeons. ' He caused a knowledge of the ' undefiled one of truth to come to be [25] [in] him. [He (or: It)] said, '[Out of] ' a foreign air, ' [from a] great aeon, [the ' great] illuminator came forth. [And he made] **83** the generation of those men ' whom he had chosen for himself shine, ' so that they should shine upon the ' whole aeon.'

"Then the seed,[5] those who will receive his ' name upon the water and (that) of them all, will fight against the power. ' And a cloud ' of darkness will come upon them.

"Then ' the peoples will cry out with a [10] great voice, saying, ' 'Blessed is the soul of those ' men because they have known ' God with a knowledge ' of the truth! They shall live forever,[15] because they have not been ' corrupted by their desire, ' along with the angels, nor ' have they accomplished the works of the ' powers, but they have stood [20] in his presence in a knowledge ' of God like light ' that has come forth from ' fire and blood.

" 'But we ' have done every deed of the powers [25] senselessly. We have ' boasted in the transgression ' of [all] our works. ' We have [cried] against [the God] ' of [truth] because all his works [...] **84** is eternal. These are against our ' spirits. For now we have known that ' our souls will die the death.' '

"Then a voice came to them,[5] saying, 'Micheu and ' Michar and Mnesinous, who ' (are) over the holy baptism ' and the living water, why ' were you crying out against the [10] living God with lawless voices ' and tongues without law ' over them, and souls ' full of blood and foul ' [deeds]? You are full of [15] works that are not of the truth, ' but your ways are full of ' joy and rejoicing. ' Having defiled the water of life, ' you have drawn it within [20] the will of the powers ' to whom you have been given ' to serve ' them.

" 'And your ' thought is not like that of [25] those men whom ' you persecute [...] [28] desire [...]. **85** Their fruit does not wither. But ' they will be known ' up to the great aeons, because the words ' they have kept, of the God [5] of the aeons, were not committed to ' the book, nor were they written. ' But angelic (beings) will bring ' them, whom all the generations ' of men will not know.[10] For they will be on a high ' mountain, upon a rock of truth. ' Therefore they will be named ' "The Words of Imperishability ' [and] Truth," for those who know [15] the eternal God in ' wisdom of knowledge ' and teaching of angels ' forever, for he knows all things.' " '

These are the revelations which [20] Adam made known to Seth his ' son. And his son taught ' his seed about them. This is the ' hidden knowledge of Adam, ' which he gave to Seth, which is the [25] holy baptism of those who ' know the eternal knowledge ' through those born of the word ' and the imperishable illuminators, who ' came from the holy seed: [30] Yesseus, Mazareus, ' [Yesse]dekeus, [the Living] Water. '

The Apocalypse of Adam

THE ACTS OF PETER
AND THE TWELVE APOSTLES (VI, *1*)

Introduced and translated by
Douglas M. Parrott and R. McL. Wilson

In spite of its present title, the *Acts of Peter and the Twelve Apostles* is not just another one of the apocryphal acts of the apostles. The work of the apostles is not at the center of the narrative, but rather the work of Lithargoel, who is actually Christ; only at the end of the narrative can the true apostolic activity begin. The identification of Lithargoel, "the god of the glistening stone," the god of the pearl, with Christ need not be too surprising. Elsewhere in ancient texts Jesus is called a pearl, and in fact the present narrative concerning Lithargoel-Christ could conceivably have been developed on the basis of a passage like Revelation 2:17.

The *Acts of Peter and the Twelve Apostles* opens with Peter and the apostles, after the crucifixion, setting off on a journey. They locate a ship and sail away, finally arriving at a city named Habitation. There Peter meets a pearl-merchant named Lithargoel, who invites the poor to come to his city and obtain a pearl. Peter and his friends successfully endure the difficult journey to the city of Lithargoel, for they do as Lithargoel has recommended: they renounce food and possessions; and hence the robbers and beasts along the way do not bother them. Finally Lithargoel disguises himself as a physician, then reveals himself as Jesus Christ, and commissions the disciples to go forth and minister to the sick and the poor.

In general the *Acts of Peter and the Twelve Apostles* seems quite consistent with the developing orthodoxy of the church of the second century, when this tractate may have been composed. The emphasis upon apostolic poverty and the polemic against the rich are even rooted in the New Testament. Though the tractate does not seem to proclaim distinctively Gnostic ideas, it is clear that Gnostic interpreters would have no trouble relating to such themes as the stranger, the journey, the hidden pearl, and the expensive garment of the world.

THE ACTS OF PETER AND THE TWELVE APOSTLES

VI 1, 1-12, 22

[...] which [...]' purpose [...: ' after ...]' us [...]⁵ apostles [...].' We sailed [...]' of the body. [Others] were not ' anxious in [their ' hearts]. And in our hearts, we were ¹⁰ united. We agreed to fulfill ' the ministry to which ' the Lord appointed us. And we made ' a covenant with each other. '

We went down to the sea at [15] an opportune moment, which came ' to us from the Lord. We ' found a ship moored at the shore ' ready to embark, ' and we spoke with the sailors of [20] the ship about our coming aboard with them. ' They showed great ' kindliness toward us as ' was ordained by the Lord. ' And after we had embarked,[25] we sailed a day ' and a night. After that, ' a wind came up behind the ship and ' brought us to a small city ' in the midst of the sea.[30]

And I, Peter, inquired about the name ' of this city from residents ' who were ' standing on the dock. 2 [A man] among [them] answered, [saying, ' "The name] of this [city is ' Habitation, that is], Foundation [...] ' endurance." And [5] the leader [among them ... ' holding] the palm branch at the edge of [the dock]. ' And after we had gone ashore [with the] ' baggage, I [went] ' into [the] city, to seek [advice] [10] about lodging.

A man came out ' wearing a cloth ' bound around his waist, ' and a gold belt girded [it]. ' Also a napkin was tied over [his] [15] chest, extending over ' his shoulders and covering his head ' and his arms.

I was staring at the ' man, because he was beautiful in his ' form and stature. There were four [20] parts of his body which ' I saw: the tops of his ' feet, and a part of his ' chest, and the palm of his ' hand, and his visage.[25] These things I was able to see. ' A book cover like (those of) my ' books was in his left hand. ' A staff of styrax wood was in ' his right hand. His [30] voice was resounding as he slowly spoke, ' crying out in the city, ' "Pearls! Pearls!"

I, ' indeed, thought he was a man [of] ' that city. I said [35] to him, "My brother and my friend!" 3 [He answered] me, [then, saying, ' "Rightly] did you say, '[My brother ' and] my friend.' What is it you [seek] ' from me?" I said to him, "[I [5] ask] you [about] lodging for me ' [and the] brothers also, because we ' are strangers here." He said [to] me, ' "For this reason have I myself just said, ' 'My brother and my friend,' [10] because I also am a fellow stranger ' like you."

And ' having said these things, he cried out, ' "Pearls! Pearls!" ' The rich men of that [15] city heard his voice. ' They came out of their hidden storerooms. ' And some were ' looking out from the storerooms ' of their houses. Others [20] looked out from their ' upper windows. And they did not see (that they could gain) ' anything from him, because ' there was no pouch on his back, nor ' bundle inside his cloth [25] and napkin. And because of their ' disdain they did not ' even acknowledge him. ' He, for his part, did not reveal himself to them. ' They returned to their [30] storerooms, saying, ' "This man is mocking us." '

And the poor [of that city] heard **4** [his voice, ' and they came to] the man [who sells ' pearls. They said, ' "We] beseech you to [show us [5] a] pearl [so that we may], then, [see] ' it with our (own) eyes. For we are [poor]. ' And we do not have this price ' to pay for it. But [allow us] ' to say to our friends that [we saw] [10] a pearl with our (own) eyes." He ' answered, saying to them, "If ' it is possible, come to my city, ' so that I may not only show it ' before your (very) eyes, but give it to [15] you for nothing."

And indeed they, ' the poor of that city, heard ' and said, "Since we ' are beggars, we surely ' know that a man does not give a pearl [20] to a beggar, but (it is) bread ' and money that is usually received. ' Now then, the kindness which we want to receive ' from you (is) that you show us ' the pearl before our eyes.[25] And we will say to our friends ' proudly that we saw a ' pearl with our (own) eyes"—because ' it is not found among the poor, especially ' such beggars (as these). He answered [30] (and) said to them, "If it is ' possible, you yourselves come ' to my city, so that I may not only ' show you it, but give it ' to you for nothing." [35] The poor and the beggars rejoiced because of **5** the man [who gives for] nothing.

[The men ' asked Peter] about the hardships. ' Peter answered [that it was impossible ' to tell] those things that he had heard about the hardships [5] of [the] way, because [interpreters were] ' difficult [...] in their ministry. '

He said to the man who sells this ' pearl, "I want ' to know your name and the hardships of [10] the way to your city because we ' are strangers and servants of ' God. It is necessary for us to spread ' the word of God in ' every city harmoniously." He [15] answered and said, "If you ' seek my name, Lithargoel ' is my name, the interpretation of which is, ' the light, gazelle-like stone. '

"And also (concerning) the road to the city,[20] which you asked me about, I will tell you ' about it. No man is able to go ' on that road, except one ' who has forsaken everything that ' he has and has fasted [25] daily from stage to stage. ' For many are the robbers and ' wild beasts on that road. ' The one who carries bread with him ' on the road, the black dogs [30] kill because of ' the bread. The one who carries a costly garment ' of the world with him, ' the robbers kill **6** [because of the] garment. [The one who carries] water ' [with him, the wolves kill because ' of the water], since they were thirsty [for] it. ' [The one who] is anxious about [meat] and [5] green vegetables, the lions eat ' because of the meat. [If] he evades ' the lions, the bulls ' devour him because of the green vegetables." '

When he had said [these] things to me, I sighed [10] within myself, saying, "[Great] ' hardships are on the road! If only ' Jesus would give us power to walk it!" ' He looked at me since my face was sad, and I ' sighed. He said to me, "Why [15] do you sigh, if you, indeed, know ' this name 'Jesus' and believe him? ' He is a great power for giving strength. ' For I too believe in the Father ' who sent him."

I replied,[20] asking him, "What is the name ' of the place to which you go, ' your city?" He said to me, ' "This is the name of my city, ' 'Nine Gates.' Let us praise God [25] as we are mindful that the tenth ' is the head." After this I went away ' from him in peace.

As I was ' about to go and call my friends, I ' saw waves and large [30] high walls surrounding ' the bounds of the city. I ' marveled at the great things I saw. ' I saw an old man ' sitting and I asked him if the name of the [35] city was really 7 [Habitation]. He [. . .], ' "[Habitation . . .]." ' He said to me, "[You ' speak] truly, for we [inhabit] here [5] because [we] endure."

[I ' responded], saying, "Justly ' [. . .] have men named it ' [. . .], because (by) everyone ' [who] endures his trial,[10] cities are inhabited; ' and a precious kingdom ' comes from them, because ' they endure in the midst of the ' apostasies and the difficulties of the storms.[15] So that in this way, the city of everyone ' who endures the burden of his yoke ' of faith will be inhabited, ' and he will be included in ' the kingdom of heaven."

I hurried [20] and went and called my ' friends so that we might go to the city ' which he, Lithargoel, appointed for us. ' In a bond ' of faith we forsook [25] everything as ' he had said (to do). We evaded ' the robbers, because they did not ' find their garments with us. ' We evaded the [30] wolves, because they did not find the water ' with us for which they thirsted. ' We evaded the lions, ' because they did not find the desire ' for meat with us. 8 [We evaded the bulls . . . [3] they did not find] green vegetables. '

A great joy [came upon] us [and a] [5] peaceful carefreeness [like ' that of] our Lord. We [rested ' ourselves] in front of the gate, [and] ' we talked with each other [about that] ' which is not a distraction of this [world].[10] Rather we continued in contemplation ' of the faith.

As we discussed the ' robbers on the road, whom we ' evaded, behold ' Lithargoel, having changed, came out to [15] us. He had the appearance of a physician, ' since an unguent box was under ' his arm, and a young disciple was ' following him, carrying a pouch ' full of medicine.[20] We did not recognize him. '

Peter responded and said to him, ' "We want you to do ' us a favor, because we are ' strangers, and take us to the house of [25] Lithargoel before evening comes." ' He said, "In uprightness ' of heart I will show it to you. ' But I am amazed at how ' you knew this good man.[30] For he has not revealed himself to ' every man, because he himself ' is the son of a great king. ' Rest yourselves a little so ' that I may go and heal this man [35] and come (back)." He hurried and came (back) **9** quickly.

He said to Peter, ' "Peter!" And Peter was frightened, ' for how did he know ' that his name was Peter? [5] Peter responded to the Savior, ' "How do you know me, ' for you called my name?" ' Lithargoel answered, "I ' want to ask you who gave the [10] name Peter to you?" He ' said to him, "It was Jesus Christ, the ' son of the living God. He ' gave this name to me." He answered ' and said, "It is I! Recognize me,[15] Peter." He loosened his garment, ' which clothed him—the one into which ' he had changed himself because of us— ' revealing to us in truth that ' it was he.

We prostrated ourselves [20] on the ground and worshipped him. We ' comprised eleven disciples. ' He stretched forth his hand ' and caused us to stand. We spoke with ' him humbly. Our heads were [25] bowed down in unworthiness ' as we said, "What you ' wish we will do. But ' give us power to do ' what you wish at all times." [30]

He gave them the unguent box ' and the pouch ' that was in the hand of the young disciple. ' He commanded them like this, **10** saying, "Go into [the] ' city from which you came, ' which is called Habitation. ' Continue in endurance as you [5] teach all those who have believed ' in my name, because I have endured ' in hardships of the faith. I ' will give you your reward. To the ' poor of that city give [10] what they need in order to live ' until I give them what is better, ' which I told you that I will give ' you for nothing."

Peter answered ' and said to him,[15] "Lord, you have taught us to ' forsake the world and ' everything in it. We have renounced them ' for your sake. What we are concerned about (now) ' is the food for a single day.[20] Where will we be able to find the needs that you ask ' us to provide for the poor?" '

The Lord answered and said, ' "O Peter, it was necessary ' that you understand the parable [25] that I told you! Do you not understand ' that my name, which you teach, ' surpasses all riches, ' and the wisdom of God ' surpasses gold, and silver,[30] and precious stone(s)?" '

He gave them the pouch ' of medicine and said, ' "Heal all the sick ' of the city who believe **11** [in] my name." Peter was afraid ' [to] reply

to him for the second time. ' He signaled to the one who was beside '
him, who was John: "You ⁵ talk this time." ' John answered and said, '
"Lord, before you we are afraid ' to say many words. ' But it is you
who asks us ¹⁰ to practice this skill. We have not been ' taught to be
physicians. How then ' will we know how to heal bodies ' as you have
told us?" '

He answered him, "Rightly have you ¹⁵ spoken, John, for I know '
that the physicians of this world ' heal what belongs to the world. ' The
physicians of souls, however, ' heal the heart. Heal ²⁰ the bodies first,
therefore, so ' that through the ' real powers of healing ' for their
bodies, without medicine of ' the world, they may believe in you,²⁵ that
you have power to heal ' the illnesses of the heart also.

"The ' rich men of the city, however, those ' who did not see fit '
even to acknowledge me, but who ³⁰ reveled in their ' wealth and pride— '
with such as these, therefore, **12** do not dine in [their] house ' nor be
friends with them, ' lest their partiality ' influence you. For many in the
churches have ⁵ shown partiality to the rich, because ' they also are sinful, ' and they give occasion for ' others to do (likewise). But judge '
them with uprightness, so ¹⁰ that your ministry may ' be glorified, and
(so that) I too, ' and my name, may be glorified in the ' churches." The
disciples ' answered and said, "Yes,¹⁵ truly this is what is fitting ' to do."

They prostrated themselves on the ground ' and worshipped him. He
caused them ' to stand and departed from ' them in peace. Amen.²⁰

The Acts of Peter '
and the Twelve '
Apostles

THE THUNDER, PERFECT MIND (VI, *2*)

Introduced and translated by

GEORGE W. MACRAE

Edited by

DOUGLAS M. PARROTT

The short tractate entitled *The Thunder, Perfect Mind* is a revelation discourse delivered by a female revealer in the first person. It is characteristic of the revelation imparted that the self-proclamation ("I am ...") is of an antithetical or paradoxical sort: "I am the whore and the holy one. I am the wife and the virgin." In addition there are added various exhortations to hear and reflect, and reproaches for failing to do so.

In terms of religious tradition *Thunder, Perfect Mind* is difficult to classify. It presents no distinctively Jewish, Christian, or Gnostic themes, nor does it seem to presuppose a particular Gnostic myth. While the Jewish wisdom literature and the Isis aretalogies provide texts which are parallel in tone and style, the particular significance of the self-proclamations of *Thunder, Perfect Mind* may be found in their antithetical character. Antithesis and paradox may be used to proclaim the absolute transcendence of the revealer, whose greatness is incomprehensible and whose being is unfathomable.

THE THUNDER, PERFECT MIND

VI 13, 1-21, 32

The Thunder, Perfect Mind '

I was sent forth from ' [the] power,
   and I have come to those who ' reflect upon me,
   and I have been found [5] among those who seek after me. '
Look upon me, you (pl.) who reflect upon me, '
   and you hearers, hear me. '
   You who are waiting for me, take me ' to yourselves.
And do not banish me [10] from your sight. '
   And do not make your voice hate ' me, nor your hearing. '
   Do not be ignorant of me anywhere ' or any time. Be on your
      guard! [15]
   Do not be ignorant of me. '

For I am the first and the last.
I ' am the honored one and the scorned one. '
I am the whore and the holy one. '

I am the wife and the [20] virgin.
I am ⟨the mother⟩ ' and the daughter.
I am the members ' of my mother.
I am the barren one '
and many are her sons.
I ' am she whose wedding is great,
and [25] I have not taken a husband.
I am the midwife ' and she who does not bear.
I ' am the solace of my labor pains.
I ' am the bride and the bridegroom, '
and it is my husband who [30] begot me.
I am the mother of ' my father
and the sister of my ' husband,
and he is my offspring. '
I am the slave of him who ' prepared me.
I am the ruler **14** of my offspring.
But he is the one who [begot me] ' before the time
on a birthday. '
And he is my offspring [in] ' (due) time,
and my power [5] is from him.
I am the staff ' of his power in his youth,
[and] ' he is the rod of my ' old age.
And whatever he wills ' happens to me.
I am the silence [10] that is incomprehensible
and the idea ' whose remembrance is frequent. '
I am the voice whose sound is ' manifold
and the word whose appearance ' is multiple.
I am the utterance of [15] my name.

Why, you who hate me, ' do you love me,
and ' you hate those who love me? '
You who deny me, confess ' me,
and you who confess [20] me, deny me.
You who tell ' the truth about me, lie about me,
and you ' who have lied about me, tell the truth about me. '
You who know me, be ignorant ' of me,
and those who have not [25] known me, let them know me. '

For I am knowledge and ' ignorance.
I am ' shame and boldness. '
I am shameless; I am [30] ashamed.

I am strength and ' I am fear.
I am ' war and peace.
Give heed ' to me.
I am the one who is disgraced ' and the great one.

Give heed to my **15** poverty and my wealth. '
Do not be arrogant to me when I am ' cast out upon the earth,
   [and] ' you will find me in [those **5** that] are to come.
And do not look ' [upon] me on the dung-heap
   nor go ' and leave me cast out, '
   and you will find me in ' the kingdoms.
And do not look **10** upon me when I am cast out among those who '
   are disgraced and in the least ' places,
   nor laugh at me. '
And do not cast me out among those who ' are slain in violence.**15**
But I, I am compassionate ' and I am cruel.

Be on your guard! '
Do not hate my obedience '
   and do not love my self-control. '
In my weakness, do not **20** forsake me,
   and do ' not be afraid of my power. '
For why do you despise ' my fear
   and ' curse my pride? **25**
But I am she who exists in ' all fears
   and strength ' in trembling.
I am she who is ' weak,
   and I am well in a ' pleasant place.
I am **30** senseless and I am wise. '

Why have you hated me ' in your counsels?
For I shall be ' silent among those who are silent, '
   and I shall appear and speak. **16**
Why then have you hated me, you Greeks? '
   Because I am a barbarian among [the] ' barbarians?
For I am the wisdom ' [of the] Greeks
   and the knowledge of [the] **5** barbarians.
I am the judgment of [the] ' Greeks and of the barbarians.
[I] ' am the one whose image is great in Egypt '
   and the one who has no image among the ' barbarians.
I am the one who has been hated **10** everywhere
   and who has been loved ' everywhere.

I am the one whom they call ' Life,
    and you have ' called Death.
I am the one whom ' they call Law,[15]
    and you have called Lawlessness. '
I am the one whom you have pursued, '
    and I am the one whom you have seized. '
I am the one whom you have scattered, '
    and you have gathered me together.[20]
I am the one before whom you have ' been ashamed,
    and you have been ' shameless to me.
I am she who does not keep festival, '
    and I am she whose festivals are many. '
I, I am godless,
    and [25] I am the one whose God is great. '
I am the one whom you have reflected upon, '
    and you have scorned me.
I am ' unlearned,
    and they learn from ' me.
I am the one whom you have [30] despised,
    and you ' reflect upon me.
I am the one ' whom you have hidden from,
    and you ' appear to me.
    But whenever ' you hide yourselves,[35]
        I myself will appear. **17**
    For [whenever] you ' [appear],
        I myself ' [will hide] from you.
Those who have [. . .] ' to it [. . .] [5] senselessly [. . .]. '

Take me [. . . ' understanding] from grief, '
    and take me ' to yourselves from understanding [10] [and] grief.
And take ' me to yourselves from places ' that are ugly and in ruin, '
    and rob from those ' which are good even though in ugliness.[15]
Out of shame, take me ' to yourselves shamelessly; '
    and out of shamelessness ' and shame, upbraid my members '
    in yourselves.
And [20] come forward to me, ' you who know me
    and you who ' know my members,
    and ' establish the great ones among the small ' first creatures.
Come [25] forward to childhood, '
    and do not despise it ' because it is small and it is little. '

And do not turn away ' greatnesses in some parts from [30] the
    smallnesses,
    for ' the smallnesses are known ' from the greatnesses.

Why ' do you curse me ' and honor me? [35]
You have wounded and you have ' had mercy.
Do not separate me from the first **18** ones whom you have [known].
[And] ' do not cast anyone [out nor] ' turn anyone away
    [. . .] ' turn you away and [. . . [5] know] him not.
    [. . . ' him].
    What is mine [. . .]. '
I know the [first ones] and ' those after them [know] me. '

But I am the mind of [. . .] [10] and the rest of [. . .]. '
I am the knowledge of my inquiry,
    and ' the finding of those who seek after me,
    and ' the command of those who ask of me, '
    and the power of the powers in my knowledge [15]
        of the angels, who have been ' sent at my word,
        and of gods ' in their seasons by my counsel, '
        and of spirits of every man who ' exists with me,
        and of women [20] who dwell within me.
I am the one who ' is honòred, and who is praised, '
    and who is despised ' scornfully.
I ' am peace,
    and war [25] has come because of me.
And I ' am an alien and a citizen. '
I am the substance and the one who ' has no substance.

Those who are ' without association with me are ignorant [30] of me,
    and those who are in my ' substance are the ones who know me. '
Those who are close to me have been ignorant ' of me,
    and those who are far ' away from me are the ones who have
        known [35] me.
On the day when I am close to **19** [you],
        [you] are far away ' [from me],
        [and] on the day when I ' [am far away] from you,
        [I am ' close] to you.

[I am [5] . . .] within.
[I am ' . . .] of the natures.
I am ' [. . .] of the creation of the [spirits]. '

[. . .] request of the souls. '
[I am] control and the uncontrollable.[10]
I am the union and ' the dissolution.
I am the abiding ' and I am the dissolving.
I ' am the one below,
    and they come ' up to me.
I am the judgment [15] and the acquittal.
I, I ' am sinless,
    and the root ' of sin derives from me. '
I am lust in (outward) appearance, '
    - and interior self-control [20] exists within me.
I ' am the hearing which is attainable to ' everyone
    and the speech which cannot be ' grasped.
I am a mute ' who does not speak,
    and great [25] is my multitude of words.

Hear ' me in gentleness, and ' learn of me in roughness. '
I am she who cries out, '
    and I am cast [30] forth upon the face of the earth. '
I prepare the bread and ' my mind within.
I am the ' knowledge of my name.
I am the one ' who cries out,
    and I listen. **20**
I appear and [. . .] ' walk in [. . .] ' seal of my [. . .].[5]
I am [. . .] ' the defense [. . .]. '
I am the one who is called ' Truth,
    and iniquity [. . .]. '

You honor me [. . .] [10] and you whisper against [me].
[. . .] ' victorious over them.
Judge them ' before they give judgment against you, '
    because the judge and partiality ' exist in you.
If you are condemned [15] by this one, who will ' acquit you?
    Or if you are acquitted ' by him, who will be able to ' detain you?
For what is ' inside of you is what is outside of you,[20]
    and the one who fashions you on the outside '
        is the one who shaped ' the inside of you.
    And what ' you see outside of you, '
        you see inside of you; [25]
        it is visible and it is your garment. '

Hear me, you hearers, '
  and learn of my words, ' you who know me.
I am ' the hearing that is attainable to everything; [30]
  I am the speech that cannot ' be grasped.
I am ' the name of the sound
  and the sound ' of the name.
I am the sign ' of the letter
  and the designation [35] of the division.
And I [. . .].
[. . .] **21**[4] light [. . .].
[. . .] [6] hearers [. . .] ' to you
[. . .] ' the great power.
And [. . .] ' will not move the name.[10]
[. . .] to the one who created me. '
  And I will speak his name. '

Look then at his words
  and all the ' writings which have been completed.
Give ' heed then, you hearers
  and [15] you also, the angels ' and those who have been sent, '
  and you spirits who have arisen from ' the dead.
For I am the one who ' alone exists,
  and I have no one [20] who will judge me.

For many ' are the pleasant forms which ' exist in
  numerous sins, '
  and incontinencies, '
  and disgraceful passions,[25]
  and fleeting pleasures, '
    which (men) embrace ' until they become sober
    and ' go up to their resting-place. '
And they will find [30] me there,
  and they will ' live,
  and they will not die ' again.

AUTHORITATIVE TEACHING (VI, 3)

Introduced and translated by

GEORGE W. MACRAE

Edited by

DOUGLAS M. PARROTT

The tractate *Authoritative Teaching* is an exposition of the origin, condition, and ultimate bliss of the soul. In describing the life of the soul, the text becomes highly metaphorical. The soul is the prostitute who drinks the wine of debauchery, the wheat which can be either pure or contaminated with chaff, the contestant who competes in the struggle of life, the invalid who makes use of the medicine of the word (the logos), the fish that the diabolical fisherman tries to catch, and the bride who finally reclines with her bridegroom in the bridal chamber.

Although it does not seem to include a Gnostic myth describing the origin of the world, *Authoritative Teaching* does presuppose certain general Gnostic ideas. Thus, as in so many other Gnostic documents, the spiritual soul is considered to be of heavenly origin, to be in conflict with the evil world of matter, and to be saved through the agency of revealed knowledge. It may also be noted that specifically Jewish or Christian themes cannot be identified with any degree of confidence or regularity, though there are a few references to "the evangelists" and "the preaching."

AUTHORITATIVE TEACHING

VI 22, 1-35, 24

[...] [6] in heaven [...] ' within him [...] ' anyone appears [...] ' the hidden heavens [...] [10] appear, and [before] ' the invisible, ineffable worlds ' appeared. ' From these the invisible ' soul of righteousness [15] came, being ' a fellow member, and a fellow ' body, and a fellow spirit. ' Whether she is in the descent ' or is in the Pleroma, [20] she is not separated from them, but they see ' her and she looks at them ' in the invisible word. '

Secretly her bridegroom ' fetched it. He presented it to her mouth [25] to make her eat it like ' food, and he applied the word ' to her eyes as a medicine ' to make her see with her mind ' and perceive her kinsmen [30] and learn about her root, ' in order that she might cling to her branch ' from which she had first come forth, ' in order that she might receive what ' is hers and renounce [matter].

[...] **23**[5] he [dwells ...] ' having [...] ' sons. The sons [...] ' truly, those who have ' [come] from his seed,[10] call the sons ' of the woman "our brothers." ' In this very way, when the spiritual ' soul was cast ' into the body, it became [15] a brother to lust, and hatred, ' and envy, and a material ' soul. So therefore the body ' came from lust, ' and lust [20] came from material substance. ' For this reason the soul ' became a brother to them.

And yet ' they are outsiders, without power ' to inherit from the male,[25] but they will inherit ' from their mother only. ' Whenever, therefore, the soul ' wishes to inherit ' along with the outsiders—for the possessions of [30] the outsiders are ' proud passions, the pleasures ' of life, hateful envies, ' vainglorious things, nonsensical things, ' accusations, [...] **24**[6] for her [... ' prostitution], he excludes her [and puts] ' her into the brothel. For [...] ' for her [debauchery. She left] [10] modesty behind. For death ' and life are set before ' everyone. Whichever of these two ⟨they⟩ wish, then, ' they will choose for themselves. '

That one (fem.) then will fall [15] into drinking much wine in ' debauchery. For wine is ' the debaucher. Therefore she does not remember ' her brothers and her father, for ' pleasure and sweet profits [20] deceive her.

Having ' left knowledge behind, she fell ' into bestiality. For a senseless person ' exists in ' bestiality, not knowing what it is [25] proper to say, and what it is proper ' not to say. But, on the other hand, the ' gentle son inherits ' from his father with pleasure, while ' his father rejoices over him [30] because he receives honor on account of him from ' everyone, as he looks again ' for the way to double the things ' that he has received. For the outsiders [...].

[...] **25**[5] to mix with the [...]. ' For if a thought [of] lust ' enters into ' [a] virgin man, he has ' [...] being contaminated. And their [10] gluttony cannot ' mix with moderation. ' For if the chaff is mixed ' with the wheat, it is not the chaff that is ' contaminated, but the wheat.[15] For they are mixed with each other. No ' one will buy her wheat because it is contaminated. ' But they will coax ' him, "Give us this chaff!", ' seeing the wheat mixed [20] with it, until they get it and ' throw it with all other chaff, ' and that chaff ' mixes with all other materials. ' But a pure seed [25] is kept in storehouses ' that are secure. All these things, then, ' we have spoken.

And before ' anything came into being, ' it was the Father alone who existed,[30] before the worlds that are in ' the heavens appeared, ' or the world that is on ' the earth, or principality, or ' authority, or the powers.

[. . .] 26⁴ appear [. . .] ' and [. . . . ' And] nothing ' came into being without his wish. '

He, then, the Father, wishing ' to reveal his [wealth] ¹⁰ and his glory,
brought about ' this great contest ' in this world, wishing ' to make the
contestants appear, ' and make all those who contend ¹⁵ leave behind '
the things that had come into being, and ' despise them with a ' lofty,
incomprehensible knowledge, ' and flee to the one who ²⁰ exists.

And (as for) those who contend with us, ' being adversaries who '
contend against us, we are to be victorious over their ' ignorance through
our ' knowledge, since we have already known ²⁵ the Inscrutable One
from whom we have ' come forth. We have nothing in ' this world,
lest ' the authority of the world that ' has come into being should detain
us ³⁰ in the worlds that are in the heavens, ' those in which universal
death ' exists, ' surrounded by the individual [. . .] 27⁵ worldly [. . .] '
we are ashamed [of the] worlds, ' though we take no interest in them
when they ' [malign] us. And we ignore ' them when they curse ¹⁰
us. When they cast shame in ' our face, we look at them ' and do not
speak.

For they ' work at their business, ' but we go about in hunger (and) ¹⁵
in thirst, looking toward ' our dwelling place, the place which ' our
conduct and our conscience ' look toward, ' not clinging to the things ²⁰
which have come into being, but withdrawing ' from them. Our hearts '
are set on the things that exist, though we are ill ' (and) feeble (and) in
pain. ' But there is a great strength hidden ²⁵ within us.

Our soul ' indeed is ill, because she dwells ' in a house of poverty, while '
matter strikes blows at her eyes, ' wishing to make her blind.³⁰ For this
reason she pursues ' the word and applies it to her eyes ' as a medicine,
⟨opening⟩ ' them, casting away [. . .] 28⁴ thought of a [. . .] ' blindness
in [. . .] ' afterwards when ' that one is again in ' ignorance, he is completely [darkened] ' and [is] material.¹⁰ Thus the soul [. . .] ' a word every
hour, to apply ' it to her eyes as a medicine ' in order that she may see, '
and her light may conceal the hostile forces ¹⁵ that fight with ' her, and
she may make them blind with ' her light, and enclose them in ' her
presence, ' and make them fall down in sleeplessness,²⁰ and she may act
boldly ' with her strength and with her ' scepter.

While her enemies look ' at her in shame, she runs ' upward into her
treasure-house— ²⁵ the one in which her mind ' is—and (into) her '
storehouse which is secure, since nothing ' among the things that have
come into being has seized ' her, nor has she received a ³⁰ stranger into
her house. ' For many are her ' home-born ones who fight against her '

by day and by night, ' having no rest **29** by day nor by night, ' for their
lust oppresses ' them.

For this reason, then, we do ' not sleep, nor do we forget [the] [5] nets
that are spread out in ' hiding, lying in wait for us to catch ' us. For if
we are caught in ' a single net, it will suck us ' down into its mouth,
while the water flows [10] over us, striking our face. And we will ' be taken
down into the dragnet, and we ' will not be able to come up from ' it
because the waters are high ' over us, flowing from above [15] downward,
submerging our heart down ' in the filthy mud. And we ' will not be
able to escape from them. ' For man-eaters will seize ' us and swallow
us, rejoicing [20] like a fisherman casting ' a hook into the water. For ' he
casts many kinds of food ' into the water because each one ' of the fish
has his own [25] food. He smells it ' and pursues its odor. ' But when he
eats it, ' the hook ' hidden within the food [30] seizes him and brings him
up by ' force out of the deep waters. ' No man is able, then, ' to catch
that fish ' down in the deep waters, **30** except for the trap ' that the
fisherman set. ' By the ruse of food he brought the fish ' up on the hook.

In this very [5] way we exist in this world, ' like fish. The adversary '
spies on us, lying in wait ' for us like a fisherman, ' wishing to seize us,
rejoicing [10] that he might swallow us. For [he places] ' many foods
before ' our eyes, (things) which belong to this ' world. He wishes to
make us ' desire one of them [15] and to taste only a ' little, so that he may
seize us ' with his hidden poison and bring ' us out of freedom ' and
take us into [20] slavery. For whenever he catches us ' with a single food, '
it is indeed necessary for ⟨us⟩ to ' desire the rest. ' Finally, then, such
things [25] become the food of death. '

Now these are the foods with which ' the devil lies in wait for us. '
First he ' injects a pain into your [30] heart until you have heartache ' on
account of a small thing of ' this life, and he seizes ⟨you⟩ ' with his
poisons. And ' afterwards (he injects) the desire [35] of a tunic so that you
will pride yourself **31** in it, and ' love of money, pride, ' vanity, envy
that ' rivals another envy, beauty of [5] body, fraudulence. ' The greatest
of all these ' are ignorance and ease. '

Now all such (things) ' the adversary prepares [10] beautifully and
spreads out ' before the body, ' wishing to make the mind of the soul '
incline her toward one of them ' and overwhelm her, like a hook [15]
drawing her by force in ' ignorance, deceiving ' her until she conceives
evil, ' and bears fruit of matter, ' and conducts herself [20] in uncleanness,
pursuing many ' desires, ' covetousnesses, while ' fleshly pleasure draws
her in ' ignorance.

But the soul— [25] she who has tasted these things— ' realized that sweet passions ' are transitory. ' She had learned about evil; ' she went away from them (and) she entered [30] into a new conduct. ' Afterwards she ' despises this life, ' because it is transitory. And she ' looks for those foods that will [35] take her into life, [32] and leaves behind her those deceitful foods. ' And she learns about her light, as she ' goes about stripping off this ' world, while her true garment [5] clothes her within, ' (and) her bridal clothing ' is placed upon her in beauty of ' mind, not in pride of flesh. ' And she learns about her depth and [10] runs into her fold, while ' her shepherd stands at the door. ' In return for all the shame and scorn, then, ' that she received in this ' world, she receives [15] ten thousand times the grace and ' glory.

She gave the body to ' those who had given it to her, and they were ' ashamed, while the dealers ' in bodies sat down and wept [20] because they were not able to ' do any business with ' that body, nor did they find ' any (other) merchandise except it. ' They endured great labors [25] until they had shaped the body of this ' soul, wishing to strike ' down the invisible soul. ' They were therefore ashamed of their ' work; they suffered the loss of the one [30] for whom they had endured labors. They did not realize ' that she has an ' invisible spiritual body, ' thinking, "We are her ' shepherd who feeds her." [35] But they did not realize that she knows [33] another way, which is hidden from them. This ' her true shepherd ' taught her in knowledge. '

But these—the ones who are ignorant— [5] do not seek after God. ' Nor do they inquire about ' their dwelling place, which exists ' in rest, but they ' go about in bestiality. They [10] are more wicked than the ' pagans, because first of all they ' do not inquire about God, for ' their hardness of heart draws ' them down to make them [15] exercise their cruelty. ' Furthermore, if they find someone else ' who asks about his salvation, ' their hardness of ' heart sets to work upon [20] that man. ' And if he is not silent as he asks, they ' kill him by ' their cruelty, ' thinking that they have done a [25] good thing for themselves.

Indeed ' they are sons of the devil! ' For even the pagans give ' charity, and they know ' that God who is in the heavens [30] exists, the Father of the universe, ' exalted over their idols, which ' they worship. [34] But they have not heard the word, that ' they should inquire about his ways. ' Thus the senseless man ' hears the call, [5] but he is ignorant of the place ' to which he has been called. And ' he did not ask during the preaching, ' "Where is the temple ' into which I should go and worship [10] my hope?" ' On account of his senselessness, then, ' he is worse than a pagan, ' for the pagans know ' the way to go to their stone temple,[15] which will perish, and they worship ' their idol, while their heart ' is set on it because it is their hope. ' But to this senseless man ' the word has been preached,[20] teaching him, "Seek and ' inquire about the ways you should go, ' since there is nothing else ' that is as good as this thing." ' The result is that the substance of hardness [25] of heart strikes a blow upon ' his mind, along with the force ' of ignorance and ' the demon of error. ' They do not allow his mind [30] to rise up, because he was wearying ' himself in seeking that he might learn about his ' hope.

But the rational soul [35] who (also) wearied herself in seeking— ' she learned about God. ' She labored with inquiring, enduring ' distress in the body, wearing out [5] her feet after ' the evangelists, ' learning about the Inscrutable One. ' She found her rising. ' She came to rest in him who [10] is at rest. She reclined ' in the bridechamber. She ate ' of the banquet for which ' she had hungered. She partook ' of the immortal food.[15] She found what she had sought after. ' She received rest from her labors, ' while the light that shines forth ' upon her does not sink. ' To it belongs the glory [20] and the power and the ' revelation for ever and ' ever. Amen. '

Authoritative '
Teaching

THE CONCEPT OF OUR GREAT POWER (VI, *4*)

Introduced by

FRANCIS E. WILLIAMS

Translated by

FREDERIK WISSE

Edited by

DOUGLAS M. PARROTT

The *Concept of Our Great Power* is a complex and somewhat inconsistent exposition of salvation history in apocalyptic form. The tractate may be called a Christian Gnostic apocalypse, or a Christian apocalypse with gnosticizing tendencies; indeed, the tractate may even have originated in Jewish apocalyptic. The Gnostic character of the document seems quite clear: the Old Testament God is portrayed as "the father of the flesh," the archons as wrathful and hostile, the flesh as defiled, and final bliss as glory in the divine light of the great Power.

Concept of Our Great Power proclaims the important moments in the history of salvation. Thus the document provides a gnosticizing perspective on the creation, the flood, the origin of evil, the Savior descending into Hades and humbling the archons, an antichrist, and the final consummation. In good apocalyptic fashion salvation history is divided into several main periods: the fleshly aeon which was ended by the flood, the natural or psychic aeon during which the Savior appears, and the indestructible aeon of the future.

The date and place of composition of *Concept of Our Great Power* remain uncertain. The mention of the Anomoean heresy probably indicates a date before or during the latter part of the fourth century; and the reference to "the East" as "that place where the Logos appeared at first" may possibly suggest that the author lived somewhere to the west of Palestine.

THE CONCEPT OF OUR GREAT POWER

VI 36, 1-48, 15

The Perception of Understanding '
The Concept of the Great Power '

He who would know our great ' Power will become invisible.[5] And fire ' will not be able to consume him. But it will ' purify and destroy ' all your (pl.) possessions. For ' every one in whom my form [10] will appear will be ' saved, from (the age of) seven days ' up to one hundred and twenty years, ' (those) whom I ⟨compelled⟩ to ' gather the whole ed-struction—and [15] the writings of our great Power, in order that ' she may inscribe your (sing.) name ' in our great light, and ' may bring to an end their thoughts ' and their works,[20] in order that they may be purified, ' and be scattered, and be ' destroyed, and be gathered in ' the place where no one ' sees ⟨me⟩. But you (pl.) [25] will see me and ' you will prepare your dwelling places ' in our great Power.

Know ' how what has departed ' came to be, in order that you [30] may know how to discern ' what exists to become: ' of what appearance ' that aeon is, or [37] what kind it is, or ' in what way [it] came into being. [Why] ' do you not ask what [kind] ' you will become,[5] (or), rather, how you came into being? ' Discern what size ' this water is, that it is incomprehensibly immeasurable, ' both its beginning ' and its end, supporting the earth (and) [10] blowing in the air where ' the gods and the angels ' are. But ' fear and light are in him who is exalted ' above all these, and [15] through him are my writings revealed. ' I have provided them as a service ' for the creation of the physical things, for ' it is not possible for anyone to stand ' without that One, nor [20] is it possible for the aeon to live ' without him, since he possesses ' what is in it, discerning (it) ' in purity.

Then ' behold the Spirit and know [25] where he is. He gave him (the Spirit) to ' men in order that they may receive life ' from him every day, ' since he has his life within ' him, giving to them all. Then [30] the darkness and Hades ' received the fire. And ' he (the darkness) will release from it what is mine. ' His eyes were not able ' to endure my light.[35] The spirits and the waters moved. [38] [And] the remainder came also into being, ' and the whole aeon of the creation, ' and their ⟨powers⟩ from which ' [the] fire came into being.[5] The Power came into ' the midst of the powers. And the ' powers desired to see my ' image. And the soul became ' its (my image's) replica. This is [10] the thing that came into being.

See ' what it is like, that ' before it comes into being it does not see, ' because the aeon ' of the flesh came to be in the great bodies.[15] And there were apportioned to them ' great days in the creation. ' For when they had been corrupted ' and had entered into the flesh, ' the father of the flesh,[20] the water, avenged ' himself. For when ' he had found Noah, who was pious ' (and) worthy, ' the father of the flesh who holds [25] the angels in subjection ' preached piety ' for one hundred and twenty ' years. And no one ' listened to him. And he [30] made a wooden ark, ' and he whom he had found entered ' it. And the flood ' took place. [39] And thus Noah was saved ' with his sons. For if, [indeed], ' ⟨the⟩ ark had not been meant for man ' to enter, then the water [5] of the flood would ' not have come. In this way he intended ' (and) planned to save the gods ' and the angels, and the powers ' ⟨of the⟩ greatness of all of these,[10] and wantonness and the way of life, ' by moving them from ' the aeon (and) nourishing them ' in the permanent places.

And the judgment ' of the flesh was unleashed.[15] Only the work of the Power stood up. '

Next the psychic ' aeon. It is a small one, ' which is mixed with bodies, ' begetting in the souls (and) being defiled.[20] For the first defilement of the creation ' found strength. And it begot ' every work: many works ' of wrath, anger, ' envy, malice, hatred,[25] slander, contempt ' and war, lying and ' evil counsels, sorrows ' and pleasures, ' basenesses and defilements,[30] falsehoods and diseases, ' evil judgments ' that they abandon according to their ' desires.

Yet you (pl.) are sleeping, **40** dreaming dreams. Wake up ' and return, ' taste and eat ' the true food! Hand out the word [5] and the water of life! Cease ' from the evil lusts and ' desires and (the teachings of) the Anomoeans, ' evil heresies ' that have no basis!

And [10] the mother of the fire was impotent. ' She brought the fire upon the soul and ' the earth, and she burned all ⟨the⟩ dwellings ' that are in it (fem.) (the soul and the earth). ' And its (fem.) shepherd perished.[15] Moreover, when she will not find (anything else) to burn, ' she will destroy herself. And ' it will become incorporeal, ' without body, and it will burn matter, ' until it has purged [20] everything and all wickedness. ' For when it will not find ' anything else to burn, it will turn ' to itself until it has destroyed itself. '

Then, in this aeon, which [25] is the psychic one, ' the man will come into being ' who knows the great Power. ' He will receive (me) and he will know me. ' He will drink from the milk of [30] the mother, in fact. He will speak ' in parables; he will proclaim ' the aeon that is to come, **41** just as he spoke to Noah in ' the first aeon of the flesh. ' Now concerning ' his words, which he uttered,[5] in all of them ' he spoke in seventy-two tongues. ' And he opened the gates ' of the heavens with his words. ' And he put to shame the [10] ruler of Hades; he raised ' the dead, and ' he destroyed his dominion. '

Then a great disturbance ' took place.[15] The archons raised up their wrath against him. ' They wanted to hand him over ' to the ruler of Hades. ' Furthermore, they knew one of ' his followers.[20] A fire took hold of his (Judas') ' soul. He handed ' him over, since no one knew ' him. They acted and seized ' him. They brought [25] judgment upon themselves. ' And they delivered him up ' to the ruler ' of Hades. And they

handed ' him over to Sasabek [30] for nine bronze coins. He prepared '
himself to go down and ' put them to shame. Then ' the ruler of Hades
took him. **42** And he found that the nature of his flesh ' could not be
seized, ' in order to show it to the archons. '

But he was saying, "Who is [5] this? What is it? His word has ' abolished
the law of the aeon. ' He is from the Logos of the power ' of life." And
he was victorious over the command ' of the archons, and [10] they were
not able by their work ' to rule over him.

The archons ' searched after that which had come to pass. ' They did
not know that this is the sign ' of their dissolution, and (that) [15] it is the
change of the aeon. The sun ' set during the day; the day ' became dark.
The evil spirits were ' troubled. And after these things he will appear '
ascending.[20] And ' the sign of the aeon that is to come will appear. '
And the aeons will dissolve. ' And those who would ' know these
things [25] that were discussed with them will become ' blessed. And they '
will reveal them, and ' they will become blessed, since ' they will come
to know the truth.[30] For you (pl.) have found rest in ' the heavens.

Then many ' will follow him, and they will ' labor in their birth-
places. **43** They will go about; they will abandon ' his words according
to their desire. ' Behold, these aeons have passed. '

What size [5] is the water of ' that aeon that has ' dissolved? ' What
dimensions do aeons have? How ' will men prepare themselves,[10] and
how will they endure, and how will they become ' indestructible aeons?

But at first, ' after his preaching, ' he proclaims the second aeon, '
and the first— [15] and the first aeon ' perishes in the course of time. '
He made the first aeon, going about ' in it until it perished ' while
preaching one hundred and twenty [20] years in number. ' This is the
perfect number ' that is highly exalted. ' He made the border of the
West ' desolate, and he [25] destroyed the East.

Then ' your (sing.) seed, and those who wish ' to follow our ' great
Logos and his proclamation—. ' Then the wrath of the archons [30]
burned. They were ashamed ' of their dissolution. ' And they fumed and
were angry ' at the life. The cities were overturned; ' the mountains
dissolved.[35] The Archon came, with the **44** archons of the western regions,
to ' the East, i.e. that place ' where the Logos appeared ' at first.

Then [5] the earth trembled, and the cities ' were troubled. Moreover,
the birds ' ate and were filled ' with their dead. The earth ' mourned
together with the inhabited world; [10] they became desolate. Then when
the ' times were completed, then wickedness ' arose mightily even until
the final ' end of the Logos.

Then ' the archon of the western regions arose,[15] and from the East '
he will perform a work, and he will instruct ' men in his wickedness. '
And he wanted to nullify ' all teaching, the words of Sophia of truth,[20]
while loving the lying Sophia. For he attacked ' the old, wishing ' to
introduce wickedness ' and to put on ' dignity. He was incapable,[25]
because the defilement ' ⟨of⟩ his garments is great. Then he ' became
angry. He appeared and desired ' to go up and to pass beyond ' that
place. Then [30] the appointed time came and drew near. And ' he changes
the commands.

Then ' the time came until ' the child would grow up. ' When he had
come to his maturity, **45** then the archons sent ' the imitator to ' that
man, in order that they may know ' our great Power. And [5] they were
expecting from ' him that he would perform for them a ' sign. And he
bore ' great signs. And he ' reigned over the whole earth and [10] ⟨over⟩
all those who are under heaven. ' He placed his throne upon the end ' of
the earth, for "I shall ' ⟨make⟩ you (sing.) god of the world." ' He will
perform signs [15] and wonders. Then they ' will turn from me, and they
will go astray. '

Then those men ' who will follow them after him ' will introduce
circumcision.[20] And he will pronounce judgment upon those who are
from the ' uncircumcision who are ' the (true) people. For in fact, he
sent many ' preachers beforehand, who preached ' on his behalf.

When [25] he has completed the established ' time of the kingdom ' of
the earth, then ' the purging of the souls ' will come, since [30] wickedness
is greater than you (pl.). ' All the powers of the sea will tremble ' and
dry up. And the firmament ' will not pour down dew. ' The springs will [35]
cease. The rivers will not flow **46** down to their springs. And the ' waters
of the springs of ' the earth will cease. Then the depths ' will be laid
bare, and they will open. The stars [5] will grow in size, and the sun will
cease. '

And I shall withdraw with ' everyone who will know me. ' And they
will enter into the ' immeasurable light, (where) there is [10] no one of the
flesh nor ' the wantonness of the fire ' to seize them. They will be un-
hampered ' (and) holy, since nothing ' drags them down. I [15] myself
protect them, ' since they have ' holy garments, which ' the fire cannot
touch, ' nor darkness nor [20] wind nor a moment, so as ' to cause one to
shut the eyes.

Then ' he will come to destroy all of them. ' And they will be chastised '
until they become pure.[25] Moreover, their period, which was ' given to
them to have power, which ' was apportioned to them, (is) fourteen '

hundred and sixty-eight years. ' When the fire has [30] consumed them all, and when ' it does not find anything else to burn, ' then it will perish by its own hand. ' Then the [. . .] will be completed. **47**

[. . .] ' the [second] power [. . .] ' the mercy will come [. . .] ' through wisdom [. . .].[5] Then the firmaments [will fall] ' down to the depth. Then [the] ' sons of matter will perish; they ' will not be, henceforth. '

Then the souls will appear,[10] who are holy through the ' light of the Power, who is exalted ' above all powers, the immeasurable, ' the universal one, I and ' all those who will know me.[15] And they will be in the aeon ' of beauty of ' the aeon of judgment, since they are ready ' in wisdom, having given glory ' to him who is in the [20] incomprehensible unity; and they ' see him because of his will, ' which is in them. And ' they all have become as reflections ' in his light. They [25] all have shone, and they have found rest ' in his rest. '

And he will release the souls that ' are being punished, ' and they will come to be [30] in purity. And they will ' see the saints and ' cry out to them, ' "Have mercy on us, O Power who art above ' all powers." For **48** [. . .] and in the tree ' [of] iniquity that exists to ' [. . .] to him their eyes. ' [And they] do not seek him [5] because they do not seek us, ' nor do they believe us, ' but they acted according to the creation of ' the archons and its other rulers. ' But we have acted according to our [10] birth of the flesh, in the creation ' of the archons, which gives law. ' We also have come to be ' in the unchangeable aeon. '

The Concept of Our Great [15]
Power.

PLATO, REPUBLIC 588B-589B (VI, 5)

Introduced and translated by

JAMES BRASHLER

Edited by

DOUGLAS M. PARROTT

The presence in Codex VI of a Coptic translation—though an extremely inept and inaccurate translation—of a section from Plato's *Republic* is something of a surprise. This excerpt may have come from a handbook of edifying quotations; it has even been suggested that it once may have been included in a collection of Hermetic writings on account of a supposed connection between Plato and Hermes. The tractate now stands as a moralistic homily proclaiming themes which are compatible with many Gnostic and Hermetic ideas. Its theme of injustice and its strict ethical tone probably had considerable appeal for those using the Nag Hammadi library. Thus the work recommends that a person "cast down every image of the evil beast and trample them along with the images of the lion"—a recommendation which surely would have struck a responsive chord in the heart of a Gnostic.

PLATO, REPUBLIC 588B-589B
VI 48, 16-51, 23

"Since we have come ' to this point in a discussion, let us again take up ' the first things that were said ' to us. And we will find [20] that he says, 'Good is ' he who has been done injustice completely. ' He is glorified justly.' ' Is not this how he was ' reproached?"

"This is certainly the [25] fitting way!"

And I said, ' "Now then, we have spoken because ' he said that he who does injustice ' and he who does justice ' each has [30] a force."

"How then?" '

"He said, 'An image that has no ' likeness is the rationality of the soul,' ' so that he who said these things will [49] understand. [...][3] or not? We [...] ' is for me. But all [...][5] who told them [...] ' ruler, these now have ' become natural creatures—even ' Chimaera and Cerberus ' and all the rest that [10] were mentioned. They all ' came down and they cast ' off forms and ' images. And they all became ' a single image. It was [15] said, 'Work now!' ' Certainly it is a ' single image that became ' the image of a complex beast ' with many heads.[20] Some days indeed it is like ' the image of a wild beast. ' Then it is able to cast ' off the first image. And ' all these hard [25] and difficult forms ' emanate from it with ' effort, since these are ' formed now ' with arrogance. And also [30] all the rest that are ' like them are formed ' now through the word. For now ' it is a single image. ' For the image of the lion is one thing [35] and the image of the man is another. **50** [. . .] single [. . .] is the [. . .] of ' [. . .] join. And this ' [. . .] much more complex ' [than the first]. And the second [5] [is small]. It has been formed. '

"Now then, join them to ' each other and make them a single ' one—for they are three—so ' that they grow together [10] and all are in a ' single image outside of the image ' of the man just like him ' who is unable to see ' the things inside him. But what [15] is outside only is what he sees. ' And it is apparent ' what creature his image is in and ' that he was formed ' in a human image.

"And I spoke [20] to him who said that there is profit ' in the doing of injustice for the man. ' He who does injustice truly ' does not profit nor ' does he benefit. But [25] what is profitable for him is this: that he ' cast down every image of the ' evil beast and trample ' them along with the images of the lion. ' But the man is in weakness [30] in this regard. And all the things that he ' does are weak. ' As a result he is drawn to ' the place where he spends time with them. **51** [. . .]. And he [. . .] [3] to him in [. . .]. ' But he brings about [. . .] [5] enmity [. . .]. ' And with strife they ' devour each other among ' themselves. Yes, all these things ' he said to every-one who [10] praises the doing of injustice." '

"Then is it not ' profitable for him who speaks ' justly?"

"And if he ' does these things and speaks in them,[15] within the man they ' take hold firmly. ' Therefore especially he strives ' to take care of them and he nourishes ' them just like the [20] farmer nourishes his ' produce daily. And ' the wild beasts ' keep it from growing."

THE DISCOURSE ON THE EIGHTH AND NINTH
(VI, 6)

Introduced and translated by

JAMES BRASHLER, PETER A. DIRKSE, and DOUGLAS M. PARROTT

Although the title for this Hermetic tractate has not been preserved in the manuscript, the *Discourse on the Eighth and Ninth* is so named on account of its contents. The reference to the eighth and the ninth indicates the eighth and ninth spheres surrounding the earth. In ancient times it was thought that the first seven spheres were the realms of the sun, moon, and planets, the lower powers whose control over human life was not necessarily benevolent. The eighth and ninth spheres thus designate the beginning of the divine realm, the levels beyond the control of the lower powers. At death the soul would journey through the seven spheres, and after successful passage it would reach the eighth and the ninth, the levels at which the soul could experience true bliss. Furthermore, the eighth and the ninth spheres can also indicate advanced stages of spiritual development. The tractate possibly assumes yet another sphere, a higher, tenth sphere, where God himself dwells, though this is not entirely clear.

The *Discourse on the Eighth and Ninth* is a dialogue between a teacher and a pupil. The mystagogue, Hermes Trismegistus (Thrice-greatest Hermes, the "father") instructs an initiate in secret knowledge, and guides him into an ecstatic experience of the eighth and the ninth. The initiate (the "son"), with the mystagogue, presents an earnest prayer and a silent hymn of praise to the divine: he has received divine light, life, and love. The tractate closes with a set of instructions for the preservation of the book; included are oaths for the careful use of these words of Hermes.

In short, the *Discourse on the Eighth and Ninth* is a document of instruction and drama. Its Hermetic character is emphasized by the name of Hermes and the similarities to other Hermetic documents; in addition the dualistic, Gnostic themes and the mystery elements should not be ignored. Finally, certain affinities with Middle Platonism suggest a date of composition in the second century C.E.

THE DISCOURSE ON THE EIGHTH AND NINTH
VI 52, 1-63, 32

[. . .] '

"[O my father], yesterday you promised me ' [that you would bring] my mind into ' [the] eighth and [5] afterwards you would bring me into the ' ninth. You said that this is the ' order of the tradition."

"O my ' son, indeed this is the order. ' But the promise was according to [10] human nature. For I told you ' when I initiated the promise, I ' said, 'If you hold in mind ' each one of the steps.' ' After I had received the spirit through the power,[15] I set forth the action for you. ' Indeed the understanding dwells ' in you; in me (it is) as though ' the power were pregnant. ' For when I conceived from the fountain [20] that flowed to me, I gave birth."

"O ' my father, you have spoken every word ' well to me. But I am amazed ' at this statement that you have just ' made. For you said, 'The [25] power that is in me—.' " '

He said, "I gave birth to it (the power), as ' children are born."

"Then, O my ' father, I have many brothers, if ' I am to be numbered among the offspring." [30]

"Right, O my son! This ' good thing is numbered by [. . .]. **53**[4] And [. . .] ' at all times. ' Therefore, O my son, ' it is necessary for you to ' recognize your brothers and ' to honor them rightly and [10] properly, because they ' come from the same father. ' For each generation I have ' called. I have named ' it, because they were offspring [15] like these sons."

"Then, O ' my father, do they have ' (a) day?"

"O my son, ' they are spiritual ones. For ' they exist as forces that grow [20] other souls. Therefore I say ' that they are immortal." '

"Your word is true; it has no ' refutation from now on. ' O my father, begin the [25] discourse on the eighth and ' the ninth, and include me also ' with my brothers."

"Let us pray, ' O my son, to the father of the ' universe, with your brothers who are my [30] sons, that he may give ' the spirit of eloquence."

"How ' do they pray, O my father, ' when joined with the generations? ' I want to obey, O my father."

"[. . .]. **54**[3] But it is [not . . .]. ' Nor [is it] a law.[5] But he is satisfied [with] it (fem.). ' [. . .] it (masc.). And it is right ' [for you] to remember the progress ' that came to you as ' wisdom in the books. O [10] my son, compare yourself to the ' early years of life. As children (do), ' you have posed senseless, ' unintelligent questions."

"O my ' father, the progress that has come [15] to me now and the foreknowledge, ' according to the books, that has come to me, ' exceeding the deficiency—these things are ' foremost in me."

"O my son, ' when you understand the [20] truth of your statement, you will ' find your brothers, who are my sons, ' praying with you." '

"O my father, I understand nothing else ' except the beauty that [25] came to me in the books."

"This is ' what you call the beauty ' of the soul, the edification that ' came to you in stages. ' May the understanding come to you,[30] and you will teach."

"I have understood, ' O my father, each one of ' the books. And especially the (fem.) **55** [. . .] which is in [a . . .]." '

"O my son, [. . .] [4] in praises from ' [those who] extol [them]." '

"O my father, from you ' I will receive the [power] of the ' discourse [that you will] give. As it was told ' to both (of us), let us pray,[10] O my father."

"O my son, ' what is fitting is to pray ' to God with all our mind ' and all our heart and our ' soul, and to ask [15] him that the gift of the ' eighth extend to ' us, and that each one ' receive from him what ' is his. Your part, then, is [20] to understand; my own is ' to be able to deliver the discourse ' from the fountain which flows to me." '

"Let us pray, O my father: ' I call upon thee, who [25] rulest over the kingdom ' of power, whose word ' comes as (a) birth of light. ' And his words are immortal. ' They are eternal and [30] unchanging. He is the one whose will ' begets life for the forms in ' every place. His nature gives form ' to substance. By him **56** the souls of [the eighth ' and] the angels are moved [. . .] [4] those that exist. His providence ' extends to everything [. . .] ' begets everything. He is the one who ' [. . .] the aeon among spirits. ' He created everything. He who is ' self-contained cares [10] for everything. He is perfect, the ' invisible God to whom one speaks ' in silence—his ' image is moved when it is directed, ' and it governs—the [15] one mighty in power, who is exalted ' above majesty, who is better than the ' honored (ones), Zoxathazo a ōō ' ee ōōō ēēē ōōōō ' ēē ōōōōōō ooooo [20] ōōōōōō uuuuuu ' ōōōōōōōōōōōōō'ōōō Zozazoth.

"Lord, ' grant us a wisdom from ' thy power that reaches [25] us, so that we may describe to ourselves the ' vision of the eighth and the ninth. ' We have already advanced to the seventh, ' since we are pious and ' walk in thy law.[30] And thy will ' we fulfill ' always. For we have walked in **57** [thy way, and we have] renounced ' [. . .], so that ' thy [vision] may come. Lord, grant ' us the truth in the image.[5] Allow us through the spirit to ' see the form of the image ' that has no deficiency, ' and receive the reflection of the pleroma ' from us through our praise.[10]

"And acknowledge the spirit ' that is in us. For from ' thee the universe received soul. ' For from thee, the unbegotten one, ' the begotten one came into being.[15] The birth of the self-begotten one ' is through thee, ' the birth of all begotten things ' that exist. Receive ' from us these spiritual sacrifices,[20] which we send ' to thee with all our heart ' and our soul and all ' our strength. Save that which ' is in us, and grant us [25] the immortal wisdom." '

"Let us embrace ' each other affectionately, O my son. ' Rejoice over this! For already ' from them the power,[30] which is light, is coming to us. ' For I see! I see ' indescribable depths. ' How shall I tell you, **58** O my son? [. . .] ' from the (fem.) [. . .] ' the places. How [shall I describe] ' the universe? I [am mind and] [5] I see another mind, the one that [moves] the ' soul! I see the one that moves me ' from pure forgetfulness. You give ' me power! I see myself! I want ' to speak! Fear restrains [10] me. I have found the ' beginning of the power that is above ' all powers, the one that has no ' beginning. I see a fountain bubbling ' with life. I have said, O [15] my son, that I am Mind. ' I have seen! Language is not able ' to reveal this. For the entire ' eighth, O my son, and ' the souls that are in it, and the [20] angels, sing a hymn in ' silence. And I, Mind, ' understand."

"What is the way to sing ' a hymn through it (the eighth)?"

"Have you become such that ' you cannot be spoken to?"

"I am silent,[25] O my father. I want to ' sing a hymn to you while I am silent."

"Then ' sing it, for I am Mind." '

"I understand Mind, Hermes, ' who cannot be interpreted,[30] because he keeps within himself. ' And I rejoice, O my father, because I see ' thee smiling. And the universe **59** [rejoices]. Therefore there is no ' creature that will lack ' thy life. For thou art the ' lord of the citizens in [5] every place. Thy providence protects. ' I call thee father, aeon ' of the aeons, great divine spirit. ' And by a spirit he gives ' rain upon everyone. What [10] are you saying to me, O my ' father, Hermes?"

"Concerning these things I ' do not say anything, O my son. ' For it is right before God ' that we keep silent about what is hidden." [15]

"O Trismegistus, let not ' my soul be deprived of the ' great divine vision. For ' everything is possible for you as master ' of the universe."

"Return to [20] ⟨praising⟩, O my son, and sing ' while you are silent. Ask what ' you want in silence." '

When he had finished praising he ' shouted, "Father [25] Trismegistus! What shall I say? ' We have received this light. And ' I myself see this same vision '. in you. And ' I see the eighth and the souls [30] that are in it and the angels ' singing a hymn to the ninth and ' its powers. And I see ' him who has the ' power of them all, creating **60** those ⟨that are⟩ in the spirit."

"It is advantageous from [now on] ' that we keep silence in a reverent posture. ' Do not speak about the vision ' from now on. It is proper to [sing a hymn] [5] to the father until the day to quit (the) body." '

"What you sing, O my ' father, I too want to sing." '

"I am singing a hymn within myself. ' While you rest yourself, be active in praise.[10] For you have found what you seek." '

"But is it proper, ' O my father, that I praise because I ' am filled in my heart?"

"What is proper ' is your praise that you [15] will sing to God ' so that it might be written in this imperishable book." '

"I will offer up ' the praise in my heart, as I ' pray to the end of the universe and [20] the beginning of the beginning, to the object ' of man's quest, the ' immortal discovery, the begetter of ' light and truth, the ' sower of reason, the love of [25] immortal life. No ' hidden word will be able to speak about thee, ' Lord. Therefore my mind ' wants to sing a hymn to you ' daily. I am the instrument [30] of thy spirit. Mind is thy ' plectrum. And thy counsel ' plucks me. I see **61** myself! I have received power from thee. ' For thy love has reached us." '

"Right, O my son."

"O grace! ' After these things I give thanks [5] by singing a hymn to thee. For I have ' received life from thee ' when thou madest me wise. I ' praise thee. I call ' thy name that is hidden within me: [10] a ō ee ō ēēē ōōō iii ' ōōōō ooooo ōōō'ōō uuuuuu ōō'ōōōōōōōōō'ōōōōōōōōō[15]ōō. Thou art the one who exists ' with the spirit. I sing a hymn ' to thee reverently." '

"O my son, ' write this book for the temple at Diospolis [20] in hieroglyphic characters, ' entitling it 'The Eighth ' Reveals the Ninth.' " '

"I will do it, O my ⟨father⟩, as ' you command [25] now."

"O my ⟨son⟩, ' write the language of the book on steles ' of turquoise. O my son, ' it is proper to write this book ' on steles of turquoise,[30] in hieroglyphic characters. ' For Mind himself has ' become overseer **62** of these. Therefore I command ' that this teaching be carved ' on stone, and that you place it in ' my sanctuary. Eight [5] guardians guard it with [...] ' of the Sun. The males ' on the right are frog-faces, ' and the females ' on the left are cat-faces.[10] And put a square ' milk-stone at the base of the ' turquoise tablets ' and write the name on the ' azure stone tablet [15] in hieroglyphic characters. ' O my son, you will do this ' when I am in Virgo, ' and the sun is in the first half of the ' day, and fifteen degrees have [20] passed by me."

"O my father, ' everything that you say I will ' do eagerly."

"And write ' an oath in the book, lest those who ' read the book bring [25] the language into ' abuse, and not (use it) ' to oppose the acts of fate. ' Rather, they should submit ' to the law of God,[30] without having transgressed at all, ' but in purity asking ' God for wisdom and ' knowledge. And he who **63** will not be begotten at the start by God ' comes to be by the general ' and guiding discourses. ' He will not be able to read the things written [5] in this book, although his ' conscience is pure within him, since he ' does not do anything shameful, ' nor does he consent ' to it. Rather, by stages [10] he advances and enters into ' the way of immortality. And ' thus he enters into the ' understanding of the eighth that ' reveals the ninth."

"So [15] shall I do it, O my father."

"This ' is the oath: I make him who will ' read this holy book swear by heaven ' and earth and fire and ' water and seven rulers of substance [20] and the creating spirit in them ' and the ⟨unbegotten⟩ God ' and the self-begotten one ' and him who has been begotten, that he ' guard the things that Hermes has said.[25] And those who keep the oath, ' God will be reconciled with them ' and everyone whom we have ' named. ' But wrath will come to each one [30] of those who violate the oath. ' This is the perfect one who is, ' O my son."

THE PRAYER OF THANKSGIVING (VI, 7)

Introduced and translated by

JAMES BRASHLER and PETER A. DIRKSE

Edited by

DOUGLAS M. PARROTT

Previously known in Greek and Latin versions, the Hermetic *Prayer of Thanksgiving* gives thanks for the reception of deifying knowledge. Since this tractate follows directly after the *Discourse on the Eighth and Ninth*, it is possible that the scribe understood the *Prayer of Thanksgiving* as a prayer of gratitude for the knowledge which had just been revealed in the previous tractate. This short prayer is particularly important for the question of Hermetic cultic practices; the prayer provides evidence for liturgical prayer, a ritual embrace or kiss, and a cultic meal. Thus the *Prayer of Thanksgiving* may once have been at home in a Hermetic Gnostic community committed to the presentation and transmission of the sort of knowledge celebrated in this prayer.

A scribe added a note located between the *Prayer of Thanksgiving* and *Asclepius 21-29* (VI, 8). He may have been the one who wrote Codex VI or the one responsible for an earlier copy of one of these two tractates. This note, written within a neatly drawn and decorated rectangular area, indicates that the scribe had a large number of documents he could have copied and that those by whom he was commissioned had an extensive library.

THE PRAYER OF THANKSGIVING

VI 63, 33-65, 7
65, 8-14

This is the prayer that they spoke: ' "We give thanks to Thee! Every soul [35] and heart is lifted up to Thee, ' O undisturbed name, **64** honored with the name ' 'God' and praised ' with the name 'Father,' ' for to everyone and everything [5] (comes) the fatherly kindness and ' affection and love ' and any teaching there may be that is sweet ' and plain, giving ' us mind, speech, [10] (and) knowledge: mind, ' so that we may understand Thee, ' speech, so that we may ' expound Thee, knowledge, ' so that we may know Thee. [15] We rejoice, having been illumined ' by Thy knowledge. We rejoice ' because Thou hast shown us Thyself. We rejoice ' because while we were in (the) body, Thou hast made us ' divine through Thy knowledge. [20]

"The delight of the man who attains ' to Thee is one thing: that we know ' Thee. We have known Thee, ' O intellectual light. O ' life of life, we have known Thee. [25] O womb of every creature, we have ' known Thee. O womb pregnant with ' the nature of the Father, we have known ' Thee. O eternal permanence ' of the begetting Father, thus have we [30] worshipped Thy goodness. ' There is one petition that we ask: ' we would be ' preserved in knowledge. ' And there is one protection that we **65** desire: that we not stumble ' in this kind of life." '

When they had said these things in prayer, they ' embraced each other and [5] they went to eat their ' holy food, which has no blood ' in it. '

* * * * * * *

I have copied this one discourse of his. ' Indeed, very many have come to me. I have not [10] copied them because I thought that they had come to you (pl.). ' Also, I hesitate to copy these for ' you because, perhaps, they have (already) come to you, and ' the matter may burden you, since ' the discourses of that one, which have come to me, are numerous.

ASCLEPIUS 21-29 (VI, *8*)

Introduced and translated by

JAMES BRASHLER, PETER A. DIRKSE, and DOUGLAS M. PARROTT

A Hermetic tractate, the Coptic *Asclepius 21-29* was previously known from a Latin version and some brief quotations from the original Greek. Only a portion of the entire *Asclepius* is to be found in Codex VI, and this excerpt may very well have been meant to be juxtaposed with the Hermetic *Discourse on the Eighth and Ninth* (VI, *6*).

Asclepius 21-29 is a dialogue between the mystagogue, Hermes Trismegistus, and an initiate, Asclepius. The tractate opens with a comparison of the mystery and sexual intercourse: both are accomplished in secret and involve intimate interaction. There follows a discussion of piety as knowledge and impiety as ignorance. With the acquisition of knowledge human beings become better than the gods, for then they are both mortal and immortal. Hermes Trismegistus next suggests that just as the Lord of the universe creates gods, so also humanity creates gods according to human likeness. In an apocalyptic section, with significant Egyptian and Jewish parallels, the speaker predicts that woes will come upon Egypt, but also promises that finally God the Creator will restore order again. The tractate closes with a discussion of individual eschatology; after death the soul is judged, and rewarded or punished accordingly.

This Coptic excerpt from *Asclepius* shows both Hermetic and Gnostic traits. On the one hand, certain passages seem to be quite pantheistic: God is in every place, and beholds every place. Yet dualistic emphases also occur, as in the discussion of the two human natures. This dualism, together with the theme of the importance of knowledge for salvation, may suggest that the tractate has certain Gnostic characteristics.

ASCLEPIUS 21-29

VI 65, 15-78, 43

"And if you (sing.) wish to see the reality of ' this mystery, then you should see the wonderful representation ' of the intercourse ' that takes place between ' the male and the female. For when [20] the semen reaches the climax, it leaps forth. ' In that moment ' the female receives the strength ' of the male; the male for his part ' receives the strength of the female, while [25] the semen does this. '

"Therefore the mystery of intercourse ' is performed in secret, ' in order that the two sexes ' might not disgrace themselves in front of many who do not experience [30] that reality. ' For each of them (the sexes) contributes its (own part in) begetting. ' For if it happens in the presence of those who do not understand the reality, ' (it is) laughable ' and unbelievable. And, moreover, [35] they are holy mysteries, ' of both words and deeds, ' because not only are they not heard, ' but also they are not seen.

"Therefore **66** such (people—the unbelievers) are blasphemers. ' They are atheistic and impious. ' But the others are not many; ' rather, the pious who are counted are few. [5] Therefore ' wickedness remains among (the) many, ' since learning ' concerning the things which are ordained does not exist among them. ' For the knowledge of the things which are ordained [10] is truly the healing of the passions ' of matter. Therefore learning ' is something derived from knowledge. '

"But if there is ' ignorance, and learning [15] does not exist in the soul of man, ' (then) the incurable passions persist in it (the soul). ' And additional ' evil comes with them (the passions) in the ' form of an incurable sore. [20] And the sore constantly gnaws at the soul, ' and through it the soul produces worms from ' the evil and stinks. But God ' is not the cause of ' these things, since he sent to men [25] knowledge and learning." '

"O Trismegistus, ' did he send them to men ' alone?"

"Yes, O Asclepius, ' he sent them to them (men) alone. [30] And it is fitting that we tell ' you why to men ' alone he granted ' knowledge and learning, ' the allotment of his good. [35]

"And now listen! God ' and the Father, even the Lord, created ' man subsequent to the gods, ' and he took him from **67** the region of matter. [Since] matter ' is involved in the creation of [man] ' of [. . .], the passions are ' in it. Therefore [5] they continually flow over his ' body, for this living creature would not exist ' in any other way except that he take this ' food, since ' he is mortal. It is also inevitable [10] that inopportune desires ' which are harmful dwell in him. ' For the gods, since ' they came into being out of a pure matter, ' do not need [15] learning and knowledge. ' For the immortality of the gods ' is learning and knowledge, ' since they came into being out of pure matter. ' It (immortality) assumed for them [20] the position of knowledge and learning. ' By necessity he (God) ' set a boundary for man; he placed him ' in learning and knowledge. '

"Concerning these things (learning and knowledge), which we have mentioned [25] from the beginning, he perfected them ' in order that by means of these things ' he might restrain passions and evils, ' according to his will. ' He brought his (man's) mortal existence into [30] immortality;

he (man) became ' good (and) immortal, just as ' I have said. For he (God) created (a) twofold nature ' for him: the immortal and ' the mortal.

"And it [35] happened this way because of the will **68** of [God] that men ' be better than the gods, since ' indeed [the] gods are ' immortal, but men alone [5] are both immortal and mortal. ' Therefore man has ' become akin to the gods, ' and they know the affairs ' of each other with certainty. The [10] gods know the things of ' men, and men ' know the things of the gods. ' And I am speaking about men, O Asclepius, ' who have attained learning [15] and knowledge. ' But (about) those who are more vain than these, it is not fitting ' that we say anything base, ' since we are divine and are ' introducing holy matters. [20]

"Since we have entered ' the matter of the communion between the ' gods and men, know, ' O Asclepius, that in which man ' can be strong! [25] For just as the Father, the Lord of ' the universe, creates gods, ' in this very way man too, ' this mortal, earthly, living creature, ' the one who is not like [30] God, also himself ' creates gods. Not only ' does he strengthen, but he is also strengthened. ' Not only is he god, but ' he also creates gods. Are you astonished, [35] O Asclepius? Are you yourself ' another disbeliever like the many?" **69**

"O Trismegistus, [I agree with] the words (spoken) ' to me. [And] I believe these things ' as you [speak]. But I have also been astonished ' at the discourse about [this]. And I have [5] decided that man is blessed, ' since he has enjoyed this great power." '

"And that which is greater than all these things, ' O Asclepius, is worthy of admiration. ' Now it is revealed to us [10] concerning the race of the gods, ' and we confess it ' along with everyone else, that it (the race of the gods) has come into being ' out of a pure matter. And ' their bodies are heads only. [15] But that which men create ' is the likeness of the gods. They (the gods) are from ' the farthest part of matter, ' and it (the object created by men) is from the outer (part) of the being ' of men. Not only [20] are they (what men create) heads, but (they are) also all the other members ' of the body and according to ' their likeness. Just as ' God has willed that the inner man ' be created according to [25] his image, in the very same way ' man on earth creates gods ' according to his likeness."

"O Trismegistus, ' you are not talking about idols, are you?" '

"O Asclepius, you yourself are talking [30] about idols. You see that again you yourself, ' O Asclepius, are also a ' disbeliever of the discourse. You say ' about those who have soul and ' breath, that they are idols—these who ³⁵ bring about these great events. ' You are saying about these who give prophecies ' that they are idols—these who give **70** [men sickness and] healing ' that [. . .] with them. '

"Or are you ignorant, O Asclepius, ' that Egypt is (the) image ⁵ of heaven? Moreover, ' it is the dwelling place of heaven and all the forces ' that are in heaven. If ' it is proper for us to speak the truth, our ' land is (the) temple of the world. ¹⁰ And it is proper for you not to be ' ignorant that a time ' will come in it (our land) ' (when) Egyptians will seem ' to have served the divinity in ¹⁵ vain, and all their activity ' in their religion will ' be despised. For all divinity ' will leave Egypt and will ' flee upward to heaven. And Egypt ²⁰ will be widowed; it will be abandoned by the ' gods. For foreigners ' will come into Egypt, and they will rule ' it. Egypt! Moreover, ' Egyptians will be prohibited ²⁵ from worshipping ' God. Furthermore, they will come ' into the ultimate punishment, especially whoever ' among them is found worshipping ' (and) honoring God. ³⁰

"And in that day the country ' that was more pious than all countries ' will become ' impious. No longer will it be full ' of temples, but it will be full of tombs. ³⁵ Neither will it be full of gods, ' but (it will be full of) corpses. O Egypt! ' Even Egypt will become like the ' fables. And your religious objects **71** will be [. . .] the marvelous things ' and [. . .], ' and if your words are ' stones and are wonderful. ⁵ And the barbarian will be ' better than you, O Egyptian, ' in his religion, whether ' (he is) a Scythian, or the Hindus, or some other ' of this sort.

"And what is this that I say ¹⁰ about the Egyptian? For they (the Egyptians) will ' not abandon Egypt. For (in) the time ' (when) the gods have abandoned the land ' of Egypt, and have fled upward to ' heaven, then all Egyptians ¹⁵ will die. And Egypt will be ' made a desert by the gods and the Egyptians. ' And as for you, O River, there ' will be a day when you will flow ' with blood more than water. And ²⁰ dead bodies will be ' (stacked) higher than the dams. ' And he who is dead will not be mourned ' as much as he who is alive. Indeed the latter will be ' known as an Egyptian ²⁵ on account of his language in ' the second period (of time). O Asclepius, ' why are you weeping? He will seem ' like (a) foreigner in regard to ' his customs. Divine Egypt ³⁰ will suffer evils greater ' than these. Egypt, lover of God, ' and the dwelling place of the gods, ' school of religion, ' will become an example of ³⁵ impiousness.

"And in that day ' the world will not be marveled at, **72** [. . .] and [immortality, ' nor] will it be worshipped ' [. . .] since we say that it

is ' not good [...]. It has become neither [5] a single thing nor ' a visiou.
But it is in danger ' of becoming a burden ' to all men. Therefore, ' it
will be despised—the beautiful world [10] of God, ' the incomparable
work, ' the energy that possesses ' goodness, the many-formed vision, '
the abundance [15] that does not envy, that is full ' of every vision. '
Darkness will be preferred to light ' and death will be preferred to '
life. No one will gaze [20] into heaven. And the pious man ' will be counted
as insane, ' and the impious man will be honored ' as wise. The man
who is afraid ' will be considered as strong. And [25] the good man will
be punished ' like a criminal. '

"And concerning the soul and the things ' of the soul and the things
of immortality, ' along with the rest of what I have said [30] to you, O
Tat, Asclepius, ' and Ammon, not only will they ' be considered ridiculous, ' but they will also be thought of as a vanity. ' But believe [35] me
(when I say) that people of this kind will ' be endangered by the ultimate
danger ' to their soul. And ' a new law will be established. [...] **73**[3]
they will [...] [5] good. [The] wicked angels ' will remain among ' men,
(and) be with them ' (and) lead them into wicked things ' recklessly, as
well as into [10] atheisms, wars, ' and plunderings, by teaching them '
things contrary to nature.

"In those days ' the earth will not be stable, ' and men will not sail
the sea, [15] nor will they know the stars in heaven. ' Every sacred voice '
of the word of God will ' be silenced, and the air will be diseased. '
Such is the senility of the world: [20] atheism, ' dishonor, and the
disregard ' of noble words. '

"And when these things had happened, O Asclepius, ' then the Lord,
the Father and [25] only primal God, God ' the Creator, when he looked
upon ' the things that happened, established his design, ' which is
good, ' against the disorder. He took away [30] error, and cut off evil. '
Sometimes ' he submerged it in a great flood, ' at other times he burned
it in a ' searing fire, and at still other times [35] he crushed it in wars '
and pestilence, until he brought [...] **74**[5] of the work. ' And this is the
birth of the world. '

"The restoration of the ' nature of the pious ones who are good ' will
take place in a [10] period of time that ' never had a beginning. ' For the
will of God has no ' beginning, even as his nature, ' which is his will,
(has no beginning). [15] For the nature of God is will. ' And his will is
the good." '

"O Trismegistus, ' is purpose, then, will?" '

"Yes, O Asclepius, since will [20] is (included) in counsel. ' For what is (the case with) what he has? ⟨He⟩ does not will it ' from deficiency. Since he is ' complete in every part, he wills ' what he (already) fully has. 25 And he has every good. ' And what he wills, he wills. ' And he has the good ' that he wills. Therefore he has ' everything. And God 30 wills what he wills. ' And the good world ' is an image of the Good One." '

"O Trismegistus, ' is the world good?"

"O Asclepius, 35 it is good, as ' I shall teach you. For just as [... **75** 3 of soul and] life ' [...] of the [world ...] 5 come [forth] in matter, [those that are good], ' the change of the climate, and [the] beauty ' and the ripening of the fruits, and ' the things similar to all these. Because of this, ' God has control over the heights 10 of heaven. He is in every place and he looks out ' over every place. And (in) his place there is neither ' heaven nor star. And ' he is free from (the) body.

"Now the creator ' has control in the place that is 15 between the earth and heaven. He ' is called Zeus, that is, ' life. Plutonius Zeus ' is lord over the earth ' and sea. And he does not possess the nourishment 20 for all mortal living creatures, ' for (it is) Kore who bears ' the fruit. These forces ' always are powerful in the circle ' of the earth, but those of others 25 are always from Him Who Is. '

"And the lords of the earth will withdraw themselves. ' And they will establish ' themselves in a city that is in ' a corner of Egypt and that will be built 30 toward the setting of the sun. ' Every man will go into it, ' whether they come on the sea ' or on the shore." '

"O Trismegistus, 35 where will these be settled now?"

"O Asclepius, ' in the great city that is on the [Libyan] mountain [... **76**3 it frightens ... ' as a] great [evil, 5 in] ignorance of the matter. ' For death occurs, [which] is ' the dissolution of the labors of the body ' and (the dissolution of) the number (of the body), when it (death) completes ' the number of the body. 10 For the number is the union of ' the body. Now the body dies ' when it is not able to support ' the man. And this is death: ' the dissolution of the body and the destruction 15 of the sensation of the body. ' And it is not necessary to be afraid ' of this, nor because of this, but because of ' what is not known ' and is disbelieved (one is afraid)."

"But what is 20 not known ' or is disbelieved?"

"Listen, ' O Asclepius! There is a great ' demon. The great God has ' appointed him to be overseer 25 or judge over the souls ' of men. And God has placed him ' in the middle of the air between the earth ' and heaven. Now, when ' the soul comes forth from (the) body, it is necessary [30] that it meet this ' demon. Immediately he (the demon) will surround ' this one (masc.), and he will examine him in regard to the character that he has ' developed in his life. And if ' he finds that he piously performed [35] all of his actions ' for which he came into the world, ' this (demon) will allow his 77 [...] ' turn him [...]. ' But [if he sees ' ...] in this one [...] he brought [5] his life into [evil] deeds, ' he grasps him, as he [flees] upward ' and throws him down ' so that he is suspended between heaven and earth ' and is punished with a great punishment [10]. And he will be ' deprived of his hope, and ' be in great pain.

"And that soul ' has been put neither ' on the earth nor in heaven. [15] But it has come into the open sea of the air ' of the world, the place where there is a great ' fire and crystal water ' and furrows of fire ' and a great upheaval. The bodies [20] are tormented (in) various (ways). ' Sometimes they are cast ' upon raging waters; at other times ' they are cast down into the fire ' in order that it may destroy them. Now, I will not say [25] that this is the death of the soul, ' for it has been delivered from evil, ' but it is a death sentence. '

"O Asclepius, it is necessary to believe ' these things and to fear them [30] in order that we might not encounter them. For ' unbelievers are impious and ' commit sin. Afterwards they will be compelled ' to believe, ' and they will not hear by word of mouth only, [35] but will experience ' the reality itself. For they kept believing that they would ' not endure these things. Not only 78 [...]. ' First, [O Asclepius], ' all [those of the earth die ' and those who are of the] body [cease ...] [5] of evil [...] ' with these of this sort. For those who are here ' are not like those who are ' there. So with the demons who [...] ' men, they despise [...] [10] there. Thus it is not the same. But ' truly the gods who are here ' will punish more whoever has hidden it here ' every day." '

"O Trismegistus, what [is the] character of [15] the iniquity that is there?"

"Now you think, ' O Asclepius, that when one takes ' something in a temple, he is impious. ' For that kind of a person is a thief and ' a bandit. And this matter concerns [20] gods and men. ' But do not compare those here with those of the other place. ' Now I want to speak ' this discourse to you confidentially; ' no part of it will be believed. For the souls [25] that are filled with much evil will not come and go ' in the air, but they will be put ' in the places of the demons, which ' are filled with pain, (and) which are always ' filled with blood and slaughter. And their [30] food is weeping, mourning, ' and groaning."

"O Trismegistus, ' who are these (demons)?"

"O Asclepius, they are the ones who ' are called stranglers, and '
those who roll souls down on [35] the dirt, and those who ' scourge them,
and those who cast ' into the water, and those who cast into the fire, '
and those who bring about the pains ' and calamities of men. For [40]
such as these are not from a ' divine soul, nor from a ' rational soul
of man. Rather, ' they are from the terrible evil."

THE PARAPHRASE OF SHEM (VII, *1*)

Introduced and translated by

FREDERIK WISSE

The *Paraphrase of Shem* is the first of the five tractates contained in Codex VII, the best preserved of all the codices in the Nag Hammadi library. This tractate takes the form of a revelation given by Derdekeas, the son and likeness of the perfect Light, to Shem (the spelling in the tractate is consistently "Sēem"), who is "from an unmixed power," and is "the first being upon the earth." Interestingly, the tractate has the same sorts of phrases and general outlook as the report of the heresiologist Hippolytus concerning the Sethian Gnostics. Hippolytus refers to his source as the "Paraphrase of Seth," apparently a Christianized version of a tractate similar to the *Paraphrase of Shem*.

The revelation from Derdekeas to Shem is introduced by Shem's rapture to heaven. Shem tells about an ecstatic experience during which his mind was separated from his body as if in sleep. He was caught up to the top of creation close to the supreme being, the Light. This framework is apparently terminated when he "awakens," though additional revelation to him occurs later in the tractate. The revelation includes discussion of cosmogony, soteriology, and eschatology. According to the *Paraphrase of Shem*, there are three basic "roots," three primeval powers: Light, Darkness, and Spirit between them. The mixing of these three powers triggers the cosmic drama: Darkness, realizing his inferiority and yearning for equality, directs his attack at the Spirit, since the Darkness is ignorant of the Light. The mind of Darkness is the prime tool of Darkness to accomplish his evil schemes in the world; yet at the same time the mind of Darkness, together with the light of the Spirit, is the object of the salvific efforts of the redeemer Derdekeas.

The description of this Gnostic redeemer Derdekeas is particularly significant. Moved by pity, Derdekeas descends to the realm of evil to rescue the fallen and entrapped light of the Spirit and of the mind of Darkness. During his stay in Hades, Derdekeas experiences the hostility of the powers of Darkness, and goes unrecognized. He puts on "the beast," apparently the body, and in that disguise he advances the cosmic work of salvation. After his stay on earth he receives honor from his amazing garments, which provide both protection and glory. Finally, he reveals his saving work as life-giving knowledge to his elect.

The *Paraphrase of Shem* is a non-Christian Gnostic work which uses and radically transforms Old Testament materials, especially from Genesis. The tractate proclaims a redeemer whose features agree with those features of New Testament Christology which may very well be pre-Christian in origin. As such, the *Paraphrase of Shem* is important for the study of Christian origins, and may contribute significantly to the understanding of the development of Christology in the New Testament.

THE PARAPHRASE OF SHEM

VII 1, 1-49, 9

The Paraphrase of Shem '

[The] paraphrase which was about ' the unbegotten Spirit. '
What Derdekea⟨s⟩ revealed to me, Shem, [5] according to ' the will of
the Majesty. ' My mind which was in my body ' snatched me away
from my race. It ' took me up to the top of the world, [10] which is close
to the light ' that shone upon the whole area ' there. I saw no ' earthly
likeness, but there was light. ' And my mind separated [15] from the body
of darkness as ' though in sleep.

I heard ' a voice saying to me, ' Shem, since you are from ' an unmixed power [20] and you are the first being upon ' the earth, hear and
understand ' what I shall say to you first ' concerning the great Powers
who ' were in existence in the beginning, before [25] I appeared. There '
was Light and Darkness ' and there was Spirit between ' them. Since
your root ' fell into forgetfulness—he who was [30] the unbegotten Spirit—
I ' reveal to you the truth about ' the Powers. The Light ' was mind
full of ' attentiveness and reason. They were [35] united into one form. '
And the Darkness was **2** wind in [. . .] waters. ' He possessed the mind '
wrapped in a chaotic fire. ' And the Spirit between them [5] was a gentle,
humble light. ' These are the three ' roots. They reigned each in '
themselves, alone. And they covered ' each other, each one with [10]
its power.

But the Light, ' since he possessed a great ' power, knew the abase-
ment ' of the Darkness and his disorder, ' namely that the root was
not straight. [15] But the crookedness of the Darkness ' was lack of
perception, namely (the illusion that) there is no one ' above him. And
when he was able ' to bear up under his evil, he was ' covered with the
water. And he [20] stirred. And the Spirit was frightened ' by the sound.
He lifted himself ' up to his station. And ' he saw a great, dark water. '
And he was nauseated. And [25] the mind of the Spirit stared ' down; he
saw the infinite Light. ' But he was overlooked ' by the putrid root. '
And by the will of the great Light [30] the dark water separated. ' And
the Darkness came up ' wrapped in vile ignorance, ' and (this was) in
order that the mind ' might separate from him because he prided [35]
himself in it.

And when he ' stirred, **3** the light of the Spirit appeared to him. '
When he saw it he was astonished. ' He did not know that another '

Power was above him. And when he [5] saw that his likeness was ' dark compared with the Spirit, he felt hurt. ' And in his pain he lifted up ' to the height ' of the members of Darkness his mind which [10] was outside the bitterness of evil. ' He caused his mind to take shape ' in a member of the regions of the ' Spirit, thinking that, by staring (down) ' at his evil, he would be able [15] to equal the Spirit. But he ' was not able. For he wanted to do ' an impossible thing. And it did not ' take place, so that ' the mind of Darkness, which [20] is outside the bitterness of evil, might not be destroyed. ' Since he was made partially similar, ' he arose and shone ' with a fiery light upon ' all of Hades, in order that [25] the equality to the faultless Light ' might become apparent. For the Spirit ' benefited from every form ' of Darkness because he appeared ' in his majesty. [30]

And the exalted, infinite Light ' appeared, ' for he was ' very joyful. He wished to reveal ' himself to the Spirit. And the likeness [35] of the exalted Light appeared ' to the unbegotten Spirit. **4** I appeared. [I] ' am the son of the ' incorruptible, infinite Light. ' I appeared in the likeness [5] of the Spirit, for I am the ray ' of the universal Light. ' And his appearance to me (was) ' in order that the mind ' of Darkness might not remain in Hades. [10] For the Darkness made himself like his ' mind in a part of the ' members. When I, (O) Shem, appeared ' in it (the likeness), in order that ' the Darkness might become dark to himself, [15] according to the will of the Majesty—' in order that the Darkness might become free ' from every aspect of the power ' which he possessed—' the mind drew the chaotic fire, with which [20] it was covered, from ' the midst of the Darkness and the water. ' And from the Darkness the water ' became a cloud. And from ' the cloud the womb took shape. [25] The chaotic fire ' which was a deviation ' went there.

And when the Darkness ' saw it (the womb) he became unchaste. ' And when he had aroused [30] the water, he rubbed the womb. ' His mind dissolved ' down to the depths of Nature. ' It mingled with the power of ' the bitterness of Darkness. And [35] her (the womb's) eye ruptured at the wickedness ' in order that she might not again bring forth ' the mind. For it was **5** a seed of Nature ' from the dark root. ' And when Nature had taken to herself ' the mind by means of the dark power, [5] every likeness took shape ' in her. And when the Darkness ' had acquired the likeness of the mind, ' it resembled the Spirit. ' For Nature rose up to expel it; [10] she was powerless against it, since ' she did not have a form from the ' Darkness. For she brought it forth in the cloud. ' And the cloud shone. ' A mind appeared in [15] it like a frightful, harmful fire. ' It (the mind) collided ' against the unbegotten Spirit ' since it possessed ' a likeness from him, in order that [20] Nature might become emptier ' than the chaotic fire. '

And immediately Nature ' was divided into four parts. ' They became clouds which varied [25] in their appearance. They were called ' Hymen, Afterbirth, ' Power, (and) Water. ' And the Hymen and the Afterbirth ' and the Power were [30] chaotic fires. And ' it (the mind) was drawn from the midst ' of the Darkness and the water—since ' the mind was in the midst of Nature ' and the dark power—[35] in order that the harmful waters ' might not cling to it. **6** Because of this Nature was divided, ' according to my will, in order that ' the mind may return ' to its power which the [5] dark root, which was mixed ' with it (the mind), had taken from it. And ' he (the dark root) appeared in the womb. ' And at the division of ' Nature he separated from the dark power [10] which he possessed from ' the mind. It (the mind) went into the midst ' of the power—this was ' the middle region of Nature.

And the Spirit ' of light, when the mind [15] burdened him, was astonished. ' And the force of his astonishment ' cast off the burden. And it (the burden) ' returned to its heat. It ' put on the light of the Spirit. [20] And when Nature moved ' away from the power of the light ' of the Spirit, the burden returned. ' And the astonishment ⟨of the⟩ light ' cast off the burden. It stuck [25] to the cloud of the Hymen. And ' all the clouds of Darkness ' cried out, they who had separated from Hades, ' because of the alien Power. ' He is the Spirit of light who has come [30] from them. And by the will of ' the Majesty the Spirit gazed up ' at the infinite Light, ' in order that ' his light may be pitied. And [35] the likeness was brought up from Hades.

And ' when the Spirit had looked, I flowed **7** out—I, the son of the Majesty—' like a wave of light ' and like a whirlwind of the ' immortal Spirit. And I blew from [5] the cloud of the Hymen upon the astonishment ' of the unbegotten Spirit. It ' (the cloud) separated and cast light upon the clouds. ' These separated in order that ' the Spirit might return. Because of this the mind [10] took shape. Its repose was shattered. ' For the Hymen of Nature ' was a cloud which cannot be ' grasped; it is a great fire. ' Similarly, the Afterbirth [15] of Nature is the cloud of silence; ' it is an august fire. ' And the Power which was mixed ' with the mind, it, too, was ' a cloud of Nature which [20] was joined with the Darkness that ' had aroused Nature ' to unchastity. And the dark water ' was a frightful cloud. ' And the root [25] of Nature, which was below, ' was crooked, since it is burdensome and ' harmful. The root was ' blind with respect to the light-bondage ' which was unfathomable since ³⁰ it had many appearances. '

And I had pity on ' the light ⟨of⟩ the Spirit which ' the mind had received. I returned ' to my position in order to pray ³⁵ to the exalted, infinite Light **8** that ' the power of the Spirit might be suspended ' over the place and might be filled ' without dark defilement. And ⁵ reverently I said, ' "Thou art the root of the Light. ' Thy hidden form has appeared, ' O exalted, infinite ' one. May the whole power of ¹⁰ the Spirit spread and may it be filled '.with its light, O infinite Light. ' (Then) he will not be able to join ' with the unbegotten Spirit, and ' the power of the astonishment will not be able to ¹⁵ mix with Nature according to the will ' of the Majesty." My prayer ' was accepted.

And the voice ' of the Word was heard saying ' through the Majesty ⟨of⟩ the ²⁰ unbegotten Spirit, "Behold, the ' power has been completed. What was revealed ' by me ⟨originated⟩ from ' the Spirit. Again I shall appear. ' I am Derdekeas, the son ²⁵ of the incorruptible, infinite Light." '

The light of ' the infinite Spirit ' came down to a feeble nature for ' a short time until ³⁰ all the impurity of nature ' became void, and in order that ' the darkness of Nature ' might be exposed. I put on my ' garment which is the garment of the light ³⁵ of the Majesty—which I am. ' I came in the appearance of the **9** Spirit to consider the whole light ' which was in the depths ' of the Darkness, according to the will ' of the Majesty, in order that the Spirit ⁵ by means of the Word might be filled with his ' light independently of the power of ' the infinite Light. ' And at my wish the Spirit ' arose by his (own) power. ¹⁰ His greatness was granted to him ' that he might be filled ⟨with⟩ his whole light ' and depart from the whole burden ' of the Darkness. For what (was mentioned) before ' was a dark fire which blew ¹⁵ (and) pressed on the Spirit. And ' the Spirit rejoiced because he was protected ' from the frightful water. But ' his light was not equal to ' the Majesty—but he who was favored ²⁰ by the infinite Light—' in order that in all his members ' he might appear as ' a single image of light. ' And when the Spirit arose above the water, ²⁵ his black likeness became apparent. ' And the Spirit honored ' the exalted Light: "Surely thou ' alone art the infinite one, ' because thou art above ³⁰ every unbegotten thing, for thou hast protected ' me from the Darkness. And at thy ' wish I arose above the power ' of darkness."

And that ' nothing might be hidden from you, Shem, the mind, ³⁵ which the Spirit from the ' greatness had contemplated, came into being, **10** since the Darkness was not able [to] ' restrain his evil. But when ' it (the mind) appeared, ' the three roots became known as they ⁵ were from the beginning. If ' the Darkness had been able to bear ' up under his evil, the ' mind would not have separated from him, and ' another power would not have appeared. ¹⁰

But from the time it appeared ' I was seen, the son ' of the Majesty, in order that ' the light of the Spirit might not become faint, ' and that Nature might not reign ¹⁵ over it, because it gazed at me. ' And by the will of the greatness ' my equality was revealed, that ' what is of the Power might ' become apparent. You ²⁰ are the great Power which came into being, ' and I am the perfect Light ' which is above the Spirit ' and the Darkness, the one who puts to shame the Darkness ' for the intercourse of the impure ²⁵ practice. For through the division ' of Nature the Majesty wished ' to be covered with ' honor up to the height of the mind ' of the Spirit. And the Spirit received ³⁰ rest in his power. ' For the image of the Light ' is inseparable from the unbegotten Spirit. ' And the lawgivers did not name ' him after all the clouds ³⁵ of Nature, nor is it ' possible to name him. ' For every likeness **11** into which Nature had divided ' is a power of the ' chaotic fire which is the ' hylic seed. The one who took to himself ⁵ the power of the Darkness imprisoned it ' in the midst of its members. '

And by the will of the Majesty, ' in order that the mind ' and the whole light of the Spirit might be protected ¹⁰ from every burden and (from) the toil of ' Nature, a voice came forth from ' the Spirit to the cloud of the Hymen. ' And the light of the astonishment ' began to rejoice with the voice ¹⁵ which was granted to him. ' And the great Spirit of light was ' in the cloud of the Hymen. He honored ' the infinite Light ' and the universal likeness ²⁰ who I am, the son of ' the Majesty, saying, ' "Anasses Duses, thou art ' the infinite Light ' who was given by the will ²⁵ of the Majesty to establish ' every light of the Spirit ' upon the place, and to separate ' the mind from the Darkness. ' For it was not right ³⁰ for the light of the Spirit to remain ' in Hades. For at thy wish ' the Spirit arose to ' behold thy greatness." '

For I said these things to you, ³⁵ Shem, that you might know **12** that my likeness, the son of the Majesty, ' is from my ' infinite mind, since I ' am for him a universal likeness ⁵ which does not lie, (and) I am above ' every truth and origin ' of the word. His appearance is in ' my beautiful garment of light ' which is the voice of the immeasurable mind. ¹⁰ We are that ' single, sole light which came into being. ' He appeared in another root ' in order that the power ' of the Spirit might

be raised from the [15] feeble Nature. For by the will of the ' great Light
I came forth from the ' exalted Spirit down to the cloud of ' the Hymen
without my universal ' garment.

   And the Word took [20] me to himself, from the Spirit, in the first '
cloud—of the Hymen—of ' Nature. And I put on ' this of which the
Majesty and the ' unbegotten Spirit made me worthy. [25] And one third '
of my garment appeared ' in the cloud, by the will ' of the Majesty, in
a single form. ' And my likeness was covered [30] with the light of my '
garment. And the cloud was disturbed, ' and it was not able to tolerate
my likeness. ' It shed the first power ' which it had taken from [35] the
Spirit, that which shone ' on him from the beginning, before ' I appeared
in the word ' to the Spirit. The cloud **13** would not be able to tolerate
both of them. ' And the light which came forth from the cloud ' passed
through the silence, until ' it came into the middle region. And, [5] by the
will of the Majesty, ' the light mixed with him, ' ⟨i.e.⟩ the Spirit which
exists in the silence, ' he who had been separated from the Spirit ' of
light. It was separated from the light [10] by the cloud of the silence. '
The cloud was disturbed. It was he ' who gave rest to the flame ' of
fire. He humbled the dark womb ' in order that she might not reveal [15]
other seed from the darkness. He ' kept them back in the middle region '
of Nature in their ' position which was in ' the cloud. They were
troubled since they did [20] not know where they were. For still ' they
⟨did⟩ not possess the ' universal understanding of ' the Spirit.

   And when I prayed ' to the Majesty, toward the [25] infinite Light,
that ' the chaotic power ' of the Spirit might go to and fro, and ' the
dark womb might be idle, ' and that my likeness might appear [30] in the
cloud of the Hymen, ' as if I were wrapped in the light ' of the Spirit
which went ' before me—. And by the will ' of the Majesty and through [35]
the prayer I came in the cloud ' in order that through my garment—'
which was from the power **14** of the Spirit of the pleroma ' of the word,
from the members ' who possessed it in the Darkness. ' For because of
them I appeared [5] in this insignificant place. ' For I am a helper ' of
every one who has been given a name. ' For when I appeared ' in the
cloud, the light [10] of the Spirit began to save itself ' from the frightful
water, and (from) the clouds ' of fire which had been separated ' from
dark Nature. And ' I gave them eternal honor [15] that they might not
again engage ' in the impure practice.

   And the light ' which was in the Hymen was disturbed ' by my power,
and ' it passed through my middle region. It [20] was filled with the
universal mind. ' And through the word of ' the light of the Spirit it

returned to ' its repose. It received ' form in its root and shone [25] without deficiency. And the light ' which had come forth with it from the silence ' went in the middle region ' and returned to the place. ' And the cloud shone. [30] And from it came ' an unquenchable fire. ' And the part which separated from ' the astonishment put on forgetfulness. ' It was deceived by [35] the fire of darkness. And the shock ' of its astonishment cast ' off the burden of the **15** cloud. It was evil ' since it was unclean. And ' the fire mixed with the water in ' order that the waters might become harmful. [5]

And Nature which had been disturbed ' immediately arose ' from the idle waters. ' For her ascent was shameful. ' And Nature took to herself the [10] power of fire. She became strong ' because of the light of the Spirit which ' was in Nature. Her ' likeness appeared in the water ' in the form of a frightful beast [15] with many faces, which ' is crooked below. A light ' went down to chaos filled ' with mist and dust, in order to ' harm Nature. [20] And the light of the astonishment which is ' in the middle region came to it ' after he cast off ' the burden of the Darkness. He rejoiced ' when the Spirit arose. For he looked [25] from the clouds down ' at the dark waters upon ' the light which was in ' the depths of Nature.

Therefore ' I appeared that I might [30] get an opportunity to go ' down to the nether world, to the light ' of the Spirit which was burdened, ' that I might protect him from the evil ' of the burden. And through [35] his looking down at the dark region ' the light once more **16** came up in order that the womb might again ' come up from the water. ' She (the womb) came up by my will. ' Guilefully the eye opened. [5] And the light ' which had appeared in the middle region ' (and) which had separated from the astonishment ' rested and shone upon ' her. And the womb saw [10] things she had not seen, ' and she rejoiced joyfully in ' the light, although this one which ' appeared in the middle region, in her ' wickedness, is not hers. When he (the light) shone [15] upon her, and ' the womb saw things she had not seen, ' and she was brought down ' to the water, she was thinking that ' she had reached to the power of light. [20] And she did not know that ' her root was made idle by ' the likeness of the Light, and that it was to her (the root) ' that he had run.

The light was astonished, ' the one which was in [25] the middle region and which was ' beginning and end. Therefore ' his mind gazed ' directly up at the exalted Light. ' And he called out and said, [30] "Lord, have mercy on me, ' for my light and my effort went astray. ' For if thy goodness does not establish ' me—, for I do not know ' where I am." And when the Majesty [35] had heard him, he had mercy on him. '

And I appeared in the cloud ' of the Hymen, in the silence, 17 without my holy garment. ' With my will I honored ' my garment which has three ' forms in the cloud of the Hymen. [5] And the light which was in ' the silence, the one from the rejoicing ' Power, contained me. ' I wore it. And its ' two parts appeared [10] in a single form. Its ' other parts did not appear ' on account of the fire. I became ' unable to speak in the cloud of the Hymen, ' for its fire was frightful, [15] lifting itself up without ' humility. And in order that ' my greatness and the word ' might appear, I placed likewise ' my other garment in the cloud of the silence. [20] I went into the middle region ' and put on the light ' that was in it, that was sunk in forgetfulness ' and that was separated from the Spirit of ' astonishment, for he had cast off the burden. [25] At my wish ' nothing mortal appeared ' to him, but they were all immortal ' things which the Spirit granted ' to him. And he said in [30] the mind of the Light, ai eis ' ai ou phar dou ia ei ou: ' I have come in a great rest ' in order that he may give rest ' to my light in [35] his root, and may bring it out of 18 harmful Nature.

Then, ' by the will of the Majesty, I ' took off my garment of light. ' I put on another garment [5] of fire which has no form, which ' is from the mind of the power, ' which was separated, and which was ' prepared for me, according to my will, in ' the middle region. For the middle region [10] covered it with a dark power ' in order that I might come ' and put it on. I went down ' to chaos to save ' the whole light from it. For without [15] the power of darkness I could not oppose ' Nature. When I came into ' Nature she was not able to tolerate ' my power. But I rested ' myself upon her staring eye [20] which was a light ' from the Spirit. For it had been prepared ' for me as a garment and a rest ' by the Spirit. Through me ' he opened his eyes down to [25] Hades. He granted Nature ' his voice for a time. '

And my garment of fire, according to the will ' of the Majesty, went ' down to what is strong, and to the [30] unclean part of Nature ' which ⟨the⟩ power of darkness ' was covering. And my garment ' rubbed Nature in her ' covering. And her unclean [35] femininity was strong. And ' the wrathful womb came up 19 and made the mind dry, ' resembling a fish which has ' a drop of fire and ' a power of fire. And when Nature [5] had cast off the mind, ' she was troubled and she ' wept. When she was hurt, and in ' her tears, she cast off ' the power of the Spirit [10] (and) remained as I. I put on ' the light of the Spirit and I ' rested with my garment on account of ' the sight of the fish.

And in order that ' the deeds of Nature might be condemned, [15] since she is blind, manifold ' animals came out ' of her, in accordance with - the number of the ' fleeting winds. All of them came into being in ' Hades searching for the light [20] of the mind which took shape. They were not ' able to stand up against it. ' I rejoiced over their ignorance. ' They found me, ' the son of the Majesty, in [25] front of the womb which has ' many forms. I put ' on the beast, and laid ' before her a great request ' that heaven and earth [30] might come into being, in order that the whole ' light might rise up. ' For in no other way could the power ' of the Spirit be saved from bondage ' except that I appear [35] to her in animal form. ' Therefore she was gracious to me **20** as if I were her son. '

And on account of my request, ' Nature arose since she possesses of ' the power of the Spirit and the Darkness [5] and the fire. For she had taken off ' her forms. When she had cast ' it off, she blew upon the water. ' The heaven was created. And from ' the foam of the heaven [10] the earth came into being. And at my wish it ' brought forth all kinds of food in accordance with ' the number of the beasts. And it ' brought forth dew from ' the winds on account of you (pl.) and those [15] who will be begotten the second time ' upon the earth. ' For the earth possessed ' a power of chaotic fire. ' Therefore it brought forth [20] every seed.

And when ' the heaven and the earth were created, ' my garment of fire arose in the midst ' of the cloud of Nature (and) ' shone upon the whole world [25] until Nature became ' dry. The Darkness which was ' its (the earth's) garment was cast into the ' harmful waters. ' The middle region was cleansed from the Darkness. [30] But the womb grieved because of ' what had happened. She perceived in ' her parts what was ' water like a mirror. When she ' perceived (it), she wondered [35] how it had come into being. Therefore she ' remained a widow. It also was **21** astonished (that) it was not in her. ' For still the forms ' possessed a power ' of fire and light. It (the power) remained [5] in order that it might be in Nature ' until all the powers are taken ' away from her. For just as ' the light of the Spirit was completed ' in three clouds, it is neces-sary [10] that also the power ' which is in Hades will be completed at the ' appointed time. For, because of the grace ' of the Majesty, I came forth to her ' from the water for the second time. [15] For my face pleased ' her. Her face also was glad. '

And I said to her, "May ' seed ' and power come forth from you [20] upon the earth." And she obeyed ' the will of the Spirit that ' she might

be brought to naught. And when ' her forms returned, they rubbed '
their tongue(s) with each other; they copulated; [25] they begot winds
and ' demons and the power which ' is from the fire and ' the Darkness
and the Spirit. But the form ' which remained alone cast the [30] beast
from herself. ' She did not have intercourse, but ' she was the one who
rubbed herself alone. ' And she brought forth a wind which ' possessed
a power [35] from the fire and the Darkness ' and the Spirit.

And in order that the **22** demons also might become free ' from the
power which they possessed ' through the impure intercourse, ' a womb
was with the winds [5] resembling water. And an ' unclean penis was '
with the demons in accordance with the example ' of the Darkness, and
in the way he rubbed with ' the womb from the beginning. And after [10]
the forms of Nature had been ' together, they separated from ' each
other. They cast off the power, ' being astonished about ' the deceit
which had happened to them. They grieved [15] with an eternal grief.
They covered ' themselves with their power. '

And when I had put them to shame, I arose ' with my garment in the
power and—' which is above the beast which is a light, [20] in order that
I might make Nature ' desolate. The mind which had appeared ' in the
Nature of Darkness, (and) which ' was outside the heart of Darkness, '
at my wish reigned over [25] the winds and the demons. And I ' gave him
a likeness of fire: light, ' and attentiveness, and a share ' of guileless
reason. Therefore ' he was given of the greatness [30] in order to be strong
in his ' power, independent of the power, ' independent of the light of
the Spirit, and ' intercourse of Darkness, in order that, at ' the end of
time, when **23** Nature will be destroyed, he may rest ' in the honored
place. ' For he will be found ' faithful, since he has loathed [5] the unchastity of Nature with ' the Darkness. The strong power ' of the mind
came into being from ' the mind and the unbegotten Spirit. '

But the winds, which are demons [10] from water and fire ' and darkness
and light, had ' intercourse unto perdition. And through ' this intercourse the winds received ' in their womb [15] foam from the penis ' of
the demons. They conceived ' a power in their vagina. From ' the
breathing ' the wombs of the winds girded each other [20] until the times
of the birth came. ' They went down to the water. ' And the power
was delivered, through ' the breathing which moves the birth, ' in the
midst of the practice. And [25] every form of the birth received shape ' in
it. When ' the times of the birth were near, ' all the winds were gathered '
from the water which is near the [30] earth. They gave birth to all kinds
of unchastity. ' And the place where ' the wind alone went was per-

meated with ' the unchastity. ' Barren wives came from it [35] and sterile husbands. **24** For just as they are born, ' so they bear.

Because of you (pl.), ' the image of the Spirit appeared ' in the earth and the water. [5] For you are like the Light. ' For you possess a share ' of the winds and the demons, ' and a mind from the Light ' of the power of the astonishment. [10] For everything which he brought forth from ' the womb upon the earth ' was not a good thing for her, ' but her groan and her pain, because ' of the image which appeared in [15] you from the Spirit. For you are ' exalted in your heart. ' And it is blessedness, Shem, if ' a part taken from ' the soul is given to the mind [20] of the Light. For the soul ' is a burden of the Darkness, and ' those who know where the root ' of the soul came from will be able ' to grope after Nature also. [25] For the soul is a work of ' unchastity and an (object of) scorn to the ' mind of Light. For I ' am the one who revealed concerning ' all that is unbegotten. [30]

And in order that the sin ' of Nature might be filled, I made the ' womb, which was disturbed, pleasant—' the blind wisdom—that I might ' be able to bring (it) to naught. And at my **25** wish, he plotted with the water ' of Darkness and also the Darkness, ' that they might wound every form ' of your (pl.) heart. For by [5] the will of the light of the ' Spirit they surrounded you; they bound ' you securely. And in order that ' his mind might become idle, ' he sent a demon [10] that the content of ' her wickedness might be proclaimed. And he caused ' a flood, and he destroyed ' your (pl.) race, in order to ' take the light and to take from [15] Faith. But I proclaimed ' quickly by the mouth of ' the demon that a tower ' come to be up to the ... of the light, ' which was left in the demons and [20] their race—which was ' water—that the demon might be protected ' from the turbulent chaos. ' And the womb planned these things ' according to my will in order that she might [25] pour forth completely. A tower ' came to be through the demons. The ' Darkness was disturbed by his loss. ' He loosened the muscles of the ' womb. And the demon [30] who was going to enter the tower was protected ' in order that the races might ' continue and might acquire coherence ' through him. For he possesses ' power from every form. [35]

Return henceforth, **26** O Shem, and rejoice [greatly] ' over your race and ' Faith, for without body and ' necessity it is protected from [5] every body of Darkness, bearing witness ' to the holy things of the greatness ' which was revealed to them in their ' mind by my will. And ' they shall rest in the unbegotten Spirit [10] without grief. ' But you, Shem, because of this, you ' remained in (the) body outside the cloud ' of light that you might remain ' with Faith. And Faith [15] will come to you. Her mind will be taken ' and given to you with a consciousness ' of light. And I ' told you these things for the benefit of your ' race from the cloud of light. [20] And likewise what I shall say to you ' concerning everything, I shall reveal ' to you completely that ' you may reveal them to those who ' will be upon the earth the [25] second time.

O Shem, the disturbance ' which occurred at my wish ' happened in order that Nature might ' become empty. ' For the wrath of the Darkness subsided. [30] O Shem, the Darkness' mouth was shut. ' No longer does the light which ' shone for the world appear in it, ' according to my will. And when ' Nature had said that [35] its wish was fulfilled, then every form ' was engulfed by the waters 27 in prideful ignorance. ' She (Nature) turned her ' dark vagina and cast from ' .her the power of fire [5] which was in her from the beginning ' through the practice of the Darkness. It (masc.) ' lifted itself up and shone upon ' the whole world instead of the righteous one. ' And all her forms [10] sent forth a power ' like a flame of fire up ' to heaven as a help to the ' corrupted light, which had lifted itself up. ' For they were members of the [15] chaotic fire. And she did not ' know that she had harmed herself. ' When she cast forth the power, ' the power which she possessed, ' she cast it forth in the . . . . The demon [20] who is a deceiver, who ' stirred up the womb to every form—. '

And in her ignorance, ' as if she were doing a great ' thing, she granted the demons [25] and the winds a star each. ' For without wind and star ' nothing happens upon the earth. ' For every power is filled ' by them after they were [30] released from the Darkness and the fire ' and the power and the light. ' For in the place where their darkness and ' their fire were mixed with each other ' beasts were brought forth. And in the place [35] of the Darkness, and the fire, and the power 28 of the mind, and the light, ' where human beings came from the ' Spirit, the mind of the Light, my eye, ' exists not in every man. [5] For before the flood ' came from the winds and the ' demons, . . . came to ' men that as yet the power ' which is in the tower might be brought forth, [10] and might rest upon the earth. '

Then Nature, which had been disturbed, ' wanted to harm the seed ' which will be upon the earth after ' the flood. [15] Demons were sent to them, and ' a deviation of the winds, and ' a burden of the angels, and ' a fear of the prophet, a ' condemnation of speech, that I may [20] teach you, O Shem, from ' what blindness your ' race is protected. When I have ' revealed to you all that has been spoken, ' then the righteous one will [25] shine upon the world with my garment. ' And the night and the day will ' be separated. For I shall hasten down to the ' world to take the light ' of that place, the one which [30] Faith possesses. And ' I shall appear to those who will ' acquire the mind of the light ' of the Spirit. For because of them my ' majesty appeared.

When [35] he will have appeared, O Shem, ' upon the earth, [in] the place which will be **29** called Sodom, (then) ' safeguard the insight which I ' shall give you. For those whose ' heart was pure will congregate to you, [5] because of ' the word which you will reveal. ' For when you appear ' in the world, dark Nature ' will shake against you, [10] together with the winds and a demon, ' that they may destroy ' the insight. But you, proclaim ' quickly to the Sodomites ' your universal teaching, [15] for they are your members. ' For the demon of human form ' will part from that place ' by my will, since he is ignorant. ' He will guard this utterance. But the [20] Sodomites, according to the will of the ' Majesty, will bear witness to the ' universal testimony. They ' will rest with a pure conscience ' in the place [25] of their repose, which ' is the unbegotten Spirit. ' And as these things will happen, ' Sodom will be burned unjustly ' by a base nature. [30] For the evil will not cease ' in order that your ' majesty may reveal ' that place.

Then **30** the demon will depart with ' Faith. And then he will appear ' in the four regions ' of the world. And when [5] Faith appears ' in the last likeness, then will ' her appearance become manifest. ' For the first-born is the demon ' who appeared in the union [10] of Nature with many faces, ' in order that Faith might ' appear in him. For when he ' appears in the world, ' evil passions will arise, [15] and earthquakes, and ' wars, and famines, and ' blasphemies. For because of him the whole ' world will be disturbed. ' For he will seek the power [20] of Faith and Light; he will ' not find it. For at that time ' the demon will also ' appear upon the river ' to baptize with an [25] imperfect baptism, ' and to trouble the world with a bondage ' of water. But it is necessary ' for me to appear in the members ' of the mind of Faith to [30] reveal the great things of my ' power. I shall separate it ' from the demon who is Soldas. ' And the light which ' he possesses from the Spirit I shall mix [35] with my invincible garment, ' as well as him whom I shall reveal **31** in the darkness for your sake ' and for the sake of your race which ' will be protected from the evil ' Darkness.

Know, O Shem, that without [5] Elorchaios and Amoias and ' Strophaias and Chelkeak ' and Chelkea and Aileou, no ' one will be able to pass by this wicked region. ' For this is my testimony [10] that in it I have been ' victorious over the wicked region. And ' I have taken the light of the Spirit ' from the frightful water. ' For when the [15] appointed days of the ' demon draw near—he who will baptize ' erringly—, then I shall appear ' in the baptism ' of the demon to reveal [20] with the mouth of Faith ' a testimony to those ' who belong to her. I testify ' of thee, Spark the unquenchable, ' Osei, the elect of [25] the Light, the eye of heaven, and ' Faith, the first and the last, ' and Sophia, and Saphaia, and ' Saphaina, and the righteous ' Spark, and the [30] impure light. And you (sing.), east, ' and west, and ' north, and south, ' upper air and lower air, and ' all the powers and authorities, [32] you (pl.) are in Nature. ' And you (sing.), Moluchtha ' and Soch are from every work ' and every impure effort of [5] Nature. Then I shall come ' from the demon down to the water. ' And whirlpools of water ' and flames of fire will rise ' up against me. Then I [10] shall come up from the water, having put ' on the light of Faith ' and the unquenchable fire, ' in order that through my help ' the power of the Spirit may cross, [15] she who has been cast in the world ' by the winds and the demons ' and the stars. And in them ' every unchastity will be filled. '

Finally, O Shem, consider [20] yourself pleasing in the mind ' of the Light. Do not let ' your mind have dealings with ' the fire and the body of Darkness ' which was an unclean [25] work. These things which I teach ' you are right. '

This is the paraphrase: '—For you did not remember ' that it is from the firmament that [30] your race has been protected.—Elorchaios ' is the name of the great Light, ' the place from which I have come, the Word ' which has no equal. ' And the likeness is my honored garment. [35] And Derderkeas ' [. . .] speaks [33] with the voice of the Spirit. And ' Strophaia is the blessed glance ' which is the Spirit. ' And Chelkeach, who is my garment, [5] who has come from the astonishment, ' who was in the cloud of the Hymen ' which appeared, he is ' a trimorphic cloud. ' And Chelkea is my garment [10] which has two forms, he ' who was in the cloud of silence. ' And Chelke is my garment which ' was given him from every region; ' it was given him in a single form [15] from the greatness, he ' who was in the cloud of the middle region. ' And the star of the Light ' which was mentioned is my ' invincible garment which [20] I wore in Hades; ' this (the star of the Light) is the mercy which surpasses ' the mind and the testimony ' of those who bear witness, and ' the testimony which has been mentioned, [25] the first and the last, Faith, ' the mind of the wind of darkness. And ' Sophaia and Saphaina are in ' the cloud of those who have been separated ' from the chaotic fire. [30]

And the righteous Spark is ' the cloud of light which has shone ' in your (pl.) midst. For ' in it (the cloud of light) my garment will go ' down to chaos.

But the **34** impure light, which appeared ' in the Darkness (and) which belongs to ' dark Nature, is a power. ' And the upper air and the lower air, and the [5] powers and the authorities, the ' demons and the stars, these possessed ' a ... of fire ' and a light from the Spirit. ' And Moluchthas is a wind, [10] for without it nothing is brought ' forth upon the earth. He has ' a likeness of a serpent and ' a unicorn. His protrusion(s) ' are manifold wings. [15] And the remainder is the womb ' which has been disturbed. You are blessed, ' Shem, for your race ' has been protected from the dark wind which is ' many-faced. And they will [20] bear witness to the universal ' testimony and to the impure ' practice of Faith. And ' they will become high-minded through the ' reminder of the Light.

O Shem, [25] no one who wears the body ' will be able to complete these things. But through ' remembrance he will be able to grasp ' them, in order that, when ' his mind separates from the body, [30] then these things may be revealed to him. ' They have been revealed to your ' race. O Shem, it is difficult for someone ' wearing a body to complete ' [these things, as] I said to you. **35** And it is a small number that will ' complete them, those who possess ' the ... of the mind ' and the mind of the light of the [5] Spirit. They will keep their mind ' from the impure practice. ' For many in the race of Nature ' will seek the security ' of the Power. They will not find it, nor [10] will they be able to ' do the will of Faith. ' For they are seed of the ' universal Darkness. And those who ' find them are in much suffering. The winds [15] and the demons will hate ' them. And the bondage of the body is ' severe. For where ' the winds, and the stars, ' and the demons cast forth from the power [20] of the Spirit, (there) repentance ' and testimony will appear ' upon them, and mercy ' will lead them to ' the unbegotten Spirit. [25] And those who are repentant ' will find rest ' in the consummation and Faith, ' in the place of the Hymen. ' This is the Faith which will [30] fill the place which has been ' dug out. But those who do not share ' in the Spirit of light and ' in Faith will ' dissolve in the [Darkness], the place **36** where repentance did not come. '

It is I who opened the eternal gates ' which were shut from the beginning. ' To those who long for the best of [5] life, and those who are worthy of the ' repose, he revealed ' them. I granted ' perception to those who perceive. ' I disclosed to them [10] all the thoughts and the teaching ' of the righteous ones. And I did not become ' their enemy at all. But ' when I had endured the wrath ' of the world, I was victorious. There was not [15] one of them who knew me. ' The gates of fire ' and endless smoke opened against me. ' All the winds rose ' up against me. The thunderings and the [20] lightning-flashes for a time will rise ' up against me. And they will bring ' their wrath upon me. ' And on account of me according to the flesh, they ' will rule over them according to kind. [25]

And many who wear ' erring flesh will go down ' to the harmful waters through ' the winds and the demons. ' And they are bound by the water. [30] And he will heal with a ' futile remedy. He will lead astray, ' and he will bind the world. ' And those that do the will of Nature, their part will [. . .] [37] two times in the day of the water ' and the forms of Nature. ' And it will not be granted them, when ' Faith disturbs them [5] in order to take to herself the righteous one. '

O Shem, it is necessary that ' the mind be called by the word in ' order that the bondage of the power ' of the Spirit may be saved from the frightful [10] water. And it is blessedness ' if it is granted someone to contemplate ' the exalted one, and to ' know the exalted time ' and the bondage. For the water is an [15] insignificant body. And ' men are not released, since ' they are bound in the water, just as from ' the beginning the light of the Spirit ' was bound.

O Shem, they are deceived [20] by manifold ' demons, thinking that through ' baptism with the uncleanness ' of water, that which is dark, ' feeble, idle, [25] (and) disturbing, he will take away the sins. ' And they do not know ' that from the water to ' the water there is bondage, ' and error and unchastity, [30] envy, murder, adultery, ' false witness, ' heresies, robberies, ' lusts, babblings, ' wrath, bitterness, [35] great [. . .]. [38] Therefore there are many deaths ' which burden their minds. ' For I foretell ' it to those who have a heart. [5] They will refrain from the impure ' baptism. And those who ' take heart from the light ' of the Spirit will not have dealings ' with the impure practice. [10] And their heart will not expire, ' nor will they curse. ' And the water—⟨nor⟩ will they be given ' honor. Where ' the curse is, there is the deficiency. [15] And the blindness is ' where the honor is. ' For if they mix with the evil ones, ' they become empty in the dark water. ' For where the water has been [20] mentioned, there is ' Nature, and the oath, and ' the lie, and the loss. For only ' in the unbegotten Spirit, ' where the exalted Light rested, [25] has the water not ' been mentioned, ' nor can it be mentioned. '

For this is my appearance: ' for when I have [30] completed the times '
which are assigned to me upon the earth, then ' I will cast from me '
[my garment of fire (?)]. And **39** my unequalled garment will ' come
forth upon me, ' and also all my garments which I ' put on in all the
clouds [5] which were from ' the astonishment of the Spirit. ' For the air
will tear my garment. ' For it (my garment) will shine, and it will divide '
all the clouds up to [10] the root of the Light. The repose ' is the mind and
my garment. ' And my remaining garments, ' those on the left and those
on the ' right, will shine [15] on the back in order that ' the image of the
Light may appear. ' For my garments which I put ' on in the three '
clouds, in the last day they [20] will rest in their ' root, i.e. in the unbegotten ' Spirit, since they are without ' fault, through the division of (the) '
clouds.

Therefore I have appeared, [25] being faultless, on account of the '
clouds, because they are unequal, in order that ' the wickedness of
Nature ' might be ended. For she wished ' at that time [30] to snare me.
She was about to establish ' Soldas who is the dark ' flame, who
attended ' on the [. . .] of error, **40** that he might snare me. ' She took
care of her faith, ' being vainglorious. '

And at that time [5] the light was about to separate ' from the Darkness,
and a voice ' was heard in the world, saying, ' "Blessed is the eye which
has ' seen thee, and the mind which has [10] supported thy majesty at '
my desire." It will be said by ' the exalted one, "Blessed is ' Rebouel
among every race ' of men, for it is you (fem.) alone [15] who have seen."
And she will listen. And ' they will behead the woman ' who has the
perception, ' whom you will reveal ' upon the earth. And according to [20]
my will she will bear witness, and she will ' cease from every ' vain
effort of Nature ' and chaos. For the woman ' whom they will behead
at that [25] time is the coherence ' of the power of the demon ' who will
baptize the seed ' of darkness in severity, ' that it (the seed) may mix
with unchastity. [30] He begot a woman. She was ' called Rebouel.

See, ' O Shem, how all the things I have said ' to you have been
fulfilled. ' [And . . . . And the things which] you **41** lack, according to
my will ' they will appear to you ' at that place upon the earth ' that
you may reveal them [5] as they are. Do ' not let your mind have dealings '
with the body. For I have said these ' things to you, through the voice
of the fire, ' for I entered through [10] the midst of the clouds. And I '
spoke according to the language of each one. ' This is my language
which I spoke to you. ' And it will be taken from you. And ' you will
speak with the voice of the world [15] upon the earth. And it will appear ' to

you with that appearance ' and voice, and ' all that I have said to you.
' Henceforth proceed with Faith ²⁰ to shine in the depths of the world. '
And I, Shem, awoke ' as if from a long sleep. ' I marveled when I
received the ' power of the Light and his whole mind. ²⁵ And I proceeded
with Faith ' to shine with me. And ' the righteous one followed us
with ' my invincible garment. And ' all that he had told me ³⁰ would
happen upon the earth ' happened. Nature was handed over ' to Faith,
that she (Faith) might overturn ' her and that she (Nature) might stand
in the Darkness. ' She brought forth a [. . .] which **42** separated itself
(and) which wanders ' night and day without ' receiving rest with the
souls. ' These things completed her ⁵ deeds.

Then I rejoiced ' in the mind of the Light. ' I came forth from the
Darkness and I walked ' in Faith where ' the forms of ¹⁰ Nature are,
up to the top of the ' earth, to the things which are prepared. Thy
Faith ' is upon the earth the ' whole day. For all night ' and day she
surrounds ¹⁵ Nature to take to herself ' the righteous one. For Nature
is ' burdened, and she is troubled. ' For none will be able to open the
forms ' of the door except the mind ²⁰ alone who was entrusted ' with
their likeness. For frightful is ' their likeness of the two forms ' of
Nature, the one which is blind. '

But they who have ²⁵ a free conscience ' remove themselves from '
the babbling of Nature. ' For they will bear witness ' to the universal
testimony; ³⁰ they will strip off the burden ' of Darkness; they will put
on ' the Word of the Light; and ' they will not be kept back **43** in the
insignificant place. ' And what they possess from ' the power of the
mind they ' will give to Faith. They will ⁵ be accepted without ' grief.
And the chaotic ' fire which they possess they ' will place in the middle
region of ' Nature. And they will take to ¹⁰ themselves, through my
garments, these things which are ' in the clouds. It is they ' who guide
their members. They ' will rest in the Spirit ' without suffering. And
because of this the ¹⁵ appointed term of Faith appeared ' upon the
earth for a ' short time, until ' the Darkness is taken away from her,
and ' her testimony is revealed ²⁰ which was revealed ' by me. They
who will prove ' to be from her root ' will strip off the ' Darkness and
the chaotic fire. ²⁵ They will put on the light ' of the mind and they will
bear witness. ' For all that I have said ' must happen.

After ' I cease to be upon the earth and ³⁰ withdraw up to my rest, ' a
great, evil error ' will come upon ' the world, and many evils ' in
accordance with the number of the forms of **44** Nature. Evil times '
will come. And when ' the era of Nature is approaching ' destruction,

darkness will [5] come upon the earth. The number will ' be small. And a demon ' will come up from the power who ' has a likeness of fire. ' He will divide the heaven, (and) he will rest [10] in the depth of the east. ' For the whole world will quake. ' And the deceived world ' will be thrown into confusion. Many ' places will be flooded because of [15] envy of the winds and the demons ' who have a name ' which is senseless: Phorbea, Chloerga. ' They are the ones who govern the world ' with their teaching. And they lead astray [20] many hearts because of their ' disorder and their unchastity. ' Many places will be sprinkled ' with blood. And five ' races by themselves [25] will eat their ' sons. But the regions of the south ' will receive the Word of the Light. ' But they who are from ' the error of the world [30] and from the east—. ' A demon will come forth ' from (the) belly of the serpent. He was **45** in hiding in a desolate place. ' He will perform many wonders. Many ' will loathe him. A ' wind will come forth from his mouth with [5] a female likeness. Her name will ' be called Abalphe. He will ' reign over the world from the ' east to the west.

Then ' Nature will have [10] a final opportunity. And the stars ' will cease from the sky. The mouth ' of error will be opened in order that ' the evil Darkness may become idle and ' silent. And in the last day [15] the forms of Nature ' will be destroyed with the winds and ' all their demons; they ' will become a dark lump, ' just as they were [20] from the beginning. And the ' sweet waters which were burdened ' by the demons will perish. ' For where the power ' of the Spirit has gone [25] there are my sweet ' waters. The other works ' of Nature will not be manifest. ' They will mix with the ' infinite waters of darkness. [30] And all her forms ' will cease from the middle region.

I, ' Shem, have completed these things. And ' my mind began to separate ' from the body of darkness. My **46** time was completed. And ' my mind put on the immortal ' memorial. And ' I said, I agree with thy [5] memorial which thou hast revealed ' to me, Elorchaios. And ' thou, Amoiaiai, and thou, ' Sederkeas, and thy guilelessness, ' Strophaias, and thou, Chelkeak, [10] and thou, Chelkea, and ' Chelke and Elaie, you (pl.) are ' the immortal memorial. ' I testify to thee, Spark, ' the unquenchable one, who is an eye [15] of heaven and a voice of light, ' and Sophaia, and Saphaia, ' and Saphaina, and the righteous ' Spark, and Faith, the first ' and the last, and the upper air and lower [20] air, {and thou, Chelkeak, and ' Chelke and Elaie, you (pl.) ' are the immortal memorial. ' I testify to thee, Spark, the ' unquenchable one, who is an eye of heaven [25] and a voice of light, and ' Sophaia, and Saphaia, and

Saphaina, ' and the righteous Spark, ' and Faith, the first and the last, '
and the upper air and the lower air,} and [30] all the powers and the
authorities ' that are in the world. ' And you, impure light, ' and you
(sing.) also, east, ' and west, and south, and [35] north, you (pl.) are the
zones **47** of the inhabited world. And ' you (fem. sing.) also Moluchtha
and Essoch, ' you (pl.) are the root ' of evil and every work and [5] impure
effort of Nature. '

These are the things which I completed ' while bearing witness. I am
Shem. ' On the day that I was to come forth ' from (the) body, when
my mind [10] remained in (the) body, I awoke as if ' from a long sleep.
And ' when I arose as it were from the burden ' of my body, I said, '
Just as Nature became old, [15] so is it also in the day of ' mankind.
Blessed ' are they who knew, when they ' slept, in what power ' their
mind rested. [20]

And when the Pleiades ' separated, I saw clouds ' which I shall pass
by. ' For the cloud of the Spirit is ' like a pure beryl. [25] And the cloud
of the hymen ' is like a shining ' emerald. And the cloud ' of silence
is like a ' flourishing amaranth. And [30] the cloud of the middle region is
like ' a pure jacinth. ' And when the righteous one ' appeared in
Nature, ' then—when Nature [35] was angry—she felt hurt, and she
granted **48** to Morphaia to visit ' heaven. The righteous one visits '
during twelve periods ' that he may visit them during one [5] period, in
order that his ' time may be completed ' quickly, and Nature ' may
become idle.

Blessed are ' they who guard themselves against the [10] heritage of
death, which is ' the burdensome water of darkness. ' For it will not
be possible to conquer them in a ' few moments, since they hasten '
to come forth from the error of the [15] world. And if they are conquered, '
they will be kept back from them ' and be tormented in the darkness '
until the time of the consummation. ' When the consummation [20] has
come and Nature has been ' destroyed, then their minds will ' separate
from the Darkness. Nature ' has burdened them for a ' short time. And
they [25] will be in the ineffable ' light of the unbegotten ' Spirit without
a form. ' And thus is ' the mind as I have said from [30] the first.

Henceforth, O Shem, ' go in grace and continue in ' faith upon the
earth. For every ' power of light and fire ' will be completed by me **49**
because of you. For without you ' they will not be revealed until ' you
speak them openly. ' When you cease to be upon the earth, they will [5]
be given to the worthy ones. And apart from ' this proclamation, let
them speak ' about you upon the earth, since they will ' take the carefree
and ' agreeable land.

THE SECOND TREATISE OF THE GREAT SETH
(VII, *2*)

Introduced by
JOSEPH A. GIBBONS

Translated by
ROGER A. BULLARD

Edited by
FREDERIK WISSE

The *Second Treatise of the Great Seth* is a revelation dialogue allegedly delivered by Jesus Christ to an audience of "perfect and incorruptible ones," that is, Gnostic believers. Apart from the title, the name "Seth" never occurs in the text, though perhaps Jesus Christ is meant to be identified with Seth. The treatise presents, in a brief and simple way, the true story of the Savior's commission by the heavenly Assembly, his descent to earth, his encounter with the worldly powers and apparent crucifixion, and his return to the Pleroma. To this story of the Savior are added an exhortation to the Savior's followers and a promise of future blessedness. As the Savior says to the Gnostic believers at the close of his discourse, "Rest then with me, my fellow spirits and my brothers, for ever."

There is no doubt that the *Second Treatise of the Great Seth* is a work that is both Christian and Gnostic. On the one hand, Christian elements are tightly woven into the fabric of the treatise. The tractate accepts the New Testament or parts of it, and claims to be the revelation of Jesus Christ. Furthermore, the crucifixion figures prominently in the tractate; in fact, it is described in three separate scenes within the tractate. On the other hand, the *Second Treatise of the Great Seth* is also clearly Gnostic: knowledge is the means of salvation. The God of this world is evil and ignorant, and can be identified with the God of the Old Testament; in addition, all his minions are mere counterfeits and laughingstocks. The interpretation of the crucifixion is that of the Gnostic Basilides as presented by the heresiologist Irenaeus: Simon of Cyrene is crucified in the place of the laughing Jesus.

The purpose for which the *Second Treatise of the Great Seth* was written is plainly polemical. The entire first part (49, 10-59, 18) describes the true history of Jesus Christ and emphasizes, over against orthodox Christianity, his docetic passion. The second part of the tractate (59, 19-70, 10) is a refutation of orthodoxy's claim to be the true church. Despite the trials and persecutions apparently instigated by the orthodox church, by those ignorant and imitative persons "who think that they are advancing the name of Christ," the Gnostic believers will enjoy true brotherhood on earth, and bliss in the joy and union of eternal life.

THE SECOND TREATISE OF THE GREAT SETH

VII 49, 10-70, 12

And the perfect Majesty is at rest ' in the ' ineffable light, ' in the truth of the mother ' of all these, and all of you [15] that attain to me, ' to me alone who am perfect, because of ' the Word. For I exist with all the ' greatness of the Spirit, which is a ' friend to us and our [20] kindred alike, since I brought ' forth a word to the glory ' of our Father, through ' his goodness, as well as an ' imperishable thought; that is, the Word [25] within him—' it is slavery that we shall die with ' Christ—and an imperishable ' and undefiled thought, an ' incomprehensible marvel, the writing [30] of the ineffable water ' which is ' the word from us. It is I who am in ' you (pl.), and you ' are in me, just as the [35] Father is in you **50** in innocence.

Let us ' gather an assembly together. ' Let us visit that creation ' of his. Let us send someone [5] forth in it, just as he visited ' ⟨the⟩ Ennoias, the regions ' below. And I said these things ' to the whole multitude of the ' multitudinous assembly of the [10] rejoicing Majesty. ' The whole house of the Father of Truth rejoiced ' that I am the one who is ' from them. I produced thought ' about the Ennoias which came [15] out of the undefiled Spirit, ' about the descent upon the water, ' that is, the regions below. ' And they all had ' a single mind, since it [20] is out of one. They charged ' me since I was willing. ' I came forth to reveal ' the glory to my kindred ' and my fellow spirits. [25]

For those who were ' in the world had been prepared by the will ' of our sister Sophia—' she who is a whore—' because of the innocence which [30] has not been uttered. And she did not ' ask anything from ' the All, nor from the greatness ' of the Assembly, nor from the ' Pleroma. Since she was first she came forth **51** to prepare monads and ' places for the Son of Light, ' and the fellow workers ' which she took from [5] the elements below ' to build ' bodily dwellings from them. ' But, having come into being in an ' empty glory, they ended [10] in destruction in the dwellings ' in which they were, since they were ' prepared by ' Sophia. They stand ready ' to receive [15] the life-giving word of ' the ineffable Monad ' and of the greatness of the assembly ' of all those who persevere ' and those who are [20] in me.

I visited a ' bodily dwelling. I cast ' out the one who was ' in it first, and I ' went in. And [25] the whole multitude ' of the archons became troubled. ' And all the matter of the archons ' as well as all the begotten powers of the earth ' were shaken when [30] it saw the likeness of the Image, ' since it was mixed. And I am the one who ' was in it, not resembling ' him who was in it ' first. For he was an **52** earthly man, but I, ' I am from above ' the heavens. I did not refuse ' them even to become ⁵ a Christ, but I did not reveal ' myself to them in the love ' which was coming forth from me. ' I revealed that I am a ' stranger to the regions ¹⁰ below.

There was a great ' disturbance in ' the whole earthly area with ' confusion and flight, as well as (in) the plan ' of the archons. And some ¹⁵ were persuaded, when they saw ' the wonders which were being accomplished by ' me. And ' all these, with the race, that came ' down, flee from him ²⁰ who had fled from the throne ' to the Sophia of hope, ' since she had earlier given the sign ' concerning us and all the ones ' with me—those of the race ²⁵ of Adonaios. Others ' also fled, as if ' from the Cosmocrator ' and those with him, ' since they have brought every (kind of) punishment ³⁰ upon me. And there was a flight ' of their mind ' about what they would counsel ' concerning me, thinking ' that she (Sophia) is the whole greatness, and ³⁵ speaking false witness, ' moreover, against the Man and the whole greatness **53** of the assembly. ' It was not possible for them to know ' who the Father of ' Truth, the Man of the ⁵ Greatness, is. But they who received ' the name because of contact with ' ignorance—which (is) a burning ' and a vessel—having created ' it to destroy Adam ¹⁰ whom they had made, in order to ' cover up those who are theirs ' in the same way. But they, ' the archons, those of the place of Yaldabaoth, ' reveal the realm of ¹⁵ the angels, which ' humanity was seeking ' in order that they may not know the Man of Truth. ' For Adam, ' whom they had formed, appeared to them. ²⁰ And a fearful motion came about ' throughout their entire dwelling, lest ' the angels ' surrounding them rebel. For without those ' who were offering praise—I did ²⁵ not really die lest ' their archangel become empty. '

And then ' a voice—of the Cosmocrator—' came to the angels: ³⁰ "I am God and ' there is no other beside me." But I ' laughed joyfully ' when I examined his empty glory. ' But he went on to ³⁵ say, "Who **54** is man?" And the entire host ' of his angels who had ' seen Adam and his dwelling were laughing ' at his smallness. And ⁵ thus did their Ennoia come to be ' removed outside the Majesty ' of the heavens, i.e. the ' Man of Truth, ' whose name they saw since he is ¹⁰ in a small dwelling place, ' since they are small (and) senseless ' in their empty Ennoia, ' namely their laughter. It was ' contagion for them.

The whole greatness ¹⁵ of the Fatherhood of the ' Spirit was at rest in ' his places. And I am he ' who was with him, since I have ' an Ennoia of a single emanation [20] from the eternal ones ' and the ' undefiled and immeasurable incomprehensibilities. ' I placed the small Ennoia ' in the world, [25] having disturbed them and ' frightened the whole multitude of the ' angels and their ruler. And I ' was visiting them all ' with fire and [30] flame because of my Ennoia. And ' everything pertaining to them was brought about ' because of me. And there came about a disturbance ' and a fight around ' the Seraphim and Cherubim, [35] since their glory will fade, **55** and the confusion around ' Adonaios on both sides ' and their dwelling—to the Cosmocrator ' and him who said, [5] "Let us seize him"; others ' again, "The plan will certainly not materialize." ' For Adonaios knows me ' because of hope. ' And I was [10] in the mouths of lions. And ' the plan which they devised ' about me to release ' their Error and their senselessness—' I did not succumb to them as [15] they had planned. But I was ' not afflicted at all. Those who were there punished ' me. And ' I did not die in reality ' but in appearance, lest [20] I be put to shame by them ' because these are my kinsfolk. I ' removed the shame from me ' and I did not become fainthearted in the face of what ' happened to me at their hands. [25] I was about to ' succumb to fear, and I ' ⟨suffered⟩ according to their sight ' and thought, in order that ' they may never find any word to speak [30] about them. For my death ' which they think happened, ' (happened) to them in their ' error and blindness, ' since they nailed their [35] man unto their death. ' For their Ennoias did not see **56** me, for they were deaf ' and blind. ' But in doing these things, they condemn ' themselves. Yes, they saw [5] me; they punished me. ' It was another, their father, ' who drank the gall and the vinegar; ' it was not I. They struck ' me with the reed; it was another, Simon, [10] who bore the cross on ' his shoulder. ' It was another upon whom they placed ' the crown of thorns. ' But I was rejoicing in the height [15] over all the wealth ' of the archons and the offspring ' of their error, of their ' empty glory. And I was ' laughing at their ignorance. [20]

And I subjected all their powers. ' For as I came ' downward no one saw me. ' For I was altering my shapes, ' changing from [25] form to form. And ' therefore, when I was at their gates ' I assumed their likeness. ' For I passed them by ' quietly, and I was viewing the [30] places, and I was not afraid ' nor ashamed, ' for I was undefiled. And I was ' speaking with them, mingling with ' them through those who are [35] mine, and trampling on those who **57** are harsh to them with zeal, ' and quenching the flame. ' And I was doing all these things ' because of my desire [5] to accomplish what I desired ' by the will of the Father above. '

And the Son ' of the Majesty, who was hidden ' in the region below, [10] we brought to the height where I ⟨was⟩ ' in all these aeons with them, ' which (height) no one has seen ' nor known, where ' the wedding of the wedding robe is, [15] the new one and ' not the old, nor does it perish. ' For it is a new and perfect bridal chamber of the ' heavens, as I ' have revealed (that) there are [20] three ways: an ' undefiled mystery in a ' spirit of this aeon, which does not ' perish, nor is it fragmentary, ' nor able to be spoken [25] of; rather, it is ' undivided, universal, ' and permanent. For the soul, the one ' from the height, will not speak ' about the error which is here, nor [30] transfer from these aeons, ' since it will be ' transferred when it becomes free and when it ' is endowed with nobility ' in the world, standing **58** before the Father without weariness ' and fear, always mixed ' with the Nous of power (and) ' of form. They will see me [5] from every side without hatred. ' For since they see me, they are being seen (and) ' are mixed with them. Since they ' did not put me to shame, they were not ' put to shame. Since they were not afraid [10] before me, they will pass by ' every gate without fear and ' will be perfected in the third ' glory.

It was ' my going to [15] the revealed height which the world did not accept, ' my third baptism in a revealed image. ' When they had fled from ' the fire of the ' seven Authorities, and [20] the sun of the powers of ' the archons set, darkness took them. ' And the world became poor ' when he was restrained with a multitude ' of fetters. They nailed him [25] to the tree, and they fixed him with ' four nails of brass. The ' veil of his temple ' he tore with his hands. It was a ' trembling which seized [30] the chaos of the earth, ' for the souls which were ' in the sleep below were released. ' And they arose. They went about ' boldly, having shed **59** zealous service of ignorance ' and unlearnedness ' beside the dead tombs, ' having put on the new man, [5] since they have come to know ' that perfect Blessed One of ' the eternal and incomprehensible Father ' and the infinite light, ' which is I, since I came to [10] my own and united ' them with myself. There is no need ' for many words, ' for our Ennoia was with their Ennoia. ' Therefore they knew what [15] I speak of, for we took counsel ' about the destruction of the ' archons. And therefore I did ' the will of the Father, who is I. '

After we went forth from our home, [20] and came down to this world, ' and came into being in the world ' in bodies, we were hated ' and persecuted, not only ' by those who are ignorant, but [25] also by those who think that ' they are advancing the name of Christ, ' since they were unknowingly empty, ' not knowing ' who they are, like dumb animals. [30] They ' persecuted those who have been liberated ' by me, since they hate them—' those who, should they shut ' their mouth, would weep with a [35] profitless groaning because **60** they did not fully know me. ' Instead, they served two masters, ' even a multitude. But you will become ' victorious in everything, in [5] war and battles, ' jealous division ' and wrath. But in the ' uprightness of our love we are ' innocent, pure, [10] (and) good, since we have a mind ' of the Father in an ' ineffable mystery. '

For it was ludicrous. It is I ' who bear witness that it was ludicrous, [15] since the archons do not know ' that it is an ' ineffable union of ' undefiled truth, as exists ' among the sons of light, [20] of which they made an imitation, ' having proclaimed ' a doctrine of a dead man ' and lies so as to resemble the freedom ' and purity of [25] the perfect assembly, ' (and) ⟨joining⟩ themselves with their doctrine ' to fear and slavery, ' worldly cares, ' and abandoned worship, [30] being small (and) ignorant since they do not ' contain the ' nobility of the truth, ' for they hate the one in whom ' they are, and love [35] the one in whom they are not. ' For they did not know the **61** Knowledge of the Greatness, ' that it is from above ' and (from) a fountain of truth, and that ' it is not from slavery [5] and jealousy, ' fear and love of ' worldly matter. For that ' which is not theirs and that which ' is theirs they use [10] fearlessly and freely. ' They do not desire because ' they have authority, and (they have) a ' law from themselves over ' whatever they will wish. [15]

But those who have not are poor, ' that is, those who do not possess him. ' And they desire him and ' lead astray those, who through ' them have become like those who possess [20] the truth of their freedom, ' just as they bought us for ' servitude and constraint of ' care and fear. This person is ' in slavery. [25] And he who is brought by ' constraint of force and threat ' has been guarded by ' God. But the entire nobility ' of the Fatherhood [30] is not guarded, since he guards only him ' who is from him, without ' word and constraint, since he is united ' with his will, he who belongs only to the ' Ennoia of the Fatherhood, [35] to make it perfect ' and ineffable through **62** the living water, to be ' with you mutually in wisdom, ' not only in word ' of hearing but in deed [5] and fulfilled word. ' For the perfect ones are worthy to be established ' in this way and to be ' united with me, in order that they may not share ' in any enmity, in [10] a good friendship. I ' accomplish everything through the Good One, ' for this is the union of the truth, ' that they should have no adversary. ' But everyone [15] who brings division—and ' he will learn no wisdom at all ' because he brings division and ' is not a friend— is hostile to ' them all. But he who lives [20] in harmony and friendship ' of brotherly love, ' naturally and not artificially, ' completely and ' not partially, this person is truly the desire [25] of the Father. He is the ' universal one and perfect love. '

For Adam was a laughingstock, ' since he was made a counterfeit ' type of man [30] by the Hebdomad, ' as if he had become stronger ' than I and my brothers. We ' are innocent with respect to him, ' since we have not sinned. [35] And Abraham and Isaac ' and Jacob were a laughing- stock, since they, ' the counterfeit fathers, were given a name ' by the Hebdomad, as if **63** he had become stronger than I ' and my brothers. We are ' innocent with respect to him, since we have not sinned. ' David was a laughingstock [5] in that his son was named the Son ' of Man, having been influenced ' by the Hebdomad, ' as if he had become stronger than I ' and the follow members of my race. [10] But we are innocent with respect to him; ' we have not sinned. Solomon was a laughingstock, ' since he thought that he was Christ, ' having become vain through ' the Hebdomad, as if he had become [15] stronger than I and my brothers. ' But we are innocent with respect to ' him. I have not sinned. ' The 12 prophets were laughingstocks, ' since they have come forth as imitations of [20] the true prophets. They came into being ' as counterfeits through ' the Hebdomad, as if ' he had become stronger than I ' and my brothers. But we are [25] innocent with respect to him, since we have not sinned. ' Moses, ' a faithful servant, was a laughing- stock, ' having been named "the Friend," ' since they perversely bore witness concerning him [30] who never ' knew me. Neither he ' nor those before him, from ' Adam to Moses and ' John the Baptist, [35] none of them knew me nor **64** my brothers.

For they had a ' doctrine of angels ' to observe dietary laws and ' bitter slavery, since they never [5] knew truth, ' nor will they know it. ' For there is a great deception ' upon their soul making it impossible ' for them ever to find a Nous of [10] freedom in order to know ' him, until they come to know the Son ' of Man. Now concerning my Father, ' I am he whom the world ' did not know, and because of this, [15] it (the world) rose up against me and my brothers. ' But we are innocent with respect to ' him; we have not sinned. '

For the Archon was a laughingstock because he said, ' "I am God, and [20] there is none greater than I. I ' alone am the Father, the Lord, and ' there is no other beside me. I ' am a jealous God, who ' brings the sins

of the fathers [25] upon the children for three and ' four generations."
As if he had ' become stronger than I and my brothers! ' But we are
innocent ' with respect to him, in that we have not sinned, [30] since we
mastered his teaching. Thus ' he was in an empty glory. ' And he does
not agree ' with our Father. And thus ' through our fellowship [35] we
grasped his teaching, since he ' was vain in an ' empty glory. And he
does ' not agree with our Father, ' for he was a laughingstock and **65**
judgment and false prophecy. '

O those who do ' not see, you do not see your ' blindness, i.e. this
which was [5] not known, nor ' has it ever been known, nor ' has it been
known about him. ' They did not listen to firm obedience. ' Therefore
they proceeded [10] in a judgment of error, ' and they raised their '
defiled and murderous hands against him ' as if they were beating the
air. ' And the senseless and blind ones [15] are always senseless, ' always
being slaves ' of law and ' earthly fear.

I am Christ, ' the Son of Man, the one [20] from you (pl.) who is among
you. ' I am despised for your sake, in ' order that you yourselves ' may
forget the difference. ' And do not become female, [25] lest you give
birth to evil ' and (its) brothers: jealousy ' and division, anger ' and
wrath, fear ' and a divided heart, and [30] empty, non-existent desire. '
But I am ' an ineffable mystery to you. '

Then before the ' foundation of the world, [35] when the whole multitude ' of the Assembly came together ' upon the places of the Ogdoad, **66**
when they had taken counsel about a ' spiritual wedding which is in
union, ' and thus he was perfected ' in the ineffable places [5] by a living
word, ' the undefiled wedding was consummated ' through the Mesotes '
of Jesus, who inhabits ' them all and possesses [10] them, who abides in
an ' undivided love of power. ' And surrounding him, he ' appears to
him as ' a Monad of all these, [15] a thought and a father, since he is '
one. And he stands ' by them all, since he ' as a whole came forth alone.
And ' he is life, since he came from the [20] Father of ineffable ' and
perfect Truth, ' (the father) of those who are there, the union ' of peace
and a friend ' of good things, and life [25] eternal and undefiled joy, ' in a
great harmony ' of life and faith, ' through eternal life ' of fatherhood
and [30] motherhood and sisterhood ' and rational wisdom. ' They had
agreed with Nous, ' who stretches out (and) will stretch ' out in joyful
union [35] and is trustworthy **67** and faithfully listens to ' someone. And
he is in fatherhood ' and motherhood ' and rational brotherhood [5] and
wisdom. And this is a ' wedding of truth, ' and a repose of incorruption, '
in a spirit of truth, ' in every mind, and a [10] perfect light in an ' un-

nameable mystery. ' But this is not, nor ' will it happen among us ' in any region or place [15] in division and breach ' of peace, but (in) union ' and a mixture of love, all of which ' are perfected in the one who is. '

It (fem.) also happened in the places [20] under heaven for their reconciliation. ' Those who knew me ' in salvation and undividedness, ' and those who existed ' for the glory of the father [25] and the truth, having been separated, ' blended into the one ' through the living word. ' And I am in the spirit ' and the truth of the [30] motherhood, just as he has been there; ' I was among those ' who are united in the friendship ' of friends forever, ' who neither know [35] hostility at all, ' nor evil, but who are united **68** by my Knowledge ' in word and peace ' which exists in perfection ' with everyone and in [5] them all. And those who ' assumed the form of my type will ' assume the form of my word. Indeed, these ' will come forth in light forever, ' and (in) friendship with each other [10] in the spirit, since they have known ' in every respect (and) indivisibly ' that what is is One. And ' all of these are one. And thus ' they will learn about the One, as (did) [15] the Assembly and those dwelling ' in it. For the father ' of all these exists, being immeasurable ' (and) immutable: Nous ' and Word and Division [20] and Envy and Fire. ' And he is entirely one, being ' the All with them all in a ' single doctrine because all these ' are from a single spirit. [25] O unseeing ones, why ' did you not know the mystery ' rightly? '

But the archons ' around Yaldabaoth were disobedient because of [30] the Ennoia who went down to him ' from her sister Sophia. ' They made for themselves a union ' with those who were with ' them in a mixture of **69** a fiery cloud, which ' was their Envy, and the rest ' who were brought forth by ' their creatures, as if [5] they had bruised the noble pleasure ' of the Assembly. ' And therefore they revealed ' a mixture of ignorance ' in a counterfeit [10] of fire and ' earth and a murderer, since ' they are small and untaught, ' without knowledge having dared ' these things, and not having understood [15] that light has fellowship ' with light, and darkness ' with darkness, and the ' corruptible with the perishable, ' and the imperishable with the incorruptible. [20]

Now these things I have presented to you (pl.)—' I am Jesus Christ, the Son of ' Man, who is exalted above the heavens—, ' O perfect and incorruptible ones, ' because of the [25] incorruptible and perfect mystery ' and the ineffable one. ' But they think that we decreed ' them before the foundation ' of the world in order that, [30] when we emerge from the places ' of the world, we may present there ' the symbols of ' incorruption from the ' spiritual union unto **70** knowledge. You (pl.) do not know ' it because the fleshly cloud ' overshadows you. ' But I alone am the friend of Sophia. ⁵ I have been in the bosom ' of the father from the beginning, in the place ' of the sons of the truth, and ' the Greatness. Rest then with me, ' my fellow spirits and my brothers, ¹⁰ for ever. '

Second Treatise '
of the Great Seth

APOCALYPSE OF PETER (VII, *3*)

Introduced by

JAMES BRASHLER

Translated by

ROGER A. BULLARD

Edited by

FREDERIK WISSE

The *Apocalypse of Peter* is a pseudonymous Christian Gnostic writing that contains an account of a revelation seen by the apostle Peter and interpreted by Jesus the Savior. The persecution of Jesus is used as a model for understanding early Christian history in which a faithful Gnostic remnant is oppressed by those "who name themselves bishop and also deacons."

This document belongs to the literary genre of the apocalypse. It is organized around three vision reports attributed to Peter. The visions are explained by the Savior, who functions as the interpreting angel commonly found in apocalyptic literature. In a series of prophecies that actually reflect past events, the early Christian church is portrayed as divided into various factions which oppose the Gnostic community. The world is a hostile environment for the immortal souls (the Gnostics), who outwardly resemble the mortal souls (non-Gnostics) but inwardly differ from them by virtue of their immortal essence. Having been given knowledge of their heavenly origin, the Gnostics long for the return of the heavenly Son of Man, who will come as the eschatological judge to condemn the oppressors and vindicate the Gnostics.

The apocalyptic form of this tractate has been employed to present a Gnostic understanding of Christian tradition about Jesus. The traditional material is skillfully interpreted in accordance with Gnostic theology. The first visionary scene, depicting the hostile priests and people about to kill Jesus (72, 4-9) is interpreted in terms of at least six groups characterized as "blind ones who have no guide." Many of these groups appear to be from the orthodox church, but some of them may be better understood as rival Gnostic sects. The second scene (81, 3-14) describes Peter's vision of the crucifixion of Jesus. The accompanying interpretation by Jesus makes a distinction between the external physical form and the living Jesus; the latter stands nearby laughing at his ignorant persecutors. The third visionary scene (82, 4-16) corresponds to the resurrection of Jesus in orthodox tradition, but it is interpreted in Gnostic terms as a reunification of the spiritual body of Jesus with the intellectual light of the heavenly pleroma.

The *Apocalypse of Peter* is significant in several respects. It contains important source material for a Gnostic Christology that understands Jesus as a docetic redeemer. The view of the Gnostic community, including its relationship to Peter as its originator, is another key theme of this document. Of considerable interest are the identity of the Gnostic group to which the writing is addressed, and the stage of the controversy, between emerging orthodoxy and heresy, presupposed by the tractate. It would appear that the *Apocalypse of Peter* was written in the third century, when this distinction between orthodoxy and heresy was rather clearly drawn.

APOCALYPSE OF PETER

VII 70, 13-84, 14

Apocalypse of Peter [1]

As the Savior was sitting in [15] the temple in the three hundredth (year) of [1] the covenant and the agreement of [1] the tenth pillar, and [1] being satisfied with the number [1] of the living, incorruptible Majesty, [20] he said to me, "Peter, [1] blessed are those [1] above belonging to the Father [1] who revealed life [1] to those who are from the life, through [25] me, since I reminded (them), [1] they who are built [1] on what is strong, [1] that they may hear my word [1] and distinguish words [30] of unrighteousness and [1] transgression of law [1] from righteousness, as **71** being from the height of [1] every word of this pleroma [1] of truth, having [1] been enlightened in good pleasure by [5] him whom the principalities sought. [1] But they did not find [1] him, nor was he mentioned [1] among any generation of [1] the prophets. He has [10] now appeared among these, [1] in him who appeared, [1] who is the Son of Man [1] who is exalted above the heavens in [1] a fear of men of like essence. [15] But you yourself, Peter, [1] become perfect [1] in accordance with your name with myself, [1] the one who chose you, because [1] from you I have established a base [20] for the remnant whom I have [1] summoned to knowledge. [1] Therefore be strong until the [1] imitation of righteousness—[1] of him who had summoned you, [25] having summoned you [1] to know him in a way which is [1] worth doing because of the rejection [1] which happened to him, and the sinews [1] of his hands and his feet, [30] and the crowning [1] by those of the middle region, [1] and the body of [1] his radiance which they bring [1] in hope of **72** service because of a reward [1] of honor—as he was about to reprove [1] you three times [1] in this night."

And as he was saying [5] these things, I saw the priests [1] and the people running up [1] to us with stones, as if they [1] would kill us; and I was afraid [1] that we were going to die.

And [10] he said to me, "Peter, I have told [1] you many times that [1] they are blind ones who have [1] no guide. If you want [1] to know their

blindness, [15] put your hands upon (your) eyes—' your robe—and say '
what you see." '

But when I had done it, I did not see ' anything. I said, "No one sees
(this way)." [20]

Again he told me, ' "Do it again."

And there came ' in me fear with ' joy, for I saw a ' new light greater
than the [25] light of day. Then ' it came down upon the Savior. ' And I
told him about those things ' which I saw.

And ' he said to me again, "Lift up [30] your hands and ' listen to
what 73 the priests and the people are saying."

And ' I listened to the priests as they sat ' with the scribes. The
multitudes were ' shouting with their voice.

When he [5] heard these things from me ' he said to me, "Prick up
your ears ' and listen ' to the things they are saying." '

And I listened again. "As you sit [10] they are praising you."

And ' when I said these things, the Savior said, ' "I have told you
that these (people) ' are blind and ' deaf. Now then, listen to [15] the
things which they are telling you ' in a mystery, and ' guard them. Do
not tell them to the ' sons of this age. ' For they shall blaspheme [20]
you in these ages since they ' are ignorant of you, ' but they will praise
you in knowledge. '

"For many ' will accept our teaching in the beginning. [25] And they
will turn ' from them again by the will ' of the Father of their error, '
because they have done what he wanted. ' And he will reveal them [30]
in his judgment, i.e. ' the servants of the Word. ' But those who became
74 mingled with these shall become ' their prisoners, ' since they are
without perception. ' And the guileless, good, [5] pure one they push ' to
the worker of death, ' and to the kingdom of ' those who praise Christ '
in a restoration. [10] And they praise the men ' of the propagation of
falsehood, ' those who will come after you. ' And they will cleave to the
name ' of a dead man, thinking [15] that they will become pure. But '
they will become greatly defiled and they will ' fall into a name of error, '
and into the hand of an ' evil, cunning man and a [20] manifold dogma,
and they will be ' ruled ' heretically.

"For some ' of them will ' blaspheme the truth and [25] proclaim evil
teaching. And ' they will say evil things ' against each other. Such '
will be named: ' (those) who stand in (the) strength [30] of the archons,
of a man ' and a naked woman ' who is manifold ' and subject to much '
suffering. And 75 those who say these things will ' ask about dreams.
And if they ' say that a dream ' came from a demon [5] worthy of their

error, then ' they shall be given perdition instead ' of incorruption.

"For evil ' cannot produce ' good fruit (cf. Luke 6:43). For [10] the place from which each of them is ' produces that which is like itself; ' for not every soul is ' of the truth, nor ' of immortality. [15] For every soul of these ages ' has death assigned to it ' in our view, because ' it is always a slave, ' since it is created for its desires [20] and their eternal ' destruction, in which ' they are and ' from which they are. ' They (the souls) love the creatures [25] of the matter which came forth ' with them.

"But ' the immortal souls are not like these, ' O Peter. But indeed, as long as ' the hour is not yet come, (the immortal soul) [30] shall ' resemble a mortal one. ' But it shall not reveal ' its nature, that it ' alone is the **76** immortal one, and thinks about ' immortality, having faith, ' and desiring to renounce ' these things.

"For people do not gather [5] figs from thorns or from ' thorn trees, if they ' are wise, nor grapes ' from thistles (cf. Luke 6:44). ' For on the one hand, that which is [10] always becoming is in that ' from which it is, being ' from what is not good, which ' becomes destruction for it (the soul) and ' death. But that (immortal soul) which comes to be [15] in the Eternal One is in the One of ' the life and the immortality of ' the life which they resemble. '

"Therefore all that which exists ' not will dissolve into what [20] exists not. ' For deaf and ' blind ones join only with ' their own kind. '

"But others shall change [25] from evil words ' and misleading ' mysteries. Some ' who do not understand mystery ' speak of things which [30] they do not understand, ' but they will boast ' that the mystery ' of the truth is theirs ' alone. And [35] in haughtiness **77** they shall grasp at pride ' to envy the ' immortal soul which has become a pledge. ' For every authority, rule, [5] and power of the aeons ' wishes to be with ' these in the creation of ' the world, in order that those who ' are not, having been forgotten [10] by those that are, ' may praise them, ' though they have not been saved, nor have they ' been brought to the Way by them, ' always wishing [15] that they may become ' imperishable ones. ' For if the immortal soul ' receives power in an ' intellectual spirit—. But immediately [20] they join with one ' of those who misled them. '

"But many others, ' who oppose the ' truth and are the messengers [25] of error, will ' set up their error and ' their law against ' these pure thoughts of mine, ' as looking out [30] from one (perspective), thinking ' that good and evil ' are from one (source). ' They do business in **78** my word. And they will propagate ' harsh fate. ' The race of immortal ' souls will go in it [5] in vain ' until my Parousia. ' For they shall come out of them—' and my forgiveness of ' their transgressions [10] into which they fell through ' their adversaries, ' whose ransom I got ' from the slavery in which ' they were, to give them [15] freedom that they may create ' an imitation remnant ' in the name of a dead man, ' who is Hermas, of the ' first-born of unrighteousness, [20] in order that the light which exists ' may not be believed ' by the little ones. ' But those of this sort are the workers ' who will be cast into the outer darkness, [25] away from the sons ' of light. For neither will they ' enter, ' nor do they permit ' those who are going up to [30] their approval for ' their release.

"And still others ' of them who suffer think ' that they will perfect **79** the wisdom of the brotherhood ' which really exists, which is the ' spiritual fellowship with those ' united in communion, [5] through which ' the wedding of ' incorruptibility shall be revealed. ' The kindred race ' of the sisterhood will appear [10] as an imitation. ' These are the ones who oppress ' their brothers, saying ' to them, 'Through this ' our God has pity, [15] since salvation comes ' to us through this,' not knowing ' the punishment of those who ' are made glad by those who ' have done this thing to the little ones whom [20] they saw, (and) whom they took ' prisoner. '

"And there shall be others ' of those who are outside our ' number who name themselves [25] bishop and also ' deacons, as if they have received ' their authority from God. ' They bend themselves under the ' judgment of the leaders. [30] Those people are ' dry canals." '

But I said, "I am afraid because ' of what you have told me, that **80** indeed little (ones) are, in our view, the ' counterfeit ones, ' indeed, that there are multitudes that will mislead ' other multitudes of living ones, [5] and destroy them among ' themselves. And when they speak your name ' they will be believed." '

The Savior said, "For a time ' determined for them in [10] proportion to their error they will ' rule over the little ones. And ' after the completion of ' the error, the ' never-aging one of the immortal understanding [15] shall become young, and they (the little ones) shall rule over ' those who are their rulers. ' The root of their error ' he shall pluck out, and he shall ' put it to shame so that it shall be manifest [20] in all the impudence which it ' has assumed to itself. And ' such ones shall become ' unchangeable, O Peter.

"Come ' therefore, let us go on with the completion [25] of the will of the ' incorruptible Father. ' For behold, those who will ' bring them judgment are coming, and they ' will put them to shame. But me [30] they cannot touch. ' And you, O Peter, shall ' stand in their midst. Do not be ' afraid because of your cowardice. **81** Their minds shall be closed, ' for the invisible one ' has opposed them."

When ' he had said those things, I saw him [5] seemingly being seized ' by them. And ' I said, "What do I see, ' O Lord, that it is you yourself ' whom they take, and that you are [10] grasping me? Or who is this one, ' glad and laughing on the tree? ' And is it another one ' whose feet and ' hands they are striking?" [15]

The Savior said to me, "He whom you saw ' on the tree, glad ' and laughing, this is the ' living Jesus. But this one ' into whose hands and [20] feet they drive the nails is his fleshly part, ' which is the substitute ' being put to shame, the one ' who came into being in his likeness. ' But look at him and me." [25]

But I, when I had looked, said, ' "Lord, no one is looking at ' you. Let us flee this ' place."

But he said to me, ' "I have told you, [30] 'Leave the blind alone!' ' And you, see how ' they do not know what they are saying. **82** For the son of ' their glory instead of my servant ' they have put to shame." '

And I saw someone about to approach [5] us resembling him, even him ' who was laughing on the tree. ' And he was ⟨filled⟩ with a ' Holy Spirit, and he is the ' Savior. And there was a great, [10] ineffable light around them, ' and the multitude ' of ineffable and ' invisible angels ' blessing them. [15] And when I looked at him, ' the one who gives praise was revealed. '

And he said to me, ' "Be strong, for you are the one to whom ' these mysteries have been given, [20] to know them through revelation, ' that he whom they crucified is ' the first-born, and the home ' of demons, and the stony vessel (?) ' in which they dwell, of Elohim, [25] of the cross ' which is under the Law. ' But he who stands near him ' is the living Savior, the first ' in him, whom they seized [30] and released, ' who stands joyfully ' looking at those who did him ' violence, while they are divided among themselves. **83** Therefore he laughs ' at their lack of perception, ' knowing that they are born blind. ' So then [5] the one susceptible to suffering shall come, since the body ' is the substitute. But what they ' released was my incorporeal ' body. But I am the intellectual ' Spirit filled with [10] radiant light. He ' whom you saw coming to ' me is our intellectual ' Pleroma, which unites ' the perfect light with [15] my Holy Spirit.

"These things, then, ' which you saw you shall present ' to those of another race ' who are not of this age. ' For there will be no honor [20] in any man ' who is not immortal, ' but only (in) those who were chosen ' from an immortal substance, ' which has shown [25] that it is able to contain him ' who gives his abundance. Therefore ' I said, 'Every one ' who has, it will be given to him, and ' he will have plenty' (Matthew 25:29). [30] But he who does not have, that is, ' the man of this place, who is ' completely dead, who ' is removed from the planting ' of the creation of what is begotten, **84** whom, if one ' of the immortal essence appears, ' they think that ' they possess him— [5] it will be taken from him and ' be added to the one who is. You, ' therefore, be courageous and do not ' fear at all. For I shall be ' with you in order that none [10] of your enemies may prevail over you. ' Peace be to you. Be strong!" '

When he (Jesus) had said these things, he (Peter) came ' to himself. '

Apocalypse of Peter

THE TEACHINGS OF SILVANUS (VII, *4*)

Introduced and translated by

MALCOLM L. PEEL and JAN ZANDEE

Edited by

FREDERIK WISSE

The *Teachings of Silvanus* is a unique tractate in several respects. Not only is it the only non-Gnostic document in Codex VII; it also is a rare example of an early Christian Wisdom text, and a portion of it is known to have been appropriated later for the tradition of teachings attributed to St. Anthony, founder of the anchoritic type of monasticism in Egypt. The evidence indicates that the tractate was known and used in monastic circles, and may actually have been written by a forerunner of a monastic community.

The non-Gnostic character of the *Teachings of Silvanus* is apparent. Its theology is not dualistic, its Christology is not docetic, and it implicitly denies that only some persons are saved "by nature." God, the Father of Jesus, is the Creator of all things. Moreover, Christ's humanity is manifested in his "bearing of affliction for sins," "dying" as a "ransom for sins," putting on "humanity." Because all persons possess the divine "mind" and "reason," potentially all can be saved.

The "teachings" set forth in the tractate are presented in the framework of a literary genre which is deeply indebted to classical and especially Hellenized Jewish Wisdom. Many Wisdom forms are utilized, including the address of the reader as "my son," negative and positive admonitions, descriptive proverbs and didactic sayings, hymns and prayers, and contrasts between the wise and the foolish. Furthermore, like Hellenized Jewish Wisdom, the *Teachings of Silvanus* displays some eclectic tastes, with influences from the Bible, the exegesis of Philo of Alexandria, Middle Platonism, and late Stoicism.

Among the more striking ideas found in the *Teachings of Silvanus* are those having to do with ethics, anthropology, theology, and Christology. Attainment of the goal of being "pleasing to God" involves, in the main, rational control of baser impulses from flesh and body. Achievement of such control entails fortifying oneself with the teachings of a good teacher, with the "light" of truth that Christ provides, and with a correct balance of power between the mind, the soul, and the body—the major constituent parts of every person. God contains all things without being contained by anything. Thus, he is not confined to a place—a view contrary to Stoic pantheism. He is difficult to know except through his "image," Christ. Christ, in turn, is viewed as the incarnate Wisdom of God. He has descended into the "Underworld" (that is, this earth), to free its captives and vanquish its Ruler (Satan) by deceit. He seems capable of joining forces with human reason, and of becoming the indwelling Logos.

The "Silvanus" to whom the text is attributed would seem to be the companion of the apostle Paul, or possibly the amanuensis of the apostle Peter (cf. 1 Peter 5:12). The use of a prominent New Testament name was a common practice in early Christian apocryphal literature. That the document was written much later than the first century, however, is clear, and internal evidence suggests a date of composition in the late second or early third century, probably in Egypt, in the vicinity of Alexandria.

A scribal note between tractates *4* and *5* (118, 8-9) seems integrally related to neither. It is in Greek, and includes the "fish" acrostic as well as a few scattered letters and signs.

THE TEACHINGS OF SILVANUS
VII 84, 15-118, 7
118, 8-9

The Teachings of Silvanus '

Abolish every childish time of life, ' acquire for yourself strength ' of mind and soul, ' and intensify the struggle against [20] every folly of the passions ' of love and base wickedness, ' and love of praise, ' and fondness of contention, ' and tiresome jealousy and wrath, [25] and anger and the desire ' of avarice. Guard ' your (pl.) camp and ' weapons and spears. Arm ' yourself and all the soldiers [30] which are the words, and the commanders ' which are the counsels, and your **85** mind as a guiding principle.

My ' son, throw every robber ' out of your gates. Guard ' all your gates with torches [5] which are the words, and ' you will acquire all these things for a ' quiet life. But he who will not guard ' these things will become like a ' city which is desolate since it has been [10] captured, and all kinds of wild beasts have ' trampled upon it. For thoughts which ' are not good are evil wild beasts. ' And your city ' will be filled with robbers, and you [15] will not be able to acquire peace, ' but only all kinds of savage wild beasts. ' The Wicked One, who is ' a tyrant, is lord over these. While ' directing this, he (the Wicked One) is beneath the great [20] mire. The whole city ' which is your soul will perish. '

Remove all these, O ' wretched soul. ' Bring in your guide and [25] your teacher. The mind is the guide, ' but reason is the teacher. ' They will bring you ' out of destruction and dangers. '

Listen, my son, to my [30] advice! Do not show your back ' [to] your enemies and flee, but ' rather pursue them as a [strong one]. **86** Be not an animal, with men ' pursuing you; but ' rather, be a man, with you pursuing ' the evil wild beasts, lest somehow [5] they become victorious

over you and trample ' upon you as on a dead man, ' and you perish
due to ' their wickedness.

O wretched ' man, what will you ¹⁰ do if you fall into their ' hands?
Protect yourself ' lest you be delivered into the hands of your ' enemies.
Entrust yourself to this ' pair of friends, reason ¹⁵ and mind, and no one '
will be victorious over you. May God ' dwell in your camp, ' may his
Spirit protect your ' gates, and may the mind of divinity ²⁰ protect the
walls. Let holy reason ' become a ' torch in your mind, burning ' the
wood which is the entirety of sin. '

And if you do these things, O my son, ²⁵ you will be victorious over
all your enemies, ' and they will not be able to wage war ' against you,
neither will they be able ' to stand firm, nor will they ' be able to get in
your way. ³⁰ For if you find these, you will despise ' them as deniers of
truth. ' They will speak with you, [cajoling] ' you and enticing (you), not
because they are [afraid] **87** of you, but because they are afraid of ' those
who dwell within you, ' namely, the guardians of the divinity ' and the
teaching.

My son, ⁵ accept the education and the teaching. ' Do not flee from
the education and ' the teaching, but when you are taught, ' accept (it)
with joy. And if ' you are educated in ¹⁰ any matter, do what is good. '
You will plait a crown of ' education by your guiding principle. ' Put
on the holy teaching ' like a robe. Make yourself noble-minded ¹⁵ through
good conduct. ' Have the austerity of ' good discipline. Judge ' yourself like a wise judge. ' Do not lose my teaching, ²⁰ and do not acquire
ignorance, ' lest you lead your people astray. ' Do not flee from the
divine ' and the teaching which are within ' you, for he who is teaching ²⁵
you loves you very much. ' For he shall bequeath to you a worthy
austerity. ' Cast out the animal nature ' which is within you, ' and ³⁰ do
not allow base thought to enter you. ' For . . . you ' know the way which
I teach. '

If it is good to rule over the [few], ' as you see it, ³⁵ [how] much better
is it that you **88** rule over everyone, since you are exalted ' above every
congregation and every people, ' (are) prominent in every respect, ' and
(are) a divine reason, having ⁵ become master over every power ' which
kills the soul.

My son, does anyone ' want to be a slave? ' Why, then, do you trouble
yourself wrongly? '

My son, do not ¹⁰ fear anyone except ' God alone, the Exalted One. '
Cast the deceitfulness of the Devil ' from you. Accept the light ' for your
eyes, and cast ¹⁵ the darkness from you. Live ' in Christ, and you will

acquire ' a treasure in heaven. Do not become ' a sausage (made) of many things ' which are useless, and do not ²⁰ become a guide ' on behalf of your blind ignorance. '

My son, listen to my ' teaching which is good and useful, ' and end the sleep which weighs heavy upon you. ²⁵ Depart from the forgetfulness ' which fills you with darkness, ' since if you were unable ' to do anything, I would not have said these things ' to you. But Christ came in order to give you ³⁰ this gift. Why do you ' pursue the darkness though the light ' is at your disposal? Why ' do you drink stale water though ' sweet is available for you? ³⁵ Wisdom summons [you], **89** yet you desire folly. ' Not by your own desire do you do ' these things, but it is the animal nature ' within you that does them. ⁵

Wisdom summons you ' in her goodness, saying, ' "Come to me, all of you, ' O foolish ones, that you may receive a ' gift, the understanding which is ¹⁰ good and excellent. I am giving to you ' a high-priestly garment ' which is woven from every (kind of) wisdom." What else ' is evil death except ' ignorance? What else is ¹⁵ evil darkness except familiarity ' with forgetfulness? Cast your anxiety ' upon God alone. Do not become ' desirous of gold and silver ' which are profitless, but ²⁰ clothe yourself with wisdom like ' a robe, put knowledge ' upon you like ' a crown, and be seated upon a throne ' of perception. For these are yours, ²⁵ and you will receive them again on high ' another time.

For a foolish man ' puts on folly ' like a robe, and ' like a garment of sorrow ³⁰ he puts on shame. And ' he crowns himself with ignorance ' and takes his seat ' upon a throne of ' [nescience]. For while he is [without reason], **90** he leads only himself astray, for ' he is guided by ignorance. ' And he goes the ways ' of the desire of every passion. ⁵ He swims in the desires ' of life and has foundered. ' To be sure, he thinks that he finds profit ' when he does all the things ' which are without profit. The ¹⁰ wretched man who goes ' through all these things will die because ' he does not have the mind, ' the helmsman. But he is like ' a ship which the wind tosses ¹⁵ to and fro, and like ' a loose horse which has no rider. ' For this (man) ' needed the rider which is reason. ' For the wretched one went astray ²⁰ since he did not want ' advice. He was thrown to and ' fro by these three evil things: ' he acquired for himself death as ' a father, ignorance ²⁵ as a mother, and evil counsels—' he acquired them ' as friends and brothers. ' Therefore, foolish one, you should mourn for yourself. '

From now on, then, my son, return ³⁰ to your divine nature. ' Cast from [you] these evil, ' deceiving friends! ' [Accept] Christ, [this true friend], **91** as a good teacher. Cast ' from you death, which has ' become a father to you. ' For death did not exist, nor [5] will it exist at the end.

But ' since you cast from yourself ' God, the holy Father, ' the true Life, the Spring ' of Life, therefore you have [10] obtained death as a father ' and have acquired ignorance ' as a mother. They have robbed ' you of the true knowledge. '

But return, my son, to [15] your first father, God, ' and Wisdom your mother, ' from whom you came into being ' from the very first in order that you might fight against ' all of your enemies, the powers [20] of the Adversary.

Listen, ' my son, to my advice. ' Do not be arrogant in opposition to ' every good opinion, ' but take for yourself the side of the divinity [25] of reason. Keep the holy ' commandments of Jesus Christ, and ' you will reign over every place ' on earth and will be ' honored by the angels [30] and the archangels. ' Then you will acquire them as friends and ' fellow servants, and you will acquire ' places in [heaven ' above].

Do not bring **92** grief and trouble to the divine [which is] ' within you. But when you will care for ' it, will request of it ' that you remain pure, and will become [5] self-controlled in your soul ' and body, you will become ' a throne of wisdom and ' one belonging to God's household. He will ' give you a great light through [10] it (wisdom).

But before everything (else), ' know your birth. Know ' yourself, that is, from what substance you are, ' or from what ' race, or from what species. [15] Understand that you have come into being ' from three races: ' from the earth, from the ' formed, and from the created. ' The body has come into being from [20] the earth with an earthly substance, ' but the formed, for the sake of ' the soul, has come into being from the thought ' of the Divine. The created, however, is the mind, ' which has come into being in conformity with the image [25] of God. The divine mind ' has substance ' from the Divine, but the soul ' is that which he (God) has formed for their ' own hearts. For I think [30] that it (the soul) exists as wife of that which ' has come into being in conformity with the image, ' but matter is the substance ' of the body which has come into being from the earth. '

[If] you mix yourself, you will acquire the **93** three parts as you ' fall from virtue into ' inferiority. Live according to ' the mind. Do not think about things pertaining to [5] the flesh. Acquire strength, ' for the mind is strong. ' If you fall from ' this other, you have become male-female. ' And if you cast out of yourself the substance of the mind, [10] which is thought, ' you have cut off ' the male part and turned yourself to the

female part ' alone. You have become psychic ' since you have received
the substance of the [15] formed. If also you cast out the smallest part of
this ' so that ' you do not acquire again a ' human part—but you have
accepted for ' yourself the animal thought and [20] likeness—you have
become fleshly ' since you have taken on animal nature. ' For (if) it is
difficult to find a psychical man, ' how much more so to find ' the Lord.

But I say that [25] God is the spiritual one. ' Man has taken shape from '
the substance of God. ' The divine soul ' shares partly in this One
(God); furthermore [30] it shares partly in the flesh. ' The base soul ' is
wont to turn from side to side ' [. . .] which it imagines the truth. '

It is [good] for you, O man, **94** to turn yourself toward the human
rather ' than toward the animal nature—' I mean toward the fleshly
(nature). You ' will take on the likeness of the part toward which you
will turn yourself. [5]

I shall say something further ' to you. Again, for what ' will you
(masc. sing.) be zealous? You (fem. sing.) wished ' to become animal
when you had come into ' this kind of nature. [10] But rather, share in '
a true nature of life. ' To be sure, animality will guide you ' into the
race of the earth, ' but the rational nature will [15] guide you in rational
ways. ' Turn toward the rational nature ' and cast from ' yourself the
earth-begotten nature. '

O soul, persistent one, [20] be sober and shake off your ' drunkenness,
which is the work of ' ignorance. If you persist ' and live in the ' body,
you dwell in rusticity. [25] When you had entered ' into a bodily birth,
you were ' begotten. You have come into being inside ' the bridal
chamber, and you have been illuminated ' in mind.

My son, do not [30] swim in any water, ' and do not allow yourself to
be defiled ' by strange kinds of knowledge. ' Certainly you know
[that] **95** the schemes of the Adversary ' are not few and (that) ' the
tricks which he has ' are varied? Especially has the noetic [5] man been
robbed ' of the intelligence ' of the snake. For it is fitting for you ' to
be in agreement with the ' intelligence of (these) two: with the [10] intelligence of the snake and with ' the innocence of the dove—' lest he (the
Adversary) come into you ' in the guise of a flatterer, ' as a true friend,
saying, [15] "I advise ' good things for you." '

But you did not recognize the ' deceitfulness of this one when ' you
received him as a true friend. [20] For he casts into your heart ' evil
thoughts ' as good ones, and ' hypocrisy in the guise of ' firm intelligence, [25] avidity in the guise ' of frugality, ' love of glory ' in the
guise of that which is beautiful, ' boastfulness and [30] pride in the guise '

of great austerity, and ' godlessness as ' [great] godliness. **96** For he who says, "I have ' many gods," is godless. ' And he casts spurious knowledge ' into your [5] heart in the guise of mysterious words. ' Who ' will be able to comprehend his thoughts and ' devices, which are varied, since he is ' a Great Mind for those who wish [10] to accept him as king?

My ' son, how will you be able ' to comprehend the schemes of this one or his ' soul-killing counsel? ' For his devices and the [15] schemes of his wickedness are many. And ' think about his entrances, that is, how ' he will enter your ' soul and in what garment ' he will enter you.

Accept [20] Christ, who is able ' to set you free, and who has ' taken on the devices of that one ' so that through these he ' might destroy him by [25] deceit. For this is the king whom you have ' who is forever invincible, ' against whom ' no one will be able to fight nor ' say a word. This is [30] your king and your father, ' for there is no one like him. ' The divine teacher is with [you] **97** always. He is a helper, ' and he meets you because of the good ' which is in you.

Do not put maliciousness ' in your judgment, [5] for every malicious man ' harms his heart. ' For only a foolish man goes ' to his destruction, ' but a wise man knows [10] his path.

And a foolish man ' does not guard against speaking (a) mystery. ' A wise man, (however), ' does not blurt out every word, ' but he will be discriminating [15] toward those who hear. Do not mention ' everything in the presence ' of those whom you do not know. '

Have a great number of friends, ' but not counselors. [20] First, examine your ' counselor, for do not ' honor anyone who flatters. ' Their word, to be sure, is sweet as ' honey, but their heart is full [25] of hellebore. For whenever ' they think that they have become ' a reliable friend, ' then they will deceitfully turn ' against you, and they will cast you down [30] into the mire.

Do not ' trust anyone as a friend, ' for this whole world ' has come into being deceitfully, and ' every [man] is troubled [35] [in vain]. All things [of] **98** the world are not profitable, ' but they happen in vain. ' There is no one, not even a brother, (who is trustworthy), ' since each one is seeking [5] his own advantage.

My son, do not ' have anyone as a friend. ' But if you do acquire one, do not entrust yourself ' to him. Entrust yourself to ' God alone as father [10] and as friend. For everyone ' proceeds deceitfully, ' while the whole earth is full of suffering and ' pain—things in which there is no profit. ' If you wish to pass your [15] life in quiet, do not keep company ' with anyone. And if you do keep ' company with them, be as if ' you do not. Be pleasing ' to God, and you will [20] not need anyone.

Live ' with Christ, and he will save ' you. For he is the true light '
and the sun of life. ' For just as the sun which is manifest 25 and makes
light for the eyes of the flesh, ' so Christ ' illuminates every mind ' and
the heart. For (if) a wicked man ' (who is) in the body (has) an evil
death, 30 how much more so (does) ' he who has ' his mind blind. '
For every blind man [goes along ' in such a way] that he (?) is seen
[just] 99 as one who does not have ' his mind sane. He does not ' delight
in acquiring the light ' of Christ, which is reason. 5

For everything which is manifest ' is a copy of that which ' is hidden.
For as a fire which ' burns in a place without being confined ' to it,
so it is with 10 the sun which is in heaven, all of whose rays ' extend to
places ' on the earth. Similarly, ' Christ has a single being, ' and 15
he gives light to every place. This ' is also the way in which he speaks
of our ' mind, as if it were a lamp ' which burns and lights up the
place. ' (Being) in a part of the soul, 20 it gives light to all the parts. '

Furthermore, I shall speak of what is ' more exalted than this: the
mind, with respect to ' actual being, is in a place, ' which means it is
in the body; 25 but with respect to thought, the mind ' is not in a place.
For how can it ' be in a place when ' it contemplates every place? '

But we are able 30 to mention what is more exalted than this: ' for
do not think in your heart ' that God exists ' [in a] place. If ' you
localize the [Lord of] all **100** in a place, then it is fitting for you to ' say
that the place is more exalted than he who ' dwells in it. For that which
contains ' is more exalted than that which is contained. 5 For there is
no place which is called ' bodiless. ' For it is not right for us to say
that ' God is a body. ' For the consequence (would be) that we (must)
attribute both 10 increase and decrease to the body, ' but also that he
(God) who is subject to these ' will not remain imperishable. '

Now, it is not difficult to know ' the Creator of all creatures, 15 but
it is impossible to comprehend ' the likeness of this One. For ' it is
difficult not only for men to ' comprehend God, but it is (also) difficult '
for every divine being, (both) the angels 20 and the archangels. ' It is
necessary to know ' God as he is. ' You cannot ' know God through 25
anyone except Christ ' who has ' the image of the Father, ' for this
image reveals the true likeness ' in correspondence to that which is
revealed. 30 A king is not usually known apart from ' an image.

Consider these things about ' God: he is in every place; ' on the
other hand, he is in [no] ' place. [With respect to power], **101** to be sure,
he is in every place; ' but with respect to divinity, he is in no ' place.
So, then, it is ' possible to know God a 5 little. With respect to his

power, ' he fills every place, but in ' the exaltation of his divinity '
nothing contains him. ' Everything is in God, [10] but God is not in
anything. '

Now what is it to know God? ' God is all which is in the truth. '
But it is as impossible ' to look at Christ as [15] at the sun. God sees '
everyone; no one looks at ' him. But Christ without ' being jealous
receives and gives. He ' is the Light of the Father, as he gives [20] light
without being jealous. ' In this manner he gives light to every place. '

And all is Christ, ' he who has inherited all ' from the Existent One. [25]
For Christ is all, apart from (his) ' incorruptibility. For if you consider '
sin, it is not a reality. ' For Christ is the idea ' of incorruptibility, and [30]
he is the Light which is shining undefiled. ' For the sun (shines) on
every impure place, ' and yet it is not defiled. ' So it is with Christ:
even if ' [he is in the] deficiency, yet [he] is without deficiency. [35] And
even if [he has been begotten], **102** he is (still) unbegotten. So it is with '
Christ: if, on the one hand, he is comprehensible, ' on the other he is
incomprehensible ' with respect to his actual being. [5] Christ is all. '
He who does not possess all is unable to ' know Christ.

My son, ' do not dare to say a word about ' this One, and do not
confine the God of all [10] to mental images. ' For he (God) who condemns ' may not be condemned by the one who ' condemns. Indeed,
it is good ' to ask and to know who [15] God is. Reason and mind ' are
male names. Indeed, let him who wishes ' to know about this One '
quietly and ' reverently ask. For there is no small danger [20] in speaking
about these things, since you ' know that you will be judged ' on the
basis of everything that you say. '

And understand by this that he who is in ' darkness will not be able
to see anything [25] unless he receives the light . . . ' by means of it. Examine
yourself (to see) ' whether you actually have ' the light, so that if you '
ask about these things, you may understand [30] how you will escape. '
For many are seeking in ' darkness, and they grope about, ' wishing to
understand since ' there is no light for them.

My **103** son, do not allow your mind to stare ' downward, but rather
let ' it look by means of the light ' at things above. [5] For the light will
always come from above. ' Even if it (the mind) is upon the earth, '
let it seek to pursue the ' things above. Enlighten your ' mind with the
light of heaven [10] so that you may turn to ' the light of heaven.

Do not tire ' of knocking on the door of reason, ' and do not cease '
walking in the way of [15] Christ. Walk in it so that ' you may receive
rest from your ' labors. If you walk in another ' way, there will be no '

profit in it. For also those who walk [20] in the broad way ' will go down at their end ' to the perdition of the mire. ' For the Underworld is open wide for the soul, ' and the place of perdition is broad. [25] Accept Christ, ' the narrow way. For he is oppressed ' and bears affliction for your ' sin.

O soul, persistent one, ' in what ignorance you exist! [30] For who ' is your guide ' into the darkness? How many likenesses ' did Christ take on because of you? ' Although he was God, he [was found] **104** among men as a man. ' He descended to the Underworld. He released ' the children of death. They were ' in travail, as [5] the scripture of God has said. And ' he sealed up the (very) heart ' of it (the Underworld). And he broke its (the Underworld's) strong bows ' completely. And ' when all the powers had seen [10] him, they fled so that he might ' bring you, wretched one, ' up from the Abyss, and might die for you ' as a ransom for your sin. He saved ' you from the strong hand of the Underworld. [15]

But you, on the other hand, with difficulty give your ' basic choice to him with a hint ' that he may take you up with ' joy! Now the basic choice, ' which is humility of heart, is the gift of Christ. [20] A contrite heart is the acceptable sacrifice. ' If you ' humble yourself, you will be greatly exalted. ' And if you exalt yourself, ' you will be exceedingly humbled.

My son, [25] guard yourself against wickedness, ' and do not let the Spirit of Wickedness ' cast you down into the Abyss. ' For he is mad and bitter. ' He is a disturbance, and he casts [30] everyone down into a pit ' of mire.

It is a great ' and good thing not to love ' fornication and not even to think ' of the wretched matter **105** at all, for to think of it is death. ' It is not good for any man ' to fall into death. ' For a soul which has been found in [5] death will be without reason. ' For it is better not to live than ' to acquire an animal's life. ' Protect yourself lest you are burned ' by the fires of fornication. [10] For many who are submerged in fire are ' its servants whom ' you do not know as ' your enemies.

O my son, strip off ' the old garment of fornication, [15] and put on the ' garment which is clean and shining, ' that you may be beautiful in it. ' But when you have this garment, ' protect it well. Release yourself [20] from every bond so that you may ' acquire freedom ' when you cast out ' the desire whose ' devices are many, and when you [25] release yourself from the sins of lust. '

Listen, O soul, to my ' advice. Do not become ' a nest of foxes and snakes, nor ' a hole of serpents and [30] asps, nor a dwelling place ' of lions, or a place of refuge ' of basilisk-snakes. When these things ' happen to you, O soul, what ' will you do? For these are the powers **106** of the Adversary. ' Everything which is dead will come ' into you through them (the powers). ' For their food is everything which is dead [5] and every unclean thing. For when these ' are within you, what living thing ' will come into you? ' The living angels will detest you. ' You were [10] a temple, (but) you have made yourself a tomb. Cease ' being a tomb, and become (again) ' a temple, so that uprightness ' and divinity may remain in ' you.

Light the light within you. [15] Do not extinguish it. Certainly no one ' lights a lamp for wild beasts or ' their young. ' Raise your dead who have died, ' for they lived and have died for [20] you. Give them life. ' They shall live again.

For the Tree of ' Life is Christ. He is ' Wisdom. For he is Wisdom; ' he is also the Word. He [25] is the Life, the Power, ' and the Door. He is the Light, ' the Messenger, and ' the Good Shepherd. Entrust yourself ' to this one who became [30] all for your sake.

Knock ' on yourself as upon ' a door, and walk upon ' yourself as on a straight road. ' For if you walk on the road, [35] it is impossible for you to go astray. 107 And if you knock with this one (Wisdom), you ' knock on hidden treasuries. '

For since he (Christ) is Wisdom, ' he makes the foolish man wise. [5] It (Wisdom) is a holy kingdom ' and a shining robe. ' For it (Wisdom) is much gold ' which gives you great honor. ' The Wisdom of God [10] became a type of fool for you ' so that it might take you up, ' O foolish one, and make you a wise man. ' And the Life died ' for you when he (Christ) was powerless, [15] so that through his death ' he might give life to you who have died. '

Entrust yourself to ' reason and remove yourself from ' animalism. For [20] the animal which has no ' reason is made manifest. ' For many think that they have ' reason, but if you ' look at them attentively, [25] their speech is animalistic. '

Give yourself gladness from the true ' vine of Christ. ' Satisfy yourself with the true wine ' in which there is no drunkenness [30] nor error. ' For it (the true wine) marks ' the end of drinking since there ' is in it (the power) to give joy ' to the soul and [35] the mind through the Spirit of God. 108 But first, nurture your reasoning powers ' before you drink ' of it (the true wine).

Do not pierce yourself with ' the sword of sin. Do not burn yourself, [5] O wretched one, with the fire ' of lust. Do not surrender yourself ' to barbarians like a prisoner, ' nor to ' savage beasts which wish [10] to trample upon you. ' For they are as lions ' which roar very loudly. Be

not ' dead lest they ' trample upon you. You shall be man! [15] It is
possible for you through reasoning ' to conquer them. '

But the man who does nothing is unworthy of ' (being called) rational
man. The rational man ' is he who fears God. [20] He who fears ' God
does nothing insolent. ' And he who guards himself ' against doing
anything insolent is one ' who keeps his guiding principle. [25] Although
he is a man who exists ' on earth, he makes himself like ' God.

But he who makes himself like ' God is one who does ' nothing
worthy of God, [30] according to the statement of Paul ' who has
become like ' Christ.

For who shows reverence ' for God while not wishing ' to do things
which are pleasing [35] to him? For piety ' is that which is **109** from the
heart, ' and piety from ' the heart (characterizes) every soul which is
near to ' God.

The soul which is [5] a member of God's household is one which ' is
kept pure, ' and the soul which has put on Christ ' is one which is pure. '
It is impossible for it to sin [10] Now where Christ is, there ' sin is idle.

Let Christ ' alone enter your world, ' and let him bring to naught '
all powers which have come upon you. [15] Let him enter the temple
which is ' within you so that he may cast ' out all the merchants. Let
him ' dwell in the temple which is ' within you, and may you become [20]
for him a priest and a Levite, ' entering in purity. '

Blessed are you, O soul, if you ' find this one in your temple. '

Blessed are you still more if you perform his [25] service.

But he who will defile ' the temple of God, that one God ' will
destroy. For you lay yourself open, ' O man, if you ' cast this one out
of your [30] temple. For whenever ' the enemies do not see Christ ' in you,
then they will come into ' you armed in order to crush ' you.

O my son, I have given [35] you orders concerning these things many
times **110** so that you would always guard your ' soul. It is not you
who ' will cast him (Christ) out, but ' he will cast you out. For [5] if you
flee from him, you will ' fall into great sin. ' Again, if you flee from
him, you will ' become food for your enemies. ' For all base persons
flee from [10] their lord, and the (man) base in virtue ' and wisdom flees
from ' Christ. For every man who is ' separated (from him) falls into
the claws ' of the wild beasts.

Know who Christ is, [15] and acquire him as a friend, ' for this is the
friend who is faithful. ' He is also God and ' Teacher. This one, being
God, became ' man for your sake. It is this one who [20] broke the iron

bars ' of the Underworld and the bronze bolts. ' It is this one who attacked ' and cast down ' every haughty tyrant. It is he [25] who loosened from himself the chains ' of which he had taken hold. ' He brought up the poor from the ' Abyss and the mourners from ' the Underworld. It is he who humbled [30] the haughty powers; ' he who put to shame haughtiness ' through humility; he who has cast ' down the strong and ' the boaster through weakness; [35] he who in his contempt scorned that which is **111** considered an honor ' so that ' humility for God's sake might be highly exalted; ' (and) he who has put on humanity. [5]

And yet, the divine Word is God, ' he who bears patiently with man always. ' He wished to produce ' humility in the exalted. He (Christ) who has ' exalted man became like [10] God, not in order that he ' might bring God down to ' man, but that man might become ' like God.

> O this ' great goodness of God! [15] O Christ, King who has revealed ' to men the Great Divinity, ' King of every virtue and ' King of life, King of ages and ' Great One of the heavens, hear my words [20] and forgive me!

Furthermore, ' he manifested a great zeal ' for Divinity.

Where is a man (who is) wise ' or powerful in intelligence, ' or a man whose devices are many [25] because he knows wisdom? ' Let him speak wisdom; let him utter ' great boasting. ' For every man has become a fool and has spoken out of ' his (own) knowledge. For he (Christ) confounded the [30] counsels of guileful people, and ' he prevailed over those wise in their own ' understanding.

Who will be able ' to discover the counsel of the ' Almighty, or to speak of the [35] Divinity, or to proclaim it correctly? **112** If we have not even been able to ' understand the counsels of our companions, ' who will be able to comprehend the Divinity ' or the divinities of [5] the heavens? If ' we scarcely find things on earth, ' who will search for the things of ' heaven? A Great Power ' and Great Glory has made the world [10] known.

And the Life ' of Heaven wishes to renew all, ' that he may cast out that which is ' weak and every black form, ' that everyone may shine forth with great brilliance in [15] heavenly garments in order to make manifest ' the command of the Father, ' and that he may ' crown those wishing to contend ' well—Christ, being judge of the contest, [20] he who crowned every one, ' teaching every one ' to contend. This one who contended ' first received the crown, gained dominion, ' and appeared, giving light [25] to everyone. And all were ' made new through the Holy Spirit ' and the Mind.

O Lord Almighty, ' how much glory shall I give Thee? ' No one has been able [30] to glorify God adequately. ' It is Thou who hast given glory ' to Thy Word in order to save ' everyone, O Merciful God. (It is) he who ' has come from Thy mouth and has risen from [35] Thy heart, the First-born, the Wisdom, ' the Prototype, the First ' Light.

For he is a light from **113** the power of God, and ' he is an emanation of the pure glory ' of the Almighty. ' He is the spotless mirror of the working [5] of God, and he is the image of his ' goodness. For he is also the light ' of the Eternal Light. He is the eye ' which looks at the invisible ' Father, always serving [10] and forming ' by the Father's will. He ' alone was begotten by the Father's good pleasure. ' For he is an incomprehensible Word, ' and he is Wisdom [15] and Life. He gives life to and ' nourishes all living things and powers. ' Just as ' the soul gives life to all the members, ' he rules all with [20] power and gives life to them. ' For he is the beginning and ' the end of every one, watching over ' all and encompassing them. ' He is troubled on behalf of every one, and he rejoices [25] and also mourns. On the one hand, he mourns ' for those who have been appointed to the place ' of punishment; on the other, he is troubled ' about every one whom he arduously brings ' to instruction. [30] But he rejoices over every one who ' is in purity.

Then beware, ' lest somehow you fall into the hands of the ' robbers. Do not give sleep ' to your eyes nor [35] slumber to your eyelids, that ' you may be saved like a gazelle ' from snares and like a **114** bird from a trap.

Fight the ' great fight as long as the fight lasts, ' while all the powers are ' staring after you—not only the holy ones, [5] but also all the powers ' of the Adversary. Woe ' to you if they are victorious over you in the midst ' of every one who is watching you! ' If you fight the fight and [10] are victorious over the powers which fight against you, ' you will bring great joy to every ' holy one, and yet ' great grief to your enemies. Your ' judge helps (you) completely [15] since he wants you to be victorious.

Listen, my ' son, and do not be slow ' with your ears. Raise yourself ' up, when you have left your old man behind, ' like an eagle. Fear [20] God in all your acts, ' and glorify him through ' good work. ' You know that every man who is ' not pleasing to God is a son of perdition. [25] He will go down to the Abyss ' of the Underworld.

O the patience ' of God, which bears with ' every one, which desires that ' every one who has become [30] subject to sin be saved!

But no one prevents ' him (God) from doing what he wants. ' For who is stronger than he that ' he may prevent him? To be sure, ' it is he who touches the earth, [35] causing it to tremble and also causing ' the mountains to smoke. (It is) he who has ' gathered together such a great sea **115** as in a leather bag and ' has weighed all the water on his scales. ' Only the hand of the Lord ' has created all these things. [5] For this hand of the Father is Christ, ' and it forms all. ' Through it, all has come into being ' since it became the mother of all. ' For he is always [10] Son of the Father. '

Consider these things about God Almighty ' who always exists: ' this One was not always ' King for fear that [15] he might be without a ' divine Son. For all dwell ' in God, (that is), the things which have come into being ' through the Word, which is ' the Son as the image of the Father. [20]

For God is nearby, he ' is not far off. All divine limits ' are those which belong to God's household. ' Therefore, if the divine agrees with ' you partially in anything, [25] know that all of the Divine ' agrees with you. But this ' divine is not pleased with anything ' evil. For it is this which ' teaches all men what is good. [30] This is what God has ' given to the human race ' so that for this reason every man ' might be chosen ' before all the angels [35] and the archangels. '

For God does not need ' to put any man to the test. **116** He knows all things ' before they happen, and ' he knows the hidden things of the heart. ' They are all revealed and [5] found wanting in his presence. Let ' no one ever say that God ' is ignorant. For it is not right ' to place the Creator of ' every creature in ignorance. [10] For even things which are ' in darkness ' are before him like (things in) the light. '

So, there is no other one hidden except ' God alone. But he is revealed ' to everyone, and yet [15] he is very hidden. He is revealed ' because God knows ' all. And if they do not wish ' to affirm it, they will be corrected by ' their heart. Now he is hidden because [20] no one perceives the things of God. ' For it is incomprehensible and ' unsearchable to know ' the counsel of God. Furthermore, ' it is difficult to comprehend him and [25] to find Christ. For he is the one who dwells ' in every place and also ' in no place. For no one ' who wants to will be able to know ' God as he actually is, [30] nor Christ, nor ' the Spirit, nor the chorus of ' angels, nor even the archangels, **117** and the thrones of the spirits, ' and the exalted lordships, ' and the Great Mind. If you do not ' know [yourself], you will not be able [5] to know all of these.

Open ' the door for yourself that you may know ' what is. Knock on ' yourself that the Word ' may open for you. For he [10] is the Ruler of Faith and ' the Sharp Sword, having become all ' for every one because he wishes ' to have mercy on every one.

My son, ' prepare yourself to escape from the [15] world-rulers of darkness and of ' this sort of air which is full of powers. ' But if you have ' Christ, you will conquer this entire world. ' That which you will open [20] for yourself, you will open. ' That which you will knock upon for yourself, you will ' knock upon, benefiting yourself. '

Help yourself, my son, ' (by) not proceeding with things in which [25] there is no profit.

My son, ' first purify yourself toward the outward life ' in order that you may be able ' to purify the inward.

And ' be not as the merchants [30] of the Word of God.

Put ' all words to the test first ' before you utter them. '

Do not wish to acquire honors which ' are insecure, nor **118** the boastfulness which brings ' you to perdition.

Accept ' the wisdom of Christ (who is) patient ' and mild, and guard [5] this, O my son, knowing ' that God's way is always ' profitable. '

* * * * * * *

Jesus Christ, Son of God, Savior (Ichthus), Wonder '
Extraordinary

THE THREE STELES OF SETH (VII, 5)

Introduced and translated by

JAMES M. ROBINSON

Edited by

FREDERIK WISSE

In Genesis, after the tragic story of Cain and Abel, Seth was a new beginning for a human race made in Adam's likeness, as Adam was made in God's; it was when Seth's lineage developed that "men began to invoke the Lord by name" (Genesis 4:25-5:8). Thus Gnostics identified Seth as the ancestor through whom the primal revelation of God to Adam was transmitted, as in the *Apocalypse of Adam* (V, 5). The Jewish historian Josephus records the legend that Seth's descendents, who discovered astrology, knew from Adam that there would be two cosmic disasters, one by fire and one by flood. Hence they inscribed for posterity their knowledge on two steles, one of brick that would survive the fire and one of stone that would survive the flood. If the pair of disasters could lead to the concept of two steles, the triad in the nature of God in Neoplatonic theology led to the concept of three steles. The tractate *Zostrianos* (VIII, 1) reflects this development, and concludes with the remark, "I wrote three tablets and left them as knowledge for those who come after me, the living elect. ... Know those who are alive and the holy seed of Seth."

The designation of the *Three Steles of Seth* in the opening line as a "revelation of Dositheos" (whose name occurs only here in the tractate) may have in view the obscure Samaritan who came to be related to Simon Magus as a founder of Gnosticism, and perhaps reflects some relation of the Sethians to Samaritan traditions.

The opening and closing phrases of the *Three Steles of Seth* refer to it as a revelation, though it does not consist of a narrative of things shown during an ecstatic trip through the heavens, but rather of the hymnic prayers accompanying such a trip. As *Zostrianos* puts it, "I joined with all of them and blessed the Hidden Aeon and the Virgin Barbelo and the Invisible Spirit. I became all-perfect." The three subdivisions of the tractate, corresponding to the threefold nature of God, seem also to correspond to three stages or levels in the ecstatic ascent of the worshipper, since at the conclusion of the tractate one must return from the third back down to the second and first.

The Jewish and Sethian liturgical background of the tractate is remarkably merged with Neoplatonic philosophical terminology, especially the Existence-Life-Mind triad in the deity. This vocabulary is also found in other tractates such as *Zostrianos* and *Allogenes* (XI, 3), tractates listed by Porphyry in his *Life of Plotinus* as Gnostic texts refuted by Plotinus' school. Thus this cluster of Nag Hammadi tractates will illumine this aspect of the background of

Neoplatonism. Such an association will also serve to provide a dating for this material prior to Plotinus' course "Against the Gnostics" in the school year 265-266 C.E.

A scribal note following the subscript title of the tractate at 127, 28-32 is a colophon probably intended to apply to the codex as a whole.

THE THREE STELES OF SETH
VII 118, 10-127, 27
127, 28-32

The revelation of Dositheos ' about the three steles ' of Seth, the Father of the living ' and unshakable race, which ' he (Dositheos) saw and understood. [15] And after he had read them, he ' remembered them. And he gave them ' to the elect, just ' as they were ' inscribed there. [20]

Many times I joined in ' giving glory with the powers, and I became ' worthy, through them, of the ' immeasurable majesties. '

Now they (the steles) are as follows:

The First [25]
Stele of Seth.

I bless ' thee, Father, Geradama(s), I, ' as thine (own) Son, ' Emmacha Seth, whom thou didst beget ' unconceived, as a blessing [30] of our God; for I am ' thine (own) Son. And thou **119** art my mind, O my Father. And ' I, I sowed and begot; ' [but] thou hast [seen] the majesties. ' Thou hast stood, being unceasing. I [5] bless thee, Father. Bless me, ' Father. It is because of thee that I exist; ' it is because of God that thou dost exist. Because ' of thee I am with ' that very one. Thou art light, [10] since thou beholdest light. Thou hast ' revealed light. Thou art ' Mirotheas; thou art my Mirotheos. ' I bless thee as ' God; I bless thy [15] divinity. Great is the ' good Self-begotten who ' stood, the God who was first ' to stand. Thou didst come in goodness; ' thou hast appeared, and thou hast [20] revealed goodness. I shall utter ' thy name, for thou art a first ' name. Thou art unconceived. Thou ' hast appeared in order that thou ' mightest reveal the eternal ones. [25] Thou art he who is. Therefore ' thou hast revealed those who really ' are. Thou art he who is uttered ' by a voice, ' but by mind art thou [30] glorified, thou who hast ' dominion everywhere. Therefore ' [the] perceptible world too ' knows thee because of ' thee and thy seed. Thou art merciful. **120**

And thou art from another race, ' and its place is over another race. ' And now thou art from another ' race, and its [place is] over another [5] race. Thou art from another ' race, for thou art not similar. And thou ' art merciful, for thou art eternal. ' And thy place is over a race, ' for thou hast caused all these to increase, though because of [10] my seed. For it is thou who knows ' it, that its place is in begetting. But they ' are from other races, for ' they are not similar. But their place is over ' other races, for their place is in [15] life. Thou art Mirotheos. '

I bless his power which was ' given to me, who caused the ' malenesses that really are to become ' male three times, [20] who was divided into the pentad, the one who ' was given to us in triple ' power, the one who was begotten ' unconceived, the one who ' came from what is select; because of [25] what is humble, he went ' forth in the midst.

Thou art a Father ' through a Father, ' a word from a command. ' We bless thee, Thrice Male, [30] for thou didst unite the all ' through them all, for thou hast ' empowered us. Thou hast come from ' one through one; thou hast moved, ' thou hast come to one. [Thou] hast saved, [35] thou hast saved, thou hast saved us, O ' crown-bearer, crown-giver! **121** We bless thee eternally. ' We bless thee, once we have ' been saved, as the perfect individuals, ' perfect on account [5] of thee, those who [became] perfect with thee ' who is complete, who completes, ' the one perfect through all these, ' who is similar everywhere, Thrice ' Male.

Thou hast stood. Thou wast first [10] to stand. Thou wast divided everywhere. ' Thou didst continue being one. And ' those whom thou hast willed, thou hast saved. ' But thou dost will to be saved ' all who are worthy.

Thou art [15] perfect! Thou art perfect! ' Thou art perfect!

The First '
Stele of Seth '

The Second Stele '
of Seth [20]

Great is the first aeon, ' male virginal Barbelo, ' the first glory ' of the invisible Father, she ' who is called [25] "perfect."

Thou (fem.) hast seen first ' him who really preexists, ' that he is non-being. And ' from him and through ' him thou hast preexisted [30] eternally, the non-being ' from one indivisible, ' triple [power], thou a triple ' power, [thou a] great monad ' from [a] pure monad, **122** thou an elect monad, the ' first [shadow] of the holy ' Father, light from ' light.

[We] bless thee, [5] producer (fem.) of perfection, aeon-giver (fem.). ' Thou hast [seen] the eternal ' ones, that they are from a shadow. ' And thou hast become numerable. And ' thou didst find, thou didst continue being [10] one (fem.); yet becoming numerable in division, thou ' art three-fold. Thou art truly ' thrice, thou one (fem.) ' of the one (masc.). And thou art from ' a shadow of him, thou a Hidden One, [15] thou a world of understanding, ' knowing those of the one, that they ' are from a shadow. And these ' are thine in the heart.

For ' their sake thou hast empowered the eternals [20] in being; thou hast empowered ' divinity in living; ' thou hast empowered knowledge in ' goodness; in ' blessedness thou hast empowered the [25] shadows which pour from the one. ' Thou hast empowered this (one) in knowing; ' thou hast empowered another one in creating. ' Thou hast empowered him who is equal ' and him who is not equal, him [30] who is similar and him who is not similar. ' Thou hast empowered in begetting, and ' (pro-vided) forms in [that which] is ' to others. [.... ' Thou hast] empowered 123 these.—He is that One Hidden ' [in] the heart.—And [thou hast] come forth to ' these and [from] these. Thou art divided ' [among them]. And thou dost [5] become a great male [noetic] First-Appearer. '

Fatherly God, ' divine child, ' begetter of multiplicity according to a division ' of all who really are, [10] thou (masc.) hast appeared to them all in ' a word. And thou (masc.) dost possess ' them all unconceived ' and eternally indestructible ' on account of thee (fem.). [15]

Salvation has come to us; from ' thee is salvation. Thou art ' wisdom, thou knowledge; thou ' art truthfulness. On account of thee is ' life; from thee is life. [20] On account of thee is mind; from ' thee is mind. Thou art a mind, ' thou a world of truthfulness, ' thou a triple power, thou ' threefold. Truly thou art [25] thrice, the aeon of ' aeons. It is thou only ' who sees purely the first ' eternal ones and the unconceived ones. '

But the first divisions are as [30] thou wast divided. Unite us ' as thou hast been united. ' Teach us [those] things which thou dost see. ' Em-power [us] that we may 124 be saved to eternal life. ' For [we] are [each] a shadow ' of thee as thou art ' a shadow [of that] [5] first preexistent one. Hear ' us first. We are eternal ones. ' Hear us as the ' perfect indi-viduals. Thou art the aeon ' of aeons, the all-perfect one [10] who is established.

Thou hast heard! ' Thou hast heard!
Thou hast saved! Thou hast saved! '
We give thanks! We bless always! ' We shall glorify thee! '

The Second Stele [15]
of Seth '

The Third Stele '

We rejoice! We rejoice! We rejoice! '

We have seen! We have seen! We have seen the ' really preexistent one (masc.) [20] really existing, being the ' first eternal one.

O Unconceived, ' from thee are the eternal ones ' and the aeons, the all-perfect ones ' who are established, and the [25] perfect individuals.

We bless ' thee, non-being, existence ' which is before existences, ' first being which is before ' beings, Father of [30] divinity and life, ' creator of mind, ' giver of good, giver of ' blessedness!

We all bless ' thee, knower, in [35] a [humble] blessing, (thou) **125** because of whom [all these are. ' ... really, ' ...], who knows thee ' [through] thee alone. For there is no one [5] [who is] active before ' thee. Thou art an only and living [spirit]. ' And [thou] knowest one, ' for this one who belongs to thee is on every side. ' We are not able to express him. For [10] thy light shines upon us. '

Present a command to us ' to see thee, so that ' we may be saved. Knowledge of thee, it ' is the salvation of us all. Present [15] a command! When thou dost command, ' we have been saved! Truly we have been ' saved! We have seen thee by mind! ' Thou art them all, for thou dost save ' them all, he who [20] was not saved, nor was he ' saved through them. ' For thou, thou hast commanded us. '

Thou art one, thou art one, just as ' there is one (who) will say [25] to thee: Thou art one, thou art a single living spirit. ' How shall we give ' thee a name? We do not have it. ' For thou art the existence ' of them all. [30] Thou art the life of them ' all. Thou art the mind ' of them all. ' [For] thou [art he in whom they all] rejoice. **126**

Thou hast commanded all these ' [to be saved] through thy ' word [...] ' glory [5] who is before him, Hidden One, blessed ' Senaon, [he who begat] ' himself, [Asi]neu(s), ' [...]ephneu(s), Optaon, Elemaon ' the great power, Emouniar, [10] Nibareu(s), Kandephor(os), Aphredon, ' Deiphaneus, thou ' who art Armedon to me, power-begetter, ' Thalanatheu(s), Antitheus, ' thou who existeth within [15] thyself, thou who art before ' thyself—and after thee ' no one entered into activity.

As what shall we ' bless thee? We are ' not empowered. But we give thanks, [20] as being humble toward thee. For thou hast ' commanded us, as he who ' is elect, to glorify thee to the extent that ' we are able. ' We bless thee, for we were saved. [25] Always we glorify ' thee. For this reason we shall ' glorify thee, that we may be ' saved to eternal salvation. ' We have blessed thee, for we are [30] empowered. We have been saved, for thou ' hast willed always ' that we all do this.

We ' all did this. [. . .] ' not through [. . . **127** ³ aeon. . . .], ' the one who was ⁵ [. . .], we and those ' who [. . .]. He who will ' remember these and give ' glory always will ' become perfect among those who are perfect ¹⁰ and unattainable from ' any quarter. For they all bless ' these individually and together. ' And afterwards they shall be ' silent. And just as they ¹⁵ were ordained, they ascend. ' After the silence, they descend. ' From the third ' they bless the second; ' after these the first. ²⁰ The way of ascent is the way ' of descent.

Know therefore, ' as those who live, that you have ' attained. And you taught ' yourselves the infinite things. ²⁵ Marvel at the truth which is within ' them, and (at) the revelation. '

The Three Steles of Seth. '

* * * * * * *

This book belongs to the fatherhood. '
It is the son who wrote it. ³⁰
Bless me, O father. I bless '
you, O father, in peace. '
Amen.

ZOSTRIANOS (VIII, *1*)

Introduced and translated by

JOHN H. SIEBER

The longest tractate in the Nag Hammadi library, *Zostrianos* occupies the first 132 pages of Codex VIII. Many of the pages, however, have deteriorated badly. Such extensive deterioration means that a lucid translation of the entire document is often difficult or even impossible. Furthermore, the opening lines of the tractate are missing, so that the ancient title of the treatise cannot be precisely determined. Yet the name Zostrianos may very well have been a part of the original title; in any case, the text clearly presents Zostrianos as the hero of the story.

The use of the name of Zostrianos, as well as that of Zoroaster in the final cryptogram, is particularly interesting. Indeed, the name Zoroaster was a famous and important name during the Hellenistic period: Zoroaster was recognized as founder of the Persian religious tradition of Zoroastrianism, but he was also connected with all sorts of philosophical, speculative, and magical systems. In addition, a link between the names of Zoroaster and Zostrianos is known from the church father Arnobius and from the Neo-platonic author Porphyry. The latter, in his important *Life of Plotinus*, even refers to an apocalypse or book of Zostrianos, a book which almost certainly should be identified as the present tractate in Codex VIII.

Another interesting feature of the tractate is the absence of any Christian references. Such is the case even in the names of the angels and powers, though some names and ideas can be traced back ultimately to the Old Testament. Thus, *Zostrianos* is an example of non-Christian Gnosticism, a Gnosticism with a philosophical tendency and a powerful message.

Zostrianos presents a series of revelations made by exalted beings regarding the nature of the heavenly realm. After an account of the initial troubling questions raised by Zostrianos, the tractate proceeds to describe the visit of the angel of the knowledge of the eternal All, a guide for the heavenly journey which ensues. In his ascent through the various levels of the aeons, Zostrianos is baptized in the names of the heavenly powers, and is instructed in the names and relationships of the numerous inhabitants of the heavenly world. The chief divine being is the Triple Powerful Invisible Spirit; the divine emanations include the Virgin Barbelo, the three great aeons (the Hidden One, the First-Appearing One, and the Self-begotten One), and many others. After his glorious heavenly experiences, Zostrianos returns to the world of perception, writes his knowledge on three tablets, and preaches the liberating salvation of light and knowledge, "the salvation of masculinity."

ZOSTRIANOS

VIII 1, 1-132, 9

[...] the words ' [...] eternal to me, I ' [...] Zos[trianos ' ...] and Yolaos. [5]

It was for these ' [who are] like me and [those] who are after me, ' the living elect, that I was in the world. The god ' [...] truth is truly alive in righteousness ' [and] knowledge [...] and eternal light. [10]

After having separated from the somatic ' darkness in me and the ' psychic chaos in mind ' and the femininity of desire ' in the darkness, I did not use it again [15] because I had found the unattainable part ' of my matter. I reproved the ' dead creation within me ' and the divine cosmocrator ' of the perceptible world, having preached powerfully [20] of the All to those ' who have alien parts. '

Although for a little while I undertook ' their ways, such as ' the necessity of the begetting of the [25] revealer, I was never pleased ' with them; but rather I always ' separated myself from them ' because I came into being through a ' holy and mixed [...], [30] having set straight my sinless ' soul. I strengthened 2 the intellectual [...] ' and I [...] ' in the [...] ' of my god [...] [5] I having [...] ' power from a holy spirit ' higher than god.

He came ' upon me alone, after I set myself straight. ' I saw the perfect child. [10] It was he who [...]. And with one who [...] ' many times and in a multitude of [ways ' he] appeared to me like a ' willing father as I was seeking the male ' father of all these. [He is] [15] in a thought and a perception, in a ' form, a race, a region ' and an All with one who ' restrains and is restrained, ' and a body and bodiless, [20] and essence and matter, ' of them all.

And Existence ' is mixed with them and the Hidden ' God who is unborn and the power ' from them all. Now concerning Existence: [25] How do those who exist, who are from ' the aeon of those who exist, come from ' an invisible spirit and from ' the undivided self-begotten, who are three ' unborn likenesses, having [30] an origin better than existence ' and existing prior to [all these] ' but having come into being as [world]? ' And how do those opposite him and all these 3 [...] good, ' [...] and excuse? ' What is the place of ' that one there? What is his origin? [5] How does the coming forth ' exist for him and all these? How ' does [he] become a simple one differing ' only from himself, existing as ' Existence and Form and [10] Blessedness, and giving strength ' as one alive with life? How has ' Existence which does not exist ' appeared in an existing power? '

I was pondering these matters in order to understand them. [15] I kept bringing them up daily ' to the god of my fathers according to the custom of my race; ' I kept speaking the praise ' of all these, for my forefathers ' who sought found. [20] As for me, I did not cease seeking ' a place of rest worthy of my spirit, ' as I was not yet bound in the perceptible ' world. Then, while I was deeply troubled ' and gloomy because of the [25] discouragement which encompassed me, I ' dared to do something and to ' deliver myself to the beasts of the desert ' for a violent death.

There stood ' before me the messenger of the knowledge of [30] the eternal Light. He said to me, ' "Zostrianos, why have you gone mad, ' as if you were ignorant of the eternal great ones **4** who are above? [...] ' to you [...] ' and [...] ' in order that you might save now [...] [5] indeed in eternal destruction, nor [...] ' those [whom] you know in order that ' you might save others, who ' are the father of the exalted, my chosen ones. ' Do you remember that you are the father of [your race], [10] or that Yolaos is your father? [...] ' a messenger of god [...] ' to you through holy men. ' Come and pass through these ' very ones to whom you will return again, [15] to preach to a living generation ' and to save those who are ' worthy and to strengthen the elect, ' because the struggle of the aeon is great ' but the time in this place is short." [20]

When he said these things to me, ' I very quickly and very ' gladly went up with him ' to a great light-cloud. I [cast] ' my body on the earth guarded [25] by glories; I was ' rescued from the whole world ' and the thirteen aeons ' in it and their angelic beings. ' They did not see us, but their archon [30] was disturbed at [our passage], ' for the [light]-cloud **5** [...] is better ' than every worldly one. ' Its beauty is ineffable. ' With strength it provides light, [5] [guiding] pure spirits ' as a spirit-savior ' [and] an intellectual word, [unlike] ' those in the world ' [...] of changeable matter [10] and an upsetting word. '

Then I knew that the power ' within me was set over the darkness ' because it contained the whole light. ' I was baptized there and [15] I received the image of the glories there. ' I became like ' one of them. I left the ' airy [earth] and passed by the ' copies of aeons, after washing [20] there seven times ' in a living [water], one for each ' of the aeons. I did not cease ' until I saw all the waters once. '

I ascended to the Transmigration [25] which [really] exists. I was baptized and ' [...] world. I ascended to the ' Repentance which [really] exists ' [and was] baptized there ' four times. I passed by the **6** sixth [aeon ...]. ' I ascended to the [...]. ' I stood there having seen a light ' of the truth, which [really] exists from its [5] self-begotten root, and ' great messengers and glories [. . .] ' in measure.

I was baptized in the name of ' the Self-begotten God by ' these powers which are upon [10] living waters, Michar and Mi[chea]. ' I was purified by [the] ' great Barpharanges. Then [they revealed] ' themselves to me and wrote me in the glory. ' I was sealed by [15] those who are on those powers, Michar ⟨and⟩ ' Mi[ch]eus and Seldao and Ele[nos] ' and Zogenethlos. I became ' a root-seeing messenger ' and stood upon the first [20] aeon which is the fourth. ' With the souls I blessed the Self-begotten ' God and the forefather, ' Geradama(s) [. . .] ' the self-begotten, the [first] perfect [man], [25] and Seth Emmach[a Seth], ' the son of [A]damas, the [father of ' the immovable] race, and the [four ' lights . . .], [30] and Mirothea, the mother [. . .] ' and eminence [. . .] ' of the lights and De[. . .]. 7

I was ' [baptized] for the second time in the name ' of the Self-begotten God ' by these same powers. I became [5] a messenger of ' the perfect male race. I stood upon ' the second aeon which is the ' third. With the sons of ' [S]eth I blessed all these.

I was [10] baptized for the third time in ' the name of the Self-begotten God ' by these same powers. ' I became a holy messenger. ' I stood upon the third [15] aeon which is the second. I ' [blessed] all these.

I was baptized ' for the fourth time by ' these same powers. I became ' a perfect [messenger. [20] I stood upon] the fourth aeon ' [which is the first] and ' [blessed all these].

Then I sought [. . .] [28] why [. . .] ' in the power [. . .] [30] them in another way in [. . .] 8 of mankind. Are [these same ones their] ' powers? Or, are these indeed the ones but are their names ' different from one another? Is there ' soul different from soul? [5] Why are men different ' from one another? With whom and how many ' are in fact mankind?

The great one ' who rules the height, Authrounios, said to me, ' "Are you asking about those [10] whom you have passed by? Concerning ' this airy earth—why it has ' a cosmic model? ' Concerning the aeon copies—' how many they are? Why they are [not] afflicted? [15] Concerning the Transmigration and the ' Repentance and the Creation of [aeons] ' and the world which [. . .] ' really, openly [. . .] ' you. Concerning [. . .] [20] me, to them [. . .] ' nor [. . .] ' to you [. . .] ' invisible [spirit . . .]." 9

The great one who rules the height, ' Authrounios, said [to me]," The ' airy earth came into being by a ' word, but to the begotten ones and those who [5] are perishable it appears ' in imperishability. Concerning

the coming ' of the great judges, they came not in order to ' taste perception and to ' surround the creation, but it was [10] because of him that
they came and saw ' the works of the world by him, ' condemning its
ruler to destruction ' as a model of the world ' [. . .] and an origin of
matter [15] [begotten] of lost darkness. '

"But when Sophia looked at these same ones, ' she produced the
darkness, since she ' [. . .] beside the ' [. . .] he is a model [20] [. . .] of
essence ' [. . .] form ' [. . .] to an image [. . .] [24] the all [. . .] [27] darkness
[. . .] ' say [. . .] the powers ' [. . .] aeon of creation to [30] see some of the
eternal ones, **10** he saw a [reflection and] with ' the reflection which he
[saw] ' in it he created the world. ' With a reflection of a [5] reflection
he worked on the world, ' and the reflection of the ' appearance was
taken from him. ' But a place of rest was given to Sophia ' in exchange
for her repentance. [10] Thus there was within her ' no prior reflection,
pure ' in itself, beforehand.

"After they had already ' come into being through him, he ' appeared
and worked on the remainder also, [15] for the image of Sophi[a] ' was
[lost] every time because her ' countenance was deceiving. But the
Archon [. . .] ' and he becomes body [. . .] ' concerning the greater
[. . .] [20] down [. . .] ' when I saw [. . .] [29] perfect [. . .] [31] through him
having **11** [revealed] the destruction of the world ' in [immutability].
It is ' in this way that the copies of the aeons exist. ' They have not [5]
reached an appearance of a single power; ' they do have eternal glories. '
They are in ' the places of judgment of each ' of the powers.

"But when the [10] souls received light through ' the light which is in
them and ' the model which comes into being ' in them often without '
[suffering], she thought that she saw [15] [. . .] and the eternal ' [. . .] in
the blessed ' [. . .] of the single one ' [. . .] each one of ' [. . .] light
which [20] [. . .] and that one ' [. . .] every one and that one [. . .] [29] of
repentance. Souls **12** according to the power [in them] ' stand [. . .] '
humble, they are trained ' by those copies [5] which receive a model of '
their souls, still existing in the ' world after the departure ' of the aeons,
one by one. They ' come into being and are removed, [10] one by one,
first from the ' copy of the transmigration up ' to the Transmigration
which really exists, ' then from the copy of ' repentance up to the
Repentance [15] which really exists, and from the ' copy of the Self-
begotten up to the ' [. . .] which really exists, ' and so forth [. . .] ' the
souls [. . .] [20] exist in [. . .] ' all [. . .] ' copies of aeons [. . .] **13** bless god
who is above ' the great aeons and the unborn ' Hidden One, and the
great male, ' First-Appearing One and that perfect [5] Child who is
higher than god, ' and his eye, Geradama(s)." '

1 called upon the ' child of the child, Ephesech. He ' stood before me and said, [10] "It is I who am the messenger of god, the son ' of the Father, the Perfect Man. ' Why are you calling me and ' asking about those whom you know, ' when you [. . .] them?" As for me, [15] [I said], "I have asked about the ' mixture [. . .] it is perfect and gives ' [. . .] has power in which ' [. . .] were baptized ' [. . .] these names are [20] [different . . .] and why [. . .] [24] mankind ' [. . .] different [. . .]." **14**

He said, "[Zost]rianos, ' listen about these [. . .] ' for the first [. . .] ' origins are three because they appeared [5] from a single origin [. . .] the ' aeon Barbelo, not like ' some origins and powers ' nor like one from an origin ' and power, having appeared [10] as every origin. They strengthened every power ' and they appeared from that which ' is far better than they, that is, ' Existence and Blessedness ' and Life [. . .] [15] and [one another . . .] ' from [. . .]. ' Concerning the [. . .] ' after they have named [. . .] ' greater [. . .] [21] perfect [. . .].

"[. . .] **15** namely a water of ' each of them. Therefore, ' [. . .] waters are perfect. ' It is the [water] of Life which [5] belongs to Vitality in which you now ' have been baptized in the Self-begotten One. ' It is the [water] of Blessedness ' which [belongs to] knowledge in which ' you will be baptized in the First-Appearing One. [10] It is the water of Existence ' [which] belongs to Divinity ' and the Hidden One. ' The water of Life [is ' . . .] a power, the water belonging [15] to Blessedness according to Essence, and the water ' belonging to [Divinity] according to ' [Existence]. All these ' [. . .] power and some ' [. . .] those which [20] [. . .] water which ' becomes pure [. . .].

"[. . .] **16** Existence as [he] is in it. ' [He] not only [dwells] in ' thought, but he [. . .] ' them that it is he who is the [. . .] [5] in this manner, he keeping a [. . .] upon ' that which is, in order that he might not come into being ' as unattainable and formless. ' But when they have crossed [it], being truly ' young, in order that [he] might come into being [10] as someone, [. . .] has ' that which is his own [. . .] ' Existence and the [Son], he stands ' with him [seeking] with him, ' surrounding him [. . .] [15] on every side [. . .] ' from the truth [. . .] ' takes him who [. . .] ' exist [. . .] ' activity [. . .] [20] life [. . .] ' his word also [. . .] ' are these [. . .] ' they [came into being . . .]. **17**

"The power is with the ' Essence and Existence of ' Being, when the water exists; ' but the name in which they wash [5] is a word of the water. ' Therefore, the first perfect water of ' the [Triple Powerful] Self-begotten ' is a life of the perfect soul, ' for it is a word of [10] the perfect God, when he comes ' into being [. . .] that, for ' the Invisible Spirit is a fountain ' of all these who are likewise ' from knowledge, being likenesses [15] of him. [But] he who knows ' that [...] what sort of and what ' [...] live at one time ' [...] lives within a ' [...] is the [20] [...] life. In the ' [... comes into being] as ' [unattainable ...] ' the name [...] **18** he really exists; it is he who ' limits himself. Those [...] come ' up to the water according to [this] single ' power and the unborn likeness of order. [5]

"The great male invisible ' perfect Mind, the First-Appearing One, ' has his own water, ' as you [will see] when you arrive ' at his place. [10] This is also the case with the unborn Hidden One. ' In relation to each one is ' a partial first form, ' in order that they may be perfect in this way; ' for the four self-begotten aeons [15] are perfect single ones ' of the all-perfect ones [... exist] ' these as the [perfect] single ones. The ' five aeons [...] ' of the Self-begotten One [...] [20] for all these [...] ' male of [...] ' for the Alls [...] ' perfect god [... ' the triple male ...] [25] perfect single ones [...] ' in the [...] **19** perfect, those who are according to a ' form and a race and a ' totality and a partial difference. ' This is also the case with the highway [5] of ascent which is higher than perfect and the Hidden One. '

"The Self-begotten God ' is the chief archon of ' his aeons and of messengers ' as his parts; for those [10] who are four in him ' individually create the fifth aeon ' at one time. The fifth aeon exists ' in one. It is the ' four who [are] the fifth, part by part, [15] [...] they are not perfect ' individually having a ' [...] also exists ' [... male] according to one ' [...] for it is [20] [...] god ' [...] the ' [...] and invisible [...] male Mind ' [...] which exists [...] **20** living and perfect parts. '

"(Concerning) the All and the ' all-perfect race and that one who is higher than perfect ' and blessed: [5] The Self-begotten Hidden One ' pre-exists, because he is an origin ' of the Self-begotten One, a god and ' a forefather, a cause of the ' First-Appearing One, a father [10] of his parts, a ' father-god, a ' foreknowledge. Yet he is unknown, ' for he is a power and ' a father from himself. [15] Therefore he is [fatherless]. The ' Invisible Triple Powerful, the ' first Thought [of] all [these], ' is the Invisible Spirit [...] ' he is, and [...] [20] Essence [...] ' and Existence [...] ' there are [existences ...] ' life [...] ' blessed [... **21** exist] in them. [...] ' in others, they [...] ' by them all ' in many places, the place which he [5] desired and the place which he wishes, ' since they are in every place, yet ' not in any place, and since they ' make room for their spirits, ' for they are incorporeal and better than [10] incorporeal. They are undivided ' and living thoughts and a power ' of the truth with those who are purer by far ' than these, since they exist as exceedingly ' pure with respect to him and are [15] not like the bodies which exist ' in one [place]. ' Above all, they have ' a necessity either according to the All or ' according to a portion. Then the way of ascent [20] [...] pure ' [...] each [...] **22** partial aeons." '

[I said], "How can he ' contain an eternal model? ' And how does the [5] intellectual universal share ' when the self-begotten water ' is complete? ' If he knows him and ' all these, is he the water of the First-Appearing One? [10] If he joins ' with him and all ' these, does he belong to the Hidden One, ' this image again which is in ' the aeons?"

"To know [them] individually [15] and the parts [...] those ' of the All where there is knowledge. ' They were divided from him ' whom they know [and] ' a fellowship which they have [20] in one another. The All and ' all these [...] ' baptism of the [self-begotten water ...] **23** there he appears from [him], ' that is, because he knew how ' he exists for him. He has ' fellowship with their companions. [5] He washed in the washing ' of the First-Appearing One. '

"By knowing the origin of these, ' how they all appear ' in a single head and how [10] they all are joined and divided, ' and how those who ' have been divided join again, ' and how the parts ' [join] with the wholes and the [15] species and [races]—' if one knows these things, he has washed ' in the washing of the Hidden One.

"In accordance with ' each of the places he ' has a share of [20] the Eternal One. He goes ' to [...] as he ' [... pure], simple ' always [...] to ' one, the [...] [25] he being purer than single. ' He is filled [...] ' in existence [...] ' and a [holy] spirit and **24** nothing outside of him. He can ' see, and in a perfect soul he sees ' those belonging to the Self-begotten Ones. In a mind ' he sees those belonging to the Triple Male. In a [5] holy spirit he sees those belonging to the First-Appearing One. ' He hears about the Hidden One ' from the powers of the spirit from ' which they have come forth in a far better ' revelation of the Invisible Spirit. [10] It is in the thought ' which now exists in silence and in ' the First Thought.

"Concerning the Triple ' Powerful Invisible Spirit, he is a hearing ' and a power of pure silence [15] in an enlivening spirit, ' the perfect one and a perfect [...] ' and all-perfect. ' Therefore, the glories which are set over ' these are [life-givers] who have [20] received the baptism of truth and knowledge. ' Those who are worthy [guard] ' them, but those who are not from ' this race [...] ' and they [go ...] [25] their [...] ' from the fifth since he [...] ' copy ' [...] of the aeons ' [...] a baptism [30] [...].

"But if ' [one] strips off the world **25** and lays aside [knowledge]—'

on the one hand, if he is one who does not ' have a dwelling place and power, ' [then] he follows the affairs of [5] others and is a sojourner; but on the other hand, if he is one who ' has committed no sin, since knowledge ' is sufficient for them, (and) takes no ' heed of anything and repents, ' then washings are appointed [10] in these as before.

"Concerning ' the path to the Self-begotten Ones, ' into whom you have now been baptized every ' time, a path which is worthy of seeing the [perfect] individuals: ' Since it has come into being [15] from the powers of the Self-begotten, ' it is knowledge [of] the All, ' knowledge which you acquire when you pass ' through the all-perfect aeons. ' And the third washing, if you should [20] wash [...] you would hear ' [...] really there ' [...]. Because of [these] names they ' exist in this way, ' but he is one [...] [25] is like [...] ' while they exist [...] ' exist and [...] ' a word [...]. [26] It is really an existing name ' [...] which are in it. '

"Those who are [safe] ' from the one he resembles do exist. [5] His resemblance in race is within that which ' is his own. He sees and understands ' and enters it and ' receives a resemblance from it. They can ' speak and hear audibly but cannot [10] obey because they are perceptible, ' somatic beings, as ' indeed, although they can contain them, ' they will contain them in this way. ' It is a reflection which is [distorted] in this way [15] because it comes ' from perception in a word. ' It is better than material ' nature but humbler than an intellectual ' essence.

"Do not be amazed [20] on account of the difference of the souls. ' When they think that they are ' different, they do [not know ...] ' of those who [...] ' that [...] he [...] [25] audibly [...] being lost [...] [27] body. But he ' who [...] time ' [...] desire [27] their soul exists as [...] ' their body. The [pure] ones ' from the All are four [...] ' which they have. Each of the nine [5] within time ' has her form ' and her custom. Although they are alike, ' they differ because they are separated, and ' they stand.

"Other immortal souls [10] are companions with ' all these souls because of ' [So]phia who looked down; ' for there are three forms of ' [immortal] souls: those who have [15] taken root upon the transmigration ' because they cannot ' beget, an ability which belongs only to those ' who dwell in works ' of others—because he is a [20] form, he is their ' [...]—; those who ' stand upon repentance which ' [...] sin, ' she sufficing [...] knowledge, [25] they being young [...] '—and he has [...] ' difference [...]—they ' sinned with some [...] [28] they repented with others ' [...] them alone, ' for [...] form which exists ' [...]; and those who have committed [5] all sins, and they repented. ' Either they are parts, or since ' they cry out alone because of ' him, their other aeons ' are six according to the place which is reached for [10] them in each of them. '

"The third form is the one that belongs to the souls ' of the self-begotten ones having ' a word of the ineffable truth, ' which exists in [15] knowledge and [power] from ' them alone and eternal [. . .]. ' They have four ' differences as indeed there ' are the forms of the messengers, [20] and those who love the truth ' and those who [hope] and those ' who believe, having [. . .] ' and they exist [. . .] ' they exist [. . .] [25] the self-begotten ones [. . .] ' he is my [. . .] that ' [. . .] is the ' [. . .] knowledge ' [. . .] the fourth [30] [. . .] is immortal [soul]. **29**

"In this way there exist [. . .] ' four lights: [Arm]ozel, a ' division of god [. . .] of truth ' and a joining of soul, is [5] [set] over the first aeon; ' Oroiael, a powerful seer ' of the truth, is set over the ' second; Daveithe, a vision ' of knowledge, is set over [10] the third; and Eleleth, an impulse ' and a preparation for the truth, ' is set over the fourth. ' The four exist because they are ' words of the truth and [15] knowledge. They do not belong to ' the First-Appearing One but ' to the mother and a thought of ' the [perfect] Mind of ' Light, letting immortal souls [20] contain them as knowledge. ' [. . .] these the self-begotten [. . .] [23] all ' [. . .] is a word [. . .] [25] ineffable [. . .] truth, ' that one which says [. . .] appears ' because of him [. . .] ' that he exists [. . .] ' exists above in [. . .] **30** in a yoking, she ' [. . .] in a light ' [. . .] and a thought in ' a [. . .] of his.

"Adamas is the [5] [perfect] man because he is the eye of ' the Self-begotten, an ascending knowledge of his, ' because the Self-begotten God is a ' word of the perfect Mind ' of the Truth. The son of [10] Adaman, Seth, comes to ' each of the souls, because he is knowledge ' sufficient for them. Therefore, ' a living seed came ' from him.

"Mirothea is [. . .] [15] the Self-begotten God [. . .] ' from her and [. . .] ' and a thought of the perfect Mind because of ' that which is hers, [Existence]—what it is, ' how it was existing, [20] that it does exist. Therefore ' the Self-begotten God is ' word and knowledge. The ' knowledge [. . .] word ' therefore [. . .] [25] Adama[s . . .] ' of the [simple ones] when she appeared ' [. . .] a change of the ' souls [. . .] is herself ' [. . . perfect], because of the [30] [perfect ones—. . .] the angelic beings [. . .].

"[. . .] **31** [3] soul [. . .] [6] the copies ' [. . .] really ' [. . .] which exists ' [. . .] repentance [10] [. . .] to this place ' [. . .] which exists ' [. . .] aeons if ' [. . .] and she loves ' [. . .] she stands upon [15] [. . .] aeon, they ' having the light ' E[le]leth [. . .] become a ' [. . .] seer of god ' if she hopes and sees [20] [. . .] and race ' [. . .] she stands upon [. . .] **32** chosen [. . .] ' she stands [. . .] [4] the light ' Ar[mozel . . .].

"[...] [8] upon the power [...] ' you stand upon [...] [10] the light which [...] ' and the [unmeasured ...] ' the aeon is great [...] ' those alone [...] ' from the perfect [...] [15] that power [...] ' be able or [...] ' be able [...] of a [...] ' every [...] his soul [...] ' perceptible [...] [20] but you are [...] ' individually [...] ' since there is nothing [...] ' him [...] ' which he [...] 33 and [...] ' upon every [...] ' every [...] ' form [...] [5] and this one ' [...] and this model ' [...] there is nothing ' [...] either ' [...] which an All [10] [...] unceasing from this ' [...] he being light in weight ' [...] he having lacked it ' [...] the perfect Mind ' [...] undivided [15] [...] perfect light ' [...] and he exists in ' [... A]damas and ' [...] the self-begotten ' [...] and he goes [20] [...] mind ' [...] the Hidden God ' [...] knowledge ' [...] but ' [... soul ...] 34 existence ' [...] she having [...] [4] the second ' power and [...] and the ' third [...] [8] which [...] ' of a [...] [10] soul and [...]. '

"And the aeons [...] ' dwelling place [...] ' souls and some [...] ' gods [...] [15] higher than god [...] ' of the [self-begotten ones ...] ' the [Self-begotten One ...] ' first [...] ' messenger [...] [20] invisible [...] ' some [...] ' soul and [...] ' aeons [...] ' and [...] to the [soul] [25] messenger [...] 35 she [...] ' eternal [...] ' time and [...] ' she [5] but if [...] a soul ' belonging to [...] become a ' [messenger ...] ' world [...] the messengers and the ' [...] that holy one [10] [...].

"And [...] aeon which ' [the Self-begotten] has ' [...] them ' [...] ruler ' [...] they have [15] [...difference] which ' [...] this is not to say ' [...] day ' [...] and ' [... Self-begotten] God [20] [...] which exists ' [...] hear ' [...] self-begotten [...] 36 has ' [...] the [existence ' ...] mind ' [...] exist because [5] word [...] ' the child [... male], ' a form [...] ' divine [...] invisible ' spirit [...] [10] in the perfect one [...] [12] and an origin [...] ' love and a [...] ' of Barbel[o ...] [15] and a [...] ' the mind of [...] ' these are two [...] ' the thought [...] ' from the [...] [20] in Barbel[o ...] ' the Hidden One [...] ' all these [... ' virgin ...] ' she [...] [25] in a [...] 37 in that one there [...] power ' [...] that one which [...] ' from the [...] but ' one [...] from the power of that one which [5] is there [...] exist really ' [...] is his ' [...] they being first ' [...] of that one ' there [...] and he is the [10] [...] he alone ' [...] give him enough ' [...] for him ' [...] all [...] he gives ' [...] through the [15] [...] for this ' [...] in order that he may ' [...] and he who ' [...] him ' [...] indivisible [20] [... Ba]rbelo, he ' [...] in order that he might become ' [...] blessedness [...] [24] all ' [...] he comes [...] 38 of the perfect ' mind [...] and he [...] ' perfect spirit ' [...] perfect, he being alive [5] forever [...] ' him and [...] he ' exists [...] ' of the [...] he '

is a word from [. . .] [10] which exists in [. . .] ' of all these [. . .] ' forever
[. . .] ' in the [triple . . .] ' exists in the [. . .] [15] they are of those which
exist [. . .] ' perfect [. . .] ' first-appearing [. . .] ' mind, but [. . .] ' pure
[. . .] [20] and that [. . .] ' of a likeness [. . .] ' appear [. . .] ' and the [. . .] [25]
him [. . .] **39** [2] namely [. . .] [5] concerning him they ' [. . .] I mark him '
[. . .] he is simple ' [. . .] for he is ' [. . .] as if he exists [10] [. . .] how you
are one ' [. . .] that is ' [. . .] need. Concerning ' [. . .] triple male ' [. . .]
really [exists [15] . . .] a mind of the knowledge ' [. . .] those which exist '
[. . .] which he has ' [. . .] really exists ' [. . .] and [20] [. . .] and ' [. . .]
second ' [. . .] perfect which ' [. . .] appear [. . .] [25] Hidden One [. . . [28]
form . . .] [30] of these [. . .] **40** [5] form [. . .] ' for a knowledge [. . . ' First-
Appearing . . .] ' male [. . .] ' he has [. . . [10] existence . . .] ' unborn [. . .] '
third [. . .] ' since [he has . . .] ' knowledge and [. . . which] [15] exists
together [. . . ' become] all-perfect [. . . ' blessed], not being [anything
. . .] ' there [. . .] [20] divine [. . .] ' with him [. . .] [23] perfect [. . .] ' of the
[. . .] [25] Hidden One [. . .] **41** know ' [. . .] of ' [. . . First-Appearing '
. . .] the mind of [5] [. . .] the powers ' [. . .] the All ' [. . .] and he exists '
[. . .] this knowledge. '

"[. . .] Self-begotten God [10] [. . .] and the [Self-begotten God ' . . .] of
the child of ' [. . .] triple male, this male ' [. . .] and a form ' [. . .]
perfect, he not having [15] [. . .] within knowledge ' [. . .] like that one
there ' [. . .] of the individuals ' [and] a single knowledge of the '
individuals [. . .] according to the All [20] [. . .] perfect. The ' male [. . .]
mind ' [. . .] Hidden One, and the Hidden One ' [. . .] divine ' [. . .] and
a power [25] [. . .] of these all ' [. . .] really [. . . **42** First-Appearing . . .] '
mind [. . .].

"[. . .] [5] the one belonging to the all [. . .] ' unborn [. . .] ' man [. . .] '
they are [. . .] ' and the one who [. . .] [10] and the one who [. . .] ' that
one who dwells [. . .] ' in the perceptible [world] ' living and dead '
[. . .] all [. . .] [15] obtain salvation [. . .] ' he who is dead, but all of them '
did not lack salvation [. . .] ' first, but being safe ' and existing more
than humble. [20] Concerning the man [of the dead], ' his soul and his
mind and ' his body all [die] ' with suffering [. . .] ' fathers of [. . .] [25]
material [. . .] ' the fire [. . .] **43** he crosses over.

"The second ' man is the immortal soul ' in those dead ones, ' [taking]
care of itself. Then [5] [. . .] a seeking of those things ' which are profitable
[in accordance with] each ' of them. [It] perceives ' the somatic earth.
They ' [. . .] and it [10] [. . .] it has ' an eternal god. It is ' a partner with
[demons]. '

"Now concerning the man in the ' Transmigration: If [15] he discovers

the ' truth within himself, he is [far] ' from the deeds of others ' who
exist wrongly [and stumble]. ' Concerning the man who [20] [repents]—if
he renounces ' the [dead] and desires ' those things which exist, the
immortal mind ' and the immortal soul ' [...]. He hastens because of
them [25] when he first asks ' about it. You are not activity, ' but you are
the deeds [...] ' for he [...] in him ' [...] and [30] [...] and ' obtain
[...]. **44**

"The man who can be saved ' is the one who seeks after him and
his ' mind, and who finds each ' of them. How much power [5] does he
have? The one who is ' saved is the one who has not known ' these [...]
how ' they exist [...] but he ' himself is in the word in the way [10] in
which he exists [...] ' he received each [...] ' in every place, [having
become] ' as simple and one; for then ' [he is saved], being able [15] by
himself to pass through all ' these. He becomes [...] ' all these. If he
desires ' again, then he parts ' from all these and [20] he withdraws to
himself alone, ' for he can become divine. ' He withdrew to god." '

I heard this ' and brought a blessing to the [25] living and unborn [God
who ' is] in truth and the unborn [Hidden One] ' and the First-Appearing, ' invisible perfect male ' Mind, and the invisible [30] triple-male
Child ' and the [Self-begotten God]. **45** I said to the child of the child '
Ephesech, who was with me, "Send ' the powers of your wisdom to
tell me of ' the scattering of the man [5] who is saved, and ' who those
are who are mixed with him, and ' who those are who are divided from
him, ' in order that the living elect might ' know."

Then the [10] child of the child Ephesek ' told me [...] plainly, ' "If he
withdraws ' to himself alone many ' times and if he comes into being
with reference to [15] the knowledge of others, ' the mind and the immortal [origin] ' know it. Then he ' has a shortage, ' for he returns
and [20] parts from himself and ' stands [...] and comes into being '
within an alien impulse. ' Instead of becoming one, he ' bears many
[forms] once more. [25] When he turns, he ' comes into being seeking
those things ' which do not exist. When he ' falls down to these in
thought ' and, being powerless, knows [30] them in another way, unless **46**
he receives the light, he becomes ' a product of nature and thus ' comes
down to birth because of it. ' He is speechless because of the [5] pains and
the limitlessness ' of matter. Although he [has] an eternal, ' immortal
power, ' he is bound within the [...] of ' the body. He is [made] living [10]
and is bound always ' within cruel, cutting ' bonds ' through every evil
breath, until he ' acts again and begins again [15] to come into being in
himself.

"Therefore, ' (powers) are appointed over the salvation of ' them, and these same powers exist ' in the world. Within the Hidden Ones ' corresponding to each of the [20] aeons stand glories, ' in order that he who is in [the world] ' might be safe beside them. The glories ' are perfect thoughts living with ' the powers; they do not perish because they [25] are models of salvation by which ' each one is saved when he receives ' them. He receives a model ' and strength through the same (power), and ' with the glory as a helper [30] he can thus pass out from the world ' [and the aeons ...].

These **47** are keepers of the immortal soul: ' Gamaliel together with ' Strem[ps]ouchos, and Akramas ' together with Loel, and Mnesinous. [5] [These are] the immortal spirits: Yesseus, ' [Ma]zareu[s], Ye[s]sedekeus; ' he is [...] of the child ' [...] the child of the child, and ' [...] and Ormos [10] [...] on the living seed. ' Kam[ali]el is the spirit-giver. ' They stand before us, ' Isauel and Audael, and [A]brasax, ' the ten thousand Phaleris, with Phalses [15] [and] Eurios. The keeper of ' [the] glories (is) Stetheus with ' Theo[pe]mptos and Eurumeneus ' and Olsen. The helpers in ' every deed are Ba[..]mos and [20] [.]son and Eir[.]n and Lalameus ' and Eidomeneus and Authrou[n]ios. ' The judges are Sumpthar ' and Eukrebos and Keilar. ' [The inheritor] is Samblo. The [25] messenger-guides ' to the clouds of clouds are Sappho ' and Thouro."

After he said these things, ' he told me about all of those ' in the self-begotten aeons [30] and all eternal lights, **48** and the perfect ones ' perfected individually. ' Corresponding to each of ' the aeons I saw a living earth and [5] a living water and [air] made of ' light, and fire that cannot ' burn [...] all being ' simple and ' immutable with [...] [10] simple and [...] ' having a [...] in ' many ways, with trees ' that do not perish in many ' ways, and tares [...] [15] this way, and all these and ' imperishable fruit ' and living men and every form, ' and immortal souls ' and every shape and [20] form of mind, and ' gods of truth, and ' messengers who exist in ' great glory, and ' indissoluble bodies and [25] an unborn begetting and an ' immovable perception. ' He was there again, he who ' suffers although he is unable to suffer, ' for he was a power of a power. **49**

[...] ' change ' [...] indissoluble ' [...] these [5] [...] all ' [...] they ' [...] by them [...] [10] come into being [...] **50** [3] perfect [...] ' eternal [...] [5] aeon [...] ' and the [...] ' receive power [...] ' and [...] ' in a [...] [10] for [...] ' not [...] **51** in ' [...]thorso ' [...] a silence ' [...] he is [5] [...] he is god ' [...] we were blessing ' [...] Geradama[s ' ...] of ' [...] is the glory [...] [11] mother [...] ' and Plesithea ' [...] of messengers and ' [the Son] of Adamas, Se[th [15] Emma]cha Seth, the father of ' the immovable [generation] and [...] ' the four lights, Arm[ozel, ' Oroia]el, Daveithe, Eleleth. ' [...] we blessed by name. [20]

[...] see him, the self-controlled ' glory, the triple [...] child ' [...] triple male ' [...] greatness, saying, ' "You are one, you are [one], you [25] are [one], the child **52** of [the child ...] ' Yato[menes ...] ' exist [...] [6] you are one, [you are one, ...] ' Semelel[...] ' Telmachae[...] ' Omothem[...] [10] male [...] ' he begets [... the] ' self-controlled [glory ...] ' desire him whom [...] ' the all-perfect [...] [15] all.

"Akron [...] ' the triple male aa[...] ' ōōōōōb+treise[...] ' you are a spirit from ' spirit. You are light [20] from light. You are [silence] ' from a silence. [You are] ' thought from thought, ' the son of [god], ' the god seven [...] [25] let us say [...] **53** [4] word [...] [8] not a time ' [...] invisible [10] [...] Barbelo [...] [12] the [triple] male Prones, ' and she who belongs to all ' the glories, Youel." [15]

[I was] baptized the fifth ' [time] in the name of the ' Self-begotten by these ' very powers. I ' became divine. [20] [I stood] upon the fifth ' inhabited aeon of ' all [these]. I saw all [those] ' who belong to the self-begotten ones ' who really exist, [25] and I was baptized five **54** [times ...] ' and [...] ' of the [...] ' Zareu[...] [5] from [...] ' that one [...] ' perfect [...] ' and the great [...] ' glory [...] [11] god [...] ' appear [...] ' perfect which is doubled [...] ' all forms [...] [15] male. The [self-controlled] ' glory, the mother [...] ' the glories, Youel, and the [four ' perfect] Lights, ' the First-Appearing One [of the great] [20] Mind, Selmen, [and those who] ' are with him, the ' god-[revealers] Zacha[...] ' and Yachthos, Sethe[us] ' and Antiphan[te]s, [25] [Sel]dao and Ele[n]os [...] **55** [2] go ' [...] the [...] [5] likeness ' [...] exists as ' [...] of the ' [...] for ' [...] aeon [10] [...] more ' [...] Light ' [...] more glories ' [...] they are in accordance with ' each of the aeons, a [15] living [earth] and ' [living] water and air ' made of light and a ' blazing fire which ' cannot [burn], and animals and [20] trees and souls ' [and] minds and men ' [and] all those which exist ' [with] them, but not gods ' [and] powers and messengers, [25] for all these [...].

[...] **56** [12] the Self-begotten One, [and I] ' received a likeness from [all] these. ' The aeons of the Self-begotten One opened [...] [15] self-begotten, a great light ' comes forth [...] ' from the aeons of the [triple]' male, and they [glorified] ' them. The four [20] aeons were desiring [...] ' in an aeon [...] ' of the form [...] ' single one existing [...]. ' Then E[phesech ...] [25] the child of the child [... **57** [5] Yesseus] Maza[reus '

Yessede]keus [. . .] ' of [. . . ' seal] on him ' [. . .] and Gabrie[l . . .] [11]
seal ' [. . .] four races. '

There came before me she who belongs to ' [the glories], the male
and [15] [virginal] Yoel. ' [I] was deliberating about the crowns. ' She
[said] to me. "Why ' has your spirit deliberated ' [about] the [20] seals on
them? ' [. . .] are the crowns which strengthen ' every [spirit] and every
soul, ' and the seals which are ' [. . .] the races and [25] [. . .] the Invisible
Spirit. [. . .] **58** [6] virgin [. . .] [12] he enabled [. . .]. ' And the seals [. . .] '
are races belonging to the Self-begotten One [15] and the First-Appearing
One ' and the Hidden One.

"The Invisible ' Spirit is a psychic ' and [intellectual] power, ' a
knowledgeable one and [20] a foreknower. ' Therefore, since he is beside '
[Ga]briel, the spirit-giver in [. . .], ' if he gives a ' holy spirit and seals [25]
him with the [crown], ' and if he gives him a crown ' with gods [. . .] **59**
power [. . .] [8] spirit ' [. . .] to each [. . .] [11] they exist ' [. . .] and they
were not ' [. . .] in order that they might ' [. . .] simple, and [15] [. . .] not
come into being as doubled ' [. . .] any form, and ' [. . .] they are
simple ' and perfect individuals. ' [. . .] and all these [20] [. . .] aeons of the
aeons ' [. . .] all these ' [. . .] which exist together ' [. . .] all-perfect, the
one belonging to a great ' [. . .] to see them [25] for [. . .] invisible [. . .] **60** [4]
perfect [. . .] [7] every [. . .] ' exist [. . .] ' he is [. . .] [10] hear him [. . .] [12]
within a thought [. . .] ' a forethought [. . .] ' since in a power [. . .] [15]
she is perfect [. . .] ' it is fitting for you to [. . .] ' concerning every deed
and [. . .] ' those to whom you will listen ' through a [thought] [20] of
those higher than [perfect] ' and with those whom you will ' [know] in
a soul [of] ' the perfect ones."

[. . .] ' because she baptized me. [. . .] **61** [7] the first ' [. . .] I received
strength [. . .] [10] and [I] received form ' [. . .] and I received ' [. . .] he
existing on my ' [. . .] a pure spirit. ' [I] came into being really existing. [15]
Then she brought me ' into the great [aeon], ' the place where the perfect '
triple [male] is. ' I saw [20] the Invisible [Child] ' within an invisible '
light. Then [she] again ' baptized me in [. . .]. **62** [8] I became able to
[. . .] ' the great ones [. . .] [10] and perfect [. . .]. '

The one who belongs to all [the glories], ' Yoel, said to me, ' "You
have [received] all the [washings] ' in which she is worthy to [give]
baptism, [15] and you have become [perfect ' . . .] the hearing of [. . .] '
all [. . .]. Now [call] again ' upon Salamex and [Selmen] ' and the all-
perfect Ar[. . .], [20] the Lights of the aeon ' Barbelo and the unmeasured '
knowledge, and they ' will reveal **63** [. . .] ' invisible [. . .] [6] which [. . . '
Virgin B]arbelo ' [and] the Invisible ' [Triple] Powerful Spirit." [10]

[. . .] to me, the one belonging ' to all [the glories], Youel. ' She [set me down] and went and ' stood before the First-Appearing One. ' Then I was [15] [standing] above my spirit, ' praying fervently to the great ' Lights within ' [Thought]. I began to call ' upon Salamex and [20] Se[lm]en and the all-perfect ' [. . .] and I saw ' glories greater than powers, ' and they anointed me. I was able [. . .] **64** [6] she clothed herself [. . .] ' all [. . .] ' Salamex and [Selmen], ' those who have revealed [10] every deed, saying, ' "Zostrianos, [. . .] ' concerning those about whom ' you asked. [. . .] ' and a single one [. . .] [15] exists before all these ' who really exist in the ' unmeasured and ' undivided spirit [. . .] ' one of the All which [20] exists in him and the [. . .] ' and him whom [. . .] ' after him. He [alone] ' who crosses it [. . .].

"[. . .] **65** [5] all these ' [. . .] he is ' [. . .] a first ' [. . .] of every thought ' [. . .] of every power [10] [. . . downward ' . . .] he is established in ' [. . .] standing, he [passes] ' into the coming ' [. . .] and an attainable one. [15] He is higher by far ' than every untraceable one, and he ' [. . .] greater than every body; ' he is purer than every incorporeal one. ' He enters every [20] [thought] and every body ' [because he] is strength for every ' [race] and form, ' since he is their All. **66** [. . .] exist ' [. . .] really exist ' [. . .] all [. . .] [6] a partial [. . .] ' part [. . .] ' in a [. . .] ' know her [. . .] [10] from him [. . .] ' which really exists; ' which is from ' the spirit who really exists; ' the one alone [. . .] [15] for they are powers of [. . .] ' Existence [. . .] ' and Life and ' Blessedness. In ' Existence there exists [20] a simple head, a ' word of his and a form. ' Let him who finds ' it come into being. ' Existing [in] [25] Life, he is alive [. . .] **67** [3] having knowledge; ' [. . .] know all these [5] [. . .] him alone ' [. . .] for god ' [. . .] unless ' [. . .] him alone. And he ' [. . .] in him [10] [. . .] the single ' [. . .] for he exists; ' [in] that which is his ' in a form of a form, ' a single [. . .] of the [15] [. . .] and he exists as the ' [. . .] since he is in ' [the mind]. He is in ' it, not coming forth to any ' place because he is a single, [20] perfect, simple spirit, ' as a place of his and ' [. . .] coming into being in him ' and the Alls. ' [He] exists, namely he who **68** [. . .] ' and a [. . .] ' and a cause of coming into being ' in it.

"The life [. . .] [5] and [activity] of the ' inessential [. . .] ' which exists in it [. . .] ' exists in it [. . .] ' exists because of it [. . .] [10] blessed and a [. . .] ' perfect. And [. . .] ' which exists in [. . .] ' which really exists. The ' [form] of the activity [15] which exists is blessed. ' When he receives existence, ' he receives power [. . .] ' a perfection [. . .] ' eternal division. Then [20] he exists as perfect. ' Therefore, he is perfect, ' being indivisible ' with his own region, ' for nothing exists [25] before him except ' the [perfect] singleness. (pp. 69-72 probably blank) **73**

"[. . .] Existence ' [. . .] is salvation ' [. . .] all, and he ' [. . .] power or he [. . .] [5] if he ' [. . .] to him, all these ' [. . .] for he who ' [exists] in Existence ' [. . .] he exists [10] wholly as life ' and he has knowledge in blessedness. ' If he is concerned with the ' [glories], he is perfect; ' but if he is concerned with [15] [two] or one, he is drunkenness ' as he received ' from it. There are, therefore, ' those who have souls ' and those without souls; [20] those who are saved, therefore, ' and therefore those will ' [perish], if they have not ' [accepted] him. Therefore ' there is matter and [25] bodies. Therefore, a **74** [. . .] ' therefore [. . .] ' all [. . .] concerning ' [. . .] he [. . .] [5] preexist and he [. . .] ' a simple head ' [. . .] single spirit [. . .] ' he is [. . .].

"And [. . .] ' Existence, the form [. . .] [10] of his. In accordance with ' activity which is life [. . .], ' and in accordance with ' perfection which is the [intellectual] ' power, being light [. . .] [15] the three stand [at one] ' time, moving at one [time] ' in every place, but ' not in any place, he [. . .] ' to them all and [20] produces the unnamed ' ineffable one. [. . .] ' exist from it [. . .] ' resting on itself [. . .] ' in its perfection [. . .] [25] it has not received from [every] form, **75** therefore [. . .] [4] nothing [. . .] [7] in Existence ' [. . .] exist in the ' [. . .] of life; but in [10] perfection and ' truth there is blessedness. '

"All of [them] were ' [in] the indivisibility of ' the spirit, and knowledge [15] [. . .] concerning it is ' [divinity] and ' disunity and blessedness ' and life and ' knowledge and goodness [20] and a ninth ' and unity. ' In short, all of them are the ' purification of the unbornness ' which exists prior to him [25] [. . .] all of them and the [. . .] **76** [6] light [. . .] ' an aeon, a [. . .] ' within a [. . .] ' unbornness, he [. . .] [10] every time, he [. . .] ' after him, since he sees him [. . .] ' and he exists as one [. . .] ' simple; since he is a ' blessedness in a [15] perfection [. . .] ' perfect and [blessed]. '

"She lacks him ' because she was lacking [. . .] ' of his, because he was following [her] [20] and knowledge. ' A knowledge of his ' exists outside of him, and he ' who examines himself ' is in him, a [25] reflection and a [. . .] **77** is lacking [. . .] [3] simple [. . .] [6] he [believes ' . . .] him, she ' [. . .] from the pleroma ' [. . .] which she had not desired [10] for herself. She has ' [. . .] him outside of the ' [perfection] and parted from ' [. . .], for she is [. . .] all-perfect one ' [of] perfection [15] existing as decision. ' With respect to him, ' she is a begetting which follows ' him.

"I am from the ' ineffable power [20] of his which has ' a first power and ' the first unbornness ' after him, ' because, with respect to all the rest, [25] a first aeon [. . .] **78** [4] all [. . .] [6] of the [. . .] ' and him [. . .] ' to know him since he really ' exists as an aeon [. . .]. [10]

"In activity [...] ' power and a [...] ' she did not begin [...] ' time, but she [appeared] ' from eternity, [15] having stood before ' him in eternity. ' She was darkened through ' the greatness of the [...] ' of his. She stood [20] looking at him and [rejoicing] ' because she was filled with ' kindness [...] ' but she has [...] 79 [7] a first ' inessential existence, and ' [...] that [...] [10] moving from the undivided ' to existence in ' activity [and] the [intellectual] ' perfection and the intellectual life ' which was [15] blessedness and ' divinity.

"The [whole] ' spirit, perfect, simple, ' and invisible, ' having become [20] singleness in existence and ' activity and a ' simple triple-[power], ' is an invisible [spirit], ' an [image] of him who [25] really exists, the One [...] 80 [6] the really [existing] one ' who is in a [...] ' he being an image [...] ' in a turning [...] [10] able to join with his [...] ' she having seen the [...] ' because he was [...] ' the all-perfection [...] ' that, because he [...] [15] preexist and [...] ' is upon all of them, he being ' a preexistent known ' as a triple power. The ' Invisible Spirit was [20] [never] ignorant; [he always] ' knew, but he was existing ' as perfection [and] ' blessedness [...]. 81

"She became ignorant [...] ' and she [...] ' body and a [...] ' promise [...] [5] light [...] ' she exists [...] [8] in order that she may not depart any more ' and come into being apart [10] from perfection. She ' knew perfection and him, ' and she made herself stand ' and was at rest ' because of him. [15] Since she was from ' him who really exists, ' she was [from] him ' who really exists and from ' all of them. She knew herself and [20] the One who preexists. '

"They followed him and ' came into being existing ' {they came into being existing} and ' appearing through those 82 [who preexist]. And ' [...] through the ' [...] they having appeared ' [...] two [5] [...] they appeared ' [...] he who ' foreknows him as ' an eternal space, ' which came into being as his [10] second knowledge, ' moreover, as the knowledge of ' his knowledge, the unborn ' Hidden One. [They] ' stood again upon him who [15] really exists, ' for because of him she knew him, ' in order that those who follow ' her might come to being, having ' a place, and that [20] those who come forth ' might be able to precede her, but ' might become holy ' and simple. She is the ' introspection of the 83 [preexisting] God. She ' became at ease [...] ' the simple [...] ' a salvation [...] [5] a salvation [...] ' he [...] ' light which they ' [foreknew]. She was named ' Barbelo by [10] Thought, the triple, ' male, virginal, and ' perfect race. She is the ' knowledge of her through whom she came ' into being, in order that they might not [15] [...] down, and that ' she might not come forth any more ' through those ' in her and those who follow her. ' But she exists [20] as a simple one, in order to be able ' to know the preexisting ' God, because ' she came into being as a good one ' of him, having [. . .] **84** an unbornness ' [. . .] third ' [. . .] two ' [. . .] this way [5] [. . .] and male [. . .] [7] and the [. . .] ' unbornness [. . .] ' she is second [. . .] [10] she stood [. . .] ' first of the reality which really ' exists, really [. . .] ' the blessedness [. . .] ' of the Invisible [Spirit of] [15] the knowledge of the prior ' existence in the ' simplicity of the ' Invisible Spirit ' within the ninth, similar [20] within the pure ' singleness and [. . .] ' form.

"He exists, ' he who [. . .] **85** [7] and knows ' [. . .] and the ' [. . .] and perfection [10] and [. . .] works on it and ' [. . .] the first Hidden One ' [. . .] them all, ' existence and activity, ' divinity, race, [15] and form. The powers ' are one and in ' one because he is one, that is, ' not partial but ' those of the All. What [20] is the unity which is the ninth? ' And from the activity ' [. . .] life ' [. . .] of ' [. . .] and whole [. . .] **86** [8] power [. . .] ' as [. . .] [10] perceptible [. . .] ' all-perfect [. . .] ' she having said to S[olmis], ' You are great, Aphr[edon], ' you are perfect, Neph[redon]. [15] She says to his Existence, ' You are great, Deipha[neus], ' his activity and life ' and divinity. ' You are great, Harmedo[n], [20] you who belong to [all] the glories, Epiph[aneus], ' and his blessedness and ' perfection of ' singleness [. . .] ' all [. . .].

"[. . .] **87** [7] forever ' [. . .] intellectual ' [. . .] perfect [10] the [Virgin Barb]elo ' through the simplicity ' of the blessedness ' of the Triple Powerful ' Invisible Spirit. She [15] who has known him ' has known herself. He is ' everywhere, being ' undivided, having ' [. . .] and she knew [20] herself as an activity of his ' [. . .] and he knew ' [. . .] knowledge' [. . .] within [. . .] **88** [9] bless [. . .] ' Be[ritheus, Erigenaor], ' Or[imeni]os, Ar[amen], ' Alphl[ege]s, Elilio[upheus], ' Lalameu(s), Noetheu(s) [. . .], ' great is your name [. . .] [15] he is strong. He who knows ' brings truth to all. You are ' one, you are one, you are one, Siou, E[. . .], ' Aphredon, you are the ' aeon of the aeons of the [20] great, perfect, first ' Hidden One of the [. . .] ' activity, and [. . .] [24] his image [. . .] ' of his [. . . **89** [9] existence ' . . .] and he [. . .] [13] in ' [. . .] glory [15] [. . .] glories [. . .] [20] in ' [. . .] aeon. [. . .] **90** [9] exist [. . . [16] blessed . . .] **91** [9] god [. . .] [13] first ' [. . .] and powers [15] [. . . all-perfect ' . . .] of ' all of them and a cause ' of them all ' [. . .] Barbelo [20] [. . .] him and ' [. . .] all these ' [. . .] he not having ' [. . .] and his ' [. . .] become [25] [. . .] but [. . .] **92** [10] of [. . .] [14] single [. . .] [17] according to the [intellectual] who [. . .] ' really [. . .] who exists [. . .] ' name [. . .] [21] Hidden One [. . .] [23] triple [. . .] ' but [. . .] **93** name him. All these do ' likewise since they come ' from him who is ' pure. '

"If you give (glory) [5] [because of] him and if you ' [...] existence ' [...] his ' [...] of a ' [...] simple [... [15] know] him [...] [17] perfect ' he being [... perfect] ' and [...] [20] complete [...] **94** he was not able to see her. ' Therefore, there is no power to receive ' him in this way in ' a purity of greatness, [5] as a perfect head of ' him who is in a [...] two [...] [9] concerning [...] say [...] [14] together [...] [18] together [...].

"[...] **95** differences of these with ' messengers, and differences ' of these with men, ' and differences of [5] these [with] Existence [...] [8] and perception [...] [11] really [...] [13] for [...] the [perceptible] ' world [...] as [... [16] Existence ...] **96** approaches him in knowledge, ' he shall receive power, and he who is ' far from him is humble." '

I said, "Why, [5] then, have the judges come into being? ' What is the [suffering] of ' the [...], for [...] [12] but [...] [15] suffering [...] upon [...]?"

"[...] **97** male, since she is knowledge [of] ' the Triple Powerful Invisible ' Great Spirit, the image of ' [...] Hidden One, the [blessedness] [5] in the [Invisible] ' Spirit [...] the [...] [9] he knows [...] [15] she appears [...] ' knowledge [...] she ' stood [...] **98** a perfect ninth of ' a completed ninth. And ' when she divided the All ' from the All, [...] [5] Existence and [...] ' the thoughts [... [9] perception ... **99** [2] Existence ...] [5] knowledge [...] [9] she blesses [...] **100** [6] Arm[ozel ...] [11] power [...] **101** invisible [...] [5] form [...] [12] the Hidden One ' [...] undivided [...] [17] thought [...] **102** which exists [...] [3] father [...] **103** origins of [...] ' which exists [...] ' which exist [...] essence ' [...] in [5] [...] he is [...] **104** she appears ' [...] of those who [...] ' of the [...] [15] really [...] **105** are those who [stand ...] ' the aeon [...] ' come up to a [...] ' which [5] exist in [...] he [...] [9] an origin [...] [13] matter ' [...] single [... [16] exist ...] **106** and he exists ' [...] is [...] and [...] ' mark of [...] [12] number [...] [14] according to [...] **107** them in [...] [3] Existence [...] ' and [...] exist [5] as [... ' image ...] first [...] [8] first [...] **108** they are not giving [...] ' he who exists [...] ' all and ' that one who [...] a multitude [...] [5] creation [...] [9] order [...]. (pp. 109-112 missing)

"[...] **113** and messengers and ' demons and minds and ' souls and living beings and ' trees and bodies and [5] those before them—both those ' of the simple elements ' of simple origins, and ' those in confusion ' and unmixed [...] air [10] and water and earth ' and number and yoking ' and movement and [...] and ' order and breath and ' all the rest.

"There are [15] fourth powers which are ' in the fourth aeon: those '
in the [. . .] and ' [. . .] the powers ' [. . .] powers [. . .] of [. . .] [22] perfect
[. . .] soul ' [. . .] soul [. . .] living beings [. . .] ' trees [. . .] **114** his own;
and some are those ' who exist as begotten, and ' others as those in an
unborn ' begetting. Some are [5] holy and others are ' eternal and immutable ' in mutation and ' destruction in indestructibility. ' Some are
those who [10] are as alls; there are others who are ' races and those in '
order and arrangement. There are ' those in [indestructibility]. ' There
are the first who [15] stand and the second in ' all of them, all [who] are '
[from] them and ' [in] them, and from ' those who [follow] these [. . .] [21]
these [. . .] ' and they stood [. . .] ' fourth aeon [. . .] ' they existing
[. . .] **115** in them, he being scattered abroad. ' They do [not] crowd
one another, ' but they also dwell ' within them, existing and [5] agreeing
with one another as if ' they exist from a single ' origin. They are
reconciled ' because they all exist ' in a single aeon of the Hidden
One, [10] [. . .] divided in a power, ' for in accord with each of the ' aeons
they exist, standing ' in accord with the one who reaches them.

"[But] the Hidden One ' is a single aeon. [15] [They] have four different '
aeons, and in accord with ' each of the aeons ' they have powers unlike '
first and [second] [20] powers, for they all are eternal ' [. . .] they differ ',
[. . .] an order and glory ' [. . .] who is in ' [. . .] four aeons and [25] [. . .]
who [preexists ' . . .] god [. . .]. **116**

"All of them exist ' in one since they dwell together ' and are perfected
individually ' in fellowship and [5] have been filled with the aeon who '
really exists. Some among ' them are those who stand ' as if they dwell
in essence, ' and others like those as an essence [10] in function or suffering '
in a second, for in ' them exists the [barrenness] ' of the [barrenness]
who ' really exists. When the [barren ones] [15] have come into being,
their power ' stands. There is there an ' incorporeal essence and [. . .] '
imperishable [. . .] ' that [. . .] namely [. . .] [20] who really exists [. . .] '
he changing [. . .] ' change, he stands [. . .] ' namely the fire [. . .] '
imperishable [. . .] [25] one [. . .] **117** he stands.

"In that world ' are all living beings ' existing individually, yet
joined ' together. The knowledge [5] of the knowledge is there ' and an
establishment of ignorance. ' Chaos is there ' and a place [completed]
for ' them all, though they are new, [10] and true light and ' darkness
which has received light and he ' who does not really exist. ' He does
not really exist ' [. . .] the non-being which does [15] not exist as the All.

"He is ' the [good] from whom is ' the good and he who is good, '
and the god from whom ' is god and he who [20] [. . .] he who is great '

[...] for in part ' [...] form and god ' [...] that and he ' [...] god [...] ²⁵ all of them ' [... darkness ...] **118** and a race. He did not ' mix with anything; rather he remains ' alone in himself and ' rests himself in ⁵ his limitless limit. He ' is the god of those who ' really exist, a seer ' and a revealer of god. '

"When she had strengthened the one who [knew] her, ¹⁰ Barbelo, the aeon, the ' knowledge of the Invisible Triple Powerful ' Perfect Spirit, gave [...] ' to her, saying, He [...] ' a life. I am alive in a [...]. ¹⁵ You, the one, are alive. He is alive, namely [...] ' who is three. It is you who are ' three who are three [...] ' eee. The first of seven [...] ' the third [...] ²⁰ the second [...] ' eeee aaaaaa[...] ' two, and he [... four ' ...] knowledge [...] **119** a part? What kind of mind? ' What kind of wisdom? What kind of understanding ' and teaching?

"His Lights are ' given names. The first ⁵ is [Arme]don and she who is with him ' [...]. The second is ' Diphane[...] and she who is with him, ' Deiph[a...]. The third is ' [Malsed]on and she who is with him ¹⁰ [...]. The fourth is ' [Solmi]s and she who is with him, Olmis. '

"The Hidden One exists ' [...] and his Eidea. ' He is invisible to all ¹⁵ these, in order that they all might be strengthened ' by him, all ' [...] is in ' [...] the all-perfect ' because [he has] four existing ²⁰ [...] the first ' [...] nor according to a ' [...] to him alone ' [... B]arbelo [...] **120** know him and him who is appointed ' as a second. The first ' of the aeons is Harmedon, ' the father-glory. The second ⁵ Light is he who [did not know] ' him, but all the ' [individuals], wisdom [...] ' are in the fourth [aeon] ' who revealed himself ¹⁰ and all the glories. The [third] ' Light who [...] ' not him, as the word of all the ' [forms] and that other [glory], ' understanding, [who] is ¹⁵ in the third [aeon]. ' Four dwell [in] ' him, Malsedon and [...]. ' The fourth Light ' is he who [...] ²⁰ of all the forms [...] ' together, existing [...] ' teaching and glory [...] ' and the truth of the [four aeons], ' O[l]mis [...] **121** fifth.

"It is the first ' that is, the one who is the second ' who is the All-perfect Hidden One. ' For the four Lights ⁵ exist, but it is the Hidden One who has divided ' again. They exist in one ' place and [all who] know those ' who exist as glories ' are perfect. He ¹⁰ [...] knows everything ' about them all, because he is an all-perfect one ' from whom is every power ' and every one and ' their whole aeon, because they ¹⁵ all [come] to him. ' They all do come from him. ' As for the power and ' the origin of all these, ' when he had come to know ²⁰ [them], he became a ' [...] aeon and a ' [...] barrenness, ' [...] other aeons ' [in ...] **122** comes into being as a Barbelo. He ' becomes a first aeon ' because of the eternity of the ' Invisible Spirit, the second [5] barrenness.

"These are ' all the glories: the unattainable ' Aphredons, the ineffable ones, ' (are) the revealers; ' the immutable ones of all [10] these, the glory-revealers, ' (are) the Marsedons; those who are ' twice-revealed, the Solmises, the ' unattainable ones, (are) the ' self-revealers; those full [15] of glory, who wait for ' glory, the blessers, the M[arse]dons, ' (are) the hidden ones who [revealed], ' the limited [...] ' upon the limited [...] [20] those who exist [in ...] **123** ten thousand glories ' in them.

"Therefore, ' he is a perfect glory, in order that ' whenever he can join and [5] prevail he might become perfect. ' Thus, even if he enters ' a body and a change ' of matter, they do not ' receive a greater honor [10] from him because of their all-perfectness, ' though they all are perfect as are those ' with him. For each ' of the aeons has ' ten thousand aeons [15] in himself, in order that by existing together ' he may become a perfect ' aeon.

"He exists in the ' [blessedness] of the ' Triple [Powerful] Perfect Invisible [25] [Spirit ...] of the silence ' [...] which are the first ' [...] and the knowledge [...] **124** whole, a silence of the second ' knowledge, the first thought, ' in harmony with the triple ' power because he commanded her to [5] know him, in order that he might become ' all-perfect and be perfect ' in himself. He is known ' by singleness and ' blessedness. [I received] [10] goodness through that ' follower of the Barbelo aeon ' who gives being to himself. The ' power was not his own but belongs ' to him.

"The aeons who really exist [15] dwell in silence. ' Existence was inactivity, ' and knowledge of the ' [self-established] Hidden One ' was ineffable, since he came [from] [20] the fourth [...] ' thought, the First-[Appearing One], ' perfect male [...] **125** is an image of his, equal ' with him in glory and power, ' higher than him in rank, ' but not having within an [5] aeon all these living ' and dwelling together ' as he does. With the aeon ' within the aeons he has ' a fourfold difference [10] and with all the rest who ' dwell in that place.

"The ' Hidden One really exists, ' and with him is located she who belongs to all ' glories, Youel, the [15] male-virgin glory, ' through whom they saw all the ' all-perfect things. They who ' stand before him are the triple ' [...] child, the triple [20] [...] the self-begotten ' [...] he having ' [...] in one, he ' [...] he also who prevails over the ' [...] he exists in [...] **126** of countless thousands.

"The ' first aeon within ' him, from whom is ' the first Light, is

Solmis [5] and the god-revealer, ' being unattainable according to the '
type which is in the Hidden ' Aeon and Doxom[ed]on. ' The second
aeon is Akremon, [10] the ineffable one, having ' the second Light, '
Zachthos and Yachthos. The ' third aeon is ' Ambrosios the virgin,
having [15] the third Light, ' Setheus and Antiphantes. ' The fourth
aeon ' is the blesser [...] ' having the [20] fourth Light, [Seldao] ' and
Elenos. They [...] ' through [...] ' Arm[edon ...] **127** phoē zoē zēoē
[...] zōsi ' zōsi zaō zēooo zēsen ' zēsen—the individuals and the ' four
who are eightfold are alive; [5] ēooooēaēō—you who are before ' them
and in all of them. ' They are within ' the first-appearing, perfect '
male Armedon, the activity [10] of all who dwell together. ' Since all the
individuals were ' existing as perfect ones, ' the activity of all ' the
individuals appeared again. [15]

"As for the Self-begotten god, he ' stands within an ' aeon. There
are within him ' four different self-begotten ' aeons. The first [20] aeon in
him ' of the first Light ' is [Harmoze]l, Orneos, Euthrounios, ' he was
called [...]. [25] The second [aeon of ' the second Light is ' Oroiael,
...]oudas[.]os, Ap[...], **128** Arros[...]. The third aeon ' of the third
Light is ' Daveithe, Laraneus, Epiphanios, ' Eideos. The fourth aeon
[5] of the fourth Light ' is Eleleth, Kodere, ' Epiphanios, Allogenios. '

"As for all the others who exist in ' matter, [they] were all continuing
to live. [10] They came into being because ' of knowledge and greatness
and boldness ' and power, and were ' adorned; yet, because they have
been ignorant ' of God, they will fade away. [15]

"Behold, Zostrianos, you have heard ' all these things of which the
gods ' are ignorant and which are ' unattainable to messengers." ' I
became bold and said, [20] "I again ask about the Triple Powerful ' Invisible Perfect Spirit: ' [how] he exists for himself, and how he ' still
comes to all these [...] ' which really exists [...] [25] what is the [....]"
...] **129** very [...] they placed me and went. '

Apophantes and Aphrois, ' the Virgin Light, came before me ' and
brought me to the first-appearing, [5] great, male, perfect ' Mind, and I
saw how all these ' who were there dwell ' within one. I joined ' with
all of them and blessed [10] the Hidden Aeon and the Virgin ' Barbelo
and the Invisible ' Spirit. I became all-perfect ' and received strength. I
was written ' in glory and was sealed [15] and received there ' a perfect
crown.

I came ' forth to the perfect individuals, ' and all of them were
questioning ' me. They were listening to the [20] greatness of the knowledge
and ' rejoicing and ' receiving strength. When I again ' came to the

self-begotten ' aeons, I received a pure [25] form worthy ' of perception.
I came down ' to the aeon-copies ' and proceeded **130** to the airy
[earth]. I wrote ' three tablets and left them ' as knowledge for those
who come ' after me, the living elect. [5] I came down to the perceptible '
world and put on my temple. ' Because it was ignorant, ' I strengthened
it and went about ' preaching the truth to all of them. [10] Neither the
angelic beings of the ' world nor the rulers saw ' me, for I destroyed a
multitude ' of [disgraces] which brought me near death. '

But an erring multitude [15] I awakened, saying, ' "Know those who
are alive and the holy ' seed of Seth. Do not [. . .] ' disobedient to
me. [Awaken] ' your god about god. [20] Strengthen your sinless [elect] '
soul, and bring it to ' death here and ' seek after the immortal ' barrenness. The [Father] of [25] all these invites you. ' Although they reprove
you and ill-treat **131** you, he will not renounce you. '

"Do not baptize yourselves with death, ' nor entrust yourselves to
those ' lower than you instead of to those [5] who are better. Flee from
the madness ' and the bondage of femininity, ' and choose for yourselves the salvation ' of masculinity. You have ' come not [to suffer],
but to [10] escape your bondage.

"Release ' yourselves, and that which has bound ' you will be dissolved. Save ' yourselves, in order that it ' may be saved. The gentle
Father [15] has sent you the savior ' and given you strength. Why ' are
you hesitating? Seek when you are ' sought; when you are invited, '
listen. For the time is [20] short.

Do not be led ' astray. The aeon of the ' aeon of the living ones is
great, ' but the [punishment] of the ' unconvinced is great also. [25] Many
bonds and ' chastisers surround you. **132** Mature quickly ' before destruction reaches you. ' Look at the Light. Flee ' the darkness. Do not
be led [5] astray to your destruction." '

Zostrianos '
Words of truth of '
Zostrianos. God of '
Truth. Words of Zoroast[er]

THE LETTER OF PETER TO PHILIP (VIII, 2)

Introduced and translated by

FREDERIK WISSE

The *Letter of Peter to Philip* received its title from the letter which comprises the first part of the tractate. It is not unusual for the opening words of a tractate to function as the title for the whole tractate. Though the title and the letter make mention of Philip, he plays a significant role only at the very beginning of the tractate; throughout the body of the document it is Peter who is the apparent leader of the apostles.

The tractate is dominated by a dialogue of the resurrected Savior with his disciples. As in other Gnostic dialogues, much of the material is deliberately structured around several questions raised by the disciples and answered by Christ. Thus, the voice from the light explains, the deficiency of the Aeons stems from "the disobedience and foolishness of the mother"—the mother who is called Sophia in other mythological versions of the primordial fall. Fullness and restoration, however, can be attained by hearkening to the call of the heavenly redeemer Christ. The lawless and hostile Archons who rule this world can be vanquished, and the sufferings of the disciples can be overcome. The tractate tries to explain why the believers must suffer. A distinction is made between the suffering of Christ and of his disciples. Suffering is foreign to Christ, since he is divine, but he suffered because of others. The disciples suffer because of themselves, for they are involved in the fall of Sophia. The tractate closes with Jesus delivering a benediction and the apostles separating in order to preach.

The opening and closing sections of the *Letter of Peter to Philip*, particularly the narrative materials, have important parallels to the New Testament, especially to Acts. Similarly, the central part of the text contains numerous themes found in other literature. The appearance of the risen Christ as a light or a voice is common in Gnostic texts, and also occurs in the New Testament at the transfiguration in the gospels, the conversion of Paul in Acts, and the apocalyptic appearance to John in Revelation 1.

Dating perhaps from the late second or the third century C.E., the *Letter of Peter to Philip* is a document with a clearly Christian Gnostic message. It is Christ who is the heavenly redeemer, the Pleroma, the light from the Father, the illuminator; and like Christ, the disciples also are to become "illuminators in the midst of dead men."

THE LETTER OF PETER TO PHILIP
VIII 132, 10-140, 27

The Letter of Peter Which He '
Sent to Philip '

"Peter the apostle of Jesus ' Christ, to Philip our beloved ' brother and our fellow apostle [15] and (to) the brethren who are with you: greetings! ' Now I want you to know, our brother, [that] ' we received orders from ' our Lord and Savior of ' the whole world that [we] should come [together] [20] to give instruction and ' preach, in the salvation ' which was promised us by **133** our Lord Jesus Christ. But you, ' you were separate from us, and ' you did not desire us to come together, ' and to know how we should locate [5] ourselves in order that we might tell the good news. ' Therefore would it be agreeable to you, our brother, to ' come according to the orders of our ' God Jesus?"

When Philip had received these, ' and when he had read [10] them, he went to Peter, ' rejoicing with gladness. ' Then Peter gathered ' the others also. They went upon ' the mountain which is called [15] "the (Mount) of Olives," the place where they used ' to gather with the blessed ' Christ when he was in the body.

Then, ' when the apostles ' had come together and thrown themselves upon [20] their knees, they prayed, ' saying, "Father, Father, ' Father of the Light who ' possesses the incorruptions, ' hear us just as [25] [...] in thy holy ' child Jesus Christ. For he ' became for us an illuminator **134** in the [darkness]. Yea hear us." '

And they prayed again another time, ' saying, "Son ' of Life, Son of [5] Immortality who is in ' the light, Son, Christ of ' Immortality, our Redeemer, ' give us power, for they ' seek to kill us."

Then [10] a great light appeared ' so that the mountain shone ' from the sight of him who had ' appeared. And a voice called ' out to them, saying, [15] "Listen to my words that I may speak ' to you. Why are you asking ' me? I am Jesus Christ who ' is with you forever."

Then ' the apostles answered [20] and said, "Lord, ' we would like to know the ' deficiency of the Aeons and their Pleroma." ' And: "How are ' we held in this dwelling place?" [25] Further: "How did we come to this place?" And: "In what ' manner shall we depart?" Again: "How do we have **135** the [authority] of boldness?" ' [And]: "Why do the powers fight with us?" '

Then a voice came to them out ' of the light, saying, [5] "It is you

yourselves who are witnesses ' that I spoke all these things to you. '
But because of your unbelief ' I shall speak again.

"First ' of all concerning [the deficiency] of the Aeons, this [10] [is] the
deficiency. And ' when the disobedience and the foolishness ' of the
mother appeared ' without the commandment of the majesty ' of the
Father, she wanted [15] to raise up aeons. And when she ' spoke, the
Authades (Arrogance) ⟨followed⟩. ' And when she left behind a ' part,
the Authades ' laid hold of it, and it became a [20] deficiency. This is the
deficiency ' of the Aeons. Now when the Authades ' had taken a part,
he sowed it. ' And he put powers over ' it and authorities. [25] And [he]
enclosed it in the Aeons ' which are dead. And all the ' powers of the
world rejoiced ' that they had been begotten. **136** But they do not
know the ' preexistent one, since they are ' strangers to him. But this is
the one to whom ' they gave power and whom they served, [5] having
praised him. But he, Arrogance, ' became proud on account of ' the
praise of the powers. He became ' an envier and he wanted to ' make
an image in the place [of an image] [10] and a form in the place of a form. '
And he commissioned the powers within ' his authority to produce '
mortal bodies. And they ' came from an untrue copy, from [15] the
semblance which had emerged. '

"Next concerning the Pleroma, it is I. [And] ' I was sent down in the
body ' because of the seed which had fallen away. ' And I came down
to their dead product. [20] But they did not ' recognize me; they were
thinking of me that I ' was a mortal man. And I ' spoke with him who
belongs to me. And he ' hearkened to me just as you too [25] who hearkened
today. ' And I gave him authority in order that ' he might enter into
the inheritance ' of his fatherhood. And I took **137** [...] they were
filled ' [...] in his salvation. And since ' he was a deficiency, for this
reason he ' became a Pleroma.

"Next, concerning the item [5] that you are being held, the reason is that
you ' belong to me. When you strip off ' from yourselves what is corrupted, then ' you will become illuminators ' in the midst of dead men. [10]

"Next, (concerning) the item that you will fight with the Powers, '
the reason is that [they] do not have rest like ' you, since they do not
wish ' [that] you be saved."

Then the apostles ' worshipped again, saying, [15] "Lord, tell us: in
what ' way shall we fight with the Archons since ' the Archons are
above us?"

Then ' a voice called out to them from ' the appearance, saying, [20]
"Now you will fight ' with them in this way, for the Archons are '

fighting with the inner man. And you ' are to fight with them in this way: come ' together and teach in the world [25] the salvation with a promise. And ' you, gird yourselves with the power ' of my Father, and let ' your prayer be known. And he, the ' Father, will help you as he has [30] helped you having sent **138** [. . .] ' as I already [said to] ' you when I was in the body." Then ' there came lightning and [5] thunder from heaven, and ' what appeared to them in that place was taken ' up to heaven.

Then ' the apostles gave thanks to ' the Lord with every blessing. And [10] they returned to Jerusalem. ' And while coming up they spoke with ' each other on the road concerning the light ' which had come. And a remark was made ' concerning the Lord. It was [15] said, "If he, our Lord, ' suffered, then how much (must) we (suffer)?" '

Peter answered, saying, ' "He suffered because of [us], ' and it is necessary for us too [20] to suffer because of our smallness." '

Then a voice came to them, ' saying, "I have told you ' many times, it is necessary for you ' to suffer. It is [25] necessary that they bring you to synagogues ' and governors, ' so that you shall suffer. But he ' who does not suffer and does not **139** [. . . ' our Father ' . . .] in order that he may ' [. . .]."

And the apostles [5] rejoiced [greatly] and came up ' to Jerusalem. And they came up to the temple. They gave ' instruction in salvation in the name of ' the Lord Jesus Christ. And they healed ' [a] multitude.

And Peter opened his mouth, [10] he said to his disciples, ' "[Did] our Lord Jesus, when he was in the body, ' show us everything? For he ' came down. My brothers, listen to my voice." ' And he was filled with a holy spirit. [15] He spoke thus: "Our illuminator, Jesus, ' [came] down and was crucified. And he bore ' a crown of thorns. And he put on ' a purple garment. And he was ' [crucified] on a tree and he was buried in [20] a tomb. And he rose from the ' dead. My brothers, Jesus is a stranger ' to this suffering. But we are ' the ones who have suffered at the transgression of the mother. ' And because of this, he accomplished everything [25] according to a likeness in us. ' For the Lord Jesus, the Son of the immeasurable glory of the ' Father, he is the author ' of our life. My brothers, let ' us therefore not obey these lawless ones [30] and walk in **140** [. . .] ' Peter [gathered . . .] ' saying, "[Our Lord Jesus] ' Christ, author [. . .], [5] give us a spirit of understanding ' in order that we also may ' perform wonders."

Then Peter ' and the other apostles saw [him] ' and they were filled with a holy spirit. [10] And each one ' performed healings. And they separated ' in order to preach the Lord ' Jesus. And they came together; ' they greeted each other, [15] saying, "Amen."

Then ' Jesus appeared, saying ' to them, "Peace to you [all] ' and everyone who believes in ' my name. And when you depart, [20] joy be to you and ' grace and power. And be not ' afraid. Behold I am with you ' for ever."

Then the apostles ' separated from each other [25] into four words in order to ' preach. And they went ' by a power of Jesus in peace.

MELCHIZEDEK (IX, *1*)

Introduced by

BIRGER A. PEARSON

Translated by

SØREN GIVERSEN and BIRGER A. PEARSON

The work entitled *Melchizedek* deals with the mysterious priest Melchizedek, who is mentioned in the Old Testament (Genesis 14:18-20 and Psalm 110:4) as well as in the New (Hebrews 5:10-7:28). In this tractate the role of Melchizedek as an eschatological high priest and Messianic warrior reflects Jewish speculations on Melchizedek current at the turn of the Common Era; such speculations are attested most notably by the Melchizedek fragments discovered at Qumran. Furthermore, the tractate's apparent identification of Melchizedek with Jesus Christ, possibly based on an interpretation of the passage in Hebrews, is also documented elsewhere in early Christianity, particularly in Egypt. *Melchizedek* was originally written in Greek by an unknown author, possibly as early as the second century, probably in Egypt; and though the work contains obvious Sethian Gnostic elements, these may be secondary. Especially interesting is the anti-docetic tendency: the body, flesh, and suffering of Jesus Christ are indeed real.

Melchizedek contains revelations given to Melchizedek by heavenly messengers. The first revelation (1, 1-14, 15) prophesies concerning the life, suffering, death, and victory of Jesus Christ, and the future high-priestly role to be played by Melchizedek himself. An intermediate section (14, 15-18, 7) apparently discusses the priestly investiture and baptism of Melchizedek, and also reflects the cultic life of the Christian Gnostic community from which the tractate emanates. The second revelation (18, 7-27, 10) then depicts Melchizedek transported into the future. Melchizedek sees that the role of Jesus Christ as suffering savior and triumphant victor is his own future role.

MELCHIZEDEK

IX 1, 1-27, 10

Melchizedek [1]

Jesus Christ, Son [of God [1] ...] from [...] [5] the aeons that I [might tell] [1] all of the aeons, and in (the case of) [1] each one of the aeons [that I might tell [1] the] nature of the aeon, what [sort] [1] it is, and that comradeship and [10] goodness I might put on [1] as a garment, O brother [...].

[...] [19] their end [...]. [1] And he will [reveal [1] to them] the truth [...] [25] proverb(s) [... **2** from the beginning] in parables [1] [and riddles

...] proclaim [5] them, Death will [tremble] ' and be angry, not only '
he himself, but also his [fellow] ' world-rulers, and archons [and] ' the
principalities and the authorities, the [10] female gods and the male gods '
together with the archangels. And [...] [16] all of them [... ' the] world-
rulers [...] ' all of them, and all the ' [...], and all the [...]. [20]

They will say [... concerning] ' him, and concerning [...] [25] they will
[...] ' hidden [mysteries ...] ' those that [...] **3** [3] out of ' [...] the All.
They will [5] [...] this, the [lawyers] ' will overwhelm him with punishment. [And ' they will] call him ' "impious man, lawless ' [(and) im-
pure]." And [on] the [10] [third] day he [will rise ' from the] dead [... **4** [4]
holy disciples. And] ' the Savior [will reveal] to them [the word] ' that
gives life to the [All]. '

[But] those in the heavens spoke [many] ' words, together with ' those
on the earth [and those] [10] under the earth. [...]. **5**

[They] will come in his name, ' and they will say of him that he is '
unbegotten though he has been begotten, (that) he does not ' eat even
though he eats, (that) he does not drink [5] even though he drinks, (that)
he is uncircumcised ' though he has been circumcised, (that) he is un-
fleshly ' though he has come in flesh, (that) he did not ' come to suffering
⟨though⟩ he came to suffering, ' (that) he did not rise from the dead [10]
⟨though⟩ he arose from [the] ' dead.

[But] all the natures [and ' all the ...] will say [these things] ' while
they are receiving from [you] ' yourself, O [Melchizedek], [15] Holy One,
[High Priest], ' the perfect hope [and] ' the [gifts of] life. [I am ' Gamaliel]
who was [sent] ' to [...] the congregation of [the [20] children] of Seth,
who are above ' [thousands of] thousands and [myriads] ' of myriads
[of the] aeons [...] ' essence of the [aeons ' a]b[...] aiai ababa. The [25]
divine [...] of the [... ' nature ... ' the Mother] of the aeons, [Barbelo, '
the first]-born of the aeons, **6** splendid Doxomedon, Dom[...] ' the
one belonging to the washings, through Jesus Christ, ' Commander-in-
chief of the luminaries, ' Armozel, Oroiael, Daveithe, [5] Eleleth, and the
Man-of-light, ' immortal Aeon Pigeradamas, ' and the good god of the '
worlds who is beneficent, Mirocheirothetou, ' through Jesus Christ, the
Son [10] of God whom I proclaim. '

Just as the One who truly exists ' [of those who] exist [received the]
greatness ' [... ' do(es)] not [exist], Abel, Baruch [15] [... to] you (sing.)
the knowledge [...] ' that he is [from ' the] race of the High Priest '
[which is] above [thousands of thousands] and ' [myriads] of myriads of
the aeons. The [20] adverse [spirits are] ' ignorant of him and (of) their
(own) ' destruction. Not only (that, but) I have come to ' [reveal] to you

[the] truth ' [which is] within the [brethren]. He included [25] himself [in the] living ' [offering] together with your [offspring. He ' offered] them up as a [sacrifice to ' the] All. [But the cattle ...] ' you will offer up [...] 7 and the unbeliefs, [...] ' ignorances [and the] evil ' [...] which they [will do ...]. ' And they [will not attain to [5] the] Father of the All [...] ' the faith [...] [27] to receive [baptism ...] ' waters [...]. **8** For [the waters] which are above ' [...] that receive baptism ' [...]. But receive [that baptism ' which is] with the waters which [...] [5] while he is coming [... [9] baptism] as they [...] [28] pray for [...] **9** archons and [all] the angels with ' [the] seed.

It flowed [forth from ' the Father] of the All [... ' the] entire [place] from [.... [5] He] engendered the [gods and the angels] ' and the men [...] ' out of the [seed ...] ' all of them, those in [the heavens and] ' those upon the earth and [those] [10] under the [earth ...] [25] nature of the females [...] ' among those that are in the [...] ' they were bound with [...] ' true Adam **10** [...] true Eve.

[For ' when they ate] of the tree [of ' knowledge] they trampled [the ' Cherubim] and the Seraphim [5] [with the flaming sword]. They [...] ' which is in Adam ' [... the] world-rulers and ' [...] them out ' [... after] they had brought forth [10] [...] begetting of the archons and ' [their worldly things] belonging to [...] [25] light [...]. ' And the females and the [males] ' who exist with [... ' hidden] from every nature, [and they] ' renounce the archons, [that is, those **11** who] receive from him the [....]. ' For [they] are worthy of [... ' immortal], and [great ...] ' and [great ... [5] and] great [...] ' sons of [men ... ' disciples ... ' image] and [...] ' from the [light [10] ...] which is holy. ' For [...] from the ' [beginning ...] a seed [...]. **12**

But I will be silent ' [...] for we [are ' ... who] came down from ' [...] living. They will [...] [5] upon the [...] [7] of Adam ' [... Abel], Enoch, [Noah ... [10] you], Melchizedek, [the Priest] ' of God [Most High ...] ' those who [...] ' women [...].

[...] **13** these two who have been chosen. ' [At] no time nor ' [in] any place will they be convicted, ' whenever they have been begotten, [5] [by] their enemies, by their friends, ' [nor even] by strangers or their ' [own] kin, (nor) by the [impious] ' or the pious. [.... ' All of] the adverse natures will [10] [...] them, whether ' [those that] are manifest, or those that ' [are] not [manifest], together with those ' [that dwell] in the heavens and those that are ' [upon] the earth and those that are under [15] the earth. They will make [war ...] ' every one [...]. ' For [...] whether in the [...] [21] many [...]. [25] And these in the [...] ' every [one] will

[...]. ' These will [...] ' with every blow [...] **14** sufferings. These '
otherwise will be imprisoned [... ' and will] be punished [...]. ' The
Savior will take them [away] [5] and everyone will be overcome, [not
with] ' their mouths and words ' but by means of the [...] ' which they
will do to [them. He will] ' destroy Death.

[These things] [10] which I was commanded ' to reveal, these things '
reveal [as I (have done)]. ' But [those things] which are hidden, do not
reveal ' [to] anyone, unless [it is revealed] [15] to you (to do so).

And [immediately ' I] arose, [I, Melchizedek], ' and I began to [...] '
God [...] ' that I should [rejoice ...] [21] while he [is acting ...] ' living
[... ' I said], I [... [26] and I] will not cease, from [now on ' for ever], O
Father of the [All, ' because] you have had pity on me, and **15** [you have
sent the] angel of light ' [...] from your [aeons ' ... to] reveal [...] '
when he came [... [5] he raised] me up from ignorance ' and [from] the
fruitfulness ' of death to life. I ' have it as a name, ' I, Melchizedek, the
Priest [10] of [God] Most High. I ' [know] that I am truly, ' [verily], the
true High Priest ' [of] God Most High, and ' [...] the world. For it [15]
is not [a] small [thing that] ' God [...] with [...] ' while he [...]. ' And
[... the angels that ' dwell upon the] earth [...] [22] the [...] of [...] '
whom Death deceived. ' When he [died] he bound them [25] with the
natures which are [leading them astray]. ' Yet he offered up **16** sacrifices
[...] ' cattle [...] ' I gave them to [Death ... ' and the angels] and the
[...] [5] demons [...] ' living sacrifices [...] ' I have offered up myself
to you as a ' sacrifice, together with those that are mine, to ' you yourself, (O) Father of the All, and [10] (to) those things which you love, which
have come forth ' from you who are holy (and) [living], even ' the
[perfect] laws. I shall pronounce ' my name as I receive baptism [now] '
(and) for ever among the living (and) [15] holy [names], and in the '
[waters], Amen.

[Holy are you], ' Holy are [you], Holy are you, O [Father ' of the
All], who truly exist [... ' who] do(es) not exist, [Abel, Baruch [20] ...]
for ever and ever, [Amen]. ' Holy are [you, Holy are you], Holy are
[you, ' ...] before [... ' for ever and] ever, ' [Amen]. Holy are [you],
Holy are [you, [25] Holy are you, Mother of the] aeon(s), ' Barbelo, ' for
ever and ever, [Amen. ' Holy are you], Holy are you, Holy are you, '
[First]-born of the aeons, [30] Doxomedon. [... **17** for ever] and ever,
Amen. ' [Holy are you, Holy are you], Holy are you, [... [5] for ever and
ever], Amen. ' [Holy are you, Holy are you], Holy are you, [...] [8]
aeon ' [... for] ever and ever, [10] [Amen. Holy are you], Holy are you, '
[Holy are you], Commander, luminary ' [...] Oriael, for ' [ever and

ever], Amen. Holy are you, ' [Holy are you, Holy are you], Commander [15] [...] Man-of-Light, ' [...] for ever ' [and ever, Amen]. Holy are you, ' [Holy are you, Holy are you, Commander-in-chief ...] [20] aeon. [Holy are you, ' Holy are you, Holy are you, ... [25] for ever and ever], Amen. ' [Holy are you], Holy are [you], Holy are you, ' good [god of] 18 the worlds, [(you) who are beneficent], ' Mirocheirothetou, [for] ' ever and ever, [Amen. ' Holy are] you, [Holy are you, Holy are you], [5] Commander-in-chief [of the] ' All, Jesus Christ, [for ever and ever], ' Amen.

[...]. [9] Blessed [...] ' confession. [And ...] ' confess him [...] ' now [...] ' then it becomes [...] ' fear [and ...] [15] fear and [...] ' disturb [...] ' as he seeks him [...] ' in the place [which has a] ' great darkness [in it [20] and] many [...] ' appear [...] ' there [...]. 19 And ' [...] they are clothed with ' [...] all, and [...] [10] disturbances. They gave ' [...] their words ' [...] and they said to me, ' [... Melchizedek, ' Priest] of God [Most High ...] [15] speak as [... ' their] mouths [...] ' in the all [...] [24] lead astray [...] 20 with his [...] ' worship [and ...] ' faith [and ...] ' his prayers. And [...] [6] those that [are his ...] ' first [...]. [10] They did not care that [the ' priesthood] which you perform, [which] ' is from [... [14] in the] counsel of [...] ' Satan [...] ' the sacrifice ' [...] which is small [...] [20] of this aeon [... [25] which] exist(s) [in ...] ' lead(s) [astray ...] 21 and some [...] [4] he gave them to [... [6] and] thirteen [...] 22 throw [it ... ' in order that] you might [... [4] for] immediately [... ' by means of ... ' on the ground]. The [... (p. 23 almost completely missing) 24 [2] which is above ...] 25 me. And ' [...] you (pl.) struck me, ' [...] you threw me, ' [...] transgression. And [5] [you crucified me] from the third hour ' [of the Sabbath-eve] until ' [the ninth hour]. And after ' [these things I arose] from the ' [dead. My body] came out of [10] [the tomb] to me. [... [12] they did not] find anyone [...] 26 greeted [me ...]. ' They said to me, Be [strong, O Melchizedek], ' great [High Priest] ' of God [Most High ...] [5] over us who [... they] ' made war; you have [...] ' they did not prevail over you [and you] ' endured, and [you] ' destroyed your enemies [...] [10] of their [...] ' will rest, in any [...] ' which is living, which [... ' those that] exalted themselves against him in [...] ' flesh.

[... 27 with] the offerings, while he is working on that ' which is good, fasting ' with fasts.

These revelations ' do not reveal to anyone [5] in the flesh, since they are incorporeal, ' unless it is revealed to you (to do so). '

When the brethren who belong to the ' generations of life had said these things, they ' were taken up to (the regions) above [10] all the heavens. Amen.

THE THOUGHT OF NOREA (IX, *2*)

Introduced by

BIRGER A. PEARSON

Translated by

SØREN GIVERSEN and BIRGER A. PEARSON

One of the shortest tractates in the Nag Hammadi library, the *Thought of Norea* has been assigned its modern title on the basis of its contents. Possibly written as early as the late second century C.E., perhaps in Egypt or Syria, this Gnostic work focuses its attention on Norea. Opening with an invocation of the Father of the All and his heavenly companions, the tractate describes Norea's cry and deliverance, her activity within the Pleroma, and the future salvation of Norea and her spiritual progeny.

The figure of Norea occurs (with considerable variation in the spelling of the name) in a variety of Gnostic documents. Norea can be presented as the daughter of Eve and the wife-sister of Seth, or sometimes as the wife of Noah or Shem; she is apparently a Gnostic version of Na'amah, an anti-heroine in Jewish legends. Within the Nag Hammadi library, the *Hypostasis of the Archons* (II, *4*) portrays Norea in a manner very much like the portrait of Norea in the *Thought of Norea*. In the latter treatise she is a figure reminiscent of Sophia: she symbolizes the fall and redemption of the human soul. Her "thought" is the knowledge necessary for salvation, for blissful rest in the wholeness of the divine Pleroma.

THE THOUGHT OF NOREA

IX 27, 11-29, 5

Father of the All, [Ennoia] ' of the Light, Nous ' [dwelling] in the heights ' above the (regions) below, [15] Light dwelling [in ' the] heights, Voice of ' Truth, upright Nous, ' untouchable Logos, ' and [ineffable] Voice, [20] [incomprehensible] Father! '

It is Norea who [cries out] ' to them. They [heard], ' (and) they received her into her place ' forever. They gave it [25] to her in the Father of Nous, ' Adamas, as well as the voice ' of the Holy Ones, **28** in order that she might rest ' in the ineffable Epinoia, ' in order that ⟨she⟩ might inherit ' the first mind [5] which ⟨she⟩ had received, and that ⟨she⟩ might rest ' in the divine Autogenes, ' and that she (too) might generate ' herself, just as he himself [has] ' inherited the [living] Logos, [10] and that she might be joined to ' all of the Imperishable Ones, and [speak] ' with the mind of the Father.

And ' [again], speaking with words of ' [Life], ⟨she⟩ remained in the [15] [presence] of the Exalted One, [possessing ' that] which she had received before ' the world came into being. ' [She has] the [great ' mind] of the Invisible One, [and [20] she gives] glory to ⟨her⟩ Father, [and ' she] dwells within those who [. . .] ' within the Pleroma, ' [and] she beholds the Pleroma. '

There will be days when she will [25] [behold] the Pleroma, and ' she will not be in deficiency, ' for she has the four ' holy helpers who intercede ' on her behalf with the Father of [30] the All, Adamas, the one **29** who is within all of the Adams ' that possess the ' thought of Norea, who speaks ' concerning the two names which create [5] a single name.

THE TESTIMONY OF TRUTH (IX, 3)

Introduced by

BIRGER A. PEARSON

Translated by

SØREN GIVERSEN and BIRGER A. PEARSON

The *Testimony of Truth* is a Christian Gnostic tractate with homiletical and polemical characteristics; its title has been assigned on the basis of content. This treatise was written originally in Greek, probably around Alexandria, Egypt. While no definite conclusion can be drawn concerning authorship, two possibilities have been tentatively suggested: Julius Cassianus (about 190 C.E.) and Hierakas of Leontopolis (about 300 C.E.).

The rather fragmentary text of the *Testimony of Truth* may be divided into two major sections. The first section (29, 6-45, 6), a homily complete in itself, addresses a group of spiritually enlightened persons on various themes: truth in contrast to the Law, knowledge in contrast to empty hopes for martyrdom and a fleshly resurrection, virginity in contrast to carnal defilement, and the life of the wise and perfect Gnostic. For such a Gnostic, who "knows himself and God who is over the truth," there is salvation and an unfading crown. In this first section the false doctrines and practices attacked are clearly those of the catholic Christian church. The rest of the tractate is even more polemical. The bitter polemics are directed not only against catholic Christianity, but also against various Gnostic groups, such as the Valentinians, the Basilidians, and the Simonians. This section of the *Testimony of Truth* may have been intended particularly for those persons in danger of falling into catholic Christianity or some sort of Gnostic error.

The *Testimony of Truth* has utilized a number of sources, including an especially interesting midrash on the serpent of Genesis 3 (45, 23-49, 7). The tractate also quotes or refers to passages from the Old Testament, the New Testament (particularly Paul and John), and apocryphal literature. Valentinian Gnostic influence is evident throughout, despite the fact that Valentinians are attacked as "heretics." The most notable feature of the *Testimony of Truth* is its radical encratism, its unbending insistence on total renunciation of the world and all that belongs to it.

THE TESTIMONY OF TRUTH

IX 29, 6-74, 30

I will speak to those who know ' to hear not with the ears ' of the body but with the ears ' of the mind. For many have sought ¹⁰ after the truth and have not ' been able to find it; because ' there has taken hold

of them [the] ' old leaven of the Pharisees ' and the scribes [of] [15] the
Law. And the leaven is [the] ' errant desire of ' the angels and the
demons ' and the stars. The Pharisees ' and the scribes [20] are those who
belong to the archons who ' have authority [over them]. '

For no one who is under ' the Law will be able to look ' up to the
truth, for they will not be [25] able to serve two masters. ' For the defilement of the Law ' is manifest; [30] but undefilement belongs to the '
light. The Law commands ' (one) to take a husband (or) to take a wife,
and ' to beget, to multiply like the sand [5] of the sea. But passion which '
is a delight to them constrains ' the souls of those who are begotten '
in this place, those who defile ' and those who are defiled, [10] in order
that the Law might ' be fulfilled through them. And ' they show that
they are assisting ' the world; and they ' [turn] away from the light, [15]
who are unable ' [to pass by] the archon of [darkness] ' until they pay
the last [penny]. '

But the Son of Man ' [came] forth from Imperishability, [20] [being]
alien to defilement. He came ' [to the] world by the Jordan ' river, and
immediately the Jordan ' [turned] back. ' And John bore witness to
the [25] [descent] of Jesus. For he ' is the one who saw the [power] ' which
came down upon ' the Jordan river; for he knew ' that the dominion
of [30] carnal procreation had come to an end. The Jordan ' river is the
power ' of the body, that is, the senses [31] of pleasures. The water ' of
the Jordan is the desire ' for sexual intercourse. John ' is the archon
of [5] the womb.

And this is what the ' Son of Man reveals to us: ' It is fitting for
you (pl.) ' to receive the word of truth. If ' one will receive it [10] perfectly,—. But as for one who is [in] ' ignorance, it is difficult for him '
to diminish his works of [darkness] ' which he has done. Those who
have [known] ' Imperishability, [however], [15] have been able to struggle
against [passions ...] [17] I have said [to ' you], "Do not build [nor] '
gather for yourselves in the [place] [20] where the brigands break open, '
but bring forth fruit ' to the Father."

The foolish—thinking [in] ' their heart [that] ' if they confess, "We [25]
are Christians," in ' word only (but) not with power, while ' giving
themselves over to ' ignorance, to a ' human death, [30] not knowing
where they are going [32] nor who ' Christ is, thinking that they ' will
live, when they are (really) in error—' hasten towards the principalities [5]
and the authorities. They fall ' into their clutches because of the '
ignorance that is in ' them. For (if) only ' words which bear testimony [10]
were effecting salvation, the whole world ' would endure this thing '

[and] would be saved. ' [But] in this way they ' [drew] error to themselves. [... ¹⁸ they do] not [know] in order that they [might destroy] ' themselves. If the [Father ²⁰ were to] desire a [human] sacrifice, ' he would become [vainglorious]. '

For the Son of ' [Man] clothed himself with their ' first fruits; he went down to ²⁵ Hades and performed many mighty works. ' He raised the dead ' therein; and the ' world-rulers of darkness became envious ³³ of him, for they did not find ' sin in him. But ' he also destroyed their works ' from among men, so that ⁵ the lame, the blind, ' the paralytic, the dumb, (and) the ' demon-possessed were granted ' healing. And he walked ' upon the waters of the sea. ¹⁰ For this reason he [destroyed] ' his flesh from [...] ' which he [...]. And he [became ' ...] salvation [... ' his death ... ¹⁹ everyone ...] ²⁰ how many [they are! They are] ' blind [guides, like the disciples]. ' They boarded [the ship, (and) at about thirty] ' stades, they [saw Jesus ' walking] on the [sea. These] ²⁵ are [empty] martyrs, ' since they bear witness only [to] ' themselves. And yet they are ' sick, and they are not able to raise ³⁴ themselves.

But when they are ' "perfected" with a (martyr's) death, this ' is the thought that they have ' within them: "If we ⁵ deliver ourselves over to death ' for the sake of the Name we will be saved." These matters ' are not settled in this way. But ' through the agency of the wandering ' stars they say ¹⁰ that they have "completed" their [futile] ' "course," and [...] ' say, [...]. ' But these [...] ' they have [delivered ¹⁵ themselves ...]. ²³ But they resemble ' [...] them. They do not have ²⁵ the word which gives ' [life].

[And] some say, ' "On the last day ' [we will] certainly arise ³⁵ [in the] resurrection." But they do not ' [know what] they are saying, ' for the last day ' [is when] those belonging to Christ ⁵ [... the] earth which ' is [...]. When the [time] ' was fulfilled, he destroyed ' [their archon] of ' [darkness ...] soul(s) [... ²⁰ he ' stood ...] ' they asked [what they have been] ' bound with, [and how they] ' might properly [release themselves]. ²⁵ And [they came to know] ' themselves, [(as to) who they are], ' or rather, where they are [now], ' and what is the [place ³⁶ in] which they will rest ' from their senselessness, [arriving] ' at knowledge. [These] ' Christ will transfer to [the heights] ⁵ since they have [renounced] ' foolishness, (and have) advanced ' to knowledge. ' And those who [have ' knowledge ...] ²¹ the great ' [... the resurrection ' ... he has come to] know ' [the Son of Man], that ²⁵ [is, he has come to] know [himself. ' This] is the perfect life, ' [that] man know ' [himself] by means of the All. '

[Do not] expect, therefore, [30] [the] carnal resurrection, **37** which [is] destruction, [and they are not ' stripped] of [it (the flesh) who] ' err in [expecting] ' a [resurrection] [5] that is empty. [They do] not [know] ' the power [of God], ' nor do they [understand the interpretation] ' of the scriptures [on account of their] ' double-mindedness. [The [10] mystery] which [the Son of Man ' spoke about ...] ' in order that [...] ' destroy [...] [16] man who [... book] ' which is written [...] ' for [they] have [... [20] blessed ...] ' within [them, and they] ' dwell before [God under the ' light yoke. Those who do not] ' have [the word which] [25] gives life in their [heart will die]; ' and in [their] thought ' they have become manifest to [the Son] ' of Man, according to [the manner of their] ' activity and their [error ...] **38** of this sort. They ' [...] as he divides the ' [...] and they [do not] understand ' [that the Son] of Man [5] is coming from him. '

But [when they have come] up to ' [...] sacrifice, they die ' [in a] human [way], and they ' [deliver] themselves [...] [12] a death [...] [16] those who ' [...] they are many ' [...] each ' [one ...] pervert [20] [...] gain ' [... their] mind. ' [Those who receive him] to themselves ' [with uprightness] and ' [power] and every knowledge [25] [are the ones whom] he will transfer ' [to the] heights, unto ' [life] eternal.

[But] those who receive ' [him] to themselves with ' [ignorance], the pleasures **39** which defile rule over them. [Those] ' men used to [say], ' "God created [members] ' for our use, for us to [grow in] [5] defilement, in order that [we might] ' enjoy [ourselves]." ' And they cause [God to] ' participate with them [in] ' deeds of this [sort; and] [10] they are [not] steadfast [upon] ' the earth. [Nor will they reach] ' heaven, [but ...] ' place will [...] ' four [...] [18] unquenchable [... [22] word ...] ' upon [the Jordan river] ' when he came [to John at] [25] the time he [was baptized]. ' The [Holy] Spirit [came] ' down upon him [as a] ' dove [...] ' accept for ourselves that [he] was born [30] of a virgin [and] ' he took flesh; he [... **40** having] received power. ' [Were we ourselves] begotten from ' [a] virginal state ' [or] conceived by the word? [5] [Rather, we have been born] again by ' [the word]. Let us therefore strengthen ' [ourselves] as virgins in the ' [...].

The males dwell ' [...] the virgin [10] [...] by means of ' [...] in the word ' [...]. But the word of ' [...] and spirit [...] [18] is the Father ' [...] for the man [... [21] like Isaiah, who was sawed ' with a saw, (and)] he became two. ' [So also the Son of Man ' divides] us by [25] [the word of the] cross. It ' [divides the day from] the night and ' [the light from the] darkness and the corruptible ' [from] incorruptibility, and it ' [divides] the males from the females. [30] But [Isaiah] is the type **41** of the body. The saw ' is the word of the Son of ' Man which separates us from the ' error of the angels.

No one [5] knows the God of truth ' except solely the man who ' will forsake all of the ' things of the world, having renounced '.the whole place, (and) having [10] grasped the fringe of his garment. ' He has set himself up as a [power]; ' he has subdued desire every [place] ' within himself. He has [. . .] ' and he has turned to him [. . .] [15] having examined himself [. . .] ' in becoming [. . . ' the] mind. And [he . . . from] ' his soul [. . .] ' there [. . .] [20] he has [. . .] [22] in what way [. . .] ' the flesh which [. . .] ' in what way [. . .] [25] out of it, and ' how many [powers does he have]? ' And who is the one who has bound him? ' And who is the one who will loose him? And what ' is the light? And what is the darkness? [30] And who is the one who has created [the earth]? ' And who is God? [And who] **42** are the angels? And what is soul? ' And what is spirit? And where is ' the voice? And who is the one who speaks? And who ' is the one who hears? Who is the one who gives pain? [5] And who is the one who suffers? And who ' is it who has begotten the corruptible flesh? ' And what is the governance? ' And why are some ' lame, and some [10] [blind], and some ' [. . .], and some ' [. . .], and some ' rich, [and] some ' poor? And why [15] are [some powerless, ' some] brigands? [. . .] [21] he having ' [. . .] as he again ' [. . .] fighting ' against [thoughts] of the archons [25] and the powers and the demons. ' He did not give them a place ' in which to rest, ' [but] he struggled against their passions ' [. . .] he condemned **43** their error. He cleansed his ' soul from the transgressions ' which he had committed with an alien hand. ' He stood up, being upright within [5] himself, because he exists in ' everyone, and because he has ' death and life ' within himself, and he exists ' in the midst of both of them. [10] And when he had received the power ' he turned toward the parts of the right, ' and he entered into the truth, ' having forsaken all things pertaining to the left, ' having been filled with wisdom, [15] with counsel, with understanding ' and with insight, and an ' eternal power. [And] ' he broke open his bonds. [Those who had] ' formed the whole place [20] [he] condemned. [But they] ' did not find [. . .] hidden ' within him.

[And he gave command] ' to himself; he [began to] ' know [himself and] [25] to speak with his [mind], which ' is the father of the truth, concerning the unbegotten ' aeons, and concerning ' the virgin who brought forth ' the light. And he thinks [30] about the power which ' flowed over the [whole] place, **44** and which takes hold of him. And ' he is a disciple of his mind ' which is male. He began ' to keep silent within [5] himself until the day when ' he should become worthy to be received ' above. He rejects for himself ' loquacity and ' disputations, and he endures [10] the whole place; and he bears up ' under them, and he endures ' all of the evil things. ' And he is patient ' with every one; he makes himself equal [15] to every one, and he also separates ' himself from them. And that which anyone ' [wants, he brings] to him, ' [in order that] he might become perfect ' [(and) holy]. When the [... [20] he] ' grasped [him], having bound him ' upon [...] and he was filled ' [with wisdom. He] bore witness to the truth ' [...] the power, and he went [25] [into] Imperishability, the place ' whence he [came] forth, having left ' the world which has ' the appearance of the [night, ' and] those that whirl the [30] [stars in] it.

This, therefore, is **45** the true testimony: When ' man knows himself ' and God who is over the truth, ' he will be saved, and he [5] will be crowned with the crown ' unfading.

John ' was begotten by the Word through ' a woman, Elizabeth; ' and Christ was begotten by [10] the Word through a virgin, ' Mary. What is (the meaning of) this mystery? ' John was ' begotten by means of a womb ' worn with age, but Christ [15] passed through a virgin's womb. ' When she had conceived she gave birth to ' the Savior. Furthermore she ' was found to be a virgin again. ' Why, then, do you (pl.) [err] [20] and not seek after these mysteries ' which were prefigured ' for our sake? '

It is written in the Law concerning this, ' when God gave [a command] [25] to Adam, "From every [tree] ' you may eat, [but] from ' the tree which is in the midst of ' Paradise do not eat, ' for on the day that you eat [30] from it you will surely ' die." But the serpent was wiser **46** than all the animals that ' were in Paradise, and ' he persuaded Eve, saying, ' "On the day when you eat [5] from the tree which is in the midst ' of Paradise ' the eyes of your mind will be opened." ' And Eve obeyed, ' and she stretched forth her hand; [10] she took from the tree; she ' ate; she also gave to her husband with ' her. And immediately they knew ' that they were naked, ' and they took some fig leaves [15] (and) put on girdles. '

But [God] came at the time of ' [evening] walking in the midst ' [of] Paradise. When ' Adam saw him he hid himself. [20] And he said, "Adam, where are you?" ' He answered (and) said, ' "[I] have come under the fig tree." ' And at that very moment ' God [knew] that he had [25] eaten from the tree of ' which he had commanded him, "Do not ' eat of it."

And ' he said to him, "Who is it **47** who has instructed you?" And
Adam answered, ' "The woman whom you have ' given me." And the
woman said, ' "The serpent is the one who instructed me." ⁵ And he
cursed the serpent, and ' he called him "devil." ' And he said, "Behold,
Adam has ' become like one of us, ' knowing evil and ¹⁰ good." Then
he said, "Let us ' cast him out of Paradise ' lest he take from the tree '
of life and eat and live for ' ever."

But of what sort is ¹⁵ this God? First [he] ' envied Adam that he should '
eat from the tree of knowledge. ' And secondly ' he said, "Adam,
where are you?" ²⁰ And God does not have ' foreknowledge, that is, '
since he did not know this from the ' beginning. [And] afterwards ' he
said, "Let us cast him [out] ²⁵ of this place, lest he ' eat of the tree of '
life and live for ever." ' Surely he has shown ' himself to be a malicious³⁰
envier. And **48** what kind of a God is this? ' For great is the blindness '
of those who read, and they did not ' know it. And he said, "I am ⁵
the jealous God; I will bring ' the sins of the fathers upon ' the children
until three (and) four generations." ' And he said, "I will make ' their
heart thick, and I will ¹⁰ cause their mind to become blind, that ' they
might not know nor ' comprehend the things that ' are said." But these
things he has ' said to those who believe in him ¹⁵ [and] serve him!

And ' [in one] place Moses writes, ' "[He] made the devil a serpent '
⟨for⟩ [those] whom he has in his generation." ' In the other book
which is ²⁰ called "Exodus," ' it is written thus (cf. 7:8-12): "He contended against ' [magicians], when the place was full ' [of serpents]
according to their [wickedness; and ' the rod] which was in the hand
of Moses ²⁵ became a serpent, (and) it swallowed ' the serpents of the
magicians."

Again ' it is written (Numbers 21:9), "He made a serpent of ' bronze
(and) hung it upon a pole **49** [. . .] which [. . .] ³ for the [one who will
gaze] upon ' [this] bronze [serpent], none ⁵ [will destroy] him, and the
one who will ' [believe in] this bronze serpent ' [will be saved]."

For this is Christ; ' [those who] believed in him ' [have received life].
Those who did not believe ¹⁰ [will die].

What, then, is this ' [faith? Those] who do not [serve . . . ²⁸ and you
(pl.) . . .] ' we [. . . **50** and] you [do not understand Christ ' spiritually
when you say], ' "We [believe] in Christ." For [this] ' is the [way] Moses
[writes] ⁵ in every book. The [book of ' the] generation of Adam [is
written for those] ' who are in the [generation] of [the Law]. ' They
follow the Law [and] ' they obey it, [and . . .] ¹¹ together with the [. . .].
(pp. 51-54 almost completely missing)

[..., "... **55** the] Ogdoad, which is the ' eighth, and that we might receive ' that [place] of salvation." ' [But they] know not what salvation is, [5] but they enter into ' [misfortune] and into a ' [...] in death, in the ' [waters]. This [is] the baptism ' [of death which they observe ...] [17] come to death ' [... and] this is ' [...] according to [...] **56** he completed the course [of] ' Valentinus. He himself ' speaks about the Ogdoad, ' but his disciples resemble [the] [5] disciples of Valentinus. ' They on their part, moreover, [...] ' leave the good, [but] they ' have [worship of] ' the idols [...] [18] he has spoken [many words, and he has] ' written many [books ...] [20] words [... **57** they are] manifest from ' [the] confusion in which they are, ' [in the] deceit of the world. ' For [they] go to that place [5] together with their knowledge ' [which is] vain.

Isidore, also, ' [his son], resembled ' [Basilides]. He himself ' [...] many, and [he [10] ...] but he did not [...] ' this [...] ' other disciple(s) ' [...] blind [... ' but he] gave them [15] [... pleasures ...] **58** they do [not] agree [with] ' each other. For the [Simonians] ' take [wives] ' (and) beget children; but the [...] [5] abstain ' from their [...] nature ' [...] a [passion ...] ' the drops [of ...] ' anoint [them ...] [11] which we [... they ' agree] with [each other ...] ' him [...] ' they [...] **59** judgment(s) ' [...] these, on account of the ' [...] them ' [...] the heretics [5] [...] schism(s) [...] ' and the males ' [...] are men ' [...] will belong ' [to the world-rulers] of darkness [...] [11] of [the world ...] [13] they have ' [...] the [archons [15] ... power(s) ...] [17] judge [them ' ...]. But [the ...] ' word(s) of [...] **60** speak, while they [...] ' become [...] ' in a fire [unquenchable ...] ' they are punished.

[But these] [5] who are [from the generation] ' of the Son of [Man have revealed] ' to the [... in] all of [the ' affairs ...]. [11] But [it is difficult] to [...] ' to find [one ...] ' and [two ...]. [16] For the [Savior said to his] ' disciples, [...] ' one in [... **61** and] he has ' [...] wisdom as well as ' [counsel and] understanding and ' [intelligence] and knowledge [5] [and power] and truth. ' [And he has] some ' [...] from above ' [...] the place where ' [the Son of Man ...] [12] power [...] ' guard against [...] **62** he knows [...] ' understands [...] [4] worthy of him [...] ' true [...] ' alien [...]. ' But [...], together with [...] ' evil, in [...] [11] he received [baptism ...] ' and those that [... (pp. 63-64 missing) **65** in] a dream ' [...] silver [...]. ' But [...] becomes [wealthy ' ...] among the [authorities ...]. [6] But [the] sixtieth ' [...] thus ' [...] world ' [...] they [10] [...] gold [... [29] they] think, [...] [31] we have been released from **66** the flesh. [...] [3] not turn him to [...] ' Jesus [... [6] the] beginning [...] '

a son [. . .] [9] out of [. . . which ' is] the pattern [. . . ' light of . . [i] [28] to find from [. . .] ' defilement which [. . . [31] they] do not blaspheme [. . . **67** them] not, neither any [pleasure] ' nor desire, nor ' [can they] control them. It is fitting ' that they should become undefiled, [5] in order that they might ' [show] to every [one] that they ' [are from] the [generation of the] Son of Man, ' since it is about [them] that the Savior bore ' witness.

But [those that are] from [10] the seed [of Adam] are manifest ' by their [deeds which are] their [work]. ' They have not ceased [from desire which is ' wicked . . .]. ' But some [15] [. . .] the dogs ' [. . .] the angels ' for [. . .] which they beget ' [. . .] will come [. . .] with their [. . .] [28] move as they ' [. . . on] the day when they will beget [30] [children]. Not only that, but they ' have intercourse while they are giving suck. **68**

But others are caught up in the death of [. . .]. ' They are [pulled] ' ⟨every⟩ which way, (and) they are gratified ' by unrighteous Mammon. [5] They lend money [at interest]; they [waste time]; ' and they do not work. But he who is ' [father] of [Mammon is (also)] ' (the) father of sexual intercourse.

But he who ' is able to renounce them [10] shows [that] he is [from] the generation ' of the [Son of Man], (and) has ' power to accuse [them. ' . . . he] ' restrains [. . .] [15] part(s) in a [. . .] ' in wickedness [and he makes] the ' outer like the [inner. He resembles] an ' angel which [. . . [20] power . . .] ' said them. But the one [. . .]. [27] And having withdrawn [. . .] he became ' silent, having ceased from loquacity ' and disputations. **69** But he [who has] found the [life-giving word ' and he who] has come to know [the Father of Truth ' has come to rest]; he has ceased [seeking], having ' [found]. And when he found he became [silent]. [5] But few are the things he used to say to those that ' [. . .] in their heart the intellectual ' [. . .].

Some enter ' the faith [by receiving a] baptism, ' on the ground that they have [it] as a hope [10] of salvation, which they call ' "the [seal]." They do not [know] ' that the [fathers of] the world are ' manifest to that [place, but] ' he himself [knows that] he is sealed. [15] For [the Son] of [Man] ' did not baptize any of his ' disciples. But [. . . if those who] are baptized ' were headed for life, ' the world would become [20] empty. And the fathers of ' baptism were defiled. '

But the baptism of truth is ' something else; it is by renunciation of [the] ' world that it is found. [But those who] [25] say [only] with the tongue [that ' they] are renouncing it [are lying], ' and they are coming to [the place] ' of fear. Moreover they are humbled ' within it. As though those to whom it was given, [30] (once) having been condemned, ' should receive something (else)!

They become ' wicked in their action, and ' some of them fall away **70** [to the worship of] idols. [Others] ' have ' [demons] dwelling with them [as did] ' David the king. He is the one who [5] laid the foundation of Jerusalem; and his son ' Solomon, whom he begat ' in [adultery], is the one who ' built Jerusalem by means of the demons, ' because he received [their powers]. When he [10] [had finished building, he imprisoned] the demons ' [in the temple]. He [placed them] into seven ' [waterpots. They remained] a long [time ' in] the [waterpots], abandoned ' [there]. When the Romans [went] [15] up to [Jerusalem] they discovered ' [the] waterpots, [and immediately] ' the [demons] ran ' out of the waterpots as those who ' escape from prison. And [20] the waterpots [remained] pure (thereafter). ' [And] since those days ' [they dwell] with men who are ' [in] ignorance, and ' [they have remained upon] the earth.

Who, then, is [25] [David]? And who is Solomon? ' [And] what is the foundation? And what is the ' wall which surrounds Jerusalem? And who ' are the demons? And what are the ' waterpots? And who are [30] the Romans? But these [are mysteries . . .] **71** [12] victorious over [. . . the Son] ' of Man [. . . [14] undefiled . . .] [18] and he [. . .] ' when he [. . .]. [20] For [. . .] is a great [. . .] [22] to this nature [. . .] [24] those that [. . .] ' all in [a . . .] blessed ' and they [. . . like a] ' salamander. [It] goes into ' the flaming fire which burns ' exceedingly; it slithers into the [furnace . . . **72** [14] the] furnace [. . .] [16] the boundaries ' [. . .] that they might see ' [. . .] and the power ' [. . .] sacrifice. Great is the sacrifice [. . . [22] but] in a ' [. . .] aside ' [. . .]. And [25] [the Son] of Man [. . .] ' and [he has become] manifest through ' the bubbling fountain of [immortality. **73** . . .] ' he is pure, ' [and he] is [. . .]. A free man ' [is not] envious. He is set apart from [5] everyone, from [every audacity and] envy ' the [power of] which is great [. . .] ' disciple [. . .] ' pattern of law [. . .] ' these [. . .] [10] only [. . .] [13] they placed ' him under a [. . .] [15] a teaching [. . .] [17] his teaching. '

They say, "[Even if] an [angel] ' comes from heaven, and preaches [20] to you beyond that which we preached ' to you, may he be ' anathema!" (cf. Galatians 1:8). They do not let the [. . .] ' of the soul which [. . .] ' freedom [. . .]. [25] For they are still immature [. . .] ' they are not able to [keep] ' this law which works ' by means of these heresies—' though it is not they, but the powers [30] of Sabaoth—by means **74** of the [. . .] ' the doctrines [. . .] ' as they have been jealous of some [. . . ' law(s)] in Christ. Those who will [. . .] [5] power [. . .] they reach the [. . .] ' the [twelve] ' judge [. . .] them ' [. . .] the fountain of ' [immortality . . .] [13] in order that [. . . [17] good . . .] ' the whole place. ' [. . .] there the enemies. [20] He was baptized, and the ' [. . .] he became divine; he flew ' [up], (and) they did not grasp him. ' [. . .] there the [enemies ' . . .] since it was not possible [25] [for them to bring him] down again. ' Every [. . .] grasps him ' [with] ignorance, attending ' to those who teach in the corners ' by means of carved things and [30] artful tricks. They will not be able [. . .].

MARSANES (X, *1*)

Introduced and translated by

BIRGER A. PEARSON

Codex X, one of the most fragmentary of the Nag Hammadi codices, apparently consists of a single tractate whose title occurs at the end: "[M]arsanes". This tractate is an apocalypse attributed to a Gnostic prophet and visionary known from other Gnostic sources (under the name "Marsanes" and "Marsianos"). It may have been among the Gnostic apocalypses which, according to Porphyry, were discussed in Rome in the school of Plotinus.

Marsanes begins and ends with an encouraging statement on the rewards of knowledge. Though it is impossible to determine the full content of the tractate, some conclusions can be reached about the content of the best-preserved pages (1-10, 25-42). Pages 1-10 describe an intellectual and visionary ascent to the highest heaven; here the various levels of reality are revealed. The readers are given to understand that they, too, can achieve the ascent to God. The vocabulary of this section is closely related to that of *Allogenes* (XI, *3*). Pages 25-42 contain revelations concerning the mystical meaning of the letters of the alphabet: their relation to the human soul on the one hand, and to the names of the angels on the other. The closest parallel to this material from previously known Gnostic sources is Irenaeus' description of the teachings of Marcus.

The content and vocabulary of *Marsanes* show interesting points of contact with Neoplatonic philosophy, revealing a distinct trend away from the radical dualism of the earliest Gnostic systems in the direction of a monistic understanding of reality. *Marsanes* was composed originally in Greek, perhaps by a Syrian author, probably in the early third century.

MARSANES

X 1, 1-68, 18

[. . .] [11] and a [reward]. They [came to know]; they ' found him with a pure heart, ' and they are not afflicted by him ' with evils. Those who have received [15] you (pl.) will be given their ' choice reward for ' endurance, and he will ' ward off [the] ' evils from them. [But] let none [20] of us be distressed [and] ' think [in] his ' heart that the great ' Father [. . .]. ' For he looks upon the All [and] [25] takes care of them all. ' And [he] has shown to them ' his [. . .]. ' Those that [. . .] **2** [11] at first. '

But as for the thirteenth ' seal, I have established it, ' together with [the] limit of [15] knowledge and the certainty ' of rest. The first ' [and the] second and the ' [third] are the cosmic ' and the material. I have [20] [in-

formed] you concerning these, that you should ' [. . .] your bodies. And '
[a] sense-perceptible [power] ' will [. . .] those who will rest, ' and they
will be kept [25] [from] passion and division ' [of the] union.

The fourth ' [and the] fifth which are above, ' [these] you have come
to know ' [. . . divine]. 3 He exists after the [. . .] ' and the nature of the
[. . .] ' that is, the one who [. . .] ' three. And [I have [5] informed] you of
[. . .] ' in the three [. . .] ' by these [two. I have ' informed] you concerning [it, that it] ' is incorporeal [. . .] [11] and after [. . .] ' within [. . .] '
every [. . .] which [. . .] ' your [. . .]. The [fifth,[15] concerning the] repentance [of] ' those that are within me, and ' concerning those who dwell
in that place. '

But the sixth, ' concerning the self-begotten ones,[20] concerning the incorporeal being ' which exists partially, ' together with those who exist
in ' the truth of the All [. . .] ' for understanding and [25] assurance. And
the [seventh], ' concerning the self-begotten power, ' which [is the] '
third [perfect . . .] 4 fourth, concerning salvation ' [and] wisdom. And
the eighth, ' concerning the mind which is ' [male, which] appeared [5] [in
the beginning], and (concerning) the being ' [which is incorporeal] and
the ' [intelligible] world. The ninth, ' [. . .] of the power ' [which]
appeared [in the [10] beginning. The] tenth, [concerning ' Barbelo, the]
virgin [. . .] ' of the Aeon. ' [The eleventh] and [the ' twelfth] speak of
the [15] Invisible One who possesses ' three powers ' and the Spirit which
does not ' have being, belonging to ' the first Unbegotten (fem.). The [20]
thirteenth speaks concerning ' [the] Silent One who was not ' [known],
and the primacy of ' [the one who] was not distinguished. '

For I am he who has [25] [understood] that which truly exists, ' [whether]
partially or ' [wholly], according to difference ' [and sameness], that they
exist from the ' [beginning in the] entire place which is 5 eternal, ⟨i.e.⟩ all
those that have come into ' existence whether without being ' or with
being, those who are ' unbegotten, and the divine aeons [5] together with
the angels, and the ' souls which are without guile, ' and the soul-[gar-
ments], ' the likenesses of [the] ' simple ones. And [afterwards they] [10]
have been mixed with [those that resemble] ' them. But still [. . . the] '
entire being [. . . which] ' imitates the [incorporeal being] ' and the un-
substantial (fem.). [Finally] [15] the entire defilement [was saved] ' together
with the immortality of ' that one (fem.). I have deliberated ' and have
attained to the boundary of the sense-perceptible ' world, ⟨I have come
to know⟩ part by part [20] the entire place ' of the incorporeal being, and '
⟨I⟩ have come to know the intelligible world. ' ⟨I have come to know⟩,
when ⟨I⟩ was deliberating, ' that in every respect the sense-perceptible [25]
world is [worthy] ' of being saved entirely.

[For] ' I have not ceased speaking [of the] ' Self-begotten One, O [...] '
became [...] **6** part by part the entire place. ' He descended; again he
descended ' ⟨from⟩ the Unbegotten One ' who does not have being,
who [5] is the Spirit. That one who exists ' before all of them attains ' [to
the divine] Self-engendered One. ' The one having ' [being] searches [10]
[...] and he exists ' [... and] he is like ' [...] and from ' [...] dividing '
[...] I became [15] [...] for many, as it is manifest ' that he saved a
multitude. '

But after all of these things ' I am seeking the kingdom ' of the
Three-Powered One,[20] which has no beginning. Whence ' did he appear
and ' act to fill the ' entire place with his power? And ' in what way did
the unbegotten ones [25] come into existence, since they were not begotten?
And ' what are [the] differences among the [aeons? ' And] as for those
who are unbegotten, ' how many [are they]? And in what respect ' [do
they differ] from each other? **7**

When I had inquired about these things ' I perceived that he had
worked ' from silence. He exists ' from the beginning among those that [5]
truly exist, that belong to the One who ' exists. There is another, existing '
from the beginning, belonging to the One who ' works within the Silent
One. ' And the silence [...] [10] him works, ' for this [...] is [a] brother. '
That one [works from] ' the [silence which belongs to the] ' Unbegotten
One among [the aeons, and from] [15] the beginning he does not have
[being]. ' But the energy of ' that One ⟨is⟩ the Three-Powered One, ' the
One unbegotten [before] ' the Aeon, not having [being].[20] And it is possible to behold the supremacy of the ' silence of the Silent One, ' ⟨...⟩
i.e. the supremacy ' of the energy of the ' Three-Powered. And the One
who [25] exists, who is silent, [who is] ' above the [heaven ...], ' revealed
[the ' Three-Powered, First]-Perfect ' One.

[When he ...] **8** the powers they rejoiced. ' Those that are within me
were perfected ' together with all the ' rest. And they all blessed [5] the
Three-Powered, ' one by one, who ' is [the] First-Perfect One, ' [bless-
ing] him in purity, [everywhere] ' praising the Lord [10] [who exists] before
the All, ' [... the] Three-Powered. ' [...] their worship ' [...] myself, '
[and I will still go on [15] inquiring] how they had ' [become silent]. I will
understand a ' power which I hold ' in honor.

The third ' power of the Three-Powered,[20] when it had perceived him, '
said to me, "Be silent ' in order that you might {not} know; run, ' and
come before me. But ' know that this One was [25] [silent], and obtain
understanding." ' For [the power] is attending ' [to me, leading] me
into ' [the Aeon which] is Barbelo, ' [the] male [Virgin]. **9**

For this reason the ' Virgin became male, ' because she had been divided from the male. The ' Knowledge stood outside of him,[5] because it belongs to him. ' And she who exists, she who sought, ' possesses (it), just as ' the Three-Powered One possesses. ' She withdrew [10] from them, from [these] two [powers], ' since she exists [outside of] ' the Great One, as she [. . .] ' who is above [. . .] ' who is silent, [who has] [15] this [commandment] ' to be silent. His knowledge ' and his hypostasis ' and his energy ' are those things of which the power [20] of the Three-Powered spoke, ⟨saying⟩, ' We all have ' withdrawn to ourselves. We have [become] ' silent, [and] ' when we came to know [him, that is],[25] the Three-Powered, [we] ' bowed down; we [. . . ; we] ' blessed him [. . .] ' upon us. [. . .]. '

[. . . the] invisible [Spirit] [10] ran up ' to his place. The whole place ' was revealed; the whole place unfolded ' ⟨until⟩ he reached the upper region.[5] Again he departed; he caused the ' whole place to be illuminated, and the whole ' place was illuminated. And [you] (pl.) have been given ' the third part of ' [the spirit] of the power of the One [10] [who possesses] the three ' [powers]. Blessed is ' [. . .]. He said, O [you ' who dwell in these] places, it is necessary ' [for you to know] those that are higher [15] than these, and tell them to the ' powers. For you (sing.) will become ' [elect] with the elect ones ' [in the last] times, ' [as] the invisible Spirit [20] [runs] up above. And you ' [yourselves], run with him ' [up above], since you have ' [the] great crown which ' [. . .].

But on the day [25] [. . .] will beckon ' [. . .] run up above ' [. . .] and the sense-perceptible ' [. . .] visible ' [. . .] and they [. . .] (pp. 11-12 missing) 13[15] the perception. He is for ' ever, not having being, ' in the One who is, who is silent, ' the One who is from the beginning, ' [who] does [not] have being [20] [. . .] part of [. . .] ' indivisible. The [. . .] ' consider a [. . . [24] ninth . . .] 14[15] I [was dwelling] ' among the aeons which have ' been begotten. As I was permitted, [I] have ' come to be among those that were not [begotten]. ' But I was dwelling in the [great] [20] Aeon, as I [. . .]. ' And [. . . ' the] three powers [. . .] ' the One who [possesses] ' the [three] powers. The [three [25] powers . . . 15 the] Silent One and the ' Three-Powered One [. . . ' the] one that does not have breath. ' We took our stand [. . .][5] in the [. . .] 13 we entered [. . .] ' breath [. . . 16 who] does not have breath, ' [and he] exists in a [. . .] ' completely. And I saw ' [. . .] him to the great [5] [. . .] they knew him [. . .][12] limit [. . .] ' and [I . . .] ' alone [. . .] 17 is active ' [. . .] why, [again], (does) knowledge ' [. . .] ignorant, and [. . .] ' he runs the risk [5] [. . .] that he become [. . .].[15] Those ' [. . .]. But it is necessary that a ' [. . .] does not have form ' [. . .]

to this one ' [...] exists before [20] [...] remember ' [... from] the beginning ' [...] the one that [...] **18** these [...] ' look(ed) at [...] in the
nine [... the] ' world of the Seven [...] ' in a day of [...] [5] for ever
[...] [14] and [... after] ' many [years ...] ' when I saw the [Father I came
to] ' know him, and [...] ' many [...] ' partial [...] [20] for ever [...] '
the material ones [...] ' cosmic [...] ' above [...] ' in addition [...] **19**[13]
he [...] [15] out of [...] ' into those that [...] ' them into [...] ' name '
[them. And] (as for) their nomenclature, [20] [bear] witness yourselves '
[that you are] lower than [...] ' and their [hypostasis]. '

But [in addition, when ...] **20**[14] hidden [... ' the] third ' [power]. The
blessed Authority (fem.) ' said [...] ' among these and [...] ' i.e. she
who [does not have ...]. [20] For there is not glory [...] ' nor even the
one who [...]. ' For indeed the one who [...]. [24] For [...] **21**[14] and the
[signs of the Zodiac ...] ' and the [...] ' and [...] ' which do not have
[...] ' acquire for [... ' revolution ...]. [20] But [the] soul(s) [...] ' there
[...] ' body(s) of this ' [...] soul(s) of heaven [...] ' around [...] [25]
shape [...] ' which is [...] **22**[15] those that [...] ' there [... [19] all the
likenesses ...] ' them [...] ' all the forms [...] ' shape(s), so that [they
... ' and] become [...] ' themselves [...] [25] and the [...] ' the animals
[...] ' and the [...] (pp. 23-24 missing) **25** there.

But their ' powers, which are the angels, ' are in the form of ' beasts
and animals.[5] Some among them are ' [polymorphous], and contrary to '
[nature] they have [...] ' for their names which [...]. ' They are [divided]
and [...] [10] according to the [... ' and ...] in [form ...]. ' But these
that are ' [patterns] of sound according to the third ' originate from
being.[15] And concerning these, all of ' these (remarks) are sufficient, '
since we have (already) spoken about them.

For [this] ' division takes place ' again in these regions in [the man-
ner] [20] we have mentioned from the [beginning]. ' However the soul, on
the ' other hand, [has] ' different shape⟨s⟩. ' The shape of the soul
exists [in [25] this] form, ' i.e. (the soul) that came into ' existence of its
own accord. The shape ' is [the second] **26** spherical portion ' while the
first follows [it], ' eēiou, the self-begotten soul, ' aeēiouō.[5] [The] second
schema, ' eēiou, (consists) of those [having] ' two sounds (diphthongs),
the first being ' placed after them [...] [12] the light.

[Restrain] ' yourselves, receive [the] ' imperishable seed,[15] bear fruit,
and ' do not become ' attached to your possessions. '

But know that the oxytones ' exist among the vowels [20] and the '
diphthongs which are ' next to them. But the [short] ' are inferior, and
the [...] ' are [...] [25] by them. Those that [...] ' since they are inter-

mediate ' [...]. The sounds of ' [the semivowels] are **27** superior to those that do not have voice. ' And those that are double are superior ' to the semivowels which ' do not change. But the aspirates [5] are better than the inaspirates (of) ' these that do not have voice. ' And those that are intermediate will [accept] ' their combination in which they are. ' They are ignorant [of] [10] the things that are good. They ' are combined with the [intermediates] ' which are less, according to ⟨the⟩ [form] ' of the nomenclature of the [gods] ' and the angels, [not] because [15] they are mixed with each other ' form by form, but ' only (because) they have their ' good works. ' It did not happen [20] that their will was revealed. '

Do not keep on [sinning], ' and do not dare to ' make use of sin.

But [I] ' am speaking to you [concerning the ' three ... shapes] ' of the soul. [The] ' third [shape of the soul] ' is [...] **28** is a spherical one, put ' after it, from those that have a ' single vowel: ' eee, iii, ooo, uuu, ōōō.[5] The diphthongs were ' as follows: ai, au, ' ei, eu, ēu, ou, ōu, oi, ēi, ' ui, ōi, auei, euēu, oiou, ' ggg, ggg, ggg, aiau,[10] [eieu], ēu, oiou, ōu, ggg, ' [ggg], aueieu, oiou, ēu, ' three times for a male soul. ' The third ' shape is spherical.[15] The second shape, being ' put after it, has ' two sounds. The male soul's ' third shape ' (consists) of the [20] simple vowels: ' aaa, eee, ēēē, iii, ooo, ' uuu, ōōō, ōōō, ōōō. ' [And] this shape is different ' [from] the first, but [25] [they resemble] each other ' [and they] make some ' [ordinary sounds] of ' [this sort: aeē]oō. And **29** from these (are made) the diphthongs. '

So also the ' fourth and the fifth. ' With regard to them, they were not allowed to [5] reveal the whole topic, ' but only those things that are apparent. ' You (pl.) were taught ' about them, that you should perceive them ' in order that they, too, might [10] all seek and find [who] ' they are, either ' by themselves alone [...] ' or by each other, ' or to reveal [destinies] [15] that have been determined from the beginning, ' either with reference to themselves alone [or] ' with reference to one another, just as [they] ' exist with each other [in] ' sound, whether partially [20] or formally.

[They are] ' commanded [to] ' submit or their ' [part] is generated and ' formal. Either (they are commanded) by [the [25] long] (vowels) or [by] ' those of [dual time value, or] ' by [...] ' which are short [...] **30** or the oxytones or the ' intermediates or the barytones. '

And ⟨the⟩ consonants ' exist with the vowels,[5] and individually ' they are commanded, ' and they submit. ' They constitute the naming ' [of] the angels. And [10] [the] consonants are ' self-existent, ' [and] as they are changed ' ⟨they⟩ submit ' to the hidden [15] gods by means of ' beat

and ' pitch and ' silence and impulse. ' [They] summon the semivowels,[20] all of which ' submit to them with ' one [accord]; since it is
only ' the [unchanging] double (consonants) ' that coexist with the
semivowels.[25]

But the aspirates ' [and the inaspirates] and the ' [intermediates]
coexist ' [with those that have] voice. [Again ' . . . they] are combined '
[with each other, and] they are separate **31** from one another. They are '
commanded, and they submit, ' and they constitute an ' ignorant
nomenclature.[5] And they become one [or] ' two or three or [four] ' or
five or six up to ' seven having a ' [single] vowel. These that [have] [10]
two [vowels . . . ' seven consonants. Among] ' the first names [some]
are ' less. And ' since [these] do not have being,[15] either [you (sing.)] are
an aspect [of] ' being [or] you do [not] separate ' the nature [of] our
mind, ' which [is masculine] (and) which is [intermediate]. '

And you [put] in [20] those that resemble each other [with] ' the vowels
[and] ' the consonants. Some ' are: bagadazatha, ' begedezethe,
[bēgēdē][25]zēthē, [bigidizithi, bogo]'dozotho, [buguduzuthu], ' bōgōdō-
zōthō. [And] ' the rest [. . .] ' ba[. . .]. **32** But the rest are ' different:
abebēbi'bob, in order that you (sing.) might [collect] ' them, and be
separated from the [5] angels.

And there ' will be some effects. ' The first, ' which is good, is from '
[the] three. It (fem.) [. . .] [10] has need of [. . .] [12] their shapes. ⟨The⟩ dyad '
and the monad ' do not resemble anything, but [15] they are first to exist. '
The dyad, being divided, ' is divided [from the] monad, and ' [it] belongs
to the hypostasis. ' But the tetrad received (the) [elements],[20] and the
fifth ' received concord, and the ' [sixth] was perfected by ' itself. The '
[seventh] received beauty,[25] [and the] eighth ' [received . . .] ' ready
[. . .] [29] greatly. **33** And the [tenth revealed] ' the whole place. ' But the
eleventh and the ' [twelfth] have traversed [5] [. . .] not having [. . .] ' it [is
higher . . .] ' seven [. . . [15] name(s) . . .] [17] promise that [. . .] ' begin [to
separate] ' them by means of [20] a mark [and] ' a point, the [one which '
quarrels] from the one which is [an enemy]. '

Thus [. . .] ' of being [. . .] [26] the [letters . . .] ' in [a . . . **34** holy] or
according to a [bond] ' existing separately. ' [And] ⟨they⟩ exist with
each ' [other] in generation or [in [5] birth. And] according to [. . .] '
generation . . .] they do not have ' [. . .] these [. . .] [18] one [. . .] speaking '
[the] riddle.

Because within [20] [the] sense-perceptible world ' there exists the temple '
[that measures] seven hundred ' [cubits], and a river which ' [. . .]
within [25] [. . . for] ever, they ' [. . .] three ' [. . .] to the four ' [. . .] seals '

[. . .] clouds 35 [and the] waters, and the ' wax-line [images, ' and] some emerald-like things. '

For the rest, I will 5 [teach you] about them. This is ' [the] generation' of the names. She who [was not] ' begotten [. . . from the] ' beginning [. . .] 15 with regard to [. . .] 18 time(s), when [confined], when ' spread out, when [diminished].20 But there exists the gentle [word], ' and there exists another ' word which [approaches] ' being [. . .] ' in this [manner . . .].26 And he [. . .] ' the difference [. . .] ' and the [. . .] 36 the all and a [. . .] ' the [undivided] beings ' and the power [. . .] ' having [. . .] 5 intercourse with [the bridegroom] ' separately and [. . .] ' whether [. . .] 15 power ' [. . . he] exists ' [in] every place [. . .] ' them always. ' [He] dwells with the corporeal 20 and the incorporeal ones. '

This is the word of the hypostases ' that one should ' [. . .] in this way. If ' [. . .] with their 25 [. . .] helping ' [those who stir up] the ' [. . .] manifest ' [. . .] if one 37 knows him, he will ' [call] upon him. '

But there are words, some ' of which are [two 5 but others] existing ' [separately . . . 13 and] they [. . .] 15 or those that [. . .] 17 or according to [those that] have ' duration. And [these] ' either are separate from [them] 20 or they are joined to one another, ' or with themselves, either [the] ' diphthongs, or the ' single [vowels], or every [. . .] ' or [. . .] 25 or [. . . ' exist] just as [. . . ' exist . . .] ' the [consonants . . .] 38 they exist individually ' until they are divided ' and doubled. Some ' have the power 5 [. . .] according to the [letters ' that are consonants . . .] 12 become [. . .] 15 by themselves ' [. . .] and three (times) ' [for the] vowels, ' and twice ' [for] the consonants,20 [and] once for ' the entire place, and with ' ignorance for ' [those that] are subject to change ' [. . . that] became 25 [. . .] together with the [entire ' place . . .] finally.

And ' [. . .] they all ' [. . . they] exist 39 as hidden, but they were pronounced ' openly. They did not ' stop without being revealed, ' nor did they stop without 5 naming the angels. ' The vowels ' [join] the ' [consonants, whether] without ' [or] within,10 [. . .] they ' said [. . . ' teach you . . .] ' again [for ever. They were counted] ' four times, (and) they were [engendered] 15 three ' times, and they became [. . .].18

For these reasons we have acquired ' sufficiency; for it is fitting that 20 each one acquire ' power for himself to bear fruit, ' and that we ' never cast ' aspersions [on] the mysteries 25 [. . .] the [. . .]. '

For [. . .] which [is . . . ' the] souls [. . . ' the] signs of the Zodiac [. . .] 40 a new hypostasis. '

And the reward which will ' be provided for this one ' in this manner is salvation.5 Or the opposite will ' happen there to the one ' who com-

mits sin. [The one who commits] sin ' by himself [...] will be ' [in a ...
in a ...] [12] in order that ' before you (sing.) examine ' the one who
⟨...⟩, one [15] might [tell] another ' [about an] exalted power ' and a
divine knowledge ' and a might that ' cannot be resisted,[20] but that you
might examine ' who is worthy that he should ' reveal them, knowing '
that [...] down ' to [...] who commit [25] sin. They [... ' the Father
...] **41** that which is fitting. Do not desire ' to give power to the sense-
perceptible world. ' Are you (pl.) not attending to me, ' who have
received salvation [5] from the intelligible world? ' But (as for) these
⟨words⟩—watch yourselves— ' do not [...] them [... [12] he understands
...] and he takes [... ' the rest], ' I [will speak of] them. The [perfec-
tion [15] ...] in order that ' it might [not] increase. [But those] who commit sin [...] [18] the embodied souls did not understand ' them. Those that
are upon [20] the earth as well as those outside of ' the body, those in
heaven, are ' more than the angels. The place ' which we [talked] about
with ' words [.... But] these [...] [25] stars [...] [27] book(s) [...] ' whether
already [...] ' into the [...] [30] blessed is [...] **42** whether he is gazing
at the ' two or he is gazing at ' the seven planets ' or at the twelve [5]
signs of the Zodiac or at ' the thirty-[six] decans [...] [12] are invisible, '
[these reach up] ' to [...] [16] and ' [these] numbers, whether [those in
heaven] ' or those upon the earth, ' together with those that are under
the [earth],[20] according to the relationships and ' the divisions among '
these, and in the rest ' [...] parts ' [according to kind and] according to
[... [27] they] will [submit ' since] she has power ' [...] above [30] [... they
exist] apart [...] **43**[6] every [...] [20] body(s) [... ' a] place [... divine
B]arb[elo ...] **44**[4] reveal them [...] ' in this [manner ...] ' this [... [20]
intelligible angels], as she [...] ' intelligible [... ' above ...] ' save(d)
from [...] [27] them [...] **45**[3] world [...] ' and [... [6] world ...] [21] they
came [...] [24] those who [...] **46**[5] is [...] ' like [...] [20] the voice of '
[...] name(s) [and ... [23] for] ever [... ' name(s) ...]. (pp. 47-54 missing)
[...] **55**[17] I became silent. [...] ' tell [me, ...] ' what is the [power
...] [20] will wash [... ' entire generation ...] **56**[17] greatly, the ' [...]
much ' [...] he is [...], and [20] [...] all [...] ' in the [... **57**[18] knowledge
...] [20] persevere [...] ' the great [...] ' for I [became ...] **58**[20] bone(s)
of the ' [...] in the [cosmic ... (pp. 59-60 missing) **61** which is] under [...]
your daughters [...] [3] for just as ' [... the] kingdom of [...].[5] But this one
[they] have [...] [12] every [...] **62** in the one who [...] ' not. [And ...]. '
For it is [...] who [... ' you (pl.) did not] know the [...] [5] for the
[... [10] partially ...] **63** in ' [...] remainder ' down [... the] earth. And
they ' [spoke] like the angels [5] [...] he is like the ' wild [beasts].

And he said, [... 8 for] ever [...] 17 from [...] ' the number [...] '
I saw [...] 21 and his [...] a [voice ...] ' and [...] his [...] **64** I [...] '
because I [saw] all of [the lights] ' around [me, blazing ' with] fire. [And
...] 5 me in their midst [...] 16 angel(s) [who ...] ' beside me. [And
...] ' the [one ...] ' Gamaliel,20 [the one] who is in command of [the
spirits] which [...] **65** the angels ' [...] which receive ' [all of them ...] '
with those whom they [... 5 and] he [took] me ' [... he finished ... 12
her] members [...] 14 the [invisible ... 17 judgment ...] ' thrown ' [...]
every [... which is placed ... 21 source ' ...] living ' [...] the two '
[... silent 25 ... god(s)] **66** wash her from [... ' of God ...] ' the one
whom they [sealed] ' has been adorned [with the 5 seal of] heaven. [...] 11
to his [...] ' great [...].17

And I [saw ... 19 unmixed ...] ' those who [...] **67** they will become '
[...] of God / [...] a woman ' [...] while she is in [travail 5 and] when
she gives birth, [...] 10 with [...] 12 all of [...] ' thing ' [...] men [...]
and 15 [...] women [and men ' in this manner ... ' no one] ⟨of⟩ those
[that are upon the] earth ' [knew] that [...] ' every [...] them,20 [and
they will] take pity on these, [together with the] ' home-[born], for these
will [pay ' ...] God [...] 24 aeon(s) [...] **68** with those who will [...] '
who have [...] ' God [...] ' from the [beginning ...] 5 in [the ...] '
fear [... 8 name(s) ... 12 mysteries ...] ' in [...] ' God [...] 16 manifest
[...] ' those who will know [him]. '

[M]arsanes

THE INTERPRETATION OF KNOWLEDGE (XI, *1*)

Introduced by

ELAINE H. PAGELS

Translated by

JOHN D. TURNER

The *Interpretation of Knowledge* offers a unique opportunity to see how a Gnostic teacher uses New Testament writings and applies them to the church. Features of style and structure suggest that the text may present a homily intended for delivery in a service of worship. The structure of the discussion follows a common pattern of worship, in which readings from "the gospel" are followed by readings from "the apostle." Correspondingly, one section of the *Interpretation of Knowledge* (9, 21-14, 15) uses passages known from Matthew to interpret the Savior's teaching and his passion; the next section (14, 15-21, 34) uses texts from 1 Corinthians and probably Romans, Colossians, Ephesians, and Philippians to interpret the church as the "body of Christ."

The author is concerned to address a community that is torn by jealousy and hatred over the issue of spiritual gifts. Some members refuse to share their spiritual gifts with one another; others envy those who have received such gifts as prophecy and public speaking, and so stand out in the congregation. Some despise others whom they consider "ignorant" (that is, lacking gnosis); the rest feel slighted and resentful.

To rectify this situation, the author first recalls the example of the "great son," Christ, who voluntarily humbled himself to demonstrate the Father's love to his "small brothers." Next the author takes up Paul's metaphor of the body and its members, and combines it with the image of Christ as the Head of his body, the church, to remind the members that they share the "same body" and the "same Head." Despite the diversity of spiritual gifts that the members receive, each one shares in the "same grace."

Strikingly, this teacher develops an interpretation of knowledge rather similar to that of Paul in 1 Corinthians 13 or even of 1 John. Unlike Paul or the author of 1 John, however, this teacher offers a specifically Gnostic interpretation, implying that those who show jealousy and hatred betray their resemblance to the jealous and ignorant demiurge, while those who show love demonstrate the love of God the Father and of his Word.

THE INTERPRETATION OF KNOWLEDGE

XI 1, 1-21, 35

[. . . ^{14} they came to] believe by means of [signs ' and] wonders [and fabrications. And ' the likeness] that came to be through [them ' followed] him, but through ' [disgraces] and humiliations [before they received ' the apprehension] of a vision. [And they [20] fled before] they heard [that the Christ] ' had been crucified. ' [But your] generation is fleeing before ' [it believes that the Christ ' is alive in order] that our faith [25] [may be] holy (and) pure, ' [not relying upon] itself actively, but ' [maintaining] itself planted in [him. ' And it was] said, "Whence ' [is the] patience to measure faith?",[30] for each one is persuaded ' [by what] he believes. If ' he disbelieves them, then [he] would be unable ' [to be persuaded]. But it is a great event ' for a man who has [the] [35] faith. He is [not] in unfaith, ' which is the [world].

[Now] the world ' [is the place of] unfaith [and ' of death]. And death [exists as ... 2][13] said, ...] ' for [... [15] likeness ...] they will [...]. ' A holy thing is the faith [to see ' the likeness]. The opposite is [unfaith ' in the likeness]. The things that he will grant [them ' will support] them. It was impossible [for them [20] to attain] to the imperishability [...] ' will [become ...] ' loosen [... [24] those who] sent [...]. ' For [he who] is distressed [... ' is] unable to bring a [great ' Church] gathered out of [a small ' gathering].

He became an [emanation of ' the trace]. For also they say [about] [30] a likeness that it is apprehended [by means of ' his trace]. The structure [apprehends by means of ' the] likeness, but God [apprehends ' by means of] his members. [He knew ' them] before they were begotten, [and they [35] will know] him. And the one who [begot ' each] one from [the first will ' indwell] them. He will [rule over them]. ' For it is [necessary] for [each one ...] 3[26] Savior [...]. ' Indeed, [not ignorant] but [carnal ' is the] word who [took him] as a husband, ' while [it is he] that is [as a] likeness, so that [30] [the slave lives], and she ' [who took] us away [for her part] makes him aware ' [that] she is [the] Womb. [It is a] marvel of hers ' [that she] causes us to overcome [patience. ' And] the marvel is that he [loves [35] the one who] was first to [honor] a virgin ' [...]. It is fitting to [...] her [flesh ' ...] the [...] unto death ' [... desire] to practice [...]. 4[24] Therefore ' [she yielded] to him in [her path] ' and he was [first to fix] our eyes, [although a] ' virgin [will despise] the [cross] ' that is in [this world. And they] were granted [some of] ' her water, [that which] the supreme authority [granted] [30] to the one [in whom] there is [a sign. This ' is that] water of [immortality which] ' the great [powers] will grant to [him while he is] ' below [in the likeness] of [her son. ' She did not stop] on his account. She [...] [35] the [...] he became [...] ' in the [...] word that [appears] ' to the [sensible world. And] ' his [...] 5[14] in [...] ' through [...] ' come from those places. [Some fell] ' in the path. Others [fell in the rocks]. ' Yet still others he [sowed in the thorns]. ' And others [. . .] [21] and the shadow. Behold [. . .] ' he [. . . .[25] And] this [is the eternal reality] ' before the souls come forth from ' [those who] are being killed.

But he was ' being pursued in that place ' by the trace produced by [30] the Savior. And he was crucified ' and he died—not his own [death, ' for] he did [not] deserve to be [killed because ' of] the Church of mortals. [They removed ' him] so that [they] might keep [35] him in the Church. [And he answered] her ' [with] humiliations, since [in this] way he [bore] the suffering ' which he had [suffered]. ' For Jesus is for us a [likeness] on account of [. . .] **6**[15] this [. . . ' the] entire [structure] and ' [. . . the great] bitterness of the world ' [. . .] us with the ' [. . .] by thieves [20] [. . .] the [slaves] but ' [. . . down] to Jericho ' [. . .] they [received ' . . .]. For [. . . [25] down] to [. . .] to [wait] ' while the entire defect restrains [them] ' until the [final] reality that is ' [their] portion, since he [brought] us down, ' having bound us in nets of flesh.[30] Since the body is [a] ' temporary dwelling which ' the rulers and [authorities] have as [an] abode, ' the man within, [after being] ' imprisoned in the vessel, [fell] [35] into [suffering, and] they compelled [him] ' to [serve them and] they constrained him to ' serve [the] energies. They split ' the Church so as to ⟨inherit⟩ [. . .] **7**[10] able to [. . .] ' and [. . .] ' and [. . .] ' having [touched . . .] ' before [. . .] [17] it is [the] beauty that will [. . . all] ' wanted to [. . . and] ' to be with [. . .] [20] fighting with [one another . . .] ' like others [. . .] ' virgin [. . .] ' to destroy [. . .] ' wound [. . .] [26] but she [. . . likens] ' herself to the [. . .] ' her since they had struck [. . .] ' imperishable. This [. . .] [30] that he remain [. . .] ' virgin. The [. . .] ' her beauty [. . .] ' faithfulness [. . .] ' and therefore [. . .] [35] her. He hastened [. . .] ' he did not put up with [. . .] ' they despise the [. . .]. ' For when the Mother had [. . . **8**[6] the] Mother [. . .] [8] her enemy ' [. . . the] teaching to [. . .] [11] the force [. . .] [15] nature [. . .] ' behold a maiden ' [. . .] he is unable ' [. . .] first ' [. . . the] opposite [. . .].[20] But how has he ' [. . .] maiden ' [. . .] he was not able ' [. . .] he became ' [. . .] killed [him [25] . . .] alive ' [. . .] he reckoned her [. . .] ' better than life ' [. . .] since he knows that if ' [. . .] world created [him [30] . . .] him to raise ' [. . .] up from ' [. . .] upon the regions [. . .]. ' But [the one] whom they grasped ' [. . .]. But [. . .] emitted him [35] [. . .] he dwells in him ' [. . .] the Father of the All ' [. . .] be more to her [. . .] ' him. He is [. . .] **9**[9] like [. . .] ' into [. . .] he [has] ' them [. . .] ' them and he [. . .] each [one will be] ' worthy [. . .] take him and [. . .] ' to [. . . [15] the] teacher if he hides himself [as if ' he were] a god [who] would embrace [his works] ' and destroy them. For [he] also ' spoke with the Church [and] he [made himself] ' her teacher of immortality, and [destroyed] [20] the arrogant [teacher] by [teaching] ' her to [die].

[And this teacher made a] ' school of [life], for [the teacher has] ' another school [that] indeed [sets apart many] ' writings; yet, although they cause us to set ourselves apart [25] from the [surfeit] of the world, ' we were being taught about our death ' through them.

Now this is his teaching: ' Do not call out to a father upon ' the earth. Your Father, who is in heaven, is one.[30] You are the light of ' the world. They are my brothers and my fellow ' companions who do the will ' of [the] Father. For what use is it if you ' gain the world and you forfeit your [35] soul? For when we were in the dark ' we used to call many "father," since we were ' ignorant of the true Father. And ' this is the great conception of all the sins [...] **10**[9] pleasure. We are like ' [...] him to [...] ' soul [...] men who [...] ' the [dwelling] place. '

Now [what] is the [place given ' him by] the teacher [in which he put away [15] the] ignorance [and] the darkness [of the eye ' of his] heart? He reminded him of the good things ' [of his Father] and race. For he said ' [to her], "Now the world is not yours that ' [you (fem.) should receive] the form that is in it because [it is] advantageous; [20] [rather (it is) dis-advantageous] and a [punishment]. Receive ' now the [teaching of the one who was] disgraced— ' (it is) an advantage and [a profit] for the soul— ' [and] receive [his shape. It is the] shape ' [that] exists in the presence [of the Father], the word [25] and the height, that you may know him ' before you have been led astray while in the flesh ' of condemnation. Likewise I became very small ' so that through my humility I ' might take you up to the great height, whence [30] you had fallen. You were taken ' to this pit. If now you believe ' in me, it is I who shall take you ' above through this shape that you see. ' It is I who shall bear you upon my shoulders. Enter [35] through the rib whence you came ' and hide yourself from the beasts. ' The burden that you bear ' now [is] not yours. Whenever [you (fem.)] go [... **11**[13] body ...]. ' But [from] now on [...] [15] from his glory [...] ' from the first. ' From the [...] him and the woman ' in sleep [...] and the Sabbath ' which [is the] world.[20] For from the [...] of the Father [...] ' sleep [...] and [...] ' from the [...]. ' For the [world] is from [...] ' and a [...]. Therefore [he] [25] that went astray [by reason of the] enemy [comes] ' from [the beasts] that had come forth. ' [And] they put upon [him a] garment of condemnation. ' For a woman [had no] other ' garment [for clothing] her seed [30] except the one she first brought ' on the Sabbath. For no beast ' exists in [the] Aeon. For the Father does not ' keep the Sabbath but does work on the

Son, ' and through the Son he continued ³⁵ to provide himself with the Aeons. The Father has ' living rational elements ' from which he clothes ' him with my [members] as garments. The man [... 12¹² this] ' is the name. The [...] he ' emitted [himself and he] ¹⁵ emitted the [disgracer. The one ' who] was disgraced changed (his) name ' and, [along with that which would be] like the disgrace, ' he [appeared] as flesh. And ' [the scornful one has no] additional help. He has [no] need ²⁰ of the [glory that] is [not his]; he has ' [his] own [glory] with the ' [name], which is the [Son]. Now he came that we might ' become glorious. [But it is the] scornful one ' [that] dwells in the [places of the] scornful.²⁵ And through [him] who was disgraced ' we receive the [forgiveness] of sins. ' And through the [one who] was disgraced ' and the one who [was redeemed] we receive ' grace.

But who [is it] that redeemed ³⁰ the one who was disgraced? It is [the] emanation ' of the name. For just as the flesh has need ' of a name, so also is the flesh an Aeon ' that Wisdom has projected. It ' received the majesty that is descending,³⁵ so that the Aeon might enter ' the one who was disgraced, that we might escape ' the disgrace of the carcass and be regenerated ' in the flesh [and] blood of [...] 13⁹ destiny. He [...] ' and the Aeons [... ' they] received the Son [although he was] ' a complete mystery [... ' each one] of his [members ...] ' grace [...].¹⁵ They separated ' from the Church like [portions of] ' the darkness from the Mother, while his [feet] ' provided him traces, and [these] ' scorched the path of [the] ascent ²⁰ to the Father.

But [in what sort of way] ' did it (fem.) become [a Head] for them? ' Well, it (fem.) made the [dwelling place and brought forth] ' the light [to those] who dwell within ' him so that [they might] see the [ascending] Church.²⁵ For the Head drew ' itself up from the pit; it was bent upon the cross and [it] ' looked down to Tartaros so that ' those below might look above.³⁰ Hence, for example, when someone ' looks at [someone], then the face of the one ' who looked down looks up; ' so also once the Head looked ' from the [height] to its members, our ³⁵ members [went] above, where the Head ' was. And it, the cross, ' was [undergoing] nailing for the members, ' and solely that they might be able [...] 14⁸ have [...] ' because they were like [...] ¹⁰ slave. The consummation, [then, ' is thus: He to whom] she signaled ' [will be completed] by the [one who] signaled. ' And the seeds [that remain will endure] ' until the All is separated [and takes] ¹⁵ shape.

And thus the decree ' will be fulfilled, for just as the woman ' who is honored until death ' [has] the advantage of time ' [it will] give birth

[the same way]. And this offspring [20] [will] receive [the effulgence] appointed for it ' [and] it will [become perfect]. He has ' a generous [nature since]
the Son of ' God dwells in [him]. And whenever ' he acquires the All,
[whatever] [25] he possesses will ⟨be dissolved⟩ in the ' fire because it
greatly despised and ' outraged the Father. '

Moreover, when the great Son was sent ' after his small brothers, he
spread [30] abroad the edict of the Father and proclaimed ' it, opposing
the All. And he ' removed the old bond of debt, the one of ' condemnation. And this is the edict ' that was: Those who reckoned themselves [35]
enslaved have become condemned ' in Adam. They have been [brought]
from ' death, received forgiveness for their ' sins, and been redeemed by
[...] [15][10] since we are worthy [...] ' and our [...] ' but I say [...] [14]
and these [...]. ' For [...] is worthy to [...] ' God. And the Father
[... the] ' Christ removed himself [from] ' all these, since he loves [his
members] ' with all his heart [...] [20] his members [...]. ' He is [not]
jealous [...] ' they are fallen from [... the] ' good which [he] sees. [By
having a] ' brother [who] regards us [as he] [25] also is, he glorifies the [one
who gives us] ' grace. Moreover, it is fitting for [each] ' of us to [enjoy]
the gift ' that he has received from [God, and] ' that we not be jealous,
since we know that [30] he who is jealous is an obstacle in his (own) [path], '
since he destroys only himself ' with the gift and he is ignorant ' of God.
He ought to rejoice [and] ' be glad and partake of grace and [35] bounty.
Does someone have a ' prophetic gift? Share it without ' hesitation.
Neither approach ' your brother jealously nor [...] [16][9] chosen as they
[...] ' empty as they [escape ...] ' fallen from their [...] ' are ignorant
of the fact that ' [...] in [this way they] have ' [...] them in [15] [...] in
order that they may ' [reflect] perforce upon the things that you want '
[them to think] about when they ' [think about] you. [For] your brother '
[also has] the grace [20] [that is in you. Do not] belittle yourself, but '
[rejoice and give] thanks spiritually ' [and] pray for that ' [one in order
that] you might share in the grace ' [that dwells] within him. Do not
consider [him [25] foreign] to you; rather, one ' who is yours, whom each '
[of] your fellow members received. ' [If] you [love] the Head who possesses them, ' you also possess the one from whom it is that [30] these out-
pourings of gifts exist ' among your brethren.

But is someone ' making progress in the Word? Do not ' be upset by
this; do not say, ' "Why does he speak [35] while I do not?", for what he '
says is (also) yours, ' and that which discerns the Word and ' that which
speaks is the same power. The Word [... [17][14] eye] or a [hand only,
but they are] ' a [single] body. [Those who belong to] all [of us] ' serve

[the Head together]. ' For each one of [the members reckons] ' it as a member.

Now [they can] not ' all become [entirely feet] [20] or entirely eyes [or entirely hands since] ' these members will not [live alone]; ' rather they are dead. We [know that they are being put to ' death. So] why [do you love] ' the members that are still dead, [instead of those that] [25] live? How do you know [that someone] ' is ignorant of the [brethren]? ' For [you] are ignorant when you [hate them] ' and are jealous of them, thereby [not receiving] ' the grace that dwells within [them],[30] since you are unwilling to reconcile them to [the] ' bounty of the Head. You ought to [give] ' thanks for our members and [ask] ' that you too might be granted ' [the] grace that has been given to them.[35] For the Word is rich, ' generous, and kind. He ' gives away gifts in this world to ' his men without jealousy according to [... **18**[12] appeared ' in each] of the members ' [...] himself and [15] [...] since they do not fight ' [at all with one another] on account of [their] difference(s). ' [Rather] they suffer with ' [one another as they] work with one another, ' [and if] one of them [20] [turns, the others] turn with him, and ' [when each one] is saved, they are saved ' [together].

Moreover, [if they] would wait for ' [the exodus] from the (earthly) harmony, they will ' [come to the Aeon]. If they are fit to share [25] [in] the (true) harmony, how much the more ' [those who] derive from the [single] unity. ' They ought to be reconciled with one ' another. Do not accuse your Head ' because it has not appointed you as an eye but rather as [30] a finger. And do not ' be jealous of that which has been made ' as an eye or a hand or a foot, ' but be thankful that you do not exist ' outside the body. On the contrary, you have [35] the same Head on ' whose account the eye exists as well as the hand ' and the foot and the rest of the ' parts. Why do you despise **19** the one that is appointed as [...] ' it desired to [...] ' you slandered [...] ' does not embrace [...] [5] unmixed [body ...] ' elect [...] [12] dissolve [...] ' of the Aeon [...] ' descent [...] [15] however [...] ' us from the [Aeons that exist in] ' that place. [Some] ' exist in the [...] Church. ' Those who exist [...] [20] the men in a [.... Others], ' however, proclaim [...] ' the Pleroma of the [...]. ' And some exist [for the life of] ' the Church on whose account [they] [25] go. For her they exist for [death], ' but others for life. Therefore ' they [are] lovers of abundant life. And ' each of the rest [endures] ' by his own root.[30] He puts forth fruit ' that is like him, since the roots [have] ' a connection with one ' another and their fruits are undivided, ' the best of each.[35] They possess them, existing for them ' and for one another. So let us become ' like the roots since we are equal **20** [. . .] us as [. . .] ' that Aeon [. . .] ' those who are not ours ' [. . .] above the [. . .] [5] grasp him [. . .] [13] since ' [. . .] your soul. He will [. . .] [15] we gave you to him [. . .] ' if you purify [. . .]. ' If you shut ' [. . . the] Devil. If you ' [. . .] his forces that [. . .] [20] be with you. For if ' [the soul] is dead, still ' it [was acted upon] (by) the rulers and ' [authorities].

What, now, do you think ' [of] as spirit? Or [25] [why] do they persecute men of ' [this] sort to death? Aren't ' they satisfied to be with the soul ' and (so) seek it? ' For every place is [excluded] from them by [30] [the] men of God so long as they ' exist in flesh. And when they ' cannot see them, since they (the men of God) live by ' the spirit, ' they tear apart what appears [35] as if thus they can ' find them. But what is the profit for them? ' They are senselessly mad! They rend ' their surroundings! They dig the earth! [. . .] **21**[3] him [. . .] ' hid [. . .] [5] exists [. . .] ' purify [. . .] [16] however [. . .] ' the [. . .] ' after God [. . .] ' seize us [. . .] [20] but we go [. . .]. ' For if the sins [. . .]. ' Now even more the [. . .] ' of the Savior. For [each one] ' was capable of [both (types)] [25] of transgression, [namely that of a combatant] ' and (that of) an average person. It is a ' single [ability] that they possess. And ' as for us, we are combatants [for] ' the Word. If we sin against [it],[30] we sin more than barbarians. ' But if we surmount every sin, ' we shall receive the crown of ' victory, even as our Head was ' glorified by the Father.[35]

The Interpretation of Knowledge

A VALENTINIAN EXPOSITION (XI, *2*),

with

ON THE ANOINTING, ON BAPTISM A AND B,

and

ON THE EUCHARIST A AND B

Introduced by

ELAINE H. PAGELS

Translated by

JOHN D. TURNER

A Valentinian Exposition expounds the origin of the creation and the process of redemption in terms of Valentinian theology, specifically in terms of the myth of Sophia. The tractate thus offers the only original Valentinian account of that myth; the *Tripartite Tractate* (I, *5*) recounts another version that features the Logos instead of Sophia.

The author begins by promising to reveal "my mystery," and follows the account with baptismal and eucharistic prayers and benedictions. This suggests that *A Valentinian Exposition* offers a kind of secret catechism for candidates being initiated into gnosis. Following the revelation of the mystery, the candidate is invited to participate in anointing, baptism, and the eucharist, as Gnostic Christians understand these sacraments.

Besides relating the Sophia myth and referring to sacramental rituals, *A Valentinian Exposition* has a third remarkable feature: it gives firsthand evidence of theological controversies among different groups of Valentinian theologians. The heresiologists attest that Gnostic teachers disagree among themselves on the interpretation of fundamental doctrines. While the heresiologists sketch out various positions taken on important issues, the author of *A Valentinian Exposition* challenges certain views and advocates others. This author contends, apparently against Valentinus' original teaching, that the Father is single, solitary, "alone"; that Limit functions, like Christ, as savior; that Sophia erred in separating herself from her partner and rashly attempted to create "alone," which is the prerogative only of God. The account describes how Sophia, after suffering in isolation, repents and receives Christ, who descends to become her divine counterpart. Their joyful reunion symbolizes how "the All will come to be in unity and reconciliation."

Comparison with the heresiological accounts indicates that the author's viewpoint differs from that of Valentinus and his disciple Ptolemy on major issues. The most likely identification concerning the author's affiliation among known schools seems to be a western group of Valentinian theologians, such as the group represented by Heracleon.

A VALENTINIAN EXPOSITION

XI 22, 1-39, 39

[...] ' enter [...] ' the abundance [...] ' me [...] ⁵ those who [....¹⁵
I will speak] my mystery ' [to those who are] mine and ' [to those who
will be mine]. Moreover it is these who ' [have known him who] is, the
Father, that ' [is, the Root] of the All, the ²⁰ [Ineffable One who] dwells
in the Monad. ' [He dwells alone] in silence, ' [and silence is] tranquility
since, after all, ' [he was] a Monad and no one ' [was] before him. He
dwells ²⁵ [in the Dyad] and in the Pair, and his ' Pair is Silence. And he
possessed ' the All dwelling ' within him. And as for Intention and '
Persistence, Love and Permanence,³⁰ they are indeed unbegotten.

The God ' [who] comes forth, the Son, Mind of the All, ' that is, it
is from the Root ' of the All that even his Thought stems, ' since he
had this one (the Son) in ³⁵ Mind. For on behalf of the All he received '
an alien Thought ' since there was nothing before him from ' that place.
It is he who moved [... 23¹⁸ a] gushing [spring]. ' Now this [is the] Root
[of the All] ²⁰ and Monad without any [one] ' before him. Now the
second [spring] ' exists in Silence and [speaks] ' only with himself. And
' likewise the [Fourth is he who] ²⁵ restricted himself [in the] ' Fourth.
While dwelling in the ' Three Hundred Sixtieth, he first brought ' himself (forth), and in the Second [he] revealed ' his will [and] ³⁰ in the
Fourth he spread ' himself [out].

While these things are ' due to the Root of the All, let us for our part '
enter his revelation ' and his goodness and his ³⁵ descent and the All,
that ' is, the Son, the Father of the All, and ' the Mind of the Spirit; '
for he was possessing this one before [...]. 24¹⁸ He [is] a [spring]. ' He
is [one] who appears ²⁰ [in Silence], and [he is] Mind of the All. ' [He
was] dwelling secondarily with ' [Life]. For he is the projector ' [of] the
All and the [very] hypostasis ' of the Father, that is, the [true Thought] ²⁵
and his descent to [the ' place] below.

When he willed, ' the First Father revealed himself ' in him. Since,
after all, because ' of him the revelation is available to the ³⁰ All, I for
my part call the All ' "the desire of the All." And he took ' such a
thought concerning the All— ' I for my part call the thought "Monogenes." ' For now God has brought ³⁵ Truth, the one who glorifies the
Root of the ' All. Thus it is he who ' revealed himself in Monogenes, '
and in him ' he revealed the Ineffable One [...] 25¹⁸ the Truth. [They] '
saw him [dwelling] in the Monad and ²⁰ in the Dyad [and] in the Tetrad.
[He] ' first brought forth [Monogenes ' and Limit]. And Limit [is the '

separator] of the All [and the confirmation ' of the All], since they are
[. . .] ²⁵ the hundred [. . .]. ' He is the [Mind . . .] ³⁰ the Son. [He is]
completely ineffable ' to the All, and he is the confirmation ' and [the]
hypostasis of the All, the silent [veil], ' the [true] High Priest, '
[the one who has] ³⁵ the authority to enter ' the Holies of Holies,
revealing ' the glory of ' the Aeons and bringing forth the ' abundance
to fragrance. The East [. . . 26¹⁸ that is] in [him. He is the one who '
revealed himself as] the ²⁰ primal [sanctuary] and [the] treasury of ' [the
All]. And [he] encompassed the All, ' [he] who is higher [than the] All.
These for their part ' [besought] Christ [to come and ' establish them]
just as they [were] established [before ²⁵ his] descent. [And they say '
concerning] him: [. . . ²⁹ He is not manifest, but ' invisible] to [them while
he remains within Limit]. ' And he possesses [four] ' powers: a separator
[and a] ' confirmer, a form-provider [and a ' substance-provider]. Surely
[we alone] ³⁵ would discern ' their presences and the time ' and the places
which [the] ' likenesses have confirmed because they have [. . .] 27¹⁷ and
they [. . .] ' from these [places ' . . .] the love [. . .] ²⁰ emanated [. . . ' the] entire Pleroma [. . .]. ' This persistence [remains] ' always, and [. . .] ' for also
[. . .] ²⁵ the time [. . .] ' more [. . . ²⁹ that is], the proof of his [great ' love].

So why a ' [separator] and a confirmer ' and a substance-producer
and a ' form-provider as others have ' [said]? For [they] say concerning ³⁵
[Limit] that he has two powers, ' [a] separator and ' [a confirmer], since it
separates ' [Bythos] from the Aeons, in order that [. . .]. 28¹⁸ These, then
[. . .] ²⁰ of [Bythos . . .]. ' For [. . . is] the form [. . .] ' the Father of the
[Truth . . .] ' say that Christ [. . .] ' the Spirit [. . .] ²⁵ Monogenes [. . .] '
who has [. . .].²⁹

It is a great and ' necessary thing that we [with] ' great firmness and
[persistence search] ' the scriptures and [those who] ' proclaim the concepts. For about [this] ' (matter) ³⁵ the ancients say, "[They] were proclaimed ' by God." Let us ' know his unfathomable ' richness! He
[wanted . . . 29¹⁸ servitude . . .] ²⁰ he did not become ' [. . .] of their life '
[. . . they look] diligently ' [at their book] of knowledge ' and [they
regard ²⁵ one another's appearance].

[That] Tetrad ' projected the Tetrad ' [that is] Word and [Life ' and
Man and] Church. ' [Now the Uncreated] One projected ³⁰ Word and
Life. Word ' is for the glory of the Ineffable ' One while Life is for the
glory of ' [Silence], and Man is for his (Monogenes') ' own glory while
Church ³⁵ is for the glory of Truth. This, then, ' is the [Tetrad] begotten '
according to the [likeness] of the Uncreated (Tetrad). ' And [the] Tetrad
is begotten [. . . 30¹⁶ the Ten] ' from [Word and Life] ' and the [Twelve

from Man] ' and Church [became the] [20] Thirty. [Therefore the one who] '
became [single and the one who ' came] forth [are associates: ' they]
enter as [partners ' but they] come forth [singly. They [25] flee from] the
Aeons [and the Uncontainable Ones. ' And] the Uncontainable Ones,
[once they had] ' looked [at them, glorified Mind] ' since [he is an Uncontainable One that] exists ' in the [Pleroma].

[But [30] the Ten] from ' Word and Life brought forth ' Tens so as to
make the Pleroma ' become a hundred, and ' the Twelve from Man [35]
and Church brought forth and [made] ' the Thirty so as to make [the
three] hundred ' sixty become the Pleroma of the ' year. And the year
of the Lord [... 31[18] perfect ...] ' perfect [...] [20] according to [... [22]
Limit] and ' [...] Limit [... [27] the] Majesty ' [...] the ' [goodness ...]
him. Life [30] [...] suffer ' [...] by ' the face [...] in the presence of ' the
[Pleroma ...] which he wanted ' [... and] he wanted [35] to [leave the]
Thirtieth— ' being [a syzygy] of Man and ' Church, that is, Sophia—to '
surpass [the Thirty and] bring the Pleroma [...] 32[16] his [...] ' but [...
and] ' she [...] [22] the [All ...] [28] but [...] those ' who [...] the All
[...].[32] And he made [...] the thought ' and [... the] Pleroma ' through
the Word [...] his [35] flesh. These, then, [are those that] are like ' them.
After the [Word] entered ' it, just as [I] said before, ' and [ascended] to '
the Uncontainable One, it [brought] forth [...] 33[11] before they ' [...]
forth [...] ' hide him from ' [...] the syzygy and [15] [...] the movement
and ' [...] project the ' Christ [...] and the seeds ' [...] of the cross '
since [... the imprints] of the nail [20] wound [dissolved] perfectly. ' [Since
after all it is] a perfect form ' [that should] ascend into ' [the Pleroma],
he did not [at all] want ' [to] accede to the suffering,[25] [but he was]
detained. And ' he [was detained] by Limit, ' that is, by the syzygy, '
since her correction will ' not occur through anyone except [30] her own
Son, ' whose alone is the fullness ' of divinity. He willed ' within himself bodily ' to leave the powers and he descended.[35] And these things
(passions) Sophia suffered ' after her son ascended from ' her, [for] she
knew ' that she dwelt in a [... 34[10] in unity] ' and [reconciliation. They
were] ' stopped [...] ' the brethren [...] ' these. A [...] did not [...] [15]
I became [...]. ' Who indeed [are] they? [The ...] for his part ' stopped
[...] while [...] for his part came ' with these [...] ' her. These [more-
over are those who were] looking at me,[20] these that [surround me],
these ' that I thought of [credited] me with ' death. They were stopped
[...] her ' and she repented [and she] ' besought the Father of the
[truth],[25] saying, "Granted that I have [left] ' my consort. Therefore [I
am] ' beyond confirmation as well. I deserve ' the things (passions) I

suffer. ' I used to dwell in the Pleroma [30] putting forth the Aeons and '
bearing fruit with my consort." ' And she knew what she was ' and what
had become of ' her.

So they both suffered; [35] they said she laughs since she remained
alone and imitated the ' Uncontainable, while he said she [laughs] since '
she cut herself off from her consort [. . .]. 35[10] Indeed [Jesus and] Sophia '
revealed [the creature]. Since, after all, ' the seeds [of] Sophia are ' in-
complete [and] formless, ' Jesu[s contrived] a Creature of this [15] [sort]
and made it of the ' seeds while Sophia worked with ' him. [For] since
they are seeds ' and [without form], he descended ' [and brought] forth
that [20] pleroma [of aeons] which are in the ' place [of the] creation as if '
these [Aeons were of] the pattern of the [Pleroma] ' and of the [in-
effable] Father. ' The Uncreated One [25] [brought forth] the pattern of the
uncreated, ' for it is from the uncreated ' that the Father brings forth '
into form. But the creature ' is a shadow of preexisting [30] things. Moreover, this Jesus created ' the Creature, and he fashioned ' out of the
passions ' surrounding the seeds. And he ' separated them from one
another, [35] and the better passions he introduced ' into the spiritual and
the worse ones ' into the carnal.

Now ' first among [all] those passions [. . .] 36[9] nor [. . .] ' him, since,
after all, Pronoia ' brought [the] correction to ' project shadows and '
images of [those who] were [from] the ' first and [those who] are [and] [15]
those who shall be. These, [then, are] the ' dispensation of believing '
in Jesus for the sake of [him who] inscribed ' the All with [likenesses]
and ' images and [shadows].[20]

After Jesus brought [them forth] ' he brought [forth] for ' the All
those of the Pleroma ' and of the syzygy, that [is, the] ' angels. For
simultaneously with the [25] [agreement] of the Pleroma ' her consort
projected ' the angels, since he abides by ' the will of the Father. For
this ' is the will of the Father: [30] not to allow anything to happen in
the ' Pleroma apart from a syzygy. ' Again, the will of the Father is: '
always produce ' and bear fruit. That she should suffer,[35] then, was not
the will ' of the Father, for she dwells ' in herself alone without ' her
consort. Let us [. . .] 37[9] another [. . .] ' the Second [. . .] ' the son of
another [. . .] ' is the Tetrad of the world. [And] ' that Tetrad put forth
[fruit] ' as if the Pleroma [of the world were] [15] a Hebdomad. ' And [it]
entered [images] ' and [likenesses and angels] ' and [archangels, divini-
ties] ' and [ministers].[20]

When all [these things were brought to pass ' by] Pronoia [. . .] ' of
Jesus who [. . .] ' and the seeds to [. . .] ' of Monogenes [. . .].[25] Indeed

[the glories] are ' [spiritual] and carnal, ' the heavenly and the ' earthly. He made them ' a place of this sort and [30] a school of this sort for ' doctrine and for form. '

Moreover this Demiurge ' began to create a ' man according to his image on the one hand [35] and on the other according to the likeness of those who ' exist from the first. It was this sort of ' dwelling place that she used ' for the seeds, namely [. . . **38**[10] separate ' . . .] God. When they ' [. . .] in behalf of man, ' [since] indeed [the Devil] is one ' [of] the divine beings. He removed himself [15] and seized the entire [expanse] ' of the gates and he ' [expelled] his [own] root ' from [that] place ' [in bodies] and [20] [carcasses of flesh], for [they cover ' the man] of God. And [Adam ' begot] him. Therefore [he acquired] ' sons who [angered ' one another. And] Cain [killed] [25] Abel his brother, for [the Demiurge] ' breathed into [them] ' his spirit. And there [took place] ' the struggle with the apostasy ' of the angels and mankind,[30] those of the right with those of the left, and ' those in heaven with those on earth ' the spirits with the carnal, ' and the Devil against God. ' Therefore the angels lusted [35] after the daughters of men ' and came down to flesh so that ' God would cause a flood. ' And he almost ' regretted that he had created the world [. . .] **39**[9] when [. . . ' the] consort ' and Sophia [and her Son] ' and the angels [and the seeds]. ' But the syzygy is the [complete one] ' and Sophia and Jesus and [the angels] [15] and the seeds are [images ' of] the Pleroma. Moreover the Demiurge ' [cast a shadow over] ' the syzygy and [the] Pleroma, ' and Jesus and [Sophia] and the [angels] [20] and the seeds. [The complete one ' is for the glory] of Sophia; the image [is for ' the glory] of Truth. [And] the glory [of ' the] seeds and of Jesus, those belonging to [Sophia, ' is] Monogenes. [And] [25] the [angels] of the males and [the ' seminals] of the females ' [are] all Pleromas. ' And whenever Sophia [receives] ' her consort and Jesus [30] receives the Christ and the [seeds] ' and the angels, then [the] ' Pleroma will receive Sophia ' joyfully, and the All will ' come to be in unity and [35] reconciliation. For by this ' the Aeons have been increased; ' for they knew that ' should they change, they are ' changeless.

ON THE ANOINTING
XI 40, 1-29

[. . . [8] Son . . .] ' according to [. . .] [10] the type of [. . .] ' see him. It is fitting for ' [thee at this time] to send thy Son ' [Jesu]s Christ and anoint ' us so that we might be able [15] to trample [upon] the ' [snakes] and [the heads] of the scorpions ' and [all] the power of the Devil. ' [He] is like the shepherd of [the ' seed]. Through him [we have [20] known] thee. And we [glorify] thee: ' [Glory] be to thee, the Father in the [Son, the ' Father] in the Son, [the] Father [in the] ' holy [Church and in the] ' holy [angels]! From [25] now on he abides forever [in the ' fellowship] of the Aeons, [until] ' the eternities, until the [untraceable] Aeons ' of the Aeons. ' Amen.

ON BAPTISM A

XI 40, 30-41, 38

[This] is the full content of the summary ' of knowledge which ' was revealed to us by ' our Lord Jesus Christ, ' the Monogenes. These are [35] sure and necessary ' so that we may walk ' in them. But they are ' those of the first baptism [.... **41**[10] The first] ' baptism [is the forgiveness] ' of sins [...] ' ⟨who⟩ said, [...] ' you to the [...] [15] your sins. The [... is] ' a pattern of the [...] ' of the Christ [... ' is the] equal of the [...] ' within him. [...].[20] For the [...] of Jesu[s ...]. ' Moreover, the first [baptism] ' is the forgiveness of ' [sins. We] are brought [from ' those] by [it [25] into] those of the right, [that ' is] into the [imperishability ' which is] the Jo[rdan. ' But] that place is [of] ' the world.[30] So, we have been brought out [of the world] ' into the Aeon. For [the] ' interpretation of Joh[n] ' is the Aeon, while the interpretation ' of that which [is] the Jord[an] [35] is the descent which is [the upward progression], ' that [is, our exodus] ' from the world [into] ' the Aeon.

ON BAPTISM B

XI 42, 1-43, 19

[... [10] from the] world ' [into John] and from ' [the great bitterness] of the world ' [into the sweetness of] God, from ' [the carnal] into the spiritual,[15] [from] the physical ' [into the] angelic, from ' [the created] into the Pleroma, ' [from] the world ' [into the Aeon], from the [20] [slaves] into sonship, ' [from] entanglements [into ' one another], from [the road ' into] our village, from [the cold ' into] the hot, [from [25] ...] into a [...] ' and we [...] ' into the [... ' so] also we were brought [from] ' seminal [bodies into [30] bodies] with a perfect form. ' [Indeed] I entered by way of example ' [the remnant] for which the Christ ' [rescued] us in the ' [fellowship] of his Spirit. And [35] [he brought] us forth who are ' [in him, and] from now on the souls ' [will become] perfect spirits. '

Now [the things] granted to us ' [by the first] baptism are [... **43**[15] invisible ... ' which] is his, since [... [18] speak] about ...].

ON THE EUCHARIST A
XI 43, 20-38

[We give] thanks [to. thee and we ' celebrate the eucharist], O Father, [remembering ' for the sake of] thy Son [Jesus Christ ' that they] come forth [. . .] ' invisible [. . .] 26 thy [Son . . .] ' his [love . . .] 30 to [knowledge ' . . .] they are doing thy will ' [through the] name of Jesus Christ ' [and] will do thy will ' [now and] always. They are complete 35 [in] every spiritual gift and [every] ' purity. [Glory] be to thee through thy Son ' [and] thy Offspring Jesus Christ ' [from now] forever. Amen.

ON THE EUCHARIST B
XI 44, 1-37

[. . .] 16 the [word] of the [. . . ' the] holy one it is [. . .] 19 food and ' [drink . . .] Son, since thou [. . .] ' food of the [. . .] ' to us the [. . .] ' in the [life . . .] 26 he does [not boast ' . . .] that is [. . .] ' Church [. . .] ' thou art pure [. . .] 31 thou art the Lord. [When] ' you die purely, [you] ' will be pure so as to have him [. . .] ' everyone who will [guide] 35 him to food and [drink]. ' Glory be to thee forever. ' Amen.

ALLOGENES (XI, *3*)

Introduced by

ANTOINETTE CLARK WIRE

Translated by

JOHN D. TURNER and ORVAL S. WINTERMUTE

The tractate *Allogenes* is a revelation discourse in which a certain Allogenes receives divine revelations and records them for his son Messos. Allogenes, meaning "Stranger," "Foreigner," or "One of another race," is a common name in this period for semi-divine revealers and is sometimes identified with Seth as representative of the Sethian spiritual race. This tractate has attracted wide interest because the Neoplatonist Porphyry mentions a writing by this title known to Plotinus, suggesting the possibility that certain elements of Neoplatonic thought may have their origin in a philosophically oriented Gnosticism.

Although *Allogenes* presents itself as a single revelation discourse, it can be divided into two parts. Part one (45, 1-57, 23) apparently highlights five revelations of the female deity Youel to Allogenes. Her revelations are complex mythological descriptions of the divine powers, particularly the Aeon of Barbelo. Part two (57, 24-69, 19) describes in more philosophical language the ascent of Allogenes as a progressive revelation by the heavenly Luminaries. Its final stage, the "primary revelation of the Unknown One," proclaims divine transcendence in a negative theology very closely paralleled in the *Apocryphon of John* (cf. II 3, 17-4, 1). Here God is revealed as the Unknown One, invisible, unfathomable, incomprehensible, "the spiritual, invisible Triple Power" which is "the best of the best" and exists, paradoxically, as "the non-being Existence."

Allogenes shares significant features with several Gnostic and Neoplatonic texts. Among the Gnostic texts the *Three Steles of Seth* (VII, *5*), *Zostrianos* (VIII, *1*), *Marsanes* (X, *1*), and the last Gnostic tractate of the Bruce Codex have the closest affinities to *Allogenes*, especially with regard to the Triple Power, three in one, which encompasses all existence, life, and mind. This triad of Existence, Life, and Mind and the philosophical ascent through negative divine predication are also signs of a significant interchange between the Gnostic and Neoplatonic movements. Porphyry's reference to an "Allogenes" tractate, as well as certain peculiarities in this Coptic text of *Allogenes*, suggest that the original Greek text of this tractate was in existence in the third century and was translated into Coptic near Alexandria, possibly around 300 C.E.

ALLOGENES

XI 45, 1-69, 20

[..., "...] [6] since they are ' [perfect individuals and dwell] ' all [to-gether], being better [than] the ' [...]. The guardian whom I sent [10] taught you. [And] it is [the power ' that exists] within you that often [extended itself] ' as speech ' from the Triple Power, [the One ' of] all [those] who [truly] exist [15] with the [Immeasurable One], the ' eternal [Light] of the Knowledge ' that appeared, the ' male virginal [Youth, ' the first] of the Aeon from [20] [a] unique triple-[powered Aeon]; ' he is the Triple Power who ' [truly exists]. For when [he was stilled ' by extension] and ' [when he was extended], he became [perfect [25] and] he received [power] from ' all of them. He knows [himself ' and the perfect] Invisible [Spirit]. ' And he [became ' an] Aeon who knows [herself [30] and who] knows That One. ' [And] she became a Hidden One ' [who] worked in those whom she ' knows. ' He is a perfect,[35] invisible, noetic ' Pro[to]-phanes-[H]armedon. Granting power ' to the individuals, she is triple male. ' And she is individually [...] **46**[8] an existence of [hers], and she [sees] ' them all truly [existing. And] [10] she contains the ' divine Auto-genes.

"When she [knew] ' her [Existence] ' and when she stood, [she brought] ' This One (masc.), since he saw them [all] [15] existing individually in the [manner which] ' obtains, and they [shall] ' become as he is; [they shall] ' see the divine Triple Male, ' the power that is [higher than] [20] God. [He is] the [Thought] ' of all these who [exist] ' together. If he [reflects upon himself], ' he reflects upon [the] ' great, [perfect, male,[25] noetic Proto-phanes], the [procession ' for] those (who), should [they] ' see it, [(they) see ' on the one hand those who truly exist] ' and on the other hand the procession [for those who exist] [30] together. And when such a one [has seen ' these], he has seen the [Hidden One]. ' And if he [sees] ' one of the hidden ones, [he] ' sees the Aeon of Barbalo. And as for [the] [35] unbegotten offspring of [That One], ' if one [sees] ' how it [lives ... **47**[5] you have heard about the ' abundance of] each one ' of them [certainly].

"[But] concerning ' the invisible, spiritual ' Triple Power, hear! [He exists] as an [10] Invisible One who is ' incomprehensible to them all. He ' possesses them all within [himself], ' for [they] all exist because of ' [him]. He is perfect, and he is [15] [greater] than perfect, and he is ' blessed. [He is] always [One] ' and [he] exists ' [in] them all, being ineffable, ' unnameable,[20] [being One] who exists through ' [them all]—he whom, ' [should] one discern ' [him, one would not desire] anything that ' [exists] before him among those [25] [that possess] existence. ' For [he] is the [source ' from which they all flow. [. . .[30] every] divinity, ' [and] he is prior [to] ' every blessedness since he ' provides for every power. And ' he ⟨is⟩ a nonsubstantial substance,[35] a God over whom there is no ' divinity, the ' transcending of whose ' greatness and ⟨beauty⟩ (is impossible) [. . . **48**[6] power. . . .] ' to receive a [revelation of] these things ' if [they] come together. ' Since it is impossible for [10] [the individuals] to comprehend the All ' [located in the] place that is higher than perfect, ' they partake of ' a First [Thought]— ' not as (they would partake of) Being—[rather] [15] he grants both Being and [the] ' Hidden One of existence. He [provides] ' everything for [himself] since it is ' he who shall come to be when he ' recognizes himself. And he is [One] [20] who subsists as a [sort of being] ' and a source and [an] ' immaterial [material and an] ' innumerable [number and a formless] ' form and a [shapeless] [25] shape and a [. . .[28] and an inactive] ' activity. [But he is [30] a] provider of [provisions ' and] a divinity [of] ' divinity. [. . .] whenever ' they partake, they partake of ' the first Vitality and [35] an undivided Energy, ' a substance of the ' beginning of the One who truly exists. ' But a second [. . . . **49**[5] He is endowed with ' blessedness] and ' goodness, because [when he is] ' recognized [as the] traverser ' of the boundlessness of the [10] Invisible Spirit [that] ' subsists in him, it (the boundlessness) turns him to [itself ' in] order that it might know what ' is within him and ' how he exists. And [15] he was becoming salvation for ' every one by being a ' point of departure for those who truly ' exist, for through him ' his knowledge endured,[20] since he is the one who knows [what] ' he is. But they brought forth nothing ' beyond themselves, neither ' power nor rank nor ' glory nor aeon,[25] for they are all ' eternal. He is Vitality and ' Mentality and That ' Which Is. For then That ' Which Is constantly possesses his [30] Vitality and ' Mentality, and {Life has} ' Vitality possesses ' {non}-Being and ' Mentality. Mentality [35] possesses Life and That Which Is. ' And the three are one, ' although they are each three as ' individuals."

Now after ' I heard these things, O my son (Messos) [. . . **50**[6] gives] power to [those who] are able [to] know ' these things [by] a revelation ' that is much [greater]. And I ' was [capable, although] flesh was [10] upon me. [I] heard from you about these things ' and about the doctrine ' that is in them since the thought ' which is in me distinguished [the things] ' beyond measure and the unknowables. [15] Therefore I fear that ' my doctrine may have become ' something beyond what is fitting.

And ' then, O my ' son Messos, the one pertaining to all the glories,[20]

Youel, spoke to me again. She made a revelation ' to me and said, "No '
one is able to hear [these things] ' except the great powers alone, '
O Allogenes.[25] A great power was put upon you, ' which ' the Father of
the All, the Eternal, put upon you ' before you came to this place, in
order that ' those things that are difficult to distinguish [30] you might
distinguish and those things ' that are unknown to ' the multitude you
might know, ' and that you might escape in safety ' to the One who is
yours, who [35] was first to save and ' who does not need to be saved.
[... **51**[6] to] you [a] ' form [and a revelation of] ' the spiritual, invisible
Triple Power ' outside of which [is] [10] an undivided, incorporeal, '
[eternal] knowledge. '

"As with all the Aeons, ' the Aeon of Barb[el]o exists, ' also endowed
with the patterns [15] and forms of those who truly ' exist, the image of '
the Hidden One. And endowed ' with the intellectual principle of '
these, he bears the [20] noetic male Protophanes like ' an image, and he
works ' within the individuals either with ' craft or with skill ' or with
partial instinct.[25] He is endowed with the ' divine Autogenes like ' an
image, and he knows ' each one of these. He ' works successively and [30]
individually, continuing to rectify ' the failures ' from nature. He is
endowed with ' the divine Triple Male ' as salvation for them all [35] and
with the Invisible Spirit. ' He is a word from a ' counsel, ⟨he⟩ is the
Perfect Youth. ' And this hypostasis is [...]."

[... **52**[7] pure heart ...] and ' I escaped [and I was] very disturbed '
and [I] turned to myself.[10] [Having] seen the light ' that [surrounded] me
and the ' Good that was in me, I became divine. '

And ' the one pertaining to all glories, Youel, anointed (or: touched)
me again [15] and she gave power to me. She said, "Since ' your instruction
has become complete ' (and) you have known the Good that is within
you, ' hear concerning ' the Triple Power those things that you [20] will
guard in great ' silence and great mystery, ' because they are not spoken
to ' anyone except those who are worthy, ' those who are able [25] to
hear; nor is it fitting ' to speak to an ' uninstructed generation concerning ' the All that is higher than perfect. ' But you have them because
of [30] the Triple Power, the One who exists ' in blessedness ' and goodness, the One ' who is responsible for all these. '

"There exists within him [35] much greatness. ' Inasmuch as he is One
in a [...] **53**[6] of the [First Thought, which] ' does not fall away [from
those who dwell] ' in comprehension [and knowledge] ' and [under-
standing. And] [10] That One moved motionlessly ' within that which '
governs, lest he sink ' into the boundless by means of ' another activity

of [15] Mentality. And he entered ' into himself and he ' appeared, being all-encompassing, (being) ' the All that is higher than perfect. '

"In this way he is prior to knowledge,[20] (but) not through me, ' since there is no possibility for perfect comprehension. ' Yet it is in this way that he is known, ' because of the ' third silence of Mentality [25] and the second ' undivided Energy which appeared ' in the First Thought, ' that is, the Aeon of Barbelo, ' together with the Indivisible One of [30] the divisible likenesses and the Triple ' Power and the non-substantial Existence." '

⟨And⟩ the power ' appeared by means of an energy ' that is at rest [35] and silent, although having uttered ' a sound thus: zza ' zza zza. But when she heard ' the power and she was filled [..., "..] **54**[6] but thou art ' [...] Solmis! ' [...] according to the Vitality, ' [that] is [thine, and] the first Energy [10] from whom ' divinity derives: Thou art great, ' Armedon! Thou art perfect, ' Epiphaneus!

"And according to ' that Energy of thine, the second power [15] and the Mentality from whom blessedness ' derives: ' Autoer, Beritheus, ' Erigenaor, Orimenios, Aramen, ' Alphleges, Elelioupheus,[20] [L]alameus, Yetheus, Noetheus, ' thou art great! He who knows [thee] ' knows the All! Thou art One, ' thou art One, He who is good, Aphredon! ' Thou art the Aeon of [25] Aeons, He who is perpetually!" '

Then she praised ' the Entire One, saying, ' "Lalameus, No[eth]eus, Senaon, ' Asine[us, ...]riphanios,[30] Mellephaneus, Elemaoni, ' Smoun, Optaon, He Who ' Is! Thou art He Who Is, ' the Aeon of Aeons, the ' Unbegotten, who art higher than the unbegotten (ones),[35] Yatomenos, thou alone ' for whom all the unborn ones were begotten, ' the Unnameable One! [...] **55**[11] knowledge." '

[Now after I] heard these things, I ' [saw the glories of the perfect] individuals ' [and] the all-perfect (ones) [15] [who exist] together, and the ' [all-perfect] before the perfect ' [ones].

[And] again [the one ' pertaining to the] glories, Youel, said to me, ' "[O Allogenes], in an [20] [ignorant knowledge] you shall know that the ' [Triple Power] exists before ' [the glories]. They do not exist ' [among those who exist]. They do [not] exist ' [at all] with those who exist [25] [or those who] truly exist. ' [Rather all these] exist ' [as divinity] and ' [blessedness and] existence, ' [and as] non-substantiality and [30] non-being [existence]." '

[And then I] prayed that ' [the revelation] might occur to me. ' [And then ' the one pertaining to all] the [glories], Youel, said to me,[35] "[O Allogenes], of course ' [the Triple] Male ' [is something beyond] a sub-

stance. ' Yet [were the (Triple Male) insubstantial, ... **56**[9] forth ...] '
those who exist [in association] ' with the [generation of those] ' who
[truly] exist. ' [The self-begotten ones exist] ' with the [Triple Male].[15]

"If you [seek with a ' perfect] seeking, [then] ' you will know [the
Good that is] ' in you; then [you will know yourself] ' as well, (as) one
who [exists with] [20] the God who [truly preexists]. ' After [a hundred] '
years there shall [come to you] ' a revelation [of That One] ' by means of
[...] [25] and Semen [and ... the] ' Luminaries [of the Aeon of] ' Barbelo
and the [Good which] ' is fitting for you [to know] ' first, so as not
[to forfeit your] [30] kind. [And if so], ' then when [you receive] ' a conception [of That One, then] ' you are completed [by] ' the word [to comple-
tion].[35] Then [you become divine] ' and [you become perfect by receiving] '
them [...] **57**[5] the seeking [...] ' the Existence [...] ' if it [apprehends] '
anything, it is [apprehended by] ' him and by [10] the very one who is
comprehended. ' And then ' he becomes greater ' who comprehends and
knows than ' he who is comprehended and [15] known. But if ' he comes
down to his nature, ' he is inferior, for the ' incorporeal natures have not
associated with ' any superiority; having [20] this power, they are everywhere ' and they are nowhere, ' since they are superior to every superiority, ' and inferior to every inferiority." '

Now after [25] the one pertaining to all the glories, Youel, said these
(things) to me, ' she separated from me and left ' me. But I did not
despair ' of the words that I heard. ' I prepared myself [30] therein and I
took counsel ' with myself for a hundred years. ' And I rejoiced exceedingly, ' since I was in a great ' light and a blessed path [35] because
those whom I was ' worthy to see as well ' as those whom I was worthy
to ' hear (are) those whom it is fitting ' that the great powers alone
(see and hear). [...] **58**[6] of [God]. '

[When ' the completion of] the one hundred years [drew nigh, ' I
received] a blessedness [10] of the eternal hope ' full of auspicious-
ness. ' I saw the good divine Autogenes; ' and the Savior ' who is the [15]
youthful, perfect Triple Male; and his ' goodness, the ' noetic perfect
Protophanes-Harmedon; ' and the blessedness ' of the Hidden One; and
the [20] first principle of the blessedness, ' the Aeon of Barbelo ' full of
divinity; ' and the first principle of ' the one without origin, the [25]
spiritual, invisible Triple Power, the All that ' is higher than perfect.

When ⟨I⟩ was taken ' by the ' eternal Light out of ' the garment that
was upon [30] me, and taken up to ' a holy place whose ' likeness can not
be ' revealed in the world, ' then by means of a [35] great blessedness I '
saw all those about whom I had ' heard. And I ' praised all of them

and I **59** [stood] above my knowledge and [I ' inclined to] the knowledge [of] ' the Totalities, the Aeon of Barb[elo]. '

And I saw [holy] powers [5] by means of the [Luminaries] ' of the virginal male Barb[el]o ' telling me ' that I would be able to test what ' happens in the world: "O [10] Allo[g]enes, behold your blessedness ' in the manner that exists in ' silence, wherein you know ' yourself as you are, and, ' seeking yourself, ascend to the Vitality [15] that you will ' see moving. And if it is ' impossible for you to stand, fear ' nothing; but if you ' wish to stand, ascend [20] to the Existence, and you ' will find it standing and ' stilling itself according to the likeness of the One ' who truly stills himself ' and apprehends all these [25] in silence and ' effortlessness. And when you receive ' a revelation of him by ' means of a primary ' revelation of the Unknown One— [30] the One whom if you should ' know him, be ignorant ' of him—and you become ' afraid in that place, ' withdraw to the rear because of the [35] energies. And when you become ' perfect in that place, ' still yourself. And ' by virtue of the pattern that is ' in you, know also **60** [that] it is so among [all these] ' according to this form. And ' [do not] further dissipate yourself, [so that] ' you may be able to stand,[5] and do not desire to be [eternal] ' lest you fall [in any way] ' from the inactivity in you ' of the Unknown One. Do not ' [know] him, for it is impossible; [10] but if by means of an ' enlightened thought you should know ' him, become ignorant of him." '

Now I was listening to these things as ' those present spoke them. There [15] was a stillness ' of silence within me, and I heard the ' blessedness ' whereby I knew myself as ⟨I am⟩. '

And I ascended to the [20] Vitality as I sought it, and ' I joined it in entering in, ' and I stood, ' not firmly but ' calmly. And I saw [25] an eternal, intellectual, undivided motion ' that pertains to all the ' formless powers, (one which is) unlimited ' by limitation.

And when ' I wanted to stand firmly,[30] I ascended to ' the Existence, whom I found ' standing and at rest ' like an image and ' likeness of what is conferred upon [35] me by a revelation ' of the Indivisible One and the One who ' is at rest. I was manifestly filled ' by means ' of a primary revelation **61** of the Unknown One. [As though] ' I were ignorant of him, I [knew] ' him and I received power [from] ' him. Since I was permanently strengthened by [it],[5] I knew the One who ' exists in me and the Triple Power ' and the revelation of ' his uncontainableness. And ' by means of a primary [10] revelation of the First One who ' is unknown to them all, the God ' who is higher than perfect, I ' saw him and the Triple Power that exists ' in them all. I was [15] seeking the ineffable ' and Unknown

God— ' whom if one should ' know completely one would ' be ignorant of him—the Mediator of [20] the Triple Power who subsists in ' stillness and silence and is ' unknown.

And when I was confirmed ' in these matters, ' the powers of the Luminaries said to me,[25] "Cease hindering the ' inactivity that exists in you ' by seeking ' incomprehensible matters; rather hear ' about him in accordance with [30] the capability provided by a primary ' revelation and a revelation. '

"Now he is ' reified insofar as he exists in that he either ' exists and becomes,[35] or acts or knows, although he lives ' without Mind ' or Life or Existence ' or Non-Existence, ' incomprehensibly. **62** And he is reified among ' his attributes. ' He is not left over in ' some way, as if he yields [5] something that is assayed or purified or that ' receives or gives. And he is not ' diminished in some way, ' [whether] by his own desire ' or whether he gives or receives [10] through another. Neither does he have ' any desire of ' himself nor from another— ' it does not affect him. ' Rather, neither does he give [15] anything by himself ' lest he become diminished ' in another way, ' nor for this reason does he need ' Mind, or Life, or [20] indeed anything at all. He is better than the ' Totalities in his privation ' and unknowability, ' that is, the non-being Existence, ' since he is endowed with [25] silence and stillness lest ' he be diminished by ' those who are not diminished. '

"He is neither divinity ' nor blessedness [30] nor perfection. Rather ' it (this triad) is an unknowable reification of him, ' not an attribute of him; ' rather he is another one ' better than the blessedness and [35] the divinity and ' perfection. For he is not ' perfect but he is another **63** thing that is (more) exquisite. He is neither ' boundless, nor ' is he bounded by ' another. Rather he is something better.[5] He is not corporeal. ' He is not incorporeal. ' He is not great. [He is not] small. ' He is not a number. He is not a [creature]. ' Nor is he something [10] that exists, that ' one could know. But ' he is something else of his that is better, ' whom one cannot know. '

"He is primary revelation [15] and knowledge of himself, ' as it is he alone who knows himself. ' Seeing that he is not one of those ' that exist but is another thing, ' he is the best of the best.[20] But like his attribute(s) and ' non-attribute(s), he participates in neither ' aeon nor ' time. ' He does not receive anything from anything [25] else. He is not diminished, ' nor does he diminish ' anything, nor is he undiminished. ' But he is ' self-comprehending, as something [30] so unknowable ' that he exceeds those who excel ' in unknowability. '

"He is endowed with blessedness ' and perfection [35] and silence—not the blessedness ' nor the perfection— ' and stillness. Rather ' it (this triad) is a reification of him that exists, ' which one cannot **64** [know], and which is at rest. ' Rather they are ' all unknown reifications of him.'

"And he is much higher in [5] beauty than all those ' [that] are good, and he is thus ' unknown to all of them ' in any form. And ' through them all he is [10] in them all, not ' only as the unknown knowledge ' that is as he is. And ' he is joined by the ' ignorance that sees him. How [15] is he unknown? ' Whether one sees ' him as he is ' in every respect, or ' would say that [20] he is something like ' knowledge, he has sinned against him, ' being liable to judgment because he did not ' know God. He will not ' be judged by [25] That One who ' is neither concerned for anything nor ' has any desire, ' but (the judgment is) from ' himself because he did not find the origin [30] that truly exists. He was blind ' apart from the eye ' of revelation that is at rest, ' the (one) that is activated, ' the (one) from the Triple [35] Power of the First Thought ' of the Invisible Spirit. ' This one thus exists from [...] **65**[16] something [... set firmly] ' on the [...] a ' beauty and a [first emergence] ' of stillness and silence [20] and tranquility and ' unfathomable greatness. When he ' appeared, he did not need ' time or (anything) from an ' aeon. Rather of [25] himself he is unfathomably ' unfathomable. He does not activate ' himself so as to become ' still. He is not an ' existence lest he [30] be in want. He is corporeal ' insofar as he is in a place, while he is ' incorporeal insofar as he is at home. He has ' non-being existence. ' He exists for all of them unto himself [35] without any desire. ' But he is a greater summit ' of greatness. And he is ' higher than his stillness in order that [...] **66**[15] those [... ' he] saw [them] ' and [empowered them all], although they do not ' concern themselves with That One ' at all, nor, if one should [20] receive from him, does he receive power. ' Nothing activates him in accordance with ' the Unity that is at rest. ' For he is unknown, ' he is an airless place [25] of the limitlessness. Since ' he is limitless and powerless ' and nonexistent, he was not giving ' Being. Rather he contains ' all of these in himself, being at rest [30] (and) standing out of ' the one who stands ' continually, since there had appeared ' an Eternal Life, the ' Invisible and Triple-Powered Spirit [35] which is in all of these ' who exist. And it surrounds them all, being higher than ' them all. A shadow [... **67**[16] he is not ' diminished by anything. And ' he] stood [...] gave ' power to them all, he [20] filled them all."

And ' concerning all of these matters you ' have heard certainly. And do not ' seek anything more, ' but go.[25] We do not know whether ' the

Unknown has ' angels or ' gods, or whether the One who is at rest ' possessed [30] anything within himself except ' the stillness, which is he, ' lest he be diminished. ' It is not fitting to ' spend more [35] time seeking. It was ' suitable that you know only him ' and that they speak ' with another one. But you will receive them [. . . **68**[16] and he said to me], "Write down ' [the things that I] shall [tell] you and ' of which I shall remind you for the sake of ' those who will be worthy [20] after you. And you will leave ' this book upon a mountain ' and you will adjure the guardian: ' 'Come, O Dreadful One.' " '

And after he said these (things), he separated [25] from me. But I was full ' of joy, and I wrote ' this book which was appointed ' for me, O my son Messos, in order ' that I might disclose to you the (things) [30] that were proclaimed in ' my presence. And at first I received ' them in great silence and ' I stood by myself, preparing ' myself. These are the things that [35] were disclosed to me, O my son (Messos) [. . . **69**[14] proclaim ' them, O my] ' son Me[ss]os, [and make] ' (the) seal [of] all [the ' books of] ' Allo[ge]nes.[20]

Al[l]ogenes

HYPSIPHRONE (XI, *4*)

Introduced and translated by

JOHN D. TURNER

The short treatise *Hypsiphrone*, fragmentary in character, occupies the last four pages of Codex XI. This tractate features Hypsiphrone, "She of High Mind," apparently delivering in the first person a revelation narrative, which describes her descent into the world and the response of others who had already come into the world. Unfortunately, the fragmentary state of the tractate prevents a clear understanding of the nature and contents of the discourse.

HYPSIPHRONE

XI 69, 21-72, 33

Hypsiph[rone] '

The book [of visions] which were ' seen [by Hypsi]phrone, ' [and] they [are revealed] in [25] the place of [her] virginity. ' [And she listens] to ' her brethren [...] Phainops ' and [...] and ' they speak [with one another] [30] in a [mystery].

Now I ' was a [first moment] after [...] [70][14] me. I came [forth ' from the place] of my virginity ' and I went down ' to the [world. Then] they told ' [...], namely those who abide ' in [the place] of my [virginity].[20]

And I went ' down [to the world] and ' they said to [me, Behold], Hypsiphron[e ' withdrew] outside ' the place [of her] virginity.[25] Then [after] Phain[ops] heard, ' [he] breathed into ' [his fount of] blood [...]. '

[And] he said, ' [... Phainops ...] [71][18] err [...] [20] desire [...] ' also those remaining [...] ' or that I may see a [man in the likeness] ' of [blood ...] [25] of a [... and a fire] ' and a [...] his ' hands.

Then [she said these things ' to] him: [Phainops] did not [go down] to ' mine. He [did not] [30] go astray [...] see a ' man [...] he [...]. [72][18] For [...] who ' [...] Phainops [20] this [...].

I saw him ' and [he said] to me, Hypsiphrone, ' although [you dwell] outside ' me, [follow me ...] and I will ' tell [you about them]. So I [25] followed [him ...], for [I] was ' in [great] fear. And ' he [told me] about a fount of [blood] ' that is [revealed by] setting afire [...] ' he said [...].

THE SENTENCES OF SEXTUS (XII, *1*)

Introduced and translated by

FREDERIK WISSE

The version of the *Sentences of Sextus* from the Nag Hammadi library is a Coptic translation of an ancient tractate previously known through Latin, Syriac, Armenian, and Georgian translations, as well as through two manuscripts written in the original Greek. As a very early witness, the Coptic version is highly significant for the critical study of the text and character of the document.

The *Sentences of Sextus* consists of a collection of wisdom sayings, a collection, very popular in Christian circles, of maxims with a strongly ethical and ascetic tone. Although the tractate itself cannot really be considered a Gnostic treatise, its esoteric, moral asceticism seems to make it quite compatible with the other tractates from the Nag Hammadi collection. Indeed, the overwhelmingly ascetic tone of the entire Nag Hammadi library may provide important clues concerning the compilers and users of the library; the evidence indicates that the library was the property of a group which placed a strong emphasis upon sexual asceticism. In the light of this emphasis it is not at all surprising that the *Sentences of Sextus* is included among the holy books.'

The *Sentences of Sextus* thus proclaims the mastery of the passions. When the bodily passions and fleshly appetites prevail, wisdom and knowledge are unattainable. If believers zealously live lives of moral exertion, however, they will then become what they are: sons of God. Being god-like, believers must also reflect divine purity and perfection.

For additional discussion the reader is referred to Henry Chadwick, *The Sentences of Sextus: A Contribution to the History of Early Christian Ethics* (Texts and Studies 5. Cambridge, England: The University Press, 1959). The numeration of the sentences is derived from that edition.

THE SENTENCES OF SEXTUS

XII 15, 1-34, 28

(157) [. . .] is [a sign] of ignorance. '

(158, 159) [Love] the truth, and the lie ' [use] like poison. '

(160) [May] the right time precede your words.[5]

(161, 162b) [Speak] when it is not proper ' [to be silent], but [speak concerning] the things you know ' (only) then [when] it is fitting. '

(163a) [The] untimely [word ' is evidence] of an evil mind.[10]

(163b) [When it is] proper to act, do not ' [use a] word.

(164a) Do not wish ' [to speak] first in the midst of ' [a crowd].

(164b) [While it is] a skill ' [to speak], it is also [a] skill [15] [to be silent].

(165a) It is [better] for you to be defeated ' [while speaking the truth], than to be victorious ' [through deceit].

(165b) [He] who is victorious through ' [deceit] is [defeated] by the truth. '

(165c) [Untrue words] are [20] [the evidence of] evil persons.

(165d) [It is] a great [crisis ' . . .] which the lie [. . .]. '

(165e) [. . .] someone when you speak ' [the truth, . . .] even if ' [you lie . . .].

(165f) Do not deceive [25] [anyone, especially] him who needs ' [advice].

(165g) [If you speak] after ' [many (others) you will see] more the advantage. '

(166) [Faithful] is he who precedes ' all [good ones]. **16**

(167) Wisdom leads [the soul] ' to the place of [God].

(168) [There is no] ' kinsman of the [truth except] ' wisdom.

(169) [It is not] possible for a [believing] [5] nature to [become fond of] ' lies.

(170) A fearful [and slavish] nature ' will [not] be able to partake in ' faith.

(171a) When you are [believing, what] ' it is fitting to say [is not more worthy than] [10] the hearing.

(171b) When you [are] ' with believing persons, desire [to listen rather than] ' to speak.

(172) A pleasure-[loving] man ' is useless [in everything]. '

(173) When there is not [guilt . . .] [15] in anything (which is) from [God].

(174) [The] sins ' of those who are ignorant [are] ' the shame of those who have [taught them]. '

(175) Those because of whom [the name of God] is blasphemed ' [are dead] [20] before God.

(176) [A wise man ' is] a doer of good works after ' God.

(177) [May your life] ' confirm [your words before those who] ' hear.

(178) What it is [not right to do],[25] do not even consider [doing it].

(179) [What you do not] ' want to [happen to you, do not do it] ' yourself [either].

(180) [What] ' it [is] shameful [to do, is also . . .]. (pp. 17-26 missing) **27**

(307, 308) He is [a wise man who commends ' God] to men, ' [and God] thinks more highly of ' the wise man than his own [works].[5]

(309) [After] God, no one is as free ' as the wise man. '

(310) [Everything] God possesses ' the wise man has also.

(311, 312) The ' wise man shares in the [10] [kingdom] of God; an evil man ' does not want the foreknowledge ' of God to come to pass.

(313) An evil soul ' flees from God. '

(314) Everything bad [15] is the enemy of God.

(315) What thinks ' in you, say with your mind ' that it is man.

(316) Where ' your thought is, ' there is your [20] goodness.

(317) Do not seek goodness ' in flesh.

(318) He who does not harm ' the soul neither does (so) to ' man.

(319) After God, ' honor a [wise] man,[25] [since he] is the servant ! [of God].

(320) [To make] the body of your ' [soul] a burden ' is [pride], but to be able to ' [restrain] it [28] [gently] when [it is necessary ' is] blessedness.

(321) [Do not become] ' guilty [of] your own [death]. ' Do not be ' [angry] at him who will take you [out of] [5] (the) body and kill you. '

(322) If someone brings [the wise man] ' out of the body wickedly, ' he rather [does what is] ' good for him, [for] he has been released [10] from bonds.

(323) The fear of [death] ' grieves man because of ' the ignorance of the soul.

(324) ⟨It were better⟩ ' for you had the man-killing sword ' not come into being; but when it comes,[15] say with your mind that it does ' not exist.

(325, 326a) Someone who says, "I ' believe," even if he spends a long ' time pretending, ' he will not prevail, but he will [20] fall; as ' your heart is, (so) will be ' your life.

(326b) A godly heart ' produces a blessed life. '

(327) He who will plot [25] evil against another, [he is] ' the first [. . .]. '

(328) Let not an ungrateful man ' cause you to cease to do [good]. [29]

(329) [Do not say with] your mind that, (regarding) anything ' [of what has] been asked, ' [you have] given immediately the greater part to ' [him who] will receive it.

(330) You will use [5] [great] property, if you will give to the ' [needy] willingly. '

(331) Persuade a senseless brother ' [not to] be senseless; if he is mad,' protect him.

(332, 334) Strive eagerly [10] to be victorious over every man in ' prudence; maintain self-sufficiency. '

(333) You cannot receive understanding except ' you know first that you possess ' nothing.

(335) There is again this sentence. The [15] members of the body are a burden ' to those who do not use them. '

(336) It is better to serve ' others than to make others ' serve you.

(337) He whom God [20] will not bring out of (the) body, ' let him not burden himself. '

(338) Not only do not hold an opinion ' which does not benefit the needy, ' [but also] do not listen to it.

(339) He who gives [25] [something without] respect commits an outrage.' [. . .].

(340) If you take on the ' [guardianship of] orphans, you will be ' [the] father of many children since you are **30** beloved of God.

(341) He [whom you serve] ' because of [honor, you have] ' served for a wage.

(342) If you [give to] ' him who ⟨will⟩ pay you respect . . ., [you have] [5] given not to man, but [you gave] ' for your own pleasure.

(343, 344) Do not [provoke] ' the anger of a mob; [know, then], ' what is fitting for the prosperous man to [do]. '

(345) It is better to die [than] [10] to darken the soul because of [the] ' immoderation of the belly.

(346) Say with [your] ' mind that the body [is] the garment of ' your soul; keep it, therefore, ' pure since it is innocent.

(347) Whatever the soul [15] will do while she is in (the) body, she has ' as witnesses when she goes into ' judgment.

(348, 349) Unclean demons ' do lay claim to a ' polluted soul; ⟨the⟩ evil demons [20] will not be able to lay hold of a ' soul which is faithful (and) good in the ' way of God.

(350) Do not give the word of ' God to everyone.

(351) For [those who] ' are corrupted by [glory] [25] it is not assuring to [hear] ' about God.

(352, 353) It is not a small [danger] ' for us to [speak the] truth ' about God; do [not say **31** anything about] God [. . . ' what is] taught by [God]. '

(354, 356) [Do not] speak with a godless person ' [about] God; if you [. . .] [5] impure works, ' [do not] speak about God. '

(357) [The] true [word] about God ' is [the] Word of God.

(355) Speak ' concerning the word about God [10] as if you were saying it in the presence of God. '

(358) If your mind is persuaded ' first that you have been god-loving, ' then speak to whomever you wish ' about God. [15]

(359) May your pious works ' precede every word about ' God.

(360) Do not wish to speak ' with a crowd about ' God.

(361) Be (more) sparing with a word about [20] God (than) about a soul.

(362) It ' is better to dispose of a soul than to discard ' at random a word about ' God.

(363a) You conceive the body ' of the god-loving man, but you will not be able to ²⁵ rule over his speech.

(363b) The lion also ' rules over the body of ' [the wise man]; also the tyrant rules ' [over it] alone.

(364) If a tyrant **32** threatens you, [then, especially], ' remember God.

(365) [He who speaks] ' the word of God [to those for whom] ' it is not lawful, he is [the betrayer] ⁵ of God.

(366) It is better [for] ' you to be silent about the word of [God] ' than to speak recklessly. '

(367, 368) He who speaks lies about ' God is lying to ¹⁰ God; a man who does not have ' anything truthful to say about [God] ' is abandoned by God.

(369) [It is not] ' possible for you to know God when you ' do not worship him.

(370) A man who ¹⁵ does evil to someone will not be able to worship ' God.

(371) The love of man ' is the beginning of godliness. '

(372) He who takes care of men while ' praying for all of them— this is ²⁰ the truth of God.

(373, 374) It is God's business ' to save whom he wants; ' it is the business of the god-loving man ' to beseech God to save ' everyone.

(375) When you ²⁵ pray for something and it happens ' to you through God, then ' say with your mind that [you have **33** . . .]. '

(376a) [A man] who is worthy of God, ' [he] is God among ' [men], and [he is] the son of God. ⁵

(376b) Both the great one exists ' and he who is next ' to the great one exists.

(377, 378) It is better for ' man to be without anything ' than to have many things ¹⁰ while not giving to the needy; so also you, ' if you pray to God, ' he will not give to you.

(379) If you, from your ' whole heart, give your bread to ' the hungry, the gift is small, ¹⁵ but the willingness is great ' with God.

(380) He who thinks ' that no one is in the presence of ' God, he is not humble towards God. '

(381) He who makes his mind like unto ²⁰ God according to his power, he ' is the one who honors God greatly. '

(382) God does not need anything, ' but he rejoices over those who give to the ' needy.

(383) The faithful do not speak many [25] words, but their works are numerous. '

(384) It is a faithful person fond of learning ' who is the worker of the truth. **34**

(385) [Adjust the] calamities ' in order [. . .].

(386) [If you] ' do not do evil to anyone, you will not be [afraid] ' of anyone.

(387) The tyrant [5] cannot take away prosperity. ' '

(388) What it is right to do, do it ' willingly.

(389a) What it is not right to do, ' don't do it in any way.

(389b) Promise ' everything rather than [10] to say, "I am wise." '

(390) What you do well, say ' with your mind that it [is] God ' who does it.

(391) No one ' who ⟨looks⟩ down upon the earth [15] and upon tables is wise. '

(392) The philosopher who is an ' outer body, he is not the one ' to whom it is fitting to pay respect, but (the) ' philosopher according to the inner [20] man.

(393) Guard yourself from lying; there is ' he who deceives and there is he who is ' deceived.

(394, 395) Know who God is, ' and know who is the one who ' thinks in you; a good man [25] is the good work ' of God.

(396) Miserable are those ' because of whom the [word] is blasphemed. '

(397) Death will [not] be able to destroy [. . .].

FRAGMENTS (XII, *3*)

Introduced and translated by
FREDERIK WISSE

Little that is certain can be said concerning the *Fragments*. With no title and only one sizable fragment surviving, the tractate (or tractates) remains quite obscure. It seems to present ethical teaching within a religious context: the reference to "my Father" suggests that the speaker may be Jesus. The speaker contrasts himself and his followers with others, referred to in the third person plural, who live in wickedness and do evil deeds.

FRAGMENTS

XII 1A, 6-29
1B, 6-29
2A, 24-29
2B, 24-29

(Fragment 1A) [...] [10] us as it is ' [fitting. ...] each other, but ' [...] a crowd to receive ' [...] they speak ill ' [...] live by wickedness [15] [...] the [...] ' work evil things to ' [...] the good things, and they ' [...] do their own things ' [...] strangers. There are [20] [...] do their own things ' [...] works which [... ' we] ourselves do [... ' works] of those [...] ' evil works [...] [25] that which we shall [... ' the] works which [...] ' that which [...] ' every one [...]

(Fragment 1B) [...]. [9] For I speak the [...] ' know [God ...] ' gave their [...] ' error. But [...] ' they are worthy of the [...] ' into God [...]. [15] And already they have [...] ' the ignorance [...] ' the righteousness [...] ' these were worthy [of ...]. ' He [...] [20] my Father who is [...] ' not to them a father [...] ' I think that [...] ' this which the [...] ' I give again to the [...] [25] they forgive [...] ' spoke it [...] ' it [...]

(Fragment 2A) [...] [26] philosopher [...] ' they are not able to [...] ' philosopher ' [...] world [...]

(Fragment 2B) [...] [27] her [...] ' begot him [...] ' think that [...]

TRIMORPHIC PROTENNOIA (XIII, *1*)

Introduced and translated by

JOHN D. TURNER

The tractate *Trimorphic Protennoia* appears to be, in its final form, a Barbeloite treatise with Sethian influences. Presumably having a rather complex compositional history, the tractate may have attained to this final form around or shortly after 200 C.E. Thus it may be considered as roughly contemporaneous with the *Apocryphon of John*, which it resembles in certain interesting ways. The *Trimorphic Protennoia* probably survived for some time in Greek, but it was eventually translated into Coptic, and found its way into Codex XIII of the Nag Hammadi library.

The *Trimorphic Protennoia* offers philosophical and apocalyptic speculation on the nature of history and the universe. The tractate proclaims three descents of the Gnostic heavenly redeemer Protennoia, who is actually Barbelo, the First Thought of the Father. The *Trimorphic Protennoia* itself is divided into three sections, each with individual subtitles and each describing one of the descents of the heavenly redeemer. First she appears as Father, or Voice; second, as Mother, or Sound; and third, as Son, or Word (Logos). Each of these three sections, in turn, is capable of being subdivided into three parts: first, an aretalogy ("I am . . ."); second, a doctrinal presentation (on cosmogony, eschatology, and soteriology, respectively); and third, a concluding revelation. As the tractate proclaims, Protennoia is the Thought of the Father, the one born first of all beings, the one who has three names and yet exists alone, as one. She dwells at all levels of the universe; she is the revealer who awakens those that sleep, who utters a call to remember, who saves. In three descents from the realm of Life and Light, the divine Protennoia brings to the fallen world of mortality a salvation through knowledge and the "Five Seals."

The question of the Christian or non-Christian character of *Trimorphic Protennoia* deserves special mention. The name "Christ" appears a few times; and the similarities between the second subtractate (on eschatology) and the synoptic apocalypse (Mark 13 and parallels) and 1 Corinthians 15, and especially between the third subtractate (on the Son or Logos) and the Gospel of John, are extremely interesting. *Trimorphic Protennoia* may in part reflect these New Testament sources. Yet it is quite probable that the tractate has been secondarily Christianized.

TRIMORPHIC PROTENNOIA

XIII 35, 1-50, 24

[I] am [Protennoia, the] Thought that ' [dwells] in [the Light. I] am the movement ' that dwells in the [All, she in whom the] All takes ' its stand, [the first]-born [5] among those who [came to be, she who exists] before ' the All. [She (Protennoia) is called] by three names, although she ' exists alone, [since she is perfect]. I am ' invisible within the Thought of the ' Invisible One. I am revealed in the immeasurable, [10] ineffable things. I am ' intangible, dwelling in the intangible. I ' move in every creature.

I am the life ' of my Epinoia that dwells within ' every power and every eternal movement [15] and (in) invisible Lights and ' within the Archons and Angels and ' Demons and every soul dwelling ' in [Tartaros] and (in) every material soul. ' I dwell in those who came to be. I move in [20] everyone and I delve into them all. ' I walk uprightly, and those ' who sleep I [awaken]. And I ' am the sight of those who dwell in sleep. '

I am the Invisible One within the All. [25] It is I who counsel those who are hidden, since I know ' the All that exists in it. ' I am numberless beyond everyone. I ' am immeasurable, ineffable, yet ' whenever I wish, [I shall] reveal [30] myself. I [am the movement of] the All. I exist ' before the [All, and] I am the All, ' since I [exist before] everyone.

I am a Voice ' [speaking softly]. I exist ' [from the first. I dwell] within the Silence [35] [that surrounds every one] of them. 36 And [it is] the [hidden Voice] that [dwells within] ' me, [within the] intangible, ' immeasurable [Thought, within the immeasurable Silence. '

I [descended to the] midst of the underworld [5] and I shone down [upon the darkness]. It is I who ' poured forth the [Water]. I am the one hidden within ' [radiant] waters. I am the one who gradually ' dawns on the All. Within my ' Thought, it is I who am laden with the Voice. It [10] is through me that knowledge comes forth. [I] ' exist in the ineffable and ' unknowable ones. I am perception and knowledge, ' uttering a Voice by means of ' Thought. [I] am the real Voice. [15] I cry out in everyone, and they know ' that a seed dwells within [me]. ' I am the Thought of the Father and through ' me proceeded [the] Voice, ' that is, the knowledge of the everlasting things. I [20] exist as Thought for the [All]. I am joined ' to the unknowable and intangible Thought. ' (It was) I (who) revealed myself within ' all those who know me, for I ' am the one joined with everyone within [25] the hidden Thought and in an exalted Voice. '

And it is a Voice from ' the invisible Thought, and it is immeasurable, ' since it dwells in the Immeasurable One. It is a mystery; ' it is [unrestrained] [30] by [the Intangible One]. It is invisible ' [to all those who are] visible ' in the All. [It is a Light] dwelling in ' Light.

It is we [also who have separated] ' ourselves [from the] visible [world] [35] since we [are saved by the] ' hidden [wisdom mediated by the] **37** ineffable, immeasurable [Voice]. And he who is ' hidden within us pays the tributes of his fruit ' to the Water of Life.

Then ' the Son who is perfect in every respect—that is, [5] the Word who originated through that ' Voice, who was the first to leave the height; who ' has within him the Name; who is ' a Light—(this Son) revealed the everlasting things and ' all the unknowns were known. [10] He revealed the things that are difficult to interpret ' and the things that are secret, and ' he preached to those who dwell in Silence and in the First ' Thought, and ' he revealed himself to those who dwell in darkness, and [15] he explained himself to those who dwell in the abyss, ' and to those who dwell in the hidden treasuries he told ' ineffable mysteries, ' and he taught unreproducible doctrines ' to all those who became Sons of [20] the Light.

Now the Voice that originated ' from my Thought exists as three ' permanences: the Father, the Mother, the Son. A Sound ' that is perceptible, it has ' within it a Word endowed with [25] every glory, and it has ' three masculinities, three powers, ' and three names. They exist in the ' manner of the triad ☐☐☐, which are quadrangles, ' secretly within a Silence [30] of the Ineffable One.

[It is he] alone who came to be, ' that [is, the Christ. And] (it was) I who anointed him ' as the glory [of the] Invisible [Spirit] with ' [goodness]. Now [the third] I established ' [alone in] eternal [glory] over [35] [the Aeons in my living water], that ' [is, the glorious light that surrounds him] **38** who first came forth to the Light ' of those exalted Aeons, and it is in glorious ' Light that he firmly perseveres. And [he] ' stood in his own Light [5] that surrounds him who is the eye of the Light ' that gloriously shines on me. ' He gave Aeons for the Father of all Aeons, who is I, ' the Thought of the Father, for Protennoia, ' that is, Barbelo, the perfect Glory [10] and the immeasurable Invisible One who is hidden. ' I am the Image of the Invisible Spirit ' and it is through me that the All took shape, ' and (I am) the Mother (as well as) the Light which she appointed ' as Virgin, she who is called [15] Meirothea, the intangible Womb, the ' unrestrained and immeasurable Voice.

Then ' the Perfect Son revealed himself to his ' Aeons who originated through him, ' and he revealed them and glorified them and [20] enthroned them and stood in ' the glory with which he glorified himself. ' They blessed the Perfect Son, the Christ, the ' God who came into being by himself. And they gave glory, ' saying, "He is! He is! The Son [25] of God!

The Son of God! It is he who ' is! The Aeon of Aeons! He beholds the '
Aeons which he begot. For (it is) thou (who) ' hast begotten by thine
own desire! Therefore [we] ' glorify thee: ma mō ō ō ō eia ei on ei! The
[Aeon] [30] of [Aeons! The] Aeon which he gave!"

Then, ' moreover, the [God who was begotten] gave them (the Aeons) '
a power of [life for them to rely] on and he ' established [them. The]
first ' Aeon he established [over the first]: Armedon, [35] Nousa[nios,
Armozel; the] second ' he established [over the second Aeon]: [39]
Phaionios, Ainios, Oroiael; the third ' over the third Aeon: Mellephaneus, ' Loios, Daveithai; the fourth ' over the fourth: Mousanios,
Amethes, [5] Eleleth. Now those Aeons ⟨are⟩ the ones begotten ' by the
God who was begotten — the ' Christ — and these Aeons received '
as well as gave glory. They were the first to appear, ' exalted in their
thought, and each [10] of ⟨the⟩ Aeons gave 10,000 glories within ' great
unsearchable lights and ' they all together blessed the Perfect ' Son, the
God who was begotten.

Then there ' came forth a word from the great [15] Light Eleleth and
said, "I ' am King! Who belongs to Chaos and who ' belongs to the
underworld?" And at that instant his Light ' appeared, shining forth,
endowed ' with the Epinoia. The Powers of [20] the Powers did not entreat
him and immediately ' there appeared the great Demon ' who rules
over the lowest part of the underworld ' and Chaos. He has neither
form ' nor perfection, but on the contrary possesses [25] the form of the
glory of those ' begotten in the darkness. Now he is called ' "Saklas,"
that is, "Samael," "Yaltabaoth," ' he who had taken power; who had
snatched ' it away from the guileless one (Sophia); who had at first
overpowered [30] her who is the Light's Epinoia ' who had descended,
her from ' whom he (the great Demon) had come forth from the first.

Now the ' Epinoia of the Light knew that [she] had begged him
(Eleleth) ' for another [order] different from hers, and she [35] said, "Give
[me another order so that] you may become for me ' [a dwelling place
lest I become] disorderly ' [forever." And the order of the] entire house
of [40] glory [was agreed] upon her ' word. A blessing was conveyed to '
her and the higher order yielded ' to her.

And the great Demon [5] began to produce ' aeons in the likeness of
the real Aeons, ' except that he produced them out of his own power. '

Then I too revealed ' my Voice secretly, [10] saying, "Cease! Desist, '
(you) who tread on matter, for behold! ' I am coming down to the world '
of mortals for the sake of my portion that was in ' that place from the
time when [15] the guileless Sophia was conquered, she ' who descended,

so that I might thwart ' their aim which the one who reveals himself '
through her appoints." ' And everyone who dwelt in the [20] house of
the unknowable Light ' was disturbed, ' and the abyss trembled. And '
the Archigenetor of ignorance ' reigned over Chaos and the underworld
and [25] produced a man in my likeness. But he neither ' knew that that
one would become ' for him a decree of annulment nor ' does he recognize the power in ' him.

But now I have come down [30] and reached down to Chaos. And '
I was [with] my own who ' were in that place. [I am hidden] within '
them, empowering [them], giving ' them shape. And [from this day] [35]
until the [day when I will grant mighty glory] ' to those who [are mine,
I will reveal myself to] ' those who have [heard my mysteries], [41] that
is, the [Sons] of [the] Light.

I ' am their Father and I shall tell you an ' ineffable and indivulgeable
mystery ' from my Forethought: Every bond [5] I loosed from you, and
the ' chains of the Demons of the underworld I broke, ' these things
which are bound on my members as restraints. And ' the high walls of
darkness I ' overthrew, and the secure gates of [10] those pitiless ones
I broke, and I smashed ' their bars. And (as for) the evil Force and '
the one who beats you, and the one who hinders ' you, and the Tyrant,
and the Adversary, ' and the one who is King, and the real Enemy, [15]
indeed all these I explained to those ' who are mine, who are the Sons
of the Light, ' in order that they might nullify them all ' and be saved
from all those bonds ' and enter into the place where they were at [20] first.

I am the first one who descended ' on account of my portion which
is left behind, that is, ' the Spirit that (now) dwells in the Soul, but
which ' originated from the Water of Life. And out ' of the immersion
of the mysteries I spoke, [25] I together with the Archons and Authorities. '
For I went down below their ' language and I spoke my mysteries to '
my own—a hidden mystery—and ' the bonds and eternal oblivion were
nullified. [30] And I bore fruit in them, that ' is, the Thought of the unchanging Aeon, and ' my house, and their [Father]. And I went ' down
[to those who were mine] from the first and ' I [reached them and broke]
the first strand [35] that [enslaved them. Then] ' everyone [within] me
shone, and [42] I constructed [a pattern] for those Lights that are ' ineffably within me. Amen. '

The Discourse of Protennoia [§ 1] '

I am the Voice that appeared through [5] my Thought, for I am "He
who is syzygetic," ' since I am called "the Thought of the Invisible

One." ' Since I am called "the Unchanging Sound," ' I am called "She who is syzygetic."

I am a single ' one (fem.) since I am undefiled. I am the Mother [of] [10] the Voice, speaking in many ways, completing ' the All. It is in me that knowledge dwells, ' the knowledge of things everlasting. [It is] I [who] ' speak within every creature and I was known ' by the All. It is I who lift up [15] the Sound of the Voice to the ears of those ' who have known me, that is, the Sons of the Light. '

Now I have come the second time in the likeness ' of a female and have spoken with them. And ' I shall tell them of the coming end of this Aeon [20] and teach them of the beginning of the Aeon ' to come, the one without change, ' the one in which our appearance will be changed. ' We shall be purified within those Aeons from ' which I revealed myself in the Thought [25] of the likeness of my masculinity. I settled ' among those who are worthy in the Thought of my ' changeless Aeon.

For I shall tell you a ' mystery [of] this Aeon that is, and ' tell you about the forces that are [30] in it. The birth cries [out; hour] begets ' hour, [and day begets day]. The months ' made known the [month. Time] has [gone round] ' succeeding [time]. This Aeon that is [43] was completed in [this fashion], and it was estimated, and ' it (was) short, for it (was) a finger that released a ' finger and a joint that was separated from ' a joint. Then when the great Authorities knew [5] that the time of fulfillment had appeared— ' just as in the pangs of the parturient it (the time) has ' drawn nigh, so also had ' the destruction approached— all together the elements ' trembled, and the foundations of the under- world and the ceilings [10] of Chaos shook and a great fire shone ' within their midst, and the rocks and the earth ' were shaken like a reed shaken by the wind. ' And the lots of Fate and those who apportion ' the domiciles were greatly disturbed over [15] a great thunder. And the thrones of ' the Powers were disturbed since they were overturned, and their ' King was afraid. And those who pursue Fate ' paid their allotment of visits to the path, and ' they said to the Powers, "What is this dis- turbance [20] and this shaking that has come upon us through ' a Voice ⟨belonging⟩ to the exalted Sound? ' And our entire habitation has been shaken, and the entire ' circuit of our path of ascent has met with ' destruction, and the path upon which we go, [25] which takes us up to the Archigenetor ' of our birth, has ceased to be established for us." ' Then the Powers answered, saying, ' "We too are at a loss about ' it since we did not know what was responsible for it. But [30] arise, let us go up to the Archigenetor ' and ask him." And the ' Powers all gathered and went up to the Archigenetor. ' [They said to] him, "Where is your boasting ' in which [you boast]? [35] Did we not [hear you say], 'I ' am God [and I am] your Father **44** and it is I who [begot] you and there is no [other] ' beside me'? Now behold, there has appeared ' [a] Voice belonging to that invisible Sound ' of [the Aeon] that we know not. And [5] we ourselves did not recognize to whom we ' belong, for that Voice which we heard ' is foreign to us, and we do not recognize ' it; we did not know whence it was. It came ' and put fear in our midst and weakening [10] in the members of our arms. So now let ' us weep and mourn most bitterly! ' As for the future, let us make our entire flight ' before we are imprisoned perforce and ' taken down to the bosom of the underworld. For already [15] the slackening of our bondage has approached, ' and the times are cut short and the days have shortened ' and our time has been fulfilled, and the weeping ' of our destruction has approached us so that ' we may be taken to the place we recognize. [20] For as for our tree from which we grew, a fruit ' of ignorance is what it has, and ' also its leaves, it is death that dwells in them, ' and darkness dwells under the shadow of its ' boughs. And it was in deceit [25] and lust that we harvested it, this (tree) through ' which ignorant Chaos became for us a dwelling place. ' For behold, even he, the Archigenetor ' of our birth, about whom we boast, ' even he did not know this Sound."

So now, [30] O Sons of the Thought, listen to me, to the Sound ' of the Mother of your mercy, for you have ' become worthy of the mystery hidden from ' the Aeons, so that [you might be perfect]. And the consummation ' of this Aeon [that is and] of the life [35] of injustice [has approached, and there dawns **45** the] beginning of the [Aeon to come] which [has ' no change forever].

I am ' androgynous. [I am both Mother and] Father since [I ' copulate] with myself. I [copulate] with myself [5] [and with those who love] me, [and] ' it is through me alone that the All [stands firm]. I am the Womb ' [that gives shape] to the All by giving birth to the Light that ' [shines in] splendor. I am the Aeon to [come. ' I am] the fulfillment of the All, that is, [10] Me[iroth]ea, the glory of the Mother. I cast a Sound [of ' the Voice] into the ears of those who know ' me.

And I am inviting you into the exalted, perfect Light. ' Moreover (as for) this (Light), when you enter ' it you will be glorified by those who [15] give glory, and those who enthrone will ' enthrone you. You will receive robes from ' those who give robes and the baptizers ' will baptize you and you will become ' gloriously glorious, the way you first were [20] when you were ⟨Light⟩. '

And I hid myself in everyone and revealed [myself] ' within them, and every mind seeking ' me longed for me, for it is I ' who gave shape to the All when it had no form. [25] And I transformed their forms ' into (other) forms until the time when a form ' will be given to the All. It is through me that the Voice ' originated and it is I who put the breath ' within my own. And I cast into [30] them the eternally holy Spirit and ' I ascended and entered my Light. ' [I went up] upon my branch and ' sat [there among] the Sons of the [holy] Light. ' And [I withdrew] to their dwelling place **46** which [. . .] [3] become [glorious . . . . Amen]. '

[On the Heimar]mene [§ 2] [5]

I am [the Word] who dwells [in] ineffable [Silence]. ' I dwell in undefiled [Light] ' and a Thought [revealed itself] ' perceptibly through [the great] ' Sound of the Mother, although it is a male offspring [that supports me] [10] as my foundation. And it (the Sound) exists from the beginning ' in the foundations of the All.

But there is a Light [that] ' dwells hidden in Silence and it was first to [come] ' forth. Whereas she (the Mother) alone exists as Silence, ' I alone am the Word, ineffable, [15] incorruptible, immeasurable, inconceivable. ' It (the Word?) is a hidden Light, bearing a fruit of ' life, pouring forth Living Water from ' the invisible, unpolluted, immeasurable ' spring, that is, the unreproducible Voice of the glory [20] of the Mother, the glory of the offspring ' of God; a male Virgin by ' virtue of a hidden Intellect, that is, ' the Silence hidden from the All, being unreproducible, ' an immeasurable Light, the source of the All, [25] the root of the entire Aeon. It is the foundation ' that supports every movement of the Aeons that ' belong to the mighty glory. It is the founding of every foundation. ' It is the breath of the powers. It is the eye of ' the three permanences, which exist as a Voice [30] by virtue of Thought. And it is a Word ' by virtue of the Sound; it was sent ' to illumine those who dwell in the [darkness]. '

Now behold! [I will reveal] ' to you [my mysteries] since [35] you are my fellow [brethren, and you shall] know ' them all [. . .]. **47** [5] I [told them all about ' my mysteries] that exist in [the ' ineffable], inexpressible [Aeons]. I taught [them the mysteries] ' through the [Voice that ' exists] within a perfect Intellect [and [10] I] became a foundation for the All, and [I ' empowered] them.

The second time I came in the [Sound] ' of my Voice. I gave shape to those who [took] shape ' until their consummation.

The third ' time I revealed myself to them [in] [15] their tents as the Word and I ' revealed myself in the likeness of their shape. And ' I wore everyone's garment and ' I hid myself within them, and [they] did not ' know the one who empowers me. For I dwell within [20] all the Sovereignties and Powers and within ' the Angels and in every movement [that] exists ' in all matter. And I hid myself within ' them until I revealed myself to my [brethren]. ' And none of them (the Powers) knew me, [although] [25] it is I who work in them. Rather [they thought] ' that the All was created [by them] ' since they are ignorant, not knowing [their] ' root, the place in which they grew.

[I] ' am the Light that illumines the All. I [30] am the Light that rejoices [in my] ' brethren, for I came down to the world [of] ' mortals on account of the Spirit that remains [in] ' that which descended (and) came forth [from the ' guileless] Sophia. [I came] and I [founded [35] ...] and I [went] to [...] **48** [6] which he had [formerly and ' I gave to him] from the [Living] Water, [which ' strips] him of the Chaos [that dwells ' in the] uttermost [darkness] existing [inside] [10] the entire [abyss], that is, the [corporeal] ' and the psychic thought. All these I ' put on. And I stripped him of it (the inferior thought) ' and I put upon him a shining Light, that ' is, the knowledge of the Thought of the Fatherhood. [15]

And I delivered him to those who give robes— ' Yammon, Elasso, Amenai—and they [covered] ' him with a robe from the robes of the Light; ' and I delivered him to the baptizers and they ' baptized him— Micheus, Michar, [20] Mn[e]sinous—and they immersed him in the spring of the [Water] ' of Life. And I delivered him to those who ' enthrone— Bariel, Nouthan, Sabenai—and ' they enthroned him from the throne of ' glory. And I delivered him to those who glorify— [25] Ariom, Elien, Phariel—and they glorified ' him with the glory of the Fatherhood. And ' those who snatch away snatched away—Kamaliel, ' [...]anen, Samblo, the servants of the great ' holy Luminaries—and they took him into [30] the light-[place] of his Fatherhood. And ' [he received] the Five Seals from the ' [Light] of the Mother, Protennoia, and ' it was [granted] him to partake of the [mystery] of ' knowledge, and [he became a Light] in [35] Light.

So, now, [.... **49** [6] I was] dwelling in them [in the form ' of each] one. The [Archons] thought ' [that I] was their Christ. Actually I [am the Father ' of everyone]. Indeed within those in whom [I revealed [10] myself] as Light [I eluded] ' the Archons. I am their beloved, [for] ' in that place I clothed myself [as] ' the Son of the Archigenetor, and I was like ' him until the end of his regime, which is [15] the ignorance of

Chaos. And among the ' Angels I revealed myself in their likeness, ' and among the Powers as if I were one ' of them, but among the Sons of Man as if ' I were a Son of Man, even though I am [20] Father of everyone.

I hid myself within them ' all until I revealed myself among my members, ' which are mine, and I taught them about the ineffable ' ordinances, and about the brethren. But they are inexpressible ' to every Sovereignty and every ruling [25] Power except to the Sons of the Light ' alone, that is, the ordinances of the Father. These are ' the glories that are higher than every glory, that is, [the Five] ' Seals complete by virtue of Intellect. He ' who possesses the Five Seals of these [30] particular names has stripped off the garments ' of ignorance and put on ' a shining Light. And nothing ' will appear to him that belongs to the Powers ' of the Archons. Within those of this sort [35] darkness will dissolve and [ignorance] will die. ' And the thought of the creature ' which [is scattered] will present a single appearance ' and [dark Chaos] will dissolve and [...] **50** [3] and the [...] ' unattainable [...] [5] within the (fem.) [...] ' until I reveal myself [to my fellow ' brethren] and until I gather [together] ' all [my fellow] brethren within my [eternal ' kingdom]. And I proclaimed to them the ineffable [Five [10] Seals] in order that ' [I might] abide in them and they also ' might abide in me.

(As for) me, I put on ' Jesus. I bore him from the cursed ' wood, and established him in the dwelling places [15] of his Father. And those who watch over ' their dwelling places did not recognize me. ' For I, I am unrestrained together with my ' seed, and my seed, which is mine, I shall [place] ' into the Holy Light within an [20] intangible Silence. Amen. '

The Discourse of the Appearance § 3 '

Trimorphic Protennoia, in 3 parts '

A Sacred Scripture written by the Father '
with perfect Knowledge

THE GOSPEL OF MARY (BG 8502, *1*)

Introduced and translated by

GEORGE W. MACRAE and R. McL. WILSON

Edited by

DOUGLAS M. PARROTT

The *Gospel of Mary* is the first of the four tractates found in the Berlin Gnostic Codex. Although the date of composition is unknown, the Coptic manuscript itself has been dated to the early fifth century, and a Greek fragment of this gospel to the early third century.

The text can easily be divided into two distinct parts. The first part opens with a familiar scene in Gnostic literature: the resurrected Christ in dialogue with his disciples, who raise questions for him to answer. The disciples grieve at his departure, and at the awesome task of preaching the gospel to the Gentiles; but Mary strengthens them with the message that his grace will remain and give protection. Peter then asks Mary to tell the group of disciples the Savior's words which she alone knows. Here begins the second part of the *Gospel of Mary:* Mary relates a vision of the Lord, and describes a revelation of the ascending soul being interrogated by the powers. When she finishes her speech (from which, unfortunately, four pages are missing), some of the disciples react with disbelief and hostility; but Levi reminds them that the Savior made Mary worthy, knows her well, and in fact loved her more than the disciples. With this rebuke they adjourn, going forth to preach.

THE GOSPEL OF MARY

BG 7, 1-19, 5

[. . .] (pp. 1-6 missing) will matter then ' be [destroyed] or not?" The Savior said, ' "All natures, all formations, all creatures ' exist in and with one another, [5] and they will be resolved again into ' their own roots. For the ' nature of matter is resolved into (the roots of) ' its nature alone. He who has ' ears to hear, let him hear." [10]

Peter said to him, "Since you have ' explained everything to us, tell us this also: ' What is the sin of the world?" ' The Savior said, "There is no sin, ' but it is you who make sin when [15] you do the things that are like the nature of ' adultery, which is called 'sin.' ' That is why the Good came ' into your midst, to the essence of every nature, ' in order to restore it [20] to its root." Then he continued and ' said, "That is why

you ' [become sick] and die, for [. . .] **8** of the one who [. . . . He who] '
understands, let him understand. [Matter gave birth to] a ' passion that
has no equal, ' which proceeded from (something) contrary to nature. [5]
Then there arises a disturbance in ' the whole body. That is why I
said to ' you, 'Be of good courage,' ' and if you are discouraged ' (be)
encouraged in the presence of the different forms [10] of nature. He who
has ears ' to hear, let him hear." '

When the blessed one had said this, he ' greeted them all, saying, '
"Peace be with you. Receive [15] my peace to yourselves. Beware that no
one ' lead you astray, saying, ' 'Lo here!' or 'Lo ' there!' For the Son
of Man ' is within you. Follow [20] after him! Those who seek him will '
find him. Go then and preach ' the gospel of the kingdom. Do not **9**
lay down any rules beyond what ' I appointed for you, and do not give '
a law like the lawgiver lest ' you be constrained by it." [5] When he had
said this, he departed.

But they ' were grieved. They wept greatly, ' saying, "How shall we
go ' to the Gentiles and preach ' the gospel of the kingdom of the
Son [10] of Man? If they did ' not spare him, how will ' they spare us?"
Then Mary ' stood up, greeted them all, ' and said to her brethren,
"Do not weep [15] and do not grieve nor be ' irresolute, for his grace
will be ' entirely with you and will protect ' you. But rather let us '
praise his greatness, for he has [20] prepared us (and) made us into men."
When ' Mary said this, she turned their hearts ' to the Good, and they
began ' to discuss the words ' of the [Savior]. **10**

Peter said to Mary, "Sister, ' we know that the Savior loved you '
more than the rest of women. ' Tell us the words of the Savior which
you [5] remember—which you know ' (but) we do not nor have we heard
them." ' Mary answered and said, ' "What is hidden from you I will
proclaim to you." ' And she began to speak to them [10] these words:
"I," she said, "I ' saw the Lord in a vision and I ' said to him, 'Lord,
I saw you ' today in a vision.' He answered and ' said to me, 'Blessed
are you, that you did not waver [15] at the sight of me. For where the
mind ' is, there is the treasure.' I said ' to him, 'Lord, now does he who
sees the ' vision see it ⟨through⟩ the soul ⟨or⟩ through ' the spirit?'
The Savior answered and [20] said, 'He does not see through the soul '
nor through the spirit, but the mind which [is] ' between the two—that is
[what] ' sees the vision and it is [. . .].' (pp. 11-14 missing)

"[. . .] **15** it. And desire said, ' 'I did not see you descending, ' but
now I see you ascending. ' Why do you lie, since you belong to [5] me?'
The soul answered and ' said, 'I saw you. You did not see me ' nor

recognize me. I served ' you as a garment, and you did not know me.' '
When it had said this, it went away rejoicing [10] greatly.

"Again it came to the ' third power, which is ' called ignorance. [It
(the power)] ' questioned the soul, saying, ' 'Where are you going? In [15]
wickedness are you bound. '.But you are bound; do not judge!' And '
the soul said, 'Why do you judge ' me, although I have not judged?
I was bound, ' though I have not bound. I was not [20] recognized. But
I have recognized that ' the All is being dissolved, both the ' earthly
(things) **16** and the heavenly.'

"When the soul ' had overcome the third power, ' it went upwards
and saw ' the fourth power, (which) took [5] seven forms. The first form '
is darkness, the second ' desire, the third ' ignorance, the fourth is the
excitement of ' death, the fifth is the kingdom of the flesh, [10] the sixth
is the foolish wisdom ' of flesh, the seventh is the ' wrathful wisdom.
These are the seven ' [powers] of wrath. They ask ' the soul, 'Whence
do you come, [15] slayer of men, or where are you going, ' conqueror of
space?' The soul answered ' and said, 'What binds ' me has been slain,
and what turns ' me about has been overcome, and my desire [20] has been
ended, and ignorance ' has died. In a [world] I was released **17** from a
world, [and] in a ' type from a heavenly type, ' and (from) the fetter
of oblivion which ' is transient. From this time on [5] will I attain to the
rest of the ' time, of the season, of the aeon, in ' silence.' "

When Mary had said ' this, she fell silent, since it was to this point
that the Savior ' had spoken with her. [10] But Andrew answered and said '
to the brethren, "Say what you (wish to) say ' about what she has said. '
I at least do not believe that ' the Savior said this. For certainly these
teachings [15] are strange ideas." ' Peter answered and spoke concerning '
these same things. He ' questioned them about the Savior: "Did
he really ' speak privately with a woman [20] (and) not openly to us?
Are we to ' turn about and all listen ' to her? Did he prefer her to
us?" **18**

Then Mary wept and said to ' Peter, "My brother Peter, what do you '
think? Do you think that I ' thought this up myself in my [5] heart, or
that I am lying about the Savior?" ' Levi answered and said to Peter, '
"Peter, you have always been ' hot-tempered. Now I see you ' contending
against the woman like [10] the adversaries. But if the ' Savior made her
worthy, who are you ' indeed to reject her? Surely ' the Savior knows
her ' very well. That is why he loved her more [15] than us. Rather let us
be ashamed and ' put on the perfect man, ' and separate as he ' commanded us and preach ' the gospel, not laying down [20] any other rule

or other law ' beyond what the Savior said." When **19** [. . .] and they began to ' go forth [to] proclaim and to preach. '

[The] Gospel '
According to [5]
Mary

THE ACT OF PETER (BG 8502, 4)

Introduced and translated by

JAMES BRASHLER and DOUGLAS M. PARROTT

The final tractate of the Berlin Codex, the *Act of Peter*, describes the healing ministry of Peter. The crowd gathers around Peter, and he heals their sick. A bystander complains, however, that Peter's own virgin daughter is paralyzed; why does he neglect her? Peter then proceeds to heal her, but quickly turns her into an invalid again. In the long narrative section which follows, Peter offers an explanation of his daughter's paralysis: the paralysis had saved her from corruption and pollution, and had kept the lover Ptolemy from defiling a virgin. Finally, Ptolemy's eyes are opened, and his soul also sees the light.

The message of the *Act of Peter* is essentially encratite, or ascetic: through the insight and act of a man of God, the virginity of a young Christian person is preserved. The tractate thus advocates rigorous self-control of the sexual life. Though a more extreme interpretation may have been possible for those so inclined, the document itself does not necessarily condemn marriage and sexual relations as such. The emphasis of the Latin *Acts of Peter* does, in fact, seem to be more extreme; the Coptic *Act of Peter* and the Latin *Acts of Peter* may represent parts of different editions of the ancient *Acts of Peter*. Though not explicitly Gnostic in character, the Coptic *Act of Peter* would have been attractive to ascetic Gnostics and open to extensive allegorization. A deeper understanding of the text could have suggested that the tractate actually proclaims the victory of knowledge, life, and the divine, over ignorance, death, and the world.

THE ACT OF PETER

BG 128, 1-141, 7

Now on the first (day) of the week, ' which is the Lord's day, ' a crowd gathered and ' brought to Peter [5] many who were ' sick, in order that he might ' heal them. And an individual ' from the crowd made bold ' to say to Peter, [10] "Peter, behold, in ' our presence you have caused many ' blind to see, and you have ' caused the deaf to hear, ' and you have caused the lame to [15] walk. And you have helped ' the weak and have given them ' strength. But your ' virgin daughter, who ' has grown up to be beautiful and who has **129** believed in the name of God, ' why have you not helped her? ' For behold, one ' side of her is completely paralyzed and she lies [5] crippled there in the corner. ' Those whom you have healed are seen (about us); ' but your daughter ' you have neglected."

Then Peter ' smiled and said to him, [10] "My son, it is apparent to ' God alone why ' her body is not healthy. ' Know, then, that ' God was not weak or [15] unable to give ' his gift to my daughter. ' But so that your soul ' may be persuaded and those who are ' here may have more faith—." **130** Then he looked at ' his daughter and said to her, ' "Arise from your place! Let ' nobody help you except Jesus [5] alone, and walk restored in ' the presence of all these (people)! ' Come to ' me!" And she arose ' and went over to him. [10] The crowd rejoiced on account of ' what happened. ' Peter said to them, "Behold, ' your hearts have been persuaded ' that God is not powerless [15] regarding anything ' we ask of him." Then ' they rejoiced even more and praised ' God.

Peter said **131** to his daughter, ' "Go to your place, sit down, ' and become an invalid ' again. For this [5] is beneficial for you and me." ' The girl went back again, ' sat down in her ' place, and became again as she ' was before. The whole crowd [10] wept and begged Peter ' to make her healthy. ' Peter said to them, ' "As the Lord lives, this ' is beneficial for her and me. [15] For on the day she was born ' to me I saw a vision, and ' the Lord said ' to me, 'Peter, there has been born ' to you today a great **132** trial. For this (daughter) ' will wound. many ' souls if her body ' remains healthy.' [5] But I ' thought the vision ' was mocking me.

"When ' the girl became ten ' years old, many were [10] tempted by ' her. And a man rich ' in property, Ptolemy, ' after he had seen the ' girl bathing [15] with her mother, sent ' for her so that he might take her for his ' wife. Her mother was not ' persuaded. He sent for her many ' times. He could not cease [. . .]. (pp. 133-134 missing) **134**[19]

"[The men-servants of] **135** Ptolemy [returned] the girl, ' and put her down ' before the house, and departed. ' And when I and her mother realized it, [5] we went down ' and found the girl ' with one whole side of her body, ' from her toes to her ' head, paralyzed and withered. [10] We picked her up, praising the ' Lord who had ' saved his servant from defilement, ' [and] pollution, and [destruction]. ' This is the cause of [15] [the fact] that the girl ' [remains] thus to this ' day.

"Now then, it is ' fitting for you to know ' the (subsequent) deeds of Ptolemy. **136** He was smitten ' in his heart and grieved ' night and ' day on account of what [5] happened to him. And ' because of (the) many tears he ' shed he became ' blind. He intended ' to go and [10] hang himself. And behold ' in the ninth hour ' of that day, ' and when he was alone ' in his bedroom, [he] [15] saw a great light ' shining in the whole house, ' and heard ' a voice saying **137** to him, 'Ptolemy, ' God did not ' give his vessels for ' corruption and pollution. [5] But it was necessary ' for you, since you believed ' in me, that you not defile ' my virgin, whom ' you should have recognized as your sister, [10] since I have become ' one Spirit for you both. ' But arise ' and go quickly to ' the house of Peter my [15] apostle and you will see ' my glory. He will explain ' the matter to you.'

"And Ptolemy ' did not hesitate. He ' commanded his men-servants **138** to lead him ' and to bring him to me. ' And when he had come ' to me he narrated everything that [5] had happened to him ' in the power of Jesus ' Christ our Lord. Then he ' saw with the eyes ' of his flesh and the [10] eyes of his soul. And ' many hoped ' in Christ. He did ' good things for them ' and he gave them [15] the gift of God. '

"Afterwards Ptolemy ' died. ' He departed from life and ' went to his Lord. **139** And [when he made] his ' will, he wrote in a ' piece of land in the name of my ' daughter, since because of her [5] he believed in God ' and was saved. I myself ' took care of the administration ' entrusted to me most carefully. ' I sold [10] the land. And ' God alone ' knows, neither I, nor ' my daughter, {I sold the land} ' kept anything [15] back from the price of the land. ' But I sent the ' entire sum of money to the poor. '

"Know, then, O servant of ' Christ Jesus, that God **140** [watches over those who] ' are his and he prepares ' what is good for ' each one. But we [5] think that ' God has forgotten us. ' Now then, brothers, let ' us be penitent and ' watchful, and pray. [10] And the goodness ' of God will look ' down upon us—and we ' wait for it." And ' {all} other teachings [15] Peter spoke in the ' presence of them all. ' Praising the name **141** of the Lord Christ, ' he gave them all ' bread. ' When he had distributed it, ' he [5] arose and went ' into his house. '

The Act of Peter

INDEX OF PROPER NAMES

The following index, compiled by Howard M. Jackson and Marvin W. Meyer with the assistance of James E. Goehring and Joy O. Robinson, seeks to identify and locate the proper names that occur in the Nag Hammadi library as here published. The names include persons, places, powers, personified concepts, and the like. These names are listed below in alphabetical order, and are followed by the relevant codex, tractate, page, and line numbers. A Roman numeral indicates the codex, a number in italics the tractate, a number in bold type the page, and a number in regular type the line. A number within square brackets signifies that the name has been largely or totally restored; a number within pointed brackets signifies that the name has been corrected by the translator. A few names cannot be listed alphabetically because of missing letters at the beginning of the names; they are added at the very end of the list, in the order of their appearance within the library.

In most instances the identification of proper names presents no difficulties. Such is particularly true with many names of persons, places, and powers, whether historical or mythological (for example, "Mary," "Sodom," "Saklas"). The index seeks in such cases to be complete (though "God" and "Lord," because of the high frequency of their occurrence, have been omitted completely). With regard to concepts and abstractions, it remains for future research to make a definitive distinction between cases where each term is a proper name and cases where it is a common noun or an adjective. In these cases the selection provided here is only preliminary, and in some cases the quantity of occurrences has led to a selection even within those that might be considered proper names.

For complete lists of proper names and personified concepts the reader is referred to the indices in the volumes of *The Coptic Gnostic Library*.

Aachiaram   II *1:* **18**, 1
Aarmouriam   II *1:* **17**, 31
Abalphe   VII *1:* **45**, 6
Abel   II *1:* **10**, 36; **24**, 25; *4:* **91**, 14, 17, 19, 21, 22, [33]; *5:* **117**, 15; III *2:* **58**, [17]; IV *1:* **26**, 20; IX *1:* **6**, 14; **12**, [8]; **16**, [19]; XI *2:* **38**, 25
Abenlenarchei   II *1:* **16**, 18
Abitrion   II *1:* **16**, 7
Abraham   II *3:* **82**, 26; *6:* **133**, 29; VII *2:* **62**, 35
Abrana   II *1:* **17**, 29
Abrasax   III *2:* **52**, 26; **53**, 9; **65**, 1; V *5:* **75**, 22; VIII *1:* **47**, 13
Abrisene   II *1:* **10**, 37
Abyss   I *5:* **89**, 28; II *1:* **11**, 6; **14**, 26; *4:* **87**, 7; **95**, 13; *5:* **99**, 1, 34; **103**, 24;

104, 11; **126**, 22, 34, [35]; *7:* **141**, 33; V *5:* **79**, 23; VII *4:* **104**, 12, 27; **110**, 28; **114**, 25; XIII *1:* **37**, 15; **40**, 22; **48**, [10] (see also Hades, Tartaros, Underworld)
Achamoth   V *3:* **34**, 3; **35**, 9, 10; **36**, 5 (see also Echamoth)
Achchan   II *1:* **16**, 3
Achiel   II *1:* **17**, 2
Adaban   II *1:* **16**, 3
Adam   II *1:* **15**, 12; **20**, 17, 25; **22**, 11, 21; **24**, 10, 29, 35; *2:* **41**, 7; **47**, 30; *3:* **55**, 8; **58**, 18; **68**, 23; **70**, 21, 22; **71**, 16, 24, 27, [28]; **74**, 3; *4:* **88**, 16, 18, 21, 22, 24; **89**, 2, 5, 10, 13, 18; **90**, 20, 21, 28; **91**, 4, 30, 32; *5:* **108**, 21; **111**, 7; **112**, 10, 25; **115**, 2, 4, 13, 27, 34; **116**, 2, 4, 12, 20, 28, [35]; **117**, 28, 31, 34;

118, 3, 5, 17; **119**, 22, 24, 27; **120**, 8, 18, 21, 24, 26; **121**, 4, 14; **122**, 5; III *2:* **60**, 1; *3:* **81**, 12; *4:* **105**, 12; V *5:* **64**, 1, 2; **66**, 2, 17; **85**, 20, 23, 32; VII *2:* **53**, 9, 18; **54**, 3; **62**, 27; **63**, 33; IX *1:* **9**, 28; **10**, 6; **12**, 7; *2:* **29**, 1; *3:* **45**, 25; **46**, 19, 20; **47**, 1, 7, 16, 19; **50**, 6; **67**, [10]; XI *1:* **14**, 36; *2:* **38**, [21]; BG *3:* **108**, 10

Adaman VIII *1:* **30**, 10

Adamas II *5:* **108**, 23; III *2:* **49**, 19; **50**, 20; **51**, 6, 22; **55**, 18; **65**, 15; IV *2:* **61**, [8]; VIII *1:* **6**, 26; **30**, 4, 25; **33**, 17; **51**, 14; IX *2:* **27**, 26; **28**, 30

Addai V *3:* **36**, 16, 20, 22

Adonaios II *5:* **101**, 31; III *2:* **58**, 14; V *3:* **39**, 11; VII *2:* **52**, 25; **55**, 2, 7

Adonaiou II *1:* **10**, 33

Adonein II *1:* **12**, 23

Adonin II *1:* **11**, 32

Adversary VII *4:* **91**, 20; **95**, 1; **106**, 1; **114**, 6; XIII *1:* **41**, 13

Aerosiel III *2:* **62**, 16

Afterbirth VII *1:* **5**, 26, 28; **7**, 14

Agromauma II *1:* **16**, 20

Aileou VII *1:* **31**, 7

Ainios XIII *1:* **39**, 1

Ainon III *2:* **44**, 25

Akioreim II *1:* **15**, 35

Akiressina III *2:* **58**, 18

Akramas III *2:* **65**, 7; VIII *1:* **47**, 3

Akremon VIII *1:* **126**, 9

Akron VIII *1:* **52**, 15

Aldabaoth (see Yaldabaoth)

Allogenes XI *3:* **50**, 24; **55**, [19], [35]; **59**, 10; **69**, 19, 20

Allogenios VIII *1:* **128**, 7

Alphleges VIII *1:* **88**, 12; XI *3:* **54**, 19

Ambrosios VIII *1:* **126**, 14

Amen II *1:* **16**, 1

Amenai XIII *1:* **48**, 16

Amethes XIII *1:* **39**, 4

Amiorps II *1:* **17**, 32

Ammon VI *8:* **72**, 31

Amoiaiai VII *1:* **46**, 7

Amoias VII *1:* **31**, 5

Anaro II *1:* **18**, 33

Anasses Duses VII *1:* **11**, 22

Andrew BG *1:* **17**, 10

Anesimalar II *1:* **16**, 22

Anomoeans VI *4:* **40**, 7

Antiphantes VIII *1:* **54**, 24; **126**, 16

Antitheus VII *5:* **126**, 13

Aol II *1:* **17**, 25

Ap[. . .] VIII *1:* **127**, 27

Aphredon VII *5:* **126**, 10; VIII *1:* **86**, [13]; **88**, 18; **122**, 7; XI *3:* **54**, 23

Aphrodite II *6:* **137**, 2, 7

Aphropais VIII *1:* **129**, 2

Apophantes VIII *1:* **129**, 2

Apostle (Paul) I *4:* **45**, 24

Ar[. . .] VIII *1:* **62**, 19

Arabeei II *1:* **16**, 29

Arachethopi II *1:* **16**, 16

Aramen VIII *1:* **88**, [11]; XI *3:* **54**, 18

Ararim II *1:* **16**, 14

Arbao II *1:* **17**, 13

Archendekta II *1:* **17**, 33

Archentechtha II *1:* **17**, 27

Archigenetor XIII *1:* **40**, 23; **43**, 25, 30, 32; **44**, 27; **49**, 13; (see also, under Father, First Father)

Archir-Adonin III *2:* **58**, [20]

Archon I *5:* **100**, 19; **110**, 9; III *2:* **59**, 22; VI *4:* **43**, 35; VII *2:* **64**, 18; VIII *1:* **4**, 29; **10**, 17; **19**, 7 (see also Ruler)

Areche II *1:* **16**, 14

Ariael II *5:* **100**, 25

Arimanius II *1:* **1**, 9

Ariom XIII *1:* **48**, 25

Armas II *1:* **17**, 8 (see also Harmas)

Armedon VII *5:* **126**, 12; VIII *1:* **119**, [5]; **126**, [23]; **127**, 9; XI *3:* **54**, 12; XIII *1:* **38**, 34 (see also Harmedon)

Armoupieel II *1:* **11**, 1

Armozel II *1:* **8**, 5; **9**, 2; VIII *1:* **29**, 2; **32**, [5]; **51**, 17; **100**, [6]; IX *1:* **6**, 4; XIII *1:* **38**, [35] (see also Harmozel)

Aroer II *1:* **17**, 24

Arouph II *1:* **17**, 19

Arrogant One II *1:* **13**, 27 (see also Authades)

Arros[. . .] VIII *1:* **128**, 1

Arsinoe V *3:* **40**, [26]

Asaklas II *1:* **16**, 33

Asclepius VI *8:* **66**, 28; **68**, 13, 23, 35; **69**, 8, 29, 31; **70**, 3; **71**, 26; **72**, 30; **73**, 23; **74**, 19, 34; **75**, 35; **76**, 22; **77**, 28; **78**, [2], 16, 32

Asineus VII *5:* **126**, 7; XI *3:* **54**, 29

Asmenedas II *1:* **17**, 31

Asphixix II *1:* **17**, 18

Astaphaios II *1:* **11**, 29; *5:* **101**, 22, 34

Asterechme II *1:* **15**, 32

Astraphaio II *1:* **12**, 19

Astrops II *1:* **16**, 12

Athoth II *1:* **10**, 29; **11**, 26; **12**, 16; III *2:* **58**, 8

Athuro II *1:* **18**, 10

Atoimenpsephei II *1:* **16**, 26
Audael VIII *1:* **47**, 13
Authades (Arrogance) VIII *1:* **135**, 16, 18, 21; **136**, 5 (see also Arrogant One)
Authrounios VIII *1:* **8**, 8; **9**, 2; **47**, 21 (see also Euthrounios)
Autoer XI *3:* **54**, 17
Autogenes II *1:* **7**, 11, 16, 20, 24, 33; **8**, 21, 23, 26, 28, 31; **9**, 1, 10; III *2:* **41**, 5; **49**, 17; **50**, 19, 22; **52**, 8, 16; **53**, 13; **55**, 5; **57**, 26; **62**, 26; **65**, 13; **68**, 16; IX *2:* **28**, 6; XI *3:* **46**, 11; **51**, 26; **58**, 12 (see also Self-begotten One)

Ba[. .]mos VIII *1:* **47**, 19
Babylon V *2:* **23**, 17
Balbel II *1:* **16**, 10
Banen-Ephroum II *1:* **16**, 1
Bano II *1:* **16**, 21
Baoum II *1:* **16**, 13
Barbar II *1:* **17**, 15
Barbelo II *1:* **4**, 36; **5**, 13, 19, 25, 26, 31; **6**, 1, 5, 10, 22; **7**, 3, 14, 17; VII *5:* **121**, 21; VIII *1:* **14**, 6; **36**, 14, 20; **37**, 20; **53**, 10; **62**, 21; **63**, 7; **83**, 9; **87**, [10]; **91**, 19; **118**, 10; **119**, 23; **122**, 1; **124**, 11; **129**, 11; IX *1:* **5**, [27]; **16**, 26; X *1:* **4**, [11]; **8**, 28; **43**, [21]; XI *3:* **51**, 13; **53**, 28; **56**, 27; **58**, 21; **59**, 3, 6; XIII *1:* **38**, 9
  Barbalo XI *3:* **46**, 34
  Barbelon III *2:* **42**, 12; **62**, 1; **69**, 3
Barias II *1:* **16**, 18
Bariel XIII *1:* **48**, 22
Barpharanges VIII *1:* **6**, 12
Barroph II *1:* **16**, 13
Bartholomew III *4:* **103**, 22
Baruch IX *1:* **6**, 14; **16**, [19]
Basiliademe II *1:* **16**, 2
Basilides IX *3:* **57**, [8]
Bastan II *1:* **17**, 27
Bathinoth II *1:* **17**, 22
Beast II *5:* **114**, 1, 2; **118**, 26
Bedouk II *1:* **16**, 28
Begetter III *3:* **82**, 3, 15; *4:* **104**, 8; **106**, 21; V *1:* **8**, [29]
  All-Begetter III *3:* **82**, 17; **84**, 13
  First Begetter III *3:* **81**, 10; **82**, 16; **83**, 23; **85**, 13; *4:* **104**, 15; **105**, 11; BG *3:* **108**, 4
  Prime Begetter III *3:* **82**, 18; *4:* **118**, 20; BG *3:* **119**, 14
  Self-Begetter III *3:* **75**, 7

Belias II *1:* **11**, 3; III *2:* **58**, [21]
Beluai II *1:* **16**, 9
Beritheus VIII *1:* **88**, [10]; XI *3:* **54**, 17
Biblo II *1:* **16**, 23
Bineborin II *1:* **16**, 26
Bissoum II *1:* **15**, 34
Blaomen II *1:* **18**, 17
Blessed One II *1:* **4**, 5; **20**, 9; VII *2:* **59**, 6
Boabel II *1:* **17**, 4
Boundless One II *5:* **98**, 12; III *4:* **96**, 19
Bythos XI *2:* **27**, [38]; **28**, [20]

Caesar II *2:* **49**, 28, 29, 30
Cain II *1:* **10**, 34; **24**, 25; *4:* **91**, 12, 15, 20, 22, 25, 28; III *2:* **58**, [15]; IV *1:* **26**, 19; XI *2:* **38**, 24
Calypso II *6:* **136**, 30
Cerberus VI *5:* **49**, 8
Chaaman II *1:* **16**, 4
Chaos I *5:* **89**, 27; II *1:* **30**, 19, 27, 29; **31**, 19; *4:* **87**, 6; **93**, 31; **94**, 32; **95**, 25; **96**, 11, 14; *5:* **97**, 26, 29; **98**, 1, 6, 9, 31; **99**, 13, 17, 21, 25, 33; **101**, 24; **102**, 2, 30; **104**, 8, 14, 26; **106**, 10, 19, 22, 27; **109**, 8, 15; **112**, 17, 20, 26; **125**, 13, 21; **126**, 15, 21; III *2:* **56**, 25; **57**, [3], 10; **58**, [22]; *3:* **85**, 21; **89**, 14, 18; *4:* **113**, 18, 20; VII *1:* **15**, 17; **18**, 13; **25**, 22; **33**, 34; **40**, 23; *2:* **58**, 30; VIII *1:* **117**, 7; XIII *1:* **39**, 16, 23; **40**, 24, 30; **43**, 10; **44**, 26; **48**, 8; **49**, 15, [38]; BG *3:* **109**, 13; **118**, 14; **119**, 10; **120**, 9; **121**, 10
Charaner II *1:* **17**, 26
Charaxio III *2:* **68**, 13
Charcha II *1:* **17**, 23
Charcharb II *1:* **17**, 21
Chelke VII *1:* **33**, 12; **46**, 11, 21
Chelkea VII *1:* **31**, 7; **33**, 9; **46**, 10
Chelkeach VII *1:* **33**, 4
Chelkeak VII *1:* **31**, 6; **46**, 9, 20
Cherubim II *4:* **95**, 27; VII *2:* **54**, 34; IX *1:* **10**, [4]
  Cherubin II *5:* **105**, 4; **121**, 9
Chimaera VI *5:* **49**, 8
Chloerga VII *2:* **44**, 17
Chnoumeninorin II *1:* **16**, 19
Choux II *1:* **17**, 23
Christ I *1:* **B**, 12; *3:* **36**, 14; *4:* **43**, 37; *5:* **87**, 9; **122**, 18; **132**, 18, 28; **134**, 13; **136**, 1, 11; II *1:* **7**, 2, 10, 20, 31; **8**, 23; **9**, 2; *3:* **52**, 19, 35; **55**, 6, 11; **56**, 4, 7, 9, 13; **61**, 30, 31; **62**, 9, 10, 12, 15; **63**, [34]; **67**, 27; **68**, 17, 20; **69**, 7; **70**, 13; **71**, 18;

72, [31]; **74**, 16, [29]; *5:* **114**, 17; *6:* **135**,
23; III *2:* **44**, 23; **54**, 20; *4:* **104**, 22;
IV *2:* **55**, [6]; **56**, [27]; **59**, 17; **60**, 8;
VII *2:* **49**, 27; **52**, 5; **59**, 26; **63**, 12;
65, 18; *3:* **74**, 8; *4:* **88**, 16, 29; **90**, 33;
96, 20; **98**, 21, 26; **99**, 4, 13; **100**, 25;
101, 14, 17, 22, 25, 28, 33; **102**, 2, 5, 7;
103, 15, 25, 33; **104**, 19; **106**, 22; **107**,
27; **108**, 32; **109**, 7, 10, 11, 31; **110**, 12,
14; **111**, 15; **112**, 19; **115**, 5; **116**, 25,
30; **117**, 18; **118**, 3; VIII *2:* **133**, 17;
134, 6; IX *3:* **32**, 2; **35**, 4; **36**, 4; **45**, 9,
14; **49**, 7; **50**, [1], 3; **74**, 4; XI *1:* **1**, [20],
[23]; **15**, 17; *2:* **26**, 23; **28**, 23; **33**, 17;
39, 30; *2b:* **41**, 17; *2c:* **42**, 32; XIII *1:*
37, [31]; **38**, 22; **39**, 7; **49**, 8; BG *4:*
138, 12; **141**, 1
    Christ Jesus BG *4:* **138**, 19
Christian II *3:* **62**, 32; **64**, 24; **67**, 26;
74, 27; **75**, 32
    Christians II *3:* **52**, 24; **74**, 14; IX
3: **31**, 25
Chthaon II *1:* **17**, 21
Church I *5:* **57**, 34; **58**, 30; **59**, 2; **94**, 21;
122, 18; **135**, 26; **136**, 13; II *3:* **53**, 32;
55, 19; XI *2:* **29**, 28, 34; **30**, 19, 35;
31, 37
Conception II *1:* **8**, 11
Confronter III *3:* **75**, 7; *4:* **99**, 8
Corinthians II *6:* **131**, 3
Cosmocrator VII *2:* **52**, 27; **53**, 28; **55**,
3; VIII *1:* **1**, 18
Creator I *5:* **105**, 32, 35; **112**, 35; VI *8:*
73, 26; **75**, 13; VII *4:* **100**, 14; **116**, 8
(see also Demiurge)
Cross II *3:* **84**, 33

Darkness VII *1:* **1**, 26, 36; **2**, 13, 15, 31;
3, 9, 19, 28; **4**, 9, 10, 14, 16, 21, 22,
27, 34; **5**, 6, 12, 32; **6**, 26; **7**, 20; **9**, 3,
13, 17, 31; **10**, 1, 6, 23; **11**, 5, 28; **14**, 3;
15, 23; **20**, 4, 26, 29; **21**, 28, 35; **22**, 8,
22, 23, 33; **23**, 6; **24**, 21; **25**, 2, 27; **26**,
5, 29, 30; **27**, 6, 30, 35; **31**, 4; **32**, 23;
34, 2; **35**, 13, 34; **40**, 6; **41**, 33; **42**, 7,
31; **43**, 18, 24; **45**, 13; **48**, 22
Daveithe VIII *1:* **29**, 8; **51**, 18; **128**, 3;
IX *1:* **6**, 4
    Daveithai II *1:* **8**, 13; **9**, 16; XIII
1: **39**, 3
    Davithe III *2:* **51**, 19; **52**, 13, 25;
56, 22; **65**, 19
David VII *2:* **63**, 4; IX *3:* **70**, 4, [25]

De[. . .] VIII *1:* **6**, 32
Dearcho II *1:* **16**, 5
Death II *4:* **96**, 8; **97**, 7; *5:* **106**, 23, 27;
VII *4:* **91**, 2, 10; IX *1:* **2**, 5; **14**, 9; **15**,
23; **16**, [3]
Deiphaneus VII *5:* **126**, 11; VIII *1:* **86**, 16
    Deiph[a. . .] VIII *1:* **119**, 8
Deitharbathas II *1:* **17**, 34
Demiurge I *5:* **105**, 1, 18; XI *2:* **37**, 32;
38, [25]; **39**, 16 (see also Creator)
Demon, great VI *8:* **76**, 22-23, 31; XIII
1: **39**, 21; **40**, 4
Derdekeas VII *1:* **1**, 4; **8**, 24; **32**, 35
Deucalion V *5:* **70**, 19
Devil I *2:* **4**, 30; *3:* **33**, 20; III *2:* **61**, 17;
VI *3:* **30**, 27; **33**, 26; VII *4:* **88**, 12;
IX *3:* **47**, 6; **48**, 17; XI *1:* **20**, 18; *2:* **38**,
[13], 33; *2a:* **40**, 17
Diolimodraza II *1:* **17**, 10
Diospolis VI *6:* **61**, 19
Diphane[. . .] VIII *1:* **119**, 7
Dom[. . .] IX *1:* **6**, 1
Domedon III *2:* **41**, 14; **43**, 8
Dositheos VII *5:* **118**, 10
Doxomedon III *2:* **41**, 14; **43**, 9, 15;
44, 20; **50**, 5; **53**, 19; **56**, 1; **62**, 8;
VIII *1:* **126**, 8; IX *1:* **6**, 1; **16**, 30

E[. . .] VIII *1:* **88**, 17
Echamoth II *3:* **60**, 10, 11 (see also
Achamoth)
Echmoth II *3:* **60**, 10, 12
Edokla III *2:* **60**, 20
Egypt II *5:* **122**, 18, 21, 35; **130**, 19, 21;
6: **137**, 12; VI *2:* **16**, 7; *8:* **70**, 4, 18, 19,
22, 23, 36, 37; **71**, 11, 13, 15, 29, 31;
75, 29
    Egyptian VI *8:* **71**, 6, 10, 24
    Egyptians III *2:* **40**, [12]; **69**, 6;
VI *8:* **70**, 13, 24; **71**, 14, 16
Eidea VIII *1:* **119**, 13
Eideos VIII *1:* **128**, 4
Eidomeneus VIII *1:* **47**, 21
Eilo II *1:* **16**, 30
Eir[.]n VIII *1:* **47**, 20
Elaie VII *1:* **46**, 11, 21
Elainos III *2:* **64**, 21
    Elenos VIII *1:* **6**, 16; **54**, 25; **126**, 21
Elasso XIII *1:* **48**, 16
Eleleth II *1:* **8**, 18; **9**, 23; *4:* **93**, 8, 18;
94, 3; III *2:* **51**, 19; **52**, 14; **53**, 1; **56**,
24; **65**, 21; VIII *1:* **29**, 10; **31**, 17; **51**,
18; **128**, 6; IX *1:* **6**, 5; XIII *1:* **39**, 5, 15

Elelioupheus XI 3: 54, 19
    Elilioupheus VIII 1: 88, 12
Elemaon VII 5: 126, 8
    Elemaoni XI 3: 54, 30
Elien XIII 1: 48, 25
Elijah I 4: 48, 8
Elizabeth IX 3: 45, 8
Eloaios II 5: 101, 32
    Eloai II 5: 101, 19
    Eloaio II 1: 12, 18
    Eloaiou II 1: 11, 27
Elohim VII 3: 82, 24
Eloim II 1: 24, 18, 22; IV 1: 38, 5
Elorchaios VII 1: 31, 5; 32, 30; 46, 6
Emenun II 1: 16, 35
Emmacha (see under Seth)
Emouniar VII 5: 126, 9
Ennoia II 1: 4, [27]; VII 2: 50, 6, 14;
    54, 5, 12, 19, 23, 30; 55, 36; 59, 13;
    61, 34; 68, 30; IX 2: 27, [11] (see also
    Thought)
Enoch IX 1: 12, 8
Enthollein II 1: 16, 28
Ephememphi II 1: 18, 15
Ephesech (see Esephech)
Epinoia II 1: 9, 25; 20, 17, 25, 27; 21,
    15; 22, 5, 16, 28, 31, 35; 23, 6, 28, 33;
    24, 11; 28, 2; IX 2: 28, 2; XIII 1: 35,
    13; 39, 19, 30, 33 (see also Thought)
Epiphanios VIII 1: 128, 3, 7
    Epiphaneus VIII 1: 86, [20]; XI 3:
    54, 13
Erigenaor VIII 1: 88, [10]; XI 3: 54, 18
Erimacho II 1: 18, 9
Eros II 5: 109, 2, 10, 14, 16, 20, 25;
    111, 9, 19
Error I 3: 17, 14, 29, 36; 18, 22; 22, 21,
    24; 26, 19, 26; 35, 17; VII 2: 55, 13;
    BG 3: 118, 17
Esephech III 2: 50, 2; 53, 25; 55, 22;
    62, 6; IV 2: 56, 22; 59, 24
    Ephesech VIII 1: 13, 8; 45, 2; 56, [24]
    Ephesek VIII 1: 45, 10
Essoch VII 1: 47, 2 (see also Soch)
Esthensis-Ouchepiote II 1: 18, 19 (see
    also Ouchepiote)
Eteraphaope-Abron II 1: 15, 30
Eternal One VII 3: 76, 15; VIII 1: 23, 20
Eugnostos the beloved III 2: 69, 10
Eugnostos the Blessed III 3: 70, 1; 90,
    12-13
Eukrebos VIII 1: 47, 23
Eurios VIII 1: 47, 15

Eurumeneus VIII 1: 47, 17
Euthrounios VIII 1: 127, 22 (see also
    Authrounios)
Evanthen II 1: 16, 8
Eve II 1: 24, 15; 3: 68, 23; 70, 20; 4: 91,
    31, 34; 92, 21, 31; 5: 113, 33; 114, 4;
    115, 33; 116, 1, 12, 25; 117, 2, 25; 118,
    18, 28; 119, 6, 22, 24; V 5: 64, 8, 26;
    65, 3, 13; 66, 8, 13, 27; 69, 16; IX 1:
    10, 1; 46, 3, 8
Evil One I 2: 4, 30; 5, 20; 5: 135, 19;
    III 5: 137, 5
Exalted One I 5: 106, 12; 111, 27; 112,
    7; 119, 31; 130, 33; VII 1: 37, 12; 40,
    12; 4: 88, 11; IX 2: 28, 15
Existent One VII 4: 101, 24 (see also
    He Who Is, One Who Is, That Which
    Is)
Exodus, book called IX 3: 48, 20
Ezekiel II 6: 130, 11

Faith I 2: 1, 6; II 5: 107, 12; III 3: 78,
    4; VII 1: 25, 15; 26, 3, 14; 28, 30; 30,
    2, 5, 11, 20, 29; 31, 20, 26; 32, 11; 33,
    25; 34, 22; 35, 11, 27, 29, 33; 37, 4; 41,
    19, 25, 32; 42, 8, 11; 43, 4, 15; 46, 18,
    28 (see also Pistis, and under Sophia)
Fate II 1: 28, 14, 21; 5: 117, 22; 121,
    15; 123, 13; 125, 28; III 3: 70, 21; 4:
    93, 3; XIII 1: 43, 13, 17 (see also
    Heimarmene)
Father I 2: 4, 33; 7, 16; 9, 11, 16; 10,
    10, 32; 11, 5, 30; 13, 13; 14, 18, 31;
    3: 16, 33, 36; 17, 1, 10, 31; 18, 1, 2, 7,
    9, 10, 15, 26, 33, 38; 19, 3, 17, 30, 32;
    20, 1, 19, 27; 21, [1], 7, 9, 19, 29; 22,
    28; 23, 15, 18, 34; 24, 7, 9, 15, 18, 30,
    31; 26, 30, 32, 35; 27, 2, 6, 10, 19, 23;
    28, 12, 33; 30, 5, 25, 33; 31, 11, 20;
    32, 17; 33, 31, 33, 39; 34, 3, 14; 35, 11,
    15; 36, 18, 34; 37, 2, 19, 24, 34, 38;
    38, 7, 14, 22, 30, 33, 37; 39, 19, 24, 26,
    28; 40, 29; 41, 3, 15, 28; 42, 4, 27, 28;
    43, 4, 7, 14, 22; 5: 51, 3, 8, 17; 52, 3;
    53, 7; 56, 31; 57, 9; 58, 1, 10, 23, 38;
    59, 4; 60, 3, 17, 28; 61, 1, 13, 29; 62, 6,
    24; 63, 19; 64, 8, 28; 65, 11, 32; 66, 12;
    67, 11; 68, 5, 18, 30; 69, 10, 17, 19, 21,
    34, 41; 70, 7, 20, 27, 33; 71, 11, 12, 19,
    34, 35; 72, 10, 26, 34; 73, 11, 14, 25;
    75, 16, 21, 24, 26; 76, 6, 24, 28, 30, 33;
    77, 1, 13, 34; 80, 37; 81, 35; 85, 34;
    86, 16, 18, 21, 29, 31; 87, 16, 18, 34;

88, 9; **91**, 34; **92**, 16; **95**, 6, 38; **96**, 21;
97, 9; **100**, 24; **106**, 2; **108**, 11; **110**, 36;
114, 17, 22; **123**, 25, 32; **125**, 20, 24;
126, 13, 23, 32; **127**, 7, 31; **128**, 7, 15;
136, 2; **138**, 11; II *1:* **1**, [23], 24; **2**, 14,
28; **4**, 18; **6**, 3, 10, 18; **9**, 10; **14**, 21;
2: **33**, 2; **35**, 31; **38**, 20; **40**, 14, 27; **42**,
4, 5, 33; **44**, 35; **45**, 27; **46**, 14; **47**, 8,
22; **49**, 3, [7], 15, 24, 26; **51**, 17; *3:* **53**,
29; **54**, 6, 8, 9, 10; **55**, 34; **56**, 2, 3, 15;
59, 11; **61**, 31; **62**, 26; **67**, 20; **68**, 9, 11;
71, 4; **74**, 16, 21, 22, 23; *4:* **86**, 21; **87**,
22; **88**, 11, 34; **96**, 12, 20, 35; **97**, 15,
18; *5:* **124**, 5, 14, 17; **127**, 11; *6:* **127**,
23; **128**, 27, 35; **131**, 18, 19, 28; **132**, 7,
21, 22, 24; **133**, 4, 27; **134**, 6, 9, 15, 26;
135, 2, 4, 26; III *2:* **40**, 13, 18; **41**, 4, 9,
11, 12, [19]; **42**, [1], 4, 11, 20, 24; **43**, 5,
13, [21]; **49**, 14; **50**, 14, 15; **51**, 2; **52**,
3, 17; **53**, 4; **54**, 7, 10; **55**, 9; **59**, 12;
63, 21; *3:* **73**, 2; **74**, 22; **75**, 23; **76**, 17;
77, 13; **81**, 11; *4:* **95**, 18; **96**, 14; **97**,
15; **98**, 20, 23; **99**, 10; **100**, 2; **101**, 1,
19, 22; **104**, 23; **105**, 12, 19; **108**, 4, 25;
114, 19; **117**, [8], [9], 10, [12]; *5:* **121**,
1. 5; **129**, 20; **130**, [9]; **133**, 19; **134**,
[15]; **144**, 9; **145**, 11, 17; IV *2:* **55**, [5];
56, [24]; **58**, 3, 26; **59**, [1], 13; **60**, [25];
V *1:* **9**, [3]; *3:* **33**, 18, 22; **35**, 8; *4:* **48**,
24; **49**, [11]; **53**, 22; **54**, 11; **59**, 11; **62**,
16; VI *1:* **6**, 18; *3:* **25**, 29; **26**, 8; **33**,
30; *6:* **53**, 28; **59**, 6; **60**, 5; *7:* **64**, 3, 27,
29; *8:* **66**, 36; **68**, 25; **73**, 24; VII *2:* **49**,
22, 35; **50**, 11; **53**, 3; **57**, 6; **58**, 1; **59**, 7,
18; **60**, 11; **62**, 25; **64**, 12, 21, 33, 38;
66, 20; **67**, 24; **68**, 16; **70**, 6; *3:* **70**, 22;
73, 27; **80**, 26; *4:* **91**, 7; **100**, 27; **101**, 19;
112, 16; **113**, 9, 11, 12; **115**, 5, 10, 19;
5: **118**, 12, 26; **119**, 1, 5, 6; **121**, 23;
122, 3; **124**, 29; **127**, 30, 31; VIII *1:* 13,
11; **130**, [24]; **131**, 14; *2:* **133**, 21, 22;
135, 14; **137**, 27, 29; **139**, 2, 27; IX *1:* 7,
5; **9**, 3; **14**, 27; **16**, 9, 17; *2:* **27**, 11, 20,
25; **28**, 12, 20, 29; *3:* **31**, 22; **32**, [19];
40, 18; **69**, [2]; X *1:* **1**, 23; **18**, [16];
40, [26]; XI *1:* **8**, 36; **9**, 29, 33, 37; **10**,
[17], [24]; **11**, 20, 32, 35; **13**, 20; **14**, 27,
30; **15**, 16; **21**, 34; *2:* **22**, 18; **23**, 36;
24, 24; **28**, 22; **34**, 24; **35**, 23, 27; **36**,
28, 29, 32, 36; *2a:* **40**, 21, 22; *2d:* **43**,
21; *3:* **50**, 27; XII *3:* Fragment **1** B,
20; XIII *1:* **36**, 17; **37**, 22; **38**, 7, 8; **41**,

2, [32]; **43**, 36; **45**, 3; **49**, [8], 20, 26;
50, 15, 23
   First Father II *5:* **102**, 11; **103**, 4;
104, 12; **106**, 13, 19; **107**, 18; **108**, 5,
11, 31; **112**, 27; **114**, 22, 25; **117**, 20;
126, 21, 26; III *3:* **74**, 22; **75**, 2-3; *4:*
98, 24; **99**, 1; VII *4:* **91**, 15; XI *2:* **24**,
27 (see also Archigenetor)
   Self-Father III *3:* **75**, 6; *4:* **102**, 1
First-Appearer VII *5:* **123**, 5
First-Appearing One VIII *1:* **13**, 4; **15**,
9; **18**, 6; **20**, 9; **22**, 9; **23**, 6; **24**, 5; **29**,
16; **40**, 7; **41**, 3; **42**, 1; **44**, 27; **54**, 19;
58, 15; **63**, 13; **124**, [21] (see also
Protophanes)
First-begotten One I *1:* A, 38; V *1:* **9**, 7
First-Existing One III *3:* **75**, 9
Foreknowledge III *2:* **42**, 10; *3:* **73**, 15
Forethought XIII *1:* **41**, 4 (see also
Pronoia, Providence, Thought)
Form II *1:* **8**, 8

Gabriel III *2:* **52**, 23; **53**, 6; **57**, [7]; **64**,
26; VIII *1:* **57**, 9; **58**, 22
Galila III *2:* **58**, [12] (see also Kalila)
Galilee III *4:* **90**, 19; **91**, 20
Gamaliel III *2:* **52**, 21; **53**, 5; **57**, 6;
64, 26; V *5:* **75**, 23; VIII *1:* **47**, 2; IX
1: **5**, [18]; X *1:* **64**, 19 (see also Ka-
maliel)
Garden II *3:* **73**, 27, 28, 33; *4:* **88**, 25,
28; **89**, 34; **91**, 4 (see also Paradise)
Gaugelan V *3:* **30**, 20
Gentile II *3:* **52**, 15
   Gentiles BG *1:* **9**, 8
Geradama(s) VII *5:* **118**, 26; VIII *1:* **6**,
23; **13**, 6; **51**, 7 (see also Pigeradamas)
Gesole II *1:* **16**, 20
Gomorrah III *2:* **56**, 10, 12; **60**, 14, 16
Gongessos III *2:* **69**, 12
Good XI *3:* **56**, [17], [27]; BG *1:* **7**, 17;
9, 22
Good One II *7:* **145**, 14; VI *8:* **74**, 32;
VII *2:* **62**, 11
Gormakaiochlabar II *1:* **16**, 30
Grace I *2:* **1**, 5; *4:* **45**, 13; II *1:* **4**, 8; **8**,
3, 4, 7; III *2:* **52**, 9; VI *6:* **61**, 3
Greatness III *5:* **133**, 6; **135**, 20; VII *2:*
53, 5; **61**, 1; **70**, 8
Great One VII *4:* **111**, 19; X *1:* **9**, 12
Greek (language) II *3:* **56**, 9
   Greek (person) II *3:* **62**, 29; **75**, 31

Greeks I *5:* **109**, 25; **110**, 25; II *5:* **113**, 31; VI *2:* **16**, 1, 4, 6

Habitation VI *1:* **2**, [3]; **7**, [1], [2]; **10**, 3
Hades I *3:* **42**, 18; *5:* **89**, 28; II *1:* **11**, 4; **22**, 2; **30**, 26; **31**, 1, 22; *7:* **142**, 37; III *2:* **56**, 25; **57**, [11]; **58**, 22; VI *4:* **37**, 30; **41**, 10, 17, 28, 33; VII *1:* **3**, 24; **4**, 9; **6**, 27, 35; **11**, 31; **18**, 25; **19**, 19; **21**, 11; *33*, 20; IX *3:* **32**, 25 (see also Abyss, Underworld, Tartaros)
Ham V *5:* **72**, 17; **73**, 14, 25; **74**, 11; **76**, 13
Harmas II *1:* **10**, 30; III *2:* **58**, 11 (see also Armas)
Harmedon VIII *1:* **86**, 19; **120**, 3; XI *3:* **45**, 36; **58**, 17 (see also Armedon)
Harmozel III *2:* **51**, 18; **52**, 10, 22; **65**, 13; VIII *1:* **127**, [22] (see also Armozel)
Harmupiael III *2:* **58**, [19]
Hebrew (language) I *2:* **1**, 16; II *3:* **62**, 13
   Hebrew (person) II *3:* **51**, 29; **62**, 6
   Hebrews I *5:* **110**, 24; II *3:* **52**, 22; **55**, 29; *5:* **113**, 32
Heimarmene II *5:* **107**, 16; XIII *1:* **46**, [4] (see also Fate)
Helen II *6:* **136**, [35]
Hermaphrodites II *5:* **113**, 31; **117**, 33
Hermas VII *3:* **78**, 18
Hermes VI *6:* **58**, 28; **59**, 11; **63**, 24
Heurumaious III *2:* **65**, 3
He Who Is III *4:* **94**, 5; *5:* **137**, 10; V *3:* **24**, 20, 23, 25; **25**, 1, 3; **26**, 27, 29; **27**, 7, 15; **29**, 18-19; **36**, 10-11; VI *8:* **75**, 25; XI *2:* **22**, 18; *3:* **54**, 31-32, 32; XIII *1:* **38**, 25-26 (see also One Who Is, Existent One, That Which Is)
Hidden One VII *5:* **122**, 14; **123**, 1; **126**, 5; VIII *1:* **13**, 3; **15**, 12; **18**, 10; **19**, 5; **20**, 5; **22**, 12; **23**, 17; **24**, 6; **33**, 21; **36**, 21; **39**, 25; **40**, 25; **41**, 22; **44**, [26]; **58**, 16; **82**, 13; **85**, 11; **88**, 21; **92**, 21; **97**, 4; **101**, 12; **115**, 9, 13; **119**, 12; **121**, 3, 5; **124**, 18; **125**, 12; XI *3:* **45**, 31; **46**, [31]; **48**, 16; **51**, 17; **58**, 19
Hieralaias the Prophet, Seventh Cosmos of II *5:* **112**, 24
Himeros II *5:* **109**, 3
Hindus VI *8:* **71**, 8
Holy One II *4:* **92**, 34; *6:* **136**, 5; III *4:* **104**, 4; XI *2e:* **44**, 17
Hormos III *2:* **60**, 3 (see also Ormos)

Hosea II *6:* **129**, 22
Hymen VII *1:* **5**, 26, 28; **6**, 25; **7**, 5, 11; **11**, 12, 17; **12**, 18, 21; **13**, 30; **14**, 17; **16**, 37; **17**, 4, 13; **33**, 6; **35**, 28; **47**, 25
Hypneus III *2:* **65**, 2
Hypsiphrone XI *4:* **69**, 21, 23; **70**, 22; **72**, 21

Ibikan II *1:* **16**, 2
Ichthus III *1:* **69**, 15; VII *4:* **118**, 8
Idea II *1:* **8**, 16
Imae II *1:* **17**, 16
Imitator VI *4:* **45**, 2
Immeasurable One XIII *1:* **36**, 28
Immortal One III *3:* **89**, 16; BG *3:* **120**, 12
Imperishability V *4:* **46**, 8; IX *3:* **30**, 19; **31**, 14; **44**, 25
Incomprehensible One I *5:* **56**, 28; **114**, 25; **124**, 2
Inconceivable One I *5:* **56**, 29, 30; **123**, 36
Incorruptibility I *3:* **35**, 24; II *4:* **87**, 1, 2, 11, 20; **88**, 18; **93**, 29; **94**, 5
Incorruptible One I *3:* **35**, 13; II *1:* **2**, 15; **26**, 30; III *2:* **65**, 26
Indivisible One XI *3:* **53**, 29; **60**, 36
Ineffable One I *5:* **56**, 26, 27; **123**, 36; VII *2:* **69**, 26; VIII *1:* **74**, 21; **126**, 10; XI *2:* **22**, [20]; **24**, 39; **29**, 31-32; XIII *1:* **37**, 30
Inscrutable One VI *3:* **26**, 25; **35**, 7
Intangible One XIII *1:* **36**, [30]
Intellect XIII *1:* **46**, 22 (see also Mind, Nous)
Invisible One I *5:* **56**, 28; **105**, 25; **115**, 1; **124**, 1; II *1:* **2**, 29; **5**, 25; **9**, 4; **14**, 21; V *4:* **58**, 15; VII *3:* **81**, 2; IX *2:* **28**, 19; X *1:* **4**, 15; XI *3:* **47**, 10; XIII *1:* **35**, 9, 24; **38**, 10; **42**, 6
Ipouspoboba II *1:* **16**, 25
Isaac VII *2:* **62**, 35
Isaiah IX *3:* **40**, 21, [30]
Isauel VIII *1:* **47**, 13
   Isaouel III *2:* **64**, 14
Isidore IX *3:* **57**, 6
Israel II *2:* **42**, 14; *5:* **105**, 24; *6:* **136**, 6; **137**, 11

Jacob VII *2:* **62**, 36
James I *2:* **1**, 1, 35; *2*, 34; **8**, 32; **14**, 1; III *2:* **64**, 13; V *3:* **24**, 10, 13; **25**, 10, 13; **26**, 2, 6, 13; **27**, 9, 13; **28**, 5; **29**, 4, 13, 19; **30**, 10, 13, 18, 28; **31**,

15; **32**, 13, 17, 23, 29; **38**, 12; **40**, 4, [9]; **41**, 19; **43**, 21; **44**, 10; *4:* 44, [12]
James the Just V *3:* **32**, 2-3; *4:* **44**, 13-14
James the Righteous II *2:* **34**, 29
Just One V *4:* **44**, 18; **60**, 12; **61**, 14
James (the son of Zebedee) II *1:* **1**, 6
Japheth V *5:* **72**, 17; **73**, 15, 26; **74**, 11; **76**, 13
Jeremiah II *6:* **129**, 8
Jericho V *2:* **19**, 13; XI *1:* **6**, 21
Jerusalem I *2:* **16**, 9; II *3:* **69**, 15, 31, 32, 33; *6:* **136**, 9; V *2:* **18**, [5], [18]; *3:* **25**, 15; **36**, 19; **37**, 12; *4:* **44**, 15; VIII *2:* **138**, 10; **139**, 6; IX *3:* **70**, 5, 8, [15], 27
Jesus I *2:* **2**, 23; *3:* **20**. 11, 23; **24**, 8; *5:* **117**, 12; II *2:* **32**, 10, 14, 19; **33**, 5, 10, 18, 23; **34**, 3, 14, 16, 25, 27, 30; **35**, 4, 10, 15, 27, 31; **36**, 5, 9, 11, 17, 26, 34; **37**, 20, 24; **38**, 1, 10, 12, ⟨17⟩, 21, 31; **39**, 2, 5, 7, 10, 18, 20, 24, 29; **40**, 2, 7, 13, 16, 19, ⟨21⟩, 26, 31; **41**, 6, 12, 24, 27, 31; **42**, 23, 25, 30, 33; **43**, 7, 9, 23, 28, ⟨31⟩, 34; **44**, 2, 10; **45**, 17, 19, 21, 25, 29, 34; **46**, 6, 11, 13, 23, 28; **47**, 12, 15, 17, 19, 24, 29, 34; **48**, 4, 7, 13, 16, 26, 33, [35]; **49**, 2, 7, 15, 27, ⟨32⟩; **50**, 2, 5, 12, 16, 18, 22, 28, 31; **51**, 4, 6, 8, 10, ⟨14⟩, 20; *3:* **56**, 3, 5, 6; **57**, 2, 28; **62**, 8, 9, 10, 13, 16; **63**, 21, 24; **70**, 34; **71**, 12; **73**, 15, 24; **77**, 1, 8; **83**, 16; *7:* **139**, 21; **144**, 37; III *2:* **64**, 1; **65**, 17; *4:* **119**, 18; VI *1:* **6**, 12, 16; VII *2:* **66**, 8; *3:* **81**, 18; VIII *2:* **133**, 8; **139**, 11, 15, 21, 26; **140**, 13, 16, 27; IX *3:* **30**, 25; **33**, [23]; **66**, 4; XI *1:* **5**, 38; *2:* **35**, [10], 14, 30; **36**, 17, 20; **37**, 22; **39**, 14, 19, 23, 29; *2b:* **41**, 20; XIII *1:* **50**, 13; BG *4:* **130**, 4
   Jesus Christ I *1:* **A**, 13; *4:* **48**, 19; **50**, 1; *5:* **117**, 15; II *1:* **32**, 6; *3:* **80**, 1; III *2:* **69**, 14; *4:* **90**, 14; VI *1:* **9**, 11; VII *2:* **69**, 21; *4:* **91**, 26; **118**, 8; VIII *2:* **132**, 12-13; **133**, 1, 26; **134**, 17; **139**, 8; **140**, 3-4; IX *1:* **1**, 2; **6**, 2, 9; **18**, 6; XI *2a:* **40**, 13; *2b:* **40**, 33; *2d:* **43**, [22], 32, 37; BG *4:* **138**, 6-7
   Jesus the Christ I *3:* **18**, 16; II *5:* **105**, 26 (see also Christ)
Jew II *3:* **62**, 26; **75**, 30
   Jews I *5:* **112**, 22; II *2:* **40**, 24; *3:* **75**, 34

John (the Baptist) I *2:* **6**, 31; II *2:* **41**, 12; *6:* **135**, 23; IX *3:* **30**, 24; **31**, 3; **39**, [24]; **45**, 6, 12; XI *2b:* **41**, 32; *2c:* **42**, [11]
   John the Baptist II *2:* **41**, 7-8, 8; VII *2:* **63**, 34
John (the disciple) II *1:* **1**, 4, 6, [18]; **2**, 9, 10; **32**, 9; VI *1:* **11**, 4, 6, 15
Jordan (River) II *3:* **70**, 35; IX *3:* **30**, 21, 22, 28, 30; **31**, 2; **39**, [23]; XI *2b:* **41**, [27], 34
Joseph the carpenter II *3:* **73**, 9
Judas III *5:* **125**, 4; **127**, 19; **129**, 16; **131**, 16; **132**, 19; **134**, 24; **135**, 4, 7; **138**, 2, 6, 11, 20; **140**, 9; **142**, 4; **143**, 11; **144**, 12; **145**, 3; **146**, 7, 10, 13
Judea II *2:* **43**, 13
Justice II *5:* **110**, 2; III *2:* **60**, 21; **62**, 20

Kalila II *1:* **17**, 8 (see also Galila)
   Kalila-Oumbri II *1:* **10**, 32
Kamaliel VIII *1:* **47**, 11; XIII *1:* **48**, 27 (see also Gamaliel)
Kandephor(os) VII *5:* **126**, 10
Keilar VIII *1:* **47**, 23
Knyx II *1:* **16**, 35
Koade II *1:* **17**, 17
Kodere VIII *1:* **128**, 6
Kore VI *8:* **75**, 21
Kriman II *1:* **16**, 11
Krys II *1:* **16**, 8

Labernioum II *1:* **17**, 6
Lalameus VIII *1:* **47**, 20; XI *3:* **54**, 20, 28
   Lalameu(s) VIII *1:* **88**, 13
Lampno II *1:* **17**, 14
Laraneus VIII *1:* **128**, 3
Leekaphar II *1:* **17**, 15
Levi II *3:* **63**, 26; V *3:* **37**, 7; BG *1:* **18**, 6
Levite VII *4:* **109**, 20
Libyan mountain VI *8:* **75**, [36]
Life I *2:* **1**, 7; II *1:* **4**, 4; **20**, 19; **23**, 23; **24**, 15; III *2:* **53**, 8; *3:* **87**, 5; *4:* **111**, 8; VII *4:* **91**, 8, 9; **106**, 25; **107**, 13; **112**, 10; **113**, 15; XI *2:* **24**, [22]; **29**, [27], 30, 32; **30**, [17], 31; **31**, 29; *3:* **49**, 31, 35 (see also Zoe, and under Sophia)
Light VII *1:* **1**, 26, 32; **2**, 10, 26, 29; **3**, 25, 30, 35; **4**, 3, 6; **6**, 32; **7**, 35; **8**, 6, 11, 25; **9**, 7, 20, 27; **10**, 21, 31; **11**, 18, 23; **12**, 16; **13**, 25; **16**, 22, 28; **17**, 30; **24**, 5, 8, 20, 27; **28**, 3; **30**, 20; **31**, 25; **32**, 21, 31; **33**, 17; **34**, 24; **38**, 24; **39**, 10, 16; **41**, 24; **42**, 6, 32; **44**, 27

Limit   XI *2:* **25**, 22; **26**, [30]; **27**, [35]; **31**, 22, 23; **33**, 26

Lithargoel   VI *1:* **5**, 16; **7**, 22; **8**, 14, 25; **9**, 8

Living One   II *2:* **40**, 1; **43**, 10; **51**, 8

Loel   VIII *1:* **47**, 4

Logos   I *5:* **75**, 22; **76**, 3, 25; **77**, 7, 9, 11; **80**, 11, 30; **81**, 22; **85**, 12, 15, 25; **90**, 14; **91**, 3, 10, 36; **92**, 4, 22; **93**, 20; **95**, 17; **96**, 17; **97**, 3, 11, 21; **98**, 21; **99**, 18, 19; **100**, 22, 31; **103**, 15; **104**, 32; **105**, 11, 17, 31; **111**, 25; **113**, 38; **114**, 7; **115**, 21, 27; **118**, 8, 19; **119**, 28; **122**, 27; **125**, 7; **130**, 14, 31; **131**, 15; II *5:* **125**, 14; III *2:* **49**, 17; **50**, 18; **53**, 13; **60**, 6; **63**, 10; **64**, 1; VI *4:* **42**, 7; **43**, 28; **44**, 3, 13; IX *2:* **27**, 18; **28**,9 (see also Word, Reason)

Loios   XIII *1:* **39**, 3

Love   I *2:* **1**, 4; II *1:* **8**, 16; *5:* **107**, 12; III *2:* **53**, 5; *3:* **82**, 24; *4:* **104**, 20; V *1:* **9**, 6

Magdalene   II *3:* **59**, 8 (see Mary Magdalene)

Majesty   I *2:* **15**, 26; VII *1:* **1**, 6; **4**, 15; **6**, 31; **7**, 1; **8**, 16, 19, 35; **9**, 4, 19; **10**, 12, 26; **11**, 7, 21, 25; **12**, 1, 23, 28; **13**, 5, 24, 34; **16**, 34; **18**, 2, 28; **19**, 24; **21**, 13; **29**, 21; *2:* **49**, 10; **50**, 10; **54**, 6; **57**, 8; *3:* **70**, 19

Malsedon   VIII *1:* **119**, [9]; **120**, 17

Mammon   IX *3:* **68**, 4, [7]

Man   II *1:* **2**, [20], 25; **5**, 7; **6**, 4; **8**, 32; **14**, 14, 23; **15**, 10; II *4:* **91**, 2; **96**, 33; *5:* **103**, 19; **107**, 26; **115**, 22; **123**, 33; III *2:* **59**, 3; *3:* **77**, 10, 14; **78**, 3; **83**, 21; **85**, 10, 21; **88**, 6; **89**, 9; *4:* **100**, 18; **101**, 20; **102**, 1, 20; **104**, 1, 6; **105**, 5; **112**, 7; **113**, 13; V *1:* **7**, 25; **8**, 18, 28, [31]; VII *2:* **52**, 36; **53**, 4, 17; **54**, 8; VIII *1:* **13**, 11; **30**, 5; IX *1:* **17**, 15; XI *2:* **29**, [28], 33; **30**, [18], 34; **31**, 36; BG *3:* **108**, 9; **109**, 5; **120**, 16; **121**, 15

Mareim   V *4:* **44**, 16

Marephnounth   II *1:* **17**, 28

Mariam   III *5:* **126**, 17; **131**, 19; **134**, 25; **137**, 3; **139**, 8; **140**, 14, 19, 23; **141**, 12; **142**, 20; **143**, 6; **144**, 5, 22; **146**, [1]; V *3:* **40**, 25

Mariamme   III *4:* **98**, 9; **114**, 8

Marsanes   X *1:* **68**, 18

Marsedon   VIII *1:* **122**, 11,16

Martha   V *3:* **40**, [26]

Mary   II *2:* **36**, 34; **51**, 19; *3:* **55**, 23, 27; **59**, 7, 11; V *4:* **44**, [22]; IX *3:* **45**, 11; BG *1:* **9**, 12, 21; **10**, 1, 7; **17**, 7; **18**, 1; **19**, 5

   Mary Magdalene   II *3:* **63**, 33 (see also Magdalene)

Mathaias   II *7:* **138**, 2

Matthew   II *2:* **34**, 34; III *4:* **93**, 24; **100**, 16; *5:* **124**, 23; **126**, 10; **128**, 23; **132**, 6, 10, 12; **134**, 25; **135**, 8; **139**, 20; **141**, 3, 6; **142**, 9; **143**, 11; **144**, 17; **145**, 3

Meirothea   XIII *1:* **38**, 15; **45**, [10]

   Mirothea   VIII *1:* **6**, 30; **30**, 14

   Mirotheas   VII *5:* **119**, 12

   Mirotheos   VII *5:* **119**, 12; **120**, 15

   Mirothoe   III *2:* **49**, 4

Melcheir-Adonein   II *1:* **11**, 2

Melchizedek   IX *1:* **1**, 1; **5**, [14]; **12**, 10; **14**, [16]; **15**, 9; **19**, [13]; **26**, [2]

Mellephaneus   XI *3:* **54**, 30; XIII *1:* **39**, 2

Memory   II *1:* **8**, 12; III *2:* **53**, 4

Meniggesstroeth   II *1:* **15**, 31

Mesotes   VII *2:* **66**, 7

Messiah   II *3:* **56**, 8; **62**, 8, 11 (see also Christ, and under Jesus)

Messos   XI *3:* **50**, 19; **68**, 28; **69**, 16

Metanoia   III *2:* **59**, 10

Miamai   II *1:* **17**, 6

Michael   II *1:* **17**, 30

Michanor   III *2:* **65**, 6

Michar   III *2:* **64**, 15, 20; V *5:* **84**, 6; VIII *1:* **6**, 10, 15; XIII *1:* **48**, 19

Micheus   III *2:* **64**, 15, 20; VIII *1:* **6**, 16; XIII *1:* **48**, 19

   Michea   VIII *1:* **6**, [10]

   Micheu   V *5:* **84**, 5

Mind   I *3:* **16**, 36; **19**, 37; **37**, 10; *5:* **105**, 23; II *1:* **6**, 34; **7**, 1, 4, 8, 12; **8**, 29; III *2:* **42**, 9; *4:* **104**, 8; V *1:* **8**, 2; VI *2:* **13**, 1; *6:* **58**, 15, 21, 27, 28; **60**, 30; **61**, 31; VII *4:* **85**, 25; **86**, 19; **90**, 12; **92**, 25; **96**, 9; **112**, 27; **117**, 3; *5:* **119**, 1; **125**, 31; VIII *1:* **18**, 6; **19**, 22; **29**, 18; **30**, 8, 17; **33**, 13; **38**, 2, 18; **44**, 29; **54**, 20; **129**, 6; IX *2:* **28**, 4, 12, [19]; XI *2:* **22**, 31, 35; **23**, 37; **24**, 20; **25**, [26]; **30**, [27] (see also Intellect, Nous)

Mirocheirothetou   IX *1:* **6**, 8; **18**, 2

Mixanther   III *2:* **65**, 5

Mnesinous III *2:* **64**, 16; V *5:* **84**, 6; VIII *1:* **47**, 4; XIII *1:* **48**, 20

Mniarchon II *1:* **16**, 6

Moluchtha VII *1:* **32**, 2; **47**, 2

Moluchthas VII *1:* **34**, 9

Monad II *1:* **2**, 26; VII *2:* **57**, 16; **66**, 14; *5:* **121**, 33, 34; **122**, 1

Monogenes XI *2:* **24**, 33, 37; **25**, [21]; **28**, 25; **37**, 24; **39**, 24; *2a:* **40**, 34

Morphaia VII *1:* **48**, 1

Moses I *4:* **48**, 9; II *1:* **13**, 20; **22**, 22; **23**, 3; **29**, 6; VII *2:* **63**, 26, 33; IX *3:* **48**, 16, 24; **50**, 4

    Moses the Prophet, Archangelikē of II *5:* **102**, 8-9

Mother I *3:* **24**, 7; II *1:* **2**, 14; **9**, 11; **10**, 18; **13**, 13, 33; **19**, 15, 22, 29; **20**, 11, 28; **23**, 24; **25**, 3; *2:* **50**, [1]; III *2:* **41**, 9, 18; **42**, 4, 12, 17; **43**, 1; **55**, 10; **67**, 4; *4:* **104**, 18; **112**, 19; **114**, 15; *5:* **144**, 11; IV *2:* **56**, 24; **58**, [4]; **59**, [13]; V *1:* **9**, [5]; VI *4:* **40**, 10, 30; VIII *1:* **29**, 17; **54**, 16; *2:* **135**, 12; **139**, 23; IX *1:* **5**, 27; **16**, [25]; XI *1:* **7**, 38; **8**, 6; **13**, 17; XIII *1:* **37**, 22; **38**, 13; **42**, 9; **44**, 31; **45**, [3]; **10**: **46**, 9, 20; **48**, 32; BG *3:* **120**, 15

Mother-Father II *1:* **5**, 7; **6**, 16; **14**, 19; **19**, 17; **20**, 9; **27**, 33

Mousanios XIII *1:* **39**, 4

Muses, nine V *5:* **81**, 3

Nature VII *1:* **4**, 32; **5**, 1, 3, 9, 20, 22, 33; **6**, 1, 9, 13, 20; **7**, 11, 15, 19, 21, 25; **8**, 15, 32; **10**, 14, 26, 35; **11**, 1, 11; **12**, 15, 22; **13**, 17; **14**, 13; **15**, 5, 9, 12, 19, 28; **18**, 1, 16, 17, 25, 30, 33; **19**, 4, 14; **20**, 3, 23, 25; **21**, 5; **22**, 10, 20, 22; **23**, 1, 5; **24**, 24, 31; **26**, 27, 34; **28**, 11; **29**, 8; **30**, 10; **32**, 1, 5; **34**, 3; **35**, 7; **36**, 33; **37**, 2; **38**, 21; **39**, 27; **40**, 22; **41**, 31; **42**, 10, 15, 16, 23, 27; **43**, 9; **44**, 1, 3; **45**, 9, 15, 27; **47**, 5, 14, 33, 34; **48**, 7, 20, 22

Nazara II *3:* **62**, 14

Nazarene II *1:* **1**, 13; *3:* **56**, 12; **62**, 11, 15, 16

Nazorean II *3:* **62**, 8, 9

Nebrith II *1:* **16**, 31

Nebruel III *2:* **57**, [18], 22

Nenentophni II *1:* **18**, 17

Nephredon VIII *1:* **86**, [14]

Nibareu(s) VII *5:* **126**, 10

Nine Gates, city of VI *1:* **6**, 24

Noah II *1:* **29**, 3, 9; *4:* **92**, 9; V *5:* **70**, 17; **71**, 15, 17, 21; **72**, 15; **73**, 1; **74**, 17; **76**, 12; VI *4:* **38**, 22; **39**, 1; **41**, 1; IX *1:* **12**, [8]

Noetheus VIII *1:* **88**, 13; XI *3:* **54**, 20, 28

Noraia, First Book of II *5:* **102**, 10-11

    Noraia, First Logos of II *5:* **102**, 24-25

Norea II *4:* **91**, [34]; **92**, 21, 32; **93**, 6; IX *2:* **27**, 21; **29**, 3 (see also Orea)

Nous VII *2:* **58**, 3; **64**, 9; **66**, 32; **68**, 18; IX *2:* **27**, 12, 17, 25 (see also Intellect, Mind)

Nousanios XIII *1:* **38**, 35

Nouthan XIII *1:* **48**, 22

Odeor II *1:* **17**, 18

Odysseus II *6:* **136**, 28

Olives, Mount of III *4:* **91**, 20; VIII *2:* **133**, 15

Olmis VIII *1:* **119**, 11; **120**, 24

Olses III *2:* **65**, 2

    Olsen VIII *1:* **47**, 18

Omothem[. . .] VIII *1:* **52**, 9

One Who Is III *3:* **71**, 13-14; V *3:* **27**, 10; VII *2:* **67**, 18; X *1:* **13**, 17, 18

    One Who Exists I *3:* **28**, 13; **39**, 15; *5:* **74**, 34; **114**, 15; II *1:* **19**, 31; VIII *1:* **80**, 6; IX *1:* **6**, 11; X *1:* **7**, 5-6, 24-25; XI *3:* **45**, 13-14; **48**, 37 (see also Existent One, He Who Is, That Which Is)

Onorthochrasaei II *1:* **18**, 11

Optaon VII *5:* **126**, 8; XI *3:* **54**, 31

Oraios II *5:* **101**, 33

Orea II *4:* **92**, 14 (see also Norea)

Originator II *1:* **12**, 29

Orimenios VIII *1:* **88**, [11]; XI *3:* **54**, 18

Ormaoth II *1:* **16**, 34

Ormos VIII *1:* **47**, 9 (see also Hormos)

Orneos VIII *1:* **127**, 22

Oroiael III *2:* **51**, 18; **52**, 11, 24; **57**, 8; **65**, 16; VIII *1:* **29**, 6; **51**, 18; **127**, [27]; IX *1:* **6**, 4; **17**, 12; XIII *1:* **39**, 1

    Oriel II *1:* **8**, 9

    Oroiel II *1:* **9**, 14

Oroorrothos II *1:* **18**, 8

Osei VII *1:* **31**, 24

Ouchepiptoe II *1:* **19**, 1 (see also Esthensis-Ouchepiptoe)

Ouchepiptoe II *1:* **19**, 1

Oudidi II *1:* **17**, 13

Oummaa   II *1:* **17**, 35
Ouriel   II *1:* **17**, 30

Paraclete   I *1:* **A**, 17
Paradise   I *3:* **36**, 37, 38; *5:* **96**, 29; **106**, 27; II *1:* **21**, 18, 25; **24**, 7; *2:* **36**, 22; *3:* **55**, 7; **71**, 22; *5:* **110**, 3, 10, 24, 32; **115**, 29; **118**, 19; **119**, 22, 25; **121**, 1, 5; **122**, 1, 10; **123**, 1; IX *3:* **45**, 28; **46**, 2, 6, 18; **47**, 11 (see also Garden)
Paul   I *1:* **B**, 9; II *6:* **131**, 2; V *2:* **17**, 19; **18**, [9], 15, [33]; **19**, 11; **21**, 25; **23**, 2; **24**, 9; VII *4:* **108**, 30
Peace   I *2:* **1**, 3; II *1:* **8**, 20; *5:* **107**, 11; III *2:* **53**, 7
Perception   II *1:* **8**, 3, 11; III *2:* **52**, 10
Perfection   II *1:* **8**, 19
Peter   I *2:* **1**, 12; **2**, 34; **3**, 39; **13**, 26; **15**, 7; VI *1:* **1**, 30; **5**, [2], 3; **8**, 21; **9**, 1, 2, 4, 5, 10, 15; **10**, 13, 23; **11**, 1; **12**, 20; VII *3:* **70**, 13, 20; **71**, 15; **72**, 10; **75**, 28; **80**, 23, 31; **84**, 14; VIII *2:* **132**, 10, 12; **133**, 10, 12; **138**, 17; **139**, 9; **140**, 2, 7; BG *1:* **7**, 10; **10**, 1; **17**, 16; **18**, 2, 6, 7; *4:* **128**, 4, 9, 10; **129**, 8; **130**, 12, 18; **131**, 10, 12, 18; **137**, 14; **140**, 15; **141**, 7
   Simon Peter   II *2:* **34**, 32; **51**, 18
Phainops   XI *4:* **69**, 27, **70**, 25, [29]; **71**, [28]; **72**, 19
Phaionios   XIII *1:* **39**, 1
Phaleris, ten thousand   VIII *1:* **47**, 14
Phalses   VIII *1:* **47**, 14
Phariel   XIII *1:* **48**, 25
Pharisatha   II *3:* **63**, 22
Pharisee   II *1:* **1**, 8, 12
   Pharisees   II *2:* **40**, 7; **50**, 2; IX *3:* **29**, 13, 18
Phersalo   V *5:* **79**, 1
Phikna   II *1:* **17**, 5
Philip   II *3:* **73**, 8; **86**, 19; III *4:* **92**, 4; **95**, 19; VIII *2:* **132**, 11, 13; **133**, 8
Phiouthrom   II *1:* **17**, 3
Phloxopha   II *1:* **18**, 6
Phneme   II *1:* **17**, 2
Phnouth   IV *1:* **25**, 20
Phoenix   II *5:* **122**, 3, 10, 16, 27, 29, 30
Phorbea   VII *1:* **44**, 17
Phthave   II *1:* **16**, 15
Pigeradamas   IX *1:* **6**, 6
   Pigeraadamas   II *1:* **8**, 34 (see also Geradamas)
Pisandriaptes   II *1:* **17**, 16

Pistis   II *5:* **98**, 14; **99**, 2, 23, 29; **100**, 20; **102**, 5, 32; **103**, 15, 28, 34; **104**, 1, 28; **107**, 19; **112**, 3; **113**, 6; **115**, 7; III *3:* **82**, 6; *4:* **106**, 24 (see also Faith, and under Sophia)
Place of Harvest-time and Joy, mountain called   III *4:* **91**, 1-2
Pleiades   VII *1:* **47**, 20
Plesithea   III *2:* **56**, 6; VIII *1:* **51**, 12
Poimael   III *2:* **66**, 1
Power   VI *2:* **13**, 2; *4:* **38**, 5; **39**, 15; **47**, 11, 33; *6:* **52**, 14; **58**, 11; VII *1:* **1**, 19; **5**, 27, 29; **6**, 28; **7**, 17; **10**, 18; **17**, 7; **35**, 9; *4:* **106**, 25
   Great Power   VI *2:* **21**, 8; *4:* **36**, 2, 3-4, 15, 27; **40**, 27; **45**, 4; **48**, 14-15; VII *1:* **10**, 20; *4:* **112**, 8
Preexistent One   I *5:* **83**, 21; **127**, 19; V *3:* **33**, 24; **34**, 7, 11, 13; **36**, [1]; VIII *2:* **136**, 2
Prones   VIII *1:* **52**, 12
Pronoia   II *1:* **4**, [32]; **5**, 16; **6**, 5, 22, 30; **7**, 22; **30**, 12, 24, 35; **31**, 11; *5:* **108**, 11, 15; **109**, 6; **111**, 18, 32; XI *2:* **36**, 10; **37**, 21
   Pronoia Sambathas   II *5:* **101**, 27 (see also Providence, Forethought)
Protennoia   XIII *1:* **35**, 1; **38**, 8; **42**, 3; **48**, 32; **50**, 22 (see also under Thought)
Protophanes   XI *3:* **45**, 36; **46**, [25]; **51**, 20; **58**, 17 (see also First-Appearing One)
Providence   III *2:* **42**, 2; **43**, 6; **63**, 22; *3:* **70**, 20; **71**, 3; *4:* **91**, 5; **93**, 2, 14; IV *2:* **58**, [23] (see also Pronoia, Forethought)
Prudence   II *1:* **8**, 4; III *2:* **52**, 13
Psalms   II *6:* **133**, 16; **137**, 15
Pserem   II *1:* **16**, 32
Psyche   II *5:* **111**, 8 (see also Soul)
Ptolemy   BG *4:* **132**, 12; **135**, 1, 19; **137**, 1, 17; **138**, 16

Reason   VII *4:* **85**, 26; **86**, 20; **88**, 4; **90**, 18; **91**, 25; **99**, 4; **103**, 12; **107**, 18 (see also Word, Logos)
Rebouel   VII *1:* **40**, 13, 31
Redeemer   I *1:* **A**, 4; *5:* **87**, 7; **138**, 20; V *4:* **55**, 15, 18; VIII *2:* **134**, 7
Rheginos   I *4:* **43**, 25; **44**, 22; **47**, 3; **49**, 10
Riaramnacho   II *1:* **18**, 2
Richram   II *1:* **17**, 32

River (Nile) VI *8:* **71**, 17
Roeror II *1:* **16**, 24
Roman II *3:* **62**, 28
  Romans IX *3:* **70**, 14, 30
Ruler II *4:* **90**, 19, 24, 30; **92**, 8, 27;
  94, 34; *5:* **100**, 5, 19, 29; **101**, 3, 8, 10;
  7: **142**, 31; V *5:* **64**, 21; **77**, 3; VII *2:*
  54, 27

Sabalo II *1:* **17**, 20
Sabaoth II *1:* **10**, 34; **11**, 31; *4:* **95**, 14,
  23; *5:* **101**, 30; **103**, 32; **104**, 6, 19, 26;
  106, 20, 25; **107**, 5; **113**, 12; **114**, 16;
  122, 23; III *2:* **58**, 15; IV *1:* **26**, 19;
  IX *3:* **73**, 30
  Sanbaoth II *1:* **12**, 22
Sabbateon II *1:* **12**, 25
Sabbath I *3:* **32**, 18, 24; II *2:* **38**, 19;
  3: **52**, 34; IX *1:* **25**, [6]; XI *1:* **11**, 18,
  31, 33
Sabbede II *1:* **11**, 33
Sabenai XIII *1:* **48**, 22
Sakla II *4:* **95**, 7; III *2:* **57**, 16, 21, [26];
  58, 24; V *5:* **74**, 3, 7
  Saklas II *1:* **11**, 17; XIII *1:* **39**, 27
Salamex VIII *1:* **62**, 18; **63**, 19; **64**, 8
Salome II *2:* **43**, 25, ⟨30⟩; V *3:* **40**, 25
Samael II *1:* **11**, 18; *4:* **87**, 3; **94**, 25;
  5: **103**, 18; XIII *1:* **39**, 27
Samaritan II *2:* **43**, 12; *3:* **78**, 7
Samblo III *2:* **53**, 8; **64**, 27; VIII *1:* **47**,
  24; XIII *1:* **48**, 28
  Sablo V *5:* **75**, 22
  Samlo III *2:* **52**, 25
Sanbaoth (see Sabaoth)
Saphaia VII *1:* **31**, 27; **46**, 16, 26
Saphaina VII *1:* **31**, 28; **33**, 27; **46**, 17,
  26
Saphasatoel II *1:* **17**, 31
Sappho VIII *1:* **47**, 26
Sasabek VI *4:* **41**, 29
Satan I *2:* **4**, 37, 39; IX *1:* **20**, 15
Sauel V *5:* **79**, 2
Savior I *2:* **1**, 23, 31; **2**, 11, 17, 40; **4**,
  [2]; **16**, 24; *3:* **16**, 38; *4:* **43**, 37; **45**, 14;
  48, 18; *5:* **87**, 7; **95**, 35; **113**, 11, 14,
  17, 18; **114**, 9, 31; **115**, 35; **116**, 3, 19,
  26, 28; **118**, 25; **120**, 10; **121**, 2; **122**,
  15; **138**, 20; II *1:* **1**, 1, 21; **22**, 10, 12,
  21; **25**, 16; **31**, 32; **32**, 5; *3:* **63**, [33];
  64, 3; *5:* **105**, 26; **124**, 33; *6:* **130**, 29;
  134, 35; **135**, 16; *7:* **138**, 1, 4, 27, 37, 39;
  139, 24, 32; **140**, 9, [40]; **141**, 4, 25;

142, 6, 10, 26; **143**, 8; III *2:* **68**, 22;
  69, 15; *3:* **82**, 2, 7; **84**, [2], 8; **85**, 14;
  4: **91**, 7, 10, 24; **92**, 6; **94**, 4, 14; **95**, 21;
  96, 15, 18; **98**, 12; **100**, [2], 18, 20;
  105, 9; **106**, 15, 20; **107**, 22; **108**, 17,
  20; **112**, 21; **113**, 1; **114**, 13; **119**, 9;
  5: **120**, 1, 2; **125**, 1, 18; **147**, 23; VI *1:*
  9, 5; VII *3:* **70**, 14; **72**, 26; **73**, 11; **80**,
  8; **81**, 15; **82**, 9, 28; *4:* **118**, 8; VIII *1:*
  131, 15; *2:* **132**, 18; IX *1:* **4**, 5; **14**, 4;
  3: **45**, 17; **60**, [16]; **67**, 8; XI *1:* **3**, 26;
  5, 30; **21**, 23; *3:* **58**, 13; BG *1:* **7**, 2,
  13; **9**, [24]; **10**, 2, 4, 19; **17**, 8, 14, 18;
  18, 5, 11, 13, 21; *3:* **107**, 16; **108**, 6
Scythian VI *8:* **71**, 8
Sederkeas VII *1:* **46**, 8
Seldao III *2:* **64**, 21; VIII *1:* **6**, 16; **54**,
  25; **126**, [20]
Self-begotten One III *3:* **82**, 14; *4:* **106**,
  6; VII *5:* **119**, 16; VIII *1:* **6**, 8, 21; **7**,
  3; **12**, 16; **15**, 6; **17**, 7; **18**, 19; **19**, 6;
  20, 7; **30**, 6, 7, 15, 21; **34**, 17; **35**, 11,
  19; **41**, 9, 10; **44**, [31]; **53**, 17; **56**, 12,
  14; **58**, 14; **127**, 15; X *1:* **5**, 28 (see
  also Autogenes)
Self-engendered One X *1:* **6**,7
Selmechel III *2:* **62**, 16
Selmen VIII *1:* **54**, 20; **62**, [18]; **63**, 20;
  64, [8]
Semelel[. . .] VIII *1:* **52**, 7
Semen XI *3:* **56**, 25
Senaon VII *5:* **126**, 6; XI *3:* **54**, 28
Senaphim II *1:* **16**, 15
Seraphim VII *2:* **54**, 34; IX *1:* **10**, 4
  Seraphin II *5:* **105**, 19
Serpent I *5:* **107**, 11; IX *3:* **45**, 31; **47**,
  4, 5; **48**, 17 (see also Snake)
Sesengenpharanges III *2:* **64**, 18
Seth II *1:* **9**, 12, 15; **25**, 1; *4:* **91**, [31];
  III *2:* **51**, 20; **54**, 11; **55**, 17; **56**, 13,
  14; **59**, 15; **60**, 1, 8, 9, 14, 15; **61**, 16,
  23; **62**, 19, 24; **63**, 11; **64**, 2, 24; **65**,
  17, 20; **68**, 2, 10; V *5:* **64**, 3, 6; **67**, 15;
  77, 1; **85**, 20, 24; VII *2:* **70**, 12; *5:* **118**,
  12, 25; **121**, 17, 19; **124**, 15; **127**, 27;
  VIII *1:* **7**, 9; **30**, 10; **130**, 17; IX *1:* **5**,
  20
  Seth Emmacha Seth VIII *1:* **6**, 25;
  51, 14-15
  Emmacha Seth VII *5:* **118**, 28
  Telmael Telmachael Eli Eli Machar
  Machar Seth IV *2:* **59**, 19-21
  Telmael Telmael Heli Heli Machar

Machar Seth   III 2: 62, 2-4
    Heli Heli Machar Machar Seth
    III 2: 65, 9
Setheus   VIII 1: 54, 23; 126, 16
Shem   V 5: 72, 17; VII 1: 1, 1, 4, 18; 4,
    12; 9, 34; 11, 35; 24, 17; 26, 1, 11, 25,
    30; 28, 20, 35; 31, 4; 32, 19; 34, 17,
    24, 32; 37, 6, 19; 40, 32; 41, 21; 45,
    32; 47, 7; 48, 30
Silence   III 2: 40, [17], 18; 41, 10, 12;
    42, [21], [22], 23; 43, 14, 23, 24; 44, 14,
    28; 50, 15; 3: 88, 8, 9; 4: 112, 8; IV 2:
    58, [24]; 59, [17]; 60, 13, [26]; XI 2:
    22, 26; 23, 22; 24, [20]; 29, [33]; XIII
    1: 35, 34; 36, 3; 37, 12, 29; 46, [5], 12,
    13, 23; 50, 20
Silent One   X 1: 4, 21; 7, 8, 21; 15, 1
Silvanus   VII 4: 84, 15
Simon (of Cyrene)   VII 2: 56, 9
Simonians   IX 3: 58, [2]
Siou   VIII 1: 88, 17
Sir, Mount   II 4: 92, 14
Smoun   XI 3: 54, 31
Snake   II 4: 89, 32; 90, 6, 11, 31, 32;
    91, 1, 3 (see also Serpent)
Soch   VII 1: 32, 3 (see also Essoch)
Sodom   III 2: 56, 10; 60, 12, 13, 18;
    VII 1: 29, 1, 28
    Sodomites   VII 1: 29, 13, 20
Soldas   VII 1: 30, 32; 39, 31
Solmis   VIII 1: 86, [12]; 119, 11; 122,
    12; 126, 4; XI 3: 54, 7
Solomon   V 5: 78, 30; 79, 3, 10; VII
    2: 63, 11; IX 3: 70, 6, 25
    Solomon, Book of   II 5: 107, 3
Son   I 2: 9, 17; 10, 14; 14, 39; 15, 2;
    3: 24, 14; 30, 26, 32; 38, 7, 15, 24;
    39, 19, 22, 26; 40, 25; 5: 56, 24; 57,
    [13], 19, 21, 33, 37; 58, 5, 14, 23, 36;
    59, 1, 4, 15; 62, 37; 65, 25, 29; 67,
    19; 86, 36; 87, 1, 14; 93, 34; 123, 29;
    124, 32; 125, 15; 127, 31; 128, 7; 133,
    18; II 1: 2, 14; 9, 11; 2: 40, 1, 28; 3:
    53, 30; 54, 7, 8; 59, 11; 67, 20; 74, 17,
    23; 4: 97, 18; III 2: 41, 9, 17; 42, 4,
    22; 55, 10; 68, 26; 4: 108, 7; 5: 121,
    7; 131, 20-21; 134, 14; 145, 17; IV 2:
    56, [24]; 58, 4; 59, 14; V 1: 9, [2]; 4:
    49, [5], 10; VII 2: 51, 2; 57, 7; 4: 115,
    10, 16, 19; 5: 118, 27, 31; VIII 1: 13,
    10; 16, 12; 2: 134, 3, 4, 6; 139, 26;
    XI 1: 11, 33, 34; 12, [22]; 13, 11; 14,
    28; 2: 22, 31; 23, 36; 25, 30; 33, 30,

36; 39, [11]; 2a: 40, [8], 12, [21], 22;
    2d: 43, 22, [26], 36; 2e: 44, 20; XIII 1:
    37, 4, 22; 38, 17, 22; 39, 13; 49, 13
    Son of Man   I 1: A, 16; 2: 3, 14,
    18; 4: 44, 23, 30-31; 46, 14-15; II 1:
    14, 15; 25, 1; 2: 48, 2; 3: 63, 29-30;
    76, 1-2, 2; 81, 14, 15, 16, 17-18, 18-19,
    19; III 2: 59, 3; 3: 81, 13, 21-22; 85,
    11-12, ⟨13⟩; 4: 104, 2; 105, 20; 106,
    15-16; 117, 22; 118, 1; 5: 135, 16-17;
    136, 21; VII 2: 63, 5-6; 64, 11-12; 65,
    19; 69, 21-22; 3: 71, 12; IX 3: 30, 18;
    31, 6; 32, 22-23; 36, [24]; 37, [10], [27-
    28]; 38, [4]; 40, [23]; 41, 2-3; 60, 6;
    61, [9]; 67, 7; 68, [11]; 69, [15]; 71, [12-
    13]; 72, [25]; XIII 1: 49, 19; BG 1: 8,
    18; 9, 9-10; 108, 2
    Son of God   I 4: 44, 16-17, 21-22,
    29; 5: 120, 36; II 3: 78, 20-21; III 2:
    69, 14; 4: 100, 3; 104, 16; 105, 21-22;
    VII 4: 118, 8; VIII 1: 52, 23; IX 1: 1,
    2; 6, 9-10; XIII 1: 38, 24-25, 25
Sophaia   VII 1: 33, 27; 46, 16, 26
Sophia   II 1: 8, 20; 9, 25; 23, 21; 28,
    13; 3: 59, [30], 31; 4: 94, 29; 95, 18,
    19, 25, 31; 5: 98, 13; 102, 1, 26; 103,
    1; 112, 1; 113, 22; 115, 31; 122, 24;
    III 2: 57, 1; 69, 3; 3: 77, 4; 81, 23;
    82, 5, 20, 21, 22, 24; 88, 6; 89, 9; 4:
    90, 14; 101, 16; 102, 13; 104, 11, 17;
    106, 16, 22; 107, 7, 17, 24; 112, ⟨7⟩;
    113, 13; 114, 14; 119, 18; V 1: 9, 4;
    3: 35, 7; 36, 6, 8; VI 4: 44, 19, 20;
    VII 1: 31, 27; 2: 50, 27; 51, 13; 52,
    21; 68, 31; 70, 4; VIII 1: 9, 16; 10,
    8, 15; 27, 12; XI 2: 31, 37; 33, 35; 35,
    10, 12, 16; 39, 11, 14, [19], 21, [23], 28,
    32; XIII 1: 40, 15; 47, 34; BG 3: 109,
    3; 120, 16
    Pistis Sophia   II 4: 87, 7-8; 95, 6;
    5: 100, 1-2, 10, 28; 104, 3, 17; 106, 11;
    108, 29-30; III 3: 82, 8; 83, 1
    Sophia Pistis   II 5: 106, 6
    Sophia, who is called Pistis   II 4:
    94, 5-6
    Sophia Zoe   II 5: 113, 12; 115, 12;
    121, 27 (see also Wisdom)
Sorma   II 1: 16, 30
Sostrapal   II 1: 16, 21
Soul   II 5: 109, 5 (see also Psyche)
Spark   VII 1: 31, 23, 29; 33, 30; 46, 13,
    18, 23, 27
Spirit   I 1: A, 17; 2: 4, 19; 5, 22; 9, 28;

3: **30**, 17; **31**, 18; **42**, 33; **43**, 17; *4:* **45**, 13; *5:* **101**, 4, [13], 18; **102**, 32; **105**, 23; **107**, 27; II *1:* **2**, 33; **4**, [24], 35; **5**, 2, 12, 14, 18, 28, [31], 33; **6**, 1, 4, 12, 19, 26, 29, 35; **7**, 6, 14, 19, 23, 32; **8**, 25, 31, 34; **9**, 7, 24, 27, 29, 34; **14**, 5; **20**, 16; **25**, 12, 23; **26**, 9, 11, 16; **27**, 18, 29; **29**, 24; **31**, 13; *3:* **60**, 7, 8; **61**, 29; **69**, 8; **70**, 24; **71**, 17; *4:* **88**, 12, 13; **93**, 22, 30; **96**, 24, [35]; *6:* **134**, 2; **135**, 30; III *2:* **40**, 13; **44**, 12, 24, 26; **49**, 25; **53**, 17; **55**, 21; **61**, 25; **63**, 3; **65**, 12; **68**, 25; **69**, 11, 17, 19; *4:* **91**, 12; **96**, 21; **102**, 13; **105** 2; **117**, [16]; **118**, [12]; **119**, [13], [16]; IV *1:* **22**, 6; *2:* **56**, 11; **58**, 25; **60**, [11] 24; V *2:* **18**, [21]; **20**, 4; **21**, 24; **22** 1, 11; **23**, 5, 23; *4:* **55**, [4]; *5:* **69**, 24; VI *4:* **37**, 24; *6:* **52**, 14; **57**, 5; **59**, 7; **60**, 1; **61**, 16; VII *1:* **1**, 3, 27, 30; **2**, 4, 20, 25; **3**, 1, 6, 13, 15, 26, 34, 36; **4**, 5; **5**, 8, 17; **6**, 13, 19, 22, 29, 31, 36; **7**, 4, 6, 9, 32; **8**, 2, 10, 13, 20, 23, 27; **9**, 1, 4, 8, 15, 16, 24, 26, 35; **10**, 13, 22, 29, 32; **11**, 9, 12, 16, 26, 30, 32; **12**, 14, 17, 20, 24, 35, 38; **13**, 7, 8, 23, 27, 32; **14**, 1, 10, 22; **15**, 11, 24, 32; **17**, 23, 28; **18**, 21, 23; **19**, 9, 11, 33; **20**, 4; **21**, 8, 21, 28, 36; **22**, 32; **23**, 8; **24**, 3, 15; **25**, 6; **26**, 9; **28**, 3, 33; **29**, 26; **30**, 34; **31**, 12; **32**, 14; **33**, 1, 3; **34**, 8; **35**, 5, 20, 24, 32; **37**, 9, 18; **38**, 8, 23; **39**, 6, 22; **43**, 13; **45**, 24; **47**, 23; **48**, 27; *2:* **49**, 18; **50**, 15; **54**, 16; **67**, 28; *3:* **83**, 9; *4:* **86**, 18; **107**, 35; **116**, 31; VIII *1:* **17**, 12; **20**, 18; **24**, 9, 13; **36**, 9; **57**, 25; **58**, 17; **63**, 9; **79**, 23; **80**, 19; **84**, 14, 18; **87**, 14; **97**, 3, 6; **118**, 12; **122**, 4; **123**, 20; **128**, 21; **129**, 12; X *1:* **4**, 17; **6**, 5; **9**, [29]; **10**, [9], 19; XI *2:* **23**, 37; **28**, 24; *2c:* **42**, 34; *3:* **45**, 27; **49**, 10; **51**, 35; **64**, 36; **66**, 34; XIII *1:* **37**, [32]; **38**, 11; **47**, 32; BG *3:* **109**, 17; *4:* **137**, 11

    Holy Spirit I *2:* **6**, 20; *3:* **24**, 11; **26**, 36; **27**, 4; *5:* **127**, 32; **128**, 8; **138**, 22; II *1:* **5**, 7; **6**, 29; **7**, 15-16; **8**, 27; **10**, 17; **14**, 5; **27**, 34; *2:* **40**, 29; *3:* **53**, 30; **55**, 17, 24; **57**, 7; **58**, 12; **59**, 12, 16, 20, 35; **60**, 28; **64**, 26; **66**, 2; **67**, 20; **69**, 5; **74**, 21; **75**, 18; **77**, 14; **85**, 23; *4:* **91**, 11; **93**, 6, 10; **97**, 16; *5:* **105**, 30; *6:* **129**, 6; III *2:* **60**, 7; **63**, 14; V *2:* **19**, [21], 26; **22**, 15, 22; *4:* **58**, 14; **63**,

[25-26]; *5:* **77**, 18; VII *3:* **82**, 8; **83**, 15; *4:* **112**, 26; IX *3:* **39**, 26; XIII *1:* **45**, 30

Stetheus VIII *1:* **47**, 16

Strempsouchos III *2:* **65**, 8; VIII *1:* **47**, 3

Strophaia VII *1:* **33**, 2

Strophaias VII *1:* **31**, 6; **46**, 9

Sumpthar VIII *1:* **47**, 22

Sunday II *5:* **118**, 2

Synogchouta II *1:* **17**, 19

Syriac (language) II *3:* **56**, 8; **63**, 22

Taphreo II *1:* **16**, 24

Tartaros II *4:* **95**, 12; *5:* **102**, 34; *7:* **142**, 36; XI *1:* **13**, 28; XIII *1:* **35**, [18] (see also Abyss, Hades, Underworld)

Tartarouchos II *7:* **142**, 41

Tat VI *8:* **72**, 30

Tebar II *1:* **16**, 5

Telmachae[. . .] VIII *1:* **52**, 8

Thalanatheu(s) VII *5:* **126**, 13

Thaspomocha II *1:* **15**, 33

That Which Is XI *3:* **49**, 27-28, 28-29, 35 (see also Existent One, He Who Is, One Who Is)

Theopemptos III *2:* **64**, 13; VIII *1:* **47**, 17

Theuda V *4:* **44**, 18

Thomas II *2:* **35**, 2, 9, 10; **51**, 28; *7:* **138**, 4, 19, 21, 36; **139**, 12, 22, 25; **140**, 5, 37; **141**, 2, 19; **142**, 3, 18; III *4:* **96**, 14; **108**, 16

    Thomas, Didymos Judas II *2:* **32**, 11

    Thomas, Judas II *7:* **138**, 2; **142**, 7-8

    Thomas the Contender II *7:* **145**, 17-18

Thopithro II *1:* **16**, 22

Thought I *3:* **16**, 35; **19**, 37; **37**, 13; *5:* **107**, 14; **108**, 16; **115**, 26; **119**, 34; **120**, 16, 19; II *5:* **104**, 12; III *2:* **42**, 7; VIII *1:* **83**, 10; XI *2:* **24**, [24]; *3:* **46**, [20]; XIII *1:* **35**, 1, 8; **36**, [3], 9, 14, 17, 20, 21, 25, 27; **37**, 21; **38**, 8; **41**, 31; **42**, 5, 6, 24, 26; **44**, 30; **46**, 7, 30; **48**, 14 (see also Ennoia, Epinoia)

    First Thought II *1:* **5**, 4; VIII *1:* **20**, 17; **24**, 12; XI *3:* **48**, [13]; **53**, [6], 27; **64**, 35; XIII *1:* **37**, 12-13 (see also Protennoia)

Thouro VIII *1:* **47**, 27

Thunder   VI *2:* **13**, 1
Toechea   II *1:* **17**, 25
Trachoun   II *1:* **17**, 4
Treneu   II *1:* **16**, 10
Triple Power   XI *3:* **45**, 13, 21; **47**, 9;
  51, 8; **52**, 19, 30; **53**, 30-31; **55**, [21];
  58, 25; **61**, 6, 13, 20; **64**, 34-35
    Three-Powered One   X *1:* **6**, 19;
  7, 17, 24, [28]; **8**, 5, 11, 19; **9**, 8, 20,
  25; **15**, 2
Trismegistus   VI *6:* **59**, 15, 25; *8:* **66**,
  26; **69**, 1, 27; **74**, 17, 33; **75**, 34; **78**,
  14, 31
Truth   I *3:* **26**, 5, 28; *4:* **44**, 35; **45**, 4, 12,
  13; **46**, 32; **50**, 7; *5:* **60**, 34; **63**, 35;
  II *1:* **8**, 8; *5:* **98**, 24; **107**, 12; III *2:*
  40, 19; **60**, 21; **62**, 20; VII *2:* **50**,
  11; **53**, 4; **66**, 21; **67**, 25, 29, VIII *1:*
  30, 9; XI *2:* **24**, 35
Tupelon   II *1:* **17**, 1

Unbegotten One   I *5:* **54**, 25; III *3:* **73**,
  16; **82**, 13; **89**, 16; X *1:* **4**, 19; **6**, 3; **7**,
  14; XI *3:* **54**, 34
Uncontainable One   XI *2:* **32**, 39; **34**, 37
Uncreated One   XI *2:* **29**, [29]; **35**, 24
Understanding   II *1:* **8**, 3, 15; III *2:* **52**,
  11
Underworld   VII *4:* **103**, 23; **104**, 2, 14;
  110, 21, 29; **114**, 26; XIII *1:* **36**, 4;
  39, 17, 22; **40**, 24; **41**, 6; **43**, 9; **44**, 14
  (see also Abyss, Hades, Tartaros)
Unknown One   XI *3:* **59**, 29; **60**, 8; **61**,
  1; **67**, 26
Unnameable One   XI   *3:* **54**, 37

Valentinus   IX *3:* **56**, 2, 5
Verton   II *1:* **17**, 12
Virgo   VI *6:* **62**, 17

Water   VII *1:* **5**, 27
Wicked One   VII *4:* **85**, 17
  Wickedness, Spirit of   VII *4:* **104**, 26
Wisdom   II *3:* **60**, 11, 12, 13, 15; **63**, 30;
  VII *4:* **88**, 35; **89**, 5; **91**, 16; **106**, 23;
  107, 3, 9; **112**, 35; **113**, 14; XI *1:* **12**,
  33; XII *1:* **16**, 1 (see also Sophia)
Word   I *3:* **16**, 34; **23**, 20, 33; **26**, 5;
  31, 12; **37**, 7, 8, 11; *4:* **43**, 34; **45**,
  3; **50**, 7; *5:* **60**, 34; **63**, 35; II *3:* **80**,
  5; III *2:* **40**, 19; **42**, 7; **43**, 21; **44**, 21;
  60, 20; *5:* **129**, 23; **130**, [10]; **135**, 21;
  IV *2:* **58**, 26; **60**, [2]; V *5:* **82**, 14; **85**,

27; VI *3:* **22**, 22; VII *1:* **8**, 18; **9**, 5; **12**,
  19; **32**, 32; **42**, 32; **44**, 27; *2:* **49**, 17,
  24; **67**, 27; **68**, 19; *3:* **73**, 31; *4:* **106**, 24;
  111, 5; **112**, 32; **113**, 13; **115**, 18; **117**,
  8, 30; IX *3:* **45**, 7, 10; XI *1:* **16**, 32,
  37, 38; **17**, 35; **21**, 29; *2:* **29**, 27, 30;
  30, [17], 31; *3:* **32**, 34, [36]; XII *1:* **31**, 8;
  XIII *1:* **37**, 5, 24; **46**, 5, 14, 30; **47**, 15
  (see also Logos, Reason)

Yabel   II *1:* **10**, 32; **17**, 8
Yachthos   VIII *1:* **54**, 23; **126**, 12
Yakouib   II *1:* **17**, 11
Yaldabaoth   II *1:* **24**, 12; *4:* **95**, 11;
  96, 4; *5:* **100**, 14, 19, 24; **102**, 11; **103**,
  1, 33; VII *2:* **53**, 13; **68**, 29; BG *3:*
  119, 15
    Aldabaoth   II *1:* **23**, 35
    Yaltabaoth   II *1:* **10**, 19; **11**, 16, 35;
  14, 15; **19**, 23, 30; *4:* **95**, 8; XIII *1:*
  39, 27
Yammeax   II *1:* **17**, 10
Yammon   XIII *1:* **48**, 16
Yao   II *1:* **11**, 30; **12**, 20; *5:* **101**, 15, 29
Yatomenes   VIII *1:* **52**, [2]
Yatomenos   XI *3:* **54**, 35
Yave   II *1:* **24**, 18, 19, 21; IV *1:* **38**, 4
Yeronumos   II *1:* **15**, 34
Yesseus Mazareus Yessedekeus   III *2:*
  64, 10-11; **66**, 10; V *5:* **85**, 30-31;
  VIII *1:* **47**, 5-6; **57**, [5-6]
Yetheus   XI *3:* **54**, 20
Yobel   II *1:* **10**, 37; III *2:* **58**, 13
Yoel   III *2:* **44**, 27; **65**, 23; VIII *1:* **57**,
  15; **62**, 12
Yoko   II *1:* **18**, 16
Yolaos   VIII *1:* **1**, 4; **4**, 10
Youel   III *2:* **50**, 2; **53**, 25; **55**, 22; **62**,
  6; IV *2:* **56**, [20]; **59**, 23; VIII *1:* **52**,
  14; **54**, 17; **63**, 11; **125**, 14; XI *3:* **50**,
  20; **52**, 14; **55**, 18, 34; **57**, 25
Yubel   III *2:* **58**, [18]

Zabedo   II *1:* **16**, 17
Zacha[. . .]   VIII *1:* **54**, 22
Zachthos   VIII *1:* **126**, 12
Zareu[. . .]   VIII *1:* **54**, 4
Zathoth   II *1:* **17**, 8
Zebedee   II *1:* **1**, 7
Zeus   VI *8:* **75**, 16
    Zeus, Plutonius   VI *8:* **75**, 17
Zodiac   X *1:* **21**, [14]; **39**, 28; **42**, 5
Zoe   II *4:* **95**, 5, 18, 19, 32; *5:* **104**, 28;

107, 4; **115**, 32 (see also Life, and under Sophia)

Zogenethlos   VIII *1:* **6**, 17

Zoroaster   VIII *1:* **132**, 9

    Zoroaster, book of   II *1:* **19**, 10

Zostrianos   VIII *1:* **1**, [3]; **3**, 31; **14**, 1; **64**, 11; **128**, 15; **132**, 6, 8

[. . .]thos   I *2:* **1**, 2

[. . .]ephneu(s)   VII *5:* **126**, 8

[.]son   VIII *1:* **47**, 20

[. . .]oudas[.]os   VIII *1:* **127**, 27

[. . .]riphanios   XI *3:* **54**, 29

[. . .]anen   XIII *1:* **48**, 28